The Stacked Deck

Second Edition

The Stacked Deck

An Introduction to Social Inequality

Jennifer Ball
Lorne Tepperman

Oxford University Press is a department of the University of Oxford.
It furthers the University's objective of excellence in research, scholarship,
and education by publishing worldwide. Oxford is a registered trade mark of
Oxford University Press in the UK and in certain other countries.

Published in Canada by
Oxford University Press
8 Sampson Mews, Suite 204,
Don Mills, Ontario M3C 0H5 Canada

www.oupcanada.com

First Edition published in 2016

Library and Archives Canada Cataloguing in Publication
Title: The stacked deck : an introduction to social inequality / Jennifer Ball & Lorne Tepperman.
Names: Ball, Jennifer, 1969- author. | Tepperman, Lorne, author.
Description: Second edition. | Includes bibliographical references and index.
Identifiers: Canadiana (print) 20200285025 | Canadiana (ebook) 20200285041 | ISBN 9780199036752 (softcover) | ISBN 9780199036790 (ebook)
Subjects: LCSH: Equality—Canada. | LCSH: Canada—Social conditions. | LCSH: Equality—Canada—Textbooks. | LCSH: Canada—Social conditions—Textbooks. | LCGFT: Textbooks.
Classification: LCC HN110.Z9 S63 2020 | DDC 305.0971—dc23

Cover images: © MJgraphics/Shutterstock, © Ala Sharahlazava/Shutterstock
Cover and interior design: Sherill Chapman

Oxford University Press is committed to our environment.
This book is printed on Forest Stewardship Council® certified paper
and comes from responsible sources.

Printed and bound in the United States of America

2 3 4 — 24 23 22 21

Contents

Preface

Why Study Inequality?

We consider social inequality to be one of the most pressing problems facing Canada today. In the past few years, quite a few news stories and analyses have highlighted the critical nature of inequality.

Unemployment, poor health, poverty, victimization: these experiences define *social inequality* as a social problem characterized by visible, measurable features that threaten people's well-being in this country. As we will see, there are countries that do far worse than Canada—countries where inequalities are even more marked and ingrained. However, the majority of Canadians appear to care about the kind of society we live in and thus see social inequality as a problem that warrants collective, remedial action.

The study of inequality began long before this book was printed. Sociologists and philosophers have been thinking about inequality for at least 250 years. According to French philosopher Jean-Jacques Rousseau, social inequality means unequal privilege. By *privilege* we mean a right, advantage, or favour specially granted to some people and not others. Consider, for example, the advantage that children have in getting a job in an organization owned by a family friend. Rousseau noted that privileges and inequalities that do not clearly arise out of a natural difference are contrary to the laws of nature. In other words, inequality is unjustifiable privilege.

While we may disagree with Rousseau's favouring of natural privilege (for example, all people deserve access to schools, not only the able-bodied who can walk up the front steps), in this book, by *inequality* we will mean the unequal (and usually unjustifiable) privileges, rewards, or opportunities that some people receive within a given society.

Inequality is unfair, but the study of inequality is not merely the study of unfairness. There are many definitions of fairness: for example, a consistent application of the rules (or the rule of law). And as we will see in Chapter 3, sociologist Christopher Jencks offers at least five definitions of fairness. Yet a fair application of the law can lead to morally unfair and socially harmful results.

Regardless of consistency, wealth disparities may result, with harmful consequences for the majority. Some of the problem of inequality in our society is a result of prejudice and discrimination. But part is due to an intergenerational accumulation of wealth that gains size and power over time. In turn, as we will see, this tends to reduce people's opportunities for advancement, no matter how talented they are or how hard they work.

This Book

This book, *The Stacked Deck*, shows that life is a stacked deck; nobody's *life choices* are entirely conscious or free. Everyone is born with different *life chances*: unequal opportunities to be and stay healthy; to gain power, status, and education; and to achieve or be ascribed other "life prizes." Or, we might say, everyone has a different opportunity to gain the capital they need to survive, which we appropriately call "survival capital."

The Stacked Deck combines both objective and subjective views of inequality to explore the effects of inequality. In discussions throughout the book, *The Stacked Deck* explores the following subjects:

- The myths and limits of social mobility and the effect of poverty on family structure and health outcomes
- The thesis that *relative poverty*, not absolute poverty, tends to be correlated with reduced life chances
- The ways in which women suffer from unequal gender relations in the professional, public, and domestic spheres
- The harmful effects of excluding and degrading the elderly at a time when seniors are increasing at a faster rate than any other segment
- The reasons why Indigenous populations are much more likely to experience harmful inequalities in the justice system
- The reduced life opportunities available to racialized groups and immigrants
- The social and economic barriers faced by people living with a disability or chronic illness

Each of the "survival capital" chapters (Chapters 3 to 11) includes the following pedagogical tools to help students as they work through the book:

- Notable Thinkers: An introduction to a researcher who is making or has made a major impact through their research on the chapter topic.
- Test Your Knowledge: A 5- to 10-question quiz (with answers provided) that tests students' existing knowledge of a topic.
- Questions for Critical Thought: A section that challenges students to build something new with the information we have provided.
- Additional Resources: A section directing students to books, articles, movies, and so on on the chapter's topic.

All people have overlapping identities and, correspondingly, intersecting social disadvantages or advantages. *Intersectionality*, which we will discuss in Chapter 1, is the process by which these disadvantages interact with one another, and it complicates attempts to predict the effects of inequality. It can also complicate individuals' struggles for equality, as political action often requires platforms of shared experience. Nevertheless, generalizations can be and are made about the ways in which "groups" are affected by inequality, and they can help bring clarity to educational settings.

This is why the survival capital chapters will focus on these populations one by one (for example, Indigenous Peoples in Canada, immigrants, and racialized people) and focus on the nature of each population's access to the key resource under discussion. The chapters focusing on survival capital will be enhanced with boxed sections featuring excerpts from interviews with people describing *their own experience* of the effects of inequality. In the last section, *The Stacked Deck* compares Canada against other similar countries and explores strategies used around the world to decrease inequality.

To close, we hope you find this book interesting and enlightening.

Acknowledgements

Our first thank you is to the outstanding University of Toronto undergraduate students who helped us research this book: Angela Abenoja and Justine Beaule. Angela helped us get all the updated information we needed, while Justine edited and clarified our prose. It's been a privilege and a pleasure to work with them—one of the two best parts of working on this book.

The other best part of this project was working with the people at Oxford University Press and their associates. Emily Kring served as the main developmental editor, followed by Peter Chambers, and both oversaw the process of flow and standardization. Thank you, Emily and Peter, for your efforts on our behalf. You both provided a lot of helpful suggestions in a timely, interesting way. Leanne Rancourt edited the copy, clearly and carefully, forcing us always to improve our thinking and writing. Thank you, Leanne; you were great.

We also want to thank our anonymous reviewers and our undergraduate, diploma, and certificate students who have read and responded to material we have presented in the classroom. They have all given us new ideas about what to discuss and how to discuss it most effectively. If you have some ideas about how we can do that better in the next edition, send us an email at jennifer.ball@humber.ca or lorne.tepperman@utoronto.ca

Finally, we would like to acknowledge the following reviewers, colleagues, experts in their fields, and friends and family whose thoughtful comments and suggestions have helped to shape this book. They were Gordon and Jane Ball, Jonathan Ball, Alexa Carson, Jan Buterman, Jay T. Dolmage, D. Ryan Dyck, Reuben Ford, Lauren Goodman, Leigh Joseph, Tessa Lochhead, Jaybird McKechnie, Colin O'Connor, Valerie Powell, and all the hardworking people at Statistics Canada.

Jennifer Ball
Lorne Tepperman

Andrii Zastrozhnov/Shutterstock

1 Theories of Social Inequality

Learning Objectives

- To define social inequalities.
- To recognize the importance of the historical context of social inequalities.
- To understand how sociologists think about and study social inequalities.
- To identify the competing theories that clarify aspects of social inequalities.
- To understand the concepts of social justice, neoliberalism, intersectionality, and interlocking disadvantages.

Sociology and the Study of Social Inequalities

People have been arguing about social inequality and the right way to address it for at least two centuries. In fact, much of early sociology was the study of social inequality.

Accordingly, we could start this book with a discussion of Plato and his vision, in *The Republic*, of a perfect society, which was, incidentally, a very unequal society. We could start with a discussion of Ibn Khaldun and his analysis of tribal societies, which were also unequal but, as nomadic societies, less so than Plato's "republic." We could start with a discussion of Thomas Hobbes, who embraced the idea of monarchy even at the expense of severe inequality, so long as it guaranteed social stability.

Even more likely, we could start with Jean-Jacques Rousseau's famous *Discourse on the Origin and Basis of Inequality among Men* ([1755] 2009). Inequality, Rousseau argued, was possibly universal and inevitable; but he was more concerned with whether it was justifiable. Rousseau thought great rewards were justified by great abilities. People of great distinction deserved special privilege; without it, they did not. We will see a revised version of this theory when we discuss the functional theory of stratification, attributed to Davis and Moore, later in this chapter.

Beyond that, Rousseau argued that inequalities may be the result of diverse mechanisms, but these are present in all societies. Second, these inequalities tend to cumulate, and third, political authorities must manage these issues while realizing the limitation of the policies intended to reduce these inequalities. In short, Rousseau laid out the groundwork for this book two and a half centuries ago.

Space permitting, we could undertake to discuss inequality around the world. For example, we could consider the ancient caste system of India, the varieties of class structure in South American feudal societies, and the relative absence of inequality in small, tribal communities of Africa. Taking a smaller scope, we could consider how social inequality in Europe was transformed by the change from agricultural feudalism to industrial capitalism between roughly 1400 and 1900 CE. However, space does not permit any of these fascinating and ambitious undertakings. This book will begin with some general history about the sociological study of inequality, but it will focus mainly on Canada in the twenty-first century. An exception to this Canadian focus is Chapter 12, where we will compare Canada to other, similar industrial societies and consider the differences.

History has shown us that we cannot eliminate social inequality, but we can reduce it through research, planning, and legislation. In the nineteenth century, most sociologists thought that humanity could improve social life through the systematic study of social issues. Sociologists believed they could improve society by using their knowledge to expel ignorance, superstition, prejudice, and senseless custom. They believed deeply in the value of real social research as the means for diagnosing social inequalities and devising and evaluating solutions.

Today, sociologists continue to know that social inequality, even if it is inevitable, is harmful if it is too severe. Top-end inequality—inequality that preserves the inherited privilege of the rich—promotes complacency and injustice. Such unearned privilege distorts government and the just distribution of rewards throughout society. Inequality at the bottom of society, for its part, prevents upward mobility. This absence of opportunity denies people the rewards to which they are entitled, thus breaking their spirits and undermining their ambition. It also robs society of valuable talent and energy. Both distortions, from above and below, leave the large middle class feeling anxious and insecure. More than that, it promotes a cynicism about the social order and public institutions that undermines political justice and stability. It promotes demagogues in government and a polarizing between classes, regions, genders, and ethnic groups. And it robs young people of hope for the future.

Societies vary in their openness. Some societies are more open than others, meaning two things. First, there are greater overall opportunities for advancement by talented people. A classic work by Lipset and Bendix ([1959] 1991) showed, using comparative data from a wide variety of industrial societies, that the chief determinant of upward mobility in a society is structural expansion, or as we might say, economic development. The more jobs that are created—especially, good, well-paying jobs—the higher the likelihood that people will advance occupationally and financially compared to the class position into which they were born. (Ironically, another factor that increases openness is death: Upward mobility is high for survivors in times of war and other mass death.)

Second, a more open society has fewer impediments to upward mobility. For example, there is an absence of discrimination against minority job applicants or, thanks to the equity legislation found in many Canadian provinces, a positive preference for minority job applicants. For millennia, the caste system kept talented Indians born into the untouchable or other low castes from aspiring to much less entering important, well-paying jobs. It also kept them from associating with other Indians who belonged to other, higher castes. Along similar lines, apartheid in South Africa, which persisted from roughly 1948 to 1994, severely limited the freedom and opportunities of Black South Africans. It also limited the freedoms of Asians and other minorities living in the country, though to a smaller degree. And, like Black South Africans, Indigenous Peoples in Canada were subjected to laws that limited their freedom, movement, and opportunities, such as the laws requiring them to secure "passes" to leave reserves or the criminalization of spiritual practices.

Apartheid was overthrown in South Africa in 1994, and in India the caste system is gradually dying out, thanks to legislative efforts by the government. John Porter ([1965] 2015), in his classic work *The Vertical Mosaic*, was concerned to find that certain ethnic groups were overrepresented in the Canadian elite while others were underrepresented. This pointed to a prejudice against Canadians who did not descend from Canada's charter groups: the French and the English. It also pointed to an absence of opportunities for higher education that would enable minority Canadians to achieve upward mobility. For this reason, Porter argued forcefully for the expansion of higher education in Canada through the establishment of new colleges and universities and the enlargement of existing ones.

Thanks to these two strategies—equity legislation and higher education—Canada has become far more open today than it was 50 years ago. Ethnic origins no longer predict occupation, income, or social class, as they did at the time *The Vertical Mosaic* was published. That said, Indigenous Peoples and others in Canada still face barriers related to funding, education, and employment, as we will discuss at length in later chapters of this book. So, Canada is a far more open society today than it was 50 or 100 years ago, but it is still far from fully and equally open, as Porter would have wished.

As Porter did in the past, sociologists are still struggling to analyze and record the patterns of social life that cause social inequalities. So, in this chapter, we will look at how sociologists study inequalities. After that, we will examine sociological theories about social inequalities. Finally, we will briefly discuss some solutions to the problems caused by social inequalities.

Social Inequalities and the Sociological Imagination

sociological imagination Refers to the ability to see the interconnections between individual experiences and larger societal patterns, trends, or forces.

According to sociologist C. Wright Mills (1959), the **sociological imagination** is a unique way of looking at the world. It allows people to see connections between their own lives (tiny micro-events) and the social world in which they live (giant macro-events). Said another way, the sociological imagination examines the links between personal or private troubles and public issues. This micro–macro link between close-to-home aspects of social life and broad social trends is at the core of sociology. Further, this relationship is our key to understanding how social inequalities affect our lives and those around us.

To use Mills's example, unemployed people may view their lack of a job as a private trouble involving only them, their immediate family members, and their friends. But this view is short-sighted. In fact, unemployment is the source of private troubles for thousands, if not millions, of people. Causes include automation, the COVID-19 outbreak, changes in global trade, and economic recessions—all things that are beyond the control of any single worker. Thus, unemployment is not merely a private or personal trouble, even if it feels that way when it affects you and your close friends. It is also a public issue, one that sends shockwaves through the lives of many people at the same time. The same is true of other bases of social inequalities—poverty, racism, homophobia, and so on.

Using our sociological imaginations means connecting the conditions of our own lives and the larger social contexts in which we live. It means asking, "Wait a minute . . . could others be experiencing this too?" The realization that many individuals are experiencing poverty for many different reasons is, perhaps, the beginning to a sociological approach. It is the start of a realization that poverty and inequality may be beyond an individual's control.

The key thing to remember about Mills's approach is that he moved our attention away from individuals struggling separately (and often secretly) with seemingly unique problems. Instead, he asked us to consider how seemingly distinct personal troubles were actually symptoms of large, widespread social problems. They were not caused by the individuals who suffered their effects, and they could not be solved by individuals either. Only by seeing their problems as similar and connected could people come to understand that they were victims of social problems not of their own making. To solve them would require banding together to demand (and in some instances create) social change.

Following Mills, sociologists make these connections between personal troubles and public issues by closely analyzing reality at two levels: the micro and the macro. Microsociology, or micro-level analysis, focuses on the interactions among people in small groups. This approach studies people's understandings and experiences of social inequalities at the local, personal level. Macrosociology, or macro-level analysis, focuses on the whole society. It explores the ways that changes occurring within major organizations and social institutions affect populations as a whole. Sociologists apply both levels of analysis to social inequalities to connect personal, private troubles and public issues—for example, the personal experience of unemployment with the public issue of high unemployment rates.

Sociological Approaches to Inequality

Recall what you learned about sociological approaches to inequality in your introductory sociology course: Two sociologists might not understand or explore the social world in the same way. The differences in their general assumptions about the world may shape the thrust of their research and the practical applications of their findings. It helps to be familiar with the dominant sociological approaches since this will help you understand the various aspects of social inequality and public responses to them. As you read our review of some historically important perspectives in sociology, consider which one makes the most sense to you.

IN FOCUS ◆ Principles of the Main Sociological Approaches to Inequalities

Functionalism

- Elements in society are interconnected and interrelated by common values.
- Well-functioning societies need social cohesion and social control.
- Inequalities serve a social purpose. They arise out of a general agreement about the kinds of qualities and skills a society needs and values most.
- Extreme social inequalities, however, may create social disorganization and lead to deviance and crime.

Conflict Theory

- Conflict and change are basic features of social life.
- Social inequalities reflect differences in power and wealth in society.
- Groups, classes, and individuals with conflicting interests will oppose the efforts of others to impose control, often intensifying conflict.
- The conflict between classes is a basic feature of all societies as some struggle to preserve power while others struggle to gain more.

Feminism

- Gender inequality is a basic feature of most human societies.
- People learn gender through childhood experiences, and ideology perpetuates it.
- Women are typically disadvantaged both at home and in the workforce.
- Societies vary in both their extent of gender inequality and responses to it.

Symbolic Interactionism/Social Constructionism

- Society is a product of continuous face-to-face interactions.
- Accounts about social inequalities are socially constructed.
- Problematic behaviours resulting from inequalities are socially learned.
- Childhood experiences and labelling shape people's responses to inequalities.

Just like in other academic disciplines, there are different *perspectives* with which sociologists typically align themselves. Some prefer macroanalysis, while others concentrate on microanalysis, for example. The three major microanalytical approaches in sociology are the functionalist, conflict, and feminist perspectives. The major macroanalytical approach is the symbolic-interactionist perspective. The next section gives an outline of each perspective.

In the humanities and social sciences, different schools or approaches rise and fall in prominence as they gain followers and build on each other's insights. As a result, the thinking of (say) Marxist scholars today is different from the thinking of Marxist scholars a century ago—it is more complex and comprehensive. The newer version offers us a better guide to present-day social life than the older ones. However, it is no more correct or accurate than earlier versions of Marxist thought.

Because of this, theories of social inequality do not always follow a straightforward timeline. All the theories we discuss here have risen to and fallen from prominence, repeatedly. Yet all of them are still in use by present-day social scientists in various versions and combinations. That is why you need to understand and recognize them when they come up in scholarly discussion. Below, we call attention to major differences between the approaches to studying social inequality and the ideas these approaches use most often.

With this warning in mind, consider the first approach: functionalism.

Functionalism

Functionalism is concerned with understanding how different social forms and practices contribute to the survival of society. Societal institutions, organizations, and groups have a purpose, stated or otherwise, that allows society to endure in its current form without much upheaval. Accordingly, functionalists—noting that social inequality is universal—want to know what, if any, function or purpose is served by this universal inequality.

The argument, therefore, that some inequality is necessary has been referred to as the "functional theory of stratification." Functionalist theorists have proposed that social stratification recruits and motivates people into key roles in the social structure (Davis and Moore 1945). Every society has many positions and social roles to fill. For example, our society needs medical doctors, lawyers, professors, nurses, janitors, bus drivers, and so on. Some of these positions require large investments of time and money for education and preparation. To motivate people to pursue these demanding occupations, society has put a reward system in place.

This system, in theory, pays high rewards to positions that are hardest to fill, since they require specialized knowledge, skills, and often credentials. By contrast, occupations that do not require specialized credentials or skills, such as cleaning an office building or serving customers at a fast-food restaurant, will have lower status and pay, as many people can occupy these positions and so workers are more easily replaced. To summarize their position, Davis and Moore (1945) say that "the [unequal] rewards and their distribution become part of the social order, and thus give rise to stratification" (p. 243).

Thus, the "functional theory of stratification" contends that inequality can be understood as a healthy, necessary feature of a stable society. If all jobs carried the same rewards, we would have a glut of hairdressers but no brain surgeons. From a functionalist's perspective, no one would make the effort to become a brain surgeon if they could get the same rewards by being a licensed hairdresser. In effect, the functionalist perspective says people get what they deserve—nothing more or less. At first glance, this is a persuasive theory because it seems to be consistent with our everyday experiences. Besides, many famous and powerful people support this view of inequality.

Donald J. Trump
@realDonaldTrump
Follow
People often ask me the secret to my success, and the answer is simple: passion, focus and hard work. Momentum keeps it all going.
12:08 PM - 20 Jan 2014
801 Retweets 695 Likes

Much has been said about Donald Trump's rise to power. Was it the result of his own "hard work" or did enormous wealth inherited from his millionaire father play a part?

However, this theory is not without flaws. First, it ignores the role of inheritance in controlling both wealth and social status. People who inherit money and prestige from their parents do not necessarily have skills that contribute to the survival of society. A second flaw in functionalist theory is that it ignores disagreements about society's most important roles. At the extremes of the occupational system, we may all agree on justifiable rewards for brain surgeons versus unskilled labourers. But for most jobs, we are likely to disagree quite a lot. Related to this, a third flaw of the functionalist perspective on inequalities is that it fails to explain a wide range of anomalies. For example, it fails to explain why leading figures in organized crime, sports, and entertainment enjoy high incomes and social prominence.

For functionalists, the general solution to problems connected to poverty, mental illness, discrimination, addiction, and poor health is not to lessen inequality. Rather, it is to strengthen social norms and slow the pace of social change.

Conflict Theory

Whether they focus on class, gender, race, sexual orientation, or something else, conflict theories are always about the unequal distribution of power. Conflict theorists view society as a collection of varied groups struggling to dominate society and its institutions. They view conflict and change as basic, unavoidable features of social life. For them, social inequalities reflect differences in power and wealth in society.

Conflict theories grew out of the work and legacies of German philosopher and economist Karl Marx (1818–1883) and German sociologist Max Weber (1864–1920), both of whom we will discuss later in this chapter. Within conflict theory, there are two primary approaches to social conflict: (1) The Marxist tradition focuses on economic inequality (that is, wealth inequality) between social classes as the source of social conflict, while (2) the Weberian tradition stresses the role of power and views its unequal distribution within society as the source of social conflict.

Conflict theory began in the nineteenth century with the work of Marx and Weber. However, it wasn't until the mid-twentieth century that the conflict approach emerged as a full-bodied reaction against functionalism. Then it built on the work of Ralf Dahrendorf (1929–2009), Lewis Coser (1913–2003), and Randall Collins (b. 1941), among others.

In *Class and Class Conflict in Industrial Society* (1959), the German-born sociologist Ralf Dahrendorf proposed that neither functionalism nor Marxism alone gave a satisfactory understanding of advanced societies. Dahrendorf viewed society as being in a constant state of change and conflict, held together only by authority and power. Like Weber, he gave special attention to the societal role of authority and power. Dahrendorf characterized "authority" as an exercise of power in formal organizations (for example, social movements or political parties) with a recognized chain of command. These organizations, like Weber's status groups, have the potential to mobilize for conflict in ways that change society. They also have the power to preserve order and inequality.

Lewis Coser's claim that conflict has important social functions led many to identify him as the first sociologist to try to bring together functionalism and conflict theory. He did this by showing that conflict could tighten the bonds of loosely structured groups and societies. Under many conditions, groups can remain locked in conflict for long periods of time without any change occurring. In this way, conflict can preserve the social order. In a society that lacks strong bonds of consensus, conflict with another society can increase social solidarity, thus helping a society survive. Another benefit of conflict is that it helps opposing groups become more aware of another's views.

Similarly, like all sociologists, Randall Collins recognized that conflict is a result of social tensions. However, he also recognized that social conflicts are predictably patterned. Social conflicts are both unavoidable and neither good nor bad. Given that they are an unavoidable part of life, Collins urges us to remember that humans create these conflicts. What's more, Collins pointed out that humans act according to the meanings they attach to conflicts: "Life is basically a struggle for status in which no one can afford to be oblivious to the power of others around him" (1974:56–61), he explained. In short, Collins addressed the socially constructed and subjective dimension of conflict in society.

Symbolic Interactionism/Social Constructionism

Functionalist theory and conflict theory focus on large, macro elements of society, such as social institutions and major demographic groups. By contrast, *symbolic interactionism* focuses on small, micro **interactions** between people.

interactions Reciprocal behaviours between two or more people producing shared and evolving realities.

Said another way, symbolic interactionists focus on the "glue" that holds people together in social relationships. They are interested in the shared meanings, definitions, and interpretations that make interaction among people possible and meaningful. Interactionists are interested in how people create and reproduce inequalities. This means that a sociologist adopting the symbolic-interactionist perspective will analyze how certain behaviours come to be defined or framed.

Symbolic interactionism began at the University of Chicago's world-renowned Department of Sociology. The "Chicago School" has, over time, produced a long list of remarkable sociologists, including George Herbert Mead (1863–1931), W.I. Thomas (1863–1947), Everett C. Hughes (1897–1983), Herbert Blumer (1900–1987), and Erving Goffman (1922–1982). In the first half of the twentieth century especially, it produced much interesting work on ethnic groups, city life, and social deviance.

labelling theory A theory that asserts people create social realities (like "crimes," for example) when they label them as such.

Consider **labelling theory** as an example of the production of a shared reality. It rests on the symbolic-interactionist premise that any given social problem is a "problem" only because an influential group of people defines it as one. Howard Becker ([1963] 2008), for example, proposed that marijuana smoking is considered a social problem only because influential "moral entrepreneurs" made it into one. Those are people with an interest in changing other people's thoughts and actions. Yet there is nothing intrinsically harmful about marijuana in itself, affirmed Becker—at least, nothing more harmful than, say, alcohol or cigarettes, which are both legal. What's more, societies change their definitions of deviance.

Symbolic-interactionist Herbert Blumer (1971) proposed that all crime waves and other social problems develop in stages. They include (1) *social recognition*, (2) *social legitimating*, and (3) *mobilization for action*. They end with (4) the *development and implementation of an official plan*, such as a government-sanctioned "war on drugs." Throughout this book, we will further explore this idea that problems evolve in stages. At this point, what you should note is the underlying assumption of symbolic interactionism is that people collectively create shared understandings of reality: Reality is what people say it is! Not surprisingly, people adopting a symbolic-interactionist approach are also interested in the results of labelling, including branding certain groups as deviants, criminals, or rule-breakers.

Interactionists think the persistence of inequality, even on an institutional level, depends on face-to-face interactions. Inequality, then, is socially constructed. People set up narratives of blame that degrade others for their disadvantages and justify oppressing them. In turn, the people so labelled set up counternarratives—narratives of validation—to excuse and explain their disadvantaged circumstances. Every society, then, is a playhouse for the war between narratives of blame and narratives of validation. Symbolic interactionists are interested in how these narratives are constructed and promoted.

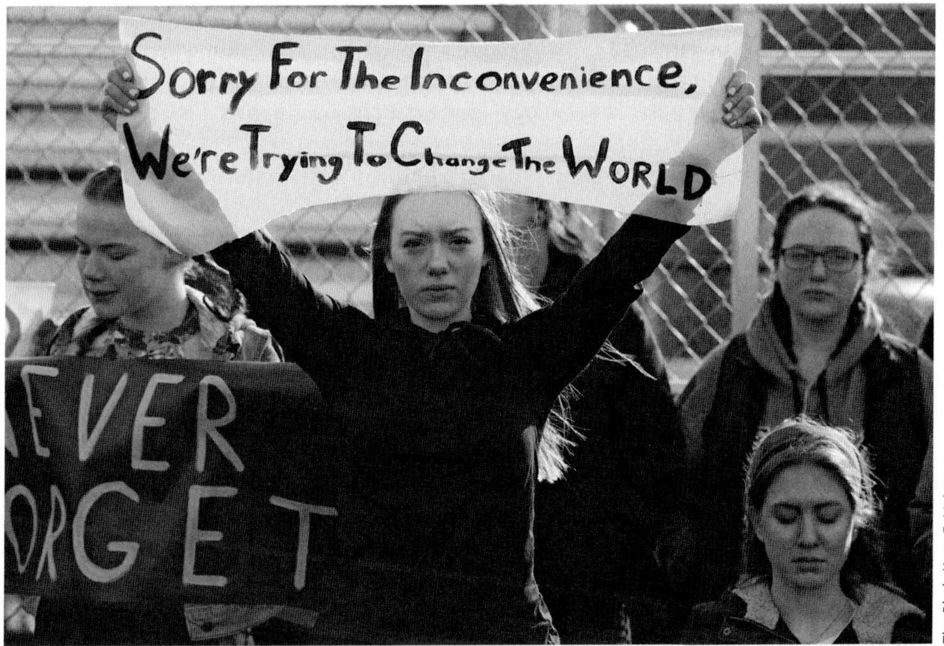

What would a symbolic interactionist think of this protestor using her sign to explain the disruption she's causing?

Feminism

Feminists study the ways gender inequality makes women's lives different from men's. They note that women often act out specific **roles** that men have defined and that shape their most important social activities at home, at work, and in the public domain. This fact also forces women to comply with their own domination or risk exclusion and even violence. Thus, accepting female roles is more costly—and even dangerous—to women than men's acceptance of male roles. Trans women especially experience this risk of exclusion and violence, given the ways in which they challenge and highlight the limits of traditional understandings of gender roles and behaviours.

role Refers to the dynamic element of status and the way in which status is performed.

The first wave of the feminist movement occurred between the mid-nineteenth century and the early twentieth century, resulting in women gaining the right to vote in many Western countries. This coincided with or was sometimes preceded by important sociological contributions by feminist women, many of whom go unstudied today.

For example, Harriet Martineau's (1802–1876) translation of Auguste Comte's seminal sociological work introduced his ideas to English speakers. Martineau is one of many women who made historically unrecognized contributions to classical theory. Her work highlighted the effect the economy, law, trade, and population could have on the social problems of contemporary society. Other early feminist thinkers included Florence Nightingale (1820–1910), Jane Addams (1860–1935), Rosa Luxemburg (1871–1919), and Mary Wollstonecraft (1759–1797), who all promoted equality and activism long before women were receiving any real recognition. Wollstonecraft, for example, is now recognized as one of history's first feminists. She wrote *A Vindication of the Rights of Women* ([1792] 1972), which challenged the subjugation of women in marriage, contending that present-day marriage was a form of legal prostitution. Feminist scholarship has also included important contributions from outside sociology—for example, writings by French philosopher Simone de Beauvoir (1908–1986).

A common theme across many types of feminism is the view that the subjugation of women is a result of socio-economic and cultural forces. They reject the idea that men and women's biological differences justify their separate social roles and responsibilities. Though feminists differ in thinking about how they might achieve change, they are all committed to erasing women's continued social inequality. As well, they tend to agree that all personal life has a political side and that women's social experiences routinely differ from men's. They also agree that patriarchy—or male control—structures the way most societies work. Both the public and private spheres of life are *gendered* (that is, unequal for men and women). And, because of different experiences and differences in power, women and men view the world differently.

LGBTQ+ An acronym referring to people who identify as lesbian, gay, bisexual, trans, queer/questioning. The + indicates that the acronym can encompass many other identities, such as Two-Spirit, intersex, pansexual, and so on. The LGBTQ+ community can encompass people who have diverse experiences of disadvantages.

intersectionality The interaction or combination of social factors that makes inequality more than the result of additive disadvantages, resulting in disadvantages that combine in unique ways.

There are three other features that characterize feminist research. First, feminists pay significant attention to *the gendering of experiences.* This is the idea that certain experiences are specifically female or male and cannot be automatically generalized to both sexes. For example, divorce is a gendered experience because men and women experience it differently: For women, it often represents a big drop in household income and in childcare support; for men, it often represents a small drop in household income and a large drop in household expenses. A second common concern is *the problem of victimization,* since women are often made the victims of crime, abuse, and discrimination.

Increasingly, different groups of feminist thinkers are interested in the experiences of other victimized groups like racialized people, the poor, and **LGBTQ+** peoples.

Following from this, some feminists are especially interested in **intersectionality**. We will have more to say about intersectionality and the related concept of interlocking disadvantages shortly.

Marx and Weber: Two Main Approaches to the Struggle for Power

Karl Marx and Max Weber—two of the founders of sociology—were both concerned with the conflicts arising out of unequal class relations. They were both writing a century or more ago, in a period when the power of early capitalists was almost uncontrolled. This privileged capitalist class exploited the working class to gain high profits and social dominance. Marx and Weber had somewhat different analyses of the situation and proposed different solutions to address it.

Marx

Karl Marx was the first theorist to place social class at the forefront of sociological thinking. Because of his politically radical views, he had to move around, first from Germany to Paris, and then from Paris to London. In Paris, he met his lifelong collaborator, Friedrich

Engels (1820–1895). In London, he and Engels co-authored their famous text *The Communist Manifesto* ([1848] 2017), a public declaration of political principles. This work offers a brief but compelling theory of history that argues capitalism carries the seeds of its own destruction. Marx proposed that class conflict drove the history of humanity. As societies moved from one form of production (or economic organization) to another and the means of production and their ownership changed, the classes in control also changed.

For example, Marxist theorist Karl Wittfogel (1896–1988) pointed out in *Oriental Despotism* (1957) that people who farm large rice paddies depend completely on irrigation systems. Often, in rice-based societies, "despots" controlled the irrigation systems and the water flowing through them. By controlling the means of production, they could control society. In contrast, in capitalist industrial societies, people who own and control factories (the source of jobs) and banks (the source of credit) make up the ruling class. In these societies, controlling the means of production means controlling the society. As the means of production change, so too do the tactics of the ruling class.

Marx identified two key classes in a capitalist industrial society: the capitalists (or the **bourgeoisie**) and the workers (the **proletariat**). The bourgeoisie own the means of production, and the proletariat must sell the bourgeoisie their labour to survive.

bourgeoisie Those who own and control the means of production in a capitalist society.

proletariat People who exchange their labour for wages and work for the bourgeoisie in a capitalist society.

In the simplest model of Marxism, capitalist society is built on a conflict between the bourgeoisie (or capitalists) and the proletariat (or working class). This binary—consisting of the "haves" and "have-nots" of society—is fundamental to all social relations and all class conflict. That is because these two classes have opposing interests and are therefore permanently locked in conflict. At the same time, the two groups are interdependent, since each gains at the expense of the other. The relationship between the bourgeoisie and the proletariat is, therefore, paradoxical. Though they need each other, they permanently oppose each other.

◆ In Their Own Words ◆

From Marx and Engels's The Communist Manifesto *(1848):*

> The bourgeoisie cannot exist without constantly revolutionising the instruments of production, and thereby the relations of production, and with them the whole relations of society. Conservation of the old modes of production in unaltered form, was, on the contrary, the first condition of existence for all earlier industrial classes. Constant revolutionising of production, uninterrupted disturbance of all social conditions, everlasting uncertainty and agitation distinguish the bourgeois epoch from all earlier ones. All fixed, fast-frozen relations, with their train of ancient and venerable prejudices and opinions, are swept away, all new-formed ones become antiquated before they can ossify. All that is solid melts into air, all that is holy is profaned, and man is at last compelled to face with sober senses his real conditions of life, and his relations with his kind.

What defines members of the bourgeoisie is their ownership of the means of production—which, in turn, gives them power to exploit the proletariat. The proletariat do not have the capital needed to own the means of production. That means they must sell to the bourgeoisie the only thing they *do* have: their time or labour power. They do so to earn the wages that allow them to survive. The bourgeoisie, in turn, buy the workers' time and labour power. They gain profits both from the goods and services that workers produce and by keeping prices high and wages (and other costs of production) as low as possible. And by ensuring a **Reserve Army of Labour** (a population of unemployed people desperate for work), their workers will accept low wages and poor working conditions upon threat of replacement.

Reserve Army of Labour Marx and Engels's term for a pool of unemployed people seeking work.

It is this exploitative work relationship that stands at the centre of capitalism and produces what Marx considered two of its central properties: exploitation and alienation.

Exploitation by the bourgeoisie involves three principles, elaborated by Eric Olin Wright (1997, p. 10). First, according to the *inverse interdependence principle*, the economic well-being of capitalists demands the economic deprivation and exploitation of workers. Second, according to the *exclusion principle*, capitalists must keep pressure on workers by excluding them from access to benefits and productive resources. They might make it difficult for them to get the capital necessary to set up their own businesses, for example. It may even mean limiting their access to jobs, housing, and other fundamental needs. Third, according to the *appropriation principle*, capitalists take advantage of the workers by buying their labour for a fraction of its real value.

This exploitation does not come without a cost. Low wages, high prices, and poor working conditions are all casualties of capitalism that harm the health and well-being of workers. To counter this, Marx proposes that workers will inevitably fight back and use every possible means to improve their wages, working conditions, and job security. To do all this, they will use unions, co-operatives, legislation, and other avenues. Under some conditions, they will form political parties or even revolutionary groups. This, then, is the class struggle under capitalism—a struggle that is unavoidable and never-ending and, according to Marx, is the driving force of history.

Clearly, people with the same relation to the means of production have an interest in banding together. Proletarians do so to protect their wages and working conditions, and capitalists do so to protect their profit, authority, and control. But such co-operative action is far from certain; rather, it calls for planning and coordination. Marx did not put much faith in significant change through peaceful methods, such as unionization and the ballot box. He sought a much more radical approach, favouring the outright elimination of capitalism via revolutionary action. For this united action to happen, however, people must develop **class consciousness**.

class consciousness An ability to see what is in the best interests of one's social class.

false consciousness An inability to see what is in the best interest for one's class, compounded by an erroneous belief that may hinder change, supporting the status quo.

Many forces prevent workers from mobilizing. For example, they may be under the influence of **false consciousness** and led astray by society's *dominant ideology*. Capitalists promote this dominant ideology to keep workers in line. It makes workers think they are powerless to organize against the capitalists. It also might make them think they are to blame for their economic condition, or that they have no right to demand higher wages and more job security. In the end, these barriers to class consciousness make it difficult for workers to mobilize toward Marx's goal of a violent rebellion against the capitalists.

Marx's theory of class conflict continues to be instrumental to studying social inequality because it provides us with a snapshot of the key contenders for social power.

However, as mentioned earlier, more complex forms of social organization call for more complex types of theories. That is where Max Weber, writing a generation after Marx, comes in.

Weber

Marx and Weber held many similar views about social class and its relation to work and workplaces. However, Weber understood power differently from Marx. He focused on the distribution of power among classes, rather than its role in the exploitation of one class by another. The two also differed on how they defined class. Marx had viewed classes as mainly economic groups defined by their relation to the means of production. Weber, by contrast, viewed classes as only one of many groups in society that contend for power. Economic class position, for Weber, depends on a person's *market position*. For Weber, that is their economic power in a given market—such as, for example, the price they could command for their labour in the labour market.

Weber thought people could gain power in various ways, only one of which was owning the means of production. From this belief, Weber distinguished economic class from two other sources of power: *parties* and *status groups*. According to Weber, *parties* are associations and organizations that give people non-economic power and influence. These include the familiar political parties of our own day. They may also include other (larger and vaguer) political formations, such as political lobbies and professional associations. By *status groups*, Weber means sets of people who share a social position in society, with a common degree of prestige, esteem, and honour. These status groups may organize around any one of many shared features, including education, religion, ethnicity, region, or even race. Their chief defining feature is that they practise exclusion to preserve the boundaries between their own group and others.

Weber's parties and status groups, in short, are related to social class but different from class. Like social class, they provide members with access to power but do so in different ways. Marx proposed that people could exercise power only by controlling the means of production. However, Weber proposed that people could gain power by entering influential parties and high-status groups. In this way, they could gain power through their social position, regardless of whether they also wielded economic control. People in such positions of power—for example, president or prime minister—would be able to dominate others, just like the capitalists Marx described.

To summarize, Marx provided the foundations of class analysis on which Weber built his own analyses of power and class. However, the modern sociological conception of social class is based more on Weber's theorizing than on Marx's, largely because Weber's is more inclusive. Further, Marx's portrayal of class cannot capture the modern complexity of class relations.

Sociologist Eric Olin Wright lists several reasons why Marx's portrayal of class relations is too simple. First, today it is no longer necessary to own a business to control the means of production. It is only necessary to manage the organization or serve on its board of directors. Second, today's working class is international because of multinational ownership and global competition. Marx would have seen the "globalization" of work as an advanced version of economic imperialism, since it imposes capitalist practices on other countries. The globalization of work has made the mass mobilization of workers in any given country much more difficult. This is because bosses can always ship the jobs overseas if the workers demand higher wages or more job security.

As a result, the "reserve army of the unemployed" is vastly larger today than it was a century ago. This makes unemployment a significantly more powerful tool for the capitalist class to use during times of labour unrest. This globalization of work also means that developing countries play an increasingly larger role in shaping the economic well-being of Canadians. This includes countries like Brazil, Russia, India, and China. Finally, the internationalization of both class differences and the capitalist division of labour has marked gender elements. Thus, globalization affects the relations between men and women.

So, as we see from this brief examination of Weber's thinking, historical context is enormously important for understanding theories of inequality. That said, both left many questions unanswered. Neither Marx nor Weber offered a thorough understanding of the role of ideology in the maintenance of social inequality. Neither offered a clear sense of how race relations might connect with class relations. Nor did either offer us an understanding of the role of advertising and consumer behaviour as new "opiates of the masses," deadening discontent with inequality. To deal with these issues, we needed to await the arrival of the neo-Marxists and the neo-Weberians. These were theorists who, in the twentieth century and afterward, built on the theories of Marx and Weber and introduced new concepts, new problems, and new solutions.

Neo-Marxism and Neo-Weberianism

We call the theorists who have adapted and developed the theories of Marx and Weber, respectively, neo-Marxists and neo-Weberians. That said, many people disagree about precisely which theorists belong in which category. Some theorists fall into a combination of both categories, while others fall distinctly within neo-Marxist or neo-Weberian thought.

Critical Theory

Let's begin with members of the Frankfurt School of sociology. People typically classify these Frankfurt School theorists as neo-Marxist because they build on essential Marxian ideas about class relations.

This school's "critical theorists" focused on how mass consumerism and mass culture promote capitalist ideals. The theorists included Theodor Adorno (1903–1969), Herbert Marcuse (1898–1979), and Walter Benjamin (1892–1940). Collectively, they viewed culture as part of class conflict in society—a means that powerful social groups use to preserve their dominance. Scholars associated with the Frankfurt School of "critical theory" thought that Marx's ideas had become too closely tied to the workings of communist parties.

critical theory An analysis of politics and society, based in Marxian theory, that focuses on the historical and ideological forces that influence culture and human behaviour.

positivism A belief that social truths can be discovered through the application of scientific methods of research.

In response to this politicization of theory, they developed a brand of Marxist theory—**critical theory**—that was less doctrinaire and more wide-ranging. Critical theory is a philosophical analysis of culture that rejects the possibility of a value-free social science. Instead, it addresses the historical and ideological forces that influence culture and human behaviour.

Critical theory's interpretation of Marxism wasn't entirely faithful to the original. The traditional version of Marxism was steeped in nineteenth-century **positivism**. This outlook supported the effort to use scientific methods to develop general "laws" about society. By contrast, critical theory under the Frankfurt School took a more subjective, less dogmatic approach to understanding society and thus bringing about change. Max Horkheimer (1895–1973), for example, looked past the revisionist, Communist Party interpretations of Marxism to explore Marx's original concerns. Other critical theorists introduced insights from Freud and from mysticism. Doing so led them to believe that a less scientific approach was necessary for understanding the modern world.

In particular, this approach focused on the contending interpretations of social life. It also called attention to the efforts of people in power to promote certain preferred ideas—dominant ideologies—to positions of prime importance. As we will see in the chapters that follow, these dominant ideologies harm all vulnerable people. Sometimes, the vulnerable even accept the victim-blaming images of these ideologies as correct, at their own cost. To correct problems of inequality in a society, we need to understand these ideologies and the conditions under which people accept or reject them.

Horkheimer, like Weber, thought the job of sociology was to explain and interpret social reality, not to predict the future using positivist models. He thought that observations and theories about society can never be fully objective, since ideologies are bound to influence researchers too. As a result, the researcher's "finding" is likely to confirm what they already believe to be true. The only clear way out of this dilemma is to admit one's goals and biases as openly as possible.

The World System

Another key thinker in the neo-Marxist tradition is Immanuel Wallerstein (1930–2019). According to Wallerstein, global inequality began many centuries ago and has persisted (mostly) in its present form for half a millennium. Wallerstein argues that today's global inequality is not the fault of poorer nations (that is, they are not poor because they have faulty values). Rather, he argued a capitalist world order keeps these nations in continuous poverty.

According to Wallerstein, the present capitalist world economy began in the late fifteenth century during economic and demographic crises in Europe. Wallerstein found that, between 1300–1450, all Europe's economies had begun to shrink for both demographic and climatological reasons. Chief among the causes was the Black Death, which killed roughly one-quarter of Europe's population.

A long economic downturn encouraged European merchants to seek wealth through long-distance trade, which gradually produced a significant buildup of capital (especially in Italy, Spain, and Holland). The main seafaring countries became wealthier and started to dominate other countries. Gradually, the capitalist world absorbed mini-systems, world empires, and competing economies by waging and winning wars against less powerful countries.

The emerging *core* nations of this "world system" had strong central governments, vast bureaucracies, and huge mercenary armies. They helped local capitalists gain control over international commerce and extract profits from their trade. They had (and still have) the economic and military power to enforce different rates of exchange between the core and the periphery.

Peripheral nations, for their part, lack strong central governments or are controlled by other states. They typically export raw materials to core nations and rely on coercive labour practices (such as slavery) to do this efficiently. Core regions use their power to exploit peripheral regions for cheap labour, raw materials, and agricultural production. Unequal trade relations allow core nations to pay significantly less for raw materials than they are worth. Through these unequal trade arrangements, core nations seize much of the surplus capital produced by periphery nations.

The Manufacturing of Consent

We noted earlier that ruling classes seek to impose their dominant ideologies on the people they rule. In doing so, they are more easily able to tame and control the members of society we describe in this book. But precisely how do they go about doing this? How do they make victimized people consent to their own victimization? How, in other words, do they "manufacture" this consent?

An influential neo-Marxist who addressed this question is the linguist and social theorist Noam Chomsky (b. 1928). Besides studying capital, resources, and trade, neo-Marxists also study language and media because of the way both influence and foster unequal power relations. This is obvious in Chomsky's book *Manufacturing Consent*, co-authored with Edward Herman (Herman and Chomsky 1988). Here, the authors propose the American mass media are powerful ideological institutions. They rely on self-censorship to produce propaganda supporting the capitalist economic system. This is because media organizations are huge, privately owned companies whose profitability needs massive advertising revenue. This means advertisers exercise control over media content. The media will therefore reflect advertisers' prejudices and interests, which often align with those of the capitalist class.

Simultaneously, large bureaucracies of the powerful—including government and business—provide and, in effect, produce the news content. They become "routine" news sources with privileged access to publication. The media are also subject to "flak" from powerful influence groups, such as privately subsidized think tanks. This may discourage the reporting of certain facts or opinions by raising the spectre of costly legal battles. Finally, certain political preoccupations provide excuses for the powerful to control, censor, and criticize anti-establishment news reporting. These preoccupations include anti-communism (before 1992) and the War on Terror (after 11 September 2001).

Neo-Weberian Approaches

Neo-Weberians, for their part, pay much more attention than neo-Marxists to non-class-based forms of power and inequality. For example, like Weber, they pay more attention to the role of race, gender, age, and social characteristics (other than class) that lead to dominance and submission. Given that racism and class and power inequality are linked, it's no wonder that Weber's theories grew to encompass analyses of race patterns.

Racialization

Take the case of race as an important variable in the neo-Weberian canon. For many years, simple, essentialist ideas about race prevailed in Western societies, supported by what we now call "scientific racism." Scientific racism is the pseudo-scientific belief in the existence and significance of racial categories and a hierarchy of superior and inferior races. It employed anthropology to classify human populations into physically distinct human races. The myth of "race" has, over the years, done an enormous amount of human and social harm.

Central to a neo-Weberian analysis of this problem is the idea of **racialization**: the differentiation or categorization of people according to their believed race or ethnicity. We will discuss racialization further in Chapter 2 and discuss its consequences throughout this book.

racialization The social processes of distinguishing or classifying people according to their believed race or ethnicity.

During the period of European colonial expansion (1870–1914), racialization was a powerful ideological tool. Politicians used it domestically and abroad as part of Britain's colonization of peripheral countries. In *Imperial Leather* (1995), neo-Weberian theorist Anne McClintock called the replacement of scientific racism within consumer capitalism "commodity racism." The ruling class used this commodity racism to mass market the "imperial spectacle" through advertisements and commodity kitsch.

According to McClintock, commodity racism appealed to people's belief in racial superiority and inferiority to sell products. For example, from the nineteenth century onward, Victorian soap advertisements equated soap with cleanliness and cleanliness with civilization. In turn, people equated civilization with whiteness, and whiteness with purity and virtue. Black people were used to represent a lack of cleanliness, civilization, purity, and virtue. White consumers saw the use of soap as daily demonstration of their evolutionary and racial superiority.

McClintock's analysis of Imperial Leather soap and the ways that goods can become ideological commodities shows the interconnection of different dimensions of social inequality. Imperial Leather served as a symbol of the moral difference between the colonial and colonized nation. Commodities like soap travelled between the metropolis and

Take a look at this advertisement from the late 1700s and the way white consumers saw the daily use of soap as a performance of evolutionary and racial superiority.

the colonies both as goods and signs (Jolly 2012). The colonial nation was clean, pure, and highly evolved, while the colonized nation was not. This difference justified the domination of one group by the other. In short, Imperial Leather had a hand in symbolizing and justifying class domination, colonial domination, racial domination, and sexual domination.

Critical Race Theory

critical race theory (CRT) A form of analysis that explores the way that beliefs about race organize all social structures.

Academics who focus on race, immigration, Indigenous Peoples, and related areas have tended to embrace the development of **critical race theory** (CRT). The thrust of CRT is that race is a performance—a social construction—rather than an innate quality. There are no meanings intrinsically attached to the colour of one's skin (James 2009); rather, people create "race" and racial inequality by imagining and performing the idea of racial differences. These ideas persist because they serve some and disadvantage others.

CRT is also concerned with the ways in which race is actively—and unproductively—ignored or erased. Certain liberal ideological concepts, including meritocracy, colour blindness, race neutrality, and multiculturalism, can actually serve to entrench racism more deeply, even if they claim to do the opposite. For example, many institutions declare themselves "colour blind" by claiming to ignore race in their decision-making processes when race does, in fact, play a role. This may occur when selecting applicants for jobs, mortgages, university admission, or scholarships. These institutions are letting race in when they're claiming not to, and they should strive *not* to let it in. Race as a biological classification is a myth, but race and racism are enduring social realities.

Despite anti-racism legislation, race still matters in our society (James 2009). In Canada, racialized people continue to face discrimination in employment, housing, education, healthcare, social services, and the legal system (Hardaway and McLoyd 2009; James 2009). In this sense, racism has become **institutionalized**. By this we mean it is deeply embedded within the power structures that dominate our society, creating patterns of social disadvantage.

insitutionalized When beliefs and behaviours are formally established in an organization and guide behaviour accordingly.

Racism is institutionalized in part because the past is hard to eradicate. Historically, the West used racist, exclusionary practices to gain advantage over people of colour throughout the world (Moshman 2007; Owen 2007). CRT seeks to challenge these practices. Despite important gains by the civil rights movement, CRT stresses that institutionalized racial oppression continues everywhere. It persists even though the blatant, unquestioned forms of racism from decades past are no longer as acceptable as they once were.

Notable Thinkers

Pierre Bourdieu

Pierre Bourdieu was born in 1930 in southwestern France. Bourdieu's early research examined the ways dominant culture preserves its power and privilege. In *Reproduction in Education, Society, and Culture* (1970), he argued the French educational system acts to reproduce the cultural divisions in society. Bourdieu's interest in the "learning of class" continued throughout his life. His central claim was that expertise and cultural competence are tools by which ruling classes transfer or reproduce social domination from one generation to the next.

Bourdieu notes that social class is "most marked in the ordinary choices of everyday existence, such as furniture, clothing, or cooking, which are particularly revealing of deep-rooted and long-standing dispositions because, lying outside the scope of the educational system, they have to be confronted, as it were, by naked taste." Further, "the strongest and most indelible mark of infant learning" would probably be in the tastes of food (Bourdieu [1979] 1984:77). Members of the ruling class teach their children aesthetic preferences to pass along class-based *cultural capital*, a resource that transfers class position across generations. Cultural capital includes "symbolic goods, especially those regarded as the attributes of excellence, . . . [as] the ideal weapon in strategies of distinction" (Bourdieu [1979] 1984:66).

In short, Bourdieu writes, "differences in cultural capital mark the differences between the classes . . . [Taste] functions as a sort of social orientation, a 'sense of one's place,' guiding the occupants of a given . . . social space towards the social positions adjusted to their properties, and towards the practices or goods which befit the occupants of that position" (Bourdieu [1979] 1984:65).

Source: Adapted from Scott 2006.

Pierre Bourdieu

We would include French social theorist Pierre Bourdieu (1930–2002) in the category of neo-Weberian theorists because he focuses on the role of symbols and non-financial capital in establishing social position. Unlike neo-Marxists, he does not see power as fully determined by class position. Even more important, he does not see class position as fully determined by ownership of the means of production. Because of the breadth and depth of his contributions to sociology, we treat Bourdieu's work separately from that of other neo-Weberians.

Bourdieu calls our attention to the powerful, class-based role of symbols in social life. Just as there is a "code" to understanding art, so too are there codes to understanding other aspects of life. They include knowing how to dress, how to talk, where to vacation, and so on. Each of these codes is part of a larger symbol system that is ideological, powerful, and controlling. They become tools that members of society use to understand and frame reality. The sharing of symbols and symbol systems help integrate society. At the same time, they distinguish us from one another and mark out the boundaries of different social classes.

To generalize, elites and dominant classes will proclaim and celebrate cultural objects (for example, beliefs and practices) that are closest to the dominant culture and its symbolic structures. Many symbol systems, including philosophical, judicial, or religious symbol systems, seem unrelated to the exercise of power. In the end, however, class conflict energizes every one of these systems.

Melissa Renwick/Toronto Star via Getty Images

This photo appeared in a 2015 *Toronto* Star article alongside the headline "Homeless to Harvard: Toronto dropout accepted to Ivy league school." If it were common for hard work to land a homeless young woman a spot at Harvard, would it make the news?

In "Forms of Capital," Bourdieu (1986) notes the existence of three types of capital: economic, cultural, and social. Bourdieu defined capital as "accumulated labour" that, when stolen by employers, turns into "social energy." Capital shapes the structure of our world socially, culturally, and economically.

cultural capital
Knowledge, material objects, and credentials that elevate status, distinguish one group from another, and perpetuate inequality.

social capital
Advantageous relationships that enable better access to key social and economic resources.

Cultural capital (learned expertise and competence, or "taste") includes all the symbols and practices that mark social distinctions. A person gains this capital by investing time into cultural communities. Bourdieu proposes that "cultural capital" signals class boundaries. It also reproduces class domination from one generation to the next. Members of the ruling class teach their children elegant taste preferences as a way of passing along class-based cultural capital. Embodied cultural capital includes human physiology—for example, good health and a healthy appearance. People gain **social capital** through membership in groups and social networks. Social networks form when people invest time into being with other group members. Important information and help flows through these social networks, helping to prop up the unequal advantages of the ruling elite. Finally, institutionalized capital includes the many credentials (degrees, certifications, and so on) one earns over a lifetime.

The unequal distribution of economic and cultural capital means that not only will there be social inequality that will be preserved, but also that there will be distinct class subcultures and lifestyles.

Sociological Approaches to Neoliberalism

In recent years, the term *neoliberalism* has been used in various ways and for various purposes. That said, people agree that neoliberalism refers to the deregulation of global markets, largely through the reduction of state power.

In a neoliberal society, the state rarely interferes with or regulates the economy. Politicians under neoliberalism ease controls, promote free trade and free enterprise, and assume that markets, working rationally, will provide the greatest good for the greatest number of people. Under this system, people (supposedly) have the freedom to seek to satisfy their private goals. In so doing, they (supposedly) create and contribute to prosperity for everyone. This view is most compatible with a functionalist approach to social organization, which (as we saw) highlights equilibrium, efficiency, and integration.

A neoliberal free market should assign prices, goods, and services more efficiently than any other method, including government planning. Central to this market system is the free choice of individuals. Ultimately, neoliberalism rests on the assumptions that humans can be economically rational and that free markets, running without state control, will enlarge human well-being.

In the Global North, neoliberalism became increasingly common and supported about forty years ago. Since then, it has shaped capitalism throughout the world. In the early twentieth century, the Great Depression shook beliefs in the free market. Many of the world's economies came to rely heavily on central planning and government intervention to recover from unregulated capitalism. However, neoliberal ideas regained currency after World War II, during the so-called Cold War, which pitted Western capitalism against Soviet communism.

In the 1980s, market deregulation received strong support from Republican President Ronald Reagan in the United States and Conservative Prime Minister Margaret Thatcher in the United Kingdom. In Canada, there was similar support for neoliberalism. Then-Prime Minister Brian Mulroney deregulated financial services, energy, transport, and telecom, among other things. He also promoted the NAFTA agreement, which was a turning point in neoliberal policy in Canada. NAFTA opened Canada to US capital far more effectively than it opened US markets to Canadian manufacturers. (See, for example, www.cfr.org/backgrounder/nafta-and-usmca-weighing-impact-north-american-trade.) Later, Conservative Prime Minister Stephen Harper's government brought market deregulation back to federal Canadian politics.

Internationally, neoliberal practices have been even more dramatic. Deregulatory reform plans were imposed on countries that sought money from the International Monetary Fund or the World Bank. These plans kept many peripheral countries poor or made them poorer.

An important assumption behind this neoliberal approach is that the market is politically neutral. Some claim that this neutrality requires a weakening of the state. They claim this is a sure result of globalization and the rise of vast multinational corporations, some of whose annual revenue exceeds the gross domestic product of most countries in the world. There is no doubt that states become less important as multinational organizations become better able to work freely across borders. Some neoliberals would even propose that even democracy is irrational, because it threatens the profitability of the market. By this reckoning, rulers must limit democracy to keep economic prosperity safe from interference from above (the state) or below (the masses). Neoliberal policies lessen the role of the state in economic activity by privatizing ownership and deregulating economic transactions.

Underlying this way of thinking is an economic Darwinism. It assumes the greatest good will *automatically* arise through survival of the fittest: the workings of an uninhibited marketplace. In this imaginary economic world, productive units will struggle for survival and transcendence. The less effective or efficient units will fail and become obsolete. The best will triumph and remain in place unchallenged because no other economic system will prove to be more productive. Liberal capitalism and embracing a free marketplace will represent the "end of history" in the sense there will be nothing more to strive for. Indeed, some neoliberals propose that, with the fall of Russian communism, we have already come to the "end of history" (see Fukuyama 2004).

In these respects, we can see a connection between neoliberalism and beliefs in a so-called "meritocratic society." The meritocratic belief that people succeed because they *deserve* to succeed helps to perpetuate inequality in modern capitalist societies, Canada included.

The neoliberal ideas we have outlined so far have been attacked from various standpoints: legal, philosophical, sociological, and otherwise. The sociological perspective is that ideal markets have never existed and never will. Markets are usually not places where people can exercise their freedoms equally. Instead, markets let people with large amounts of wealth, power, and information use their resources to gain even more power, information, and wealth. And as we will see throughout this book, information (and unequal access to it) is an extraordinarily important source of class inequality.

The extension of "free" markets under neoliberal policies, whether national or international, was assumed to increase individual freedoms. Wealth would trickle down from the top to the bottom of the social class system, conservative economists asserted. In practice, however, income inequality has increased under Western neoliberalism. Jobs have been outsourced to low-income countries, and the world economy was brought to a near meltdown by the Wall Street collapse of 2008. Author William Blum (2004) noted correctly that "the poor, who must subsist on table scraps dropped by the rich, can best be served by giving the rich bigger meals."

For example, Oxfam has reported that wealth is becoming even more concentrated. In 2018, 26 people owned the same as the 3.8 billion people who make up the poorest half of humanity, down from 43 people the year before. The world's richest man, Jeff Bezos, owner of Amazon, saw his fortune increase to $112 billion. Just 1 per cent of his fortune is the equivalent to the whole health budget for Ethiopia, a country of 105 million people (Elliott 2019). Neoliberalism is an ideology aimed at increasing the power of people who are already powerful and wealthy. It is a way of legitimating inequality and protecting people who are already at the top of society. Governments achieve this goal by reducing oversight and control in the marketplace. Compare it to building a casino where the owners use stacked decks without any supervision or control. No wonder, then, the main result of neoliberalism since 1980 has been a worldwide increase in inequality, both between and within nation-states.

Conflict theory can best explain the progression of capitalism through neoliberal policy and ideology. According to conflict theory, capitalism is an inherently expansionist economic system. It is always looking for new markets and new, lower-cost labour and resources. Capitalists and capitalism are always looking to control and even conquer other societies. Capitalists want to manipulate markets, populations, and, if necessary, governments. Neoliberalism is the perfect means by which capitalists and capitalism can chase these goals.

Neoliberalism is the economic face of modern capitalism, but, as we have discussed, capitalism is also a system of world domination. The governments of leading capitalist nations have repeatedly supported aggressive economic or military intrusions into foreign countries. Of course, capitalism did not invent imperialism. Egyptian, Persian, Greek, and Roman empires existed thousands of years before capitalism emerged and had both imperial armies and colonial wars. However, the development of capitalism after 1800 intensified these colonial, imperialistic efforts because, as Marx pointed out, capitalism has a natural tendency to extend its reach. In fact, many consider present-day globalization as just another effort by multinational organizations to extend their control of wealth throughout the world by seeking ever-cheaper labour and resources and ever-larger markets. They even use war and espionage to do so, when necessary. No wonder, then, that many people view repeated American and Russian incursions into the Middle East as veiled efforts to capture oil deposits and oil transit routes. A prime example is the repeated invasion of Afghanistan.

In effect, then, applying the debate between conflict theorists and functionalists to neoliberalism is not actually about whether there is a hierarchy of regions and nations. Western capitalist societies dominate the markets of the world, though Russia, China, and India are quickly gaining power. Instead, conflict theorists and functionalists are divided about the nature of this global system. They are divided about whether it is good or bad and about the role of force versus choice in setting up the global order. Neoliberally minded functionalists would propose that inequality arises naturally through free-market relations. Conflict theorists would disagree, saying it results from the efforts of capitalists and multinational corporations.

Social Justice

Another important idea in the study of inequality is *social justice*. Social justice refers to the fair and just treatment of members of society. This treatment includes a fair distribution of wealth, an equal opportunity for personal activity, and a justifiable sharing of social privilege. Social justice concerns actions in both the public and political spheres, as well as private individuals' and organizations' (that is, businesses') actions.

Concern for social justice grows out of the notion that all members of society have a natural right to satisfy certain basic needs. For example, they have the right to satisfy their needs for food, shelter, and safety. Over time, this list has grown to include the rights to political representation, a living wage, and unbiased treatment by the institutions of law and order. By this reckoning, it is the role of government to ensure the provision of these needed things.

Some governments have this idea woven into their constitutions. The United States, for example, proclaims it is the federal government's responsibility to ensure citizens' right to life, liberty, and the pursuit of happiness. However, this thinking did not influence the Canadian Constitution, which legislators wrote a century later than the American Constitution. As a result, we do not find such rights guaranteed in the British North America (BNA) Act of 1867. The BNA Act asserts only that the state shall provide peace, order, and good government.

In fact, it was not until 1982 that the Canadian Charter of Rights and Freedoms (a part of the Constitution added in 1982) guaranteed Canadians' basic rights and freedoms. The rights protected in this way are essential to preserving Canada as a free and democratic country. The Charter applies to all governments: federal, provincial, and territorial.

The Charter forms the first part of the Constitution Act, 1982 and guarantees seven distinct categories of political and civil rights to Canadian citizens: fundamental freedoms, democratic rights, language rights, mobility rights, minority language educational rights, legal rights, and equality rights. So, for example, the Charter prevents state institutions from discriminating against people because of sex, gender, race, age, disability, or other named grounds.

The adoption of the Charter expanded the scope of judicial review, giving courts and judges more policymaking importance than they previously had. In the last 35 years, this has allowed the courts to strike down federal and provincial statutes and regulations that treated people unfairly in the public realm. In this way, it has helped to change the way people try to ensure fair treatment under the law.

However, the Charter does not always prevent private businesses from discriminating against women, racial minorities, or sexual minorities. Nor does the Charter consider poverty or economic inequality to be, fundamentally, matters of state policymaking. Thus, the Charter does not serve as a basis for challenging laws that increase poverty or economic inequality. For example, the current laws would not think it was discriminatory for teachers to want doctor's notes from students who miss tests. Yet this practice unduly penalizes poor students, since doctors usually charge a fee for providing such notes.

Thus, social justice discussions intersect with but lie outside of traditional Marxist discussions of social class and traditional Weberian discussions of power. Social justice discussions in Canada and elsewhere are related to what people have called *identity politics*. Identity politics are concerned with social distinctions that are not economic in origin, though they may have economic consequences. They focus mainly on women, racial groups, sexual minorities, older adults, people with disabilities, immigrants, and other groups. Proponents of identity politics–based social justice are less concerned about redistributing wealth across the entire population, as Marxists are, than they are about removing discrimination against social minorities. Poverty and social inequality concerns are part of the social justice debate. However, they are only a small part, compared with issues of equal treatment, equal access, and respectful treatment.

Social justice discussions are very much concerned with fairness: with judging in ways that are unbiased and free from discrimination. In this sense, fairness is a type of equality that one often refers to as *equity*. Equity does not mean that everyone gets the same thing, however. It means that people, mostly, get what they need. Thus, the social justice viewpoint asserts that everyone deserves equal economic, political, and social rights and opportunities, but does not assert that *complete* equality of wealth, power, and status will result.

It is important to note that social inequality is about more than fairness and what some have called *distributive justice*. True, inequality and injustice are unfair, as Rousseau clearly pointed out 250 years ago. However, even a privilege that is earned meritoriously—for example, through a life-saving invention or brilliant movie career—may harm others if it deprives them of health, safety, dignity, and decent life chances. So equality is more than fairness; but we do not have space here to review the lengthy debates about what is "fair" and what is "equal."

Similarly, it is important to note that inequality is not the same as poverty. A society can be (relatively) equal and rich, like Norway, or unequal and rich, like the United States. Indeed, the experience of inequality may be especially painful in a society that is rich, even if the people experiencing inequality are not themselves poor. Inequality can shorten your lifespan, even if you have a secure, comfortable job in a rich country. This is the lesson of the so-called Whitehall Studies, which we will discuss later in the book.

Nonetheless, as we will see, social justice matters. A socially just society is a society that creates institutions and passes laws that treat people in a just, fair manner. This attention to fairness promotes a fair distribution of economic resources, sometimes called *distributive justice*. It also promotes respect for people's rights (sometimes called *rights-based justice*) and respect for morally acceptable laws (sometimes called *legal justice*). A society with these qualities will not be equal. However, it will come closer to an equitable distribution of wealth and power than Canada currently does.

Typically, societies with strong social justice practices usually have less economic and political inequality than other, similar countries. A strong social safety net, strong protections against discrimination, and well-funded public institutions all contribute to greater equality, as measured (for example) by the Gini index of income equality. A statistical representation of income inequality between the rich and the poor, the **Gini index** expresses inequality on a scale of 0 to 1, with 1 being perfect inequality (for example, if there are 100 people and $100, one person has the whole $100) and 0 being perfect equality (if there are 100 people and $100, everyone has $1).

Gini index The statistical representation of income inequality between the rich and the poor. It expresses inequality on a scale of 0 to 1, with 1 being perfect (or complete) inequality and 0 being perfect equality.

Using the Gini index, we find that Scandinavian countries like Norway, Sweden, Denmark, Finland, and Iceland do better than Canada, the United Kingdom, and the United States. Typically, the Gini index ranges between .25 and .55 for most countries of the world, with the higher-income countries (for example, the Nordic countries) scoring toward the lower (less unequal) end and lower-income countries (as well as the United States, United Kingdom, and Israel) scoring toward the higher (more unequal) end.

The Gini index made it possible for social researchers everywhere to accurately and precisely measure income inequality (as well as wealth inequality) in the same, rigorous way. This, in turn, has made it possible for researchers to compare countries to see which have higher and lower levels of inequality. And it has made it possible to track variations in income inequality over the course of time, as a consequence of other changes in the society. Regrettably there are no measures in the Gini index for measuring gender inequality, racial inequality, or other social inequalities.

One defining feature of the social justice approach to inequality is the emphasis it places on social construction—the imagining and performance of social differences. They oppose the so-called "essentialist" position, which holds that differences between men and women, white people and people of colour, and young people and older people (and so on) are natural, fundamental, important, and inescapable. Often, essentialists claim these differences are rooted in genetics and influence intelligence, rationality, and even morality.

By contrast, theorists in the social constructionist tradition assert that most social inequalities rest on differences that are socially constructed. They are not "natural"; rather, people invent and share them through social interaction. The differences that lead to inequality are not real but imagined. If they are real (for example, some bodies can give birth and some cannot), they are less consequential than people believe. As well, they may not be relevant to the aspects of social life people apply them to. Social constructionists also take relativist positions on differences between cultures. They reject social evolutionary views that certain cultures are superior to others or that certain social practices survive for evolutionary reasons.

Some people have misunderstood, or even ridiculed, social justice in present-day life. Yet social justice is linked to social equality, so we must discuss it. Social justice theorists think that sociology should reveal the underlying biases people hold about various minority or powerless groups, and we will try to do so. The job of the sociologist is to show how laws, programs, and beliefs are biased and support and promote the interests of more powerful, advantaged groups in society.

Intersectionality and Interlocking Disadvantages

Another important but often misunderstood idea in the study of social inequality is intersectionality. The theory of intersectionality recognizes that one person may face several different types of inequality that interact and influence one another in interesting ways (Choo and Ferree 2010:133). As we will see, people often fall into more than one marginalized social category. In this way, they embody what Dorothy Smith (1990) refers to as "multiple standpoints" and experience multiple kinds of social inequality.

While many Black feminist scholars had previously considered the overlapping experience of race, class, and gender, legal scholar Kimberlé Crenshaw coined the term *intersectionality* in the late 1980s while discussing the occupational implications of being both Black and a woman (Carbado 2013:811). Crenshaw had stumbled on an especially interesting legal case in which a Black woman, denied a job at an automobile plant, sued the company for discrimination. The company argued that it couldn't possibly be sexist, since they had white women working in the secretary pool. Likewise, it couldn't possibly be racist, since it had Black men working on the assembly line.

Judges dismissed the case, and that's how the term intersectionality was born. Crenshaw (1991) noted that, in this case and elsewhere, Black women were often the victims of two systems of oppression: racism and sexism. She proposed it was impossible to disentangle one type of oppression from the other, since race and gender oppression intersect in Black women. Black women experience them simultaneously, so they influence one another and are inextricably tied. We cannot understand the lives of Black women simply by understanding the lives of women (on the one hand) and Black people (on the other hand). And historically, feminist movements had underplayed or overlooked this complex experience of oppression.

Intersectionality does not work by addition; rather, it works by multiplication (Choo and Ferree 2010:135). Disadvantaging identity characteristics overlap, interact, and intersect. The intersectional approach views each person's experience of discrimination as nearly unique. That's because each life contains a nearly unique combination of social advantages and disadvantages (Lindsay 2009:8; Choo and Ferree 2010:136).

Since Crenshaw, intersectionality has come to have much broader applications (Carbado 2013:812; Hancock 2007:249). Adherents of this approach note that the identity of every individual is shaped by the intersection of multiple dimensions. People don't fit perfectly into any single identity group. Similarly, no single dimension of identity eclipses all the others (Crenshaw 1991:1299, Lindsay 2009:9). Just because an individual is a man, for example, does not mean that he has all the same experiences or sees the world in the same way as all other men do. Nor does it mean that advantages because of being a man will outweigh disadvantages that result from poverty, racial discrimination, or physical disability.

Three decades after coining the term intersectionality, Kimberlé Crenshaw (2015) reflected on how the term is used today:

> Intersectionality is an analytic sensibility, a way of thinking about identity and its relationship to power. Originally articulated on behalf of black women, the term brought to light the invisibility of many constituents within groups that claim them as members, but often fail to represent them. Intersectional erasures are not exclusive to black women. People of color within LGBTQ movements; girls of color in the fight against the school-to-prison pipeline; women within immigration movements; trans women within feminist movements; and people with disabilities fighting police abuse—all face vulnerabilities that reflect the intersections of racism, sexism, class oppression, transphobia, able-ism and more. Intersectionality has given many advocates a way to frame their circumstances and to fight for their visibility and inclusion.

While the term intersectionality can—and does—frame multiple circumstances, as Crenshaw points out, some feel it should be reserved for its original purpose: to describe the experiences of Black women who so often stand at the intersection of race *and* gender-based oppression. Therefore, we will use the term for this specific context only. For all other cases in which oppression is amplified or compounded by multiple social identities, we will instead use the term **interlocking disadvantages**, with thanks to Crenshaw who offered us a theoretical doorway into the ways in which identity characteristics overlap and intersect.

interlocking disadvantages The ways in which multiple identity characteristics can overlap and intersect to worsen life chances.

Take a classic theoretical example: Imagine you are a working-class person with a particular relationship to the means of production. That does not mean you will have the same experiences or see the world in the same way as all other working-class people. This helps explain why, historically, the working class has had such a hard time developing class consciousness. It would also help explain why other disadvantaged groups (for example, women) have had such a difficult time sharing and mobilizing a shared (feminist) consciousness.

In sum, intersectionality helps us avoid oversimplified generalizations (Nash 2008:5). One can never know what it is like to be only a woman, or only a person of colour, or only a low-income person. That's because no one can ever disentangle these identities from all the other "parts" that make up a person. However, we can use intersectional approaches to try to gain a better understanding of what it may be like to be a white, middle-class teenager, or a Black, wealthy grandfather.

Kathy Davis (2008) proposes that intersectionality is a "buzzword," the implications of which have both positive and negative aspects: "Paradoxically, it is precisely the concept's alleged weaknesses—its ambiguity and open-endedness—that were the secrets to its success and, more generally, make it a good feminist theory." Non-feminist sociologists might contest this view, though we will not do so. We will note, however, that this ambiguity and open-endedness produce an organizational problem for the present book. Consider the reasons.

Given there are so many unique combinations to explore, Crenshaw proposes that identity politics on their own are far from fruitful. Considering only a single, one-dimensional category means ignoring the intersections between that category and others (Crenshaw 1991:1242). Social justice, identity politics, and intersectionality are often linked, but they are distinct. Each idea does a separate theoretical job. However, in practice, intersectionality has dominated debate, serving to reframe gender and racial politics in the Global North.

For example, intersectionalists have criticized mainstream feminism for thinking all women worldwide can band together to protest sexism and oppression. Such an assumption relies on the false belief that women all have the same values, beliefs, perspectives, and experiences of oppression (Longino 1993). This approach fails to address how being Black, trans, or disabled may change one's experience of being a woman. Similarly, it fails to address how being a woman may change one's experience of being rich or poor (Geerts and Van Der Tuin 2013:173). Accounting for these multiple, intersecting dimensions of experience creates more nuanced pictures of how people live and experience social inequality.

Intersectionality implies a new way of looking at social inequality. It also implies a different approach to inequality, using what Canadian sociologist Dorothy Smith (1990) called "standpoint theory." This theory implies that each individual experiences the world in a subjective way, largely rooted in their gender, race, class, or other positions of disadvantage. In short, a person's experience depends on their unique combination of social categories.

But this simple idea poses a serious problem. If this theory is valid, how can we even talk about general ideas such as "class inequality" or "gender inequality"? It is almost impossible to map out every different combination of social difference. Treating every case as unique would lead to a nearly endless expansion of categories (Davis 2008:77; Geerts and Van Der Tuin 2013:172).

Just consider the math involved. Imagine there are eight categories of inequality, and each category has only two values: advantaged or disadvantaged. The number of possible combinations is $2^8 = 256$ different types of social experience to consider. No book can talk about so many different types of experience; for one thing, the resulting book would be thousands of pages long. So, to talk effectively about social inequality, we must limit and organize our thoughts more simply. That is why we organize this book around a set of different situations and populations. We isolate disadvantages one at a time.

In each chapter, we look at a single problem of unequal access as experienced by eight (or more) disadvantaged populations. This organizing principle is only a convenience. In real life, inequality is much more complicated. Consider, as an example, caregivers, almost all of whom are women, who immigrate to Canada from the Philippines. What these women show especially well is that women are not a homogenous group with identical experiences. Many caregivers are racialized immigrants who live with and take orders from other women—most often wealthy, Canadian-born, white women. In this case, a privileged woman—the employer—may even abuse her position of power to display (and enjoy) inequality.

How does a paid caregiver see the world compared with how her boss sees it? The perspective of a live-in caregiver is especially useful, given her unique circumstance. She is very much outside the dominant, privileged group and marginalized because of her race, class, and gender. However, she lives within a well-off household and is privy to her employers' private lives. So she can gain an intimate understanding of their experiences. People sometimes refer to this as the "outsider within" position (Wood 2005).

Circumstance—for example, living in someone else's house or someone else's country—also makes a difference. It was Donna Haraway who called our attention to the importance of circumstance as something that "situates" all knowledge in a concrete set of relations. Haraway (1988) suggested that our understanding of objectivity is deeply flawed, since we view it as an unbiased perspective. In fact, it is not unbiased. What most people consider to be objective is subjective—a picture of the world from their own perspective. Many of the views that we think of as neutral or unbiased belong to (and favour) white, upper-middle-class, heterosexual men.

The dominant social groups create what Haraway (1988:578) calls "disembodied scientific objectivity." These groups put forward dominant perspectives, accounts, and ways of knowing things that come to pass as common sense. We can think of this perspective as a "view from nowhere" (Hinton 2014). In fact, however, particular opinions come from particular "types" of people: women, the elderly, queer people, Indigenous people, and so on. That is why we should tie opinions, views, and attitudes to the bodies of the people who propose them. Doing so will help us remember that they are subjective and biased.

Much more could be said about intersectionality, situated knowledge, and the biases we bring to our study of society. For example, given intersectionality's history, should it be reserved for describing the specific oppression of poor, racialized (particularly Black) women? When used in other contexts, does it make invisible the experiences of those it was designed to empower? In the pages that follow, we will strive to remain aware of multiple intersections and the biases we inevitably bring to understanding them. As we advance, we will remain aware of the social construction of stories we tell ourselves about inequality. We will also remain aware of the evidence we need to support or refute these accounts.

Closing Remarks

The goal of sociology today, just as it was two centuries ago, is to understand society and to use knowledge to improve it. We sociologists are concerned about all the social inequalities that harm people—especially those that do major harm to our health and quality of life. Often the government and other powerful agencies are doing too little to address these problems. So one job of sociologists is to issue a wake-up call.

Our goal in writing this book is to explain the roots of social inequality, the problems it causes, and how we can address these problems. For this task, it is important to explore facts and theories about how social problems develop. We must also consider how they are interrelated. After all, this bridge between private problems and public problems is at the heart of the sociological tradition.

As we will see, individual social institutions—families, the economy, government, education, and others—each contribute to the work of society. Often, as functionalists suggest, the cause of social problems is a failure of institutions to deal with significant inequalities during times of rapid change. And, as conflict theorists suggest, social inequalities are the key to understanding all social life. It is also important to recognize that social inequalities are changing all the time. For example, it is too soon to how how inequality in our society will be affected by the COVID-19 epidemic. However, we can be certain it will make inequality worse, by increasing the number of low- and middle-income people thrown out of work.

Few of you reading this book will become professional sociologists, but you are all potential consumers of sociological knowledge. As knowledgeable citizens and voters, we need to know how to frame social questions and review the relevant information about these questions. As members of a society, we need to understand the political initiatives that people in authority put before us. We need to know how to read and decode newspaper editorials, political claims, and ideological declarations.

Understanding the different theoretical approaches that are foundational to sociology and social inequality can help you think critically about all the inequalities discussed in this book. By extension, it can help you start questioning your life and the lives of people around you.

Test Your Knowledge

1. Define social inequalities. How are real inequalities different from sensed or imagined social inequalities?
2. What is the sociological imagination?
3. What is the difference between macro-level analysis and micro-level analysis?
4. Name a few criticisms we might level at neoliberalism and the neoliberal way of looking at inequality.
5. What is intersectionality and how does it strengthen our understanding of social inequality while making it seemingly more complicated?
6. Match the theoretical perspective with its main points:

Theoretical Perspectives	Main Points
Functionalism	a. Conflicting groups, classes, and individuals all oppose efforts of others to impose control, and often conflict intensifies.
Conflict theories	b. We learn gender inequalities through childhood learning and ideology.
Symbolic interactionism/ social constructionism	c. Elements in society are interconnected and interrelated by common values. Well-functioning societies need social cohesion and social control.
Feminist perspective	d. Society is a product of continuous face-to-face interactions. Accounts about social inequalities are socially constructed.

See the Answer Key online to check your answers.

Questions for Critical Thought

1. Think of a time you tried to justify something unfair that happened to you or a friend. Is there a different way you can account for what happened?
2. How did you spend yesterday? How might you have spent the day differently if you were twice as wealthy? If you were twice as poor?
3. The functional theory of stratification asserts that inequality is universal because it is necessary for the survival of society, and fear of poverty motivates people to work hard. Is there a better way we could motivate people to perform necessary, valuable work?
4. Think of three places where you could meet people who try to justify inequality. Where would these people be, how would they discuss inequality, and why might they talk about it in that way?

5. Can you think of a society, anywhere in the world, where meritocratic values—that is, where the highest value is placed on talent and hard work—are not the norm? What values do people in that society give the highest priority to instead?
6. Do you think you have an objective perspective on some social issues or aspects of your life? What topics do you think you're more likely to have a subjective perspective on?

Additional Resources

Recommended Readings

Ehrenreich, Barbara. 2011. *On (Not) Getting by in America*. New York: Picador. Journalist Barbara Ehrenreich set out to discover, firsthand, how anyone survives on a wage of $6 an hour. To find out, she took the cheapest lodgings she could find and accepted whatever jobs she was offered. What she reports is startling.

Grabb, Edward, Jeffrey Reitz, and Monica Hwang, eds. 2016. 6th ed. *Social Inequality in Canada: Dimensions of Disadvantage*. Toronto, ON: Oxford University Press. This book brings together articles on inequality written by experts in the field. It covers many dimensions of social disadvantage, explaining them and looking at their consequences.

Smith, Dorothy E. 2005. *Institutional Ethnography: A Sociology for People* (Gender Lens Series). Lanham, MD: AltaMira Press. This foundational text presents sociology from women's standpoints, and in doing so reveals how social relations of inequality always look different from the top and from the bottom of the power structure.

Stiglitz, Joseph. 2013. *The Price of Inequality: How Today's Divided Society Endangers Our Future*. New York: W.W. Norton & Company. Economist Joseph E. Stiglitz exposes the efforts of powerful elites to compound their wealth at the expense of the rest of society. In doing so, he examines the effect of inequality on the economy, the political system, and the system of justice.

Svallfors, Stefan. 2012. *Contested Welfare States: Welfare Attitudes in Europe and Beyond* (Studies in Social Inequality). Palo Alto, CA: Stanford University Press. Over recent decades, European welfare states have undergone profound restructuring. This book focuses on the link between individual welfare attitudes, institutional contexts, and structural variables.

Zawilski, Valerie. 2009. *Inequality in Canada: A Reader on the Intersections of Gender, Race and Class*. Toronto, ON: Oxford University Press. Written by Canadian experts on family, education, health, justice, labour, and global inequality, this book examines the variety of domains in which people experience inequality.

Recommended Websites

Canada Without Poverty

www.cwp-csp.ca

Canada Without Poverty is an organization dedicated to reducing poverty in Canada. The leaders of the organizations are people who have experienced, firsthand, the dangers of living in poverty.

Centre for Social Justice (CSJ)

www.socialjustice.org

CSJ is a group that focuses on research, education, and advocacy in hopes of reducing inequalities related to income, wealth, and power while improving security and peace.

Equality Trust

www.equalitytrust.org.uk

Equality Trust is a registered UK Charity founded by eminent social researchers Wilkinson and Pickett to collect, analyze, and deliver up-to-date international information about social inequality and its effects.

Parliament of Canada

www.ourcommons.ca/DocumentViewer/en/41-1/FINA/related-document/6079428

This website provides links to a variety of publications related to inequalities in Canada, including ones related to policy alternatives, services available, income inequalities, support for working parents, and employment services in Canada.

Recommended Films

Inequality for All. 2013. Produced by RADIUS-TWC. United States. *Inequality for All* is an award-winning documentary directed by Jacob Kornbluth that examines the growing income gap and its implications on the US economy as well as on democracy in that country.

Benoit Daoust/Shutterstock

2 Populations under Discussion

Learning Objectives

- To identify groups in Canada that are vulnerable to socio-economic disadvantages.
- To explain the ways in which these populations are vulnerable.
- To identify the ways in which these populations suffer from multiple interlocking disadvantages.
- To recognize that they should not be viewed as merely victims.
- To explain the ways that inequality is not unavoidable and normal.

Introduction

This chapter is about the people who belong to groups that we might call vulnerable, disadvantaged, or even (sometimes) victimized. They are people whose **life chances**—the chances they will gain wealth, power, or prestige—are lower than average, often dramatically. Their successes, often hard fought, will often be modest, even when measured against

life chances A term credited to Max Weber, referring to the opportunities people have to gain wealth, power, and prestige.

low goals. And they are people who often have to overcome obstacles to live healthy, happy, and long lives. As this book's title implies, the cards are stacked against them, though they also have the power to change their lives, if they exercise it. In short, as we will see throughout this book, they are not passive victims.

In the chapters that follow, we will show how disadvantages build on one another, begetting more disadvantage. We will also examine how the concentration of power, wealth, and health in the hands of few at the expense of many—in other words, inequality—is harmful for *everyone*, not only these vulnerable populations. As we saw in Chapter 1 (and as we will underline again and again in later chapters), many of these people also suffer from multiple, interlocking disadvantages. For now, we will introduce these populations and provide information about them one by one.

agency An individual's ability to make choices.

Some people make better choices than others because they have better opportunities or more alternatives from which to choose. We call this ability to make choices **agency**—that is, the choices people make when they have choices. All our decisions, good and bad, have effects, and many of them have long-term importance for our social and economic status. However, we can't use the idea of agency to blame people—especially those belonging to the groups we discuss in this chapter—for their own disadvantaged lives. Many of them start from deprived conditions, and sometimes they might not even *know* they are disadvantaged and that they need to fight harder.

In this book, we will see that some populations fare worse and some fare better depending on the particular dimension of inequality under discussion. In each chapter, the most complex (though not necessarily most strongly affected) category for that particular dimension of inequality is addressed first, and then intersectional issues are addressed. Not every category is covered in instances where inequality against that group is not especially pronounced.

The Peopling of Canadian Society: A Thumbnail History

Why discuss Canada's history of settlement, however briefly? First, it is worth remembering that Canada is a relatively new country compared to many societies with which we might compare it. Second, in a very short period, Canada was rapidly settled by immigrants from Europe, then other parts of the world. The pattern of immigration was shaped by policies first set by the French and British governments, then set by a Canadian government dominated by French and British views. Third, Canada's economic (and therefore social) development was, until recently, shaped and controlled by outsiders.

Indigenous Peoples were the first to inhabit what is now Canada, with evidence of their presence dating to at least 14,000 years ago. One common theory is that they originally came from Siberia, over the Bering Strait and across a land bridge that has since disappeared. However, there are other theories about the initial arrival of people on the continent, and also some Indigenous perspectives holding that the presence of Indigenous Peoples on the continent has been eternal.

Around the tenth century CE, Norsemen came to present-day Canada from Scandinavia. These master sailors and warriors visited Newfoundland briefly but didn't settle here. In time, sailors and fishers also came from Portugal to catch cod in the Grand Banks off Newfoundland. However, the first European immigrants to stay and settle here in any numbers came from France, which sought to stake a claim in what they referred to as the "New World." The earliest ones came to trap beaver and collect fur pelts for sale in Europe, where they were made into stylish hats; but gradually, some settled along the St Lawrence River to farm. Women were imported from France to marry these men and set up households in Quebec; producing large families, these settlers quickly grew in number.

By this time, England had recurrently warred with France for hundreds of years. In 1763, English troops finally and decisively defeated French troops on the Plains of Abraham. This allowed them to take control of most of North America, which they shared with the Spanish, who controlled lands to the south. Shortly after this, the Americans won their independence from Britain. In the nineteenth century, immigrants came mainly from Britain, Ireland, and Scotland to settle the Maritimes, Lower Canada (later, Quebec), Upper Canada (later, Ontario), the Prairies, and British Columbia. As the settlers moved westward, investors promoted the exploitation of "staple products" for which there was a market in Europe. These products included cod from the Grand Banks; furs from Quebec; timber from the Maritimes, Quebec, and Ontario; minerals from northern Ontario and Quebec; wheat from the Prairies; and of course oil and gas from Alberta.

Canada's history reflects the goals of financiers and capitalists in Britain and later the United States whose aim was to maximize profits from Canadian resources. Vast differences in regional development resulted, leaving a residue of regional competition and conflict (for example, between Ontario and Alberta) that persists to this day. Likewise, the treatment of Indigenous Peoples has reflected the economic and political goals of the Canadian government and, underlying that, the goals of British and American capitalists. As we will see, nineteenth-century ideologies about social evolution (and what people believed to "more highly" and "less highly" evolved groups) also played a part.

These historical themes are mentioned here because they are relevant to understanding present-day global inequality—that is, Canada's relation to other countries. They also help us understand the historic role of immigrants in Canadian society and the evolving policies that affected immigration. Finally, most of all, these themes are relevant to understanding the treatment and experiences of Indigenous Peoples in Canada. It is to that topic that we will now, briefly, turn.

Colonial History and Current Issues

The National Inquiry into Missing and Murdered Indigenous Women and Girls has promoted discussion about the reasons Indigenous women and girls are disproportionately victims of death and disappearance. We will discuss this inquiry further in Chapter 10. These deaths and disappearances are not only important in themselves; they also represent the danger and neglect facing all Indigenous Peoples in Canada.

Early evidence suggested that these deaths and disappearances were largely neglected by the police. Critics say they have not been looked into with the same diligence as the deaths and disappearances of other Canadians (sociologists sometimes refer to this as the "hierarchy of victimization"). The RCMP and other police forces have denied such negligence, asserting that much of the violence against Indigenous women and girls was domestic violence by Indigenous husbands and boyfriends and other family members. Many have noted the Indigenous women and girls who died or disappeared were involved in sex

lateral violence Violence directed "sideways" at peers instead of at oppressing groups or individuals.

work or heavy drug use or both, and these practices carry high risks of harm to anyone. These assertions can be accused of either blaming the victim or of overlooking how extreme, perpetual marginalization can contribute to **lateral violence**.

Social scientists, for their part, recognize that poor and marginalized people in Canada and elsewhere face risks. They are everywhere more likely than average to die by violence or disappear. They are more likely than average to be neglected and unprotected by the police. They are more likely than average to enter the sex trade, use drugs to excess, and suffer domestic violence. Since the first classic works of the Chicago School of Sociology a century ago, these risks and dangers have been explained as results of deprivation and "social disorganization." A recent version of a similar argument by Richard Matthews (2017) characterizes the problem as "cultural erosion."

With Indigenous Peoples in Canada, another explanatory element has been added to the mix: the role of colonialism in these deaths and disappearances. Some have asserted that a colonial mentality has "othered" Indigenous Peoples—that is, Indigenous Peoples have been framed as intrinsically different from society's dominant social group—and made them seem worthless to many white Canadians.

The idea that Indigenous Peoples are more "primitive" on an evolutionary scale of social development first came into fashion in the early days of colonial conquest. These ideas were convenient for settlers as they justified the maltreatment of Indigenous Peoples. It retained its popularity, in many quarters, until the middle of the twentieth century. By then, racist ideas (such as eugenics and cultural inferiority) had been discredited, largely in reaction to the horrors of the Nazi-attempted "extermination" of Jews and others in Europe. However, many Canadians still have little patience or respect for traditional Indigenous ways of life, which they view as backward. For example, the final report of the National Inquiry into Missing and Murdered Indigenous Women and Girls (2019) notes the limited attention that mainstream media has given to violence against Indigenous women. This, the report states, "sends the message that Indigenous women, girls, and 2SLGBTQQIA people are not 'newsworthy' victims, contributing to the Canadian public's apathy toward this crisis" (390).

This historical background is critical. It helps us understand that Indigenous Peoples, over the centuries, were treated in ways that result, today, in their being impoverished and marginalized, othered and neglected, murdered and missing. It also helps us better appreciate the effort, courage, and persistence that has been required on the part of Indigenous Peoples to rise up and oppose the forces set in motion so long ago.

There has been a great deal of writing by social scientists on the long-term effects of imperial colonialism on colonized peoples, and much of it points in one direction. Defenders of colonization have historically argued that it brought "civilization" and "modernity" to previously poor and backward parts of the world. In this way, colonization allegedly improved colonized people's standards of living. It gave them access to a prosperous, post-Enlightenment future, if they chose to take it (for a general discussion of colonialism and post-colonialism, see Butt 2016).

Chief among these supposed benefits was access to Western education, which was the official motivation behind an originally voluntary and then compulsory residential school program, which we will discuss in greater detail later in this chapter.

Lest we imagine that only the Indigenous Peoples were colonized, we need to remember that French Canadians, especially in the Maritimes and Quebec, also were colonized. They were colonized by the British, first militarily and then economically. The French colonial culture would probably have disappeared if not for the tenacity of the Catholic Church, which controlled education, local politics, and much else in heavily French parts of Canada. The struggle between capitalist British (and American) forces of modernity and pre-capitalist French-Canadian forces of tradition is first recounted in Everett Hughes's classic sociological work, *French Canada in Transition* (1939). This work by a transplanted American sociologist not only captured a key moment in Canadian history, using a sociologist's camera, it also played a key role in the development of Canadian sociology; Hughes was a teacher at McGill University and then at the University of Chicago.

Much writing on the effects of colonialism on colonized people, however, has focused on the economic consequences. In principle, colonization was to bring prosperity for all, but in practice it favoured the colonizers, not the colonized. In most cases, colonization appears to have delayed the economic development and prosperity of many colonized nations around the world. Karl Marx would have predicted this. He made us aware that capitalism is an expansionary practice that encourages colonization and global competition for wealth. It was to be expected that capitalist economies (and communities) would attack and swallow pre-capitalist economies (and communities) wherever possible. Capitalism destroyed feudal societies and it even more easily destroyed pre-feudal societies of the kind that existed in the Americas in 1492.

We have been speaking about Indigenous Peoples as though they were a single group, with a single culture, location, and organization. Nothing could be further from the truth. The Indigenous Peoples within Canada—indeed, throughout the Americas—comprise thousands of communities and hundreds of cultures. From a technological standpoint, they ranged widely from nomadic hunter-gatherers to settled farmers and fishers. The more settled a group was, the more developed was its technology, the more complex its social organization, and the more prosperous its economy. And these communities, far from forming a single, peaceful group, competed and warred with one another, forming shifting empires whose fortunes rose and fell.

With all that said, none of these pre-capitalist communities could hold out long against the empire-building capitalists who sought to colonize the Americas to gain access to their raw materials and, eventually, market their goods. Some of these communities were ravaged by unfamiliar diseases against which they had no immunity. In North America, some were ravaged in wars against the invading French or British forces or, further south, against the invading Spanish and (later) US forces. Many were ravaged more gradually, by starvation and despair. Nowhere were the Indigenous Peoples major beneficiaries of progress, modernity, or prosperity.

In fact, many social scientists in the Marxist tradition have argued that capitalist colonization not only seized the land of colonized people, it also undermined the prospect of such progress and prosperity. Andre Gunder Frank (1976) has shown that the chief consequence of colonization was the creation of underdevelopment and economic dependency in colonized countries. Immanuel Wallerstein (1992) has shown that the building of a capitalist world system began with colonization in the late fifteenth century. Its goal was to centralize wealth, power, and control in so-called core countries at the expense of peripheral countries. Thus, raw materials and labour power could be extracted and finished goods could be marketed most profitably. In both formulations, the colonized countries were denied opportunities to industrialize profitably; export their goods on favourable terms; grow a healthy, highly educated population; or develop a modern division of labour. Angeles (2005) reports that income inequality is an almost inevitable consequence of colonization.

Much more could be said about these theories and the evidence supporting them. The point is, Indigenous Peoples throughout the world within post-colonial countries have entered the twenty-first century at a disadvantage. This disadvantage was built into the capitalist economy and the post-Enlightenment European culture. It was not restricted to Canada. Nor have its results been different in Canada than in other modern countries. Indigenous Peoples who live in distinct rural communities in the United States, Australia, New Zealand, Norway, Finland, and Greenland all report higher-than-average rates of poverty, unemployment, addiction, poor health, and suicidality (Axelsson, Kukutai, and Kippen 2016).

So it is with justification that many propose the problems facing Indigenous Peoples today—especially those on reserves—are a result of the colonialism they or their ancestors suffered. As noted, these current problems include poor mental health, addiction, poor physical health, family violence and fragmentation, poor housing and infrastructure, underrepresentation in graduation rates, and higher rates of unemployment. We will discuss all of these problems further in the course of this book. We will also show examples where Indigenous communities and their allies have taken steps to rectify these problems.

The problem sociologists face is knowing how to link a (possibly) distant cause—for example, colonization two centuries ago or forced residential schooling a generation ago—to present-day issues. What are the intervening variables that link these causes and effects?

Auger (2016), synthesizing a variety of qualitative sources, suggests interrupted cultural continuity itself is a source of distress. An early effort to link colonialism and mental distress, albeit not in Canada but in Algeria, was provided by Frantz Fanon in his book *The Wretched of the Earth* (1961). As a psychoanalyst, Fanon saw the problems colonized people faced in Africa, Asia, and the Caribbean in terms of powerlessness and low self-worth. This powerlessness and low self-worth (or self-esteem) kept colonized people from taking action to improve their situation. It made them apathetic and, sometimes, even self-destructive. To overcome this apathy and self-doubt, Fanon argued, the colonized peoples would have to eject their colonizers, by violence if necessary. They would have to seize freedom and autonomy through their own efforts before they could become healthy, as well as self-governing.

There is ample clinical evidence that low self-esteem (or even self-hate) is harmful to people's well-being (Okazaki, David, and Abelmann 2008:92–3). Okazaki and colleagues (2008) discuss the huge literature on racism, discrimination, prejudice, stigma, and various forms of exclusion, denigration, and othering.

A second effort to answer this question is found in the book by American social scientist Daniel Moynihan, *The Negro Family: The Case for National Action* (1965). Fifty years ago, Black communities were facing high rates of poverty, crime, addiction, unemployment, domestic violence, and school leaving. Among less-educated urban Black Americans, these problems were increasing, despite legislative efforts to improve the status and condition of Black people. The result was growing inequality, both between Black people and white people, and between Black Americans who were educated and those who were less educated. In effect, Black Americans had become an internal colony of the United States, and as colonized people, they needed to improve their condition. To solve this problem, Moynihan saw one chief remedy: strengthening Black families, which had been ravaged by generations of slavery, poverty, and racial discrimination.

At the time, Moynihan and his report were attacked on the grounds that he was "blaming the victim"—in effect, holding Black Americans responsible for their own situation or, at least, requiring that they do something to improve their situation. In this latter respect, his stance was not completely different from Fanon's: Both saw a need for the colonized people to take action in their own interest.

Moynihan's analysis comes to mind here because of the centrality of family-related issues in discussions of problems involving Indigenous Peoples in Canada. Forcing Indigenous children to attend white-run residential schools undermined Indigenous family structures and family traditions in Indigenous communities. Ties were destroyed or weakened between parents and children. Children, separated from their parents for great periods of time and forced to learn an alien culture, reported being unable to learn "how to parent." As a consequence, many struggled when parenting their own children. They were not exposed to healthy spousal relationships and, as a consequence, were unprepared to be spouses themselves when they grew up. These problems were intensified during the so-called Sixties Scoop. Then, child welfare services forcibly removed many Indigenous children from their homes and put them in foster homes on the grounds they were receiving poor care.

For the past 15 years or so there has been widespread study into the impacts of colonial trauma—that is, conquest, plunder, family fragmentation, cultural genocide, and impoverishment, among other things—on Indigenous Peoples alive today. Colonization is widely understood to be profoundly traumatic in the sense that it harms physically, emotionally, spiritually, and psychologically. Indigenous scholars describe the long-term impacts as "historical trauma" or more commonly as "intergenerational trauma": an emotional (or social) response by the *children and grandchildren* of the trauma survivor that impacts health and longevity (Marsh et al. 2015).

The traumatic event that has been the most widely studied is exposure to residential schooling. Social scientists have asked has—or *how* has—residential school attendance affected the children and grandchildren of attendees?

Barker and colleagues (2019), for example, found that young Indigenous people with a parent or grandparent who attended residential school were more likely to be involved in the child welfare system versus Indigenous youths whose families had no historic involvement with residential schools. Pearce and colleagues (2008) found some correlations between parental residential school involvement and sexual victimization. Other researchers have found increased risk of suicidality and depression (Elias et al. 2012) and lower educational outcomes (First Nations Centre 2005). And most notably, a great many Indigenous people have said in interviews that they attribute their present-day family challenges to the residential schooling of their parents and grandparents (Truth and Reconciliation Commission 2015).

The prevailing theory is that this trauma is passed down via socialization or childhood learning. In other words, parents pass along their pain, and their challenges become their children's challenges. Scholars have noted the ways in which trauma can be passed through different channels, including "cultural (through storytelling, culturally sanctioned behaviours), social (through inadequate parenting, lateral violence, acting out of abuse), and psychological (through memory processes) channels" (Wesley-Esquimaux and Smolewski 2004). Newer research is being done into the ways that historical trauma may even imprint on the genes. This is broadly referred to as *epigenetics*. We still have a lot to learn before drawing conclusions about epigenetics.

Unsurprisingly, other populations whose ancestors have survived traumas through war or other forms of extreme persecution have also been studied. In 1996, for example, Mazor and Tal (1996) found that the children of Holocaust survivors had more spousal challenges, which was also found to be true for the descendants of residential school survivors. Fossion and colleagues (2003) found that the grandchildren of Holocaust survivors demonstrated increased emotional distress, but the sample size was small and other studies on this population did not show significant difference from controls (Bachar et al. 1994). Meta-analyses of published research literature on the Holocaust find little evidence of intergenerational trauma among the children of Holocaust survivors (see, for example, Kellerman, 2001; van Uzendoorn, 2003; Schwarz, 2008).

Some have said that the traumas experienced by other populations, such as Holocaust survivors, is dissimilar to those experienced by Indigenous Peoples in that the traumatic event is limited to one or two generations versus many (O'Neill et al. 2016). By contrast, the "Four Cs" of Indigenous historical trauma have been identified as *colonial* in origin, *collectively* experienced, with *cumulative* effects, and *cross-generational* impacts (Hartmann and Gone 2014).

Some Indigenous scholars find inquiry into intergenerational trauma to be yet another manifestation of the colonial agenda, obscuring the very real, present-day oppression of Indigenous Peoples. They argue that once again, this theory frames Indigenous cultures as inferior with a focus on what is viewed as problematic parenting or personal deficits. Maxwell (2016) writes that "some contemporary mental health and child development professionals have invoked parents' and grandparents' transmission of historical trauma in ways which construct Indigenous families as pathological, promote an oversimplified, universalizing understanding of Canadian colonialism, and divert attention from the contemporary continuation of colonial structures and relations." The approach to treating social problems—like racism and colonization—with clinical, medical-style trauma therapies and remedies has been termed "the medicalization of the social" (Hartmann and Gone 2014).

Suffice it to say, research into intergenerational trauma is complex, and the diagnostic criteria for such a classification is not yet established. Are researchers, as Maxwell argues, "making meaning out of social suffering in the present by reference to the past"? Or is the goal to identify the mechanisms causing present-day problems so they can be clearly identified and mitigated?

As the authors of a broad review of the current research on intergenerational trauma conclude, the literature "has yet to cohere into a body of knowledge with clear implications for health policy or professional practice" (Gone et al. 2019). And yet there is certainly enough evidence to conclude that sustained attacks against a population may "accumulate over generations and interact with proximal stressors to undermine collective well-being" (Bombay, Matheson, and Anisman 2014).

Low-Income People in Canada

Poverty, or low income, is the condition of not having enough of the things we need for life, whether in **absolute or relative terms**—that is, not enough food, clothing, shelter, and so on. Inequality, in contrast, is a condition that can occur among rich or poor people. It marks a difference in which one person has more than another person: more food, clothes, shelter, and so on. Thus, a society can be poor but equal or poor but unequal, rich but equal or rich but unequal.

absolute poverty versus relative poverty Absolute poverty refers to how much difficulty a person has satisfying their daily survival needs. Relative poverty describes that person's economic condition compared to the average in their community.

That said, unequal societies are likely to have more people living with poverty than equal societies, both in absolute and relative terms. And the life experience of poor people is much harsher in unequal societies than it is in equal societies. In fact, one could say that it is far worse to be a poor person in a rich, unequal society than it is to be a poor person in a poor, equal society. And low-income people in Canada today are precisely that: poor in a relatively rich, relatively unequal society.

The preferred method of measuring low income in Canada today is the **market-basket measure (MBM)**. The MBM calculates how much income a household requires to meet its needs, including subsistence needs, such as basic food and shelter. After much consultation, in 2018 the Government of Canada decided to consider the MBM as "Canada's official poverty line." Some would say this shift to MBM from other measures implies that Canada is moving away from a relative measure of poverty to a more absolute (and less forgiving) measure of poverty. Others might say that it represents a shift away from a focus on social comparison to a focus on physical survival. Figure 2.1 compares the MBM to two other measures of poverty: the low-income measure and the low-income cut-off. Note that the rate for the MBM falls in the middle of the others. Using data from the 2016 Census, the MBM reveals a poverty rate of 12.9 per cent in 2016 (Statistics Canada 2017c).

market-basket measure (MBM) The method used to measure low income in Canada that calculates how much income a household requires to meet its needs. These include subsistence needs (such as basic food and shelter) and the needs to satisfy community norms.

Despite slightly different estimates of the number of Canadians experiencing poverty, experts agree on other features of this population. One widely noticed feature is that poverty is concentrated in large cities. This means you would find more poverty in

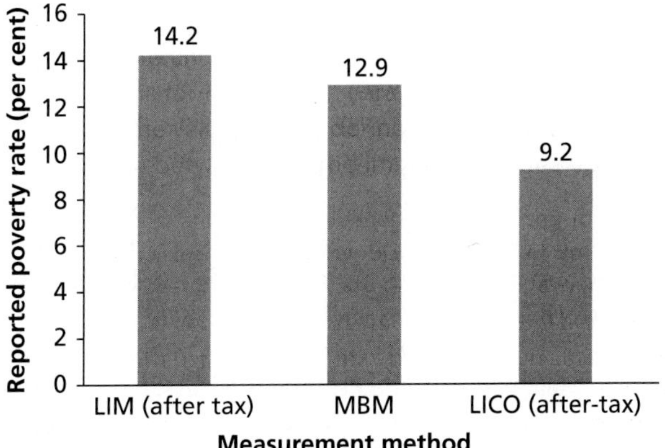

Figure 2.1 ◆ Reported Poverty Rate in Canada, by Measurement Method

Source: Statistics Canada 2017c.

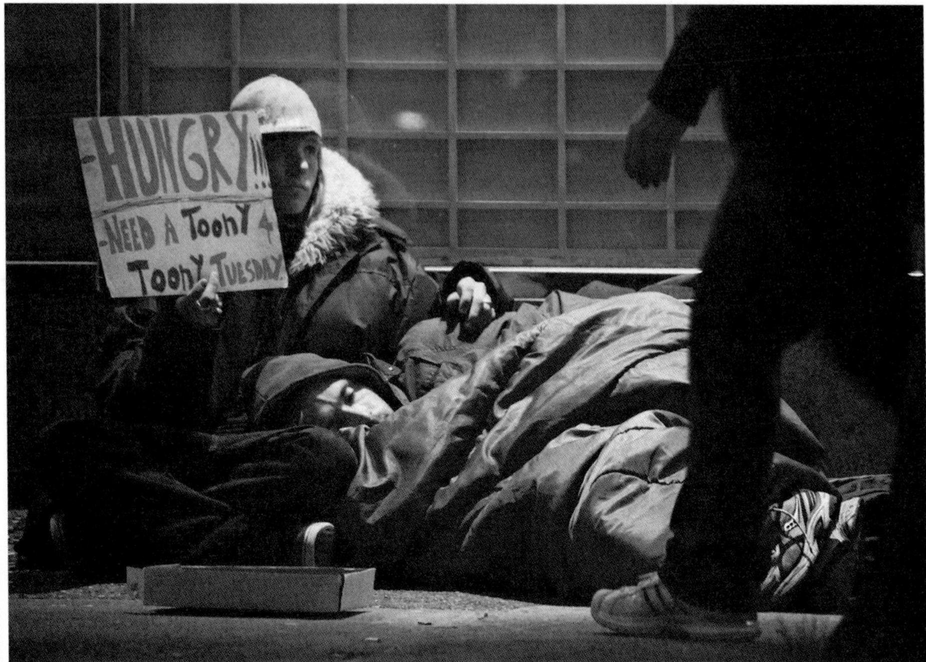

Barbara Walton/EPA/Shutterstock

The Government of Canada's recent change to the way it calculates how much income a household requires to meet its needs has little material effect for people who are well below the poverty line, such as these individuals on the streets of Vancouver. However, do you think changing the calculation might affect those living closer to the poverty line?

a random sample of 100 city-dwellers than in a random sample of 100 people living in a rural setting. In fact, the 2016 Census found that Toronto, Montreal, and Vancouver were home to three-fifths of all low-income people in Canada (Statistics Canada 2017e). Smaller cities, such as Sherbrooke and Windsor, also have high concentrations of low-income people living in low-income neighbourhoods. Why is this the case? In large part, poor people tend to live in cities because, increasingly, most Canadians live in large urban regions. Good jobs, schools, and housing opportunities not available in rural regions are often lures.

The data show that poverty rates follow shifts in the overall economy. When the economy worsens, the number of poor people swells, and they suffer most during an economic recession. Low-paying, part-time jobs *put people at greater risk* of becoming low income even if they aren't low income already (Gaetz et al. 2013). This downward shift is a common trend of our current moment, and it is not a shift for the better, as we will see.

Economic recessions hit the poorest among us the hardest (Pasma and Sears 2010). In the 2008 recession, both the cost of living and the unemployment rate rose. In other words, people needed to spend more when they earned less. Pasma and Sears (2010) note that 13 staples of a low-income diet (items such as milk, flour, and bread) rose in price by more than 5 per cent between December 2008 and December 2009. Four of the 13 items rose by more than 20 per cent! The cost of rental housing also rose during this time, hitting low-income Canadians hardest (since they are the least likely to own their home). These changes resulted in more personal debt and a larger number of bankruptcies, especially for

Notable Thinkers

Dennis Raphael

Dennis Raphael is a professor of Health Policy and Management at York University in Toronto. Most of his publications have focused on the health effects of income inequality and poverty, the quality of life of communities and individuals, and the impact of government decisions on Canadians' health and well-being. Over the course of his career, he has published 12 books, 58 book chapters, and 156 refereed journal articles. Raphael has published on the affinities between the social determinants of health and the social determinants of oral health. He has also written about health discourses among disease associations and concepts of legitimacy and competency of governing authorities in liberal welfare states.

Raphael's work leads students who are studying social inequality back to the most fundamental, life-and-death issues one can imagine. Just as Rudolf Virchow noted in nineteenth-century Europe, Dennis Raphael notes in twenty-first-century Canada that poverty and social inequality have devastating effects for the most vulnerable members of our society.

people who were financially vulnerable even before the recession. During the COVID-19 pandemic of 2020, between 15 and 20 per cent of the population lost their jobs and income, owing to the shutdown of non-essential businesses governments mandated to reduce the spread of the virus. This loss of jobs and incomes fell most heavily on hourly wage workers in service and manufacturing jobs, not on people with salaries and pensions. Thus the epidemic revealed, once again, the human cost of precarious labour in our society.

Many people move in and out of poverty during their lifetimes. This doesn't mean, however, that it's common for people to move from poverty to wealth, a subject discussed later in this book. Take Canadian seniors, for example. Historically, people's incomes tend to rise during their early years, reach a peak in late adulthood (in their forties or fifties), and then start to decline with old age. To some degree, this is still true. A report issued by Employment and Social Development Canada in 2019 notes that Canada has achieved its lowest poverty rate ever:

> The poverty rate of 9.5 percent in 2017 represents the lowest rate of poverty ever based on Canada's Official Poverty Line (formerly known as the Market Basket Measure). This historic low poverty rate represents an important step towards the Government of Canada's goal to cut poverty in half by 2030.

Racialized People in Canada

Another group that is often considered vulnerable, disadvantaged, and even victimized is the group formerly called racial or visible minorities and now called *racialized people.*

Skin colour is a significant aspect of racialization—perhaps its single most important feature. Even within racialized populations (for example, among Black people or

East Indians) people feel great concern about their skin colour. Darker shades are often considered less attractive and are given lower status than lighter shades, with the result that many racialized women use chemicals to bleach their skin (or straighten their hair). Lighter-skinned racialized women—again, using the example of Black women—are often considered more attractive than darker-skinned women. Some have called this stigmatization of darker-skinned people *shadism,* referring to the tendency to devalue darker skin shades in favour of lighter shades.

Likely, this prejudice in favour of lighter-shaded skin, as well as hair texture and colour that is common among white people, reflects the effects of European colonization. People with lighter skin, straighter hair, and lighter hair are likely to have ancestors who came from Europe. Thus, we may want to view this bias as a subtle form of self-denigration among racialized people. Many have remarked on the effects of such a bias on the stigmatization and self-esteem of Indigenous Peoples in Canada.

social construction A term used to describe how something has meaning only because it is made up or seen as such—it is not real (or biological) in nature.

In this book we use the term *racialized* because it implies a *process* rather than a *state* of being. Using a "process" word suggests that we should understand race as a continuing **social construction** rather than a biological certainty—or, said another way, as a social fact rather than a physical fact. There are many common, enduring, and harmful beliefs about race. For example, some believe that race is an important sign of a person's worth. Others believe there are a handful of discrete "racial categories" into which all people can be neatly organized and that people belonging to one supposed racial category are "naturally" the same.

Biologically (or genetically) speaking, we know that race is insignificant. Race, as it is commonly understood, is not a biological predictor of ability, intelligence, disposition, or many other things that have been examined (often under racist pretenses). The genes that control our physical appearance are independently inherited and are few compared to the sum total of our genetic makeup. They affect our skin colour, hair texture, and other markers of "racial difference." As many point out, a person may have more in common, *biologically speaking,* with someone of a "different race" than someone who looks racially identical to them.

Therefore, the term *race* has little meaning biologically. Instead, as Galabuzi (2006) explains, racial categories are socially constructed to explain and justify social inequality. "Racialized groups" are people who belong to "non-dominant ethno-racial communities who, through the process of racialization, experience race as a key factor in their identity and experiences of inequality" (Galabuzi 2006:5). The term *visible minority* is generally no longer used as it only refers to non-white people, reinforcing a problematic belief that whiteness is *not visible.* As well, the term may promote the stigmatization of certain groups. The idea that someone belongs to a "minority" group is often attached to notions of inferiority and disempowerment. These are notions that can negatively affect the way other people view a person (Galabuzi 2006).

The results of the 2016 Census reveal key features of racialized people in Canada. Roughly 22.3 per cent of the total population in Canada, or 7.6 million people, identify as belonging to a "visible minority group" (Statistics Canada 2017g). This number showed an increase from 19 per cent in 2011, and it shows no sign of decreasing (Statistics Canada 2017g). According to the National Council of Welfare (2013), Canada's racialized population is increasing much more quickly than the non-racialized population. In fact, demographers predict that one in three Canadians may be member of a racialized group by 2031 (Statistics Canada 2010).

Rawpixel.com/Shutterstock

Kids playing in a Toronto park. According to Statistics Canada, roughly 22 per cent of all Canadians identify as belonging to a "visible minority group." Does your classroom show this diversity?

Canadians who identify as racialized concentrate in some parts of the nation more than others. Most of this population live in the large cities of Ontario, British Columbia, Quebec, and Alberta. This concentration of racialized Canadians is greatest in Ontario, where almost 3 in 10 Ontarians identify as visible minorities. Data from the 2016 Census reports the following:

- In 2016, 3,885,585 Ontarians identified as members of the visible minority population.
- These individuals make up 29.3 per cent of Ontario's total population and represented more than half of Canada's total visible minorities (7.7 million).
- Most of the visible minority population live in Census Metropolitan Areas, including 3.0 million in Toronto.
- Between 2011 and 2016, Ontario's visible minority population increased by 18.5 per cent, while the population not belonging to a visible minority group declined by 0.2 per cent. Ontario's 374,395 people who self-identified as Aboriginal are not counted as part of the visible minority population.
- Of the 3.9 million Ontarians who identified as visible minority, more than one-third (36.5 per cent) were born in Canada, while 63.5 per cent were born outside Canada.

In 2016, people who identified as South Asian, Chinese, or Black made up 61.2 per cent of all racialized people in Canada (Statistics Canada 2017g). However, note the great diversity within these huge groups. For instance, some of the people who self-identified as "South Asian" on the 2016 Census reported Pakistani origins, while others reported Sri Lankan or Indian origins (Statistics Canada 2017g). Even if "Black people" or "Asian people" seem the same to outsiders, they do not accept being lumped together as though they share common values, attitudes, aspirations, or identities.

As described in Chapter 1, interlocking disadvantage especially deriving from gender, race, and class is an important factor affecting people's opportunities and outcomes in life. Consider the case of racialized people who are also low-income Canadians. Data from the 2016 Census show that racialized people are more likely than non-racialized people to live in poverty. And in the case of Indigenous Peoples, as discussed above, we can see the interlocking disadvantage of racism, classism, and xenophobia.

Young People in Canada

If you are reading this book or attending courses at an educational institution, you might be what we would call a "young person." However, young people are a diverse and variably defined group in Canada. What exactly makes a person "young"? At what age are we no longer "young" and instead classified as "adults" or even as "old"? The 2016 Census revealed that 8,884,235 respondents were between the ages of 15 and 34. That works out to about a quarter of our total population (Statistics Canada 2016).

There is significant variation in the way young people are dispersed throughout Canada. Compare Alberta with Newfoundland and Labrador, for example, where Alberta has a significantly higher population of young people than Newfoundland and Labrador does. The differences between these places reflect a higher fertility rate in the West and the North. They also reflect many young adults migrating to the province from other provinces and other countries. In contrast, many young adults have been moving out of Newfoundland and Labrador to other parts of Canada, and fewer foreign immigrants have been arriving in the province. Statistics Canada (2017b) reports

> Nationally, the ratio of people 65 years and older to children aged 0 to 14 years was 1.05, showing the first group had a slightly higher demographic weight than the second. Nova Scotia had the highest ratio, with 1.42 people 65 years and older for every child aged 0 to 14. In contrast, Nunavut had 0.13 people aged 65 and older for every child aged 0 to 14. Among the provinces, Alberta had the lowest ratio (0.67).

These facts are not surprising, given that young people move around more than anyone else in Canada. They often move for school and job opportunities and end up living in the largest Canadian cities where these opportunities are most plentiful (Clark 2007). Older people tend to stay put and do not move in pursuit of educational and employment opportunities.

Today, the pursuit of educational and employment opportunities also accounts for what many call a "delayed transition to adulthood." Finding a job, moving out of your parents' house, and getting married are usually considered markers of adulthood. However, doing all of these "adult" things is often complicated these days. As Galarneau, Morissette, and Usalcas (2013) explain, young people face a more uncertain and complicated future than they did in the past.

Finding a job right out of school and achieving social and economic stability is no longer easy. That's because of a high rate of youth **underemployment**, which is employment in a job that needs far less education and preparation than an individual has gained. It is also because of a general increase in unemployment and short-term employment and the continuing changeover to a technical and information-based economy (Clark 2007).

underemployment Employment in a job that needs far less education and preparation than an individual has earned.

As a result, young people are spending more years in school and becoming more educated to increase their chances of landing a good job (Clark 2007). Prolonged schooling has its benefits. However, these benefits come at a price, such as increased tuition fees and student debt. Feeling financially insecure, many young adults choose to continue living with their parents. Young people who focus on finding stable employment and repaying student debt tend to put things like buying a house, getting married, and having children further down on their "to-do" list.

For several reasons, it's hard to put numbers on any of these life transitions—for example, from single to attached, or from student to full-time worker. First, that's because there's more drift through statuses today than there was in the past. People drift into stable-type relationships through dating, then cohabiting, then marriage, and so on. Sometimes, they drift out of them too. Similarly, people drift in and out of education and in and out of full-time work. What's more, the two kinds of drift—marital and occupational—are highly related. Many young people, in Canada and elsewhere, delay any serious romantic commitments—even any sexual relations—until they have a steady job (Ravanera and Rajulton 2007).

That said, it's clear that people have been getting more education for the past century. So they have also been delaying marriage and full-time work for most of this period. (Of course, these tendencies vary from one region of the country to another and from one social class and ethnic group to another.) These delay patterns have been most extreme in Quebec, which, since the Quiet Revolution of the 1960s, has been open to cohabitation and out-of-wedlock births. News reports from Quebec note the following:

> Data released in Quebec last month revealed the average age of a first marriage for a man in the province in 2016 was 33.4 years and 31.9 for women. [This marked] a rise of 7.8 years for men and 8.5 for women since 1971. Across Canada, the proportion of young adults aged 25 to 29 who were never married has been steadily rising. (Canadian Press 2017)

Three vulnerable populations account for an especially large proportion of young people. These populations are Indigenous Peoples, immigrants, and racialized people. Also, this proportion is increasing. In short, Canada's young population continues to grow in both size and diversity and shows no signs of slowing down. These people's young age makes them more likely than many others to face certain types of inequalities, as we will see in the chapters that follow.

Women in Canada

Oddly, women are often called a "minority group," but not because they are a numerical minority. Indeed, in many societies they are a majority, especially at older ages. However, they are often treated like a minority in the sense that they are marginalized, excluded,

feminization of poverty The overrepresentation of women among the poor.

and stigmatized in many male-dominated activities. As a result, women are overrepresented among the poor people of the world. This is referred to as the **feminization of poverty**. High rates of female poverty are the result of women's occupational disadvantage in society and their overall subordinate position to men.

Fully up-to-date statistics on the feminization of poverty are hard to find. Statistics Canada (2016) showed that, overall, men outnumber women in the labour force (though not by much). More women aged 25 and older were working part time than Canadian men. In fact, women overall, and single mothers in particular, are more likely to be impoverished than any other demographic group. According to Statistics Canada,

> Nearly two in five children in lone-parent families (or 38.9%) lived in a low-income household in 2015. This rate was three and a half times higher than for children in two-parent families (11.2%). Further, most children living in a lone-parent family lived with their mother. The low-income rate for these children was much higher than for children who lived with their father (42.0% compared with 25.5%). (Statistics Canada 2017d)

Also, various health issues trouble women who are economically deprived. They include increased vulnerability to arthritis, migraines, stress, heart disease, stomach ulcers, and infectious diseases. They also include mental illnesses such as clinical depression and self-destructive coping behaviours.

The following statistics help us understand the extent to which the poverty of women is a significant social problem:

- *Low-wage earners*: Most poor people work full or part time. Women are in the paid working force more now than ever before. However, many women work in low-wage occupations that don't provide enough income to survive.
- *Women raising families by themselves*: Lone-parent-mother families are far more likely to live in poverty than other family types, even lone-parent-father families (Statistics Canada 2014). For example, 26 per cent of lone-parent-mother families were low income compared with 12.8 per cent of lone-parent-father families (Statistics Canada 2014).
- *Wage gaps*: Using Statistics Canada data, the CBC reported that "Canadian women earned 87 cents an hour for every dollar made by men in 2015. The data shows the gender wage gap has shrunk by 10 cents since 1981, when female workers earned 77 cents for each dollar earned by men. This reflects the hourly earnings of Canadians aged 25 to 54" (Israel 2017).
- *Racialized women*: Racialized women are more likely than racialized men to live in poverty (52 per cent versus 48 per cent). This is similar to the rates of poverty for non-racialized women compared to non-racialized men (54 per cent versus 46 per cent; National Council of Welfare 2012).
- *Senior women*: From 2003 to 2013, the median income for senior women increased from $19,300 to $21,900. However, they still have a lower median income when compared to senior men, whose income also increased over the same period from $28,700 to $32,300 This is unsurprising. Since the early 1990s, the median income

of senior men has been around 1.5 times higher than that of senior women (Hudon and Milan 2016).

- *Migrant women*: In some sectors of migrant employment, such as in-home domestic workers, women make up most of the workforce. These professions are especially vulnerable to low wages, exploitation, and lack of workplace safety enforcement. Usually, they are also ineligible for employment benefits such as employment insurance, even though money may be deducted from their salaries toward these benefits.
- *Indigenous women*: In 2010, the median income of Indigenous women (aged 15 and over) was $5,500 less than the median income of non-Indigenous women. Furthermore, when compared with the median income of Indigenous men, Indigenous women's median income was about $3,600 less (Arriagada 2016).
- *Queer women*: There is not enough research focusing on income struggles related to sexual orientation. One Winnipeg study, however, revealed that senior lesbian women were three times more likely to report being low income than senior gay men (McKee 1999). We will say more about both seniors and LGBTQ+ people later.
- *Trans women*: According to a recent report, the median income of trans people living in Ontario was $15,000 a year. This represents significant underemployment based on their levels of education and experience, with 44 per cent of individuals having a post-secondary or graduate degree (Bauer and Scheim 2014).
- *Women with disabilities*: In Canada, people with a disability are more vulnerable to poverty, and more women (14.9 per cent) than men (12.5 per cent) report a disability (Burlock 2017).

Gender issues are involved in most, if not all, aspects of Canadian social life. Gender discrimination carries social and psychological costs. For women, these costs include derogation by men, awareness of their subordinate status in society, or a failure to achieve the stereotypically ideal female body—all of which can have damaging results. These results can include decreased self-esteem, increased depression, and other psychological problems. As we have already noted, one area in which this limitation occurs is the choice of careers.

Teenage pregnancy is another big problem for women in North America. Outcomes are typically not good for teen mothers, who are more prone to issues of joblessness and poverty and have more challenges in completing an education. For *nearly all women*, for typically *30 years of fertility*, preventing pregnancy is considered their responsibility. Similarly, women, not men, mainly feel the results of unwanted pregnancy, whether those results are abortions, single parenthood, or other arrangements.

In all of these ways, and to varying degrees across regions, ethnic groups, and social classes, women often make up a disadvantaged "minority group" in Canadian society.

Seniors in Canada

When we talk about seniors in our society, we mean people who are over the age of 60 or 65. Physical quality of life declines in old age. One reason for this is **senescence**, the natural decline of physical and mental abilities during the aging process. Muscles grow weaker,

senescence The natural decline of physical and mental abilities during the aging process.

the mind becomes less sharp, and aches and pains become routine complaints. Exactly at what age and in what form this decline takes place varies from one person to the next, but decline is certain. Health problems often arise alongside and because of changes in the life course. For example, studies show that widowhood and divorce are associated with health problems. Equally important, the loss of independence as one ages can also cause emotional and physical distress. This may go with, for example, the loss of a driver's licence, the need to rely on others for help with the activities of daily living, or the loss of physical control.

An aging, longer-living adult population leads to increased demands for informal (non-professional) care. Indeed, a Statistics Canada report suggests the demand is already great (Cranswick and Dosman 2008). Seventy-eight per cent of senior primary-care receivers continue to live in their homes, and only 22 per cent live in formal care facilities. Compared with 30 years ago, the elderly today are more likely to live independently. The 2016 Census reported nearly 6 million seniors over 65. Today, "nearly 93 percent of those seniors lived in private residences with most of the remainder living in group residences for senior citizens or other health care facilities" (Norris 2017).

At the same time, more adult children in their fifties are more likely to have a surviving parent. They are also more likely than in past decades to be divorced, so they don't have a spouse present to help with eldercare. See Figure 2.2 for an illustration of the changing proportion of the population in G8 countries that is 65 years old or older.

sandwich generation Middle-aged adults who are caring for both their elderly parents and their own young children.

One result of the population's aging is the so-called **sandwich generation**, who are middle-aged adults caring for both elderly parents and for their own young children.

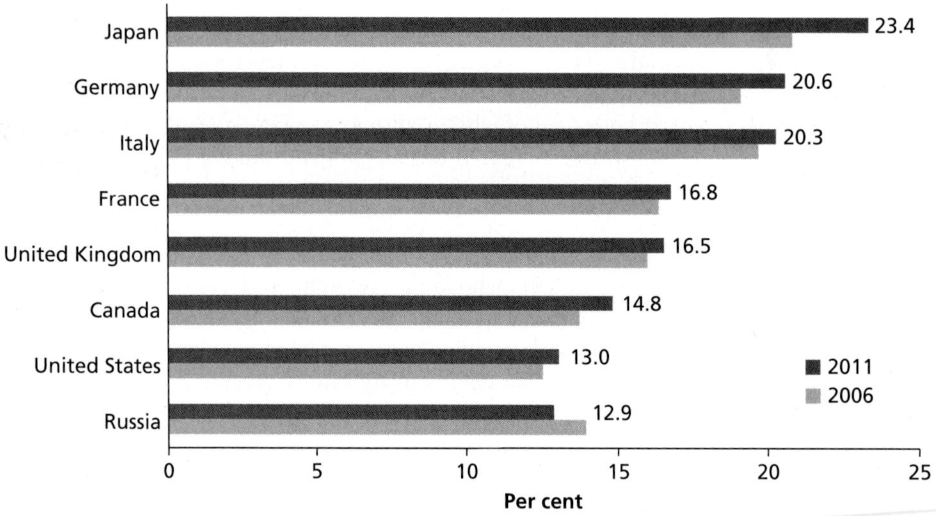

Figure 2.2 ◆ Proportion (in Percentage) of the Population Aged 65 and Over, G8 Countries, 2006 and 2011

Source: Statistics Canada, censuses of population, 2006 and 2011; US Census Bureau, 2006 and 2010; National Institute of Statistics (Italy), 2006 and 2011; National Institute of Statistics and Economic Studies (France), 2006 and 2011; Statistics Bureau of Japan, 2006 and 2011; Russian Federation Federal State Statistics Service, 2006 and 2010; and Human Mortality Database for Germany, 2006 and 2010, and for United Kingdom, 2006 and 2010.

And of course, not every senior in Canada has family living nearby with the necessary resources to support them. Other societal changes include a shift from institutional to community-based (in-home) care, a growing ideological commitment to eldercare by the state, and funding cuts by the federal government for such services.

Aging is invariably associated with some disability. However, there is great inequality in the effect that **socio-economic status (SES)** has on the extent of the disability. Countless studies have shown that seniors who are lower in SES have significantly greater disability-associated problems than their higher-SES counterparts. Higher social inequality over the life course is associated with greater likelihood of disability during the senior years. For example, in one study, some life-course social inequalities that predicted greater future disability were illiteracy and no outside income (or an inadequate outside income). Working in a low-skill occupation and poverty and hunger early in a person's life also predicted this result (Guerra, Alvarado, and Zunzunegui 2008). Despite experiences of sexism, women tend to be much more resilient to the effects of social inequalities experienced over the life course than men.

socio-economic status (SES) An important determinant of health that considers income, class, social networks, cultural capital, education, and other achieved credentials.

Living longer brings unprecedented opportunities, but it also presents serious social challenges. One of these is elder abuse. Elder abuse occurs in various settings. Typically, the abused older person is mistreated in their own home by a spouse, sibling, child, friend, or trusted caregiver (see Figure 2.3). In institutions for elderly people, staff and professional caregivers may sometimes mistreat other seniors. It's more common in rural districts (Savage 2017). Estimates of the prevalence of elder abuse vary. Statistics Canada finds that somewhere between 4 and 10 per cent of elders suffer abuse. A survey of CARP (Canadian Association of Retired Persons) members suggests the number is closer to 10 per cent (CARP 2013). One study estimates that five elder abuse incidents go unreported for every incident that is reported.

IN FOCUS ◆ The Market for Senior Care

According to the 2016 Census, most Canadian seniors—93 per cent of them—live in a private residence. We can already see a growing interest among seniors to remain in their own communities, and even in their own homes. In part, this is because many institutional arrangements are much more expensive. As well, the COVID-19 pandemic in 2020 revealed that seniors living in retirement communities run a higher-than-average risk of dying from infection compounded by neglect.

However, the trend to more homecare will require a drastic expansion of care services for the seniors who do remain at home. And, since seniors remain healthy and mobile for an ever-longer time, municipalities will need to improve public transportation for those who want to get out of the house. In addition, more businesses will want to offer seniors home delivery of their products (for example, groceries and drug store needs), as was common a century ago, and more baby boomers will move to smaller homes, looking for both condos and rental apartments in preference to full-sized houses.

Source: Adapted from Norris 2017.

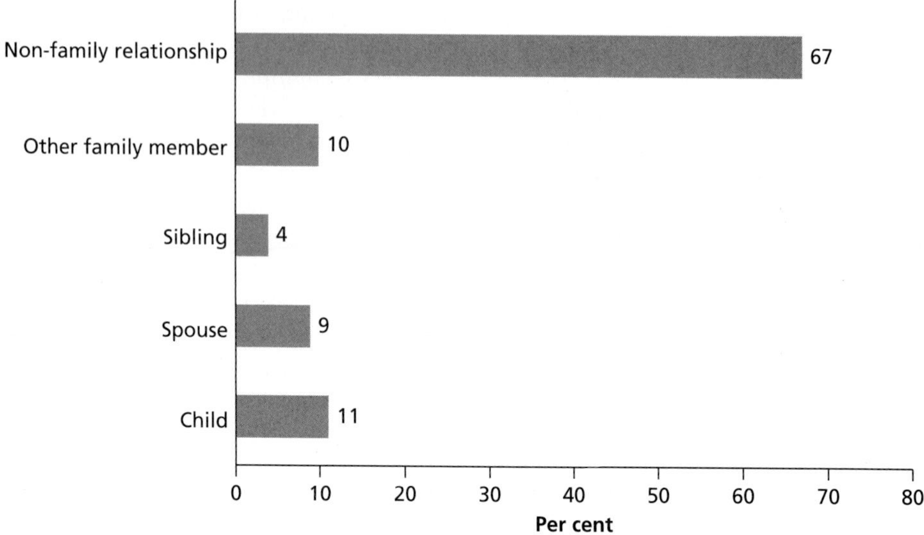

Figure 2.3 ◆ Senior Victims of Police-Reported Family and Non-family Violence, by Relationship of Accused to Victim, Canada, 2017

Source: Statistics Canada 2018c.

Immigrants in Canada

Earlier, we discussed the way Canada is a society of immigrants and their descendants. An even more revealing image of Canada—that of a great railway station—is provided by John Porter ([1965] 2015). From the beginning of its history, people have been entering Canada and leaving Canada in great numbers. So great were the numbers of emigrants leaving Canada in its first 50 years that the national population would have eventually disappeared if not for the countervailing large numbers of immigrants entering Canada. Since the 1930s, emigration (or outmigration, as it is often called) has declined significantly while immigration has continued at a very high rate.

Immigration and outmigration are important for many reasons. A low-fertility society like Canada (in which women bear few children each) tends to age rapidly. This, in turn, means that it needs large numbers of new young families to immigrate, both to enter the workforce and to reproduce the population. This has three effects: keeping the Canadian population from disappearing, keeping the population from aging too quickly, and providing tax revenues to support the dependent senior population who can no longer work. Additionally, however, immigration also gives Canada a "brain gain"—that is, an influx of some of the most talented, educated, hard-working, and ambitious people in the world. Conversely, this has the effect of a "brain drain" for the countries from which these immigrants come. What is a net gain for Canada is a net loss for many countries in the Global South.

The three main categories under which foreign-born people can apply to immigrate permanently are as economic immigrants, family class immigrants, and refugees (see Figure 2.4). Economic immigrants are people deemed to have the necessary skills and

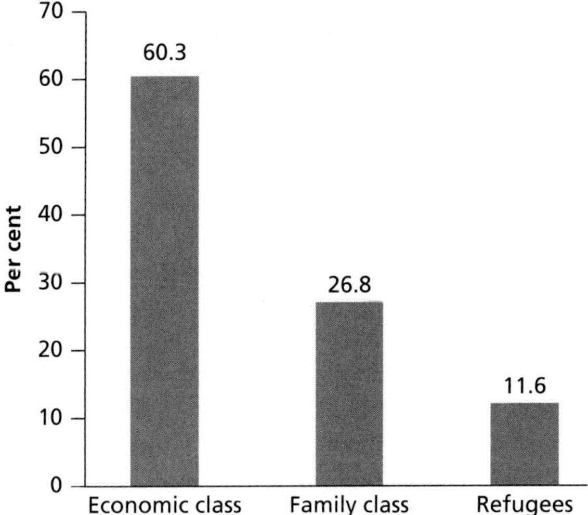

Figure 2.4 ♦ Immigrants to Canada by Type, 2016

Source: Adapted from Statistics Canada 2016.

experience to contribute to Canada's economy, whether as skilled workers, businesspeople, professionals, or otherwise. Family class refers to immigrants who are sponsored by close relatives already living in Canada, and they may or may not have useful job-related skills. Finally, refugees are those who come to Canada in need of protection from persecution in their home country. Like other immigrants, they too may or may not have job-related skills.

Immigrants have always been an important source of Canada's growing population and labour supply. The results of the 2016 Census show there were 7.5 million immigrants living in Canada, representing just over 20 per cent of the total population. The largest group of immigrants came as adults and hail from Asian countries. However, large numbers of others came from Africa, Central and South America, and the Caribbean (Statistics Canada 2016). When we describe immigrants and their children, by convention we use certain terms. "First generation" comprises the immigrants themselves, "second generation" refers to their children, and "third generation" refers to their grandchildren. Over 20 million people in Canada described themselves as third generation immigrants, meaning they are the grandchildren of immigrants.

Some economic immigrants stay only for a short while. The Government of Canada has moved to defining two classes of temporary immigrants, or those that briefly supply needed labour from outside the country without swelling the number of landed immigrants (note that a work permit or authorization to work without a permit is required for a foreign national to be allowed to work in Canada under either of the following programs):

- *Temporary Foreign Worker Program*: Employers must get a Labour Market Impact Assessment (LMIA) to hire foreign workers to fill temporary labour and skill shortages.

- *International Mobility Program (IMP)*: The IMP lets employers hire temporary workers without an LMIA. Exemptions from the LMIA process are based on the economic, cultural, or other competitive advantages for Canada and the benefits gained by Canadians and permanent residents.

Many continue to debate whether these temporary worker programs displace available Canadian workers and whether they are administered properly. Added to this, the public view of immigrants has been mixed in recent years, as revealed in the findings of several public opinion surveys. For example, a 2018 survey conducted by the Environics Institute found that most Canadians (58 per cent) do not feel the current level of immigration is too high (see Figure 2.5).

As noted earlier, the composition of Canada's recent immigrants overlaps with another population under discussion—young people. In 2016, 64 per cent of immigrants were between 15 and 44 years old (Statistics Canada 2016). A young immigrant population is great news for the federal government, who recently changed Canada's point system to recruit workers aged 18 to 35. Canada's point system is an assessment tool that scores prospective immigrants on desirable features such as age, education, work skills, and language skill in English or French (Government of Canada 2013b). See Figure 2.6 for a comparison of the growth rate of the Canadian population by births versus immigration.

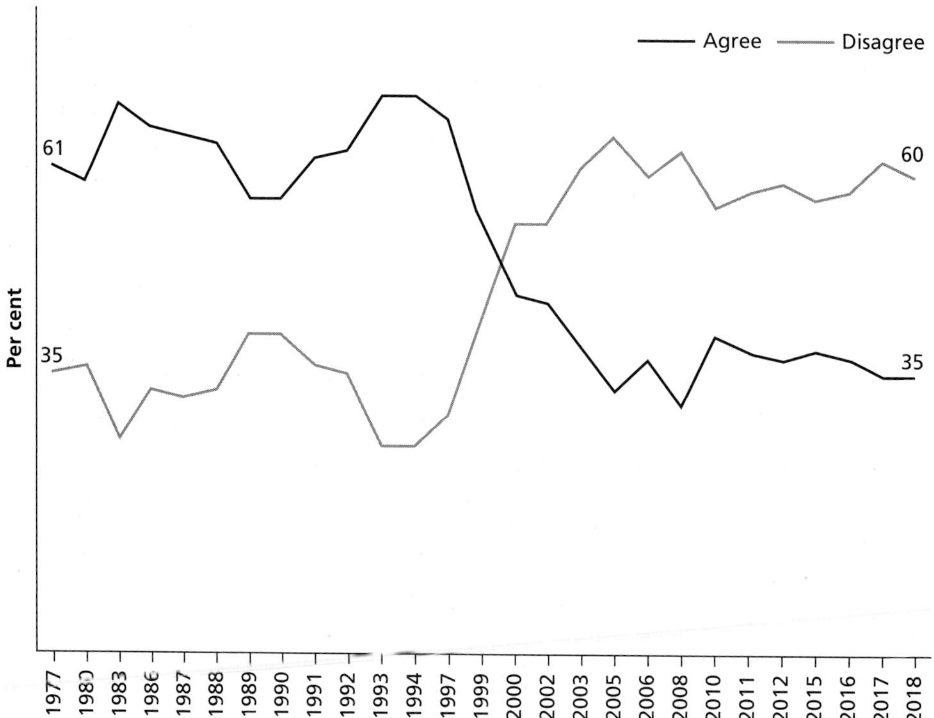

Figure 2.5 ◆ Responses in Favour or Against the Statement "Overall, There Is Too Much Immigration to Canada," 1977–2018

Source: Environics Institute 2018:2.

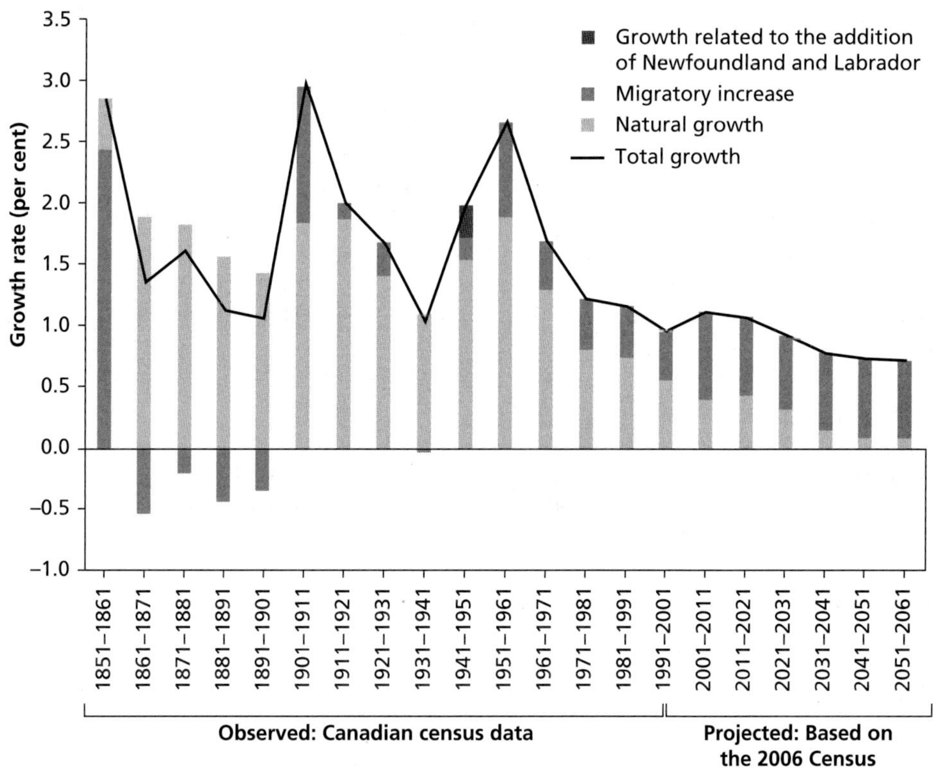

Figure 2.6 ◆ Growth Rate Comparisons—Births versus Immigration

Source: Statistics Canada 2018b:Figure 1.

◆ In Their Own Words ◆

One of the major challenges for skilled immigrants arriving in Canada is finding jobs within their fields. For example, Abdul Waheed originally hailed from Pakistan and trained as a chemist with two master's degrees. Five years ago, Waheed came to Montreal with his wife and kids. He believed he would eventually be able to find a job in his field. Despite searching dozens of job sites, sending out several résumés, taking job-finding programs offered by Emploi-Québec, and studying French, the only job he found was at a call centre. When asked about his experience, Waheed replied: "I can't express the feeling of dismay and despair I have because of this . . . I feel like a big failure. I didn't come here to live this kind of life. I just want [my kids] to be proud of me."

Source: Hendry 2018.

Indigenous Peoples in Canada

As we noted briefly in the opening section of this chapter, Indigenous Peoples are one of the most, if not the most, diversely disadvantaged groups in Canadian society. In this sense, they capture most dramatically what it means to suffer from a "stacked deck." And precisely because they illustrate so many aspects of inequality, we have left the discussion of Indigenous Peoples until now to allow for a fuller discussion of the disadvantages they suffer.

Indigenous Peoples vary widely—culturally, socially, and geographically. In Canada, the umbrella term *Indigenous* comprises three different subpopulations: First Nations, Métis, and Inuit. The term *First Nations* describes a large and diverse group. In fact, in 2018, the Government of Canada recognized over 630 First Nations communities, comprising more than 50 cultural groups and 50 different languages.

A second subpopulation of Indigenous people is the Métis. Most people agree the term describes a person who has both Indigenous and non-Indigenous ancestry. In the early years of colonization, the word *Métis* was used to describe a wide range of people who were the offspring of varied combinations of settlers and locals. Today, the term encompasses a distinct cultural or political group. The population of Métis in Canada is growing, partly because laws that officially label a person as having Indigenous ancestry are changing to include more (or different) people.

The remaining Indigenous Peoples live in what is referred to as "Inuit Nunangat." This is a vast area in the northern part of the country that stretches from the west all the way to the east. This huge region—a full third of Canada's total land mass—comprises 53 recognized communities (Government of Canada 2013a). Inuit speak different languages, practise different cultural traditions, and have different historical and present-day experiences across Inuit Nunangat.

As previously mentioned, the Indigenous population in Canada is young and growing. Children aged 14 and under make up 26.8 per cent of the Indigenous population, compared to only 16.4 per cent in the non-Indigenous population. So, there are far fewer seniors among Indigenous Peoples than among non-Indigenous people (Statistics Canada 2017a). Between the years 2006 and 2016, the Indigenous population grew by 42.5 per cent. This rate of growth is more than four times the growth rate of the non-Indigenous population during that same period.

Some Indigenous Peoples in Canada are "Registered Indians" while others are not. Indigenous Peoples who are **Registered Indians** (also called **Status Indians**) are those who are registered with the Government of Canada. People on this registry are entitled to rights and benefits as outlined in the Indian Act, which was first created in 1876.

Registered Indians (or Status Indians) Indigenous Peoples who are registered with the Government of Canada and entitled to some rights and benefits as outlined in the Indian Act. Interestingly, there is no federal register for Inuit or Métis.

Before the Indian Act was changed in 1985, a Registered Indian woman would lose her official status if she married a non-registered man, regardless of her genetic ancestry. Losing her official status would mean losing all the associated rights and benefits. As well, until 1960, any Registered Indian who wished to vote in a federal election had to abandon their Indian status. On the one hand, these Indian Act policies imply people's status derives from the genetic composition of their blood. On the other hand, they imply that same status is something they can choose to abandon or be deprived of by others. Doesn't this seem contradictory? In their own words, representatives of the Government of Canada are "the only authority under the *Indian Act* who can determine a person's eligibility for Indian status" (Government of Canada 2018). This means that many people who consider themselves to be Indigenous may *not* be included on the registry—which means our census numbers may not show the whole picture.

As noted earlier, for more than any other population in Canada, a consideration of history is crucial to understanding the present-day realities for Indigenous Peoples. The colonizer–colonized relationship in North America is over 500 years old, and over the course of those five centuries, public views of Indigenous Peoples have varied widely. Many early settlers valued Indigenous Peoples as knowledgeable partners in trade. However, other settlers considered the local inhabitants to be nothing more than a nuisance to be wiped out. In Canada, Indigenous Peoples remain the most vulnerable population on every dimension of social inequality. The United Nations (2014) puts it this way: Of the bottom 100 communities on the Canadian Community Wellbeing Index, 96 are Indigenous communities. In the top 100 communities in Canada, only one is Indigenous.

As noted earlier, a social issue that has (finally) caught the attention of the public of late has been the continued disappearance and murder of Indigenous women and girls in Canada. Reports vary based on who is doing the counting. However, the RCMP (2014) state that over 1,000 Indigenous women have disappeared or been murdered since 1980 (see Figure 2.7). The same RCMP report also noted that these murders are solved at a significantly lower rate than those of non-Indigenous women. Progress is especially slow if the victim was involved in the sex trade or associated with illegal activities. Further, female Indigenous murder victims are twice as likely to be beaten to death as their non-Indigenous counterparts.

Indigenous Peoples in Canada have never been more active in addressing the inequalities they face. Idle No More and various Indigenous-led environmental movements have seized the Canadian public's attention in unprecedented ways, drawing focus to the injustices, strengths, and opportunities in Indigenous communities.

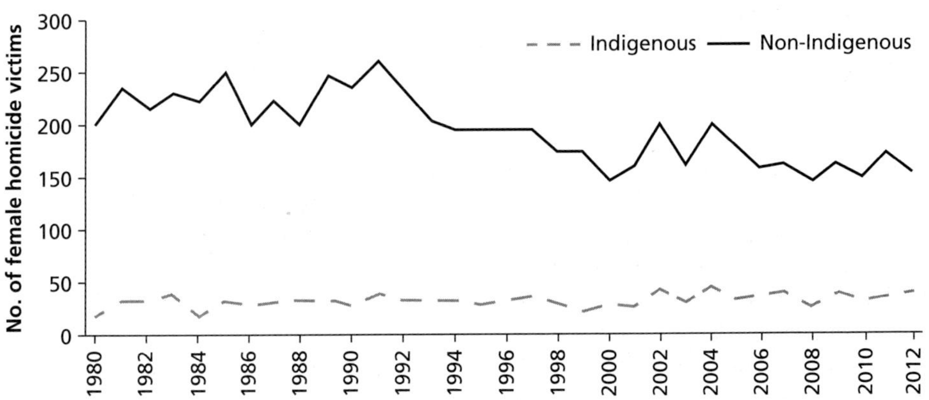

Figure 2.7 ◆ Female Homicides per Year, 1980–2012

The number of Indigenous female victims of homicide has remained relatively constant, while the number of non-Indigenous female victims has declined.

Source: © 2014 HER MAJESTY THE QUEEN IN RIGHT OF CANADA as represented by the Royal Canadian Mounted Police.

LGBTQ+ People in Canada

Some have estimated that 1 out of 10 people are LGBTQ+—lesbian, gay, bisexual, transgender, or queer; the "+" stands for all the other identities that the acronym encompasses (such as asexual, pansexual, intersex, nonbinary, or Two-Spirit, to name just a few). Before we discuss numbers, let's break down LGBTQ+, a catch-all acronym encompassing many widely differing people and populations.

LGB stands for *lesbian, gay, bisexual* and refer to a person's sexual orientation—that is, whether a person is attracted to members of the same sex, the opposite sex, or both sexes. T is for *transgender*, which relates to a person's *gender* identity (not their sexual orientation); trans masculine refers to people who are AFAB (assigned female at birth) but are actually men, and trans feminine refers to people who are AMAB (assigned male at birth) but are actually women. Q is for *queer*, a word used to represent people who don't feel a part of **heteronormative** society and reject the broad classifications of other terms.

heteronormativity The societal assumption that all people are by default heterosexual and that heterosexuality is the normal state of being.

Data from national surveys confirm that more Canadians self-identify as LGBTQ+ today than they did in the past. For example, the number of self-identified same-sex couples increased by 60.7 per cent between 2006 and 2016 (Statistics Canada 2017f). In comparison, during that same period, the number of opposite-sex couples increased only by 9.6 per cent (Statistics Canada 2017f). As a result, same-sex couples accounted for 0.6 per cent of all couples in Canada in 2006 and grew to 0.9 per cent in 2016 (Statistics Canada 2007; Statistics

Egale Canada, an organization promoting equal rights for LGBTQ+ populations, sells this teaching tool. The four different-coloured dice are "designed to support participants' understanding of four distinct and independent categories of human identity—assigned sex, gender identity, gender expression and attraction."

Egale

Canada 2017f). In addition, the 2016 Census showed that half of all same-sex couples in Canada live in Montreal, Toronto, Vancouver, and Ottawa-Gatineau. Like immigrants and young people, LGBTQ+ people tend to concentrate in the nation's largest Census Metropolitan Areas, with smaller numbers in smaller urban centres (Statistics Canada 2017f).

Non-response to survey questions about sexual orientation or gender identity results in the underrepresentation of LGBTQ+ groups. Members of this group *are* recognized in these surveys. However, some may be reluctant to reveal their sexual orientation because they have not yet come out to their friends or families (Raj 2012). This reluctance is especially evident in smaller communities, where LGBTQ+ Canadians may worry about experiencing homophobia, discrimination, and even violent victimization. A significant problem facing LGBTQ+ Canadians is the threat of homophobic bullying—a threat that is greatest among young Canadians. The 2009 Canadian Climate Survey on Homophobia shows that LGBTQ+ high school students are far more likely than heterosexual students to be bullied, including verbal harassment, physical harassment, or personal harassment on the Internet or via texting. In fact, an alarming 73 per cent of LGBTQ+ students report feeling unsafe at school, indicating just how pervasive bullying is toward LGBTQ+ youth today (*CBC News* 2010).

Other trends suggest that the public perception of LGBTQ+ individuals has changed for the better. Table 2.1 shows results from the first pan-Canadian survey of LGBTQ+ populations in 2017. This survey asked 1,897 LGBTQ+ individuals about their perceived level of acceptance within their various social circles.

One clear sign of this growing acceptance was the legalization of same-sex marriage in Canada in 2005. Giving same-sex Canadians the legal right to marry shows a more

Table 2.1 Perceived Level of Acceptance, LGBTQ+

	(%)	Age					
	Total	**15–17**	**18–24**	**25–34**	**35–44**	**45–54**	**55+**
Your circle of friends							
Very well accepted	71	85	73	78	73	65	63
Very + Rather poorly accepted	5	0	4	2	5	5	10
Your spouse/partner, your children							
Very well accepted	69	76	71	78	53	74	64
Very + Rather poorly accepted	13	7	7	7	10	12	21
The management of the company you work for							
Very well accepted	60	50	47	72	79	58	32
Very + Rather poorly accepted	7	6	15	5	1	2	16
Your co-workers							
Very well accepted	56	49	47	64	76	55	26
Very + Rather poorly accepted	7	2	13	5	1	7	15

Source: Jasmine Roy Foundation 2018:76.

positive attitude in Canadian society toward these groups than existed in the past. Knowing that other Canadians support their sexual orientation may lead more same-sex couples to come out—that is, to disclose their identities to friends, family, co-workers, and others. This trend is certainly reflected in the number of same-sex marriages in Canada, which tripled between 2006 and 2011 (Raj 2012).

Another legislative change that showed growing public support for transgender Canadians was enacted in 2017. Bill C-16 added gender identity and gender expression to the list of banned grounds of discrimination. This means a person can no longer be denied housing or education or any other right based on their gender identity. Similarly, starting in 2017 the Criminal Code protects against hate speech or propaganda based on gender identity or expression. Before Bill C-16 was enacted, actions such as these against transgender people would not technically have been illegal. Legal changes like these speak volumes about how the public perception of LGBTQ+ Canadians has changed in recent years.

However, despite the growing legal acceptance of LGBTQ+ people (in respect to marriage, for example), issues around healthcare continue to abound for this population. According to the American Cancer Society,

> Studies have found that lesbians and bisexual women have higher rates of breast cancer than heterosexual women. They also get less routine health care than other women, including colon, breast, and cervical cancer screening. The reasons for these differences include:
>
> - Many health insurance policies do not cover unmarried partners. This makes it harder for many lesbians and bisexual women to get quality health care.
> - Many women do not tell their doctors about their sexual orientation because they don't want discrimination to affect the quality of health care they receive.
> - Fear of having a negative experience with a health-care provider can lead some women to delay or avoid medical care, especially routine care such as early detection tests.

Same-sex couples tend to be younger than heterosexual couples, on average. In fact, in 2011, 25 per cent of the members of all same-sex couples were under 35 years of age, while only 6.2 per cent were over 65 years of age (Raj 2012). Further, as we will see in Chapter 6, LGBTQ+ youth are at higher-than-average risk of homelessness. These facts highlight how multiple vulnerabilities may overlap or intersect, and how the intersection of multiple vulnerabilities can increase the risk of negative outcomes.

People with Disabilities in Canada

disability The condition of having difficulty carrying out familiar tasks, according to the Canadian Survey on Disability. This includes being limited in normal daily activities because of a long-term health condition or health-related problem.

According to the Canadian Survey on Disability (CSD), a person is considered to have a **disability** if their full participation in society is limited by a long-term condition or health problem (Statistics Canada 2018a). For every five Canadians over the age of 15, roughly one of them reports one or more disabilities.

According to the most recent data available from Statistics Canada (see Figure 2.8), the percentage of Canadians with disabilities was lowest in Nunavut (6.9 per cent) and highest in Nova Scotia (18.8 per cent). Likely, this difference is due to disability's

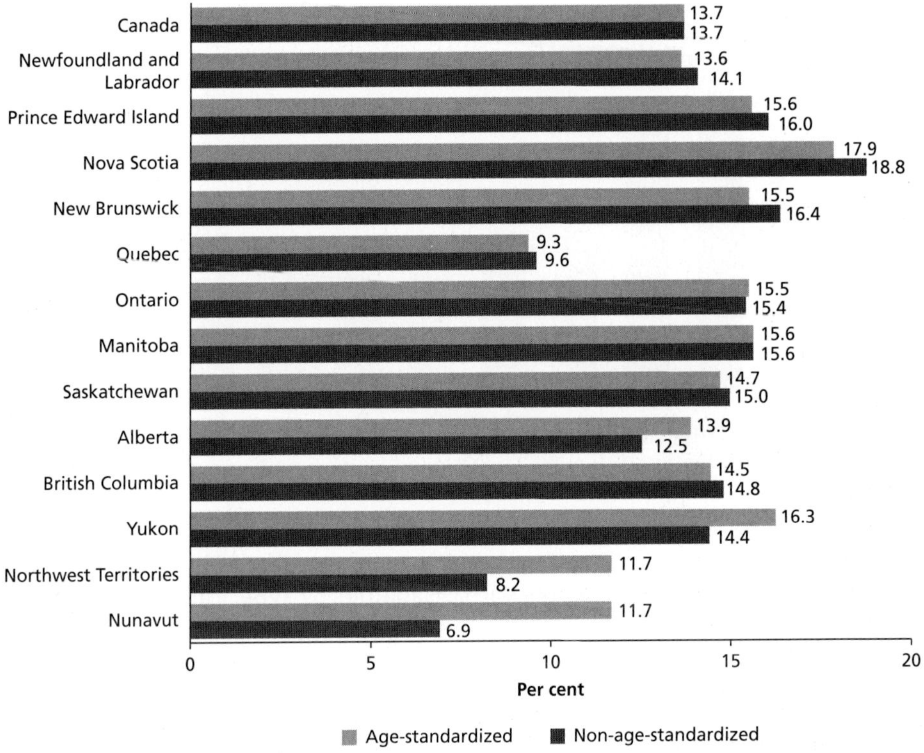

Figure 2.8 ◆ Percentage of People with Disabilities, by Province and Territory

Source: Statistics Canada 2012:Chart 1.

association with age. A much higher percentage of elderly people (over the age of 65) are disabled, compared to younger people (under 25). Further, because of immigration and fertility patterns, Nunavut is a young population while Nova Scotia is an older population.

Disabilities can range from mild to severe, and mild disabilities are typically more common than severe ones (see Figure 2.9). The CSD identifies 10 types of disabilities: pain, mobility, agility, hearing, seeing, learning, psychological, memory, speech, and developmental (Statistics Canada 2013a). Bear in mind too that some disabilities are not readily visible, so the challenges and daily struggles facing those who live with a disability often go unnoticed. That said, other disabilities are indeed visible and noticed, and historically, many people with disabilities have experienced discrimination and abuse. In the early part of the twentieth century, they were thought to be burdens and threats to society and, as a result, were often segregated and warehoused in institutions (Rogow 2002).

To fight the inequality they experienced and to gain more control over their lives, people with disabilities eventually came together. In the 1960s, they began the **disability rights movement** in Canada. This movement was motivated by the civil rights movement in the United States, and it advocated for some of the same principles, such as respect, full citizenship, and inclusion in society.

disability rights movement A Canadian movement that spoke for the respect, full citizenship, and inclusion of disabled people in society.

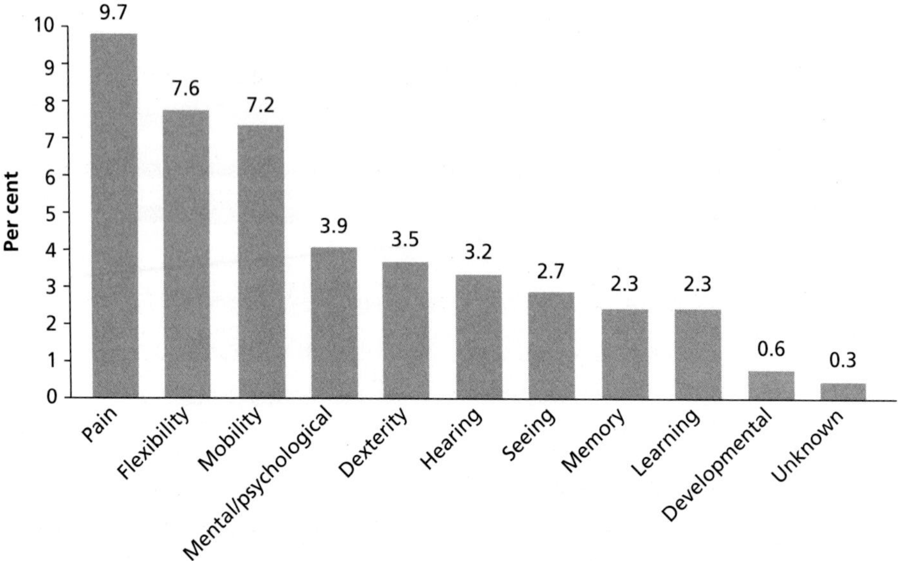

Figure 2.9 ◆ Percentage of People with Disabilities by Type, Canada, 2012

Source: Statistics Canada 2013b.

The population of people with disabilities in Canada has made great progress toward equality over the past few decades. However, it continues to face vulnerability, disadvantage, and even victimization. For example, people with disabilities earn much less, on average, than people without disabilities. The 2017 CSD reported the following demographic summary for people with disabilities in Canada:

- In 2017, one in five (22 per cent) of the Canadian population aged 15 years and over—or about 6.2 million individuals—had one or more disabilities.
- Disabilities related to pain, flexibility, mobility, and mental health were the most common disability types.
- Among youth (aged 15 to 24 years), however, mental health–related disabilities were the most prevalent type of disability (8 per cent).
- Among those aged 25 to 64 years, persons with disabilities were less likely to be employed (59 per cent) than those without disabilities (80 per cent).
- As the level of severity increased, the likelihood of being employed decreased. Among individuals aged 25 to 64 years, 76 per cent of those with mild disabilities were employed, whereas 31 per cent of those with very severe disabilities were employed.
- Among those with disabilities aged 25 to 64 years who were not employed and not currently in school, two in five (39 per cent) had potential to work. This represents nearly 645,000 individuals with disabilities.
- Persons with more severe disabilities (28 per cent) aged 25 to 64 years were more likely to be living in poverty (as measured by the market-basket measure) than

their counterparts without disabilities (10 per cent) or with milder disabilities (14 per cent).

- Among those with disabilities aged 15 to 64 years, lone parents and those living alone were the most likely to be living in poverty among any type of household living arrangements. Since eight in ten lone parents were women, the high risk of living in poverty in this group disproportionately affected women (Morris et al. 2018).

As is evident from the summary above, having a disability can make finding a job a challenging task. According to a 2013 Bank of Montreal survey, only 30 per cent of 301 small business owners in Canada have ever hired a person with a disability. It's no surprise, then, that the unemployment rate for Canadians with disabilities was higher than the rate for all Canadians in 2006. Many people with disabilities end up settling for part-time work because they are unable to find a full-time job (BMO Financial Group 2013).

Not surprisingly, almost a third of working age adults who live with a severe disability live in poverty (Statistics Canada 2018a). Someone with a mobility disability is more likely to live in poverty than someone with a hearing disability. However, they are less likely to experience poverty than a person with a cognitive disability. From this standpoint, a hearing disability (that is, slight or considerable deafness) is only a *slight* disability in its economic effects. Far more damaging is a mobility disability (for example, requiring a wheelchair) or cognitive disability (for example, being unable to make appropriate judgments in social situations).

Closing Remarks

As we have seen, there are different kinds of vulnerable populations in Canada today. Taken together, they amount to a majority of the Canadian population. Another way of saying this is to note that this book is about *most* Canadians, because most Canadians today, one way or another, are vulnerable, disadvantaged, or even victimized. There are a huge number of Canadians who are old, or poor, or young, or racialized, or have other socially stigmatized characteristics.

Yet we rarely reflect on this fact and its significance. It means that committing ourselves to studying and, perhaps, reducing inequality means studying and improving the lives of most Canadians: people who are like the readers and writers of this book. For this reason, we all have a sound, personal purpose for wanting to know more about these vulnerable, disadvantaged, and even victimized people. Namely, this book is about most of us.

The COVID-19 epidemic has driven home, more forcefully than anything else imaginable, how interdependent we are and how vulnerable we all are to massive economic disruptions of society. No one who has weathered the worldwide epidemic can be indifferent to the harm humanity suffers—and especially the most disadvantaged people suffer—when natural disasters strike with full force. We will see evidence of this throughout the book.

Test Your Knowledge

1. Can you list three groups in Canada that are vulnerable to socio-economic disadvantages and some of the reasons why each group is more vulnerable than the general population?
2. Can you give three examples of populations that face multiple interlocking disadvantages?
3. What are the differences between the low-income cut-off, market-basket, and low-income measures of poverty?
4. Why in this book do we prefer to use the term *racialized people*? Why is it preferable to the older term, *race*?
5. List and describe the three types of immigrants. What are the key distinctions among the types, and how do they affect people's experience in Canada?
6. Explain the difference between sexual orientation and gender identity. Why is this distinction important?
7. According to the Canadian Survey on Disability, when is a person considered to have a disability? List the different kinds of disabilities.
8. Fill in the blank: The ____________ refers to how women are overrepresented among low-income people around the world.
9. Fill in the blank: There is a lot of overlap between Canada's recent immigrants and ____________.
10. What does LGBTQ+ stand for?

See the Answer Key online to check your answers.

Questions for Critical Thought

1. What are strengths and weaknesses of the idea of Indigenous "intergenerational" trauma?
2. Do you agree that the feminization of poverty is a significant social problem? Why or why not?
3. What social initiatives might be beneficial in bringing about equality for the disabled community? What has been tried but has failed to work well?
4. Using what you read in this chapter, brainstorm at least one initiative aimed toward improved equality for three of the other victimized populations listed in the chapter.

Additional Resources

Recommended Readings

Adams, Christopher et al. 2010. *Métis in Canada: History, Identity, Law and Politics*. Edmonton, AB: University of Alberta Press. This set of essays provides a rich source for people who want to learn more about the history and culture of the Métis people in Canada.

Auerbach, R.P., J. Alonso, W.G. Axinn, P. Cuijpers, D.D. Ebert, J.G. Green, I. Hwang, et al. 2016. "Mental Disorders among College Students in the WHO World Mental Health Surveys."

Psychological Medicine 46(14):2955–70. Using data from the World Health Organization World Mental Health Surveys, the authors study the effects of college attendance on well-being. They find that mental illnesses are common among college students, are associated with college attrition, and are typically untreated.

Jordan-Fenton, Christy and Margaret Pokiak-Fenton. 2010. *Fatty Legs: A True Story*. Toronto, ON: Annick Press. This book is a memoir of a young Inuit girl's experience at an Indigenous residential school and chronicles her victories over her persecutors. It is written based on the experiences of author Margaret Pokiak-Fenton.

Kar, Nayan Tara 2013. *The Truth & Nothing But . . . : A Family's Ordeal!* Denver, CO: Outskirts Press. This biographical novel recounts a case of elder abuse and its effects on the family in discussion.

Recommended Films

Teo in Toronto. 2012. Directed by Min Sook Lee. Canada: TVO. In this documentary, Min Sook Lee reconnects with Teodoro Martinez, a migrant worker meeting with community activists to discuss poverty and food security. Teodoro meets a group of homeless youth in Parkdale, Toronto, growing their own food in a local garden.

The Remaining Light. 2010. Produced by Goh Iromoto, Shannon Daub, and Marcy Cohen. Canada: Seniors Care Project (BC). This documentary follows the community-based care services seniors have available to them. The film features personal interviews that explore seniors' dignity, how to prevent illness and social isolation, and how to control for healthcare costs.

Kanehsatake: 270 Years of Resistance. 1993. Directed by Alanis Obomsawin. National Film Board. This Canadian documentary portrays the 1990 showdown between the Mohawk Nation and the mainly white Quebec town of Oka, which sought to develop land judged sacred by the Mohawk.

The following films are also excellent cinematic representations of some of the difficulties faced by the disadvantaged groups discussed in this chapter:

- *For the Bible Tells Me So*. 2007. [sexuality]
- *Out of the Past: The Struggle for Gay and Lesbian Rights in America*. 1998. [sexuality]
- *Saving Face*. 2004. [racialization, immigration, sexuality, gender]
- *Summer Storm*. 2004. [sexuality]

Seika Chujo/Shutterstock

3 Employment Income

Learning Objectives

- To identify current trends in Canadian employment.
- To identify the ways in which racialization correlates with employment inequality.
- To understand how age discrimination affects younger and older Canadians.
- To understand how household and unpaid work is set apart by gender.
- To understand why foreign workers are often overqualified for their jobs.
- To identify the barriers to employment faced by Canadians with disabilities.
- To understand the Employment Equity Act.

Introduction to Survival Capital

survival capital The resources and opportunities people in a modern urban society need to survive and, perhaps, thrive.

In this and the next eight chapters, we will discuss different types of **survival capital**. By survival capital, we mean the resources and opportunities people in a modern urban society need to survive and, perhaps, thrive. Employment income, daycare and early childhood education, formal education, housing, transportation, nutritious food, healthcare, legal representation, safety, and some measure of respect are all forms of survival capital.

Like all the forms of cultural capital and social capital discussed in Chapter 1, all forms of survival capital play a huge part in people's lives. For example, survival capital affects their physical survival: their longevity and years of freedom from illness. It also affects their opportunities and their abilities to lead fulfilling lives. But more than cultural capital and social capital, which address prosperity and inclusion, survival capital is a matter of life and death. It involves resources that people need to *survive*.

Like cultural and social capital, investing in survival capital can lead to great rewards in the form of other types of capital. For example, investing in the survival capital of education by enrolling in university can result in new knowledge (cultural capital) and new friendships (social capital). But like cultural and social capital, survival capital often cannot be gained without sacrifices. Sometimes people may reluctantly leave the comfort of their home communities in pursuit of job opportunities elsewhere. More often, they must forgo or sacrifice some types of survival capital to gain other types of survival capital. For example, parents may have to forgo good health or good housing to ensure their children receive a good education. Similarly, students forgo employment income to attend school.

In this chapter, we discuss employment income. Of all the kinds of survival capital covered in this book, employment income is perhaps the most fundamental. Most of us need the income from employment to buy food, shelter, transport, and other essentials. Of course, jobs are not solely about earning money; they can also provide a sense of identity and fulfillment. But most importantly, a job provides a person with the means to live, ideally with a little left over for important, stress-relieving leisure pursuits. Some jobs may also provide a pension that helps financially support employees after retirement, while other jobs may support workers by offering health and dental benefits.

Theoretical Perspectives on Access to Employment Income

In this chapter, we will explain some of the specific barriers that vulnerable populations face when they try to access safe, secure, and reasonably compensated work. Specifically, we will do so with an eye to the theories we discussed in Chapter 1—functionalism, conflict theory, feminism, and symbolic interactionism—and how they address income and employment inequality.

Recall from Chapter 1 that the functionalist approach in sociology focuses on how social arrangement contributes to the survival of society. Functionalism might focus on how poverty or economic inequality contributes to social stability or even social improvement. On the other hand, conflict theorists focus on the struggle between more and less powerful people. Thus, conflict theory would focus on the ways that powerful people limit wages and maximize economic inequality to their own advantage.

Feminism, you will recall, focuses on the gendered nature of disadvantage in our society and the reasons behind it. Symbolic interactionism, on the one hand, focuses on how people represent advantage and disadvantage—on the ways that poor people are taught to regard and behave toward rich people, for example. On the other hand, a brand of symbolic interactionism called *social constructionism* focuses on the ways powerful people develop and use ideologies to justify their advantage. For example, it might study how people justify their right to high incomes and fancy lifestyles at the expense of poor, disadvantaged people.

With these approaches in mind, we begin with what is sometimes referred to as a "common sense perspective" on inequality, succinctly summarized by sociologist Karen Anderson (2012). A common sense understanding of unequal pay is the view that people earn what they deserve to earn. Those who work harder get more pay and more job opportunities, according to this view. However, many sociologists point to the characteristics of society, not the characteristics of individuals, to explain employment income inequality. This is a case, perhaps, where a common sense perspective doesn't make much sense at all.

You will recall from Chapter 1 that functionalism also tries to explain employment inequality. Functionalists argue that employment inequality is necessary for the functioning of society. Despite its negative effects, income inequality is useful and necessary because high rewards motivate people to work harder. In this view, hard-working people with the most talent, smarts, and skills will float up and fill the most highly paid, socially important roles.

As mentioned, this may sound similar to the common sense perspective, but the two approaches differ slightly. Functionalism focuses on how employment inequality is a result of the unequal value of jobs in society. The common sense perspective, on the other hand, focuses on how employment inequality results from the varying degrees to which people are willing to work hard. From the functionalist perspective, people have difficulty gaining employment because they are uneducated, untalented, or unskilled. From the common sense perspective, people have difficulty gaining employment because they do not work as hard as others do. Look back to Chapter 1 for the critique of the functional theory of stratification.

Conflict theorists contend that social life revolves around the unending competition for valued resources like property, power, and status. Those at the top—sometimes called "the ruling class"—use whatever is at their disposal to stay at the top, including hiring people like themselves into vacant positions. From the conflict theory perspective, many people have trouble gaining employment or climbing the income ladder. That's because the ruling class works against them to consolidate their control over valued resources.

Feminist theorists note that women and men, even within the same class, often have different experiences. Typically, men enjoy more and better employment opportunities than women, other things being equal. In large part, that is because of women's heavier responsibility to perform unpaid domestic labour. Oxfam (2019) has put a dollar figure on the unpaid work done by women around the world. It reported that "if all the unpaid care work done by women across the globe was carried out by a single company, it would have an annual turnover of $10 trillion—43 times that of Apple."

So men, who usually occupy higher-paid jobs than women, often profit at the expense of women who work for them. As a result, many women suffer from job dissatisfaction and poorer physical and psychological health outcomes and behaviours. These outcomes are especially common when working women have other disadvantaging characteristics as well, such as race, age, or physical disability (Triana et al. 2019).

Symbolic interactionists, finally, are interested in how people interpret the situations in which they find themselves. They study how people make sense of social life and how they act based on these interpretations. They also focus on small-group and face-to-face interactional settings. Symbolic interactionists, for example, would be interested in studying how workers help the bosses they like and undermine the actions of bosses they don't like. In every workplace, a culture emerges that supports certain kinds of unofficial, sometimes subversive behaviour. This is designed to make the job palatable and interesting and, sometimes, to fight against managers who are unfair or impossible to satisfy. As sociologists discovered many generations ago, workplace cultures also limit productivity, so no one stands out as especially better or worse than the rest of the group. It does so by enforcing a set of unstated but widely understood group productivity norms.

Symbolic interactionists are also interested in how workers make sense of unclear and sometimes impossible organizational rules. An example here would be the ways police officers make sense of and enforce informal (yet formally justifiable) rules about how and when to use force when catching a suspected criminal. Often, the organizational rules or formal laws are written so broadly that everything and nothing is justifiable, leaving workers to define these rules in a way that protects them against criticism.

Different Kinds of Capital

To get capital, you have to have capital. As we will see in this chapter, to get the survival capital we are calling access to employment, you need to have and spend other kinds of capital.

One type of capital we will discuss repeatedly is **human capital**, by which we mean educational credentials, job experience and skills, and physical fitness for work (also known as good health). Another type of capital we will discuss is social capital. That is the sum total of a person's social contacts—friends, relatives, and acquaintances—all or any of whom can help you land or keep a job. Finally, we will talk about cultural capital. When people hire someone for a job, they are not merely judging that person's likely ability to do the job satisfactorily. They are also judging whether and how well that person will fit into the work group and get along with other workers, clients, and customers. Often, when a person is denied a job, the reason is not an absence of credentials, skills, or social contacts. More likely, it is because of a view that this person will not fit in. However, this view of unsuitability is often related to that person's self-presentation: the way that person talks, responds to questions, or even dresses. Since these are all learned skills, they are all part of cultural capital.

human capital The skills, knowledge, and credentials that can be shared from one person to another and contribute to the productivity of society.

Let's briefly consider how clothing can affect someone's ability to get and keep a job. Most workplaces are more formal than school or home. We see this reflected in the ways people dress. Different ways of dressing at work signal different ways of thinking. Namely, how a person dresses says something about their willingness to comply with organizational rules and "fit in." For example, employees who wear suits to the office are playing by the rules. But an employee who wears flip-flops or pajama bottoms to the office may seem not to care about the rules. When everyone in a workplace is dressed similarly, it suggests the organization is trying to regiment the workers—and succeeding (Rafaeli and Pratt 1993:32; see also Massimino and Turner 2017).

Most organizations try to influence their workers' clothing choices in at least three ways (Rafaeli and Pratt 1993:32). First are the qualities of clothes—for example, formal versus informal. Second is homogeneity—that is, is everyone dressed similarly or differently? Third is conspicuousness—whether people wear attention-catching outfits or not. In most organizations, all three elements are regulated, and these rules differ for men and women. Obeying them can make the difference between landing a job or not, getting promoted or not, and getting a raise or not. In this sense, consumer choices—that is, the clothes we buy—impact our ability to consume in the future by impacting our success at work.

Clothes don't only affect others' views of you; they also affect how you see yourself. Both men and women who think workwear matters also say it makes them feel more competent (Peluchette, Karl, and Rust 2006; Roth, Kim, and Kincade 2017). In large corporations, employees feel the most authoritative, trustworthy, and ready to succeed when wearing formal business clothes (Peluchette and Karl 2007). In turn, these people take on more challenging tasks, show greater persistence, and recover from setbacks faster. So when people present themselves well, they also tend to perform well. In a sense, this makes clothing consumption a self-fulfilling prophecy.

Those who buy costly business wear, like suits and dresses, both look and *feel* the part. They become more likely to do the kinds of work and behave in the sorts of ways that help them move up in the organization. On the other hand, those who cannot afford these clothes are less likely to be noticed and respected by management. And they are less likely to feel like they fit in. Feeling excluded hinders their ability to do their best work, making it less likely they will move up.

Many people also think dressing properly helps improve their work relationships. For example, they think their colleagues will respect them and their bosses will see them as stable, obedient, and reliable. So how a worker dresses signals their willingness to fit into the organization and co-operate with other workers. It also offers workers in one branch an opportunity to distinguish themselves from those in different departments (Pratt and Rafaeli 1997; Brown 2017). The clothes we buy—and are taught to wear—therefore help preserve an office hierarchy. They reflect our status within the organization. And they show how we rank, compared with others inside the organization.

As noted, women become especially aware of their clothes if they work in the business world. They know how important it is to project specific meanings and identities through their dress. They also know how costly it can be if people misunderstand these self-presentations. To study this, Kimle and Damhorst (1997; see also Peluchette and Karl 2018) interviewed 24 businesswomen employed in various companies and agencies in an urban centre. Most were involved in management, and they were all widely experienced. These women felt they could choose different kinds of clothes to express different meanings, including credibility and competence. The ideal businesswoman's image, they said, combined a mix of conservatism, fashion, masculinity, femininity, sexuality, creativity, and conformity. Obviously, some of these elements—like conservatism and sexuality—are contradictory, causing tensions that need conscious balancing. Balancing wrongly can endanger the woman's credibility.

Broadly, job applicants and jobholders are judged on how they look, and disadvantaged people have a harder time meeting others' expectations. People who do not or cannot dress "properly" will have trouble getting and holding a job, especially in a tight job market. They are like people who do not or cannot speak or act in expected ways.

Changing Trends in Employment

The last few decades have seen many changes in the Canadian workplace. The 2007–8 global financial crisis resulted in a spike in the unemployment rate, which is the measure of the number of Canadians who are not employed and looking for work. Today, workers continue to feel the aftereffects of this recession. The COVID-19 pandemic in 2020 was even worse, bringing the rate of unemployment in Canada close to historic levels reached during the Great Depression of the 1930s.

Simply put, recessions produce unemployment because employers cannot afford to pay as many employees. In the case of COVID-19, many businesses were forced to close while workers and customers sheltered at home. However, before that, from June 2017 to June 2018, around 126,500 Canadians were unemployed, despite searching for a job for a year or more (Hardy, Lovei, and Patterson 2018). By 2018, the overall unemployment rate had fully recovered from the 2008 recession.

However, the long-term unemployment rate remained above the pre-recession levels (Hardy et al. 2018). As well, the quality of available jobs has also declined. In particular, many unionized, well-paying manufacturing jobs have been lost. Often, job loss occurs when companies move their production to another location, usually to gain access to cheaper labour. This, of course, results in local layoffs: Layoffs in Ontario and hiring in Mexico, for example. Accompanying this has been a shift from permanent to temporary work—that is, employment lasting six months or less. This growth of temporary work is another current trend in Canada. Since 1998–9, the growth in permanent jobs has been outpaced by the growth in temporary or short-term jobs. For example, the percentage of Canadians employed temporarily rose from 12.0 per cent in 2016–17 to 13.6 per cent in 2017–18 (Hardy et al. 2018). While this one-year increase may sound small, think about how large 10 or 20 such one-year increases would be and you'll get a clear idea of what young workers are facing.

Temporary work is sometimes called contract work, because employees must rely on a chain of short-term contracts to cobble together a living wage. During the period of 2016–18, around 20 per cent of employment gains came from such temporary work (Hardy et al. 2018). Temporary work is part of a broader category of work known as non-standard or **precarious employment**. This employment is the fastest-growing employment in developed countries, including Canada. It includes jobs with one or more of the following features: part-time employment, self-employment, fixed-term work, temporary work, on-call work, homework, and telecommuting. According to a report in the *Globe and Mail* (Parkinson 2019), non-standard work represents about 31 per cent of all jobs in Canada. As well, people are often underemployed, which means they are grossly overqualified for the fields they work in.

precarious employment Non-standard employment that is poorly paid, insecure, and unprotected.

Economist Francis Fong (2018) has noted difficulties in measuring the extent of this problem because it is hard to define and measure precarious employment. Fong explains that precarious employment can refer to many different things and people, "from an older, low-wage, part-time recent immigrant hired through a temp agency to a newly graduated, short-term continuous-contract worker." To measure how precarious employment impacts specific disadvantaged populations, we first need a clearer sense of what counts as precarious work and who it affects. Fong notes that part-time work has become more common in parts of the economy in which women are overrepresented. This includes "information, culture and recreation services; educational services; and accommodation and food services." As such, it's not surprising to learn that women are far harder hit than men by trends in precarious employment.

THE CANADIAN PRESS/Ted Pritchard

Canadian Union of Postal Workers members in Halifax take part in a 2018 strike over health and safety concerns, workload, staffing, and wages. The number of unionized jobs with the strong benefits that usually accompany them are getting fewer every year. During your career, do you expect you will work as part of a union?

The increase in precarious, non-standard employment results in a decrease in the benefits that have traditionally come with full-time employment, such as pensions and healthcare plans. Pension plans allow employees to contribute financially to an investment fund during employment. Between 1996 and 2016, the number of Canadians covered by a registered pension plan has fallen (Statistics Canada 2018c), as have the number of Canadians working unionized jobs (Statistics Canada 2018d). Unions—free associations of workers intended to protect and further workers' rights—are critical for encouraging (or demanding) that employers offer pensions and health benefits.

The decrease in union jobs between 1999 and 2014 was especially pronounced for young men (Statistics Canada 2018d). This decline is partly explained by shifts in employment from unionized jobs like manufacturing and construction to largely non-unionized jobs like professional services or retail.

The result is that the financial prospects for young people today are worse than they were a generation ago. Most Canadian adults today have more education, experience, and higher qualifications than they did 30 years ago. However, young Canadians still have roughly the same odds of working in a low-wage job as they did in the 1980s and 1990s. In Canada, minimum wage varies across provinces and territories, with the lowest hourly rate in Saskatchewan ($11.32 an hour) and the highest in Alberta ($15 an hour; Retail Council of Canada 2020). Many Canadians working minimum wage jobs may not be able to meet their basic needs even with full-time employment. This population is sometimes called the **working poor**. In Canada, around 746,000 individuals live in families where the main income earner meets the definition of the working poor, and sadly this number is increasing. The working poor are also less likely to have access to work-related benefits, including disability insurance or a family dental plan (Statistics Canada 2014).

working poor Low-income individuals who may be drawing an income from a part-time job or other forms of precarious work.

Those who are inclined to blame poor people for their impoverished circumstances are typically swayed by notions of the so-called urban culture of poverty, which vividly casts the urban poor as authors of their own downfall. The perspective is illustrated in the work of anthropologist Oscar Lewis (1914–1970), who first studied this culture of poverty in the slums of Mexico, Puerto Rico, and the United States. A poignant version of this worldview is found in Lewis's book *The Children of Sanchez* (1961), written from the biographical standpoint of sons and daughters of the impoverished Sanchez family, who live "from hand to mouth" in a Mexico City slum. Lewis found that many of these urban poor, like the Sanchez family, had come from rural backgrounds that provided little in the way of coping skills. Without kin or social supports, let alone a social safety net, they struggled to understand the chaotic social world. Most lacked the skills necessary to attain better lives in better communities, so they remained isolated, unemployed, and poor. The boys were often lured into violence and crime, while the girls became plunged into early pregnancy and violent marriages. Early hopes and aspirations were dashed by a cruel, unyielding reality.

This description, though too brief to capture the richness of Lewis's original analysis, is full enough to suggest why the culture of poverty theory has polarized scholarly opinion. Some say it portrays the poor as "deserving" of their poverty because they do not make enough effort to escape it. In other words, this theory appears to support stereotypical characterizations of poor people as "naturally" lazy or incapable—an idea that has long since fallen out of favour with most sociologists and anthropologists. For his part, Lewis viewed the culture of poverty as a demonstration that class disadvantage had shattered people's abilities to learn, grow, plan, and protect themselves.

As we have hinted, the quality of work has declined in the past few decades. One study looking mostly at employees with postsecondary education and incomes greater than $60,000 per year has found that flexible work arrangements have become less common since 1991. At the same time, work demands have increased, as reflected in the number of hours people spend at their jobs every week. The data also show that reported levels of stress and depression have increased, and reported levels of life satisfaction have dramatically decreased. Absenteeism due to ill health or emotional/mental fatigue has been on the rise (Duxbury and Higgins 2012). When people work hard and don't enjoy their work, they are likely to feel stressed, exhausted, or depressed.

People have different amounts of vulnerability to these changing work trends. In this chapter, we are interested in examining the Canadians who are disadvantaged when it comes to securing stable, satisfying, and reasonably compensated employment. So, in the next section, we examine some populations in Canada that are especially vulnerable to employment inequality.

As you read these examinations, we urge you to keep the idea of interlocking disadvantages in mind. Recall from Chapter 1 that one person may face several different types of inequality. They interact and contribute to a unique experience of powerlessness in society. How do the groups we address experience inequality differently? What similarities do their experiences share?

Immigrants in Canada

We begin with Canadian immigrants, an important and diverse population. Canada, like many other developed nations, relies on the flow of immigration to fill key labour roles. Since the early years of immigration policy in Canada, most immigrants have been selected based on how well their skills and experience can meet the needs of the labour market. There is an employment gap between immigrant and Canadian-born workers, but it's shrinking (see Figure 3.1). Immigrants, who make up around a quarter of workers in Canada, are usually finding jobs.

Owing to Canada's immigration selection rules, immigrants are typically more academically qualified than their Canadian-born counterparts. Roughly one-third of Canadian-born workers hold a university degree, compared to nearly one-half of immigrants (Statistics Canada 2018b). Many people think that academic qualifications are the key to finding a *good* job, but this is often not true for recent immigrants. Educated immigrants are finding work, but it is not always work that matches their skills and experience.

We have all heard about taxi drivers in Canada's major cities who are overqualified for their jobs. One might easily find a foreign-trained doctor, lawyer, or engineer behind the wheel. Overqualification rates are typically higher among immigrants than they are among Canadian-born workers, and that's especially true for women. By one account, university-educated women who were not born in Canada and did not graduate in Canada or the United States get the worst jobs. Fully 43 per cent are employed in jobs that need a high school education or less. In comparison, among Canadian-born women, only 15 per cent are employed in those low-education (and low-wage) jobs (Uppal and LaRochelle-Cote 2014).

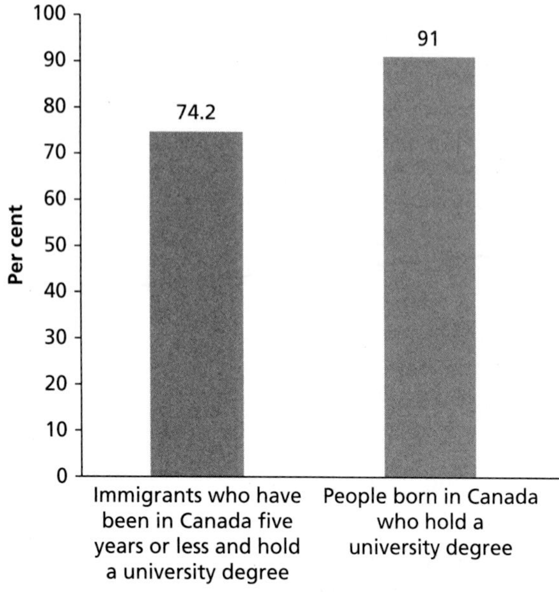

Figure 3.1 ◆ Labour Force Participation

The unequal employment trends are more pronounced if we consider immigrants who arrived recently (Statistics Canada 2019). But even in this case, we find the gap on a narrowing trend, overall.

Source: Statistics Canada 2017a.

This tendency for immigrants to secure jobs that do not reflect or benefit from their experience and qualifications is called **de-professionalization**. Often, de-professionalization occurs because Canada does not recognize credentials earned overseas. In other words, immigrants employed in de-professionalized jobs are underemployed, despite a high degree of training (and often experience). This is especially noticeable for immigrants educated in fields like nursing, medicine, engineering, law, and teaching (see Figure 3.2).

Studies have tried to quantify the gap between employment and qualification. These studies suggest that an overseas education is treated as equivalent to three-quarters of a comparable Canadian education. Similarly, one year of overseas work experience is treated as equal to only four months of Canadian experience. This means that immigrants must complete more education or receive professional certification in Canada before they can take jobs in their field of expertise—a process called *relicensing*, which we will address in more detail in Chapter 4. Studies show that some employers insist on applicants having Canadian experience even when the job doesn't need it (Finnie and Meng 2002). Relicensing is important for immigrants who hope to find jobs that they have trained for overseas. However, immigrants face significant barriers to relicensing, which is an expensive and lengthy undertaking. Even if relicensing were faster and less expensive, steady employment in a non-professional job might serve as a deterrent. An immigrant who has secured a job of any kind may no longer have the time it takes to retrain and relicense for a job that better suits their skills.

de-professionalization The tendency for immigrants to occupy jobs that underutilize their experience and qualifications.

Finally, there is a large earnings gap between the Canadian-born population and Canadian-educated immigrants who graduated from university. This gap persists both in the early years after immigration and in the long term (Hou and Lu 2017). Put another way, many immigrants who *complete their education in Canada* and gain Canadian credentials may still face large gaps in their earnings compared to Canadian-born workers. This may be because the employer thinks the foreign-born worker has less familiarity with Canadian society and culture, which poses an impediment.

Employment in de-professionalized jobs means that immigrants work jobs for which they are overqualified and poorly paid. Take a look at Table 3.1. These are the most common jobs held by foreign-born qualified nurses who can't secure nursing jobs in Canada. The list compares Canadian-born-and-educated nurses with foreign-born-and-educated nurses. You'll note that foreign-born nurses are much more likely to work lower-paying jobs.

Research often identifies a lack of language skills as a barrier to immigrants securing employment. Besides working jobs for which they are overqualified, immigrants are more likely than Canadian-born workers to unwillingly work part time. They would prefer to work full time, but, for various reasons, they cannot get a full-time job. One study showed that recent immigrants are twice as likely to work short-term contracts as their

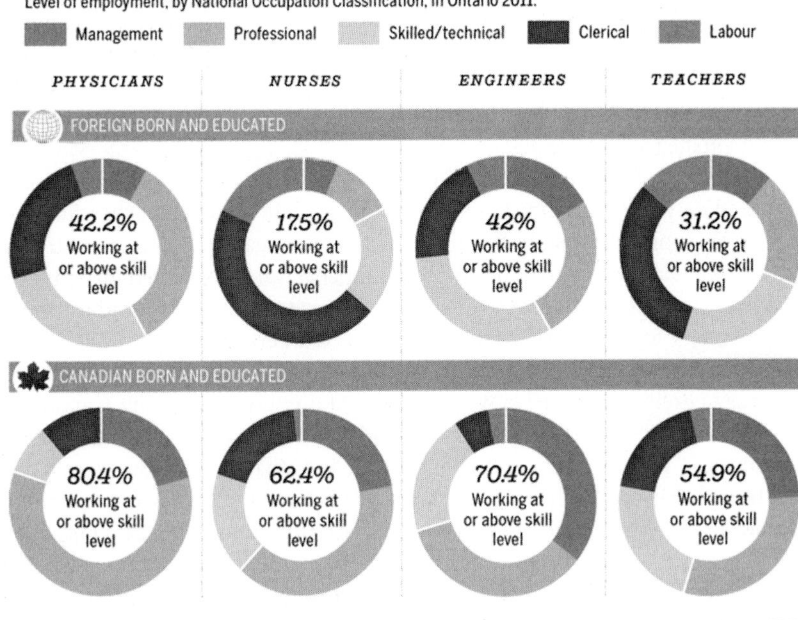

Figure 3.2 ◆ The Benefits of a Canadian Education

Source: Dharssi 2016. Material republished with the express permission of: *Calgary Herald*, a division of Postmedia Network Inc.

Table 3.1 Top 10 Alternative Jobs for Trained Nurses

Canadian Born and Educated	Foreign Born and Educated
1. Healthcare manager	1. Nurse aid/orderly
2. Head nurse	2. Homemaker/housekeeper
3. College instructor	3. Practical nurse
4. Health policy researcher	4. Babysitter/nanny
5. Nurse aid/orderly	5. Food service worker
6. Administrative officer	6. Retail salesperson
7. University professor	7. Cashier
8. Office clerk	8. Secretary
9. Retail salesperson	9. Cleaner
10. Homemaker/housekeeper	10. Labourer

Source: Office of the Fairness Commissioner 2012.

Canadian-born counterparts and less likely to work a unionized job (Statistics Canada 2009). New immigrants are also more likely to experience a non-fatal injury in their workplaces (Marni and Kosny 2012). Overall, the data paint a picture of Canadian immigrants working in dangerous, low-paying jobs for which they are often overqualified.

Immigrants, especially newly arrived immigrants, are vulnerable to precarious, de-professionalized work. As well as the reasons we have already explored, immigrants usually have fewer social contacts in Canada than Canadian-born workers do; diverse **social networks** can help people get a job (Thomas 2015), and most immigrants do not have this advantage (see Figure 3.3).

social networks Patterns of social relationships among individuals based on face-to-face interaction or mediated communication.

So far we have seen that immigrants are more likely than Canadian-born workers to be employed in de-professionalized jobs, part-time jobs, or short-term contract work. We have also touched on relicensing, the persistent income gap between immigrant workers and Canadian-born workers, and the role that social networks play in job hunts and income. The rest of this section explores two major categories of immigrant workers in Canada: temporary foreign workers and non-status workers.

The first major category, temporary foreign workers, come to work in Canada through the Temporary Foreign Worker (TFW) program. At any given moment, Canada's immigration policies allow several hundred thousand temporary foreign workers in through the TFW program. This program allows employers in Canada to hire workers from other countries temporarily to fill labour shortages they cannot fill with Canadian workers. Once the workers' contracts are up, they are legally required to leave the country.

Unfortunately, the TFW program creates ample room for exploitation. For example, many temporary foreign workers find positions through hiring agencies, and some of

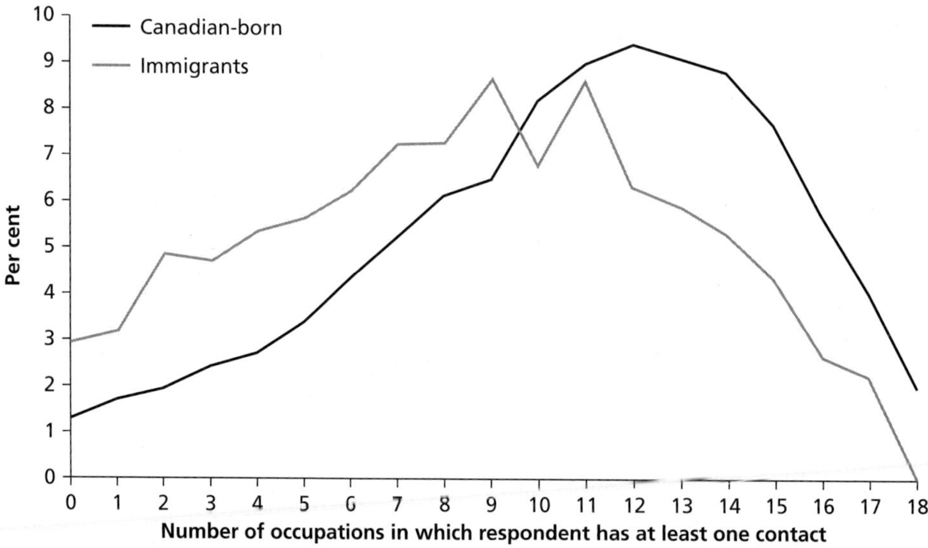

Figure 3.3 ◆ Important Social Networks

This figure shows that people who are born in Canada are more likely to have contact with people in a *diverse range* of jobs. What would your count be? The higher it is, the better your odds are of finding employment.

Source: Statistics Canada 2015a:Chart 1.

these hiring agencies want the worker to pay an excessive recruitment fee (Wright 2018). Some agencies even take a sizable cut from workers' wages. Also, some employers not only want temporary foreign workers to live in housing they provide, but also charge unreasonable rent for this housing and even withhold workers' passports.

A second major category of immigrant workers is non-status workers. These are immigrants working in Canada without the official documentation that affords them the rights and privileges of a permanent resident or Canadian citizen. People who employ non-status workers often pay them "under the table," which means the pay they receive is not formally documented. Therefore, their wages may not meet provincial minimum wage requirements because their employers are not held legally accountable. Non-status workers may also work in "3D" jobs (jobs that are dirty, dangerous, and degrading). Non-status jobs, like agricultural work or live-in caregiving, also rarely offer sick pay or vacation pay.

Further, because the work is undocumented, workers are not eligible for employment insurance or workers' compensation if they are hurt on the job or unfairly fired. Finally, non-status workers are reluctant to complain about their working conditions since doing so makes them vulnerable to deportation.

Racialized People in Canada

In this section, we will consider employment inequality for racialized people in Canada.

A useful idea for understanding employment inequality among racialized people is **racialized stratification**. Racialized stratification is the process by which the membership of an individual or a group to a race becomes the basis for unequal treatment in a society.

racialized stratification The process by which the membership of an individual or a group to a race becomes the basis for social stratification.

Statistics Canada data from 2015 reveal that the unemployment rate is higher for racialized job seekers, whether they are immigrants or Canadian-born people. The data in Figure 3.4 show that racialized men are more likely to be unemployed than white men, and racialized women are more likely to be unemployed than white women.

Here are some other troubling statistics about race-based inequalities in the labour market:

- Racialized men earn 76 cents for every dollar non-racialized men earn (Block and Galabuzi 2018).
- Racialized women earn 85 cents for every dollar non-racialized women earn (Block and Galabuzi 2018).
- Racialized Canadians are more likely to be employed in insecure, temporary, or low-paying jobs than non-racialized Canadians (Block and Galabuzi 2011).

Drawing Connections

Think about the sequencing of this chapter, which is deliberate: many newcomers to Canada are seen and classified according to their race. So they may experience another layer of employment inequality because of this racialization. Recall that this compounding of inequalities (in this case, immigrant status and race inequality) is explained by the principle of interlocking disadvantages.

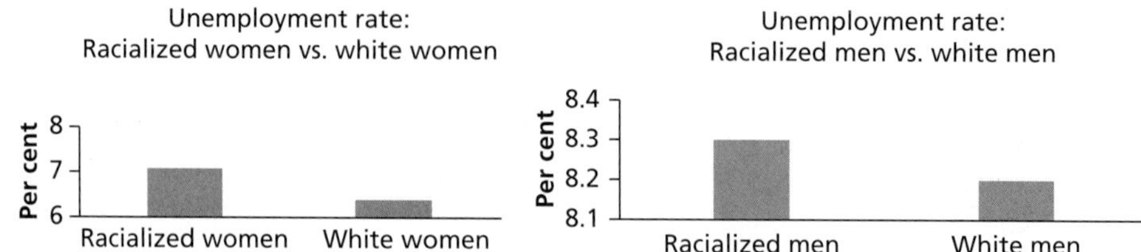

Figure 3.4 ◆ How Does Racialization Impact Job Hunting?

Source: Statistics Canada 2016.

The data on these disparities lumps together people with different amounts of education, so it masks the educational differences between Canadian-born racialized people and non-racialized Canadian-born people. Note that racialized people in Canada are more likely to have a postsecondary certificate, diploma, or degree than non-racialized people. In fact, they are 15 per cent more likely to have a bachelor's (university) degree than non-racialized Canadian people (Statistics Canada 2019). Let that sink in for a minute: Racialized people are, on average, *more* educated than non-racialized people in Canada, yet they are more likely to be unemployed! How can that be?

Well, before we try to answer that question, let's examine some more data. Let's consider immigrants. Figure 3.5 shows that not all immigrants have the same odds of employment. For example, immigrants from the Philippines have the highest employment rate among immigrant groups; their employment rate is even higher than for Canadian-born workers. Immigrants from Latin American countries fare a little worse, and those from African countries are lower than the rate of all immigrant groups. These differences are be explained in part by differences in education systems, languages, and credentials, which can favour immigrants from one country over another. Statistics Canada points to the Live-In Caregiver Program, which historically employs an overrepresentation of women from the Philippines. Racism alone does not cause unemployment, even if it is a contributing factor for many people seeking work. Could these differences in employment also be explained by other forces, such as anti-Black racism?

The data in Figure 3.6 show that unemployment rates of Canadian-born workers have remained flat (that is, they are unchanged) over the past 10 years. Yet the unemployment rates of all immigrants have been declining. So, while immigrants are disadvantaged when they arrive, they gradually catch up with the employment status of longer-term immigrants and, eventually, even with Canadian-born workers. As well, the children and grandchildren of immigrants do better as time passes. This fact is evident in Figure 3.7.

However, unemployment and employment rates may disguise inequalities in the jobs people hold. In Canada, racialized people are overrepresented in low-paying, precarious jobs such as administrative support, waste management, and remediation services. As well, Block and Galabuzi (2011) point out that racialized Canadians earn only 81 cents for every dollar paid to non-racialized Canadians. When we apply the principle of interlocking inequalities, we see the added economic disadvantage of gender (see Figure 3.8).

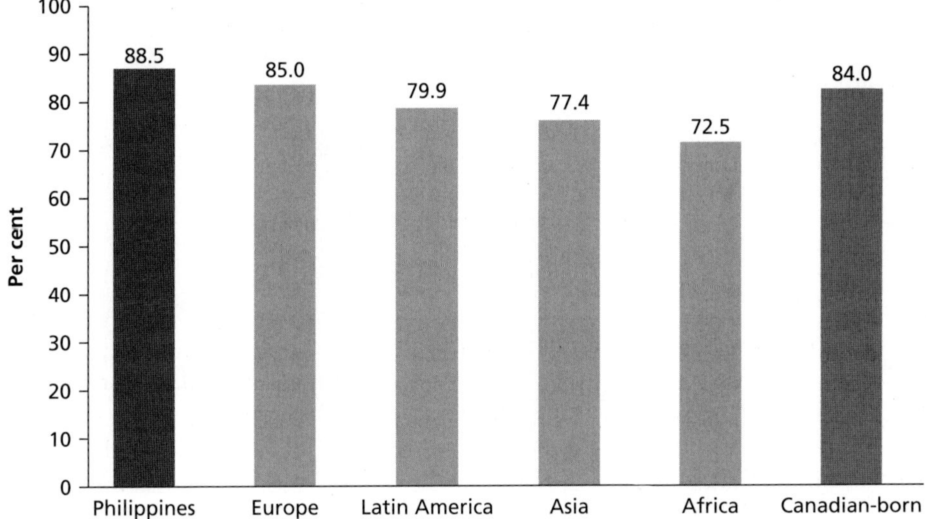

Figure 3.5 ◆ Employment Rate by Birthplace, 2017

Note that the employment rate is highest for people born in the Philippines.

Source: Statistics Canada 2018b.

In fact, racialized women are paid 63 cents for every dollar paid to a non-racialized man. It would be useful to know how Canada compares with other Western societies; however, comparative data of this sort are hard to come by.

Both immigration status and race affect people's employment and income. For example, Figure 3.9 shows that racialized immigrants fare more poorly than white immigrants, Canadian-born white people, and Canadian-born racialized people when it comes to average income. Racialized immigrants also earn less, on average, than their non-racialized counterparts. As above with the cents-per-dollar example, we can see the added effect of

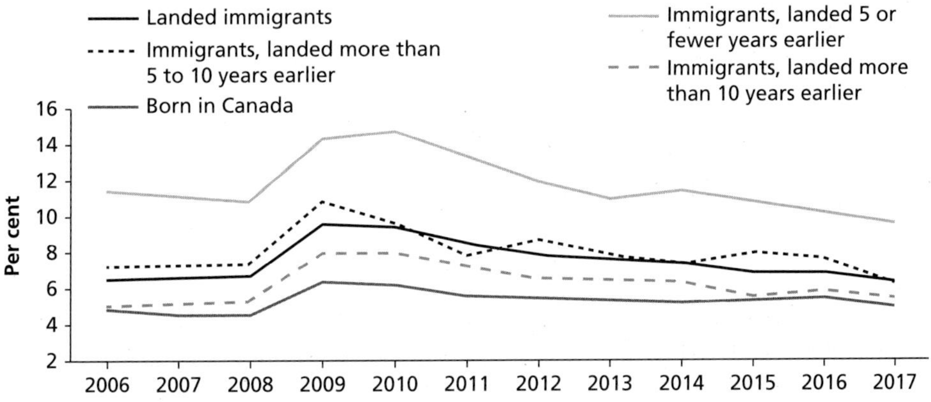

Figure 3.6 ◆ Unemployment Rates of Recent Immigrants

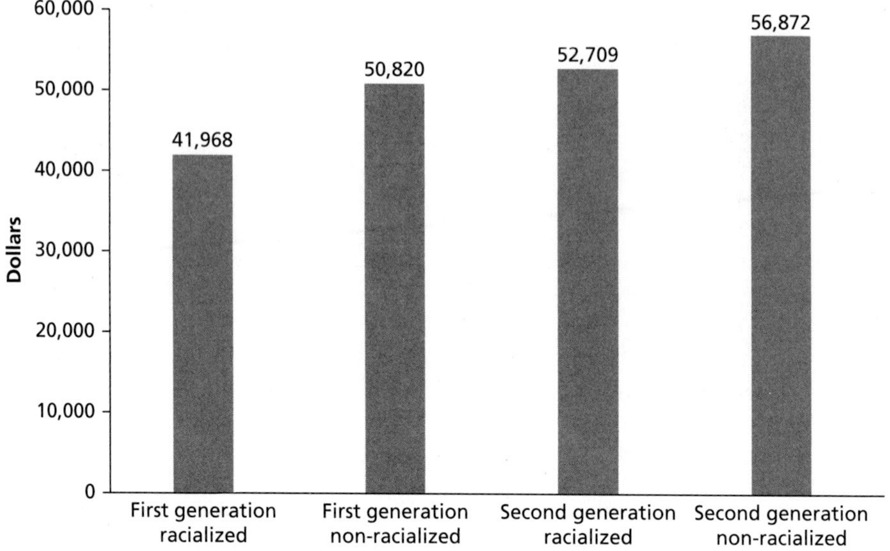

Figure 3.7 ◆ Average Income in Canadian Dollars of Immigrants by Generation and Racialization, 2016

Source: Statistics Canada 2016.

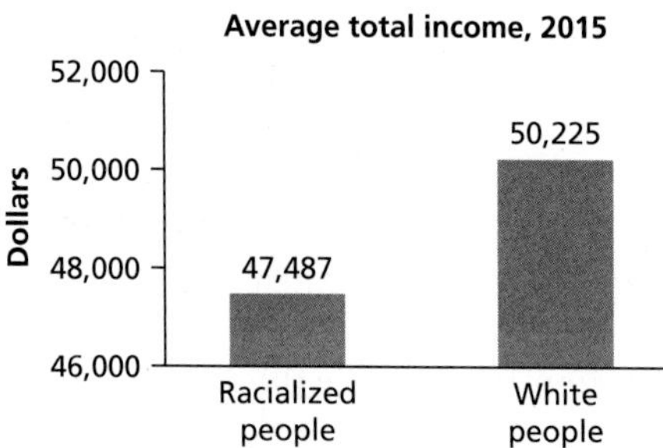

Figure 3.8 ◆ Does Racialization Impact Income?

Source: Statistics Canada 2016.

gender when we compare the annual average incomes of men and women.

The Government of Canada has tried to encourage fair representation of racialized people at all levels of the workforce, which we will discuss later in this chapter. Despite these efforts, however, wage and representation disparities are obvious even in the federal service. There, the population of federal employees who describe themselves as racialized still falls well below their labour market availability (Government of Canada 2011).

Young People in Canada

For many young people, it is increasingly difficult to transition smoothly from school to a satisfying, long career with a single employer.

Data show that the 2008 recession was especially hard on young workers, and economic recovery "has been almost non-existent" for them (Fong 2012). Today, postsecondary education requirements are more demanding, education, and housing are more expensive, the debt load is larger, and the job market is more competitive than ever. As a result, young people are delaying or forgoing typical life transitions like buying a home, starting a family, and staying put in a single community (O'Rourke 2012).

These economic and social changes create unique barriers for young people trying to get jobs. More rigorous requirements for postsecondary education plus increasing

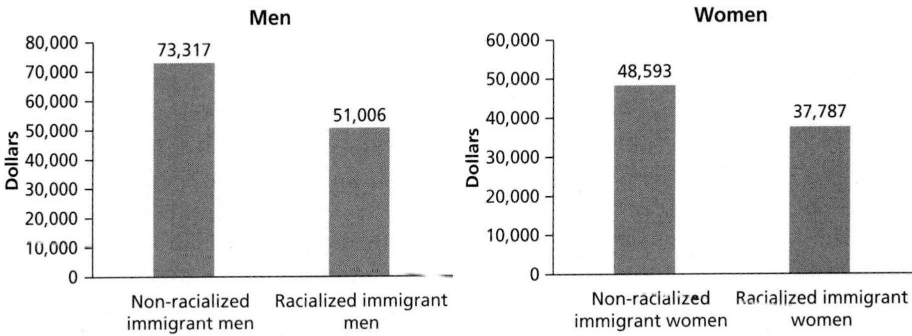

Figure 3.9 ◆ Average Annual Income in Canadian Dollars: Non-racialized versus Racialized First-Generation Immigrants, 2015

Source: Statistics Canada 2016.

tuition costs have increased the lag time between high school and postsecondary program enrolment (Liu 2013). Since postsecondary education provides the educational qualifications that people increasingly need to get a job, a lack of education reduces the likelihood of youth employment. Student debt loads have also increased: Fifty-seven per cent of Canadian students carry student debt, compared to 49 per cent 10 years ago. Today, Canadian students have an average debt load of $20,000 to $30,000 (Usher 2018).

A report on the indebtedness of Canadian graduates (Ferguson and Wang 2014:36) reveals that students' debt loads upon graduation depend on their programs and how they pay for their education. College students were more likely to graduate with small debt loads than university undergraduate students, for example. Similarly, large debt loads were more likely for some programs—like health, recreation, and fitness—than others—like business, management, and public administration.

Since the recession, Canada's labour market has also undergone a demographic shift. More seniors are leaving retirement and returning to work as term employees, mentors, or consultants (O'Rourke 2012). They are also increasingly working jobs traditionally held by youth—for example, as delivery people, fast-food workers, and grounds workers. Age discrimination may be contributing to this demographic shift and acting as a barrier to employment for young people. In an Ipsos Reid poll, 41 per cent of respondents aged 18–34 felt they had been victims of workplace prejudice based on their age (Hiltz 2012a).

Women in Canada

More women in Canada are working in paid jobs today than they were 30 years ago. Figure 3.10 shows the increase in women's participation over the last 30 to 40 years.

Over decades, the gap between men's and women's labour market participation has continued to narrow. Today, more women are working, and they are increasingly working in positions previously held by men. As well, women in the labour force are less likely than men to be unemployed, in part because the 2008 recession hit men harder than women (see above). Also, women who became unemployed during the 2008 recession were more likely than men to drop out of the labour force and work other, nonpaid jobs like

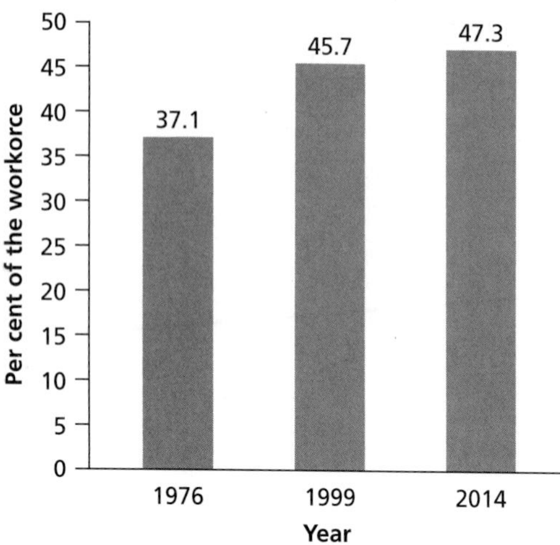

Figure 3.10 ◆ What Percentage of Paid Workers Are Women?

Source: Statistics Canada 2017d.

caregiving. Leaving the labour force in this way means you are not counted as unemployed, since you must be actively seeking paid employment to be considered unemployed. Similar counting problems arose in efforts to enumerate the unemployed during the COVID-19 pandemic.

Women and men also differ in the employment they secure. As noted above, women are more likely than men to hold precarious jobs. In 2013, 70 per cent of the part-time workers in Canada were women, and this number has been increasing (Statistics Canada 2015b). Part of this can be credited to parental responsibilities. As we will see in Chapter 4, parental responsibilities can be a barrier to women's employment. Women who have children are less likely to work than women who don't, and single mothers are less likely to secure employment than mothers with domestic partners (Statistics Canada 2015b). Single mothers are also more likely to make $10 or less per hour and to live below the low-income cut-off than other workers.

emotional work Paid work that demands not only face-to-face contact with customers but also the continued expression or non-expression of certain emotions; also known as "commodified emotions."

feminization The increasing presence and influence of women in previously male-dominated jobs or institutions.

Besides being excessively represented in precarious work, women also contribute disproportionally to the field of "emotional work." **Emotional work** refers to service jobs that require managing and hiding emotions every day. One example is service work, which can be precarious, exploitive, and occasionally even dangerous. Most service workers are disadvantaged women. The increase of women in the workforce, combined with their increasing employment in precarious jobs previously held by men, is referred to as **feminization**. The feminization of poverty refers to the overrepresentation of women among the poor.

Further, the wage gap between men and women is a continued topic of debate, with discussions centring on its causes and how best to approach reducing it. Possible explanations for and causes of the wage gap include gendered employment, hostile and unfriendly work environments, differences in education, impostor syndrome, and the work of social reproduction.

If you ask a 90-year-old woman how she imagined her career prospects when she was younger, she would probably name four paid professions that were typically accessible for women in the mid-1900s: secretary, teacher, retail worker, and nurse. The numbers of women working in fields traditionally dominated by men are increasing. However, women still work mainly in female-dominated fields such as healthcare, education, sales, and service jobs (Moyser 2017). Some of these jobs pay less than jobs traditionally held by men, which partially explains why women in Canada earn less per year, on average, than men.

Jobs are gendered in ways that reflect a society's expectations of how someone of a certain gender should act and work. If a society associates caregiving, child-minding, and service with women and expects these things of them, then work that fulfills those behaviours will be associated with women. This means more women may take up such work and men may avoid it for fear that it might undermine the qualities associated with *their* gender. In the same way, women may hesitate to pursue gendered jobs typically associated with men because they feel, or are made to feel, unwelcome or unsuitable for them.

Women also earn less than men for the same work. Pay gaps are least pronounced in healthcare and in art, culture, recreation, and sport; they are greatest in jobs that are unique to primary industries. Primary industries are concerned with extracting natural resources or with converting natural resources into commodities. They are typically male driven and male oriented, so when women do enter them, their work contributions may be undervalued and compensated less than the contributions of their male counterparts.

There are different ways to measure the gender pay gap in Canada, and Figure 3.11 shows three of them. The first two bars compare all workers in Canada, both full time and part time. You'll note that this gap is the largest, because most part-time workers are women. The second two bars compare the average total annual earnings of full-time workers only. The size of this gap shows, in part, that male full-time workers put in more hours, on average, than women, and thus earn more. So, for a more precise depiction of the wage gap, the last two bars boil it down to the hourly wages of full-time workers (for example, $26 per hour versus $29 per hour).

Women know that competing with men requires disproportionate effort, and some don't feel up for the job. Women are more likely than men to experience what is referred to as *impostor syndrome* in the workplace. Clance and Imes (1978) define impostor syndrome as a funny feeling that one is "faking" skills (no matter how qualified one may be). A person imagines that it is only a matter of time before the rest of the work team clues into the ruse. Women who experience impostor syndrome are less likely to ask for raises and are less likely to apply for promotions (Desmarais and Curtis 1997).

Even highly educated women experience the impostor problem, as Ivie, White, and Chu (2016) revealed in a study of women with Ph.D.s in astronomy and astrophysics. These researchers found that, among other problems (like mentorship and finding careers post-graduation), impostor syndrome affected women's thoughts on leaving their field of study.

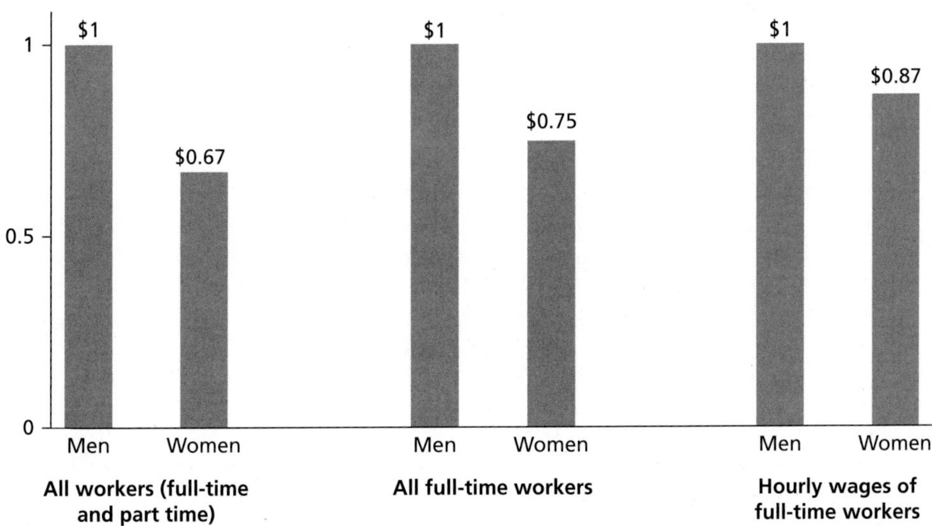

Figure 3.11 ◆ The Gender Wage Gap, 2016

Sources: Statistics Canada 2020a, 2020b; Moyser 2017.

Notable Thinkers

Jean Wallace

Jean Wallace is a professor of sociology at the University of Calgary. Part of her research concerns gendered experiences in law firms. In the 2001 publication "Gendered Inequalities in Earnings: A Study of Canadian Lawyers" that she co-authored (Robson and Wallace 2001), Wallace examines if and why male and female lawyers in Canada are rewarded to different degrees.

She found that a lawyer's gender does not *directly* influence their earnings, but women are disadvantaged by many factors that play a role in increasing earnings. The first of these factors is that female lawyers have less experience practising law, work shorter hours, and are more likely to have preschool-aged children. They also have less job autonomy than their male counterparts or equals. Finally, they are also more likely than men to leave the workforce, temporarily or permanently, for childcare reasons.

In her publication "Can Women in Law Have It All? A Study of Motherhood, Career Satisfaction and Life Balance," Wallace (2006) responded to studies that suggested women in law are generally dissatisfied because of the difficulties of balancing work and family. Wallace, however, showed that some women *can* have it all, meaning that the career satisfaction and life balance are similar for both mothers and non-mothers alike. Wallace provides some reasons for this. For one, women are more likely than men to work in law firms that are "family friendly." This means they have more control over their work hours, greater availability of alternative work arrangements, and they work fewer hours than non-mothers in the law profession.

Drawing Connections

Not all women experience the gendered wage gap equally. Older women, for example, experience a wider pay gap than younger women. Similarly, women with no high school diploma earn much less than men with no high school diploma. Women in Canada are also more likely to have secured a university degree (Statistics Canada 2019), and yet the pay gap persists. Consider the connection between this disparity and this chapter's earlier discussion about how racialized people are likely to receive less compensation than their education and experience would justify.

social reproduction
The biological reproduction of the labour force, including the provision of food, shelter, clothing, and healthcare.

Finally, the wage gap can also be explained by the work that women do. In contrast to the "productive work" that most men do, which involves the exchange of money and the production of goods and information, it is women who mainly perform the work of **social reproduction.** Social reproduction involves tasks like planning and cooking meals, caring for children or the elderly, preserving the home, and transporting people to and from social activities, such as soccer and ballet. This work is almost always unpaid, and for various reasons social reproduction is not framed as actual "work." It is work, and it is essential to the smooth functioning of society.

When referring to social reproduction, we often hear the expressions "the double day" or "the second shift." These expressions refer to a work-sharing arrangement between spouses in which women take on most domestic labour, even when they are also working outside the home. Time-use surveys show that men are taking a more active role in the home than in previous generations, but the division of domestic labour is still unequal. A European study suggests that this has something to do with men's increasingly uncertain and demanding work outside the home (Sani 2014). It shows how today's shifting economy ripples outward to affect workers both at and outside their jobs.

In 1984, Marxist theorist Christine Delphy considered the material benefits of the labour-sharing arrangement in the home, arguing marriage is, in essence, a badly paid labour contract (Delphy and Leonard 1984). She suggested that heterosexual relationships make wives exploited workers with no defined limit to the hours they work—and no agreed-on wages. Delphy expanded this analysis to include sisters, daughters, or other unmarried women, who also often labour for the men in their lives.

Take childcare, for example. In 2015, women in heterosexual domestic partnerships, on average, still did twice as much childcare as their male counterparts (Moyer and Burlock 2018). This difference was especially pronounced in families with stay-at-home moms, who spend, on average, 81 hours a week providing childcare. (Surprisingly, stay-at-home dads only spend roughly 37 hours a week on childcare [Statistics Canada 2012b].)

Yet caring for children is only one home-based duty. Canadian women in heterosexual domestic partnerships work, on average, one-and-a-half times longer than their male counterparts completing household chores, regardless of their working arrangements (Moyer and Burlock 2018). This is because the household chores that women are typically responsible for, especially carework, are more time intensive than the chores for which men are responsible. Figure 3.12 shows the disparities in childcare and household chores.

There are also organizational duties involved in domestic labour. They include tasks like securing before-and after-school care for children, scheduling medical and dental appointments, and managing school paperwork. Women in Canada do more than their share of organizational work. As well, women do more of the "kin keeping" labour: for example, remembering birthdays and anniversaries, nurturing relationships with friends and neighbours, and organizing play dates. None of this important, time-consuming work earns an employment income, and none is typically valued in the same way as men's labour.

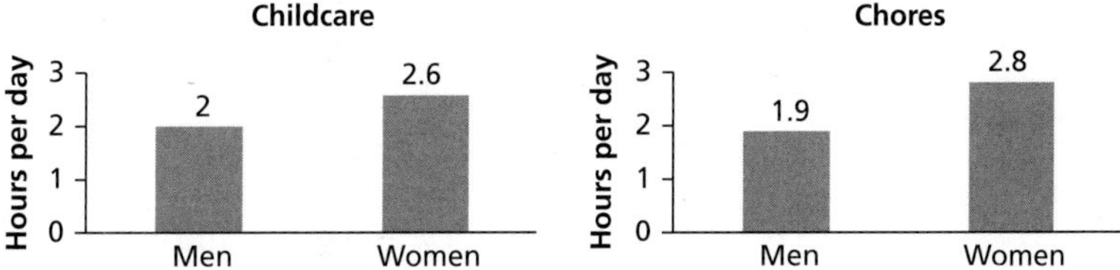

Figure 3.12 ◆ Labour Disparities in the Home

These graphs show the 2015 labour disparities in childcare and household chores.

Source: Moyer and Burlock 2018.

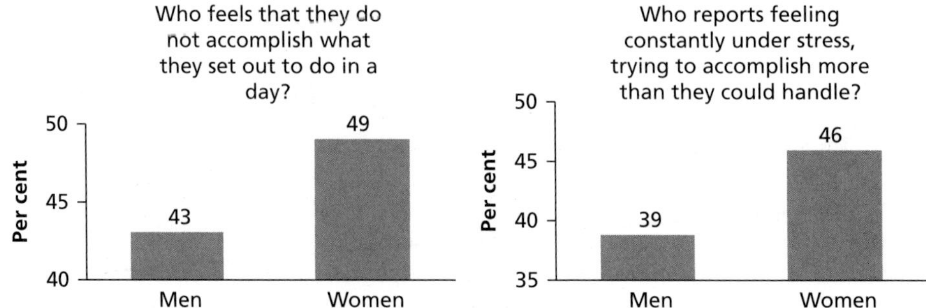

Figure 3.13 ◆ Emotional Impacts by Gender

Source: Moyer and Burlock 2018.

Coordinating and performing unpaid labour like childcare, chores, organizational work, and kin keeping takes a mental toll on women, as you can see in Figure 3.13.

One reason that women suffer more mental health and well-being challenges is because they enjoy less leisure time (see Figure 3.14). Moreover, when women engage in leisure activities, they are likely to bring their children with them (Moyer and Burlock 2018). This enables them to perform the unpaid work of childcare simultaneously. It also prompts the question: How restorative is an afternoon workout or walk through the park when you have a five year old in tow?

Many sociologists are curious about the division of unpaid work in the domestic sphere. Understanding this division is important because the burden of domestic responsibilities can force women to leave the workforce or take lower-paying jobs. The second shift can also make it difficult for women to fully engage with their paying jobs, harming their chances of earning promotions or raises (Creese and Beagan 2009; Kurtz 2012). Some theories suggest that fathers are socially pulled toward paid work while mothers are pulled toward childcare. Andrea Doucet's interviews with fathers and mothers, for example, show that early socialization about gendered parenting roles may partly explain mothers' feelings of moral responsibility for their children (Doucet 2012).

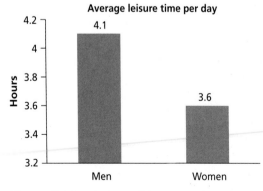

Figure 3.14 ◆ Leisure Discrepancies

Source: Moyer and Burlock 2018.

Seniors in Canada

As you've learned, Canada's population is aging. This means that even though many seniors are coming out of retirement, more people in Canada have retired or are closer to retirement than in previous generations. Increased life expectancy and all-round better healthcare for older Canadians may mean that people will stay in jobs longer, often working past the age of retirement. Thus, the proportion of working seniors has increased (see Figure 3.15).

Senior employees have much to offer workplaces. Specifically, they can mentor younger employees and share their views of how past successes and failures will influence present-day workplace choices. Older employees can also draw from wide social networks they have built from years of forming relationships at work.

However, older workers who have lost a job through automation or outsourcing may have trouble finding a new job. Some older workers spend years refining a specific set of skills. If they become unemployed, it can be challenging to find another role that needs those same skills. Data from Statistics Canada showed that 58 per cent of older, unemployed job hunters were pessimistic about their likelihood of finding a job within three months. This is nearly twice the percentage of young, unemployed Canadians who were asked the same question (Statistics Canada 2012a). In an Ipsos Reid survey of roughly 1,000 Canadians, nearly 75 per cent of respondents believed that older job applicants aren't being considered for jobs because of their age (Hiltz 2012a).

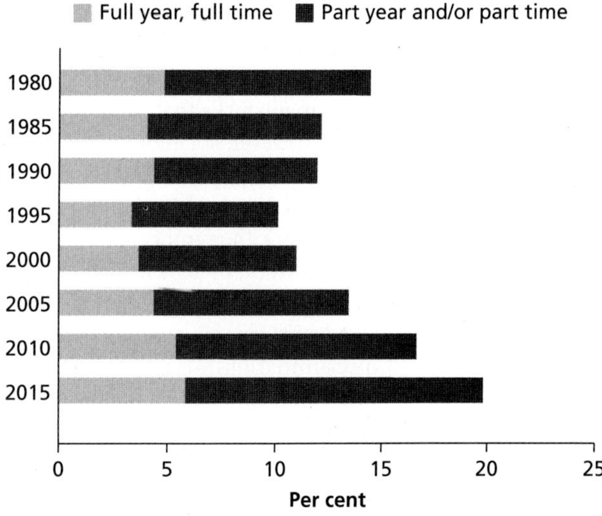

Figure 3.15 ◆ Seniors in the Workforce

Source: Statistics Canada 2017c.

Second, workplace technology has changed at an incredibly fast rate over the last few decades. As a result, older workers may face what is called **skill obsolescence**: Their skills may no longer be applicable in rapidly changing technological environments. In another Ipsos Reid poll, half the respondents felt that older workers were harder to train on new technology than younger workers (Hiltz 2012b). This may be true or the result of a "self-fulfilling prophecy." That is, older workers may be offered fewer training opportunities because of this belief, causing their skill obsolescence to grow—regardless of their aptitude and ability to learn necessary and new workplace skills.

skill obsolescence The degree to which professionals lack the up-to-date knowledge or skills necessary to preserve effective performance in their current or future work roles.

Drawing Connections

Note how young people's struggles with employment intersect and are complicated by seniors' struggles (and vice versa). Younger people like to think that they will be working in safe, stable, satisfying, and reasonably compensated jobs until retirement. However, as they grow older, they may find themselves applying to new employment opportunities. Since more people are leaving retirement to go back to work, it is also important to consider the unique employment barriers and challenges that people over 55 face. Similarly, recall this chapter's note about a poll of young people finding that 41 per cent of respondents felt they had been overlooked because of their young age. The problem of age discrimination can show itself against both older and younger individuals; it may also vary with the job or industry.

The employment challenges facing older Canadians may reflect wider social values about the "usefulness" of seniors. Some feel the older someone is, the less valuable they may be in the workplace. Indeed, it's true that older workers may experience a declining ability to perform job tasks that need physical strength, mobility, vision, hearing, speed, and reaction time. However, sociological research has revealed that older employees can offset or "make up for" these physical challenges. They do so "through other qualities, such as caution, experience, and leadership skills as well as through minor adjustments in their job and the nature of the work they undertake" (Gunderson 2003:318). Studies have also found that in many fields of work, there is no correlation between productivity and age (Gobel and Zwick 2012).

There is both provincial and federal legislation in place to combat the barriers faced by Canadian seniors. Sometimes, however, discrimination (including age-based discrimination) is not illegal. In other words, the courts have decided that discrimination can be legally justified in specific circumstances—even if employees are qualified, experienced, and wish to remain at work. The decision to overrule age discrimination laws may stem from beliefs that with age comes a decreased ability to perform one's duties effectively. For example, an older firefighter or paramedic may struggle to safely or adequately perform the hard, physical duties demanded of them.

phase out The process of gradually exiting a workforce, so an individual works part time or part year before leaving the workforce.

Older workers must make important decisions about when to stop working. Studies have shown that people can better adapt to retirement when they **phase out**—gradually working fewer and fewer hours over a long period of time instead of stopping suddenly. However, studies have found that older workers who wish to phase out often face barriers, including pension penalties, lessened pay, and lower organizational status (Gunderson 2003).

ageism Discrimination, or the holding of irrational and damaging views about individuals or groups, based on their age.

Typically, Canadians elect to stop formal, paid work around the age of 65. And yet many older Canadians are not ready to retire at 65. Some may have emotional or physical reasons to delay retirement. For many, their jobs are more than just a paycheque: They feel socially engaged, intellectually stimulated, and physically active because of their jobs.

Other older workers may have financial reasons to remain employed. For example, many workers don't begin saving for retirement early enough in their career, so they may

IN FOCUS ◆ Compulsory Retirement

Can you guess which Canadian province is the only one to ban compulsory retirement practices? Manitoba! In Manitoba, the human rights legislation that protects employees from age discrimination does not "cap out" at 65. That means that if an 80-year-old Manitoban were forced to retire, they would have grounds to contest the dismissal as forming discrimination.

Do you think older firefighters should be forced to retire? **Ageism**—another word for discrimination against older people—does not attract the same levels of outrage as does other forms of employment discrimination. Industrial relations expert Morley Gunderson suggests that this lack of moral outrage reflects a belief in the "social benefit" of forced retirement. This is the belief that forced retirement creates opportunities for younger, cheaper workers (2003).

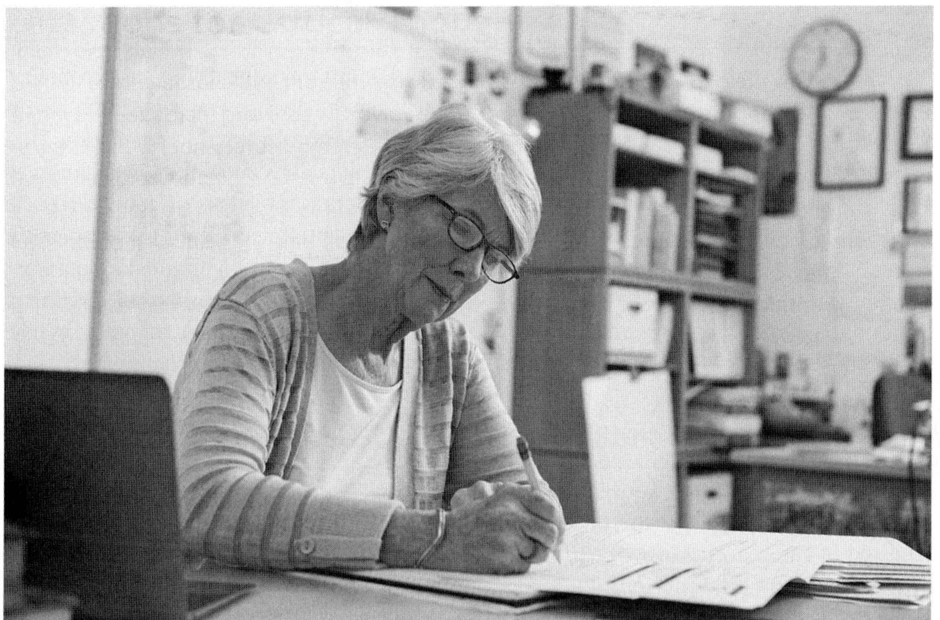
Monkey Business Images/Shutterstock

Some older workers stay employed into their late sixties and seventies not because they need income, but because they derive social and emotional benefits from their work. Do you think this is fair to other unemployed or underemployed workers who do need the income?

Drawing Connections

Sociologists Grant and Wong Grant have looked specifically at older immigrants and retirement. They note that "since many immigrants arrive relatively late in their working life and with little personal wealth, denying them the right to employment may unintentionally create an undue economic hardship by limiting their capacity to collect enough savings for retirement" (Grant and Wong-Grant 2002:v). This is yet another example of the value of considering interlocking disadvantages. In this case, it is the intersection between age and immigrant status that creates a unique experience of inequality.

not be able to afford to retire at age 60 or 65. Similarly, workers who have held jobs that are neither full time nor come with pension plans may not have been able to plan for retirement.

Indigenous Peoples in Canada

As we saw earlier in this book, there is no single, uniform Indigenous identity in Canada. The intersections of age, economic class, ability, gender, sexual orientation, and so on may affect an Indigenous person's employment differently.

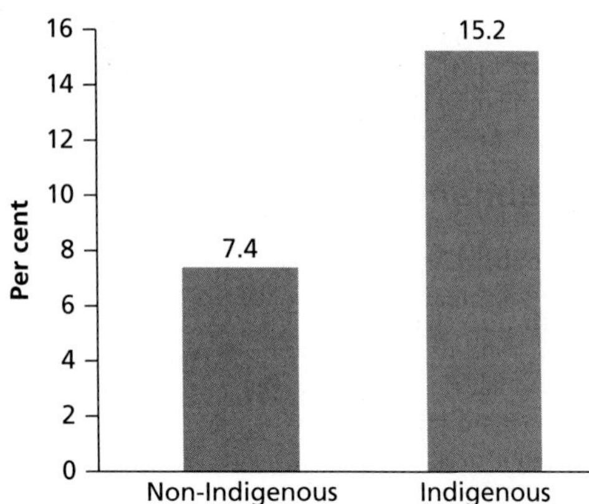

Figure 3.16 ◆ Canadian Unemployment Rate: Non-Indigenous versus Indigenous

Source: Statistics Canada 2018a.

We know that, on average, Indigenous Peoples have higher unemployment rates than non-Indigenous people (Statistics Canada 2018a; see Figure 3.16). For example, during the latest economic recession, the employment rate for Indigenous Peoples fell nearly three times as much as that of the non-Indigenous population. This was especially true for older Indigenous Peoples, showing another example of interlocking disadvantages (Statistics Canada 2011).

We will consider a few potential reasons for this inequality: family structure, the long-term impacts of residential schools, access to education, and finally **structural discrimination**. Structural or systemic discrimination refers to any set of rules or practices that disadvantages some groups while advantaging other groups.

structural discrimination Any set of rules or practices that disadvantages some groups while advantaging other groups.

Indigenous Family Structure

Indigenous Peoples living on reserves have higher unemployment rates than those living off-reserve. This has been credited to the scarcity of work in reserve contexts. As well, the data suggest that another factor may influence employment (and the lack of it) in Indigenous populations: family structure.

White, Maxim, and Obeng Gyimah (2003) found that Indigenous women with children were far less likely to work than non-Indigenous mothers, and Indigenous women who were solo parents were even less likely. Indigenous women often become mothers at a younger age than non-Indigenous women, and a significantly higher proportion of Indigenous women are single parents—twice as many as in the non-Indigenous population. Single parents, young ones especially, face significant challenges securing employment. Further sociological research might explore how the multiple identities of being young, single, a mother, and Indigenous combine to create added challenges to finding stable work. Figure 3.17 compares the employment rates of Indigenous early mothers with non-Indigenous early mothers and childless non-Indigenous women.

The Legacy of Residential School Experience

Sociologists have also explored the long-term impacts of residential schools on the employment of Indigenous youth today. As noted in Chapter 2, residential schools forcibly prevented several generations of Indigenous Peoples from parenting their children. In time, many residential school survivors became parents themselves. Some, having grown up without role models, have reported struggling to understand their parental roles in helping their children find pathways to employment (Marshall et al. 2011).

Indigenous Education

As discussed earlier, higher educational attainment usually means a higher chance of getting a job. The higher unemployment rate among Indigenous Peoples has been explained

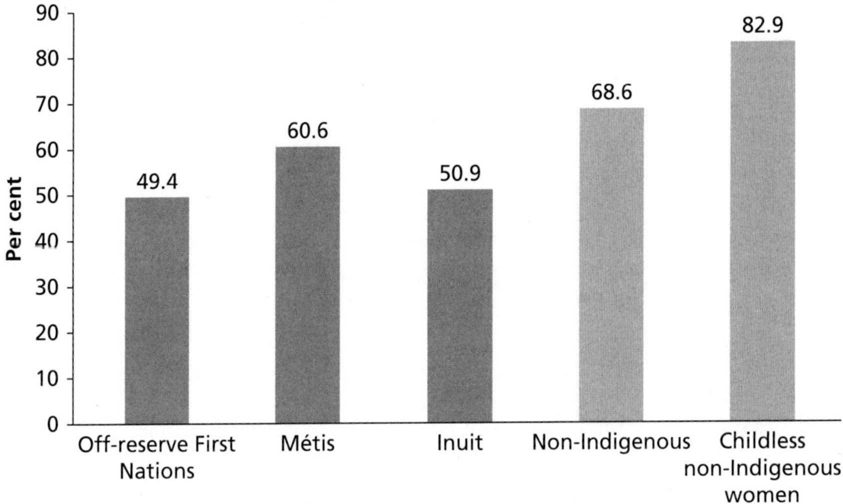

Figure 3.17 ♦ Employment Rate, Recent Mothers: Non-Indigenous versus Indigenous

Source: Boulet and Badets 2017.

by the fact that fewer Indigenous youth finish high school or go on to complete a postsecondary degree or diploma (Hango and de Broucker 2007). The number of Indigenous youth enrolled in or having completed postsecondary education has almost doubled since 1986 (*Maclean's* 2012), yet this population is still far less likely to earn the postsecondary credentials that are often needed to secure employment. Chapter 5 addresses some of the reasons for this, including sensed discriminatory practices in the education system and the fact that Indigenous students are more likely to leave school sooner than non-Indigenous students.

As human capital theory would argue, this lack of education has unavoidable results for Indigenous Peoples. Human capital theory proposes that wage differences reflect differences in the value that different workers bring to a job (Sweetland 1996). From this perspective, a relative lack of education, qualifications, or job experience is the reason that Indigenous populations are underemployed and earn less.

Hossain and Lamb (2012:440) find that human capital factors play a significant role in accounting for the employment and pay received by Indigenous workers in Canada. However, they note that social capital is just as important. If Indigenous Peoples in Canada were able to form the same kinds of networks and social relations as non-Indigenous people in Canada, their employment outcomes and earnings may improve. However, social capital can be difficult to measure.

Structural Discrimination against Indigenous Peoples

In contrast to human capital theory, researchers have pointed to larger structural social problems that account for the underemployment and wage inequality facing Indigenous populations.

Relative deficiencies in education, health, and job experience are not enough to explain the differences in wages and employment numbers between Indigenous and non-Indigenous people in Canada. For example, a gap persists between Indigenous university-educated men and non-Indigenous university-educated men in Canada, although this gap has shrunk significantly in the past 20 years. However, White, Maxim, and Obeng Gyimah have pointed out that "other factors, including discrimination, operate to occupationally segregate and under-reward Indigenous workers" (2003:412). These other factors are often called structural factors. They include the negative characterization of Indigenous workers as "deficient, that they are a problem to be fixed, and that they are outside of the working class" (Mills 2011). These structural factors often lead to part-time and part-year work, layoffs, poor pay, and unsatisfying work. White and colleagues (2003) suggest that these employment realities "both marginalize and discourage the workers, and can produce less labour force involvement" (412).

The Indigenous population has the largest group of young people in Canada, and almost half of the population are under the age of 25. It is also the fastest-growing population in Canada (Guimond, Robitaille, and Senécal 2009). Statistics Canada (2018a) reports that the Indigenous population has grown because of increased life expectancy, high fertility rates, and an increase in the number of people identifying as Indigenous on the Census.

Because of this, the Indigenous labour force has been referred to as "untapped" and full of "boundless potential" (Burke 2008, *Maclean's* 2012). Marshall and colleagues (2011) note that "Indigenous people in Canada have historically had inequitable access to resources that promote opportunities to participate in the labour force and education institutions" (555). Indeed, this unequal access to employment income could potentially become more pronounced as today's young Indigenous Peoples begin to seek tomorrow's jobs.

LGBTQ+ People in Canada

Compared to other marginalized populations in Canada, little research has explored the employment barriers faced by lesbian, gay, bisexual, trans, and queer people. This is even though people from these diverse groups report facing gender- or sexuality-based discrimination in their jobs or job hunts (Gates and Viggiani 2014; Parnell, Lease, and Green 2012; Ragins 2004). Apart from potentially affecting employment, sexual orientation may also impact wages. One American study, for example, found that gay men earned less than their married heterosexual counterparts (Antecol, Jong, and Steinberger 2008).

Trans people experience several issues with employment that are important to address. For example, they can experience anti-trans or transphobic attitudes and actions during the hiring process and once employed. There can be many troublesome elements of work for trans people, such as the enforced use of gender-binary washrooms and change rooms. Some trans people undergo medical procedures to align their bodies with their gender. These procedures can require travel to other places (patients in Alberta, for example, may need to travel to Montreal to undergo gender-confirmation surgery). The procedures themselves typically require considerable preparatory time spent completing assessments and securing referrals. Then, there is the recovery time after these complex procedures, which can be long and painful and require time off of work, which is not always paid. At least partly for this reason, trans people are especially susceptible to unemployment when they are engaged in a process of gender confirmation. Also, since some aspects of gender confirmation are expensive, their experience of inequality can pose another challenge.

People with Disabilities in Canada

Roughly one in five Canadians over the age of 15 report a disability. On average, the employment rate of Canadians who report a disability trails behind that of their non-disabled counterparts (Morris et al. 2018). Figure 3.18 compares both populations. Data indicate that the greater the reported severity of the disability, the greater the likelihood of unemployment.

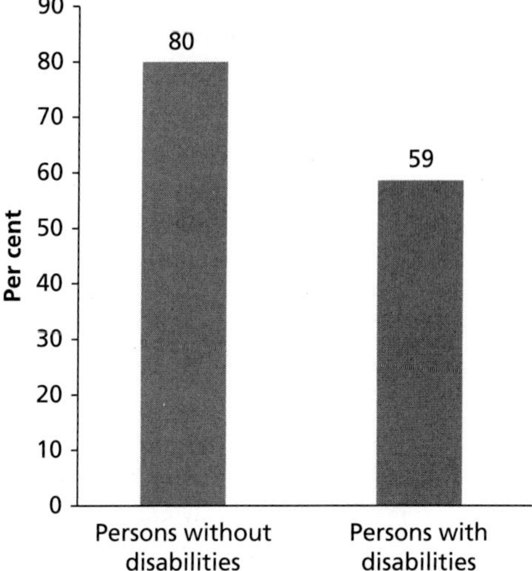

Figure 3.18 ◆ **Employment by Disability Status, 2016**

Source: Morris et al. 2018.

As you might imagine, studies show that type and degree of disability affect employment outcomes differently. Those who report a more severe disability also report incidents where they were refused employment, denied a promotion, denied necessary training, or fired because of their disability (Williams 2006). Hiring discrimination may result from an employer's lack of knowledge about the degree of limitation and anxiety about the expected costs of workplace adjustment (Turcotte 2015). Figure 3.19 shows the way opinions of employment discrimination worsen according to the severity of the disability. The wage gap also increases with the severity of the disability.

People with severe disabilities earn half the income of those with no reported disabilities (Morris et al. 2018). These factors may contribute to the fact that Canadians with a disability are far more likely to live in poverty. This problem is amply illustrated in Table 3.2.

Workers with disabilities often have less education and fewer qualifications than the general population, which may show a barrier to employment because of education. What might be preventing Canadians with disabilities from reaching their full potential in school? We will discuss this in Chapter 5.

Another barrier to employment may be that workplaces do not meet the diverse needs of Canadians working with a disability. Workplace adjustments could require physical changes to the workplace (for example, installing ramps or elevators) or adaptive technology (for example, providing access to voice-activated writing software). It could also

Critical Thinking Question

Canadians live—and work—with an enormous variety of disabilities. The jobs held by Canadians with a disability were similar to those without. However, Canadians with a disability were slightly more likely to work in healthcare and social assistance and less likely to work in management or retail trade (Williams 2006). Why do you think that might be?

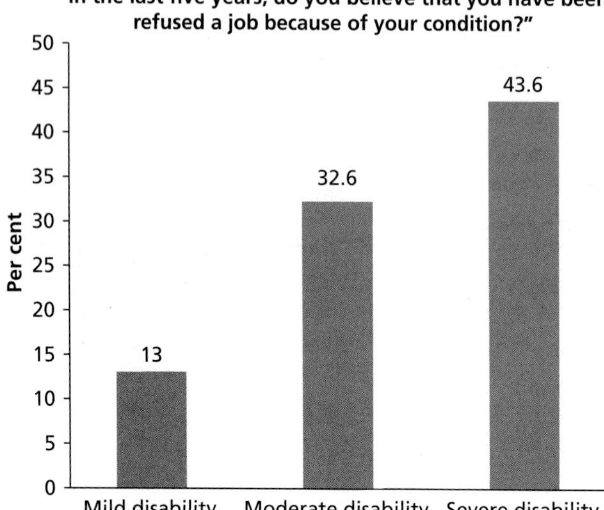

Figure 3.19 ◆ Disability and Job Discrimination: Per Cent Being Refused a Job

Source: Turcotte 2015.

require flexible work hours or the presence of a support animal. Employers who view some of these adjustments as costly or troublesome may be disinclined to hire people with disabilities.

Finally, **stigma** may be one more barrier to employment. Stigma is a social fear or disapproval directed at certain populations based on the belief that certain characteristics make that population morally, mentally, physically, or emotionally inferior. The Canadian Mental Health Association (n.d.) notes that Canadians with a severe mental illness face the most stigmatization in the workplace. As a result, they experience the highest levels of unemployment among people with disabilities.

In 2010, Canada approved Article 27 of the United Nations Convention on the Rights of Persons with Disabilities. This article calls for recognition of "the right of persons with disabilities to work, on an equal basis with others." This could be achieved by providing work environments that are "inclusive and accessible to persons with disabilities." We have shown that much is still to be done to carry out this commitment. The same can surely be said about the other disadvantaged groups we've discussed in this chapter.

stigma Visible or invisible social distinctions that disqualify individuals from full social acceptance.

Effects of Unequal Access

As we've mentioned in previous chapters, an increasing number of people are studying how unequal access to survival capital is disadvantageous for all of society—it is not just disadvantageous for those at the bottom of the employment food chain. Richard Wilkinson and Kate Pickett (2010) show that countries that score poorly on income equality measures also perform poorly on various health and social measures. These measures range from infant mortality, levels of stress, the proportion of the population in prison, levels of obesity, numbers of teenaged pregnancies, and more. Among the roughly 40 developed economies that Wilkinson and Pickett studied, Canada lands around the middle where inequality is concerned, ending up around the mid-point when assessed for health and social problems (see Figure 3.20).

So why (and how) does income inequality cause poor health and social problems? Wilkinson and Pickett suggest that more unequal societies foster heightened stress and anxiety; they call this *social evaluation anxiety*. In unequal societies, being at the bottom is terrifying. Perhaps as a result, people cling desperately to their status, push others down, and compete for opportunities to move up to positions with more power, status, and wealth.

Many of the impacts of income inequality found by Wilkinson and Pickett affect, in some way, all members of society—not just the poor. Interestingly, the health of men declines in societies where women's status is low. The same is true for infant mortality.

Table 3.2 Disability and Income

Per cent living in poverty (using after-tax low-income measure) by sex, disability status, and type, persons aged 25–64*

	CIS 2013	LISA 2014
	Per cent	
Both sexes		
Without a disability	8.9	8.6
With a disability	23.5	23.2
Physical–sensory disability	16.1	16.8
Mental–cognitive disability	22.8	26.6
Combined disabilities**	37.9	35.3
Women		
Without a disability	9.8	9.3
With a disability	25.0	23.1
Men		
Without a disability	8.0	7.9
With a disability	21.6	23.3

This table displays the results of after-tax low-income measure (LIM–AT) by disability status and type CIS2013 and LISA2014. It is calculated using per cent units of measure (appearing as column headers).

*Disability status refers to the collection period in both surveys. Both surveys were conducted in early 2014 and are linked to the 2013 income tax records.

**Combined disabilities refer to persons who have both a physical–sensory disability and a mental–cognitive disability.

Source: Statistics Canada 2017b.

Data suggest that in countries of the Global North, infants die more often in the richest populations of unequal societies than in the poorest populations of more equal societies.

So how might this broader social inequality relate to employment? You might know or meet a professional who describes starting their career clearing tables in a restaurant and then moving up to waiter, and then manager, and then owner. The ability of individuals to move within a social hierarchy is called **social mobility**.

social mobility The ability of individuals to move within a social hierarchy; often used in terms of job or class.

One of the ways we can measure inequality is through the use of **wealth deciles**. No society has a completely open system, meaning that all members move freely from one wealth decile to the next. And no society has a completely closed system either, where members are forever locked in the wealth decile into which they were born. Cultural and political realities, like caste systems and persistent structural xenophobia or racism, can worsen social mobility. The differences between the richest and the poorest in a given society can be calculated using the Gini index: Stay tuned for a deeper discussion of this calculation in Chapter 12.

wealth deciles Wealth expressed in terms of tenths of the population, ranked from bottom to top; so the wealthiest Canadians are in the top decile of the population.

In Canada, sociologists have documented "stickiness at the poles." This means that those in both the highest (tenth) decile and those in the lowest (first) decile have, metaphorically speaking, glue on their feet: these people don't step out of their decile easily. This happens when the poorest don't have enough to build "ladders" out of poverty—like education, decent attire for job interviews, and so on. And the richest are protected from slippage even if they drop out of school or choose not to work.

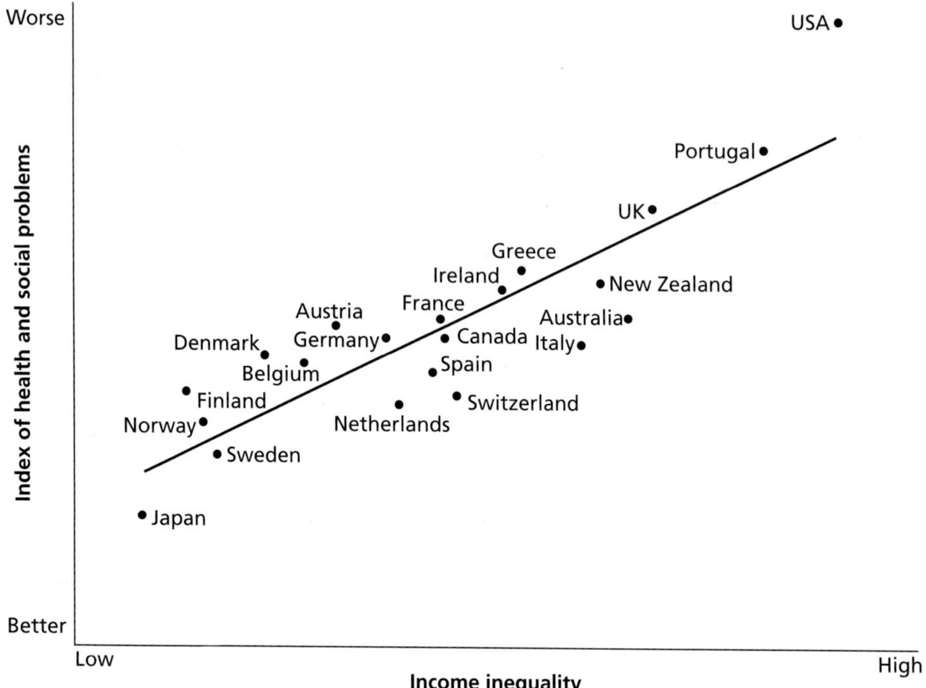

Figure 3.20 ◆ Income Inequality Correlates with Health and Social Problems

Source: Wilkinson and Pickett 2010.

Wilkinson and Pickett (2010) show that social mobility decreases as inequality increases. As the potential to move up an economic class decreases, income becomes more stagnant. Stagnant income means that individuals are increasingly likely to earn the same, if not less, than their parents made. As living costs and inflation lessen the buying power of income, social inequality will increase. So, in a self-perpetuating cycle, inequality decreases social mobility and increases income inequality. In turn, income inequality compounds and worsens the effects of other inequalities, especially for vulnerable populations.

Similarly, Wilkinson and Pickett (2010) show that inequality also reduces children's educational performance, which can affect their job prospects. This leads them to argue that "great inequality wastes the talents of a large proportion of the population" (57).

Strategies of Resistance

We have seen how a lack of education, effort, talent, and smarts are often not the reason that people are denied opportunities to work in safe, stable, reasonably compensated jobs. Many people feel frustrated about unequal access to employment income and so devote their time and energy to this cause. Similarly, the Government of Canada has tried to promote equal access to employment income.

This next section will look at a few strategies of resistance that individuals and groups are undertaking to address the unequal access to this form of survival capital. This list is by no means exhaustive—there are many, many individuals, organizations, and governmental efforts working to improve access to employment income.

Government-Level Strategies of Resistance

The Employment Equity Act asserts that treating people equally may mean treating them differently. If **employment discrimination** did not exist in Canadian society, it is reasonable to expect the socio-demographic makeup of all workers would reflect that of the general population. Yet, as we have seen in this chapter, it does not—and historically, it has not.

employment discrimination Refers to the unequal treatment by employers based on ascriptive characteristics such as gender, race, ethnicity, accent, and skin colour.

In the 1970s, the Government of Canada began to address the fact that the composition of the public service did not reflect the composition of the country. White, English-speaking, non-disabled men vastly outnumbered all other public service employees. A debate began—and continues today—about the best way to address and equalize those differences. This debate has revolved around divergent understandings of equality.

Christopher Jencks (1988), for example, has shown there are at least five different interpretations of equality and fairness where "equal" opportunity is concerned. He shows this by asking us to imagine how a schoolroom teacher, Ms Higgins, should split her time among better and worse readers.

1. Democratic equality requires Ms Higgins to give everyone equal time and attention. She is to disregard how well they read, how hard they try, how deprived they have been in the past, what they want, or how much they or others will benefit.
2. Moralistic justice requires Ms Higgins to reward virtue and punish vice. In the classroom, virtue involves effort, and moralistic justice means rewarding those who make the most effort to learn whatever Ms Higgins is trying to teach.
3. Weak humane justice requires Ms Higgins to compensate those students who have been shortchanged by giving them more than their proportionate share of her attention while they are in her classroom. She is to do this especially for those who have been shortchanged at home or in their earlier schooling.
4. Strong humane justice requires Ms Higgins to compensate those who have been shortchanged in any way in the past.
5. Utilitarianism means that competitions must be open to all, run on a level field, and judged solely on the basis of performance. Thus, insofar as Ms Higgins's attention is a prize, it should go to the best readers. (Adapted from Jencks 1988:519–20)

As you can see, one model of fairness—utilitarianism—suggests we must treat everyone the same way. In a schoolyard race, this might mean lining up all the kids at the same start line before blowing the "go" whistle. Another model of fairness, sometimes called equity-based equality, suggests the best way to be fair is to take extra steps to help those who lag behind to catch up. In that same schoolyard race, this might mean allowing the younger, smaller students to begin at a start line set a little ahead of the bigger, faster students. That way, they may all have equal opportunity to finish the race together.

By the mid-1980s, proponents of the equity-based equality theory succeeded in influencing lawmakers, and the first Employment Equity Act was passed in 1986. Read the stated purpose of the Act and note the clear reference to this equity-based equality approach:

> The purpose of this Act is to achieve equality in the workplace so that no person shall be denied employment opportunities or benefits for reasons unrelated to ability . . . [E]mployment equity means more than treating persons in the same way but also requires special measures and the accommodation of differences. (Section 2 of the Employment Equity Act)

Refusing to hire someone, firing them, or denying them a promotion based on their sex, race, age, ability, or other grounds is employment discrimination. Such discrimination is illegal in Canada, as outlined in the Canadian Human Rights Act of 1977. Provinces also have their own legislation in place to combat discrimination. For example, the Ontario Human Rights Code bans discrimination based on a large number of grounds, including race, ancestry, place of origin, colour, ethnic origin, citizenship, creed, sex, sexual orientation, gender identity, gender expression, age, record of offences, marital status, family status, or disability. Another important piece of legislation is the Canadian Charter of Rights and Freedoms (1982), which enables people to take legal action against the government by challenging discriminatory governmental action or discriminatory legislation. Simply put, laws at both the provincial and federal levels make various kinds of discrimination in the workplace illegal.

There is, however, an important difference between the Canadian Human Rights Act and the Employment Equity Act. The latter requires employers to actively recruit employees from certain historically disadvantaged populations. Also, it only applies to federally regulated employers, such as banks and Crown corporations like the CBC, Canada Post, and so on. This entire group makes up only 6 per cent of all employees in Canada. The remaining Canadian employers must decide on their own what employment strategies they may (or may not) undertake to promote the full representation of Canadians among their workforce.

It is also worth noting that not everyone supports the Employment Equity Act. Some believe the Act promotes employment opportunities for the wrong populations. Others argue it does not promote opportunities for enough populations. The first objection to the Employment Equity Act is grounded in the belief that hiring aimed at improving access to employment for vulnerable populations limits opportunities for other deserving candidates—that is, it limits opportunities for white, non-disabled men and women. Sometimes, these are popularly named "reverse racism" objections. The second objection suggests the list of historically disadvantaged populations included in the Act should be expanded. For example, in 2010 the Public Service Alliance of Canada (one of Canada's largest labour unions) recommended "the designated groups should be expanded to include lesbians, gay men, bisexual groups and the transgendered." They have made similar recommendations for older workers.

For now, despite these objections, the Employment Equity Act remains.

Organization-Level Strategies of Resistance

Some of the groups we have discussed in this chapter are better able than others to develop and carry out collective strategies of resistance. That is because some of them live in self-segregated communities while others do not.

For example, immigrants often self-segregate in ethnically homogeneous communities with institutional completeness. Immigrants who settle in Canada often access some form of settlement services. These are small, medium, or large organizations staffed by both paid workers and volunteers who help immigrants in various ways. Immigrant Services Association of Nova Scotia (ISANS) in Halifax, Nova Scotia, is one such organization. By no means the only one of its kind, ISANS was the first organization in Atlantic Canada to deliver many important settlement programs. Some of the ways that ISANS assists immigrants to access the labour market include the following:

- English-language instruction
- Practice job interviews
- Job search workshops
- Professional mentorships
- Work placements
- Computer and technical training

ISANS also targets the de-professionalization of immigrants by helping those who need Canadian licensing to follow careers in their fields (for example, engineers, teachers, or healthcare professionals). It offers them help as they navigate through what can be a complicated system.

Individual-Level Strategies of Resistance

Recall this chapter's earlier discussion of the importance of clothing for employment outcomes. Affording the professional clothes that most interviewers expect is just one barrier someone might face when seeking employment. Other barriers include a lack of transportation to and from interviews and the inability to access a computer and printer to put together application packages.

Just as institutional solutions are important in reducing barriers to employment, individual-level solutions also have a role to play. One such initiative is the "Dress for Success" organization, founded by Nancy Lublin in 1996. Lublin inherited $5,000 when her great-grandfather passed away. She decided that she wanted to use the money to help poor people build cultural capital so they would stand a better chance of getting a job. So she used her inheritance to start Dress for Success Vancouver (2011). Dress for Success provides low-income women with suits (and accessories) to wear to their job interviews. If they get the job, they can return to Dress for Success for further professional wardrobe staples. Lublin's idea has spread to more than 10 countries. For over 12 years,

◆ In Their Own Words ◆

Liz Struijf-Mandishora immigrated to Canada in 2011. She made use of the settlement programs offered at ISANS. Here's an excerpt from her story:

> I arrived in Canada in November 2011 with my husband, 18-month-old son, and expecting our second son. I was obviously excited about our new life but like any newcomer I was aware of the challenges of settling down in our adopted country and finding a job while having an addition to the family.
>
> The first activity I took part in was the intake process. I was positively surprised by the amount of information I received, and it was a great help in arranging practical things such as getting health cards, where to get a SIN number, etc. I was especially impressed by how the intake coordinator addressed the issues that were specific to me and provided resources to help me handle any challenges or specific concerns I had.
>
> My intake worker referred me to an employment specialist who helped me to set short- and long-term goals regarding my job search. We identified the training courses and workshops that I needed to attend which would be helpful in my job search. Initially I had thought I would just look for a job, but I soon realised that I needed someone with experience in the Nova Scotia Job market. Once again she was able to provide resources that were useful in my line of work including job search websites specific to my line of work. Through these resources and contacts I actually got my first job interview.
>
> My employment specialist also referred me to the mentorship program. The objective of the program was to meet with a professional in the field I wanted to work in and gain contacts, potential references and learn about the industry. This was definitely another fantastic experience. It was a great opportunity meeting with someone who has a wealth of experience in the banking industry. Not only was it a great learning opportunity but I ended being hired by one of the branches at the end of the program. (Struijf-Mandishora 2012)

What are three or four of the barriers to employment present in Liz's story? How were these barriers addressed by ISANS' settlement programs?

the Vancouver Dress for Success organization has helped women aim for employment opportunities.

Working to improve access to employment can come in many forms. As we have shown, institutional-level, organizational-level, and individual-level solutions are all important in improving access to this form of survival capital. Creating better access to employment has massive benefits for society as a whole, not just for the individuals receiving help. As such, it is imperative that we continue to support and participate in such initiatives.

Dress for Success® Vancouver

A Dress for Success® volunteer helps a low-income woman find proper clothes for her job interview. Imagine not having suitable clothes for an important job interview. What impression would you make? How would it affect your chances of securing the position?

Closing Remarks

In the long run, the chance of creating better opportunities is greater for a group of people working together than for an individual working alone. Bringing about equalizing legislation requires banding with others who suffer discrimination and joining forces across ethnic, class, gender, and regional boundaries where necessary. It also means electing sympathetic legislators to push for changes. If successful, the result will be a more equitable, less discriminatory society.

A second approach is to mobilize within one's own group—whether class, ethnic, religious, or regional—to increase community organization. This group mobilization can counter the discrimination the group faces in society. Many groups use this tactic today, notably class-based political parties, unions, lobbies, and associations.

Group mobilization, however, carries the risk of increasing intergroup conflict without removing the underlying conditions that caused it. Pitting one group against another—women against men, racialized people against non-racialized people, LGBTQ+ people against cisgender, heterosexual people—increases the risk of misunderstanding and injustice. As such, it is important to consider how to form intergroup relationships and solidarities that draw and build on connections across different kinds of disadvantage and experience.

It is also important to understand the various inequalities and difficulties faced by different populations in seeking employment. As we have seen, populations can struggle with problems such as discrimination, difficulties juggling work and family, technological advances, and worker exploitation. In addition, the risk of unemployment, which can cause health problems, depressive disorders, and thus a higher mortality rate, can pose difficulties for various populations. We have also learned that inequality in general is harmful for entire societies, not just those who directly experience inequality. As current or future members of the workforce, it is likely that many of you reading this book will come up against some of these issues during your own careers. That fact alone makes it all the more important that you have a solid understanding of the issue and how to critique and mobilize against it.

Test Your Knowledge

1. What is de-professionalization and why does it happen?
2. Why might non-status workers be reluctant to complain about working conditions?
3. What is skill obsolescence and what group does it apply to?
4. Explain how stigma may influence rates of employment for Canadians with disabilities.
5. What is the "common sense perspective" and how does it differ from the functional theory of stratification?
6. What are the two models of fairness?
7. Complete the table:

Name of Theory for Inequality	Sociologist	Main Points
Common sense perspective		
Functional theory of stratification		
Functional theory—the ethnicity paradigm		
Conflict theory		
Conflict theory—the equity paradigm		
Symbolic interactionism	None named in this chapter	
Feminist theory	Jean Wallace	

8. Fill in the blanks:
   a. One government-level strategy of resistance is the ____________________.
      It aims to prevent ____________________.
   b. One organizational-level strategy of resistance is the ____________________.
   c. One individual-level strategy of resistance is ____________________.

See the Answer Key online to check your answers.

Questions for Critical Thought

1. How do the theoretical perspectives presented by Karen Anderson and feminist sociologists like Jean Wallace differ? Which theory would you argue is most applicable to present-day Canada?

2. Have you faced any discrimination or barrier when applying for work? Think about how your experience may have reflected interlocking disadvantages.
3. Consider group mobilization and individual change. Can you provide an instance in which a group has succeeded in its goal and an instance in which group mobilization had harmful effects?

Additional Resources

Recommended Readings

Doucet, Andrea. 2004. "'It's Almost Like I Have a Job, but I Don't Get Paid': Fathers at Home Reconfiguring Work, Care, and Masculinity." *Fathering* 2(3):227–303. Fathers who stay at home doing carework find ways to remain connected to traditionally masculine sources of identity. They develop new sets of relations between home and work and often develop a new sense of self and time use.

Hochschild, Arlie and Anne Machung. 1989. *The Second Shift.* New York: Penguin Group. A classic discussion of gendered inequality in the home, which forces women to face (sometimes) more hours more of paid and unpaid work a day than their spouses.

Recommended Websites

International Labour Organization

www.ilo.org

The first specialized agency of the UN, the main goals of the ILO are to promote rights at work, encourage decent employment opportunities, improve social protection, and strengthen discussion on work-related issues.

Ontario Ministry of Labour

www.labour.gov.on.ca

This ministry was set up in 1919 to develop and enforce labour legislation. It aims to advance safe, fair, and harmonious workplace practices.

Aboriginal Futures

www.aboriginalfutures.com

Training and employment services for urban Indigenous Peoples.

Recommended films

As I Am. 2010. Directed by Nadia Myre. Canada: National Film Board. This short, four-minute experimental documentary challenges stereotypes about Indigenous Peoples in the workplace.

Between the Laughter. 1984. Directed by Barbara K. Lee. Canada: National Film Board. This documentary looks at the life of a deaf stand-up comedian who discusses the challenges of work among other things.

Doctors Without Residency. 2010. Directed by Tetchena Bellange. Canada: National Film Board. This documentary looks at the experiences of foreign-trained doctors in Canada with a focus on systemic racism.

The Interview. 2010. Directed by Claire Blanchet. Canada: National Film Board. This two-minute animated video demonstrates how racial stereotypes and prejudices deprive a highly qualified candidate of a fair interview.

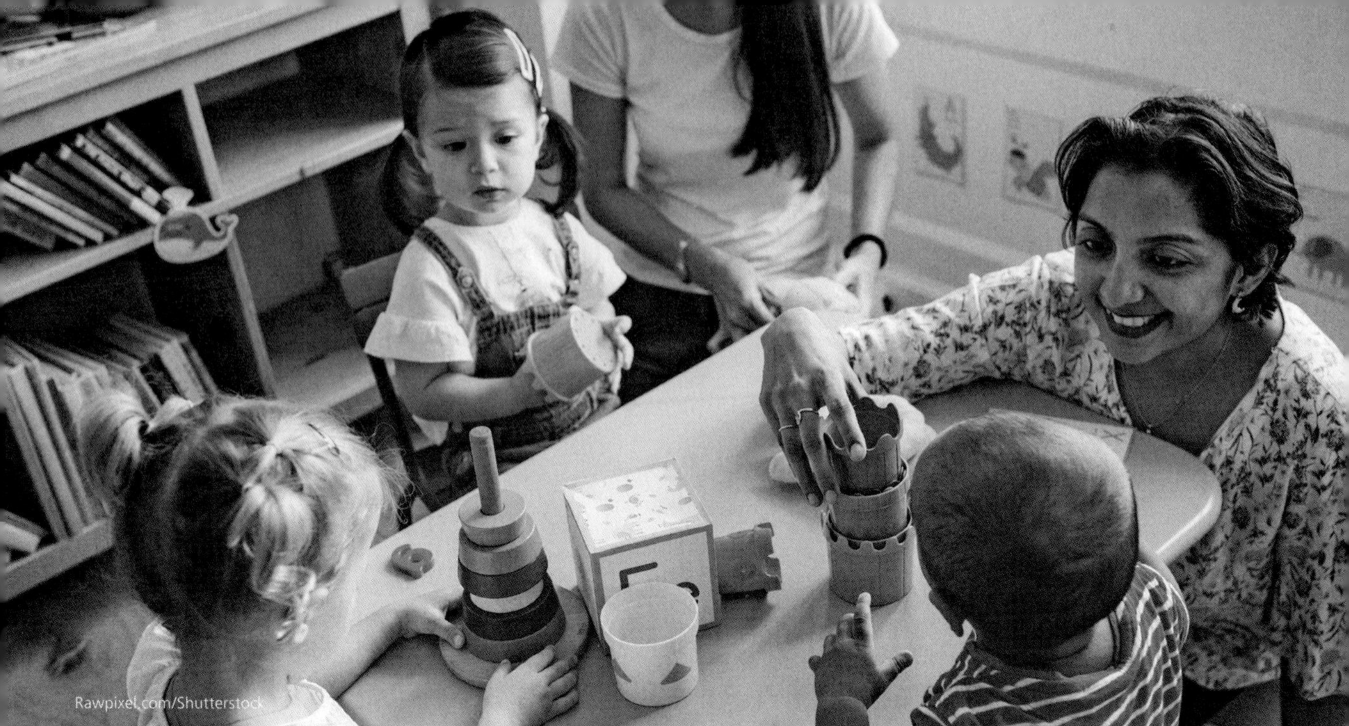

4 Access to Daycare and Early Childhood Education

Learning Objectives

- To recognize different theoretical approaches to daycare and early childhood education.
- To interpret the facts about childcare in Canada.
- To explain why the early years matter the most to children.
- To identify the ways in which children, parents, and the general population can benefit from improvements to early childcare.
- To recognize barriers to daycare and early childhood education.
- To identify the results of unequal access to daycare and early childhood education.

Introduction

In this chapter, we will explore why quality childcare is an important dimension of inequality for children, mothers, and society in general. We will then look at the populations in Canada that are most likely to experience unequal access to high-quality daycare and early childhood education.

IN FOCUS ◆ Are Families Doing What They Need to Do?

Some of the problems facing young children are caused by a lack of access to early childhood education and quality daycare. But as Sean Reardon, a professor at Stanford University, has written, parents need to step up too. Emphasizing the role of families in passing along cultural capital, Reardon (2013) writes "Even though middle-class and poor families are also increasing the time and money they invest in their children, they are not doing so as quickly or as deeply as the rich."

Economists Richard Murnane and Greg Duncan report that from 1972 to 2006, high-income families increased the amount they spent on enrichment activities for their children by 150 per cent, while the spending of low-income families grew by 57 per cent over the same time period (cited in Reardon 2013). Likewise, the amount of time parents spend with their children has grown twice as fast since 1975 among college-educated parents as it has among less-educated parents.

The nature of the problem—a growing educational gap between the rich and the middle class—is unfamiliar. After all, for much of the last 50 years conversations about educational inequality have focused almost exclusively on strategies for reducing inequalities between the educational successes of the poor and the middle class, and it has relied on programs aimed at the poor.

We will see that families without adequate support from daycare face serious problems. Happily, daycare opportunities are increasing and improving, though they are still far from perfect. Moreover, as we see below, families vary dramatically in their ability to provide children with good-quality care and enrichment opportunities.

As we saw in the discussion in Chapter 1 of theories of inequality, people who enjoy social and economic advantages take steps to maintain their advantage. More than that, they take steps to pass these advantages along to their children, thus maintaining the class structure from one generation to the next. They do this by passing along capital in its many forms: their wealth, their social capital (in the form of social connections), and their cultural capital. In Chapter 1 we explored the varieties of cultural capital and how people come to master it, gaining both "taste" and an ability to distinguish "good" things from "bad" things, culturally speaking. We also learned that the acquisition of cultural capital for privileged classes begins at birth. It involves sending one's children to the best and most suitable schools; but even before that, it involves sending them to the best preschools. The process of what sociologist Annette Lareau (2003) has called "concerted cultivation" begins immediately after birth and involves costly tutors, teachers, courses, programs, holidays, parties, and playdates. "Concerted cultivation" allows no room for what Lareau has called "natural growth," let alone parental neglect. Instead, the privileged child must be honed by the best influences that money can buy to ensure their continued advantage.

These influences include the best, most expensive daycare and preschool experiences. These then lead to the best school experiences, then the best college and postgraduate experiences, and so on. Thus, these parents provide their children with survival capital that, throughout their lives, will increase the likelihood of advantage and good treatment.

However, people of privilege typically have no desire to provide such preschool education to all children in Canada—only to their own children. This leaves ordinary people—people without wealth—to seek the best alternatives they can afford. In this chapter, we explore these alternatives and compare the different childcare arrangements available in different parts of Canada—indeed, in different parts of the Global North. Within Canada specifically, we will explore

- the differences between family supervision by grandparents or other relatives, in-home nannies, and institutions, both regulated and unregulated;
- the differences between not-for-profit and for-profit childcare organizations;
- the regulatory role of federal, provincial, and municipal governments; and
- the significant variations in childcare delivery that result from this.

Throughout this chapter, we will see that many different preschool and childcare arrangements have been imagined and many have been tried, with varying results. We argue that it is critically important that all Canadians, not merely people of privilege, enjoy the benefits of high-quality preschool and childcare. It is important to children, their parents, and Canadian society as a whole that all children receive attention, affection, and cultural capital in their preschool years.

As usual, however, sociologists differ somewhat in their views of childcare and early education, mainly because their views about family life differ. In particular, functionalists differ the most from other sociologists because they see traditional family as playing a key role in all childcare and childhood learning.

Theoretical Perspectives on Childcare and Early Education

Functionalists see the family as a microcosm of society, with individual family members coming together to form a productive unit. In Talcott Parsons and Robert Bales's seminal functionalist analysis (1955), the family's gendered division of labour is the key to its success (see Figure 4.1). In the functionalist's dream family, the husband performs an instrumental role as the breadwinner, decision maker, and source of authority and leadership. Meanwhile, the wife fulfills an expressive role as the homemaker, nurturer, and emotional centre of the family.

Though gendered roles in families have changed dramatically since the 1950s, functionalists still tend to believe that this traditional family model accomplishes several vital functions better than any other social institution. Specifically, functionalists view the family as chiefly responsible for socializing children, with mothers chiefly responsible for (and capable of) fulfilling this function.

To this end, functionalists suggest that a stable source of home-based education and care will, presumably, provide a child with the sense of security (or attachment) they need to develop into a healthy, secure adult. This belief implies, first, that the family itself must be stable and, second, that the mother must be reliably present and available. Implicit in this idyll of childhood is the notion that sending a child off to daycare will possibly harm the child's development.

Present-day research does not support this concern about working mothers and daycare. However, we can see how this functionalist thinking traces back to the origins of sociology—from Émile Durkheim's classic work, *Suicide* (1897). There, he argues that, other things being equal, clear social rules and expectations are better for people than a

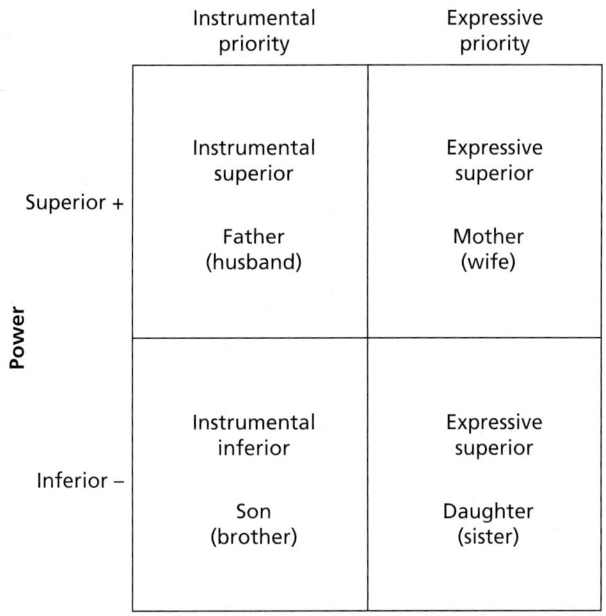

Power	Instrumental priority	Expressive priority
Superior +	Instrumental superior Father (husband)	Expressive superior Mother (wife)
Inferior –	Instrumental inferior Son (brother)	Expressive superior Daughter (sister)

Figure 4.1 ◆ Parsons and Bales's Basic Role Structure of the Nuclear Family

This figure is from Parsons and Bales's influential 1955 book *Family Socialization and Interaction Process*. The chart outlines the roles that mothers and fathers assume in the family. Note that one sex is "superior" in one domain and "inferior" in the other. Do you agree with this theory?

Source: Parsons and Bales 1955.

lack of rules (Durkheim called this state *anomie,* or normlessness) and social integration is better than isolation or extreme individualism.

That said, questions remain about the importance of family stability. Functionalists argue that the traditional, nuclear family form is natural and better than any other, largely because it provides steady integration and a set of rules to live by. That's why some researchers suggest that departures from traditional monogamy might cause long-term harm. These researchers point out that communities in which people have multiple sexual partners also have increased rates of sexually transmitted infections. Moreover, they note that out-of-wedlock births, infant morbidity, and lower educational attainment are connected to departures from monogamous, nuclear families (Immerman and Mackey 1999). Other researchers have noted that cohabitating relationships are often less permanent than legal marriages (Waite 2000). From a functionalist perspective, this would mean that these relationships fail to provide the stability, regulation, and integration that marriage offers. They are also less likely to engage help from extended families and offer less support to partners during a crisis.

There is some support for these concerns. Osborne, Manning, and Smock (2007), for example, report that children born to cohabiting versus married parents are five times more likely to experience their parents' separation. Yet such studies assume that a marriage that doesn't end is stable or positive, or that parental separation is destabilizing, when perhaps it isn't for many families. However, this assumption opens up a number of important questions. For example, how do functionalists account for permanent marriages that are neither healthy nor stable? And how do these perspectives respond to suggestions that relationships ending might illustrate a greater sense of freedom for female partners than the decay of social institutions? Of course, people in harsh and abusive relationships are well-advised to leave them. In short, functionalism has an escape clause: Other things being equal, stable, integrative, and inclusive relationships are best for children's development. But things are not always equal. In today's society, people will not settle for relationships that fail to deliver opportunities for dignity, fairness, and self-expression even if they fall short on stability, integration, and rules and expectations.

With these things in mind, the injunctions of functionalists against non-traditional unions and childcare arrangements do not hold up under scrutiny. But important questions remain about what kinds of childcare and preschool education are best for children and for their parents.

Unlike functionalists, *conflict theorists* do not assume that families are unchanging and unchangeable or that children require only one kind of care to thrive. Instead, conflict theorists accept that with industrialization, families moved from being self-sustaining economic units (for example, a farming household) to consumption units (a dual-income household that buys shelter, food, clothing, services, and luxuries). This meant that working-class men had to sell their labour power to the bourgeoisie (capitalists) in exchange for a salary. In this way, women gained exclusive control over, and thus responsibility for, the home.

Women's dependence on their wage-earning husbands easily turned into patriarchal subordination—domination by a male household head. These patriarchal tendencies are older than industrialization. However, the capitalist economy affirmed them by providing men with both preferential access to and treatment within the labour market, as well as control over many of the family possessions. With this history in mind, feminist sociologists have looked at the issue of childcare from two different angles. First, they highlight the unpaid work that women do when taking care of their children (that is, reproductive work), which you'll recall from Chapter 3 is known as the "second shift." Household work is exploitive in the sense that it is often unchosen and usually unpaid. As Ann Oakley (1974) found out in the first and classic study of housework, most stay-at-home housewives hate housework but feel morally obliged to do it. For many, it seemed such work was their destiny.

Second, feminist sociologists note that childcare is an assumed household responsibility of women. It may not be as soul-crushing as other types of housework—laundry, dusting, vacuuming, and so on—but it limits women's aspirations and job opportunities. It may stand in the way of employment, promotions, and general well-being. As such, feminists often support policies that lessen the gendered load of childcare and give women more freedom to choose. Such policies include flexible work arrangements, parental leave policies, and a universal childcare program. We will discuss these strategies and reproductive work in greater depth later.

Regarding childcare and early education, *social constructionists* focus on the development and use of family ideologies. For example, they focus on the "family values" promoted by right-wing religious leaders and social conservatives in both the United States and Canada. Most people care enormously about their family life. So moral and political entrepreneurs take advantage of this care to channel popular anxieties into hostility against certain groups. The groups targeted include single mothers, LGBTQ+ people, and divorced people. Typically, such entrepreneurs encourage people of a traditional bent to criticize families that deviate from the traditional norm and women who take paid work, at the supposed expense of their children's well-being.

These criticisms and hostilities produce support for political initiatives that reduce social welfare spending and coercively control the behaviour of other disadvantaged groups—for example, people of colour or Indigenous Peoples in Canada. By scapegoating these groups, critics of the disadvantaged undermine the ability of activists to put the issue of quality childcare and early childhood education on the public agenda. This scapegoating, fuelled by a supposed need to protect family values, then distracts the public and fragments the support that childcare activists need to make change.

All parents want the best for their children, but few parents can afford the kind of expensive childcare and childrearing practices wealthy parents can provide. With this in mind, we will now look at current childcare needs in Canada and how they illustrate social inequality.

Ten Facts You Need to Know about Childcare in Canada

Danish sociologist Gøsta Esping-Andersen gave us a useful way to think about social benefits, from daycare up through healthcare and unemployment insurance. His book, *The Three Worlds of Welfare Capitalism* (1990), questioned existing ways of thinking about the differences among welfare states in high-income capitalist democracies. In the book, he argued that earlier theoretical models of the welfare state were inadequate because they relied too heavily on comparing total welfare state spending.

According to Esping-Andersen, welfare states vary in terms of which particular egalitarian justice principles they accentuate and which specific notions of social solidarity they pursue. Some welfare states, for example, have embraced a notion of equality that invites co-operation and collective achievement. Others, however, have embraced a notion that invites competition and the opportunity for individual achievement. As a result of these different goals, welfare states fell into three main categories, which reveal fundamentally different views about the state, the market, and family. He also argues that public spending should no longer be a measure of comparison and that we should seek to replace it with other measures.

The three main categories (or "worlds") of welfare capitalism are liberal regimes, conservative regimes, and social democratic regimes. "Welfare regimes" refer to institutional arrangements between the market, the state, and the family in which the state has a central role in protecting individuals against market risks. Esping-Andersen distinguishes the three regimes by the degree of de-commodification and the stratification they produce in society. *De-commodification* occurs when vital services are provided by right, not as market goods, and when people can survive without relying on the market. *Stratification* refers to the result of redistribution and the universality of solidarity that is imposed by the welfare state, and it reflects inequality in society. Using just these two variables, Esping-Andersen distinguished between (1) liberal, (2) conservative-corporatist, and (3) social democratic welfare states.

Liberal regimes typically provide modest aid to low-income, usually working-class, recipients. This aid, which is means-tested and based on strict claim rules, is often stigmatizing. This regime encourages market solutions (like private health insurance, for example) to personal problems (like poor health). It does this either by guaranteeing only a minimum of aid, wanting the recipient to co-pay for services received, or by directly encouraging and supporting private welfare plans as well as charities.

Conservative regimes also typically provide modest aid to low-income, usually working-class, recipients. However, instead of relying on the market to provide the rest, they rely on families to do so. So these regimes encourage family life through traditional family values and family benefits that encourage motherhood and social insurance that excludes non-working wives. They encourage families to care for their own members, with the state stepping in only when the family is no longer able to aid its members. Here too charities are encouraged as sources of aid to families and individuals.

Social democratic regimes typically provide more generous aid to every citizen. This promotes equally high standards for all, removes stigma to aid recipients, and gives individuals—especially women and children—more agency in their families. By socializing the costs of caring for children, the aged, and the infirm, these regimes relieve many women of what is often a crushing burden of care. Doing this, however, means turning welfare services—such as healthcare and employment insurance—into costly public responsibilities to be paid out of general taxes. Doing so also encourages states to reduce social problems such as bad health and unemployment through state policies that include public health promotion and full employment. Here, charities play only a small role in aiding individuals and families.

As should be obvious, these three models (or "worlds") help us to think about different societies, but they are incomplete. As well, real societies are often a mix of types. Canada, for example, contains some elements of social democratic regimes, such as universal public healthcare. However, it lacks many other elements (for example, universal public daycare for children or universal public care for older adults), leaving these to the market or the family. Thus, it is a mix of social democratic and liberal or conservative regimes. What's more, wide regional variations are possible within countries. In Canada, for example, we find variation in welfare regimes from one province to another. That is because education and social services are largely under the control of provinces (not the federal government). So, for example, daycare in Quebec largely follows a social democratic model, while daycare in Ontario follows a liberal model.

With Esping-Andersen's characterization of liberal welfare regimes in mind, here are 10 things we know for certain about childcare in Canada today.

1. The Early Years Set the Stage for Life

The earliest years of life are among the most important. Most of us have trouble remembering years 0–5 of our own lives, and yet it is during these years that important brain functions form. These formative years can either aid or impair our intellectual, social, and emotional abilities for the rest of our lives. An entire semester in your sociology course will likely matter less in your life than one week you spent, at age three, under the care and guidance of your long-forgotten childhood educator. We will discuss what the research tells us on this topic later in the chapter. For now, remember this: Most experts from different fields agree the first few years of life are critical, and thus the quality of care children receive during this time really matters.

2. Childcare in Canada Is Market Determined

While the quality of childcare matters a great deal, there is still no national childcare policy in Canada to ensure that all childcare meets certain quality standards. This means the federal government, with a few exceptions, does not directly pay for or oversee the provision of childcare. Instead, it transfers money to the provinces and territories, which then manage and deliver these funds in different ways.

In contrast to many other countries in the world, and in absence of government-led delivery of early childcare, Canada has adopted a **market-determined childcare model**. In this model, childcare providers are essentially entrepreneurs who sell a product (childcare) to consumers (parents and guardians). In some regions and in Quebec, governments have set fee caps, and childcare is fully subsidized. But in most of the country, childcare providers set their fees at the level determined by the market. This typically means they charge the maximum their customers are willing and able to pay.

market-determined childcare model An arrangement under which childcare providers sell childcare to parents and guardians, just like any other providers of goods and services on the open market.

Childcare providers are diverse. One may be a cutting-edge educational institution with over a hundred children and many trained caregivers. Another may be a babysitting service in someone's basement, with only one caregiver for five or six children who sit anesthetized in front of a TV. As such, quality of care varies accordingly.

Some childcare providers are not-for-profit, while others are profit based. When money is tight, providers may cut back on expenses and compromise their overall quality of care. Cutbacks on staff training, upgrades to the facility, and the quality of food served to the children are all common. Except in Quebec, most of the working costs are borne by parents.

3. Some Facilities Are Regulated, but Many Are Not

Many childcare facilities in Canada receive effectively no **regulation**. Regulation, in this case, means that each province/territory can set health and safety standards and sporadically inspect childcare providers to make sure these standards are being met. So childcare—like eldercare and long-term healthcare—can be more heavily regulated than many organizations. These standards may include specifying the following:

regulation Official oversight ensuring that childcare centres meet health, safety, and educational standards.

- The ratio of caregivers to children
- The training caregivers must have
- The outdoor and indoor space
- The safety of the equipment, and more

In ideal circumstances, more standards are specified and rigorously applied. Sometimes, however, inspections fail to identify weaknesses and failures.

Health and safety standards vary from province to province. For example, in Ontario all childcare providers with more than five children must be regulated to the same standards. In Prince Edward Island, the rules apply only to facilities with more than seven children; in Manitoba, childcare providers can care for up to eight children without being regulated. In all of these jurisdictions, it is illegal for any unlicensed (that is, unregulated) childcare provider to care for more than the allowable number of children; however, these offenders are rarely caught. This is because childcare providers attract the attention of the authorities only when someone has complained, and public complaints are rare.

Regulation sounds like a good idea for all childcare centres. However, running an unregulated (also called unlicensed) childcare centre is *not illegal* in Canada. In fact, *most* children in Canada receive care in non-regulated childcare settings that mostly run without government oversight. In 2013, the CBC television show *Marketplace* looked into 20 unlicensed daycares in Vancouver and Toronto. They found "unqualified providers with substandard facilities that included missing baby gates on stairways, cramped, windowless rooms with no fire exits and unfenced outdoor play areas" as well as caregivers "driving children as young as 11 months through snowy streets without car seats" (*CBC News* 2013). No parent would feel comfortable leaving their child in such care. Yet many have no choice because of the shortage of good-quality daycare spaces.

Given that childcare centres run with no oversight, parents aren't always aware if theirs is the former or the latter. So why would a parent choose an unregulated centre? This brings us to our next known fact about childcare in Canada.

4. There Are Not Enough Regulated Childcare Spots in Canada

The demand for good childcare far outstrips the supply of good childcare. Because fewer parents stay at home with their children full time, more childcare is also needed than ever before (see Figure 4.2). Yet increases in Canada's available regulated childcare spots have not kept up with this change; in fact, less than a quarter of children aged three to five can get a regulated place (HRSDC 2012). As a result, unregulated childcare remains an essential aspect of Canada's childcare system (Macdonald and Friendly 2014). This childcare arrangement is the most common in the Atlantic and Prairie provinces (Sinha 2015).

As you've already learned, childcare in Canada is market determined. This means that entrepreneurs are not likely to start businesses that aren't profitable. So childcare

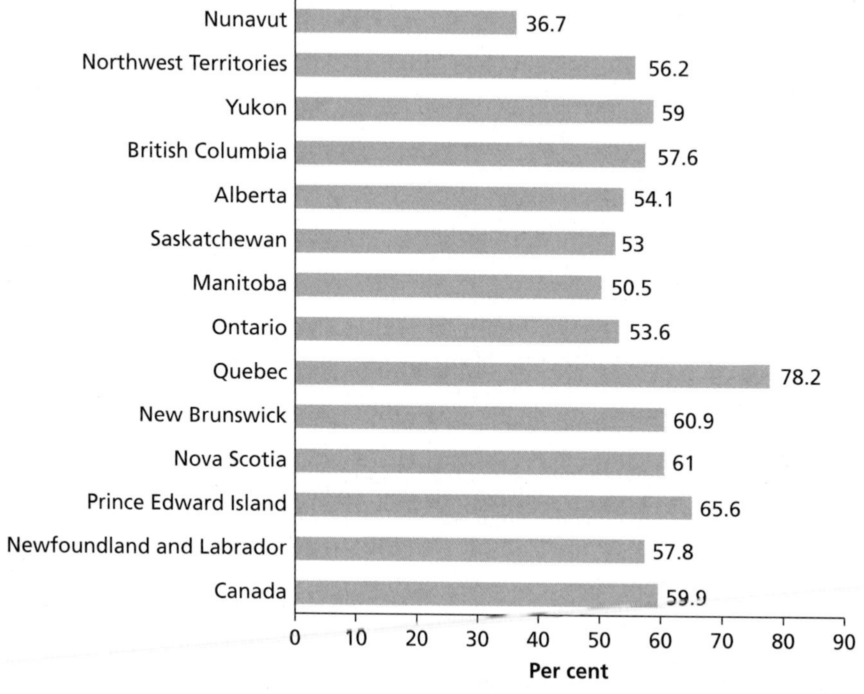

Figure 4.2 ◆ Percentage of Parents Using Childcare by Province and Territory, 2020

The province of Quebec is a childcare anomaly in Canada, and as we will point out, there are good reasons to think that the best and most affordable daycare is found in Quebec. Unsurprisingly, daycare-use rates are also highest there.

Source: Statistics Canada 2020b.

centres are rare in poorer neighbourhoods where few families can afford the cost of tuition. Similarly, in northern or remote regions, entrepreneurs know that working costs are high and, therefore, are less inclined to set up shop. When costs are high, paying customers are few, and profits are low, new daycare spaces will not appear. The province with the lowest number of children (aged 0–12 years old) in regulated care is Saskatchewan, at 8.1 per cent (Friendly et al. 2015). This is much lower than the 50.8 per cent of kids in regulated care in Quebec, which has the country's highest rate.

5. Childcare Is Expensive

Good childcare costs a lot of money. Of course, the cost of childcare differs widely from province to province. Some provinces, like Manitoba and Prince Edward Island, set caps on the fees charged by qualified, licensed, not-for-profit childcare facilities.

As noted above, user fees pay for most childcare in Canada. In other words, parents typically have to pay the full cost themselves. On average, this comes to about 22 per cent of a family's income. Compare this to say, Sweden, where parents pay, on average, 4 per cent of their family income on childcare (OECD 2016).

This is not so different from the problem students (or parents) face when they graduate from high school. If parents want their child to attend the University of Toronto medical school, they'll need to pay a base tuition fee of $25,660 a year. If they want to send their infant to the onsite University of Toronto childcare centre, they'll pay $26,616 per year—nearly $1,000 more than a year of medical school tuition! Not every child gets concerted cultivation, nor can every parent afford these kinds of fees.

Some parents can afford to pay their children's postsecondary tuition. When their children are ready to attend, they may have saved enough money through a Registered Education Savings Plan or other plan. By this time, parents are at the peak earning period of their careers. However, there are no registered childcare savings plans. This means that many parents with toddlers do not have enough time to prepare for the high costs of childcare. To do so, they would have had to start saving long before their children had been born—say, at the age of 13, perhaps with their own babysitting money!

The yearly cost of sending an infant to a daycare in Toronto (roughly $21,540) is not much less than the after-tax income of a minimum wage salary (approximately $24,088). After paying for daycare, a parent working full time at minimum wage would pocket only $212 per month in a city where the cost of living is estimated to be closer to $3,000 per month (see Figure 4.3).

Consider how this would affect a single mother working a minimum wage job. She can work full time, needing full-time childcare, and have no money left over for food. Or, she can care for her child full time at home and rely on government aid, which barely covers her basic needs and weakens her attachment to the labour force. This is why the City of Toronto subsidizes childcare for many families.

6. Some Families Are Eligible for Subsidies

Some families are able to defray the expenses of childcare with government subsidies. And that is good, because we are talking about a form of survival capital.

The high cost of childcare is a burden for most families with young children, especially low-income families. So provincial and territorial governments set aside a

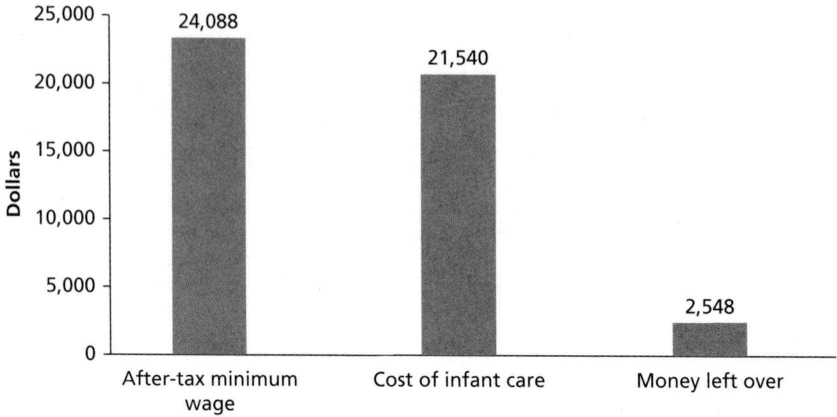

Figure 4.3 ◆ Childcare Fees in Toronto Compared to After-Tax Minimum Wage, 2020

Source: YMCA 2020.

small sum of money for parents who show economic need and require a subsidy to pay for regulated childcare. Sometimes these governments also provide grants for parents who are job seeking when they need childcare or for parents of children with special care needs.

This approach is called funding the "demand side" of childcare: subsidizing parents directly, instead of parents paying some or all the working costs of childcare centres (the "supply side").

7. Many Families Who Need Subsidies Don't Get Them, and Some That Do Still Can't Afford Childcare

Subsidized childcare spots are hard to get. Most come with waiting periods, and eligibility is typically tied to low family income. For example, as of April 2017, Toronto's waiting list for subsidies included over 15,000 children (City of Toronto 2017).

By the time they reach the top of the waiting list, many of these families will have outgrown the need for childcare. As well, the application for a subsidy can be complicated and alienating. It poses unique problems for those with low literacy levels or little time. It also poses problems for people who might have difficulty getting to and from their workplaces to meetings, who lack a phone or computer, or who are new to the country. Even people who *can* show that they have a low income often don't get subsidized care.

Some families that receive childcare subsidies still find the cost of childcare unaffordable. For example, in British Columbia, the most a family can receive (for a child under 19 months of age in a licensed group childcare facility) is $600 per month (Government of British Columbia, n.d.). However, in Vancouver, the median fee for infant childcare is $1,400 per month (Macdonald and Friendly 2018). By contrast, the province of Quebec funds childcare directly, offering a wide-ranging (and popular) childcare program, so fees are much lower. We will look at Quebec's policies later in this chapter.

8. Parents Are Forced to Find Alternatives

Because subsidized, regulated childcare spots are hard to come by, many parents spend more than they can afford on childcare or they compromise on quality, location, or reliability. Many parents would like subsidies but don't qualify, so they find more affordable, unregulated childcare. As noted above, without the regular inspections that only accompany regulated centres, it's hard to be sure how good many of these operations are.

9. Canada Lags Behind in Support for Early Childhood Care and Education

Canada is one of the few remaining industrialized countries without an effective, public childcare system. The most recent data show Canada places dead last in a ranking of 25 developed countries in their commitment to early childcare (Decter 2011). This means that Canada supports early childcare at rates lower than are recommended by international child welfare organizations like UNICEF (Adamson 2008). And this, in turn, means that survival capital is unfairly shared among Canadians.

10. People Are Calling for a Universal Childcare Program

Finally, we need to solve problem 9. As activist Ann Decter (2011) writes, "childcare services in Canada today are an inadequate patchwork that fails to meet the needs of children, families, communities and the nation" (10). This failure has led many to call for a "national" childcare program. But what does this mean? This refers to something that does not yet exist—a national policy with principles, guidelines, and standards that provinces and territories are obliged to meet to receive federal funding. The principles, guidelines, and standards could include the following:

- *Affordability*: The cost of childcare must be free, low, or geared to income.
- *Quality control*: Childcare workers must show that they have completed certain training, the child–worker ratios must be low, and the facility must pass regular health and safety inspections.
- *Appropriateness*: The facility must meet the needs of developmentally and culturally diverse children of all ages.
- *Universally accessible*: There must be space for all the families in Canada who wish to place their children in regulated daycare.

In stressing the importance of good-quality, affordable childcare, we are not arguing it is "The Great Equalizer," the magic bullet for ending disadvantage in our society or any other. But quality childcare does influence the way young people's lives unfold and can predict children's success in formal education, which will be discussed in the next chapter.

If all of this makes sense, you may be ready to ask three critical questions: (1) If you don't have children—and if you're not a child—why does equal access to early childhood education matter? (2) Which populations are especially vulnerable to barriers to this survival capital, and why? (3) What do sociologists have to say about this problem?

To start answering these important questions, we look at the value good-quality childhood experiences can have for children. Then we will look at how it affects other family members, and finally we will look at how it benefits society in general. Remember, problems of social inequality and challenges to them impact society as a whole, not just the groups directly impacted. Social inequality is a pervasive issue, and early childhood education is only one domain in which it manifests.

Children

We noted above that the early years of life matter a lot for children's development. Let's expand on that point a little further.

Young children who are nurtured in reliable, kind, stimulating, and caring environments reap multiple benefits. Essential brain functions, like language development and sensory and perceptual development, are established in the early years of life. For example, Tierney and Nelson (2009) explain that positive stimuli in children's early years "create the scaffolding upon which development depends," with "studies of institutionalized children [suggesting] that quality psychosocial experiences are necessary for the development of a healthy brain" (12).

Children who receive quality care often have higher intelligence scores, better nutrition and health, and show improved social and emotional behaviour (World Bank 2013; Harvard University 2010). Research has also suggested that a child's **sense of agency**—their feeling of confident independence—is formed through positive adult responses during this early period (Adamson 2008).

sense of agency A person's feeling of confident independence.

Furthermore, children who had good-quality early childhood care are less likely to drop out of primary or secondary school and generally stay in school longer. As adults, they tend to be more active citizens, secure better jobs, earn more, and achieve financial stability. Quality childcare is especially important for troubled infants. On this, Belsky and Pluess (2011) have noted that infants who show negative emotional behaviour are more likely to externalize that behaviour as children if they received low-quality childcare.

As well, good-quality early childhood care especially benefits children from low-income or other disadvantaged backgrounds (Decter 2011). This is because it can offset some of the problems that come with living as a member of a disadvantaged group, including exposure to poverty and maternal depression (Shonkoff and Phillips 2000). One notable study conducted in the United States, the Perry Preschool Project, found the economic benefits of free childcare for low-income, high-risk families had a return of over $12 for each dollar invested in early childcare (Berrueta-Clement et al. 1984).

These benefits included better health, better academic performance, and higher earnings. With higher incomes, families could spare a parent or two for work because they no longer needed to watch over their children. When these children held jobs of their own, they enjoyed these benefits too. Conversely, researchers have found that children raised in stressful or unstimulating environments or with non-responsive caregivers do not tend to have the same life chances or positive sense of agency as other children (Adamson 2008).

The adverse effects of a stressful early childhood are more than just intellectual or social. Negative early childhood experiences undermine the development of the body's immune, metabolic, and cardiovascular systems, affecting future health. As researchers from Harvard University (2010) put it, "early experiences are built into our bodies" (1).

While it is widely accepted that a child's early learning environment contributes to a healthy future, not everyone sees a role for childcare in achieving this aim. Some believe the best place for young children is at home with their parents. John Bowlby (1960, 1973) and

◆ In Their Own Words ◆

From an International Women's Day address by Professor Joellen Riley, 8 March 2013:

> Is a child the property of her parents, so that it is the parents who are receiving services from the childminder? Should we not treat the child herself as a citizen who is receiving services? Why not allow a childhood pension, to enable children to pay for their own care? When we consider the broader economic benefit of greater female participation in the labour market, it is reasonable to consider the whole community as the "user" who benefits from the childcare services.

Source: Riley 2013.

Mary Ainsworth (1969; Ainsworth et al. 1978), for example, developed an influential theory of infant attachment to support this view. Their theory proposes that attachment between a child and at least one adult at the beginning of life is critical for healthy psychological development.

This kind of thinking leads people to believe that children are best cared for at home even beyond their first year. So they lobby the government to make staying home easier and more attractive for parents. Increasing and extending parental leave payments or requiring employers to hold work positions for multiple years are just some of the measures they campaign for. Recently, the federal government extended parental leave, inviting parents to stretch their 12-month benefit over 18 months, during which time their employer is obliged to hold their position. However, this choice may only be feasible for the better off, as the parental leave benefits are scarcely enough to live on.

Some also call for more resources for stay-at-home parents, such as early childhood centres. These centres help stay-at-home parents get their children together and enjoy the benefits of broader social interaction, something often missing from stay-at-home arrangements. Conversely, others suggest that young children are cared for just as well (or better) in childcare centres staffed by professionals trained in early childhood education and care. Moreover, they propose that children learn and grow best when exposed to well-equipped facilities, group interaction, and routine. They say that children should be exposed to the diverse personalities of their peers and regularly challenged by new social interactions. For this reason, they may say the best environment for child development is *rarely* found in homes.

So are children better off at home or at a childcare facility? In a thorough literature review, Lamb and Ahnert (2006) conclude that no sweeping generalization can be made about this issue. Rather, research shows that young children need consistent care from sympathetic, engaged adults who lovingly encourage their development. Children who receive that care will do better than if they were to receive care that is discouraging or neglectful. All children, when they're ready, need opportunities to interact socially. They must be challenged intellectually and given spaces to explore and learn independently, without emotional or physical risk. They all need toxin-free, safe places; some time each day to run around outside; and consistent and healthy snacks and meals. They need someone to change their diapers, apply sunscreen, tie their shoelaces, tell them they are worthy and unique, and make them feel loved and accepted.

Many would agree with Canadian childcare researchers Cleveland and Krashinsky (2003) when they argue that

> there needs to be a range of good quality educational and care services to choose from at reasonable cost. Further still, these services should be available to children whose parents have decided to stay at home, as well as to those whose parents are employed. (26)

We know that children benefit from good-quality early childhood education. But parents benefit from good-quality early education programs, too. In the next section, we'll focus on the advantages childcare offers parents.

Parents

People live in different and diverse family types. Increasingly within many families, men as well as women provide loving, attentive caregiving and share childcare tasks with their partners. Researchers have found that family intimacy, support, and affection are far more critical in shaping the quality of family life and parenting than family structures (as opposed to what functionalists might argue). Family arrangements include nuclear or extended, single parent or two parent, married or common law, same-sex or different-sex spouses.

◆ In Their Own Words ◆

A new term you might hear is "Mommune." A Mommune refers to a living arrangement in which multiple single mothers live together and share the work of parenting: It's a commune for moms.

One mom reflects on her time in a Mommune:

> My son called [my housemate] Mama Judi and her daughter called me Mama Ramona. It was okay [to my son] for her to read them both bedtime stories. [Judi] had to be up before her daughter was up two days a week and I dropped them off at school . . . It was great getting to do a Christmas tree together in matching pajamas and opening presents . . . It took some pressure off us [moms]. [The kids] could get into a three-hour make-believe game making a tent cave.

Family structures are always evolving. Cases like the Mommune challenge limited expectations surrounding what kinds of family arrangements/structures are beneficial for children.

Source: Crowe 2018.

In most (heterosexual) families, both mothers and fathers benefit from quality, reliable, and affordable childcare. However, in the last 50 years childcare provision has changed the lives of mothers more than the lives of fathers. This is why this section mainly discusses mothers and their need for quality childcare.

There are two reasons the provision of childcare impacts women more than men. The first is that women are more likely to be lone parents. Single mothers rely on childcare because the social assistance they would otherwise get is not enough to live on (and neither, for that matter, is minimum wage). This means that single mothers often do not have the choice of staying home to care for their child or children, even if they would like to.

The second reason is that childcare has played an essential role in helping the entry of *all* mothers (not just single women) into the labour force. The "flooding" of the labour force by women has fittingly been called "the most dramatic social change in the latter half of the twentieth century" (Cleveland and Krashinsky 2003). Forty years ago, only one in six mothers with children under the age of six were in the paid labour force. Today, more than three-quarters of mothers with children under the age of six are in the paid workforce (Ferns and Friendly 2014). As growing numbers of mothers have taken on work outside of the home, the need for childcare choices has also risen to unprecedented levels.

Census responses show that when one parent cuts back on paid work hours or stays home to care for children, most of the time it is mothers who do so. More generally, women are more often tasked with carework than men, whether the care recipients are children, seniors, sick family members, or otherwise. So even with women's entry into the workforce, childcare is still a gendered responsibility. See Figure 4.4 for a breakdown of men and women reporting "caring for children" as a reason for working part time in 2018. This,

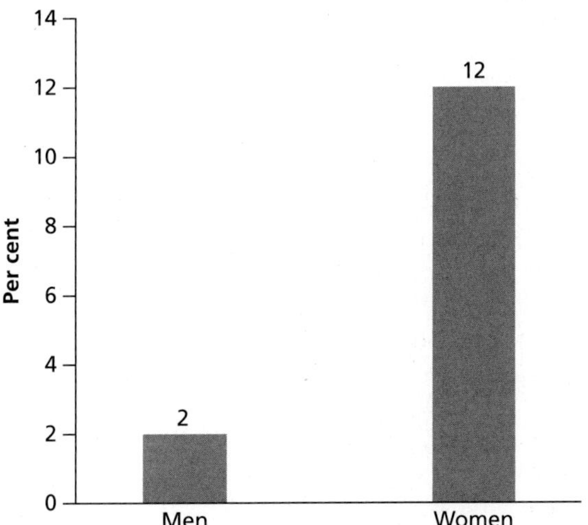

Figure 4.4 • Caring for Children as a Reason for Part-Time Work, 2018

Source: Statistics Canada 2020a.

in part, serves to explain the enduring gender wage gap. As economist Carole Vincent (2013) argues,

> providing better access to high-quality, affordable early childhood education and care is the best way to address the large gender wage gap and boost female labour participation. Just over half of the earnings penalty experienced by Canadian mothers can be explained by fewer years of work experience and more hours devoted to unpaid work.

The "parenting penalty" is not only visible among lower-paid, part-time workers. A survey of those earning salaries in the top 1 per cent revealed that women are less likely to have children or have fewer children than their male counterparts (Richards 2019). Fortin, Bell, and Böhm (2017) point out that an important contributor to the gender wage gap is women's underrepresentation in top-earning management and leadership positions. This wage gap is due, in part, to difficulties mothers face juggling work and childcare. In short, children and childcare limits women's ability to climb the corporate ladder far more than it does for men:

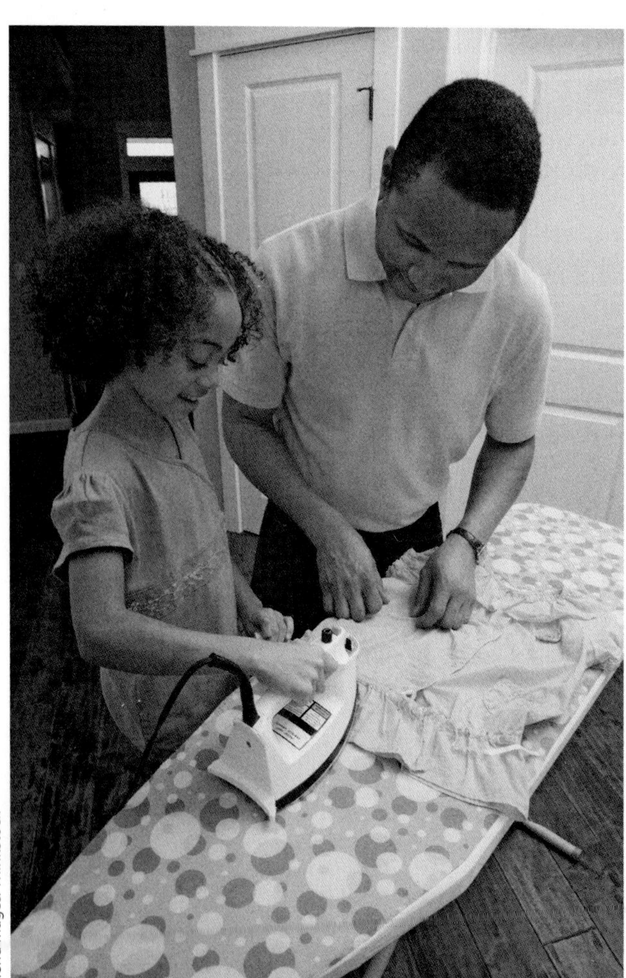
Blend mages/Thinkstock

Today, men are more likely than they were a few decades ago to do housework, and some are even stay-at-home dads. Are these changing trends producing equality in Canadian households?

> For women, economic inequality is still a reality three decades after the 1970 report of the Royal Commission on the Status of Women. [Even today,] women's equality is undermined as women continue to make up for the lack of public services to care for their young children, and—increasingly—ageing parents as well. Mothers cannot afford to stay home but without access to good childcare, may be forced into lower wage jobs or part-time work with little prospects for benefits or a pension. Childcare . . . is a key women's issue and is fundamental to . . . women's equality. (Friendly and Halfon 2012)

An added problem is male rigidity—a continued unwillingness to pitch in and help out their wives. Many men—notably those raised in patriarchal, traditional cultures—refuse to help out more at home. Even in societies with progressive attitudes about gender equality, men often fail to take on as much domestic labour as women. Even where the law mandates paternity leaves, many men do not use them fully for fear of seeming uncommitted to their jobs (Bruning and Plantenga 1999; Lappegard 2008).

Time-use studies show that men's contributions to housework have increased but are still far from equal (see Figure 4.5). Sociologists find the most equal contributions are among younger spouses, so this trend to equality will likely continue. More fathers are also choosing to be stay-at-home dads while more mothers are becoming the primary income earner for their families.

Changes at work have also contributed to mothers' increased involvement in the labour force. Workplace discrimination against women and mothers has significantly decreased, while postsecondary enrolment for women is at an all-time high. Also, parental leave, which has increased in duration since the 1970s and is predominantly taken by mothers, oblige employers to hold positions.

But most importantly, many mothers report that they *want* to work outside the home, and they have fought long and hard to secure the right to do so. Many mothers who work for pay report a sense of purpose and satisfaction from their employment. Work is a source of social stimulation and intellectual challenge, and women value their contributions to society and to their children. Your grandmothers and great-grandmothers may have had many of the same ambitions, but their options would have been more limited.

Two-parent families enjoy the financial benefits of dual incomes. Dual-income families can afford to give their children more opportunities, such as summer camp attendance and postsecondary education. Mothers reportedly feel financially independent when they work outside of the home; moreover, they feel protected in the case of divorce or other forms of sudden, unexpected single parenthood. When their children are in quality,

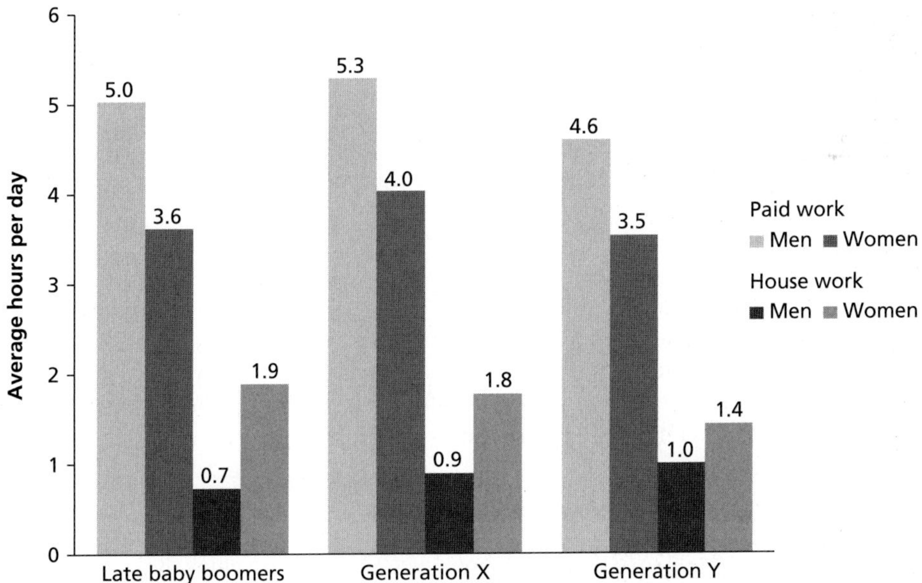

Figure 4.5 ◆ Hours of Paid Work and Housework Are the Most Similar for Men and Women of Generation Y

This chart shows that the division of labour is getting more equitable, with those born between 1980 and 1996 (Generation Y) sharing the load most equitably—but still not equally.

Source: Statistics Canada 2015.

◆ In Their Own Words ◆

Here is a quote excerpted from an interview with a mom who chooses to work outside of the home:

> I enjoyed my maternity leave but [after a] year was starting to feel intellectually understimulated and bored. I was craving the opportunity to use my professional skills again and be appreciated for my intelligence and abilities instead of for clean laundry and singing silly songs. [Luckily,] I was able to arrange to start back at work part-time for the first few months . . . I got the benefits of working but also had a couple of days a week alone with my daughter [and] appreciated our time together so much more once back at work.

Source: Carson 2013.

reliable childcare, parents feel comfort knowing that their children are growing and learning in a safe and nurturing environment.

The increase in demand for childcare is not only the result of women's increased employment. It is also because—and this may sound shocking to some readers—many parents feel that early childhood educators do a better job teaching their children than they could. Sure, parents could educate their children, but not all parents have equal means, ability, or motivation to do so. As Friendly and Prentice (2009) put it,

> [a] breathtaking myth . . . is that women naturally know how to care for children. This myth is damaging to quality [of childcare] because it promotes the notion that good-quality programs are possible without early childhood education training or ongoing professional development. (9–10)

Many parents genuinely feel that the best educators of their children are people trained to do the work. That doesn't mean those parents don't play a key role in their children's development. Rather, it shows they recognize and value the unique skills required of early childhood educators—skills that don't come "naturally" to anyone.

While the need for good-quality childcare has a vast impact on the lives of parents—particularly women, but increasingly men, too—childcare matters for everyone.

Who Is Everyone?

Other family members, like fathers and school-aged siblings, also enjoy the economic advantages of a dual-income family when one parent is not obliged to stay home and care for a young child. Children also tend to benefit when parents feel they are doing what they want with their lives—happy parents are often good parents.

Many Canadians demand that the government create a fully subsidized, nationally regulated childcare program. This would be an arrangement that sees *all* Canadians pay for the care of young children, not just parents paying for their own children.

Critical Thinking Question

Do you think someone who doesn't have children should have to financially contribute toward the care of other people's young children? Before you continue reading, try to imagine some reasons that quality, reliable, and affordable early childhood care and education may benefit everybody.

Not everyone can have children or chooses to do so. So some people feel that having children is like buying a dog or a cat: a personal decision the rest of society should not be accountable for. For example, many would say the government should not subsidize dog food or cat litter—and similarly, having children is a "private matter." However, many others argue that quality childcare is a public interest worthy of public management.

There are two "good" reasons used to defend the argument that childcare is a public interest: the "social good" and "economic good" of quality early childhood education and care. The "social good" reason argues that we all have an interest in healthy, well-adjusted children because they will become healthy, well-adjusted adults. And these adults, presumably, will be the ones removing our appendixes, managing our life savings, policing the streets, and running the country. If early years matter, then it matters that we, as a country, collectively ensure good learning and growing conditions for the adults of tomorrow. This would, theoretically, allow everyone to benefit from a smarter and healthier society.

The "economic good" reason argues that good childcare centres improve the economy. As a business venture, childcare centres stimulate the economy. Economists like it when money changes hands—this is sometimes called the "velocity" of money. If you make money, you'll probably spend it, causing somebody else to make money too. The wish to earn money motivates people to provide their communities with needs like food, shelter, and clothing (and childcare). As economist Adam Smith wrote, "it is not from the benevolence of the butcher, the brewer, or the baker that we expect our dinner, but from their regard to their own interest" (Smith, [1776] 1991).

Governments also seize the opportunity to collect some money for the collective pot when money changes hands. This leads us to the second reason why good childcare centres improve the economy: Widespread employment leads to more taxable income and thereby more tax funds. When you earn money, the government gets a portion of it. You also pay a tax to them when you purchase something, and theoretically, the government reinvests those taxes in social goods like roads, schools, and hospitals. That's a simple explanation of why the current economy relies on people earning money and spending it. If nobody had any earnings to give to the government, the roads would be in pretty bad shape.

Similarly, more available childcare has freed up women to both earn and consume actively, driving the wheels of the economy and contributing taxes to the government. For example, in Canada in 2017, the economic contribution of working mothers was estimated to be around $250 billion (Tencer 2018).

Let's think long term about the future economic contributions of the children in care. From this standpoint, childcare is an investment in the future. An "investment" is something you buy now with the hopes of gaining something in the future. As noted above,

knowledge economy An economic system based on intellectual capital.

children who are well cared for in their early years tend to stay in school longer and secure better jobs. They become more productive workers in what is increasingly known as a **knowledge economy**. Some of those children may grow into adults who hire other workers or invent new products. They'll pay taxes through their own earnings but also via their employees. With this in mind, economists have estimated that future generations will enjoy a $1.50–$3.00 return for every dollar invested in early childhood education today (TD 2012).

Another economic argument concerns parents (often single parents, and often women) who receive social assistance. These parents usually weigh the costs and benefits of returning to work with those of staying home. Recall the earlier example of a minimum wage earner paying for childcare: With so little leftover, it sometimes isn't affordable to work.

Subsidized childcare and social assistance both cost the government money. But when someone chooses to remain on social assistance instead of working, the government loses in three ways: First, it loses the parent's current income tax. Second, it loses the parent's greater future income tax, which will likely reflect her number of years in the workforce. Third, the government loses any consumer tax on the purchases the parent could have bought with their earnings.

The above social and economic reasons justify a universal, regulated, low-fee childcare system. Not surprisingly, one province in Canada has set up such a system: Quebec. In Quebec, childcare costs range from $8–$21 per day, depending on a family's income. The provincial government pays the rest of the costs. It costs the government a fortune, but economists show that these costs are recouped by the economic contributions of working parents.

Let's pause for a moment. We've known for some time that critical human development occurs in the first few years of life. We also know that there are social and economic benefits to investing in quality early childhood care and education. So why don't all municipal, provincial, and federal governments invest in early childhood education? Why does direct government funding for and management of education only kick in for elementary and secondary schooling? Here's why:

1. These outdated policies emerged when early childhood care largely came from mothers at home.
2. When these policies were created, not much was known about this critical stage of human development.
3. There has been a lack of political will to create a federally regulated program through which all Canadians would have equal access to quality childcare.

Balancing work and family life is a huge problem worldwide, and Canada is no exception. This problem, and the need for government intervention, will not disappear. As women enter the labour force, whether by choice or necessity, the work traditionally assigned to women—what we have elsewhere called *reproductive work*—must be accomplished somehow.

Single-women households, especially those with young children, experience the highest levels of poverty. With this in mind, we need to consider what kinds of government policies are most effective for alleviating poverty among single mothers. Misra, Budig, and

Moller (2007) identified four strategies states use to help women combine employment and care. Each carries specific assumptions about the role of women and men in the household:

1. *The **carer strategy***: This is closest to the traditional model of family and work. Here, the husband is seen as the breadwinner and the wife as the caregiver. Caregiver allowances, parental leaves, and flex time may be provided, but part-time employment is considered the best way for women to combine work and care. Here, women's caregiving is the primary source of care. Countries in this category include the Netherlands, Germany, and Luxembourg.

carer strategy Part-time employment, plus assistance, is considered the best way for women to combine work and care.

2. *The **earner strategy***: This strategy is based on the dual breadwinner model, where men and women are equally encouraged to take part in the labour market through policies against gender discrimination in employment. However, little or no effort is made by the government to directly address the tension between work and family brought on by childcare responsibilities. The United States is unique among industrialized countries in its lack of public help for childrearing mothers. For example, it does not offer state-guaranteed minimum payments or employment policies that would help mothers increase their earnings. Other countries in this category are Canada and the United Kingdom. (Quebec is somewhere between the choice strategy and the earner-carer strategy).

earner strategy Men and women are equally encouraged to participate in the labour market through policies against gender discrimination in employment.

3. *The **choice strategy***: States that employ this strategy provide women with more freedom to choose between providing care or engaging in full-time employment. In France, for example, the state offers childcare, generous parental leave, and homecare allowances that support parental care for two or more young children. Belgium also employs this strategy. In both countries, there is little focus on equalizing men's contribution to childcare and housework.

choice strategy Women are given many opportunities to exercise choice to either provide care or engage in full-time employment.

4. *The **earner-carer strategy***: States that employ this strategy envision a society where informal carework and employment is equally shared between men and women. Both are encouraged to take parental leave, and men's involvement in the household is promoted through paternity leaves that only men can take. These states also provide high-quality childcare outside of the home to simplify women's maintenance of full-time employment. Sweden, Norway, and Finland employ this strategy.

earner-carer strategy Unpaid carework and paid work are equally shared between men and women.

The earner strategy is associated with the highest levels of family poverty. As Misra and colleagues (2007) point out, "a focus on the market provision of care does not appear to

Critical Thinking Question

Take a moment to reflect on what you think would be the "ideal" government support for families with young children. Perhaps you imagine a version of the carer strategy where one parent steps away from the labour market to rear their children, with little support from or interference by the state. Or perhaps you imagine a world where childcare facilities are fully subsidized, top-of-the-line educational facilities.

Many models are possible, but which one is best? Why?

address the roots of poverty for mothers and their children. Without generous benefits, leave policies, or childcare, families with children must precariously balance care against employment" (815). Therefore, state policies are needed to decrease the degree of gendering in domestic work. This is a worthwhile endeavour - in Sweden, more paternal involvement in childcare has resulted in higher female workforce participation (Misra et al. 2007).

Earlier in the chapter we asked: Why should we be concerned about equal access to early childhood education and care? By now, you've learned the answer to this question: Because children, mothers, families, and the rest of society benefit from its provision. You have also learned that most families in Canada have difficulty accessing regulated, quality childcare. But which populations are especially vulnerable to barriers to this survival capital, and why? We will answer this second question by taking a look at low-income families, parents with unusual jobs, rural families, recently arrived immigrant families, Indigenous families, and families of children with special needs.

Low-Income Families

Childcare costs are an especially challenging barrier for low-income families. The sad irony is that many low-income families are the ones that need quality childcare the most. High-quality childcare can set children on a path to an education that may allow them to rise above their parent's economic status. Recall our earlier discussion of the need to demystify meritocracy as the key to breaking the cycle and rising through social classes: Receiving high-quality care from a young age can set children up for success in ways that their individual merits cannot.

High childcare fees can make family poverty worse. Many low-income families have at least one unemployed parent, and the cost of childcare may prevent that parent from seeking employment. This harms the entire family by perpetuating poverty. Cleveland and Krashinsky (2003) also point out that when parents are not employed, "children lose the benefits of seeing within their families the regular attachments that most adults have to the labour force. Enabling single parents to look for jobs—while providing high-quality care to their children—may be an important way to break the cycle of poverty" (21).

Some low-income families can only afford to pay for substandard care. Often, the caregivers in lower-cost facilities are unlicensed and unqualified. As mentioned earlier, substandard care is often the result of a lack of employee training and low earnings.

In general, early childhood educators' (ECEs) salaries are lower than other kinds of teachers. Take a look at Figure 4.6, which compares ECE salaries against teachers' salaries in each province. This gives a sense of how this important work is valued and rewarded. If we consider Alberta, for example, we see that ECEs earn, on average, only 47 per cent of what teachers earn. Figure 4.7 zooms in on this province's salary comparison and adds that ECEs in Alberta earn only 61 per cent of a zookeeper's salary! This low wage contributes to rapid turnover in this field. This is not good for children, who need stable, consistent adult relationships. The low salary also deters qualified job seekers with the necessary training because they cannot afford to pay down their student loans with a minimum wage salary. A report from the Organisation for Economic Co-operation and Development on childcare found that "tuition costs to gain an additional diploma are high, and for childcare staff, the opportunity costs are far greater than any conceivable payback in future earnings" (OECD 2003).

As noted earlier, childcare fees are subsidized for low-income families in all Canadian provinces and territories. However, families in different provinces receive different

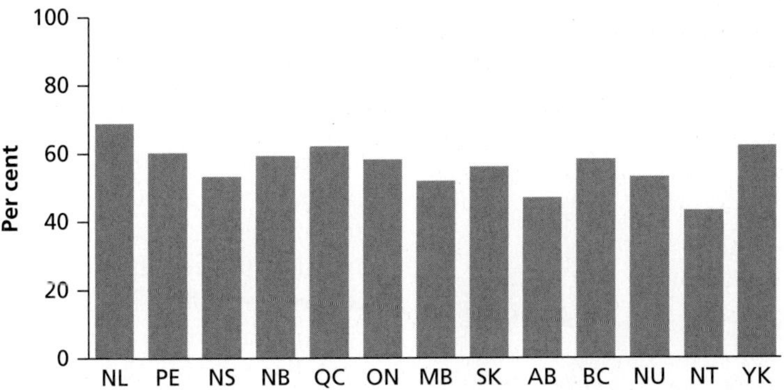

Figure 4.6 ◆ ECE Salaries

This chart shows how much early childhood educators earn as a percentage of teachers' salaries.

Source: Akbari and McCuaig 2019.

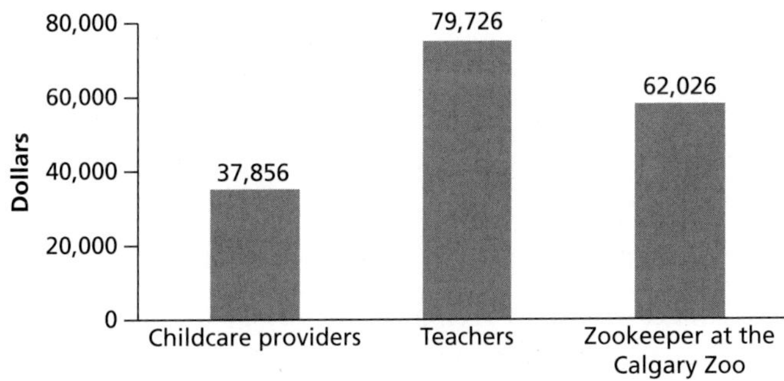

Figure 4.7 ◆ Salary Comparison: Alberta

Sources: Statistics Canada 2016a; City of Calgary 2018.

subsidies. This affects whether these families can afford childcare. This is shown by comparing the out-of-pocket costs paid in different provinces by a "sample" low-income families, consisting of two parents and two children and earning $30,823. (This is the average amount earned by Canadian families with young children living below the poverty line; Macdonald and Friendly 2018). In Toronto, this "sample" family would have an out-of-pocket cost of $90 a month post-subsidy. However, in Saskatoon, that same "sample" family would have an out-of-pocket cost of $497 a month post-subsidy. With such high extra fees, it is unlikely that this family could even afford licensed childcare, despite already receiving government assistance.

Parents with Unusual Jobs

As you may recall from Chapter 3, Canadians are increasingly working non-standard or precarious jobs. Many of these jobs may require irregular hours or rotating shifts. Others may be seasonal and require intense periods of childcare at specific times, instead of the same number of hours every day of the year. Yet most childcare centres do not offer extended or flexible hours to meet the needs of parents working these kinds of jobs.

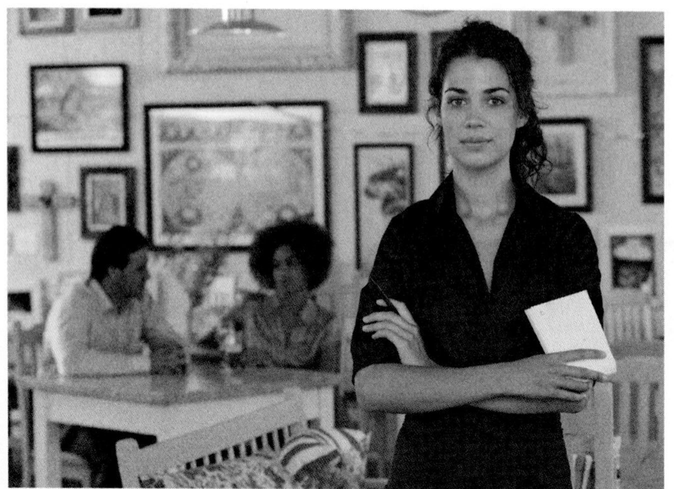
Goodshoot/Thinkstock

Parents that work rotating shifts, in factories or restaurants, for example, need flexible childcare to meet the needs of their changing schedules. Consider the barriers that they might face in accessing safe and suitable childcare.

Also, most subsidy arrangements are tied to employment, and parents who are unemployed or not enrolled in school are ineligible for most subsidies. Further, a self-employed parent must earn a certain amount each year for their employment status to be recognized and thus to keep the grant. This may be challenging for parents whose incomes rise and fall widely from one year to the next. For example, they may make a lot of money one year and then very little the following year.

Rural Families

Rural Canadian families face unique barriers to securing quality childcare. For one thing, they may have special scheduling needs: They are more likely to be engaged in seasonal work like fishing, farming, or tourism. As a result, they will have a greater need for care during some periods and less need in others. Parents in rural communities may have a long commute if they work in urban areas, and so would need extended care before and after the workday.

Finally, since childcare centres spring up mainly at the whim of entrepreneurs, well-regulated, good-quality childcare options may not be available in rural areas. Remember, this is because high working costs and low numbers of paying customers may discourage entrepreneurs. This leaves rural families looking for care out of luck (*CBC News* 2010). Some farming families have no choice but to keep young children at home while both parents continue the farm work. Working farms are full of hazards that may present safety issues for young children. Moreover, remaining at home in a rural area may also limit children's ability to develop social/cultural capital.

Recently Arrived Immigrant Families

Immigrants make up one-fifth of the Canadian population. Often, children of recently arrived immigrants don't know how to speak English or French. Currently, there is no national program in place to help train caregivers to deliver important language skill development programs. Nor is there a training program to help childcare providers work with the increasingly varied cultural backgrounds present in childcare centres. Parents may have to make tough decisions between quality, cost, and culturally appropriate care. This is what faced the parents of Eva Ravikovich, a two-year-old who died of heat stroke in 2013 at an unlicensed, unsafe daycare in Ontario. Her parents were initially attracted to the daycare because of its location, low cost, and Russian program delivery.

Drawing Connections

Other things being equal, immigrants tend to earn less than their Canadian-born counterparts. As a result, immigrants face many of the same barriers to early childhood education and care as low-income Canadians do. Further, immigrant families may be faced with a unique set of choices. The relicensing that many immigrants need to be hired in a well-paying job is an expensive process. Low-income immigrant families may, therefore, be forced to choose between childcare or the relicensing that could lift them out of poverty.

Indigenous Peoples in Canada

With some exceptions, the federal government does not directly fund or oversee the delivery of childcare in Canada. Indigenous children are one such exception. The federal government supports childcare programs on-reserve and in Inuit communities and funds some off-reserve Indigenous childcare as well.

Despite this support, there are still not enough regulated childcare spaces for Indigenous children (whose population, as you'll remember from previous chapters, is booming). Further, the available spots may not meet the unique cultural needs of this population, especially with regard to the inclusion of their traditional languages and cultural practices.

Problems related to Indigenous childcare illustrate the connectedness of disadvantages we discuss throughout this book, where we explore how many Indigenous communities in Canada face barriers related to many dimensions of inequality. These include safe, reliable housing; good health and healthcare; nutritious food; income from employment; and so on. Childcare programs offered to all marginalized populations—not just Indigenous Peoples living in Canada—would be uniquely positioned to address some of those other problems.

For example, since a higher-than-average number of Indigenous mothers are teen mothers, more childcare centres could offer culturally appropriate parenting support while also supporting mothers' continued engagement in education or job training. This kind of programming could stimulate economic return while also investing in the prosperity of a population that has been historically mistreated. Due to the effects of colonization, single parents, young ones especially, face significant challenges securing employment.

Parents of Children with Special Needs

Children with special needs also experience significant barriers to quality childcare. As you have learned from previous chapters, special needs range from physical accommodations like ramps or adjusted bathrooms to personal considerations like a specially trained caregiver. Despite the benefit of high-quality early childhood care, it can be challenging for parents to find high-quality care for their children with special needs.

Legislation in all provinces and territories requires that children with special needs be guaranteed access to public school. However, no such law exists for childcare. This ignores the UN Convention on the Rights of Persons with Disabilities (2006). That document, which Canada signed, clearly requires signatories to "ensure the full enjoyment by children with disabilities of all human rights and fundamental freedoms on an equal basis with other children" (Article 7).

All provinces and territories have voluntarily set up different ways to support children with disabilities. For example, all provinces and territories offer subsidies to provide funding for families with children that need special supports (physical accommodations and staffing) in childcare environments. Parents of children with special needs face the same scarcity of options other parents do *plus more*: There are simply not enough childcare centres able to accommodate children with special needs. Statistics Canada (2008) data show that one-fifth of families with a child or children with special needs reported being refused care. Moreover, recent news reveals that "54 per cent of families applying for . . . exceptional needs benefits" in Quebec have been turned down, despite promises from the Quebec government to help parents of children with special needs (Leclair 2017).

Childcare directors may turn away children with special needs because they cannot afford the necessary upgrades to their facility. They may be unable to provide extra staff training or the cost of hiring more staff. In Alberta, for example, Wiart and colleagues (2011) found that 36 per cent of childcare programs were "unable to accept children with special needs into care" (352). So parents of these children must travel farther or make uncomfortable compromises when securing care for their children. As a result, many children with special needs miss opportunities for the best early learning and growth, some of which might affect the opportunities available to them in the future.

Concerns surrounding inclusion don't end the moment a child is registered at a childcare centre. SpeciaLink: The National Centre for Child Care Inclusion, an organization committed to fighting for childcare for children with special needs, has established a quality scale to assess the inclusivity of children with special needs (Hope 2009). This six-point scale illuminates inclusion benchmarks that our current system should meet:

1. Zero rejection—all children should be included.
2. The proportion of children with disabilities is roughly that of their natural proportion in the general population (10–15 per cent).
3. The same hours/days of attendance that are available to other children should be available (not just half-days).
4. Full participation in all activities and routines should be possible.
5. Maximum parental involvement should be welcomed.
6. Childcare centres should work with other organizations and all levels of government to promote ongoing development in early years support for children with special needs.

Consequences of Unequal Access to Daycare and Early Childhood Education

What happens if we don't deal with this issue of inequality-from-birth by providing more affordable, quality childcare opportunities for children whose parents cannot pay out of pocket? The results are apparent: Inequality continues throughout life and society. Little improves for those who are disadvantaged, because they are limited—incapacitated—by what they didn't get when they were young. Here's an interesting quote that puts the problem in its broadest perspective:

> We are not really "all in the same boat" if high income and wealth allow some to secede from the common institutions of society . . . The rich will have little interest in the quality of community parks and playgrounds, public transit, public education, and public health care if they live in gated communities, send their children to private schools and elite universities, and meet their health care needs in exclusive, for-profit clinics. They will also tend to oppose paying fair taxes to promote the public good. [Thus,] high income inequality threatens social sustainability. (Broadbent Institute 2012:7)

As mentioned above, good-quality childcare and early childhood education is not the cure-all to social inequality. However, it plays an essential role in solving the problem and, compared to many other approaches, returns benefits far more significant than the money invested.

Strategies of Resistance

As we have seen in this chapter, childcare presents a large financial burden for most families. It is crucial that we work to improve access to this survival capital for everyone. The data in Figure 4.8 show us that other countries have managed to do this better than Canada has.

Government-Level Strategies of Resistance

In British Columbia, the 2018 budget called for sweeping changes to make early childhood education much more available than ever before. Many needed changes have already begun. As reported by Jennifer Saltman (2019) in the *Vancouver Sun*:

> In July 2017, a $237-million fund was announced to create 22,000 new, licensed child-care spaces across the province over the next three years . . . Over the past year, the government has introduced a number of programs, including the child-care fee-reduction initiative, which cut day-care costs by up to $350 a month per space depending on the age of the child and whether they are in licensed family or group day care. According to the government, 88 per cent of eligible child-care spaces are now participating in the program . . .
>
> The affordable child-care benefit was introduced in September 2018 to replace the existing child-care subsidy, saving eligible families up to $1,250 a month per child. In the fall, the government began a $60-million pilot project to convert about 2,500 child-care spaces at more than 50 facilities into spaces that cost $200 a month or less per child. The pilot will last until spring 2020. These programs will continue to be funded into 2022. The goal is to ensure universal daycare at a cost to parents of $10 a day per child.

In Ontario, the NDP under Andrea Horwath is promising a comparable plan:

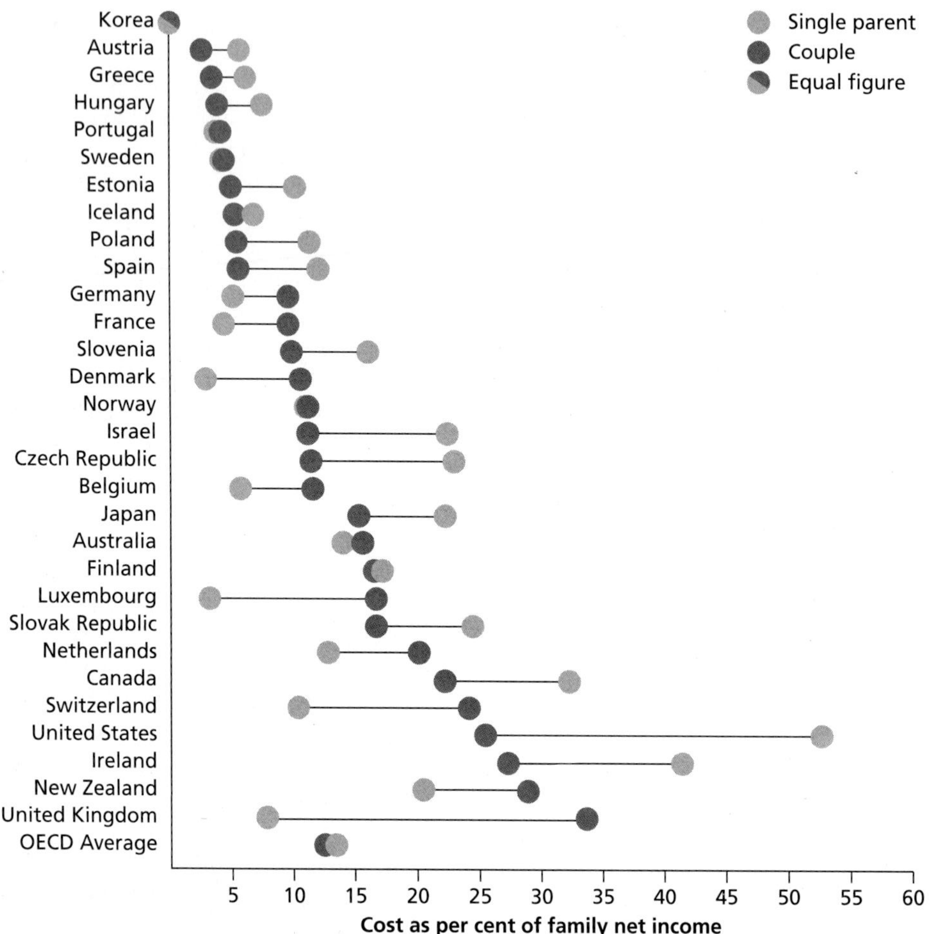

Figure 4.8 ◆ Childcare Costs in Wealthy Countries

Source: *CTV News* 2018.

> Andrea Horwath's plan will make child care easier to find and more affordable for every Ontario family. As part of Horwath's Change for the Better platform, the NDP will create 202,000 new licensed, not-for-profit childcare spaces. For families making less than $40,000 per year, licensed, non-profit care will be free, and the average cost for all other families will be just $12 per day. (Ontario NDP 2018)

However, a *Global News* report notes that

> [f]ees for full-time, regulated child-care spaces have risen faster than inflation in 61 per cent of cities reviewed. The fees were highest in Toronto and the surrounding area, where fees for children under 18 months average $1,685, and $1,150 a month for older preschoolers. Cities in Quebec had the lowest fees for full-time, regulated spaces across the country, followed by Winnipeg and Charlottetown—in the three provinces that have fixed fees for years.

David MacDonald, a senior economist with the Canadian Centre for Policy Alternatives, explained to *Global News* that three provinces have intervened in child care and set fees at lower costs than the market rate. Quebec, Manitoba and PEI have lowered the costs for residents by setting a maximum price, MacDonald said. (Abedi 2019)

Organization-Level Strategies of Resistance

To some degree, the private sector has done what the public sector has so failed to do. Over the last 20 or so years, large corporations have become more sensitive to the needs of families. As a result, many have adjusted their policies, provided new employee benefits and services, and even reformed their organizational cultures—the way they think and talk about work issues. The changes have paid off. The more an organization supports its employees with family responsibilities, the more productive their workforce is and the less expensive per-employee startup costs are. Moreover, employees will experience less strain between their paid work and family roles.

How do these workplace policies improve productivity and reduce startup costs? A combination of parental leave laws, organizational policies, and the cost and quality of childcare jointly control how soon a mother will begin (or return to) working outside the home after giving birth. Per-employee startup costs are reduced through such policies because they make mothers more likely to return to work. Workplaces, therefore, don't need to hire and train a permanent replacement. These policies are also expected to boost morale, which can improve productivity. Mothers' family circumstances and their family's attitudes also matter in deciding how soon she will return to work.

Unfortunately, family-friendly workplace policies are only available to a minority of families. The Workplace and Employee Survey, updated in 2005, suggested that most companies' practices do not promote the integration of work and family (Statistics Canada 2016b). While roughly one-third of Canadian employees have *flextime*, access to other family-friendly work arrangements is rare. Flextime involves working the same number of hours but having some freedom to decide when to work these hours. It is popular among parents, especially women, since it does not reduce one's chances for a promotion or lead to pay cuts.

Access to family-friendly practices depends on the company's size and industry, as well as on the type of work performed. Well-educated managers and professionals make the most significant use of the program, and use is almost unrelated to the personal needs or family characteristics of its employees. Jann Lee (2018), in a report published by Benefits Canada, notes that

> [p]art-time telecommuting is becoming the norm for many global workplaces, with 50 per cent of Canadian employees working at least 2.5 days a week outside the office, according to a new survey by IWG. The survey, which polled more than 18,000 professionals in 96 countries, found 74 per cent of Canadians work away from the office at least one day a week, and one-fifth work offsite every day of the work week.
>
> Current technology and changes in employee expectations has increased mobility within the workforce, noted the study. "Canadian employees no longer need

> so much time in a particular office," said Wayne Berger, chief executive officer of IWG Canada and Latin America, in a press release. "We're entering the era of the mobile workforce and it's a game-changer—not just for employees, but for employers too."

Since most working people do not want the difficulties associated with home offices or self-employment, they increasingly value flextime. Unions have played a large part in pressing for more workplace benefits and gender equality, including more flextime. Overall, firm size and unionization are the most potent determinants of family-friendly policies in North American (especially American) companies (Glass and Fujimoto 1995). Corporate cutbacks and falling union membership in Canada do not bode well for family-friendly policies. And bear in mind that we have already (in Chapter 3) pointed out the decline of unionized jobs in Canada; in effect, this means a decline of supports for family life.

One popular family-friendly workplace initiative is onsite daycare for young children. This program does not change how parents work, but it does relieve some anxieties. Collectively, services sponsored by employers, groups of employees, or unions are called work-related childcare centres. Daycares do not necessarily have to be onsite; any support to childcare, whether community based or in the form of offsite, consortium centres, is helpful to working parents (Barbeau 2001).

Individual-Level Strategies of Resistance

In response to the growing costs of early childhood education and the difficulty of finding quality childcare spaces, parents have started turning to alternative childcare models. For example, daycare co-operatives and collectives have sprung up in Toronto and Montreal. These organizations are created when a group of parents come together to provide accessible early childcare to their community.

One exciting example is the Montreal Childcare Collective (MCC). Founded in 2004, the MCC is run by volunteers and aims to "provide free childcare for community groups during meetings and demonstrations" (Ebbels 2008). Although the MCC doesn't provide full-time childcare, it plays an important role by giving people who cannot afford nannies or daycare a chance to participate in political movements. This is important because the families most in need of political change are the least likely to be able to afford childcare while they campaign for it. The MCC works alongside other social organizations, such as the Filipino Women's Centre, the Immigrant Workers Centre, and Solidarity Across Borders. According to Selena Ross, a volunteer for the MCC, "It's also about making community organizing more accessible to women, especially single moms. It's a class struggle. So many people can't afford babysitters" (Ebbels 2008).

The movement for equal access to early childhood education is slowly gaining momentum in Canada and in other parts of the world. We have seen that different levels of government are starting to take a more progressive attitude when it comes to these issues. That said, we still need a strong popular movement in support of universal early childcare for these proposals to become a reality. This is why individual-level strategies have an important role to play—they can create and mobilize support for universal early childcare.

Notable Thinkers

Susan Prentice

Susan Prentice is a professor of sociology at the University of Manitoba. Her research focuses on social inequality and social change as well as public policy and systematic discrimination. In particular, her research examines both contemporary and historical childcare policies and advocacy.

In her paper "Less Access, Worse Quality," Prentice (2007b) examines the long-term implications of growing up in straitened environments because of a lack of access to quality childcare. Her national overview and closer examination of Winnipeg, Quebec City, and Vancouver reveal great inequalities in access to quality childcare. This is because, in a free-market system, neighbourhoods with higher levels of social and other capital are at an advantage. This unequal access to childcare reproduces neighbourhood socio-economic positions of class and racialization. Further, she proposes that policies targeting only the vulnerable children will not be effective in correcting this relationship between socio-economic status and access to childcare. Instead, regular funding by the government is the only method of guaranteeing equal access to quality childcare for all groups.

In another publication, "Childcare, Justice and the City" (2007a), she explores the connection between childcare and where an individual lives. Her study concludes that access to and distribution of childcare services is unequal and inequitable across neighbourhoods. She found that in licensed childcare spaces throughout Winnipeg, childcare services are characterized by inequality in all neighbourhoods. Poor and Indigenous neighbourhoods suffer particular disadvantages (namely, less access and fewer services) than the more wealthy and suburban communities. However, even the most affluent neighbourhoods were characterized by inadequate and unequal services.

Closing Remarks

Data from the General Social Survey (Sinha 2015) reveal that most parents—up to 86 per cent—rely on the regular availability of daycare for their children. As we have seen, investments in daycare for vulnerable children have large returns over time. They can reduce unemployment, crime, and dependency on social welfare and increase tax revenue. Without quality universal daycare, the care that working parents can provide to their children depends on their financial, cultural, and educational backgrounds. Parents with the most resources—the wealthiest 5 per cent of the population—may hire nannies to provide at-home childcare.

The important note is that all children need rich and stimulating experiences to support healthy development. So what makes daycare "good" or "bad"? Research based on the National Longitudinal Survey of Children and Youth (Kohen, Hertzman and Willms 2002) has identified three factors that make daycare most useful to children: low child-to-adult ratios, educated staff with specialized training, and resources to provide stimulating activities. High-quality daycare centres increase children's linguistic, cognitive, and social competencies. This, in turn, has long-lasting benefits for children, especially those from low-income families who might otherwise be unable to build social and cultural capital and break out of poverty. The COVID-19 epidemic made amply clear how very important quality daycare—and its discontinuation—can be for working parents.

As mentioned, there are not enough spaces at high-quality daycare centres to house all children, and waiting lists are common. Various advocacy groups are pressing for better childcare and fairer policies that will benefit all types of families. Good-quality care arrangements need to be accessible and affordable so that all children can take part, regardless of their race, ethnic background, needs, or income. To achieve this, Canada will need to have a national standard of quality and universal access to childcare that is set up across the provinces in a coordinated way. A failure to do this will result in long-term losses—social, cultural, and economic—to Canadian society.

Test Your Knowledge

1. What are the unique barriers faced by rural families in accessing quality childcare?
2. What barriers do Indigenous Peoples in Canada face in obtaining childcare?
3. Name five reasons that children benefit from high-quality, reliable early childhood education and care.
4. Name five reasons why more mothers are working today than ever before.
5. Fill in the blank: Some ________________ families can afford to pay for care, but the care they can afford is often substandard.
6. Fill in the Blank: ________________ require physical accommodations, lower caregiver–child ratios, or a caregiver who is specially trained to deliver their program.
7. What are three different strategies for connecting families and childcare?
8. Why are rules and integration good for people's health?
9. Why are families good providers of rules and integration, compared to other social institutions (for example, schools, workplaces)?
10. In the table below, correctly match each theoretical perspective with its main points:

Theoretical Perspectives	Main Points
1. Functionalism	a. With industrialization, men became dependent on outside sources of income to meet survival needs, and women gained exclusive control of the home without pay.
2. Conflict and feminist theories	b. There is a naturalness or inevitability of certain family forms. For instance, all marriage systems across the world support monogamy. Cohabitation is inferior to traditional (legal) marriage because it is less permanent, fails to provide the benefits of marriage and is less likely to involve extended families.
3. Symbolic interactionism	c. The promotion of "family values" by right-wing religious leaders and social conservatives appeals to people's interests and concerns about their family life. It also channels anxieties against groups such as single mothers, LGBTQ+ people, and divorced people.

See the Answer Key online to check your answers.

Questions for Critical Thought

1. Do single fathers face the same problems as single mothers? Explain why or why not.
2. If all Canadian provinces provided free childcare, should refugees and undocumented or non-status immigrants be entitled to it?
3. What theoretical perspective(s) on unequal access to daycare and early childhood education do you subscribe to?
4. Should all childcare and childhood education providers be trained to meet the unique cultural needs of the Indigenous population? Why or why not?
5. Should the government subsidize parents directly or pay some or all the operating costs of childcare centres?

Additional Resources

Recommended Readings

Blackstock, Cindy and Eddy Robinson. 2017. *Spirit Bear and Children Make History: Based on a True Story.* Nanaimo, BC: Strong Nations. Cindy Blackstock is a Canadian-born Gitxsan activist for child welfare and the executive director of the First Nations Child and Family Caring Society of Canada. She is also a professor for the School of Social Work at McGill University. This book is about Spirit Bear's long train trip to Ottawa to stand up for Indigenous children in foster care.

Dietz, Beverlie. 2006. *Foundations of Early Childhood Education: Learning Environments and Children in Canada*. Toronto, ON: Pearson Canada. This book offers insight into how the physical environment, the people a child interacts with, and the child's experiences impact the development of a child's ability to learn. Further, it offers strategies, examples, and exercises to help create beneficial learning environments for children and families.

Doucet, Andrea. 2006. *Do Men Mother? Fathering, Care and Domestic Responsibility.* Toronto, ON: University of Toronto Press. Doucet sheds light on the lives of stay-at-home dads and single fathers. This book illustrates the radical change in childcare and domestic responsibilities in this century.

Howe, Nina and Larry Prochner. 2013. *Recent Perspectives on Early Childhood Education in Canada.* Toronto, ON: University of Toronto Press. These authors address the history, social policies, economic aspects, and provincial rules related to early childhood education in Canada. It also discusses issues related to early childhood learning, education, and curriculum. Finally, this book examines recent developments undertaken by the Canadian government related to early childhood education and care.

Langford, Rachel, Susan Prentice, and Patricia Albanese. 2017. *Caring for Children: Social Movements and Public Policy in Canada*. Vancouver, BC: University of British Columbia Press. This book examines how the government's childcare policies have favoured professional, nuclear families while ignoring the needs of the most vulnerable, including low-income, immigrant, and Indigenous families.

Lloyd, Eva and Helen Penn. 2013. *Childcare Markets: Can They Deliver an Equitable Service?* Chicago, IL: Policy Press. This book offers a comparison of the childcare systems in eight different countries, including Canada and the United States.

McDaniels, Susan, Lorne Tepperman, and Sandra Colavecchia. 2018. *Close Relations: An Introduction to the Sociology of Families*. Toronto, ON: Pearson Canada.

Prochner, Larry. 2010. *A History of Early Childhood Education in Canada, Australia, and New Zealand.* Vancouver, BC: University of British Columbia Press. In England during the early nineteenth century, specialized education programs were developed by the government as a way to give kids a "head start" in life. This book explores how early childhood education subsequently spread from England to three of its colonies.

Recommended Websites

Canadian Childcare Federation

www.cccf-fcsge.ca

The Canadian Childcare Federation is committed to protecting and improving children, promoting the health and safety of children, and providing Canadians with the best knowledge about childcare and childcare practices. This website addresses many topics related to childcare, including the state of Indigenous childcare.

Child Care Canada: Childcare Resource and Research Unit

www.childcarecanada.org

The Childcare Resource and Research Unit is a research institute that examines policies related to early childhood education and childcare. The website features up-to-date news, videos, and publications.

Child Care Now

https://timeforchildcare.ca

Child Care Now (formerly the Child Care Advocacy Association of Canada) is a not-for-profit organization dedicated to promoting publicly funded, inclusive, quality, not-for-profit childcare. This website includes links to a variety of publications as well as information on how to join.

Recommended Films

Experiences Build Brain Architecture. United States: National Scientific Council on the Developing Child. This short two-minute video describes the neurological processes of learning in the early years of life.

The Motherload. 2015. Canada: CBC. This documentary follows several working mothers at different levels of the workforce as they struggle to balance their professional and personal lives.

Toxic Stress Derails Healthy Development. United States: National Scientific Council on the Developing Child. This short two-minute video explains the effects of stressful environments in early childhood.

Recommended Podcasts

"The Preschool Podcast" by HiMama. Through conversations with leading professionals in early childhood education, this podcast by HiMama discusses recent successes and challenges within the childcare and preschool setting. Some topics covered include managing autism spectrum disorder in preschools, creating an open classroom for all kids regardless of their socio-economic background, and using storytelling to nurture resilience in children living with family substance-use disorder.

Marc Bruxelle/Shutterstock

5 Access to Formal Education

Learning Objectives

- To identify barriers to formal education.
- To recognize the importance of equalizing access to formal education.
- To recognize the effects of unequal access to formal education.
- To analyze how the education system perpetuates inequality.
- To examine how the impact of gender has changed in education.
- To evaluate strategies of resistance in equalizing access to formal education.

Introduction

With a few minor exceptions, education falls under provincial jurisdiction in Canada. While each province is responsible for the delivery of its own curriculum, the federal government provides cash through transfer payments and supports students through federal student loans. The exceptions are Indigenous Peoples living on reserves, members of the Armed Forces and their families, and inmates in federally run correctional facilities.

◆ In Their Own Words ◆

Ask anyone about inequality, and you're likely to hear three words in response: education, education, education. Oh, and education. And it's true: school should be the ladder out of poverty, but too often it is not.

—Matthew O'Brien

Source: O'Brien 2013.

Canadians are among the most educated people in the world. In a ranking of postsecondary graduation rates among all 40 countries in the Organisation for Economic Co-operation and Development (OECD), Canada comes in first place: 56 per cent of Canadian adults hold a postsecondary degree or diploma. With 6 per cent of our gross domestic product devoted to educational institutions, Canada pours more money into formal learning than the OECD average (Statistics Canada 2018b).

As we noted in the previous chapter, Canada has what Esping-Andersen (1990) would call a "liberal welfare regime." That means, in this case, that people usually have to pay for their own postsecondary education, though society as a whole will benefit. Of course, the costs of postsecondary education vary somewhat from province to province and institution to institution. But generally speaking, tuition fees have been rising since 1980 with the flowering of neoliberal political views in Canada. The hikes in tuition have been especially marked in professional faculties (medicine, law, and business, among others.) Meanwhile, governments have been supplying proportionally less financial support to postsecondary institutions year after year. This has made it harder for low-income children to attend these institutions.

Yet, despite increasing tuition costs, enrolment at colleges and universities has increased consistently over the last four decades (Statistics Canada 2018a). More Canadians and international students are recognizing the value of Canadian postsecondary education. This recognition of education's value is also clear at the secondary school level. Ninety-three per cent of 25–34 year olds have completed high school, a number significantly higher than the previous generation of Canadians and higher than most other first-world economies (Statistics Canada 2018b). Since you are currently reading a textbook, we will assume you are probably a student, one of the 2 million Canadians enrolled right now in some postsecondary program.

Did you aim for a diploma, certificate, or degree to increase your future earnings? Good for you—your education will probably do that too. Figure 5.1 compares the median annual earnings for full-time workers in Canada based on their highest educational attainment.

Drawing Connections

Note that the median earnings for women with a bachelor's degree are only slightly higher than the median earnings of men with a college diploma. This reminds us that, although formal education usually helps disadvantaged people do better, it does not eliminate all disadvantages, whether based on gender or otherwise.

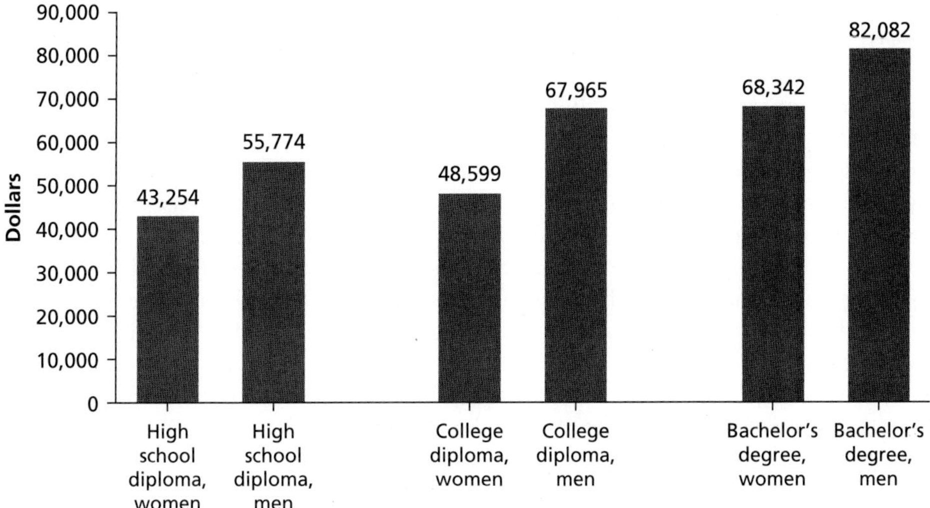

Figure 5.1 ◆ Median Annual Earnings Based on Highest Educational Level, Canada, 2016

Source: Based on Statistics Canada 2016.

But besides economic and professional benefits, formal education can lead to other personal gains. Did you know that your education, in some ways, benefits your neighbour, your barber, and the strangers on your morning trip to campus? We will discuss this in more detail later, but sociologists have been telling us for years about the proven value of education as a true "equalizer." It is one of the most effective ways to increase an individual's social mobility. That makes education another form of survival capital: Something critical to satisfying life's most fundamental needs. If life were a game of Snakes and Ladders, education would be a ladder . . . if you can grasp the first rung, that is. Not everybody can.

This chapter explores barriers to formal education. While the most significant barriers are at the postsecondary level, the roots of educational inequality begin much earlier. Some Canadians are more vulnerable than others to these barriers. For example, Canadians are half as likely to drop out of high school today than they were 20 years ago. However, young men, low-income students, Indigenous students, students with a disability, and racialized students are overrepresented among the 8 per cent who do drop out (HRSDC 2013).

In this chapter, we will consider financial barriers and the barriers presented by different living circumstances. These include living in a rural setting, being a person with a disability, being Indigenous, being an older student, being LGBTQ+, being a young male, and being a non-status immigrant.

Theoretical Perspectives on Access to Formal Education

Let's begin this theoretical discussion with a very non-theoretical observation: Young people in North America know almost nothing about how to spend or save money. This is because primary and secondary schools do not teach young people much, if anything, about saving money, spending money, comparison shopping, using credit cards, figuring out interest charges, or looking for hidden costs. Some parents teach their children about these things, but parents are often quite uninformed as well. The result is not merely financial illiteracy on a local scale. As Lusardi and Mitchell (2011) have shown with comparative international data, financial illiteracy exists on a worldwide scale, especially among people with the least money to spend.

This is important because buying a higher education is likely one of the most expensive items you will ever purchase. With tuition, fees, books, living expenses, and forgone income, it can easily run into the hundreds of thousands of dollars. So most young people and their families make this costly, momentous decision without sufficient information. Typically, they hope that it will all pay off in the end, and often it does. However, even on this matter of the usefulness of higher education, sociologists differ in their views and emphases.

socialization The processes surrounding the internalization and learning of culture, most of which occurs during childhood.

Functionalist sociologists view "the school" as a social institution that performs the important role of **socialization**. From junior kindergarten to the Ph.D., schools "help prepare new adults for generational succession—they are the major means by which one generation prepares its own replacement" (Davies and Guppy 2010:23). This makes the education system one of society's most important institutions: It contributes to preserving social order and provides opportunities for social mobility.

In this context, schools are fair, neutral testing grounds that are designed to socialize, educate, and classify people on the basis of ability. This view of schools is predicated on another functionalist theory: that the market for talent is also fair. That is, the job market will recognize and reward individuals according to their academic achievement (and credentials). Because schools are considered fair and neutral, academic performance can be credited to a student's merit or ability, not to class origins, gender, or other defining characteristics. If you succeed in school, it is because you worked hard and earned it. But if you do not succeed, it is because of a personal flaw or weakness.

credentialism The organization of education to ensure that students receive the formal qualifications (that is, diplomas and degrees) they need to get jobs.

In the functionalist view, schools create equal opportunity and social mobility and provide the basis for a meritocracy. They provide rewards (educational credentials) that are proportional to an individual's ability and effort, their merit. As a consequence, some have said that modern education is preoccupied with **credentialism**—that is, with handing out degrees and diplomas that attest to people's job qualifications.

manifest functions These are the stated, intended purposes of a particular social institution.

latent functions Unintended consequences of the norms of a particular social institution.

From the *functionalist* perspective, social problems related to education occur when schools fail to perform their **manifest functions**—the visible and intended goals, consequences, or effects of social structures and institutions. For schools, this includes socialization, transmission of knowledge, and change and innovation. In a multicultural society like Canada, it also includes cultural assimilation: the learning of new ways of think and behaving in a culturally diverse context. Functionalists also point out the **latent functions** of the education system: those unintended consequences that result from the norms of a particular social institution. For example, when children are in school, they are not being physically active outside. A latent function of the education system is a disconnection from natural, wilderness spaces. Functionalists think that many of the social problems discussed in this book, such as poverty and unemployment, can be linked to the failure of educational systems to carry out their manifest functions. In their intended form, schools should create social equality, not worsen it.

Conflict theory, on the other hand, highlights social inequalities in education, arguing that certain groups are favoured over others based on class, race, and gender. Rather than providing equal opportunity, formal education brainwashes students under the guise of socializing them, stigmatizes certain students to "assimilate" them, and regulates people rather than integrates them. Formal education also makes certain kinds of knowledge exclusive to different people (for example, based on class). For conflict theorists, students' defining characteristics (such as their gender) are deeply tied to their academic performance—the opposite of the functionalist view.

From this standpoint, schools are far more likely to promote the status quo and stifle innovation. Consider the issue of student dropouts. We know that having parents with a low educational attainment level and low family income are key reasons that young people drop out of high school (Statistics Canada 2017). This is evidence that our social class position directs our educational pursuits. Rather than providing a universal and equal mechanism for success, educational systems support and perpetuate existing inequalities in society.

The *symbolic-interactionist* perspective is more concerned with individuals—for example, the ways people interact in small groups—and the meanings people attach to schooling and education. For example, symbolic interactionists are interested in the structure of favouritism in classrooms, in cliques and bullying, and in the "code" or subculture that defines who is popular or unpopular.

Symbolic interactionists are also interested in the labels society attaches to education and to "educated people" versus "uneducated people." The value placed on education is sometimes used to mask and justify the degradation and stigmatization of less-educated people. For example, educational attainment may be used to justify someone's high income and prestige even if their education has played little or no part in determining the income and prestige they enjoy. They may have gained it through inheritance, for example.

Feminist theory, for its part, is concerned with the gendering of educational experiences, especially in schools. More than two centuries ago, English philosopher and social critic Mary Wollstonecraft contested popular attitudes toward women and education in *The Vindication of the Rights of Women* ([1792] 1997). Wollstonecraft argued that women deserve social equality and should be given the education necessary to earn it (Zeitlin 2001). Overall, she expressed the view that men and women, by sharing the same virtues, should be treated the same and given the same opportunities.

Feminist theorists and researchers who study education today have focused on the extent to which the school system produces and perpetuates social and economic disadvantages for girls and women. Historically, in educational opportunity and result, young boys received greater advantages over young girls. According to Dillabough and Arnot (2002), "the long-term goal of feminism here was to empower women to take up their rightful place throughout the development of female autonomy" (34). In education, feminism has focused on the removal of barriers toward subject preference, occupational choice, and decisions surrounding sex and gender roles.

The Present-Day Inequalities of Access

Today, many working- and middle-class families do not experience significant intergenerational mobility. The few who do move upward typically move a shorter distance than their counterparts did a generation ago.

Drawing Connections

The Canadian job market has become crowded by people with similar skills and credentials competing for a limited number of jobs. Over the past 50 years, the demand for specialized knowledge and skills has risen. In response, the number of people enrolled globally in higher education has more than doubled. In 2000, there were 100 million postsecondary students, and by 2014 this number had risen to 207 million (UNESCO 2017).

The crowding that results from the increased pursuit of higher education is especially severe in developed nations with large urban middle classes. In these nations, higher education is a norm and working-class jobs are scarce, mostly moved offshore or erased by technological advances. As more people become educated in these nations, an "opportunity trap" emerges. When everyone seeks the "advantage" of a higher education to get ahead, it is no longer an advantage. This way of getting ahead is a "trap" in that it *causes* the social congestion it seeks to relieve. Because of this congestion, universities raise entry requirements and employers increase the number of hurdles you have to get over to get hired, such as demanding more work experience from new graduates.

So as more people have gained qualifications, traditional middle- and upper-income jobs have become less widely available. Not only is there less room for upward mobility from the working to the middle class, but we are starting to see some *downward* mobility out of the middle class (Byrom and Lightfoot 2013).

Nevertheless, hopes of securing financial success through education persist. Attending college or university is such a standard choice for today's youth that those who choose alternative routes often become alienated from their peers, viewed as having made the "wrong choice" (Byrom and Lightfoot 2013). Young North Americans are encouraged to feel personally responsible for their future and are told they will be entitled to certain rewards if they have paid the price of postsecondary education. But many are set up for disappointment. In the labour market, only some will succeed, leaving the "failures" to be blamed for their own misfortune. This complacent belief in the power of individual decision making permeates the entire class structure. Even many of those disadvantaged by such beliefs approve of this way of thinking.

Expanding educational opportunities has not erased occupational or income inequality. Instead, it has led to the "massification" of education, increasing the average level of educational attainment (Iannelli, Gamoran, and Paterson 2011). More people are getting an education, and that is a good thing. However, the proportions of students from working-, middle-, and upper-income backgrounds remain skewed. Educational expansion has benefited people from all social classes, but it did not and cannot create social equality.

Academics have refuted complacent views of education (and the meritocratic view of the marketplace) as a solution to our increasingly rigid social hierarchy (Scherger and Savage 2010). When every candidate for a job has a postsecondary degree, employers take other variables into account when deciding whom to hire. Besides the "hard currencies" of credentials, scholarships, and work experience, employers consider the "soft currencies" of professional bearing, punctuality, dependability, persistence, and networking skills. They

Drawing Connections

Advantaged people are right to note that higher education remains a young person's best investment in eventual job success. But scholars have shown that it is more challenging for lower-income youth to complete a college or university degree, let alone excel in their studies.

interpret these and other "soft skills" (that is, cultural capital) as signs of a candidate's ability to "perform" at work. As we have seen, white, middle- and upper-income parents are usually better able to pass on these soft skills.

Many of these students must work while in school, cutting into their time to study. They are thus placed at a disadvantage compared with more privileged youth whose parents pay for their tuition. Many working-class students also struggle to use the resources available to them and may not feel as though they "belong" within postsecondary institutions. Middle- and upper-income students are used to—and may even feel entitled to—receiving guidance from authority figures, including teachers, librarians, and counsellors.

Many advantaged people credit the lower academic performance of working-class students to their supposed lack of motivation and poor work ethic. But research shows that many universities are a poor academic and social fit for these young adults. They often fail to find a place for themselves in environments that devalue their class-based customs, values, experiences, and identities. Despite the unpleasant experiences they often face, many working-class students show great resilience and commitment.

Views of education diverge on how just they view the existing system to be. Advantaged people hold that the system is fair. Children from wealthier families typically succeed academically, and therefore deserve to gain stable, well-paying jobs. But when lower-income youth try to level the playing field by earning the same academic credentials as their wealthier counterparts, they still suffer a competitive disadvantage. The massification of education allows employers to select job candidates from more well-off backgrounds, candidates whose cultural capital sets them apart. In this way, class background and childhood socialization, not education, remain the key factors controlling one's career and class destinations (Scherger and Savage 2010).

As long as people think the education system is just and their hard work and determination will pay off, they are unlikely to protest the status quo. But young people in developed countries are now highly educated, frustrated, and disappointed. They were promised a better standard of living in return for their hard-earned education, but not all have received a return on their investment. Limited career opportunities, combined with mounting student debt, have led to youth unemployment and underemployment. These trends may lead to a resurgence of **class politics** in Canada, as it has in other countries, and to rising rates of crime, addiction, and mental illness.

class politics Political speech focused on class position, as distinct from "identity politics," which focuses on gender, racial, regional, or other non-class affiliations.

For example, students attending Ontario colleges and universities staged a mass action against the province's Progressive Conservative government in March 2019 to express their anger against changes to postsecondary funding. Further uproar occurred a month later in secondary schools, where students and parents protested funding cutbacks, mandatory online learning, and larger class sizes.

Shawn Goldberg/Shutterstock

Students across Ontario walked out of classes in 2019 to demonstrate against the provincial government's changes to the education system.

Low-Income People in Canada

Consider the problems faced by low-income families. Family income can affect access to (and quality of) formal education at all levels: postsecondary, secondary, and even primary. Someone is paying handsomely for your current education. It is either you, a family or friend, or partly Canadian taxpayers. Those who took out loans will pay more for their education than those who didn't in the form of future interest payments. This is one way that some will struggle more than others, depending on family income. Public primary and secondary education is paid for by everyone, through their taxes, so it feels "free." And yet even in the lower grades, family income can still result in advantages and disadvantages.

These advantages and disadvantages start in the diaper years, as we saw in Chapter 4. From the beginning, wealthy families can afford all the out-of-school resources their children need to be physically and mentally prepared to learn. These include nutritious meals, suitable clothing, school supplies, and extracurricular lessons, among other things.

In Canada, kindergarten teachers use a tool called The Early Development Instrument, or the EDI for short, developed by Dr Dan Offord and Dr Magdalena Janus at the Offord Centre for Child Studies at McMaster University (Janus & Offord, 2007). The EDI is a 103-item questionnaire completed by kindergarten teachers in the second half of the school year that measures children's ability to meet age-appropriate developmental expectations in five general domains. It focuses on the overall outcomes for children as a health-relevant,

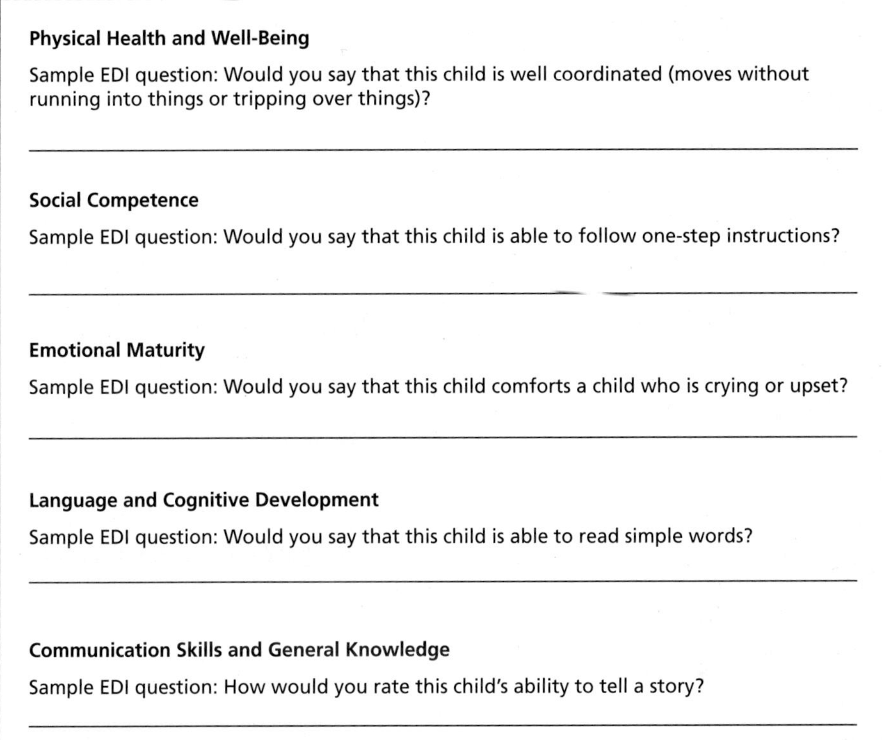

Physical Health and Well-Being

Sample EDI question: Would you say that this child is well coordinated (moves without running into things or tripping over things)?

Social Competence

Sample EDI question: Would you say that this child is able to follow one-step instructions?

Emotional Maturity

Sample EDI question: Would you say that this child comforts a child who is crying or upset?

Language and Cognitive Development

Sample EDI question: Would you say that this child is able to read simple words?

Communication Skills and General Knowledge

Sample EDI question: How would you rate this child's ability to tell a story?

Figure 5.2 ◆ The Early Development Instrument

Some sample EDI questions.

Source: Early Development Instrument 2020.

measureable concept that has long-term consequences for individuals and populations. Figure 5.2 shows a snapshot of some of the questions on the EDI.

What the EDI data reveal is that 25 per cent of kindergarten students in Canada are considered "vulnerable" on one or more EDI domains. Numerous studies have shown that early vulnerability predicts a child's lifelong health, learning, and behaviour. Vulnerability on the EDI is strongly associated with family income (Janus 2007), and neighbourhood socioeconomic variables across Canada (Forer et al. 2019) for typically developing children as well as those with special needs (Zeraatkar et al. 2020). This matters for the child, but it also matters for the rest of us. Economists and others have shown that reducing these vulnerabilities will likely result in widespread economic gains (Hanushek and Woessman 2008). So how do we decrease the number of vulnerable children in kindergarten? Many suggested strategies involve increasing the economic status of low-income families to lift and flatten the social gradient. Studies in British Columbia have also found EDI vulnerabilities among the middle class, who are also stretched thin with the cost of quality early childhood education and care.

Some primary school children get homework help from skilled tutors in addition to their parents and teachers. A provincial survey conducted by the Ontario Institute for Studies in Education showed that 35 per cent of parents hired a private tutor for their child (Hart and Kempf 2015). Kids from wealthier families are also more likely to engage

◆ In Their Own Words ◆

Using EDI survey data, public health researchers in British Columbia found that

> for virtually every measure of health, including early child development, individuals or neighborhoods lower down the socioeconomic scale experience, on average, less well-being. In terms of EDI results, neighborhoods where proportionately more families have sufficient access to private wealth to compensate for the social determinants of early vulnerability report lower EDI vulnerability rates. Conversely, those neighborhoods that report higher rates of poverty suffer higher vulnerability levels.

Source: Kershaw et al. 2009.

in extracurricular activities, possibly because they or their families do not rely on income from a part-time job that takes up after-school time. After-school sports or other physical activities have been correlated with higher academic performance in math (McIsaac, Kirk, and Kuhle 2015) and reading (Fedewa and Ahn 2011). They are especially helpful for children with special needs (Fedewa and Ahn 2011).

Family income has also been linked to home environments that promote learning. Wealthier homes tend be less stressful, environmentally healthier, more stable, and less crowded. Imagine trying to learn trigonometry—or even fractions—in a room full of people while coping with, say, mould-aggravated untreated asthma. Enough sleep and limited screen time have also been correlated with higher academic performance (Faught et al. 2017). These are some reasons why resource-poor students from low-income families are sometimes academically disadvantaged before they even step foot in the classroom.

Both poverty and wealth often concentrate in certain regions. You can probably name the "rich" and "poor" parts of your town or city. This means that schools in some catchment areas can have student populations that trend one way or another. Low-income students are especially vulnerable to certain learning challenges. Therefore, teachers who teach mainly low-income students spend less time on instruction and more time on classroom management (Desimone and Long 2010). This is another clear example of the cycle of poverty. Students with more barriers to academic achievement are given fewer opportunities to achieve—their teachers are often too busy to teach!

Finances aren't everything, however, and having money in a bank account doesn't guarantee academic achievement. This is where the "socio-" in "socio-economic" comes in. There are learning advantages found in wealthier homes that do not result directly from purchasable learning supports. Recall the importance of social and human capital: They often correlate with income but don't necessarily carry a price tag.

Let's not forget about the role of social and cultural capital in this process. One study found that parents from lower-income families were less likely to engage themselves in activities at their child's school. For example, they were less likely to be members of a parent–teacher association or attend a parent–teacher meeting. They were also less likely to attend a school event, take part in a fundraising initiative, or volunteer for a parent committee (Herrold and O'Donnell 2008). Busy low-income parents, who are also more likely to be single parents, must often work long hours to keep a household. This is one reason they might miss opportunities to engage with their kids' school communities.

Human capital, on the other hand, refers to the skills and knowledge that can be shared from one person to another. Human capital theory looks at how investment in training and education contribute to productivity. People gain skills and knowledge in various settings. For example, an experienced plumber has a certain set of skills that look a lot different from an accountant's.

Being a student also needs a particular set of skills. Wealthy parents, especially those who have spent a considerable amount of time in school themselves, are better able to pass on these necessary academic skills to their children. Studies show that richer parents have more time to spend with their kids (Gayle, Golan, and Soytas 2018), to read to their kids (Reardon 2013), and generally speak more to their kids (Fernald, Marchman, and Weisleder 2013). All of these skills learned at home benefit a child at school.

How many generations in your family have attended postsecondary school? The percentage of Canadians with a postsecondary education is gradually increasing. However, students whose parents completed university are more than twice as likely to complete university themselves as people whose parents did not (Statistics Canada 2011). Parents with higher incomes—those more likely to have achieved higher levels of education themselves—are more likely to save for their children's education (Statistics Canada 2013b). This makes tuition fees less of a burden for their children. Other studies suggest that parents who attended college or university are more likely to promote a "family culture" that channels their children toward higher education. Figure 5.3 shows that postsecondary participation increases with family income.

The costs of an education extend beyond tuition and textbooks. Typically, a student will spend years studying instead of actively earning an income. Spending money and not earning any is what economists call an **opportunity cost**. Students from low-income families are at risk of sinking into dangerous levels of poverty when they abandon earning to learn. To mitigate this threat, some opt to work while attending school. When work hours cross a "high-intensity" threshold, work has been associated with lower marks (Marsh and Kleitman 2005), lower levels of engagement at school, and delayed graduation (Neyt et al. Baert 2018).

opportunity costs The value of opportunities a person forgoes to take advantage of other opportunities.

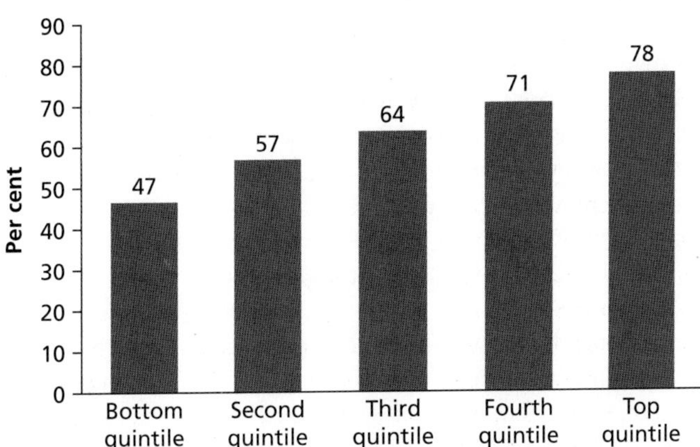

Figure 5.3 ◆ Postsecondary Participation Rate by Parental Income

Source: Based on Frenette 2017.

◆ In Their Own Words ◆

Some Canadian university grads recall the influence of their family culture on their educational paths:

> Somehow even though the "choice" was mine I think the unspoken expectation was that postsecondary education would follow high school. Just like many other values that are shaped by your parents, I think that this expectation was ingrained long before the time came to make this decision.
>
> —Melanie

> I remember my mother saying to me, "Oh when you go to university, you'll have such a great time in residence." Not going to university was never discussed—instead, we just talked about all the fun things I'd do when I inevitably went.
>
> —Sam

Source: Personal interviews.

And then, of course, there are tuition costs to consider. Which field of undergraduate study is the most expensive? Is it pharmacy, medicine, or dentistry? If you guessed dentistry, you're right! From 2018–19, the average cost of yearly tuition for a dentistry undergraduate degree in Canada was $23,474. Medical students paid $14,780, and law students paid $13,332. For graduate students, a master's program in business has the most expensive tuition, averaging $30,570 per year (Statistics Canada 2018d).

One common way that lower-income students finance their postsecondary education is by borrowing money. Some borrow from friends and family, and some borrow from banks. Most students, however, borrow from the government. The federal government co-operates with provincial governments to deliver what is called "student financial assistance programs" (that is, student loans). Quebec, the Northwest Territories, and Nunavut coordinate their own loan programs.

Every year, more and more students take out one of these student loans. This growth in student need is partly because of rising tuition fees. Tuition rates have been steadily increasing for many years now. Some people think the annual increases in tuition fees reflect

◆ In Their Own Words ◆

The cost of postsecondary education becomes an issue only if these non-financial barriers are overcome in the first place.

Source: Senate Standing Committee on Social Affairs, Science, and Technology 2011.

increases in the cost of living, and that tuition simply keeps pace with inflation. However, since 1998, the increases in tuition fees have, at times, doubled that of inflation (Statistics Canada 2012).

As a result, it is becoming more and more difficult for students to pay for a year's tuition with their earnings from a summer job. In 1995, a person needed to work 330 hours at minimum wage to pay a year's university tuition. Today, someone would need to work 525 hours.

In principle, students can make up the shortfall in their earnings by borrowing from the government. However, eligibility for student loans is dependent on family income. If a family earns above a certain amount, their child will not be eligible to receive a loan. For example, for a full-time student from a family of four, the threshold is set at roughly $61,200, compared with $68,424 for a family of five (Government of Canada 2018).

This, presumably, ensures the poorest among us have "first dibs" on the available loans. However, students who hover just above these family thresholds—upper-lower-income or lower-middle-income families—may not qualify. As well, some parents who earn more than the threshold choose not to support their children's education with their personal earnings. These children would be ineligible for most student loans, even though they are paying for their education without any parental help.

Then there's the problem that loans have to be repaid. Loans can be a blessing for lower-income students, but debt can be a curse. Figure 5.4 shows the average debt at graduation for students at different levels of education.

What does it mean to carry a student loan? People who are paying one off in their adult years—typically lower-income students—are less able to invest or begin saving for retirement, making them more financially vulnerable later in life. They are also less able to buy their own homes. After all, who can afford a mortgage when you have a big loan to repay? And while the benefits of education outweigh the obvious financial disadvantages

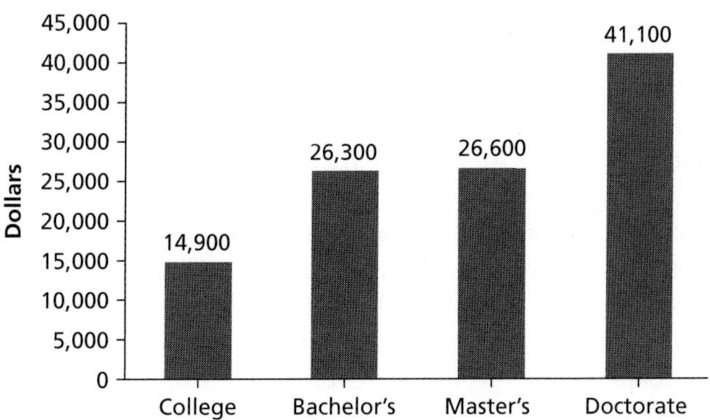

Figure 5.4 ◆ Average Debt at Graduation, 2010

Students from lower-income families often must rely on government help to complete a postsecondary education. After graduation, they must pay off their loans, which can delay their retirement savings. Will they be able to support their own children's education, or will their children have to repeat the same cycle?

Source: Based on Statistics Canada 2019b.

of student debt, the burden of debt may be passed along to their children, depriving them of chances at higher education.

Andruska and colleagues (2014) find that many postsecondary students have only a foggy idea of the student debt they are amassing over their educational career. They note that

> although the majority of students are aware that they owe on student loans, many underestimate the amount they owe. One eighth of students in the current study reported no student debt when, in fact, they had a loan. Over a quarter of the students underestimated the amount they owed by less than $10,000, and nearly one tenth of students underestimated the amount that they owed by more than $10,000. (125)

Hoping to better understand this confusion, Johnson and colleagues (2016) studied online focus groups of postsecondary students. Their results showed that "(a) students relied heavily on advice from parents, guidance counselors, and friends; (b) attending college was not possible without student loans; and (c) students knew very little about the loans they would be responsible for repaying" (184)

Yet despite the confusion surrounding loans and repayment, many students do not have other options and so take on significant debt. From US research on this topic, Cho, Xu, and Kiss (2015) conclude that "[a]s of 2012, more than 38 million people in the U.S. had outstanding student loan debt totaling over 1.1 trillion dollars . . . Those who complete a 4-year degree, or beyond, can generally anticipate greater lifetime earnings than those who do not" (239). Similarly, in 2018 the Canadian Federation of Students (n.d.) asserted that Canadian students owe $28 billion to all levels of government. The interest on this debt is a significant source of revenue, bringing in $862.6 million from the Canada Student Loans Program in 2018 alone.

Shockingly, however, the availability of such loans has not levelled the playing field among people from different social class backgrounds or improved college graduation (Cho et al. 2015). Instead, "[f]amily and parental contributions toward the expenses of educational investment, including even small amounts in a child's savings account, have been identified as the most significant influences on both college enrollment and graduation" (Cho et al.:239). This means that wealthier families have retained their advantage.

Sociologists have known the importance of family support and encouragement for at least 45 years. Raymond Breton (1974) carried out the first major study of educational ambitions and attainments in Canada in the early 1970s, when the baby boom generation was passing through colleges and universities. Fifty years later, educational access and educational quality remain major problems in both Canada and the United States. Perhaps this suggests that, in solving our social problems, we do not lack information and insight but rather political commitment to do so.

That said, the question of "who should pay for higher education" remains hotly contested. This is shown by political turmoil over the issue in Ontario, where the election of a Progressive Conservative provincial government under Doug Ford in 2018 has led to the elimination of free tuition for low-income students and severe cuts to education at every level (*CBC News* 2019)

In Canada as a whole, postsecondary education is still a good way to get ahead. Earning a postsecondary degree helps ensure that you will earn a comfortable, living income, and if you don't get a postsecondary education, you are more likely to struggle. This may be less and less true in the United States, however. Economists have shown that in the United States, students from rich families who *don't* get a degree are still 2.5 times more likely to wind up wealthy than low-income students (PEW Charitable Trusts 2012). In other words, inherited wealth and status may be more powerful and persistent in terms of economic standing than educational credentials. This hinders movement between economic classes (that is, social mobility) and leads to what some have called "stickiness at the poles." Stickiness means that social mobility is sluggish for people at the top and those at the bottom of the income distribution.

As journalist Timothy Noah (2012) so aptly puts it, "it's harder to climb a ladder when the rungs are farther apart." As we have noted, children from poorer families are less likely than children from middle-class or wealthy families to attend institutions of postsecondary education. Also, of those who do go on with education after high school, children from middle-class and wealthy families are more likely to attend universities and less likely to attend community colleges. Though the reasons are varied, cost and potential debt are especially important.

Rural Students in Canada

Educational opportunity and the quality of available education are unequally distributed across Canada. As of 2011, there were 175 community colleges in Canada; however, these colleges are not evenly distributed geographically (Senate Standing Committee on Social Affairs, Science, and Technology 2010). They are overwhelmingly in and around large Canadian cities, especially in the most-populated provinces. So while cost helps to explain some barriers to postsecondary education, geography and location are also important.

In a government study by Marc Frenette (2003), Statistics Canada found that distance from a university often decreases university participation, especially for people from low-income families. Studies done in the United States (Combs 2016) show these factors still operate. When potential students are asked to explain their choices, researchers discover that their reluctance to attend the further university has nothing to do with academic achievement or motivation. Rather, distance is the problem, and distance translates into cost. Researchers found that it was the cost of living far away from home that deters potential students (Statistics Canada 2007).

Might the results today be affected by the growth of online learning? Students can enroll at many colleges and universities in Canada and attend "classes" without leaving their home communities. However, research on online postsecondary courses highlights limitations. Online courses eliminate the factor of geographic distance, but they also reduce student involvement, course completion, and grades attained. In general, students are less committed to online courses (see Jaggars, Edgecombe, and Stacey 2013).

Arkorful and Abaidoo (2015) note that online learning comes with many disadvantages, including congested websites and difficulty monitoring plagiarism and cheating. They explain that the lack of face-to-face interaction in online learning makes the

IN FOCUS ◆ Francophone Students

A significant barrier to postsecondary education exists for francophone students in Canada—the relative shortage of French-language universities and colleges. Most of the French-language schools are located in Quebec, but remember—not all francophones live in *la belle province*!

learning process more difficult for both teachers and students. It also can negatively impact students' socialization and communication skills. This is because students do not have the opportunity to interact with and practise delivering information to their peers and teachers.

Boys and Young Men

One of the most pronounced changes in postsecondary education over the past few decades has been the tipping of the scales in terms of gender balance. Next time you're in class, take a look around you. You are among the first few generations to count more women in the postsecondary classroom than men. Figure 5.5 shows the gender difference in postsecondary enrolment.

Across the country, women are outnumbering men at the postsecondary level by over 10 per cent. This number has increased dramatically since the 1970s but has remained constant over the past decade or so (Statistics Canada 2013a). More women are graduating from postsecondary programs, and those with degrees earn higher incomes. Nonetheless, an income gap of 72 cents to the dollar persists between men and women (Statistics Canada 2016). Ironically, even at universities female professors in Canada (who now outnumber male professors) are earning less than their male counterparts (see Figure 5.6).

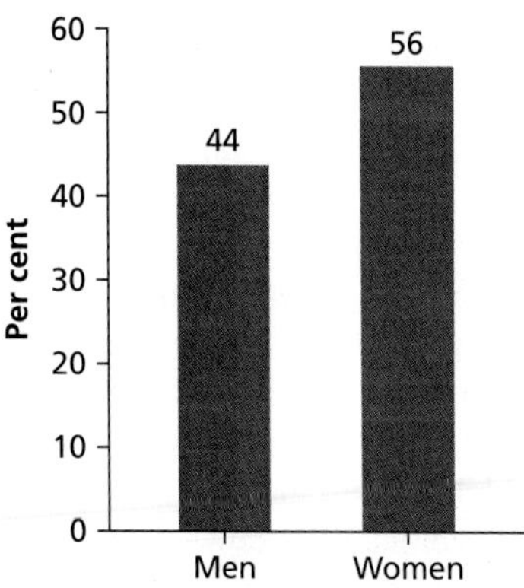

Figure 5.5 ◆ Postsecondary Enrolment by Gender

Source: Based on Statistics Canada 2018a.

Women face fewer barriers in this institutional setting than in the past, even though their academic achievements do not always translate into equal earnings in the workplace. So many sociologists and scholars from other fields have begun to turn their attention to the evidence of missing men to understand why fewer young men are pursuing postsecondary education. The population of men enrolled at university has been increasing, but the increase has not kept pace with the increase of women.

This gender difference—the growing educational supremacy of women—begins at primary and secondary school. In other words, we need to understand the gendering of educational attainment almost from birth. What we see in postsecondary institutions is merely the last step in a decades-long

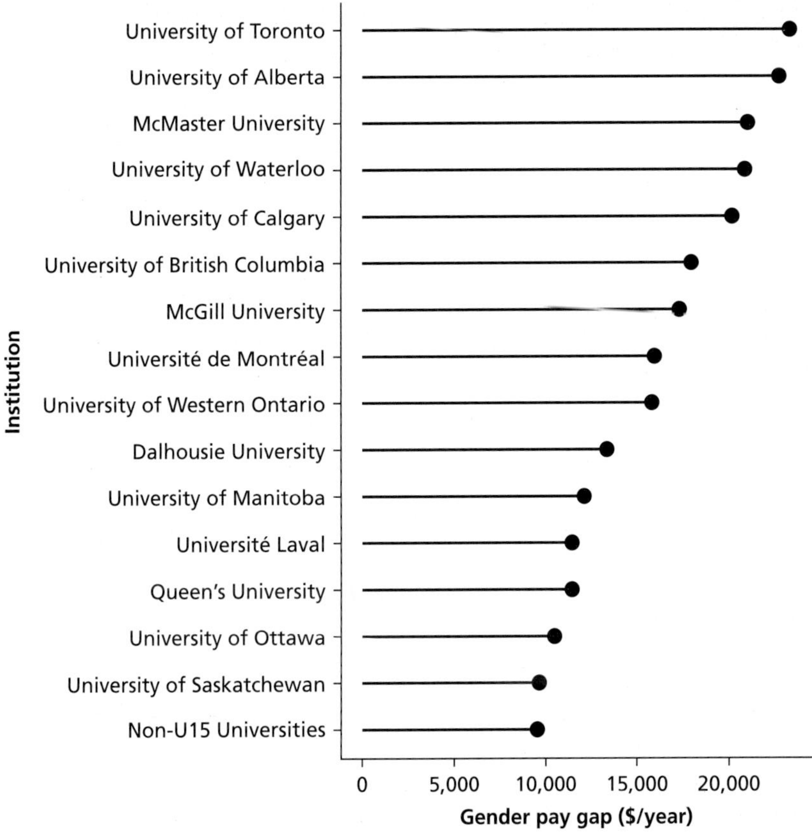

Figure 5.6 ◆ Earnings Gap per Year, Male and Female University Faculty

This gender pay gap explains why, in April 2019, the University of Toronto gave a 1.3 per cent salary increase to 800 women faculty members. The U of T president, Meric Gertler, announced that this move is "immediate action to close the pay gap between men and women professors who are tenured or in the tenure stream based on the comprehensive, in-depth analysis of the issue undertaken by the advisory group" (*U of T News* 2019).

Sources: Based on Frederickson 2018; Statistics Canada 2018c.

process of inequality. So why are boys and young men lagging behind their female counterparts beginning in their primary years?

Sociologists note that many boys are already floundering in primary school. Interestingly, this is being tracked in most OECD countries. An OECD (2015) report concluded that

> [y]oung men are significantly more likely than young women to be less engaged with school and have low skills and poor academic achievement. They are also more likely to leave school early, often with no qualifications. Boys in OECD countries, for example, are eight percentage points more likely than girls to report that school is a waste of time. (18)

Drawing Connections

Remember the feminization of poverty discussed in Chapter 2 and the feminization of employment and wages discussed in Chapter 3. With this in mind, is the inequality caused by natural differences between boys and girls or social and cultural performances of gender—that is, is it "nature" or "nurture"? In general, efforts by social scientists to assign these differences to either nature or nurture fail, but we do know that nature and nurture interact. People are born with certain inclinations or tendencies, and their social environment either encourages or discourages the development and display of these tendencies.

A six-part series in the *Globe and Mail* studying this topic compiled data suggesting that boys are falling behind their girl counterparts by "nearly every measure of scholastic achievement" (Abraham 2010a). Girls are earning higher grades overall while boys are scoring much lower on standardized tests. Boys do not show the same aptitudes in reading and writing. They are also "more likely to be picked out for behavioural problems, more likely to repeat a grade and to drop out of school altogether" (Abraham 2010a).

feminization of education The growing educational focus on developing skills of girls and women in middle and higher education, which risks alienating and disadvantaging boys and men.

Why are boys struggling in primary school? One theory suggests that the (new) interest in promoting girls' skills has resulted in a **feminization of education** that alienated young boys. For example, one scholastic area in which boys trail behind girls is reading. In the OECD (2015) international comparison, researchers found that boys spend one hour less on their homework each week than girls, more time playing video games, and less time reading. In schools with many disadvantaged students, boys are more likely to underachieve.

Some commentators point to the shortage of male primary school teachers as part of the problem. Their numbers are so low that sightings of male teachers have been likened to sightings of spotted owls, the leatherback turtle, and Beluga whales (Abraham 2010b). In 2016, Statistics Canada's national Census revealed low numbers of male teachers at the preschool, elementary, and high school levels. The disparity between the proportions of male and female teachers has become a professional and public concern (Ontario College of Teachers 2004). Some credit boys' poor academic performance to a lack of male role

Drawing Connections

Women have dominated the field of teaching for decades, and for decades if not centuries teaching was one of the only professions open to women. Recalling what we discussed in Chapter 3, how do you account for this and the fact that, over this long period, boys seemed to perform much better than girls?

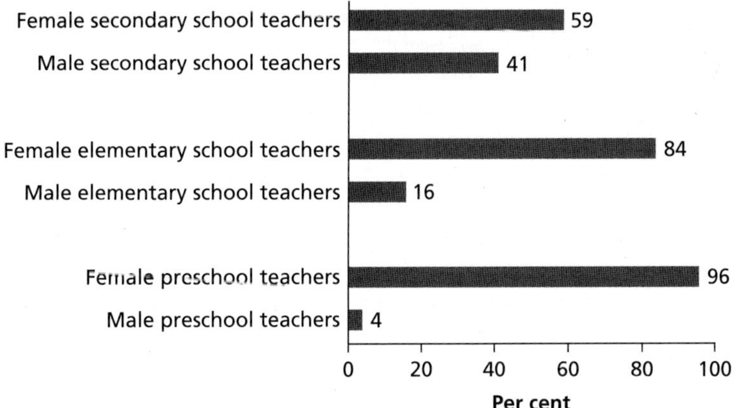

Figure 5.7 ◆ Gender Disparities in Three Levels of Education

Source: Based on Statistics Canada 2016.

models at the blackboard. When it goes on long enough, boys may begin to imagine education as a "girls' thing." Figure 5.7 shows the differences between men and women in the educational professions.

There are many reasons men are not gravitating toward primary teaching. Many sociologists believe this is due to lingering ideas about which jobs are "best suited" for which gender. Jobs that involve the nurturing and care of young children—especially what sociologists have called *emotional work*—have historically been associated with women. Therefore, sociologists propose that men and women—either consciously or subconsciously—avoid jobs that violate common gender norms. In their study of undergraduate students in Western Canada, Block, Croft, and Schmader (2018) found that men were less likely than women to value jobs that involved "helping others, serving humanity, working with people, connecting with others, attending to others, caring for others, and intimacy." Men who responded were also more likely to assign lower salaries to jobs like healthcare and early childhood education and higher salaries to STEM professions. Men who would make happy, excellent teachers are limited by these gendered ideas surrounding the teaching profession.

Finally, some theorize that boys' underperformance results from their overmedicalization. More boys are being diagnosed and treated for learning disabilities like attention-deficit hyperactivity disorder. The Canadian Paediatric Society (2018) recently expressed concern about this issue, noting that prescription rates of drugs like Ritalin are rising in Canada, the United States, and the United Kingdom. With this in mind, they recommend that such drugs only be used (1) as part of a larger, multimodal treatment approach, and (2) when not using them will result in significant educational and interpersonal impairment.

Males are more prone to some neurological disorders (and women more prone to others). Most agree that many of the boys prescribed these drugs do in fact need them. Boys often display hyperactivity and poor impulse control in school more often than girls do, and some attribute this to neurological differences. And yet others think that these behaviours are largely a result of the teaching techniques or parenting approaches used and not evidence of a neurological disorder (see Meyer and Lasky 2017). This debate is important, because the unnecessary use of these powerful drugs includes side effects like insomnia and headaches that may make learning more difficult.

Boys are also struggling at the level of secondary education. To repeat, sociologists have tracked fewer dropouts over the past 20 years, but in doing so they have noted that young men leave school more often than young women (Statistics Canada 2017). Regardless of boys' motivations for not spending more time on homework or not pursuing career paths associated with female labour, we know that poor performance in secondary school affects the strength of college and university applications. This further limits the academic pursuits of young men and tips the gender scales of postsecondary enrolment. In the end, failing to bring the best out of boys and girls, men and women, means throwing away enormous human potential: the resources with which we build a future society.

Older Students

For various reasons (including cost), some people delay their postsecondary education. Some choose to "take time off" and explore the world a little (or a lot). Some decide to enter the working world for a while to gain experience, explore their long-term career goals, or save enough money to pay for future tuition (instead of taking out a loan). Some people take a few years before deciding that postsecondary education is something worth seeking. Others have to deal with life events, such as illness, pregnancy, or family duties, that delay college or university attendance.

Whatever the reason, about one-third of Canadians aged 18–64 report having unmet educational needs or wants (Statistics Canada 2015). What's more, these needs or wants are most commonly reported among women. Likely, this points to women taking time off from education (and work) to have children. Interestingly, people who already have some form of postsecondary education report the same unmet needs—they want more education too. Here, researchers speculate, "the exposure to learning may lead to an increased awareness of knowledge or skills that they may still lack" (Knighton et al. 2009). In other words, it takes some learning to be astounded at what could be left to learn!

Entering postsecondary education as an older student presents some unique obstacles. As you learned from the short quiz above, family responsibilities are the most common reason that older students do not return to school. This is especially true of people aged 25–45, who cited this reason twice as often as people in the 18–24 age range (Knighton et al. 2009). In the 25–45 age range, people are busiest bearing, raising, and paying for children—so they have less time and money to spend on higher education.

Many people reading this book will, at some point, likely become older students. More people are getting more formal education: The economy demands it. And, as we have seen, for various reasons many people delay their higher education to pay off debts, start a family, or start a career. Increasingly, middle-aged people find themselves unemployed or working poor and in need of more education to start a new career or upgrade their employability.

Critical Thinking Question

For various social and psychological reasons, such as discomfort around young people, many adults are reluctant to seek further education (Goto and Martin 2009) However, practical reasons are important as well. In the most recent available study, Statistics Canada (2008) surveyed a large group of older Canadians who wished to pursue further education but felt they could not. The reasons these Canadians gave were ranked from most common to least common. Here is the list the below, out of order. Can you guess the correct order?

- Wasn't able to secure a loan for tuition and other expenses
- Need to work
- Family responsibilities
- Cost
- Work schedule

Answer: 1. Family responsibilities (27 per cent); 2. Need to work (26 per cent); 3. Work schedule (25 per cent); 4. Cost (21 per cent); 5. Wasn't able to secure a loan for tuition and other expenses (2 per cent).

Source: Knighton et al. 2009.

Drawing Connections

Consider the overlapping effects of barriers to childcare, as discussed in Chapter 4. If Canadians age 25–45 could freely access reliable, affordable, quality childcare for their children, what effect do you think this would have on post-secondary enrolment for this population? How does this relate to interlocking disadvantages?

People with Disabilities in Canada

Disabilities differ greatly in the way they affect a person's access to education. Not all disabilities are equally disabling, and some may have greater or lesser impacts at different times during a person's life. As well, some barriers to education are related to the disability itself, and some are related to the way that others understand (and respond to) the disability.

A disability may require a person to enroll in school part time instead of full time. This means that completing their education will take longer and be more expensive. Similarly, a disability may result in unplanned school absences, either short term or long term, and absences often lower marks. Long-term absences force students to relearn material they have forgotten since their last engagement with school.

Some students with disabilities struggle to get the support they need. Increasingly, postsecondary institutions are developing new services for students with disabilities, but many students still face obstacles. There may be a shortage of note-takers, an absence of ramps or elevators, or not enough computers with adaptive software. In fact, there may be a shortage of all manner of other accommodations that a particular student might need to learn.

Also, securing these accommodations can be lengthy and complicated, especially at the beginning of a semester when accessibility support services are flooded with applications. Some students may have to struggle for weeks without the necessary accommodations while they wait for their paperwork to be processed. Ironically, the organization, time management, and attention to detail needed to complete some accommodations applications can be especially challenging—impossible, even—for students with some types of learning disabilities (Lindsay, Cagliostro, and Carafa 2018). These students, understandably, can get frustrated and give up.

Students with disabilities may also face added educational costs. They may have to pay for tutors, adaptive software, interpreters and note-takers, special transportation to and from school, and other accommodations (Senate Standing Committee on Social Affairs, Science, and Technology 2011). While there is some funding available at the level of the school, the government, and through private sponsorship, many feel that it does not meet the growing need.

Some students with disabilities also need more time to complete their schoolwork, and this means less time for part-time jobs that might help offset the cost of tuition and other expenses. These students must repay a greater debt load after they graduate, incurred during the longer stay in school with greater expenses. Repaying debt is especially challenging for the precariously employed, an all-too-common experience for people with disabilities (see Chapter 3).

Postsecondary institutions are reporting an increase in the number of students with disabilities. And it's not just the numbers of students with disabilities that are changing; the types of reported disabilities are changing, too. Just a few decades ago, mobility and sensory-related disabilities were less commonly reported among students. Today, students are much more likely to seek support for a wide variety of learning disabilities, both mental and physical. Increasingly, mental health disabilities are being reported at the postsecondary level (Standing Senate Committee on Social Affairs, Science and Technology 2010). Data from the 2016 National College Health Assessment survey show that conditions are getting worse, not better. Many students are exhausted from a multiplicity of demands at school, at home, and at work (if they have a paid job as well). The survey noted that the percentage of Canadian students who had seriously contemplated suicide had increased by about 3.5 per cent since 2013 (Chiose 2016).

Indeed, schools are learning that they must react quickly and effectively to mental health issues, such as depression and anxiety, given that mental illness may often present in early adulthood when intervention is especially critical. Figure 5.8 shows the Canadian population aged 15 to 24 years with a disability who are in school.

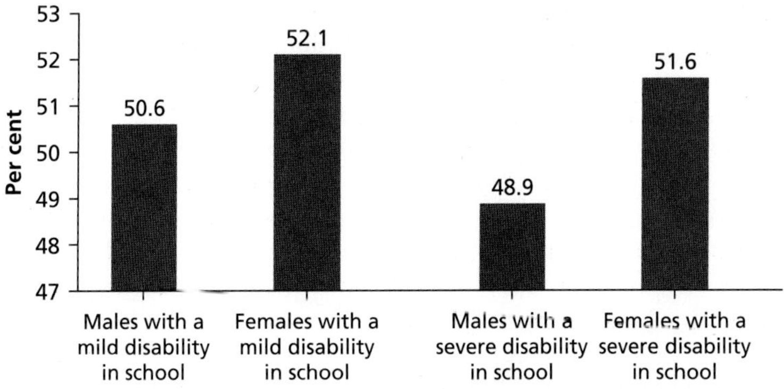

Figure 5.8 ◆ Canadian Population Aged 15 to 24 Years with a Disability Who Are in School

Source: Based on Morris et al. 2018.

Mental health and learning disabilities are the most common disabilities affecting youth in Canada. These types of disabilities, when mild or severe, are correlated with lower school enrolment (Statistics Canada 2018a). The increased reported rates of youth disability are due in part to improved diagnostic tools and more support in schools. They are also because of the efforts of educators and disability activists to de-stigmatize disability so more people openly seek the help they need. We understand more today about the complex and diverse ways that people learn, one being no better than the next. Even the term *disability*, which some believe connotes inability, is being challenged in educational settings, where you might instead meet the term *accessibility*, which focuses

◆ In Their Own Words ◆

One Canadian with a visual impairment reflects on his experiences in high school:

> In 1975, I was diagnosed with a rare eye disease. I could no longer see the boards or read books. So the principal told me to tell the teachers to read out loud as they were writing on the board. But teachers forgot or didn't care to try. There were no book-reading services, so I was unable to answer questions or write book reports. Eventually, teachers stopped asking me questions in class and I became invisible. I showed up daily to get whatever education I could. But in the end, I fell three credits short of graduating.

Source: Personal interview.

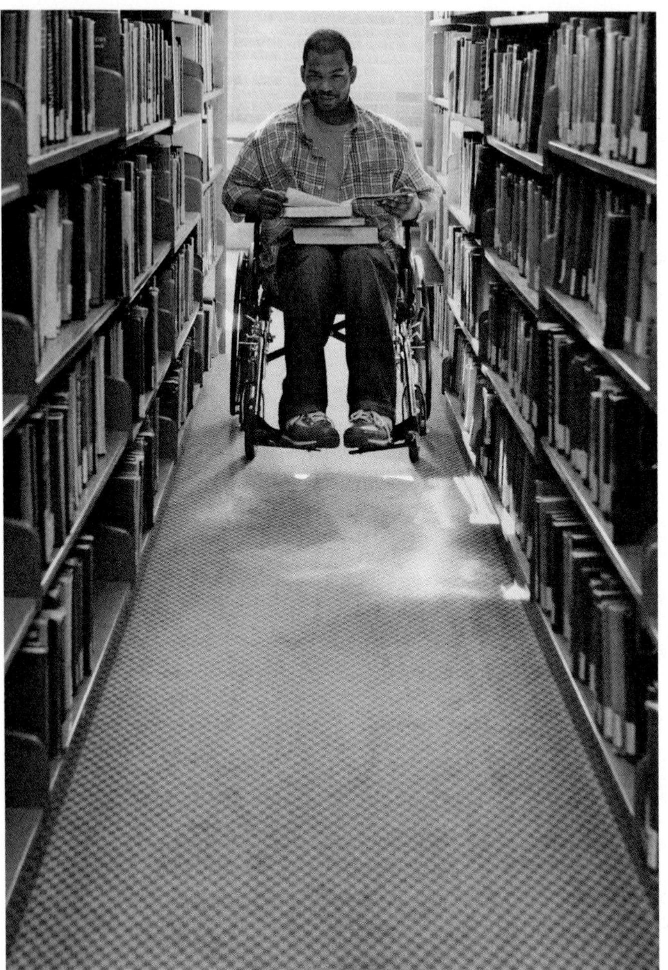

What technological advances have you witnessed at your own educational institution that aid students with disabilities? Can you think of any improvements that are needed in this domain? Spend a day noting whether every building, room, facility, service, and mode of transportation you use is accessible for people with different abilities.

on the end goal. So, many educational institutions are stressing differentiated instruction or individual learning plans that target each student's unique needs and learning style.

Schools are increasingly adapting to students' diverse learning needs, but it has not been enough to fully level the playing field. More Canadians who live with a disability are enrolling in postsecondary education, and more students are reporting and registering with schools' disability support services (Association of Universities and Colleges of Canada 2011). In Ontario, a survey of parents of children with disabilities revealed that "68 per cent . . . had participated in college or university by age 21, with 46 per cent in college and 22 per cent in university" (McCloy and DeClou 2013:9).

Yet the postsecondary participation rate among Canadians with a disability is still much lower than for other Canadians. As well, only half as many graduate from high school (Senate Standing Committee on Social Affairs, Science, and Technology 2011).

Across Canada, people with disabilities encounter barriers that stem from how society perceives and treats disabilities and the people who live with them. And views about disability impact government funding. Each province and territory independently manages its own funding programs for students with disabilities, so there are no consistent standards. This means that a student who qualifies for funding in one place may not qualify in another, limiting their mobility should they wish to transfer provinces mid-degree or mid-diploma. The lack of consistent standards also means that some students are only eligible to receive funding for their disabilities if they are also eligible for other types of funding.

There are other ways that views about disability can affect a student's access to and experience of formal education. For example, other students may have prejudiced and stereotypical ideas about the accommodations that students with a disability are entitled to. They may feel these students are unfairly advantaged and treat them differently or disregard their academic contributions. Teachers might expect "perfect" work from students who are granted learning accommodations. Some students must prove how "broken" they are in order to access the accommodations they need. They are then expected to prove the opposite when it comes to their schoolwork. In short, students with disabilities may be stigmatized and stereotyped by their peers and mentors, just as conflict theorists would predict.

Finally, people with invisible disabilities often don't get the support they need. Invisible disabilities are not immediately obvious in social interactions. Examples include mental health–related disabilities, sickle cell anemia, and undiagnosed sources of physical pain. Invisible disabilities prevent barriers because people don't see them, but they are disabling nonetheless.

dre
@badtrvp
#InvisiblyDisabledLooksLike being denied medical attention because you don't 'seem' to be in crippling pain @ the ER.#sicklecellstrong

Some people who live with invisible disabilities recently took to Twitter to raise awareness about this type of disability.

◆ In Their Own Words ◆

In April 2010, Claudette Larocque, director of Public Policy and Programs, Learning Disabilities Association of Canada, reflected on the impact of learning disabilities to the Standing Senate Committee on Social Affairs, Science and Technology (2010):

> Learning disabilities are invisible; they are lifelong and they may run in families. Learning disabilities can occur with other disorders—mental health conditions or any other mobility disabilities as well. Learning disabilities are not the same as mental retardation, autism, deafness, blindness, behavioural disorders, or laziness. Learning disabilities are not the result of economic disadvantage, environmental factors, or cultural differences. Living with a learning disability can have an ongoing impact on friendships, school, work, self-esteem, and daily life. People with learning disabilities can succeed when solid coping skills, accommodations, and strategies are developed.

Immigrants in Canada

The barriers to education for immigrants, especially those who have recently arrived in Canada, are cultural, linguistic, and financial. Many immigrants have firsthand experience of the employment limitations resulting from a lack of education—or from an education that goes frustratingly unrecognized in Canada. This may partially explain why young immigrants and the children of immigrants (second generation Canadians) often seek postsecondary education at higher levels than non-immigrant Canadians. They are often more educated than their parents, especially when comparing second generation women with their mothers (Chen and Hou 2019).

There are also differences in the university completion rate among people of different national origins. As Chen and Hou (2019) report, "the education progress across generations is especially salient among Chinese, South Asian, and Korean Canadians, but rather moderate among Black and Latin American men, and absent among Filipino men."

The higher rates of postsecondary participation are especially impressive given the financial barriers to education for immigrants, a population that tends to be low income. For example, one study found the children of families who had arrived in Canada since 1980 were more likely to take out a student loan. This is partly because their parents earned lower incomes than those of other students (Statistics Canada 2006).

In short, many immigrant children are highly motivated to study hard and pursue a university degree. At the same time, those with the highest motivation and expectations are also most likely to suffer from anxiety, loneliness, and depression. The Toronto District School Board's (2018) 2017 Student and Parent Census showed that "students' emotional well-being has dropped incrementally by age and over time" (2), with more students "nervous and under a lot of stress and pressure often or all the time, and [having] multiple worries especially about their own future and their school marks" (2).

So we must remain alert to the implications for mental health when pushing children to excel at school, even when these students are healthy and highly motivated to succeed.

IN FOCUS ◆ Refugees and Non-status Immigrants

Children who are refugees or refugee claimants may attend school in Canada. The Immigration and Refugee Protection Act states that "every minor child in Canada, other than a child of a temporary resident not authorized to work or study, is authorized to study at the pre-school, primary or secondary level" (section 30(2)).

This means that, theoretically, non-status immigrants also have the right to attend school. And yet studies show that in some regions of Canada non-status immigrants encounter barriers to public education (Education Without Borders 2013; Sidhu 2008). Enrolment may be (illegally) denied outright. Enrolling your child in school often requires documentation, such as proof of citizenship or passports, that non-status immigrants cannot provide. Non-status parents may fear that enrolling their children in school may alert authorities to their non-status and make the family vulnerable to deportation. Others who can successfully enroll their children may limit their involvement in extracurricular activities or other school community events for this same reason. Participation in school trips often require that students have provincial health insurance, which non-status immigrants struggle to get (Sidhu 2008).

Indigenous Peoples in Canada

Another population that lags behind in postsecondary participation is Indigenous Peoples in Canada. Figure 5.9 shows that Indigenous men and women in Canada are far less likely to have a diploma or degree at or above the bachelor level.

These gaps begin to form in the primary grades, where young Indigenous students often score much lower than other Canadian students on performance indicators. They widen in secondary school, where the dropout rate for Indigenous students living off-reserve is three times that of non-Indigenous students. School completion rates are even lower for Indigenous youth living on-reserve (Richards and Scott 2009; Statistics Canada 2013a).

Indigenous Peoples in Canada encounter many overlapping barriers to education. One such barrier is the legacy of residential schools. The lasting effects of residential schools include "a deep mistrust among some Indigenous people of mainstream educational institutions. The importance of getting a good education becomes secondary to what may be seen as a further assimilative assault on Indigenous culture, language and traditions" (Chalifoux 2003).

The Indigenous population in Canada is also, in general, at higher risk of having a low income than the non-Indigenous population. As we have seen, low-income status is in itself a barrier to education, especially at the postsecondary level. Indigenous youth in Canada are also more likely to have parents who did not attend postsecondary education themselves. The Canada Council on Learning (2009) reports that students who are the first in their families to attend postsecondary institutions "are more likely to be sceptical of the benefits potentially conferred by a post-secondary education and are, therefore, less motivated to pursue post-secondary studies." So while these effects are seen in other, non-Indigenous families, they are especially pronounced in the Indigenous population.

The lack of employment opportunity on Canadian reserves is another factor that influences the educational gap between Indigenous and non-Indigenous populations. Researchers John Richards and Megan Scott (2009) note, "on-reserve, investing in education

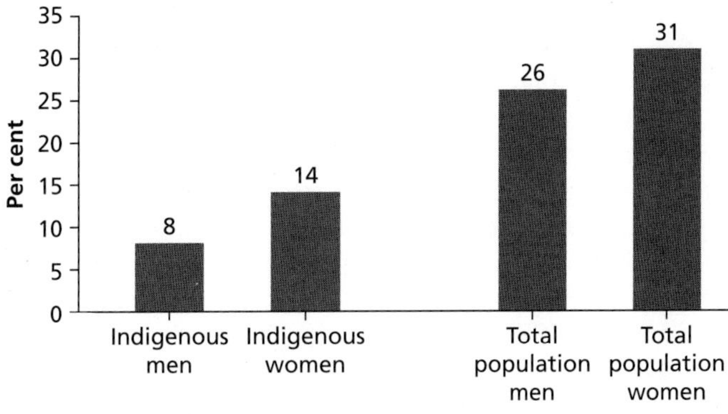

Figure 5.9 ◆ Indigenous Postsecondary Education Level

Source: Statistics Canada 2019a.

United Church of Canada Archives

In Canadian residential schools, Indigenous children were stripped of their culture, language, and traditions and forced to adopt Euro-Canadian and Christian customs. As a result, even today, Indigenous Peoples share an understandable mistrust of the education system.

is less rewarding because of the scarcity of nearby jobs, especially jobs requiring higher education levels." In other words, people—Indigenous or otherwise—often aren't inclined to seek a postsecondary education if they don't feel it will be useful professionally.

Earlier in this chapter we saw that students with disabilities face barriers to education. Socially disadvantaged populations of many kinds often show higher levels of disabilities such as learning disabilities, fetal alcohol spectrum disorder, visual or hearing impairments, behaviour disorders, and physical disabilities. Among some Indigenous populations in Canada the rate of people with these special needs are triple that of the non-Indigenous population (Richards and Scott 2009). Schools therefore would require triple the resources to provide comparable educational opportunities to this population. Ideally, some of these special needs would be addressed in the early years of childhood. This is why access to quality early childhood education and care is especially important in some regions of Canada (see Chapter 4).

Many think that education works best when it is culturally appropriate, and that's why many Indigenous communities in Canada today are incorporating Indigenous culture in their school curriculum. Some educators are working to sustain and revitalize the diverse Indigenous languages in Canada, since many of them have been devastated by the residential school system (Richards and Scott 2009). A culturally responsive curriculum may also mean hiring Indigenous teachers and engaging family and community members. Some of these initiatives cost money—money that many Indigenous schools do not have (Richards and Scott 2009).

As we have already seen, Indigenous Peoples are at a much higher risk of poverty, unemployment, and poor health. This is partly because of their lower social status and the lack of respect they receive from others. Education, especially postsecondary education, is understood by many to be an important strategy to alleviate some of these conditions.

IN FOCUS ◆ First Nations University

First Nations University of Canada (FNUniv) was established in 1976 as the Saskatchewan Indian Federated College through a federated partnership with the University of Regina. It was founded "to enhance the quality of life, and to preserve, protect and interpret the history, language, culture and artistic heritage of First Nations people." Today, FNUniv continues to fulfill this shared vision. FNUniv provides a unique opportunity to study in an environment that supports First Nations cultures, languages, and values. FNUniv students can participate in and learn through ceremonies with Elders as well as through classroom-based experience on three university's campuses in Regina, Saskatoon, and Prince Albert. FNUniv is a unique Canadian institution that specializes in Indigenous knowledge, providing postsecondary education for Indigenous and non-Indigenous students alike within a culturally support environment.

Source: First Nations University website: http://fnuniv.ca.

LGBTQ+ People in Canada

Ensuring that all people have equal and free access to a quality educational experience is beneficial to our society. That's partly why school communities are required to uphold the Canadian Charter of Rights and Freedoms and actively preserve environments that are free of discrimination. Many schools have safe school policies that further underline their commitment to inclusion. However, studies have shown that schools are often not safe spaces for LGBTQ+ students.

There is little information about LGBTQ+ students' attendance rates for postsecondary schooling. For that reason, this section focuses more on primary and secondary education. In their survey of 3,700 high school students across Canada, researchers Taylor and Peter (2011) found that LGBTQ+ students are routinely subjected to discrimination. This includes the casual use of disparaging and homophobic language, belittlement, sexual taunting, and verbal, physical, and sexual harassment. Here are some of the results of the cross-Canada survey:

- Six times as much verbal harassment, and up to three times as much physical and sexual harassment about their sexual orientation compared with non-LGBTQ+ students.
- Twice as much verbal harassment and three and a half times more physical harassment about their gender identity compared with non-LGBTQ+ students.
- Trans students reported verbal harassment at rates that were twice as high as LGBTQ+ students and four times higher than non-LGBTQ+ students.
- Students with one or more LGBTQ+ parents are more likely to report verbal harassment than their peers (even if they themselves are heterosexual and have a conventional gender identity).
- In general, female LGBTQ+ students experience higher levels of harassment than their male counterparts.

Social and institutional practices support and may even encourage these discriminatory practices. Among students, the use of homophobic or transphobic language is so widespread that it structures the social interaction of students (Taylor and Peter 2011). Students who witness harassment or discrimination may not intervene to stop it, likely because they are aware of the possible social effects of sticking up for the bullied. Victims of harassment, on the other hand, often choose not to report incidents, likely because they can't rely on a proper response. There is also the fear that reporting harassment will only increase their vulnerability to repeat attacks. Often teachers who witness homophobic incidents do nothing, and when they intervene, they appear ineffective. Yet their failure to intervene appears to condone this behaviour (Taylor and Peter 2011).

Some believe that the media focus on the effect of these negative experiences has increased hopelessness, and in that way increased youth suicides. Happily, however, it has also led to some changes in policies centred on detecting and addressing homophobic bullying, violence, and exclusion. LGBTQ+ students are now specifically addressed in Manitoba's Public Schools Act (2014) and Newfoundland's Safe and Caring Schools Policy (2013). As of 2012 and 2015, respectively, Ontario and Alberta now compel schools to support students if they wish to create Gay–Straight Alliance groups or clubs. The Government of New Brunswick, going one step further, now requires schools to create Gay–Straight Alliances when requested by teachers, parents, or other members of the community, not just students. And public schools in Quebec must now develop concrete action plans to end LGBTQ+-based bullying (Taylor et al. 2015).

Parents also contribute to hostile educational environments for LGBTQ+ students. Researcher Gerald Walton (2004) writes, "although some parents are supportive, many express concern that discussions about homosexuality might have some undue influence on their children or that educational administrators are undermining what their children are taught at home" (28). Children may carry these attitudes with them to school, harming LGBTQ+ students.

◆ In Their Own Words ◆

An LGBTQ+-identified teen describes an experience of discriminatory education:

> I am discouraged when every day I sit in class and hear mean homophobic remarks, and the teachers just ignore it or perhaps even have a laugh with the students who said it!! I have lost faith in the supposed "teacher role model" crap. Yeah right. These people only conform to their own beliefs of religion and such, and rarely do I see a teacher stick up against homophobic remarks. I would love it if classrooms could be videotaped or recorded. Some of these "qualified" teachers should not be teaching if they are not going to do their jobs.

Source: Teacher, interview subject from Taylor et al. 2015

Because of the hostile educational climate they face, many LGBTQ+ students report spending as little time as possible in the school environment, becoming isolated and disconnected. LGBTQ+ students who are targeted by harassment also "often have lower grades, lower progress to post-secondary education, higher rates of skipping school because of safety concerns, higher rates of risky behaviour, and higher rates of depression and suicidal ideation than non-LGBTQ+ students" (Taylor and Peter 2011).

Consequences of Unequal Access to Education

Why should we care about unequal access to education? The answer is simple: Educated people are healthier, more securely employed, and more prosperous than less-educated people. And healthy, securely employed, and prosperous people are good for society.

Employment aside, education involves learning how to learn and passes on a capacity for self-reliance and self-development. People expect education to provide them with a wide range of skills to prepare them for an uncertain future, and usually they gain that benefit.

In Canada and other industrial societies, formal education helps people gain valuable credentials—entry tickets into top occupations. Formal education is supposed to be a fair way of assigning unequal economic positions to people. However, as we have seen, access to educational credentials is unequal from the start. People from wealthier, more educated families are more likely to both be encouraged to get a higher education and receive financial support that allows them to meet this goal. Besides, postsecondary education is not doing everything it could to ensure that schooling educates people adequately. Today, most top North American universities are designed to train researchers and produce research findings with only a small emphasis on undergraduate teaching.

At the same time, a persisting problem for secondary schools and universities is youth subculture. In his classic work, *The Adolescent Society* (1962), James Coleman questioned the socialization that takes place in schools and its importance for higher education. What Coleman found from this survey is that most high school students hated learning in school, caring more about "good looks" and "being an athlete" than they did for "good grades" and "being smart."

Of course, schools are different now than they were 60 years ago. Garner and colleagues (2006) attempted to revisit Coleman's research using qualitative research methods and found three major differences between high schools today and high schools at the time of Coleman's survey:

1. There is more racial and ethnic diversity, which leads to greater pluralism and fragmentation.
2. There are more oppositional cultures, like Goths, stoners, and so on. These oppositional cultures replicate dominant values (like coolness) while repudiating conventionality and conformity.
3. There is increased tension in schools than in the past.

Generally, schools today reflect the communities and community values in which they are embedded. Since society is more diverse, fragmented, and even conflict-laden today than it was two generations ago, students and student bodies are also more diverse, fragmented, and conflictual. Often, students from different socio-economic, religious, or ethnic backgrounds do not get along well with one another.

Teens who do focus on academic achievement face problems of their own. The increased parental (and societal) pressure on children, teenagers, and young adults to excel in school is beginning to take a toll. As mentioned earlier with data from the Toronto District School Board (2018), levels of stress and anxiety are high among high school and university students.

Strategies of Resistance

Access to formal education has improved significantly over the past 50 years, but, as we have seen throughout this chapter, we still have a long way to go until it is truly equitable. The following section explores a few strategies being used to ensure everybody has the chance to receive formal education.

Government-Level Strategies of Resistance

In the Northwest Territories, the territorial government is working to improve access and quality of education for Indigenous youth. To that end, they have been implementing the Indigenous Student Achievement Education Plan since 2011. This plan aims to close the gap in education between Indigenous students and other students in the Northwest Territories. It focuses on getting more Indigenous families involved in educating their youth and integrating Indigenous languages and culture into the education system. Finally, it hopes to have Indigenous youth meet the admission requirements for university or college education at the same rate as non-Indigenous students.

The initiative's four main focuses are on (1) early childhood development and care, (2) student and family support, (3) Indigenous language and culture curricula, and (4) resource development and literacy.

Organization-Level Strategies of Resistance

In 2011, a campaign named "Breaking Barriers: A Strategy for Equal Access to Education" was launched by three student groups in Ontario. The campaign showed how certain groups in society are often underrepresented in postsecondary education. These include low-income students, Indigenous students, first generation Canadians whose parents did not gain postsecondary education, rural and northern students, and students with dependents, such as a parent caring for a child. According to one of their policy papers, "because of the complex interaction and overlap between barriers to post-secondary education, a successful access strategy must simultaneously address different needs" (College Student Alliance et al. 2011). Thus, the campaign works to address multiple barriers to education at the same time. To that end, Breaking Barriers promotes the following initiatives:

- Early outreach programs to engage youth in learning about the importance of higher education

- Primary and secondary school outreach, such as equipping students with a "success team" and guidance counsellor
- Enrichment programs for at-risk students
- Bridging programs to help students who lack university and college prerequisite courses to transition to higher education

This approach works well—often much better than individual approaches to the problem. Their approach to student engagement shows the value of reaching out, from organization to organization, to share information, ideas, and resources.

Individual-Level Strategies of Resistance

Despite the importance and power of organizational or collective strategies, we should not ignore the contribution of individuals to the solution of school-related problems. All of us, as individuals, can take actions to make our little corner of the world better.

Consider the problem of bullying and what individuals can do about it. As noted above, schools can be a place of bullying and harassment for many LGBTQ+ youth. In response to a rash of teen suicides, sex-columnist Dan Savage created a YouTube video to inspire hope for LGBTQ+ youth who face harassment. The project has now become a worldwide movement, receiving approvals from celebrities and important figures such as Rick Mercer, Barack Obama, Hillary Clinton, and Ellen DeGeneres. Their website, ItGetsBetter.org, is a place where LGBTQ+ youth can come together and receive support from others who share their experience. In the hopes of ending the bullying of LGBTQ+ youth, the project published a book called *It Gets Better: Coming Out, Overcoming Bullying, and Creating a Life Worth Living* (Savage and Miller 2011). The book includes essays, personal stories, and recommendations on how to make the world a safer place for LGBTQ+ people.

Closing Remarks

Historically, people have argued that schooling outcomes reflect differences in personal abilities (the functionalist view). This perspective has encouraged the view that students who are low achievers will underperform and that underperforming schools are a "lost cause."

However, the evidence sociologists have collected suggests a different conclusion. Teachers, for example, can make a difference. While social and economic disadvantage hinder student performance, schools can make a measurable impact on the life chances of all students. Exceptional schools in disadvantaged areas can succeed in helping students against unequal odds. When schools and teaching practices become successful, we must learn how and why this has occurred. From this, we can spread educational successes throughout society, not just among dominant and wealthy groups.

The COVID-19 epidemic, by interrupting part-time and summer jobs, and other paid work, may have significantly delayed and disrupted the education plans of hundreds of thousands of Canadian post-secondary students.

As we have seen, the success of our schools—especially our publicly funded, public access schools, colleges, and universities—is critically important to our society. More education is better for society than less, and more equal access to education is not only fairer, but also produces a healthier, more prosperous society for all.

Notable Thinkers

Ross Finnie

Ross Finnie is an associate professor at the Graduate School of Public and International Affairs at the University of Ottawa. His research focuses on postsecondary education, namely access and barriers to postsecondary education. He also focuses on the experiences of underrepresented and minority groups and the outcomes of postsecondary education.

Finnie and Mueller (2009) have explored the relationship between access to postsecondary education and being a child of an immigrant in Canada. Their findings show that both first and second generation immigrants are more likely to attend a postsecondary institute than their non-immigrant counterparts. This difference is explained by demographic factors, the high education level of immigrant parents, and parents' hopes for their children. In another study, "Access and Barriers to Post-Secondary Education: Evidence from the YITS" (Finnie, Mueller, and Wismer 2012), parental education was correlated to an increased likelihood of attending university, decreased likelihood of attending college, and increased access rates to university. Those who did not attend a postsecondary institution cited that they did not have ambitions or faced barriers, namely financial, related to accessing postsecondary education.

Further, his research shows that certain groups run a greater risk of leaving a postsecondary institution. These are students from low-income families, single-parent households, rural backgrounds, and Indigenous Canadians. Students cited financial difficulties, the need to work, having low grades, or personal reasons for leaving.

Test Your Knowledge

1. Name three benefits of having an education.
2. How are parents "paying" for public primary and secondary education? And how does this disadvantage some more than others?
3. How does human capital support education?
4. How do demographic elements impact the likelihood of enrolling in university?
5. Why are boys and men lagging behind their female counterparts at the earliest levels of education?
6. Why are Indigenous Peoples in Canada less likely than their non-Indigenous counterparts to participate in postsecondary education?
7. Fill in the blank: Parents from ________________ families are less likely to be members of a parent–teacher association, attend parent–teacher meetings, attend school events, participate in fundraisers, and volunteer for a parent committee.

8. Fill in the blank: The most common reason older students do not return to school is because of ________________.
9. Fill in the blank: Immigrants face cultural, ________________ and financial barriers to education.
10. Fill in the blank: ________________ students often have lower grades, lower progress to postsecondary education, higher rates of skipping class because of safety concerns, higher rates of risky behaviour, and higher risk of depression.
11. Match the theoretical perspectives with its main points.

Theoretical Perspectives	Main Points
1. Structural functionalism	a. The student role requires someone to infer meanings and impressions from the verbal and non-verbal expressions of teachers.
2. Conflict theory	b. Certain groups are favoured over others and inequalities are perpetuated based on class, race, and gender in education systems. The quality of education is far from equal in Canada.
3. Symbolic interactionism	c. Focuses on the extent to which the school system produces and perpetuates social and economic disadvantages for girls and women.
4. Feminist theory	d. Schools are "great equalizers" that give everyone a fair and equal chance to succeed and help socialize children. Social problems related to education occur when schools fail to perform their manifest functions.

See the Answer Key online to check your answers.

Questions for Critical Thought

1. Have you experienced any barriers associated with accessing formal education? Do they relate to the barriers mentioned in this chapter?
2. Do you think the gendered shifts in education will change workplace inequality in the future? Explain why or why not.
3. Can you think of any other disadvantages associated with higher educational attainment?
4. Do you think increasing government funding for education is enough to knock down the barriers associated with education?
5. What are the manifest and latent (hidden or unintended) functions of education?

Additional Resources

Recommended Readings

Finnie, Ross, Richard Mueller, and Arthur Sweetman. 2008. *Who Goes? Who Stays? What Matters? Accessing and Persisting in Post-Secondary Education in Canada*. Kingston, ON: School of Policy Studies Queen's University. This book addresses the dynamics of choice, opportunity, and barriers in accessing postsecondary education. Furthermore, it explains why policy initiatives must extend beyond simply making school affordable.

Fisher, D., K. Rubenson, and T. Shanahan. 2014. *The Development of Post-Secondary Education Systems in Canada*. Montreal, QC: McGill-Queen's University Press. This book compares how different policies, influenced by public investment and economic development, have led to the divergent evolution of postsecondary education in British Columbia, Ontario, and Quebec.

Organisation for Economic Co-operation and Development. 2013. "Education at a Glance 2013" (http://dx.doi.org/10.1787/eag-2013-en). This online report, published by the OECD, provides a country-by-country comparison of different facets of education, including access to education, its quality, and its relevance to the workforce.

Stonechild, Blair. 2006. *The New Buffalo: The Struggle for Indigenous Post-Secondary Education in Canada*. Winnipeg, MB: University of Manitoba Press. This book examines the history of Indigenous postsecondary education, beginning from its time as a tool for assimilation and a means to control this population. This book incorporates firsthand knowledge from Indigenous Peoples to reveal the vast inequalities between Indigenous and non-Indigenous Canadians in education.

Widdowson, Frances and Albert Howard. 2013. *Approaches to Indigenous Education in Canada: Searching for Solutions*. Edmonton, AB: Brush Education. Widdowson and Howard present issues related to Indigenous education from two distinct perspectives to examine this complex and emotional problem from different angles.

Wotherspoon, Terry. 2017. *The Sociology of Education in Canada: Critical Perspectives*, 5th edn. Toronto, ON: Oxford University Press. This book provides an introduction to the sociology of education, providing information about relevant debates, issues, and theories. Wotherspoon examines education-related issues caused by gender, race, and globalization.

Recommended Websites

Academic Matters: The Journal of Higher Education

www.academicmatters.ca

Academic Matters is a magazine that publishes information related to higher education in Ontario, other provinces of Canada, and internationally. The magazine and its website is intended to be a thought-provoking forum for discussion on current events related to postsecondary education and the future of academia.

Canadian Federation of Students

https://cfs-fcee.ca/campaigns/fight-the-fees

This website provides information about the Canadian Federation of Students' efforts to fight for free or at least lower tuition fees in postsecondary institutions.

Council of Ministers of Education, Canada (CMEC)

www.cmec.ca/en

The CMEC is an intergovernmental body that represents provinces and territories and develops publications on education indicators. It also helps in producing education-related statistics and consults and acts on various issues related to all levels of education. The CMEC is currently involved in activities related to Indigenous education, literacy, and access to postsecondary education. This website provides an overview of their programs and initiatives as well as various relevant publications.

Ontario Undergraduate Student Alliance (OUSA)

www.ousa.ca

OUSA represents over 140,000 undergraduate and professional students in eight student associations across Ontario. Their goal is to make university accessible, affordable, and of high quality across Ontario through developing solutions, lobbying the government, and creating policy alternatives. This website offers information about OUSA, related research, and how to get involved.

Statistics Canada: "New Perspectives on Access to Postsecondary Education"

www.statcan.gc.ca/pub/81-004-x/2010001/article/11152-eng.htm

This website provides information related to the determinates of postsecondary participation, factors that impact access to postsecondary education, as well as factors that influence the likelihood of remaining in postsecondary education.

University Affairs

www.universityaffairs.ca

This website is a resource for and about Canada's university community. University Affairs publishes up-to-date information regarding several Canadian institutions while also providing practical tools to help jumpstart one's career in academia.

Recommended Films

Certain Proof: A Question of Worth. 2010. Directed by Ray Ellis and Susan Ellis. United States: Footpath Pictures. This award-winning documentary shows the experiences of three students with disabilities as they strive for integration in public schools.

Women Are the Answer. 2015. Directed by Fiona Cochrane. Spain. This award-winning feature-length documentary makes the connection between women, education, population growth, and the climate crisis.

Eric Buermeyer/Shutterstock

6 Access to Housing and Transportation

Learning Objectives

- To examine emerging housing trends in Canada.
- To identify barriers to accessing safe and healthy housing.
- To find out the social effects of unequal access to housing and transportation.
- To recognize barriers that impact access to transportation.
- To understand how access to housing and transportation are interconnected.
- To identify and evaluate strategies that equalize access to housing in Canada.

Introduction

Most animals have "nests" of some sort, and humans are no exception. What makes us unique among animals, however, are the many social benefits we gain from our housing. Housing is not only shelter but can influence our sense of dignity and belonging. The maintenance and decoration of a home gives us opportunities to be creative, useful, and expressive—to personalize our surroundings. Our homes also support healthy social interaction (try hosting a birthday party in a homeless shelter). Without a home, people have difficulty securing and keeping a job, gaining custody of their children after a marital breakup, or even achieving and staying in good health.

So a home is useful for what it keeps out: a roof to keep out the rain and a locking front door to keep out strangers. However, it is also useful for what it can contain. Most homes have a place to store and prepare food and furniture on which to seek quiet rest and recovery. But all of this comes at a price. Housing is typically the single largest expense borne by Canadian households. And while money and the lack of it is the most significant barrier to housing, there are other social factors that make it difficult for people to secure housing. In this chapter, we will explore unequal access to housing and transportation and how this inequality affects us all.

Theoretical Perspectives on Access to Housing and Transportation

Thinking about housing requires us to think about cities—those huge communities where most people in Canada set up a home and try to lead their lives in the company of strangers.

Functionalists are interested in how cities are useful or disadvantageous to society and how urbanization produces new types of social balance. The peculiar features of cities—growth, specialization, and disorganization, in particular—often bring social benefits but also social problems. Cities promote creativity, diversity, and individuality but can also create and aggravate crime, addiction, and mental illness.

Modern city life is different from the way most people lived in the past. Urbanization has changed how people connect with one another. Pre-industrial communities were mainly small, rural settlements in which members shared a **common (or collective) conscience** and **mechanical solidarity**. Émile Durkheim ([1893] 2014) coined these terms to describe the sense of community that arose from common values, norms, and identity. In urban–industrial societies, social bonds are preserved by what Durkheim referred to as **organic solidarity**. This solidarity emerges from the division of labour. We are no longer self-sufficient; rather, we depend on one another for survival and prosperity. So while relations are less intimate in cities than in rural societies, social bonds still exist thanks to the interconnectedness between individuals. (For a more detailed discussion of these concepts, see the *Oxford Dictionary of Sociology* [Scott 2014].)

common (collective) conscience A shared state of mind, including common values, in a small stable community.

mechanical solidarity Social integration or cohesion that is rooted in a common conscience.

organic solidarity Social integration or cohesion that is rooted in a recognition and appreciation of difference and interdependence.

From the functionalist standpoint, housing and transportation issues are "growth pains" in the gradual evolution of a perfect social form: the modern city. The existence of housing issues in cities is merely a sign of the normal workings of a competitive market in real estate. Because our society is organized around a market economy, people with less money and social capital have a more difficult time buying the houses they want in the neighbourhoods they want.

At the same time, functionalists regard the lack of housing as a social problem. The modern city, as a perfect social form, should have little social problems. So functionalists would see the need to help disadvantaged people by, for example, increasing public housing and public transit through taxation. They would support these programs to solve social problems, increase social cohesion, and prevent crime and disorder.

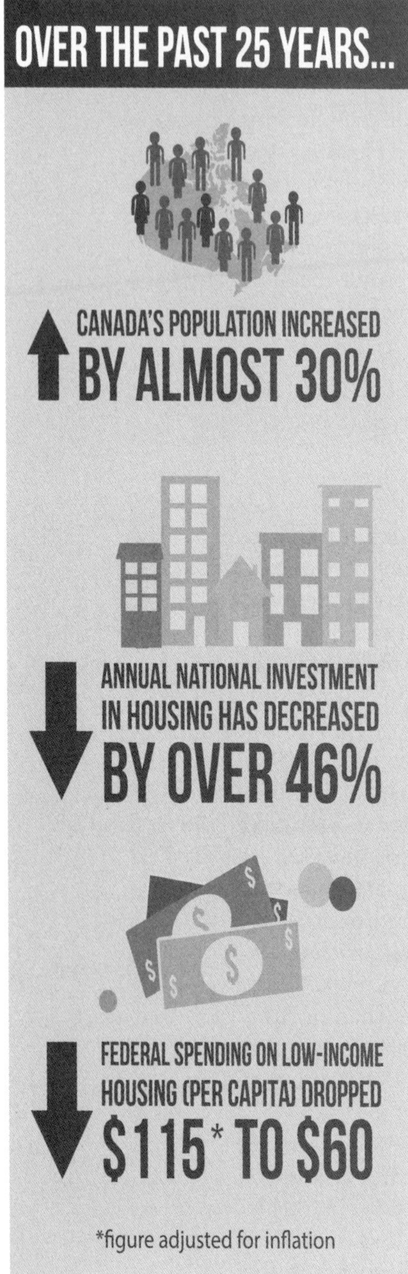

OVER THE PAST 25 YEARS...
CANADA'S POPULATION INCREASED
BY ALMOST 30%
ANNUAL NATIONAL INVESTMENT
IN HOUSING HAS DECREASED
BY OVER 46%
FEDERAL SPENDING ON LOW-INCOME
HOUSING (PER CAPITA) DROPPED
$115* TO $60
*figure adjusted for inflation

Figure 6.1 ◆ The State of Homelessness in Canada, 2014

Adequate housing for all could take years to achieve. Projects funded in 2014 could be housing underhoused people *today*.

Source: Gaetz, Gulliver, and Richter 2014.

Unlike functionalists, *conflict theorists* are interested in the role of power and influence in how urban environments are composed. They would credit urban problems such as homelessness, poor housing, and faulty transportation not to universal effects of city size, variety, and fluidity, but to the specific workings of capitalism. From this perspective, capitalist cities suffer urban problems because no powerful group cares enough to prevent them. And unlike functionalists, conflict theorists believe that solving urban problems needs more than housing—as important as this may be. They argue the ideal way to minimize and solve urban problems is not by dealing with the disorganization in cities, but rather by dealing with problems of inequality.

It is the unequal distribution of wealth and power in cities (that is, economic inequality) that creates most of its problems, argue conflict theorists. It controls whether city-dwellers will live or die, stay or leave. In many cities (especially in the United States), well-off residents have fled the inner city to distant suburbs, suggesting a lack of interest in solving the urban problems facing poor people. In other cities of the world, well-off residents may isolate themselves in gated compounds or homes protected by walls and electronic security. In the cities of societies with better social welfare legislation like Sweden, well-off residents are less likely to flee the downtown core or barricade themselves in gated communities. They feel confident that low-income residents are being adequately helped by social housing and welfare programs and are therefore less likely to cause them problems.

The problem facing poor people in Canadian cities is a lack of public investment in housing and public transportation (Figure 6.1). Instead, investments are made in the development of roads, not public transit. The interests of the wealthier are also represented in biased practices in the zoning of land use. Decisions about the location of new roads and subway lines, new major business complexes, or condominium developments protect their interests.

Finally, *symbolic interactionists* study how people experience and adapt to city life. Georg Simmel (Simmel and Wolff 1950), one of the earliest writers to take this approach, argued that cities are often too stimulating and quick paced. To prevent sensory overload, inhabitants reduce their sensitivity to events and people around them, detaching themselves from each other and social interactions.

However, symbolic interactionists doubt that everyone has this experience. Herbert Gans (1982), among others, focuses on how the meaning of city life varies among groups and communities. People in different neighbourhoods have different city experiences, because they take part in different subcultures. A subculture will share some cultural traits of the larger society but will, as a group, have its own distinctive values, beliefs, norms, style of dress, and behaviour. Subcultures rest on the kind of shared values—the kind of collective conscience—that Durkheim associated with "mechanical solidarity."

Urban subcultures allow people in an impersonal city to form connections with others—often with neighbours who are share economic, ethnic, linguistic, or other similarities. An ethnic urban community is one common example of a subculture; youth gangs are another kind. For obvious reasons, housing and transportation opportunities are important influences on the creation and survival of urban subcultures. Symbolic interactionists, unlike conflict theorists, are not so much interested in explaining how these different districts come into being. They are more interested in describing the urban experience in these different districts and the populations these subcultural districts serve.

Affordable Housing and Homelessness

One of the most dramatic urban experiences imaginable is homelessness, and every major city has an area where the homeless are most likely to gather. In Canada, any "individual or family without stable, permanent, suitable housing or the immediate prospect, means and ability of acquiring it" is considered homeless (Gaetz et al. 2014). The risk of becoming homeless is not limited to a certain population; homelessness is periodic, widespread, and transitional for many Canadians.

There are four categories of homelessness. First, at one extreme end is what we might call the *unsheltered*—those people living on the street. Second, some homeless people can secure occasional shelter in buildings designed to house them; this group is known as *emergency sheltered.* However, because of overcrowding, they are never able to settle in but must move from one shelter to the next, sleeping wherever they can find space. A third group of homeless people is *provisionally sheltered.* These individuals stay as long as they can with friends or relatives, or live in institutions such as hospitals or prisons, but lack a permanent home of their own. A fourth group consists of people at risk of becoming members of the absolute homeless. Also known as being *at risk of homelessness,* these people experience unstable housing conditions and, as a result, health and safety concerns.

Climate change is also affecting these categories. Because of climate change, Canadians are experiencing extreme weather events more often. In Central and Eastern Canada these have often taken the form of flooding, and in Western Canada, wildfires. In 2016, a wildfire destroyed many homes in Fort McMurray, displacing over 80,000 people—many of whom were rendered homeless when their homes were destroyed. While some evacuees secured new housing, others did not.

Many people slip in and out of these different states of homelessness. Some are chronically homeless (street affiliated for a long duration), some are episodically homeless (long series of on-and-off homelessness), and some are transitionally homeless (shorter-term homelessness). As a result, it is difficult to count the total number of homeless people in Canada. Most homeless counts are based on the number of people in shelters on a given night and do not consider the provisionally sheltered or at-risk population (Richter et al. 2011). This means a large fraction of our homeless population remains uncounted and "hidden."

Bearing such complications in mind, the Homeless Hub (2016), Canada's most authoritative source of information on the homeless, estimates that at least 235,000 Canadians experience homelessness in a given year, and over 35,000 on a given night. The actual number is potentially much higher, given that many people who are unhoused live with friends or relatives and do not come into contact with emergency shelters. An up-to-date assessment of youth homelessness in Canada is provided in the October 2019 edition of *Parity*, a journal published by the Council to Homeless Persons in Melbourne, Australia. This journal issue is guest edited by Stephen Gaetz (York University), an international expert on youth homelessness (see Council to Homeless Persons 2019). Of special interest to our readers, it contains a fascinating article by Eric Weissman (University of New Brunswick), Jeannette Waegemakers-Schiff (University of Calgary), and Rebecca Schiff (Lakehead University) on the causes, extent, and consequences of postsecondary student homelessness in Canada (Weissman et al. 2019). Youth homelessness is especially interesting because of its connection to family problems and domestic violence. Many youth end up on the street because, no matter how bad life on the streets may be, for some it's better than living at home.

Taking homeless people as a whole, one-third report they became homeless because they could no longer afford their rent (Aubry et al. 2012). So the homelessness crisis in Canada can be traced back to cuts to affordable and social housing projects that began in the 1990s. During this time, few new subsidized housing units were built and many existing ones were sold to private owners. Often, previously affordable rental units were converted into more expensive condominiums (Jones et al. 2012; Richter et al. 2011). At the same time, federal income support programs lost some if not all of their funding (Leo and August 2006).

Because social (as opposed to individual) factors have driven up homeless rates, the homeless population is far from demographically homogenous (Richter et al. 2011). Single males between the ages of 25 and 55 are the most numerous, making up 47.5 per cent of the identified homeless population. Young people account for an increasing fraction of the homeless at 20 per cent. First Nations, Métis, and Inuit people are heavily overrepresented among the homeless (Gaetz et al. 2014), and newly arrived immigrants also make up a large fraction at 23 per cent. The most vulnerable of the homeless—those who suffer the most—include the young, women, the mentally ill, families, single parents, minorities, and seniors.

The mainstream media fail to capture this population's diversity, portraying the homeless as a homogeneous group composed only of drug and alcohol addicts and the mentally ill. For example, one study examined the representation of homelessness in four Canadian newspapers. It found a unified narrative where readers are urged to be sympathetic toward the struggles faced by homeless individuals (Schneider, Chamberlain, and Hodgetts 2010). However, homeless individuals were also depicted as needing to be controlled and regulated to preserve social order, which affects their inclusion within society.

It is true that some homeless people suffer from diagnoses that range from schizophrenia to more manageable affective or mood disorders, just like the rest of the population (Roos et al. 2013). As well, some do indeed have addiction problems. Mental illness and addiction do not, however, necessarily cause homelessness, nor do they necessarily prevent a person from escaping it. The main cause and obstacle to exiting homelessness is poverty (Aubry et al. 2012). For example, in an analysis of the Toronto housing market, the

Canadian Centre for Economic Analysis and the Canadian Urban Institute (2019) found most homeless individuals report unaffordable rent or eviction as the reason they are on the streets. In the end, most homelessness is caused by broad social structures rather than by personal variables like addiction and mental illness.

Efforts to reduce homelessness are well intentioned but usually underfunded. Consider the National Homelessness Initiative, introduced in 1999, and renamed the Homelessness Partnering Strategy in 2007. Local governments and community organizations were granted $135 million a year to address the homelessness problem. Different cities used their funding in different ways, with varying success. In Vancouver, government officials and community actors worked together to set goals and divide funding. Their Community Advisory Board—a panel of experts on homelessness in the city—came to be widely recognized as fair, inclusive, and transparent (Doberstein 2012). Perhaps as a result, Vancouver has seen a 68 per cent drop in unsheltered people since the program's implementation (Gaetz et al. 2014).

Besides a city's choice of strategy, poor success of the Homeless Partnering Strategy can also be credited to the federal government. Often the federal government steps in to fund programs that solve national problems but are beyond the budget capacities of particular cities or provinces. In 2019, the Government of Canada released its National Housing Strategy, a "10-year, $55 billion+ plan that will create 100,000 new housing units and remove 530,000 families from housing need, as well as repair and renew more than 300,000 community housing units and reduce chronic homelessness by 50 percent" (CMHC 2019). In this way, the National Housing Strategy will give more Canadians a place to call home. It will prioritize the vulnerable Canadians we discuss in this book: women and children fleeing family violence, Indigenous Peoples, seniors, people with disabilities, those dealing with mental health and addiction issues, veterans, and young adults, among others.

Municipalities have been quick to applaud this strategy. Federation of Canadian Municipalities President Jenny Gerbasi was quick to highlight what the mayors liked:

> The federal government took our advice to focus on the fundamentals. Replacing expiring social housing rent subsidies is a breakthrough for thousands of families who fear losing their homes as long-term operating agreements wind down. Investing to repair and renew that social housing will keep more people in their homes and help secure tomorrow's supply. And getting back to investing in affordable housing construction is the breakthrough we needed to start tackling the supply crunch. (quoted in Gossage 2018)

So Canada's towns and cities are onboard with this new initiative. But there's a lot more to be done, including lots of research on preventative solutions. The National Housing Strategy, in hopes of reducing chronic homelessness by 50 per cent, will help local communities fund and deliver a variety of housing measures. These measures will draw on the lived experience of people who have been homeless. Besides support for practical interventions, it will encourage researchers to find ways of stemming the flow of people into homelessness. In particular, it will stimulate what it calls "evidence-based housing"—that is, housing interventions based on research, data, and demonstration projects. All of this, and more, will be part of a $241-million National Housing Strategy Research Agenda.

While affordable housing projects provide a lasting solution, such programs only help the already homeless to cope. They do not protect lower-income people from falling into poverty

We're #BuildingCanada and investing to reduce homelessness, improve housing for Indigenous peoples, and make sure every Canadian has a place to call home – now and for generations to come.

In 2017 the Liberal government launched the National Housing Strategy, which, if successful, will ensure that all Canadians have access to stable, safe, and healthy housing in the foreseeable future. It will do this through a variety of means that include research and institutional lending.

and homelessness or develop plans to prevent this. The National Housing Strategy promises a new approach to this problem—a way of ensuring that the housing needs and concerns of vulnerable Canadians are kept in the forefront. It does this through a type of planning they call GBA+, meaning gender-based analysis (and more). Developed by Status of Women Canada, the GBA+ provides a step-by-step process that starts by identifying the housing needs of vulnerable populations in particular.

Too often in the past people have been blamed for their own problems. For example, homeless people have often been said to deserve their fate (Belcher and Deforge 2012). The individuals who promote this view rationalize their own privilege by claiming that their hard work justifies their wealth (Robertson and Williamson 2012). Millionaire Steve Siebold supports this perspective, writing: "While the masses are waiting to pick the right numbers and praying for prosperity, the great ones are solving problems." Such reasoning allows the well off to view class inequality as an acceptable result of a meritocratic society, writing off political action that tries to reduce inequality as unnecessary and wasteful (Hollis 2004; Wachocki 2014).

This focus on individual, personal failings is often criticized for victim blaming. Victim blaming has two effects in this case. According to Gerald and Patricia Gurin (1970), who developed *expectancy theory*, victim blaming reduces expectations among the disadvantaged. So when the advantaged blame the poor for their conditions, they internalize that blame, lose hope, and begin to think that their conditions are inescapable.

Second, victim blaming diverts attention from systemic inequalities (Wright 2005). By focusing on individual behaviours, we fixate on symptoms of the illness rather than its root cause (Hollis 2004). However, such a systemic perspective is discouraged in competitive societies like ours (Carr and MacLachlan 1998; Robertson and Williamson 2012). This is partly because the changes in policy that could potentially address systemic disadvantages also threaten the status of society's most privileged.

Emerging Trends in Housing

gentrification When property in old downtown areas are bought by businesses and middle-class homeowners and upgraded to better condition and attractiveness, pushing out long-time residents who are often low-income people.

Many North American neighbourhoods are undergoing or have already undergone **gentrification**, meaning that businesses and middle-class homeowners are moving into old downtown areas. This is the reverse of what happened in the middle of the twentieth century, when middle-class people left cities for the safety of suburbia. The gentrification of older areas can drive up housing prices and drive out poorer residents who cannot afford the new prices.

Another trend impacting housing costs is the introduction of increasingly popular home-sharing platforms like Airbnb. Landlords see the opportunity to make more money with potentially less hassle and more flexibility by renting to a series of temporary guests instead of full-time tenants. This creates a market where the demand for full-time housing far exceeds the supply, driving up prices. Corporate asset management or private equity firms also get into this game, buying up entire multi-residential buildings or city blocks and turning them into "ghost buildings" occupied by rotating tourists.

So some cities have explored ways to limit homeowners' ability to rent on Airbnb, with varying degrees of success. Some homeowners have undertaken a massive expensive renovation of their basement to make it Airbnb ready. Others who have taken on huge mortgages in an overheated market are now relying on that extra income and are resistant to settling for the lower rents of full-time tenants. This debate about Airbnb shows yet another way the free market makes some people (the owners of Airbnb properties) wealthy at the expense of many other people (the owners of nearby homes). This is a pattern that conflict theorists consistently point out.

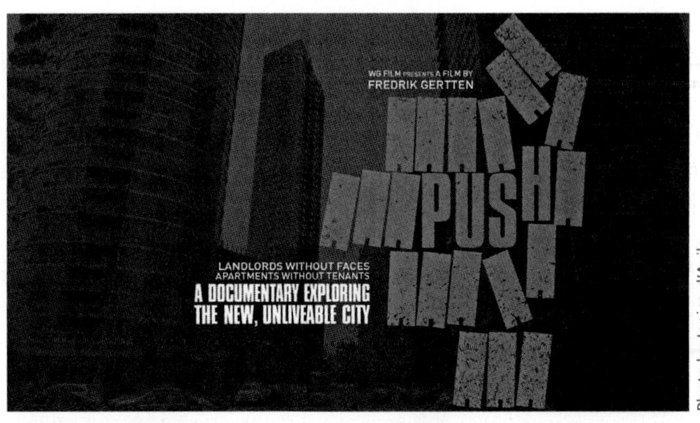

Photo by Janice d'Avila

The documentary *PUSH* (2019) explores the way that private equity firms like Blackstone or Starlight invest in private asset firms that buy up low-income housing and subsequently evict pension-holders.

Another trend affecting housing in Canadian cities is **ghettoization**—a pattern evident in the United States for over a century. This is the tendency for certain neighbourhoods to be settled mainly by people of one particular class (often poor) and ethnicity (often racialized). This term comes from the word *ghetto*, which describes the gated Jewish quarter in medieval Italian cities where Jews were forced to live and were locked in every night when the sun went down. This history reminds us that some people are forced to live in certain neighbourhoods based on their economic need. Figure 6.2 illustrates how Vancouver is experiencing a process of ghettoization in some of its neighbourhoods.

ghettoization Occurs when certain neighbourhoods are settled mainly by people of one particular class, race, or ethnic group.

In many North American and European cities, efforts have been made to fight both gentrification and ghettoization. These efforts include the development of not-for-profit public housing that are owned, regulated, and preserved by the city or province. This provides housing for people with limited incomes and has often provided an effective alternative to slum housing or even homelessness. Among the various types of not-for-profit housing are co-op housing, which places management and ownership in the hands of the residents.

Another housing trend has to do with homeownership, which has declined in recent years. In Canada, there are typically three ways to secure housing: Either you buy a place to live, you rent a place to live, or someone else, like a parent or other benefactor, buys or rents the place you are living in. (There are a few exceptions—like prisoners—who don't fit into any of these three categories.)

The first way is the most common; over two-thirds of Canadian households own a home (Statistics Canada 2017). Housing buys rose between the 1970s to the early 2000s and then levelled off. However, 30-year-old millennials today have lower homeownership rates than previous generations did at their same age. Today's 30 year olds are also more likely to live in apartments—that is, if they aren't living with their parents well into their late twenties, as one-third of millennials do. Six out of 10 Canadians who have mortgages are financially overextended. And we are increasingly living with this stress all

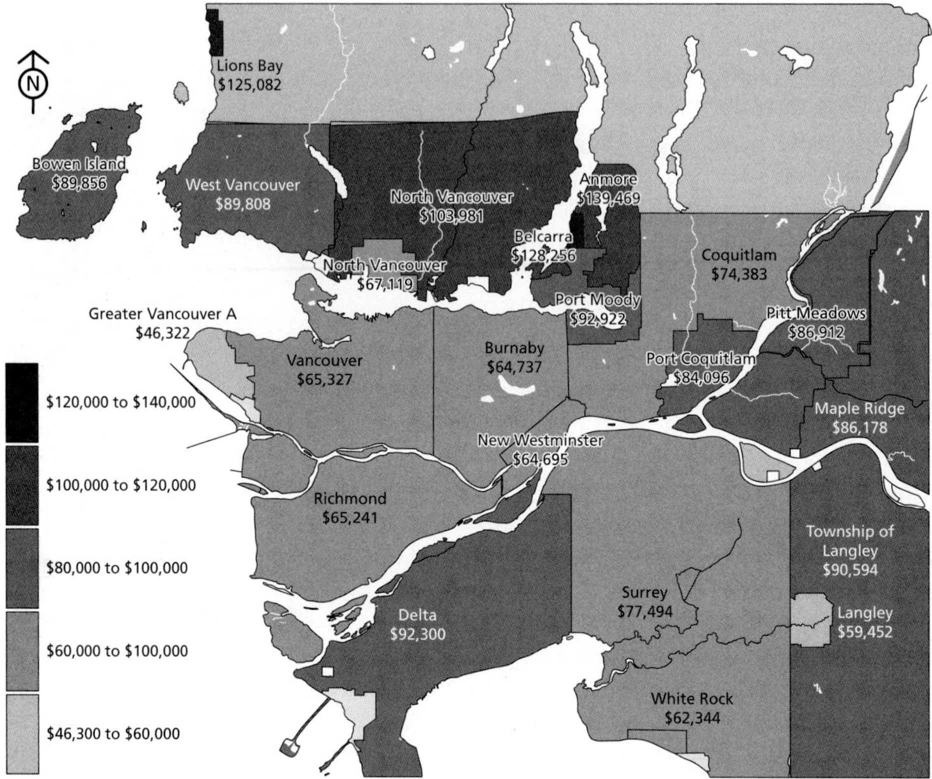

Figure 6.2 ◆ Household Income by Neighbourhood in Vancouver, 2016

This figure shows the various neighbourhoods in Vancouver, organized by income. This map demonstrates ghettoization: The tendency for the people of similar incomes to live in the same neighbourhood.

Source: Kelley 2017. Copyright 2020 City of Vancouver and reproduced with the permission of the City.

by ourselves—more Canadians are living alone than ever before. In that sense, we have been spreading themselves over more housing units and bearing the cost of those units independently.

discrimination The unjust or prejudicial treatment of different categories of people, especially on the grounds of race, age, sex, or sexual orientation.

Some barriers prevent people from securing safe, satisfactory, and reliable housing. One powerful barrier, especially in the rental market, is **discrimination**. The Oxford dictionary defines discrimination as "the unjust or prejudicial treatment of different categories of people, especially on the grounds of race, age, or sex." At the root of discrimination are beliefs related to the social value of individuals or groups of people and their right to needed resources.

So with housing, as with jobs, some "kinds" of people enjoy advantages while other "kinds" of people suffer disadvantages. They are disadvantaged simply because of their sex, age, class, race, ethnicity, religion, or sexual orientation. Note that all of these barriers are what sociologists call "ascribed" characteristics—unchangeable characteristics no one chose and for which one is not to blame. Nonetheless, these characteristics have important effects for the housing of many Canadians.

Steve Russell/Toronto Star via Getty Images

A group of residents of a licensed rooming house in Parkdale, a mixed-income, gentrifying neighbourhood in Toronto, saved their home from being sold on the open market. They teamed up with Neighbourhood Land Trust, a local charity, and secured funding from the city to purchase the property and remain in their low-income housing.

Housing discrimination is only one form of discrimination. Typically, it occurs in rental housing arrangements when a potential tenant is unfairly denied an opportunity to rent an accommodation. It may also occur when a tenant already living in the rental unit is treated differently than other tenants.

housing discrimination Any practice or policy that systemically causes harm through inequitable access to housing based on prejudiced or biased assumptions about would-be residents.

To be treated differently does not necessarily mean to be treated unfairly—sometimes it's fair to treat someone differently. For example, a person who uses a wheelchair may need a ramp to access their front door. It would be fair to install one for them and not for someone who doesn't need one.

However, sometimes treating everyone the same way is unfair. Some landlords want all potential tenants to agree to a check of their credit score (a number that reflects a person's ability to repay loans on time). Such a check may look like a neutral requirement. However, it discriminates against some populations that may not have a credit history. For example, it discriminates against young people who are only recently financially independent from their parents or people whose ex-spouses were the household borrower.

Housing discrimination is "officially" recognized as a problem, and all provinces and territories contain in their Human Rights Code specific prohibitions against it. Some banned grounds of discrimination include citizenship, disability, age, sexual orientation, race, and religion. Most provinces' and territories' human rights codes also clearly forbid housing discrimination against family status (in other words, if a potential tenant has children, lives alone, has no children, and so on) and income source (if a potential tenant is collecting an income from social assistance, for example).

IN FOCUS ◆ Housing Discrimination

"Housing discrimination consists of any behaviour, practice, or policy within the public or market realm that directly, indirectly, or systemically causes harm through inequitable access to, or use and enjoyment of, housing for members of social groups that have been historically disadvantaged" (Novac et al. 2002)

For more on this topic, watch a short animated introduction to housing discrimination produced by the Centre for Equality Rights in Accommodation: http://vimeo.com/31499918.

In some provinces, grounds of housing discrimination do not apply if a tenant shares a bathroom or kitchen with their landlord. In Ontario and Saskatchewan, for example, a landlord who shares these spaces with a tenant may legally discriminate against a potential tenant because of, say, their sexual orientation.

Discrimination does not need to be intentional to be considered discriminatory. Sometimes a landlord may even be "acting in good faith" and still be discriminatory. For example, imagine if a landlord were to refuse tenancy to a family because the backyard wasn't thought large enough for the family's children to play and have fun in. Doing that would be discrimination because of family status.

Rental housing discrimination is not the only barrier to housing in Canada. People may face discrimination while applying for a mortgage, when applying for insurance coverage, or when they are subject to discriminatory land-use planning. Proposals for new housing developments, for example, are sometimes subject to resistance from local residents. This resistance may stem from legitimate concerns such as loss of green space, environmental impact, or worries about noise levels. However, sometimes resistance grows out of discriminatory beliefs about the new residents that are likely to move into the new development.

Low-Income People in Canada

Low-income Canadians face barriers, including prejudice and stigmatization, when trying to secure safe, satisfactory housing. In this section, we will see a few ways that these barriers contribute to what is commonly referred to as the **cycle of poverty (or deprivation)**. These are the factors or events by which poverty, once started, is likely to continue unless there is outside intervention.

cycle of poverty (or deprivation) The set of factors or events by which poverty, once started, is likely to continue unless there is outside intervention.

Many people cannot afford to buy a house outright, since doing so requires a large lump of money. Those who can, however, will pay less each year on their housing than even those who can't afford a mortgage! Consider this: If you own a house without a mortgage, you pay, on average, about $4,000 per year. You will use this money to pay taxes, insurance, and so on and to improve or repair your investment, which normally increases in value every year.

If you rent, on the other hand, you pay on average three times that much: $12,000 (Statistics Canada 2017). Your rental payments are not investments; your money is gone forever, into the pockets of a landlord. What does this mean? It means those who are already ahead preserve their lead. It means that renters spend more of their income on housing, leaving less for other costs of living and less for saving or investment. Homeowners see their investments hold or gain value. Renters don't, and to make things worse, their costs often rise and their income doesn't keep pace. While homeowners can enjoy watching their net value increase, renters are often caught in a discouraging downward spiral. It's like playing a rigged game that you're bound to lose; in other words, it's a cycle of poverty.

Many low-income Canadians are low income because of employment issues: Either they are unemployed, precariously employed, or are earning only minimum wage. You could understand, then, why an unemployed, low-income person might consider moving to a region where there are many jobs. Unfortunately, few can afford to! Studies have found that housing regions that offer more job opportunities also have higher housing and rental prices. For example, a report by CBRE Group (2019) showed that Toronto, a city with one of Canada's biggest job markets, also has the world's twelfth-most-expensive housing market.

Stable housing has historically been associated with better employment results. Studies have shown that women, for example, typically "set down roots" in stable housing and build important social networks. These networks can help them access the workforce, increase self-confidence, and build self-esteem (CMHC 2009). Settling down in one place also makes sense job wise. But low-income tenants are most vulnerable to displacement for reasons outside of their control, such as rent increases, pests, flooding, and so on. So housing stability contributes to employment, and low-income Canadians often seek employment . . . but can't afford the stable housing. The cycle of poverty strikes again.

Homeownership has been positively correlated with higher educational attainment for children because it is positively correlated with higher-than-average income (CMHC 2009). You may also notice another "cycle" here: a **cycle of opportunity**. Consider this: Homeowners' children typically achieve higher levels of education. Higher levels of education contribute to higher incomes. Higher incomes ensure that those children get to buy their own homes one day. And so the cycle continues. Housing, on its own, "is not the root cause of advantage and disadvantage; rather, it is only one element in a set of interrelated factors that determine the outcome" (CMHC 2009).

cycle of opportunity The set of factors or events by which advantage, once started, is likely to continue unless there is outside intervention.

There is often a scarcity of rental units in rural areas. This is partly because housing is harder to build. Empty plots of land or multi-unit homes typically need expensive water, electrical, and sewer installation or upgrades. (You'll learn more about infrastructural issues in rural, northern Indigenous communities later in this chapter.) When there is a scarcity, the competition for rental units increases and can drive up prices relative to local incomes. That's why one of the main barriers to housing reported by rural, low-income Canadians is affordability (Waegemakers-Schiff et al. 2015).

As well as being expensive for local residents, rural housing also tends to be a lot older than urban housing and is more likely to need major repairs. We find yet another contributor to the cycle of poverty: Low-income Canadians can only afford rental homes that cost more to run. They spend so much on repairs that they can't save for a down payment on a house of their own. So the question is: Who can afford to be poor?

Many low-income Canadians receive social assistance like welfare, employment insurance, or disability payments. There is a social stigma associated with these kinds of income sources or low-income status—a stigma so pronounced that it can interfere with access to housing. Novac and colleagues (2002) write, "perceived causes of poverty are frequently based on moral explanations, such as lack of responsibility, that blame poor people for their own misfortune and ignore structural explanation, such as structural unemployment . . . Systemic

IN FOCUS ◆ Housing Discrimination Based on Income Source

Olivia is a 39-year-old woman who lives in Hamilton. She has a physical disability and cannot work. As a result, she receives Ontario Disability Support Program (ODSP) benefits. Olivia saw an advertisement for a basement bachelor apartment with a monthly rent of $500. She felt she could afford this and made an appointment to see the apartment. When she saw the place, she liked it and asked for an application. The landlord asked what Olivia did for a living. Olivia replied that she is on ODSP. The landlord said he "doesn't rent to those kinds of people." When asked why, the landlord replied, "those kinds of people trash the apartments and are bad tenants."

Source: CERA 2011.

issues of credit-worthiness assessment, deposit requirements, and co-signer requirements often pose barriers to housing access for people living in poverty."

However, Canadian human rights law forbids housing discrimination based on income source. In other words, a landlord cannot legally deny someone a rental opportunity or treat a tenant differently just because their income comes from a form of social assistance. Quebec, New Brunswick, and the Northwest Territories go a little further in their human rights laws. These provinces and territory forbid housing discrimination based on "social condition," which includes not only income source but also education level and occupation. People cannot be denied housing just because the landlord disapproves of the work they do or the fact they haven't finished secondary school (CERA 2008).

Young People in Canada

Most Canadians live with their parents or guardians until the age of 18 or so. Feeling financially insecure, many young adults choose to continue living with their parents. In 2011, fully 42 per cent of young people between the ages of 20 and 29 lived in their parents' homes (Milan 2016). The number of young adults living with parents has increased dramatically in the 30 years between 1981 and 2011, as we see in Figure 6.3.

Recent data from the 2016 Census of Canada (Statistics Canada 2017) reveals the following:

- More than one in three (34.7 per cent) young adults aged 20 to 34 were living with at least one parent in 2016, a share that has been increasing since 2001 (indeed, since 1981, as mentioned earlier).
- Over the same period, the share of all young adults living with their own family decreased from about one-half, or 49.1 per cent in 2001, to 41.9 per cent in 2016.
- More than two in five (42.1 per cent) young adults in Ontario were living with their parents, by far the largest share observed in the provinces and territories. This proportion has increased by 20.3 per cent since 2001.

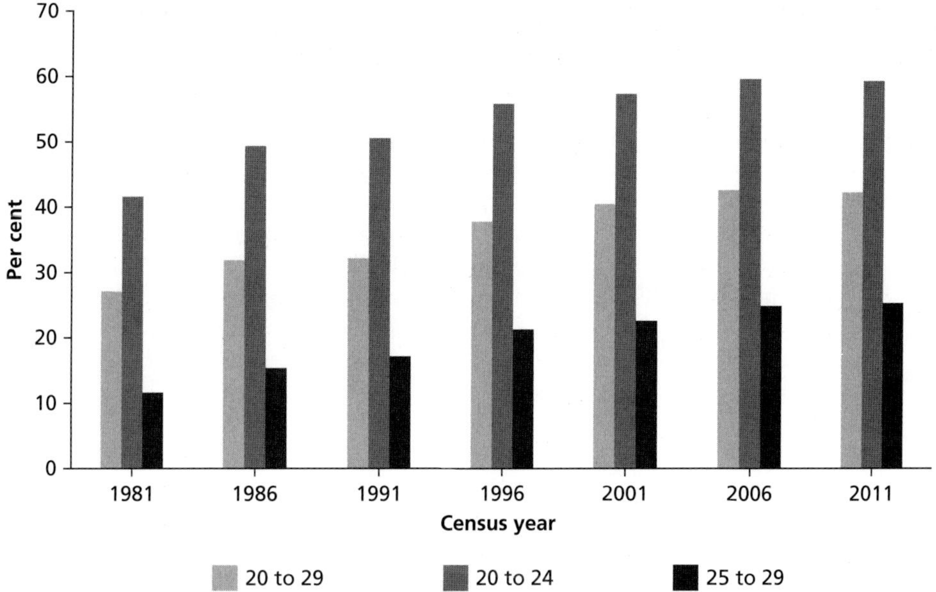

Figure 6.3 ◆ Proportion of Canadians Aged 20 to 29 Living with Their Parents

Source: Statistics Canada 2016.

Among the 35 Census Metropolitan Areas in the country, Toronto (47.4 per cent) and Oshawa (47.2 per cent) had the largest shares of young adults living with their parents—almost one in two young adults. One reason young people continue to live at home is the cost of rent versus income. Teenagers, especially those who wish to remain in school, don't typically make a lot of money—some don't earn any at all. Without support from their parents, it can be difficult for them to afford their own home.

To make matters worse, teenagers are often not eligible for many income support programs. Often they lack the savings they would need to cover living expenses on their own as they attend school. There is no minimum age requirement for the federally managed employment insurance, but young people would likely have to sacrifice school to work the hours needed to qualify.

The beliefs of potential landlords—beliefs about young people's reliability and responsibility—form another barrier. Landlords may worry that younger tenants will be noisy, will not pay rent, or will damage the property. Many landlords want a young person to provide a *guarantor*: Someone who pledges to cover the rent should the young person be unable or unwilling to pay it. Typically, landlords insist the guarantor live in the same building. If the guarantor lives elsewhere, landlords may be less willing to accept the tenant. The reason is "probably because of the extra cost or nuisance for landlords who may have to contact or pursue the guarantor for payment in situations of default" (Novac et al. 2002).

In most provinces, some forms of housing discrimination based on age are allowed. For example, in Ontario landlords are legally entitled to discriminate against people under the age of 16. It is not obvious why some Canadian provinces or towns allow discrimination

◆ In Their Own Words ◆

Lindsay and her daughter spent months without proper housing, steadily losing hope as the rejections piled up. "I had to sleep on couches. My daughter had to stay with my parents. I had to settle for slumlords, places that smelled like rat piss," she said. Widespread prejudice against single mothers had further complicated the situation, she said, with landlords asking prying questions, lecturing her, and questioning her parenting ability and why she was not looking for a larger unit for herself and her daughter.

Source: Pflug-Back 2016.

against young people when they don't allow discrimination based on sex, race, or ethnicity. This just goes to show that in Canada there can be great regional variations in culture, economy, and legislation where people's rights and opportunities are concerned. Symbolic interactionists are especially interested in these variations and the difficulties they cause for federal co-operation. They are especially interested in understanding the difficulties people encounter when they try to make sense of one another's concerns.

Feminists, for their part, recognize the entwined, interlocking disadvantages of youth plus gender when it comes to homelessness. Paradis, Wilson, and Logan (2014), for example, remind us that "a gendered understanding of homelessness takes into account the effects of inadequate housing on children, and the difficulties lone-parent mothers face in securing housing that is safe, affordable, and appropriate for themselves and their children" (3).

Youth homelessness continues to rise rapidly, with roughly 20 per cent of Canadian youth between the ages of 13 and 24 experiencing homelessness (Gaetz et al. 2016). As a result, on any given night at least 6,000 youth are homeless. On average, when youth become homeless, they have already experienced stressful events in their short lives. These events

IN FOCUS ◆ Housing Discrimination Based on Age

Ashley, a 17-year-old woman, left her parents' home because it was unstable. She applied for a bachelor apartment that rented at $625 per month. Ashley and her worker from the Children's Aid Society (CAS) went to see the apartment. The superintendent asked Ashley's age, and when told that she was 17 years old he said he could not rent to anyone under 18. He said he had once rented to students and they were "too loud." Ashley and her CAS worker successfully filed a human rights complaint with the Human Rights Tribunal of Ontario. Today, 16 and 17 year olds are legally entitled to rent an apartment in Ontario.

Source: CERA 2011.

can include abuse, assault, neglect, bullying, or trouble with the law, any combination of which might drive them to flee home. After becoming homeless, youth experience an average of 6.4 more stressful events. This lasting trauma makes them more likely to experience long-term homelessness (Roos et al. 2013).

Research confirms that most homeless young people—as many as 70 per cent in some areas of Canada—do not currently attend school (Klodawsky et al. 2006). However, this is usually a result rather than a cause of homelessness. Many homeless youth *want* to return to school and are eager to put their existing work experience to use. However, because of a lack of funding, most shelters and programs can only provide a fraction of homeless youth with temporary food and shelter. With finding their next meal or bed their top concern, most homeless young people report being forced to set aside academic and career ambitions. Usually they are unemployed school dropouts because they are homeless, not because they have no goals or motivation. Once again, structural inequalities (such as poverty) provide a more convincing explanation of homelessness than individual choice or characteristics.

Women in Canada

When women look for satisfactory and affordable housing, they often face various overlapping issues. As we have seen in previous chapters, women experience varying degrees of sex-based discrimination in the workplace. This contributes to a lower average income than men and makes them more vulnerable to poverty. And as we have seen in this chapter, it can be a challenge to secure satisfactory housing when a person is poor.

Women are also more likely to be single parents, and many report a "lack of social support" to offset the financial burden of caregiving roles (OHRC 2008). Also, while it is illegal in all jurisdictions in Canada, some landlords will refuse accommodation because of family status with statements such as "no children" or "adults only." These actions disproportionately discriminate against women, since women are more likely to be the ones with children.

IN FOCUS ◆ Ying v. Star Developments Ltd. (2003)

The Human Rights Tribunal of Ontario ruled that Star Developments and landowner Stanley Morris discriminated against Maria Ying based on family status. Morris refused to rent Ying a three-bedroom apartment to her and her two teenage sons. Ms Ying's appeal went to a tribunal, and it was found that Mr Morris had a general guideline that he used to match rental units with families. By this measure, he did not consider Ms Ying and her sons an "ideal family." The Tribunal pointed out to Mr Morris the law requires landlords to rent to families with teenage children, regardless of the size of the rental unit. They must do so unless there are compelling and lawful reasons not to. Ms Ying won a settlement of $4,000 for the loss arising out of the "infringement of her rights," and Mr Morris was ordered to stop discrimination on the base of family status.

Mothers of children with special needs face even more barriers to housing. In 2008, the Ontario Human Rights Commission (OHRC) undertook a province-wide consultation with the public to better understand the experiences of victims of housing discrimination. In these consultations, the commission heard that "parents of children with mental disabilities may be under particular scrutiny from neighbours and landlords with regard to noise or other manifestations of their children's disabilities. Sometimes, these kinds of issues can lead to eviction."

Women are also disproportionately the victims of domestic violence. As a result, women need to secure emergency housing for themselves and their children at higher rates than men; single women head most homeless families (Maki 2017). Victims of domestic violence who are not financially independent often have few housing choices, and this is uniquely damaging to mothers. Mothers who are victims of violence "are at an increased risk of having their children removed by child welfare authorities because of housing that is unsuitable" (OHRC 2008). Indigenous women, who suffer higher rates of both domestic violence and barriers to safe, secure, and satisfactory housing, are also disproportionately at risk of having their children removed (OHRC 2008).

Women are also more likely to be victims of sexual violence and harassment. In public consultations, women reported "inappropriate behaviour by landlords and property managers, especially when women are at risk of losing their tenancy due to financial difficulty or a personal crisis . . . The Commission was told that some landlords may seek sexual favours from low-income women in lieu of rent if they have fallen into debt, to prevent eviction or if they require maintenance services" (OHRC 2008). Some women said that they preferred homelessness to the threatened or real harassment they faced from landlords.

Since there are few choices for low-income women escaping sexually, physically, or emotionally abusive households, many remain in unsafe living conditions. Women with disabilities who are victims of domestic violence have even fewer choices; often, emergency shelters are not equipped to house women with mobility problems. Landlords may also hold discriminatory beliefs about housing women escaping abusive relationships. These landlords may fear the atmosphere of violence may "follow" the women to the new accommodation and make life difficult for neighbours or for the landlords themselves.

Table 6.1 shows some cited reasons women seek shelter in Canada.

Did you ever think that low-income status might affect a person's right to privacy? Some low-income women seek accommodation in "social housing" units (or subsidized housing) where rent is tied to household income. This means that if household income changes in any significant way, the rent also changes. In other words, if a working spouse moves into the house, the rent should increase similarly (CLEO 2017). Women, who make up most single parents in social housing, are sometimes subject to increased "spouse-in-the-house" scrutiny when they have guests. "Is the partner moving in?" the neighbours or superintendent might wonder. "Does he live there? How many nights has he stayed over this week?" This impedes residents from living normal, private lives. Feminists recognize that, in raising these questions and concerns, landlords and others are applying gendered standards to their tenants. They would not, likely, be raising the same concerns about male tenants.

Table 6.1 Reasons Women Seek Shelter

Reason	Frequency Reason Was Cited	Percentage of Women
Abuse		
Emotional abuse	2,933	66
Physical abuse	2,193	50
Threats	1,593	36
Financial abuse	1,671	38
Harassment	1,183	27
Sexual abuse	925	21
Other abuse	590	14
Protecting children from		
Witnessing abuse of mother	1,158	26
Psychological abuse	784	18
Physical abuse	428	10
Threats	348	8
Neglect	267	6
Sexual abuse	72	2
Housing		
Unable to find affordable housing	1,311	30
Short-term housing problem	767	17
Housing emergency	428	10
Mental health	1,087	25
Drug/alcohol addiction	862	19
Other	482	11
Unknown	53	. . .
Total reasons for admission	19,135	. . .

Source: Beattie and Hutchins 2015.

Seniors in Canada

As people age, they are likely to live through the following experiences:

- A decline in health, which requires more time and resources to preserve quality of life
- A change in finances from relying on savings and pensions instead of a regular salary from work
- A change in family composition as family members move elsewhere or die
- A change in neighbourhood priorities; these include neighbourhood walkability, ease of access to public transportation, and moving to be closer to family either to help care for grandchildren or to be cared for by children and grandchildren

As we have previously learned in this book, the proportion of seniors in Canada is increasing every year (CMHC 2011). This is because of several factors. First, healthcare is improving and people are living longer. Second, the generation born in Canada immediately following World War II (known as the "baby boom" generation) is large and is aging all at once. Third, many immigrants came to Canada as young adults and are now getting old. Finally, younger immigrants have sponsored their aged parents as part of the family reunification program. As immigrants age, they may find themselves isolated from many of the social and family supports that native-born Canadians, living in the community where they grew up, take for granted.

And while many of us like to imagine that our eldest Canadians are living comfortably in the final years of life, one in six senior households are in core housing need (CMHC 2011). Core housing need means the seniors' home is either in need of major repairs, is too small, is too costly, or is not well equipped for the senior's needs.

Let's consider just a couple of the barriers that are unique to seniors. First, landlords may (illegally) deny an older tenant housing because of a belief the tenant will not have the ability to care for themselves. Or they may think the senior cannot adequately keep up a property or may die while owing them rent. Since older people are more likely to experience disability, older tenants may also experience disability-related discrimination. For example, a landlord might deny a person a rental unit for fear that accommodation laws may require them to install ramps or lifts in the unit.

Did you know that if a lease is continuous, a landlord may only increase a person's rent by a small fraction every year? As soon as a new lease is signed with a new tenant, the landlord can "reset" the rental price according to their preference (or what the market dictates). Some older Canadians have lived in a rental unit for a long time, and as a result their landlord may be earning much less from their rental fee than the current market would allow. This may encourage the landlord to evict the older tenant just to fill the space with a new tenant and a new, more profitable lease.

There are various housing choices for seniors. Some live independently in condos, apartments, or houses. Others share a home with friends or family, while others still rent a room in a retirement home or long-term care home, among others.

One residential alternative that many seniors choose is called a *secondary suite*. A secondary suite is a small "coach house" built near the principal house on a property. The senior can live in the secondary suite while their family occupies the principal house (allowing "close-enough" family contact and support). Or the senior can live in the main

Drawing Connections

Remember our discussion of the growing market for senior care in Chapter 2. In particular, remember the link between inequality and people's ability to choose their preferred housing (based on income). Seniors, like everyone else, want to live in particular ways and don't like others telling them why doing so isn't possible or desirable.

house—perhaps with a spouse—and house a caregiver in a secondary suite. This arrangement is ideal for many Canadian seniors.

But many seniors are not in an economic position to choose what they prefer. In many cities, zoning bylaws prevent or limit the construction of a secondary suite. This comes from the legitimate concern that too many structures on a single property will tax the municipal infrastructure. Unfortunately, this prevents many seniors from choosing this housing alternative. Happily for many seniors, some Canadian towns recognize the social value of secondary suites. They are making special age-related amendments to existing bylaws to make this housing available for seniors. The city of Victoria is even offering financial incentives to encourage the construction of secondary suites (CMHC 2011).

Immigrants in Canada

New immigrants tend to have lower rates of homeownership in their first few years in Canada. The longer they stay, however, the more likely they are to own a home at the same or higher rates as people born in Canada. This holds true even if they must take out a larger mortgage to finance the purchase (Morissette 2019).

Many recently arrived immigrants rent their home. Next time you visit Toronto, Canada's most popular destination for new immigrants, gaze up at the high-rise rental units. Fully three-quarters of their residents are immigrants (Toronto Community Foundation 2012). In all jurisdictions in Canada, it is illegal to discriminate against a potential tenant because of nationality (that is, the place where a person was born). And yet recently arrived immigrants report higher-than-average levels of housing discrimination (Nangia 2013; Ibraham 2018). Experiences of discrimination are worsened when the immigrant is also racialized.

Discrimination might occur at the first point of contact with a potential landlord, at which point the recently arrived immigrant is turned away. One survey of 20 multi-property landlords in Ontario's Kitchener-Waterloo region found that half

IN FOCUS ◆ Chauhan v. Sunshine Seniors Housing Cooperative Assn. (2004)

Sai Bhatnagar was born and raised in India and now lives in Canada in a seniors' housing co-operative. In 2002, the family that lived above her began to complain that Bhatnagar's ethnic cooking produced "offensive smells" and complained to the Sunshine Seniors Housing Cooperative Association. For five years prior, Ms Bhatnagar had cooked both "ethnic" and "Western" food with no complaint from other residents. Ms Bhatnagar was informed by the Association that she must stop creating the "offensive" smells or be evicted. The Human Rights Tribunal of Ontario, however, found that Ms Bhatnagar was cooking dishes that were an expression of her ethnicity. They felt she should not be forced to choose between cooking them and being evicted. The Tribunal ruled the Association did indeed discriminate against Ms Bhatnagar. It ordered them to pay her $2,500 for injury to dignity and feelings and repay her for the cost of her legal fees and other related expenses.

were reluctant to rent to immigrants. In this study, landlords reported that their reasons for refusal included "communication difficulties, lack of cleanliness, and cooking aromas (presumably considered unpleasant)" (Shaftoe and Alcade 1991). Immigrants' housing decisions are influenced by both a mixture of positive and negative forces. The positive forces include attraction to same-ethnicity neighbours, and the negative forces include rejection or exclusion by other-ethnicity neighbours (Andersen 2010; Murdie 2008; Texeira 2008).

Another common form of housing discrimination occurs when a landlord requires a potential tenant to pay more than first and last month's rent as down payment. This is a common human rights complaint emerging from Canada's immigrant population (Keung 2012). Forcing tenants to pay more than first and last month's rent is illegal. So why are immigrants asked to provide enormous down payments on rental properties? Some landlords may collect an inflated down payment because they worry the tenant will leave without giving the required two-month notice. These fears grow out of faulty assumptions that immigrants are flighty, unreliable, and won't or can't pay rent on time.

Other landlords want inflated down payments. They demand this regardless of whether a two-month departure notice is given by the tenant. They even demand it if the tenant is forced to move because of flooding, insect infestation, or fire. Clever landlords may invest the lump sum and earn interest from it throughout the rental period. In all of these scenarios, it's likely that many landlords are capitalizing on the fact that some recently arrived immigrants may not be aware of their rights as tenants. Other immigrants may feel too unsteady in their new country to lodge complaints even if they know they are being treated illegally and unfairly.

The effect of housing discrimination for immigrants may mean that immigrants must search for housing for longer periods of time while paying for expensive, short-term housing like hotels or hostels. They may settle in less desirable neighbourhoods with poorer access to public transportation, employment opportunities, or schools for their children. Those undocumented workers or refugees may not make formal complaints against landlords for fear they will be deported. Newcomers in general may not seek social supports or legal representation if they aren't aware such things exist or that their rights have been violated in the first place.

IN FOCUS ◆ Mohammed v. Novtek Corporation (2002)

Mr Mohammed, born and educated in Bangladesh, moved to Canada with his wife and daughter in 1989. He took a job as a bilingual secretary, where he earned $28,000 a year, and had $25,000 in savings. When he applied to rent an apartment in Mississauga, owned by the Novtek Corporation, at $879 per month, he did not have a credit card; this form of payment was rarely used in Bangladesh. Mr Mohammed's application was refused because he did not have a credit rating and his income was deemed inadequate. As well, his wife's employment record was inadequate, as she had only been working a few weeks. The Ontario Board of Inquiry ruled that Novtek Corporation's tenant-selection policy is discriminatory, especially for newcomers to Canada. It ordered the Novtek Corporation to pay $5,000 to Mr Mohammed for general losses and to stop any discriminatory action of this nature in the future.

Racialized Populations and Ethnic Minorities in Canada

Of course, not all immigrants are racialized, and not all racialized people are immigrants. These are common misconceptions. For that reason, it can be useful to compare the experiences of racialized versus non-racialized immigrants to better isolate—and thus understand—how racialization affects how one experiences barriers to housing and housing inequality.

For example, researchers set out to examine the housing experiences among recently arrived members of three ethnic groups in Toronto: people from Somalia, Poland, and Jamaica. The research found that of the three groups, Somali immigrants reported the greatest levels of housing discrimination, followed by Jamaicans and then Polish immigrants. The researchers speculated that discrimination based on race accounted for the different experiences reported by the Somali and Jamaican group (who were mainly Black) and the Poles (who were mainly white) (Murdie 2003).

Another survey found that Black respondents (not necessarily immigrants) reported being less satisfied with their housing than Italian, South Asian, or Portuguese respondents (Dion 2001). Another study found that Black lone parents were twice as likely to be discriminated against when seeking housing than non-Black lone parents (CERA 2009).

Historically, as Black people moved to northern US cities from the rural south, they encountered all of these difficulties and more. They encountered what sociologists have referred to as *white flight*. As the migrants moved in—usually in rundown neighbourhoods of the central city, where generations of immigrants had lived—white residents moved out of the city to nearby or sometimes even distant suburbs. This process repeated itself as upwardly mobile Black Americans moved into working-class and middle-class white suburbs, again prompting the white residents to move out to even more distant suburbs.

This process has been less marked in Canadian cities, where it is often the poorer residents who live in distant suburbs and the more affluent residents who live downtown.

◆ In Their Own Words ◆

In 2008, the Ontario Human Rights Commission consulted with people who had experienced housing discrimination. Here's testimony they heard from one man who identified his skin colour as "brown":

> [When] I called to book an appointment . . . I used a Canadian accent and the superintendent gave me the interview and was cordial. Once I showed up for the viewing with my family, the superintendent was making various excuses, which seemed unusual at that particular time. He claimed the apartment was already rented out. Later in the week, I had my white friend call and go in for a viewing [of] the same apartment that I was supposed to view. My white friend was successful in viewing and applying for the apartment.

Source: OHRC 2008.

As in US cities, there is some degree of residential segregation by ethnicity and race in Canadian cities. However, there has never been the degree or form of white (or even middle-class) flight as has been repeatedly witnessed in US cities.

Housing discrimination based on racialization is illegal throughout Canada. Similarly, discrimination based on association with a racialized individual—such as a mixed-race marriage—is equally illegal. Rarely, however, do landlords openly admit to discriminating against racialized housing seekers. Instead, racialized populations may discover the "apartment has already been rented" or the "landlord changed their mind." This hidden discrimination is what sociologists call "adverse discrimination," and it is no less harmful for being hidden or even sometimes unconscious.

Indigenous Peoples in Canada

Of all Canadian populations vulnerable to barriers to satisfactory housing, the most vulnerable are First Nations, Inuit, and Métis people living in Canada. Remember, Indigenous Peoples in Canada may live on-reserve or off-reserve. Housing on many reserves in Canada does not meet the necessary conditions for health. Figure 6.4 shows how many people living on-reserve are in suitable housing, defined as housing that is not in need of major repair and not crowded.

Many Indigenous Peoples in Canada live in remote regions where housing services like sewer pipes, gas lines, and electricity are costly and difficult to install. In these regions, the prices are also higher for oil and fuel, which often translates into higher running costs. One study noted the annual utility cost for a three-bedroom unit in Coral Harbour, a small community in Nunavut, was $12,000 (Bruce 2003). Recall that unemployment is also higher in northern, remote communities, and median annual income can be as low as $15,000 per year. Once again, we see how the cost of living can be higher in regions where income is typically lower.

News reports suggest that "thousands" living on reserves across Canada are without safe or satisfactory water or sewage. In many reserves, water must be boiled before consumption to remove harmful bacteria. The federal government has recently announced an initiative to end boil water advisories by 2021, but this goal has yet to be completed (Government of Canada 2019).

In addition, overcrowding occurs at six to ten times the rate it does off-reserve (Stastna 2011; see also Figure 6.4). The United Nations special rapporteur on the rights of Indigenous Peoples, James Anaya (2014), describes the housing as a "crisis." He reported that in the North,

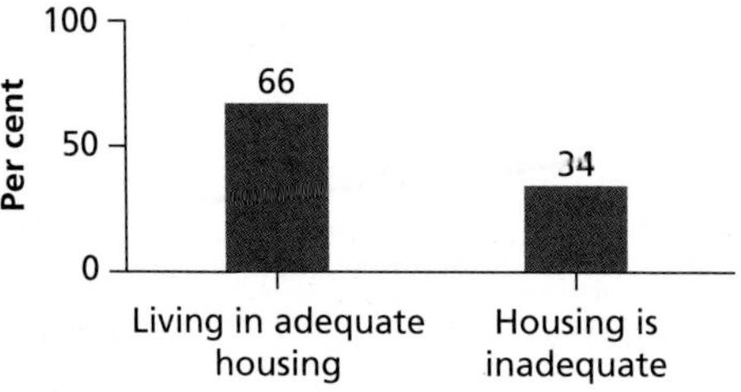

Figure 6.4 ◆ Percentage of Indigenous People Living in Adequate Housing

Source: Based on CMHC 2018.

> overcrowded housing is endemic. Homes are in need of major repairs, including plumbing and electrical work. These conditions add to the broader troubling water condition in First Nations reserves, in which more than half of the water systems pose a medium or high health risk to their users . . . Overcrowding contributes to higher rates of respiratory illness, depression, sleep deprivation, family violence, poor educational achievement and an inability to retain skilled and professional members in the community.

People offer many reasons to explain the housing crises on Indigenous reserves. One reason is the shortage of cash for infrastructural development. The largest source of revenue for reserves in Canada is transfer payments from the federal government. These transfer arrangements are left over from the British North America Act of 1867, which made reserves and Indigenous policies a federal responsibility. However, provinces are generally responsible for infrastructure and transportation. Today, many feel that transfer payments have not kept pace with the rapidly expanding Indigenous population or rate of inflation. In large part, progress on this matter has been impeded by squabbling between the federal and provincial governments over responsibility and cost-sharing for planning and service delivery.

But some of the problem is squarely because of federal disorganization. One CBC journalist pointed out the federal funding "is allocated on a year-to-year basis, which makes the kind of long-term planning that is essential for building infrastructure difficult" (Stastna 2011). Further, "the timing of federal budgets is not conducive to a construction window that is short and limited by weather and geography" (Stastna 2011). Some reserves with natural resources to sell or other commercial ventures (for example, casinos or a tourism industry) supplement government transfer payments. But those without another source, who also typically experience a high unemployment rate, just can't afford to preserve the infrastructure needed to support safe and satisfactory housing.

Another reason is that many reserves are small; 80 per cent of reserves in Canada have fewer than 1,000 residents. Just like food, prices for building materials decrease when they are purchased and assembled "in bulk." In other words, shipping 50,000 nails instead of 2,000 nails works out to a lower cost per nail. This cost advantage of bigger building projects (sometimes referred to as **economies of scale**) is rarely enjoyed by these tiny reserves.

economies of scale The per-unit cost advantage of building something bigger rather than smaller.

Many reserves also face unique challenges in constructing adequate housing because of their location. In June 2019, a special Senate committee released a report called "Northern Lights: A Wake-Up Call for the Future of Canada." The report outlines the ways in which northern communities have been historically underserved and are uniquely vulnerable to the effects of climate change. The report makes several recommendations:

> Understanding that Arctic communities deserve better, the committee recommends that the Government of Canada: 1) complete a building code adapted to Arctic conditions and the effects of climate change; 2) implement an action plan to mitigate the effects of climate change on existing and new infrastructure, including housing; 3) take immediate measures to address the housing crisis in the Arctic by funding a complete continuum of Arctic housing; and 4) report on the effects of its investments on housing annually to local, Indigenous and territorial governments. (Patterson and Bovey 2019)

◆ In Their Own Words ◆

The Ontario Human Rights Commission reports that:

> The impact of colonization, the legacy of Indian Residential Schools and several resulting factors has led to higher rates of addictions, substance abuse and mental illness among the Indigenous population. Indigenous people who suffer from addictions and/or mental illness have a particular difficulty obtaining social and rental housing and are often at a great risk of homelessness.

Source: OHRC 2008.

political will The desire and ability to mobilize people politically behind a particular policy or program.

Finally, a significant cause of housing inadequacies on Indigenous reserves is the lack of **political will**. This neglect stems from systematic racism enduring from colonization. We see this when problems in Indigenous communities, such inadequate housing, lack of safe drinking water, and critical health issues endure without the appropriate resources, support, and action on the part of the federal, provincial, territorial, and municipal governments. We see this when the media turns their cameras away from the substandard living conditions on Canadian reserves to focus instead on those in remote corners of the world. We even see this in over-the-fence conversations with our neighbours. There, we are likely to discuss the weather and the latest celebrity gossip, not the tuberculosis that continues to ravage the damp, mouldy, crumbling excuses for homes mere hours away.

Many Indigenous Peoples living off-reserve face barriers to satisfactory housing. Perhaps as a result they are more likely to move from place to place (referred to as *residential instability*). They are also more likely to spend more than 30 per cent of their household income on shelter and are more likely to be in core housing need. A study of the housing experiences of First Nations, Métis, and Inuit people living in northwestern Ontario

◆ In Their Own Words ◆

Here is what some respondents had to say in Motz and Currie's study on the effects of housing discrimination experienced by Indigenous postsecondary students:

> "Couldn't find a home because of being First Nations. Great difficulty because of my last name."
>
> "Some landlords said no after hearing I was an Aboriginal person."
>
> "When I have tried to rent a place, people would often tell me that the place had been unavailable as soon as they knew where I was from."

Source: Motz and Currie 2019.

revealed that these groups were discriminated against on multiple grounds: Indigenous status, receipt of social assistance, race/ethnic origin, disability, and family status (CERA and MNO 2015). Again, we see the overlapping effects of multiple marginalized identities.

LGBTQ+ People in Canada

Discriminatory beliefs about sexual orientation or gender identity make securing safe housing more challenging for some people in Canada. Same-sex partners may be denied housing based on a landlord's belief about their marriage. LGBTQ+ people may be asked inappropriate questions about their sexual practices or family status. Trans people may be subject to mistreatment in the form of increased scrutiny and lack of privacy or outright neglect (for example, landlords who ignore requests for repairs or routine maintenance).

LGBTQ+ youth are at higher risk of homelessness. This may be influenced by family conflict related to the disclosure of their sexual orientation or gender identity. Studies have shown that many young people have experienced physical abuse or were kicked out of their home when they came out (NGLTFPI 2006). The overrepresentation of LGBTQ+ in the youth homeless population "may reflect the harassment and rejection experienced at school and/or at home by their peers and/or their caregivers" (Duncan et al. 2000:15).

In June 2012, Ontario became the first province in Canada to include "gender identity" in the list of banned grounds of discrimination. This amendment to the Ontario Human Rights Code grew out of testimonies from the trans (and non-trans) population testifying to experiences of discrimination, including when seeking jobs, healthcare, and housing. Today, all of Canada's provinces and territories offer such protection against discrimination based on gender identity (Canadian Centre for Diversity and Inclusion 2018:36).

Gender identity and sexual orientation may also present challenges and barriers when people are seeking "shared" living arrangements, like student residences or seniors' homes. Some organizations are working to specifically support awareness-raising in this area. QMUNITY, for example, a queer resource centre based in Vancouver, works with seniors' homes to ensure that staff have had enough training to support the needs of LGBTQ+ residents. Another "shared" living arrangement is emergency or temporary shelters for homeless people. Trans individuals often have difficulty feeling safe in shelters that are segregated according to binary gender.

IN FOCUS ◆ Housing Discrimination Based on Sexual Orientation

The Centre for Equality Rights in Accommodation reports a story about Eva's housing experience.

Eva, a 29-year-old woman, lives in a one-bedroom apartment on the top floor of a house, with the landlord living on the main floor. After moving in, Eva began dating Jennifer, who would stay overnight twice a week. The landlord soon became less friendly and complained about the sound of footsteps on the stairs. He also said two parking spaces in front of the house were reserved for "family," not overnight guests. Eva challenged this and, the next month, she received an eviction notice. Believing she was facing discrimination because of her sexual orientation, she filed a formal complaint.

Source: CERA 2008.

People with Disabilities in Canada

By now, we have looked at a wide range of disabilities experienced in Canada. We have also seen how disabilities interact with other aspects of identity and how the particular combination of these multiple identities affects each person's life chances in unique ways.

Let's begin this section by discussing the two important barriers to housing for people with a disability: accessibility and affordability. Some people with disabilities need changes to be made to their home. This might involve ramps, adapted bathrooms, lowered kitchen countertops, and wider doors. These changes are expensive to install and preserve. (In some condos, for example, these renovations are not always permitted.) A study by Giesbrecht and colleagues (2017) revealed that walk-in baths/showers, lift/elevators, and ramps were the most common unmet needs among people with mobility disabilities. The primary barrier to these home modifications was the cost.

If a person owns a house and has money, they can afford these necessary renovations. However, if a person cannot afford to renovate, there are few homes available that already feature these important accessibility adjustments. MLS (Multiple Listing Service), the website devoted to real estate searches, does not even include a search option for these features.

Those units that meet the needs of mobility-related disabilities are often not competitively priced. Remember from previous chapters that people with disabilities are more likely to be low income. Despite this, their safe-housing needs are likely to cost more.

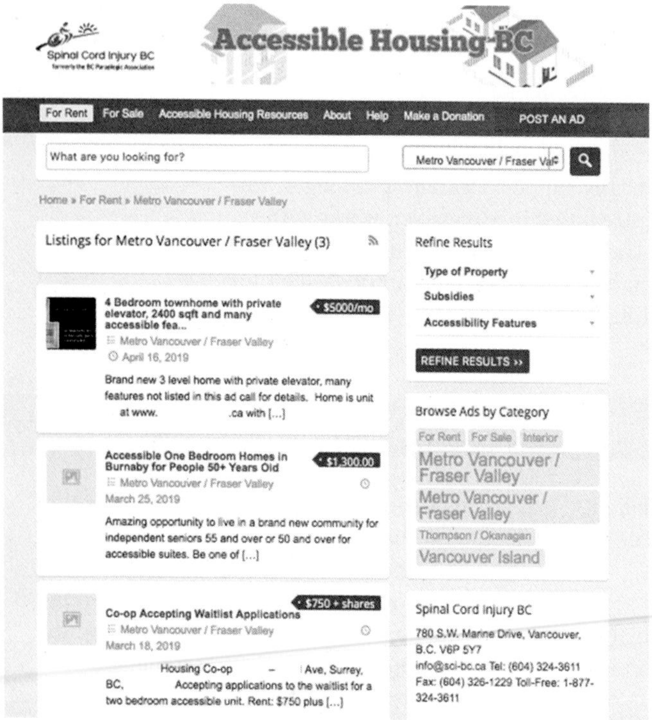

Discrimination is another barrier to housing for people with disabilities. Landlords may deny a person an accommodation based on misguided beliefs about the ability for some people to live independently. For example, they may resist taking in a guide dog for a tenant with a visual impairment. Housing discrimination based on disability is illegal in all jurisdictions in Canada. Landlords have a duty to house a person with a disability, but only to the point of "undue hardship."

Consider Nova Scotia's clear prohibition against discrimination based on an "irrational fear of contracting a disease or illness" (CERA 2008). Is this irrational fear merely a misguided effort to protect rental property values? Or does it point to a discrimination against minority groups? An Ontario-based study found that one-third of their respondents who live with HIV/AIDS experience discrimination when trying to find housing (OHRC 2008). Similarly, people who live with mental illness report higher-than-average levels of discrimination and harassment.

Housing problems associated with disability are especially pressing because, as a

Spinal Cord Injury BC

Spinal Cord Injury BC has created a site dedicated to helping people find accessible rental housing. Note that they have only three listings for the entire Vancouver metropolitan area.

◆ In Their Own Words ◆

The Ontario Human Rights Commission reports that:

> People with mental illnesses who have been involved in the criminal justice system are at a particular disadvantage in obtaining and keeping suitable housing. Some people get stuck in the hospital or in substandard housing because they are unable to obtain housing from community agencies.

Source: OHRC 2008.

IN FOCUS ◆ Housing Discrimination Based on Disability

A car accident left Carlton unable to walk. In his wheelchair, Carlton cannot climb the set of steep stairs at the front of his building, so Carlton asked the landlords to install a ramp. As an alternative, they suggested Carlton enter the building through the garbage room in the back, where there are no stairs. Instead, an accessibility consultant suggested a wheelchair lift costing $12,000. The landlords said this was too expensive, but CERA told them landlords have a duty to make room for Carlton's disability. Unless they can prove "undue hardship," they will have to install the lift for Carlton.

Source: CERA 2011.

society, we are seeing more—not fewer—disabilities. This is because more people are living longer under conditions of disability, and this means housing more disabled people for more years. Our society has not yet figured out how to solve that problem in an economical, humane way.

Transportation

Like housing, transportation is about location. And, as we will see, people suffer barriers and disadvantages where transportation is concerned, just as they do with housing.

Throughout this book we have explored the different types of survival capital; the things that everybody needs to live safe, happy, and healthy lives. Unlike food, education, housing, or healthcare, transportation doesn't directly contribute to one's survival. Nobody "needs" to sit in a car. In fact, sitting in a car tends to make a person less healthy. A minute in a car is a minute less engaged in important social or leisure activities. A minute in a car also costs money that could be better spent building other forms of survival capital (think about this while looking at Figure 6.5).

In these ways, you might think of transportation as a "reverse" survival capital: the less you need of it, the better off you are. In this way, transportation is unique on our list of survival capital.

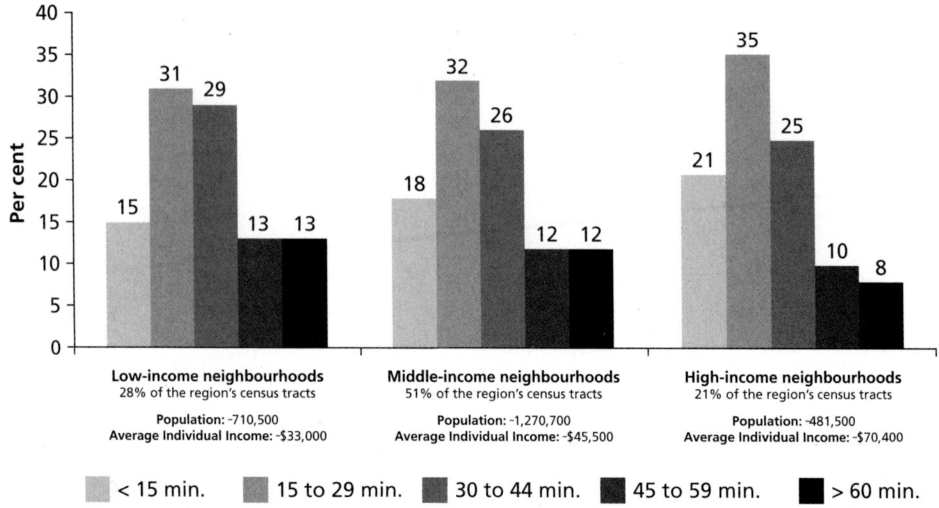

Figure 6.5 ◆ Duration of Commute to Work of Metro Vancouver's Population

As you can see from this figure, higher-income people are likely to spend the least amount of time commuting to work every day.

Source: Cheung 2018.

One of the most typical reasons a person needs transportation is to get to work. Some commute because the giant, richly appointed, expensive properties they live on are located outside major, more densely populated metropolitan areas. But for most others, it's too costly to live close to work, or the limited work opportunities near their homes force them to work someplace else.

Low-income Canadians often fall into this second category. The cost of living is usually cheaper in rural areas or at the outer limits of large metropolitan areas. Unfortunately, the work opportunities are often concentrated elsewhere. These commuters must pay more to get to work (as a fraction of their income) and have to spend more time getting there (see Figure 6.5). Those who can't afford to drive a car typically spend twice as much time in transit.

Driving a car to work is still typically the fastest way to get there. However, we've known for some time that inactivity—like the inactivity borne of driving to work—is at the root of many health problems. Inactivity can be worsened by what is called the **built environment**—the design of cities and the associated transportation infrastructure (like the roadway) that allows us to get from place to place (Figure 6.6). In recent years, building **walkable neighbourhoods** has become a goal of urban planners. This has grown especially as we have discovered that certain populations are more likely than others to live in less-walkable neighbourhoods.

built environment The city design (for example, zoning), housing, and associated transportation infrastructure that enables us to get from place to place.

walkable neighbourhood A neighbourhood that is safe enough to walk around at almost any time of day or night.

One Canadian study found that poorer neighbourhoods were less walkable than wealthier ones. These poorer neighbourhoods had fewer banks, pharmacies, grocery stores, biking and walking paths, parks, and recreational facilities than the wealthier neighbourhoods. They were also more unsafe for walkers: The researchers counted more

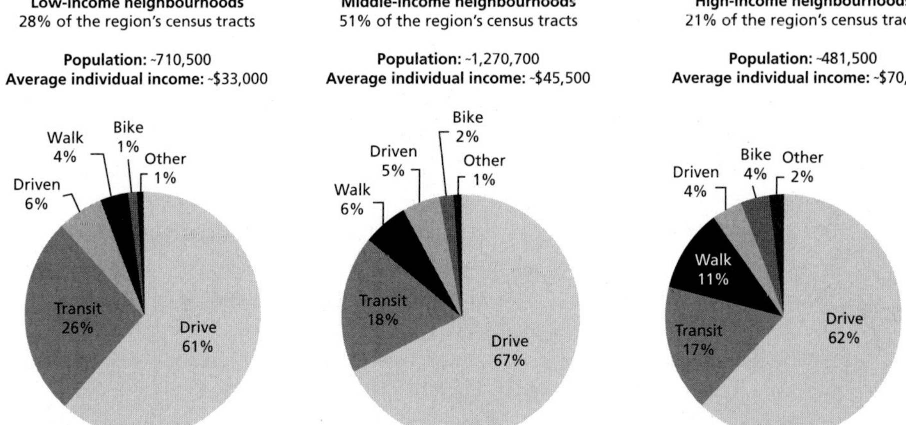

Figure 6.6 ◆ How Metro Vancouver's Population Gets to Work, 2016

Take a look at who is most likely to use the healthiest modes of transportation (walking and bicycling) people from high-income neighbourhoods. Could it be that their commute is shorter, safer, and more bike friendly? Their equipment more reliable? And their workplaces more supportive of cyclists?

Source: Cheung 2018.

than twice as many pedestrian–vehicle collisions in poorer neighbourhoods compared with wealthier ones (Grant et al. 2010). This study suggests that poorer people are unequally deprived of the health benefits from walking as a form of transportation.

Poorer people are not the only ones unequally experiencing the negative effects of few or no healthy transportation choices related to their built environment. Other studies have shown that recently arrived immigrants living in less-walkable neighbourhoods were 50 per cent more likely to develop inactivity-related health problems (Taylor 2012).

This is also true of ethnic groups who concentrate in certain neighbourhoods. In most North American and European cities, immigrants from the same region often live together in the same neighbourhood. Fearing discrimination, they isolate themselves for protection. Lacking fluency in the English language, they look for shops and services in their native language. Missing the familiarity of their home customs, they often set up churches, schools, and newspapers that help them uphold their traditions. Sociologist Raymond Breton (1964) has called these practices **institutional completeness**, noting that ethnic communities with the most institutional completeness last the longest and preserve the strongest identities.

institutional completeness A community characteristic featuring a full array of necessary services and goods, including schools, churches, and media.

On the other hand, some ethnic residential segregation is not voluntary but a result of discrimination or the need for inexpensive housing. People from the same families and ethnic backgrounds move to the same neighbourhoods in a process sociologists call **chain migration** because they hear about the housing opportunities from their friends and relatives.

chain migration Migration to communities or countries that results from information about opportunities received from friends and relatives.

Often, however, low-priced neighbourhoods are inconveniently located. Not only are these neighbourhoods far from work, they have too few grocery stores, schools, and other key destinations, forcing a reliance on transportation. A recent study found that levels of diabetes are dramatically increasing among people of Chinese origin in Ontario

◆ In Their Own Words ◆

In her study of immigrants and precariously employed people in Toronto, Stephanie Premji (2017) noted that "participants sometimes found it difficult to decide whether the number of hours worked on a particular day would make the commute worthwhile, since work hours were unpredictable." To study this, Premji collected testimonials from people struggling with transportation and heard the following:

> "And he [temporary agency representative] said 'I'm telling you to go if you want to get a job just go' and I said OK because I needed a job. Then I went and it takes 1 hour and 45 minutes and there I worked for 2 hours with seniors . . . After two hours finished and I came back it also take 1 hour and 45 minutes. Then that guy again phoned me 'Next Tuesday you have to go' and I say OK, but I don't know how much I will get and he said 'For 1 hour you will get $14.' So $28 . . . To go and come back, I have to spend on the way more than 3 hours and I will work 2 hours. It is almost I will get paid less than . . . normal wage."

> "We were living in [one] area and the work was in [another area] . . . But this job, it was 7 days and we had to start I think . . . 7:00, but we have to wake up I think 4:00 because it took us like 2 hours to get there. And on some days, because there was no subway, we had to take a taxi . . . At the end we make our account, our math, we were gaining like $5 per hour . . . And wasting like 4 hours, yeah, per day. It was too much. So then we, we quit."

Source: Premji 2017.

(Alangh, Chiu, and Shah 2013). The main researcher noted that Chinese communities have shifted "from urban-core Chinatowns to suburban regions. So they are moving away from urban, walkable neighbourhoods to more car-requiring, sprawling suburban areas" (Taylor 2013).

As well as health problems, a lack of transportation can have negative effects on emotional well-being. Studies have shown that seniors who don't have access to the survival capital of transportation are socially cut off. They are less likely to visit friends, take part in activities, and volunteer. This is especially pronounced with elderly women. They tend to lose or give up their drivers' licences sooner than elderly men and as a result experience more social exclusion (Statistics Canada 2006; Wasfi, Levinson, and El-Geneidy 2012).

As we have seen, problems associated with transportation are intimately connected to problems related to housing. People who live in inconveniently placed, low-cost locations are often poorly served by low-cost public transportation. This makes it hard for them to get and keep jobs, use social services, and shop for healthy, reasonably priced food. Thus they are doubly disadvantaged: They suffer discrimination in their search for housing and are then undermined by the only housing they can afford (Figure 6.7).

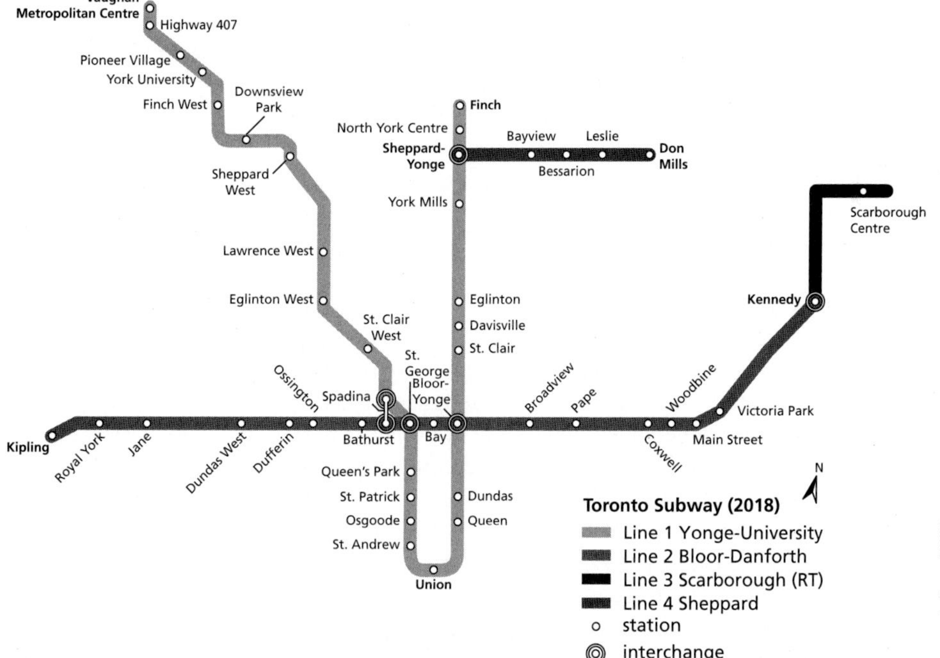

By permission of TTC

Figure 6.7 • Toronto Subway Maps, Showing (Top) All Stations and (Bottom) Accessible Stations

Compare the two maps above. The first is the Toronto subway map. The second map shows only the stops that are wheelchair accessible. What differences do you notice?

Consequences of Unequal Access to Housing and Transportation

Research has shown that many poor neighbourhoods lack parks and green space, libraries, social services, hospitals, shops, restaurants, and movie theatres. In short, the "quality of life" is worse in poorer neighbourhoods. And a poor quality of life causes stress and does predictable harm to people's physical and mental health. So poor housing and transportation are part of a large network of interlocking disadvantages that lead to results—unemployment, crime, stress, poor health—that put people at a further disadvantage.

Ensuring that everyone in Canada has access to satisfactory housing would be incredibly expensive. But so too is the cost of homelessness and other social effects of housing instability like crime, stress, poor health, interrupted education, and community instability. In fact, some studies have shown that for every $10 spent on housing, more than $20 is recovered in savings (Goering et al. 2012).

Strategies of Resistance

People employ various strategies to overcome their housing and transportation disadvantages. As urbanization continues, the demand for affordable housing and transportation within our cities will continue to rise. Innovative ideas are necessary to meet these new needs and improve housing and transportation equity. The following section will examine what various actors, at the government, organizational, and individual levels, are doing to improve access to these services.

Government-Level Strategies of Resistance

In Portland, Oregon, a bold new strategy for combating homelessness has been considered by the municipal government. By building micro-houses, the city hopes to offer a new form of affordable housing that will give individuals the stability and dignity they need to get back on their feet. Micro-houses are small (192 square feet) individual housing units that can be built cheaply and quickly to help meet the growing demand of transitional housing. One prototype being considered, designed by TechDwell, costs only $20,000 and can be built in days. They would be "made of prefab materials available at Home Depot and Lowe's, [and] include two sleeping pods joined by a kitchen, bathroom and eating area" (Hamilton 2014). The houses do not require training to assemble, are easily replicable, and can be adjusted to better suit families or other needs.

For years now, the city of Portland has seriously considered building dozens of these units. They would be distributed throughout the city to ensure mixed-income neighbourhoods and mitigate social inequality. Micro-housing has the potential to be more effective at reducing the volume of homelessness than traditional shelters because it provides people with a permanent address and a place that is their own. This is more attractive to many who are reluctant to enter shelters that offer little privacy and are often stigmatized. Further, by offering a permanent address to put on résumés, micro-housing gives individuals a better chance at finding employment and improving their lives.

The local reaction to micro-housing has been far from welcoming. A newspaper article by Janet Easton (2017) in *The Oregonian* allegedly lists 77 reasons critics give for opposing micro-houses, regardless of who is going to live there.

However, Emily Brown (2016), in a report titled "Overcoming the Barriers to Micro-Housing: Tiny Houses, Big Potential," sees the opposition more in terms of the people who will most benefit from such housing. Brown writes that communities can encourage the spread of tiny homes and micro-villages by developing "an ethic that supports, rather than discourages, nonconventional living situations." Brown explains that the biggest challenge for projects like Portland's micro-housing villages is "developing the political and social will to make projects happen." Without challenging existing attitudes, solutions will encounter roadblocks and resistance. New ideas often run afoul of "mechanical solidarity," Durkheim might have noted. More systematic change is clearly needed.

Micro-housing is but one part of a satisfactory public housing system and would exist alongside community housing projects and traditional shelters. Studies have shown that governments save money in the long term by investing in infrastructure to house the homeless. This is because reducing homelessness can save a lot of money. It eases the burden on the health and justice systems, which more than offset the cost of the investment (Zaretzky, Flatau, and Brady 2008). So beyond being moral, initiatives like micro-housing have the potential to even be frugal.

Organization-Level Strategies of Resistance

Consider as an example of organizational-level strategies the case of Habitat for Humanity. Founded in 1976, Habitat for Humanity is an international organization whose mission is to provide newly built houses for low-income families. They achieve this by partnering the low-income families with volunteer builders and (mostly) donated land and supplies. The future homeowners must commit to spending at least 500 hours of labour on house construction. Once completed, the houses are sold to the low-income "partner" family at no profit. Those who cannot pay for the house outright may pay for their home with affordable monthly no-interest mortgage payments tailored to the household income.

So far the organization has provided shelter for 3 million people worldwide, including 2,200 families in Canada (Habitat for Humanity 2013). A recent study showed that after moving into a Habitat house, the children of partner families did better in school. They also showed greater overall well-being, including improved behaviour and more enjoyment at school. Families also reported better health.

Individual-Level Strategies of Resistance

By comparison, individual efforts to solve housing and transportation problems are small. Take the decision to give up using your car in favour of walking or bicycling. Owning a car has become much more costly in recent years. Gas prices have gone up and our cities have made little progress in lessening gridlock. Cars are becoming less attractive as we become more aware of their negative environmental impact, and for many individuals owning a car is simply not financially feasible. This has caused an increasing number of Canadians to turn to bicycling as their primary means of travel. Even though cycling can be difficult during snowy Canadian winters, the other benefits are becoming too hard to ignore for many individuals. Cycling offers a cheap, fast, and consistent (no never-ending bus delays or gridlock) way to get around the city. With that in mind, it's no surprise that more people are hopping on bikes if they live in these areas.

Biking is especially popular with the younger, urban population that lives downtown, but it is also gaining traction with those who live further away from the city centre. Bike sharing networks allow people to rent bikes as they need them. They make cycling even more accessible to individuals with low incomes and have been established in major cities like Toronto, Montreal, and New York.

Unequal access to housing and transportation can seem like an insurmountable problem. As we have seen, however, there are many ways that we can address these issues and make them more equitable.

Consequences of Poor Housing

For most of us, "home" is where we spend most of our time, where we are most comfortable, and where we are most familiar with our surroundings. Because we know this personal space so well, we feel safe and protected there. However, research suggests that it may not be as safe as we think. In addition, the houses of disadvantaged people are more likely than average to be dangerous. This is because disadvantaged people are less likely to have the time and money needed to keep their homes in safe, healthy condition. Never were the consequences of poor housing so evident than during the enforced social isolation of the COVID-19 epidemic.

Injuries in the home can vary in cause and severity. Minor examples include burns from kitchen stoves or hot water from a kettle, electrical shocks from outlets, and falls down slippery hardwood stairs. Other domestic accidents are fatal, such as drowning in bathtubs or swimming pools.

Much research on unexpected injuries at home focuses on stairs. Insurance companies are especially interested in the underlying causes of fall-related injuries, given the expensive compensation they often draw (Bux, Parzeller, and Bratzke 2007). Many insurance policies state that if a client falls down their stairs as the result of intoxication, for example, their insurance is rendered void. These injuries affect different populations and vary in their causes and circumstances. To reduce the rates of these domestic injuries, we need to design living spaces that are conducive to people's health and safety. We can start by regulating and enforcing building codes to make sure living spaces are being built up to standard. (For more information about these issues, see Tepperman and Meredith's book *Waiting to Happen: The Sociology of Unexpected Injuries* [2016].)

Closing Remarks

Many of the social problems people experience are affected by the characteristics of our built environments. In this chapter, we have focused on housing and transportation inequality; where it comes from and what people's different experiences of it have to tell us about how best to confront/challenge it. What we have tried to show in this chapter is that people experience built environments differently, depending on their social advantages and disadvantages. We do not all occupy the same social world. Social inequality means we occupy different social worlds with only passing acquaintance or contact between them. Nowhere is this clearer than with housing and transportation.

Notable Thinkers

Carlos Teixeira

Carlos Teixeira is an associate professor of geography at the University of British Columbia. His research interests include urban and social geography, community formation, housing and neighbourhood change, ethnic entrepreneurship, and the social structure of Canadian cities. Currently, he is the leader of the Housing and Neighbourhoods domain at Metropolis, a global network that examines public policy related to migration, diversity, and the integration of immigrants.

Teixeira's research provides insight into the barriers faced by immigrants, refugees, and ethnic minority groups in getting housing. In "Finding a Home of Their Own," Teixeira (2011) examines the housing experiences of new immigrants in Vernon, Penticton, and Kelowna in British Columbia. These are cities with some of the highest real estate market rates in Canada. His interviews with immigrants revealed that affordability was one of the primary issues related to housing. Many were forced to share housing with family or rent basements. This was associated with issues of overcrowding, a lack of privacy, and increased family tension. Immigrants also faced difficulty accessing complete and reliable information. Some experienced discrimination from landlords, who refused to rent because of reasons related to large family sizes and immigrant customs (for example, cooking habits).

In another study, Teixera and McEwan (2012) identified barriers students faced in accessing rental houses. Affordability, followed by transportation and location, availability, and discrimination, are the greatest barriers faced by students. Many students are forced to take out loans to pay rent or are forced to rely on food banks after paying rent. Others become part of the "hidden homeless," which entails "couch-surfing" or sharing houses temporarily with other students, family, or friends. Some students live in other cities due to the high costs of living but must then pay for extra travel costs or must settle for low-quality housing. Further, students are often denied housing because of the belief they will be partying excessively and will be loud and disruptive.

Teixeira proposes the federal government should fund affordable housing projects, regulate and co-operate with developers, encourage communication between land holders and renters, and assist community organizations.

Test Your Knowledge

1. Define the cycle of poverty.
2. Why is there a scarcity of rental units in rural regions? What is the impact of this?
3. What factors contribute to the housing crisis on Indigenous reserves?
4. What are two major barriers Canadians with disabilities face in accessing housing?

5. True or false: Treating two people in the same way can be discriminatory.
6. True or false: Low-income Canadians often live in metropolitan areas to increase their chances of finding work opportunities
7. True or false: Low-income Canadians are the most vulnerable to inadequate housing.
8. Fill in the blank: ______________ refers to the tendency in some North American cities for certain areas or neighbourhoods to be settled mainly by people of one particular class (often poor) or one particular racialized group of people.
9. Fill in the blank: ______________ are not eligible for many income support programs, do not have the savings needed to cover living expenses, and are thought of as unreliable and irresponsible by landlords.

See the Answer Key online to check your answers.

Questions for Critical Thought

1. In this chapter, we discussed how access to transportation and housing are related. Do you think solutions for one problem is enough? Explain why or why not.
2. Have you faced any discrimination or barrier in accessing safe and satisfactory housing? Do your experiences relate to those of the groups discussed in this chapter?
3. Do you think increasing funding for affordable housing is enough to end the housing-related challenges in Canada? Why or why not?
4. What can we do to decrease the discrimination faced by the vulnerable populations discussed in this chapter?
5. How does living in a rural or urban region impact an individual? Do you think these effects will persist into the future? Why or why not?

Additional Resources

Recommended Readings

Anderson, Alan. 2013. *Home in the City: Urban Indigenous Housing and Living Conditions.* Toronto, ON: University of Toronto Press. This book provides an in-depth analysis of urban Indigenous housing, living conditions, issues, and trends.

Gutentag, Daniel. 2018. "What Airbnb Really Does to a Neighbourhood." *BBC News*, August 30 (https://www.bbc.com/news/business-45083954). This article presents a thorough examination of problems related to Airbnb rentals, as well as attempted solutions throughout the urban world.

Hulchanski, David and Michael Shapcott. 2004. *Finding Room: Policy Options for a Canadian Rental Housing Strategy*. Toronto, ON: University of Toronto Press. This book examines the nature and scope of the problems and issues that an affordable housing policy must address by examining specific policies and programs.

Johnson, R. 2019. "Navigating the Toronto Housing Crisis as an Indigenous Person." *CBC News*, February 24 (https://www.cbc.ca/news/indigenous/urban-housing-rental-market-toronto-1.5029653). This article highlights the discrimination faced by Richard Peters, an Indigenous man, as he searches for a home in Toronto.

McCallion, David. 2007. *Housing for the Elderly: Policy and Practice Issues*. New York: Routledge. McCallion examines the key aspects of issues faced by the elderly during housing transitions, evaluates housing programs for the elderly, and examines the aid provided by social workers.

Silver, Kim. 2011. *Good Places to Live: Poverty and Public Housing in Canada*. Black Point, NS: Fernwood Publishing. This book examines how the stereotypes and stigma related to public housing, particularly its association with poverty, illegal activity, and violence, reduces the availability of affordable housing.

Recommended Websites

Canada Mortgage and Housing Corporation (CMHC)

www.cmhc-schl.gc.ca

CMHC is Canada's leading house agency and premier provider of mortgage loan insurance, mortgage-backed securities, housing policy and programs, and housing research. They work with community organizations, the private sector, not-for-profit agencies, and all levels of government to help create innovative solutions to housing issues.

Canadian Housing and Renewal Association (CHRA)

www.chra-achru.ca/en

The CHRA is an association that aims to bring issues of affordable housing and possible solutions to the agenda of decision makers. This website includes up-to-date news about the affordable housing in Canada, publications, and potential solutions related to housing and homelessness.

Government of Canada: Affordable Housing Initiative

http://actionplan.gc.ca/en/initiative/investment-affordable-housing

This website, created by the Government of Canada, provides access to information about two publications: Canada's Economic Action Plan and Investment in Affordable Housing.

Habitat for Humanity Canada

www.habitat.ca

Habitat for Humanity Canada is an organization with the goal of preparing families for homeownership, providing Habitat homes, and holding partner family mortgages. This website includes information about the organization, their initiatives, and how one can get involved.

Recommended Films

Home Safe Toronto. 2009. Produced by Skyworks Charitable Foundation. Toronto: Vtape. This documentary follows two families facing challenges associated with housing, particularly finding adequate funds to pay their monthly rent.

The People of the Kattawapiskak River. 2012. Directed by Alanis Obomsawin. Canada: National Film Board. In this documentary on First Nations' housing issues, we see something we face repeatedly in this book: namely, the intersection or overlapping of multiple disadvantages where Indigenous Peoples are concerned.

Push. 2019. Directed by Fredrik Gertten. Sweden: WG Film AB. This documentary explores the ways in which private equity firms are purchasing bulk housing stock and impacting housing in cities.

Tony's Story. http://vimeo.com/27214019. This video profiles Toni's experience of discrimination as a disabled person in a subsidized co-operative housing unit.

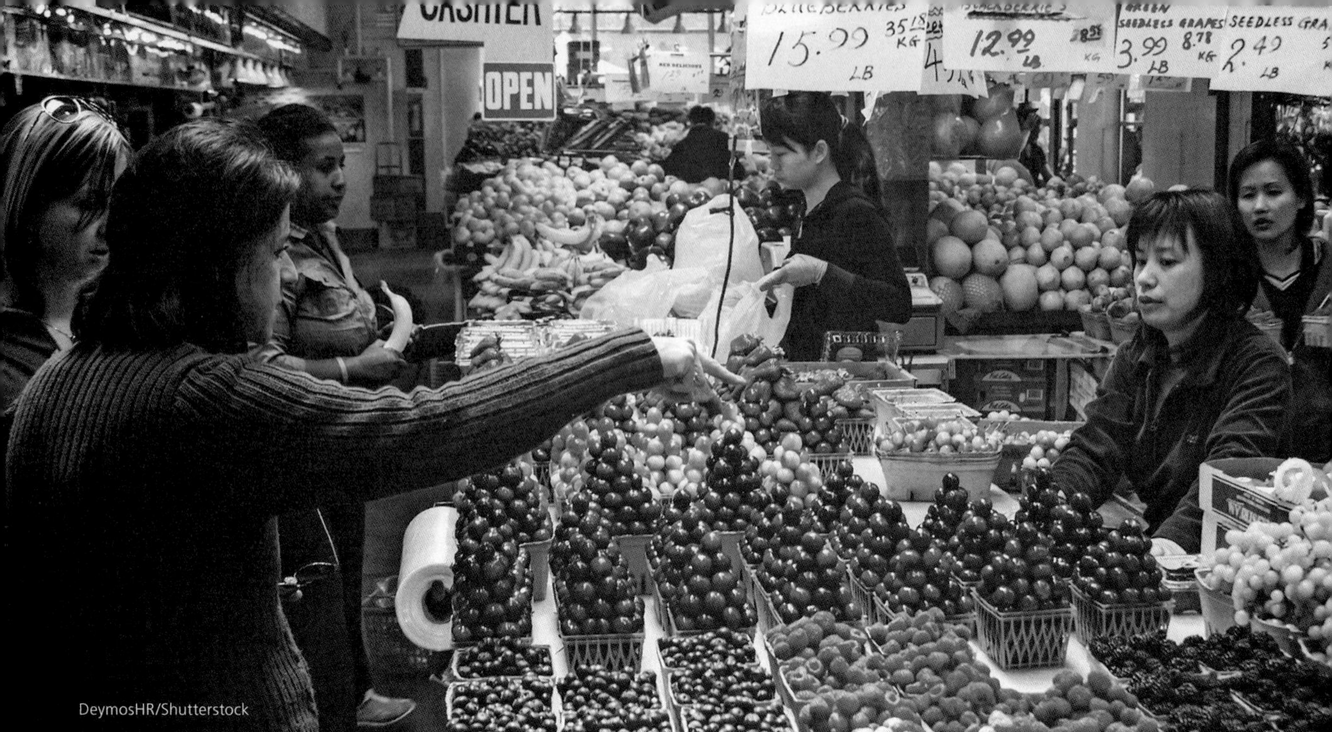

DeymosHR/Shutterstock

7 Access to Nutritious Food

Learning Objectives

- To examine changing food trends in Canada.
- To identify the various populations in Canada that have unequal access to food.
- To recognize the physical and emotional effects of food insecurity.
- To understand the societal effects of food insecurity.
- To consider different theoretical perspectives that address unequal access to nutritious food.
- To evaluate strategies of resistance at the governmental, organizational, and individual levels.

Drawing Connections

When reading through this chapter, think about the principle of interlocking disadvantages. How might some populations be more vulnerable to food insecurity than others? For example, the food insecurity of a recently immigrated, low-income, racialized person with a disability might be different from a settled white, wealthy person with the same disability.

Introduction

> It is fatal to look hungry. It makes people want to kick you.
> —George Orwell, *Down and Out in Paris and London* ([1933] 2001)

Food keeps all living creatures alive, so the absence of enough food will obviously pose a physical problem. People in every society are divided into two main classes: Those with enough (or even too much) to eat, and those without enough to eat. The difference between this social inequality and the others we have explored is a more immediate matter of life and death. Food security is perhaps the most important kind of survival capital; its absence means the risk of death.

In this chapter, we discuss food inequality. Often when sociologists talk about food and access to it (or lack thereof), they use the term **food security** or **food insecurity**. Households with food insecurity, the opposite of food security, do not have consistent access to enough safe and nutritious food. Think about the word *security*: It means freedom from danger, stress, risk, and anxiety. It is dangerous, stressful, and risky to have limited or inconsistent access to safe, nutritious food.

food security When a household has consistent access to enough safe, nutritious food.

food insecurity When a household does not have consistent access to enough safe, nutritious food.

We will begin this chapter with a general outline of some key themes related to food security. Next we will look at some changing food trends in Canada. After that, we will examine various populations in Canada that have unequal access to this vital resource.

Theoretical Perspectives on Access to Nutritious Food

Issues about access to nutritious food are different from the issues of survival capital we discussed in earlier chapters. We eat food for more than symbolic purposes: We eat to stay alive.

That isn't to say there are no symbolic issues around eating. Wealthy people tend to eat better and more stylishly than low-income people. They enjoy a wider range of food possibilities. Because money is no object, they can conspicuously consume food. Some of them make this consumption part of their identities as "foodies." Foodies are people who display a refined interest in food, eating not only out of hunger but also as a hobby and to show their social status. Often, foodies also express concern for environmental sustainability, organic cultivation, and fair labour practices.

Some businesses offer these wealthy food consumers an opportunity to strive for sustainable practices by buying products that align with these values. For these businesses, ethical consumption is mainly an elite social practice. Consider the Whole Foods Market chain. Whole Foods Market offers a wide variety of organic and sustainable foods, but they are usually more expensive than conventional products. Johnston and Baumann (2014) argue that this high-pricing practice limits citizenship by narrowing the range of choices available to lower-income people. It also hinders environmental sustainability, in part, by stimulating an increased consumption of food products.

Johnston and Baumann find that people with high incomes and a Euro-Canadian background are the most likely to indulge in these costly ethical eating practices. People who are not socially privileged do not engage in the same degree of ethical eating as their privileged counterparts, largely for financial reasons. By overpricing sustainably grown foods, producers hinder consumers from unprivileged backgrounds who want to engage in ethical eating.

However, most people are not foodies. For poor people especially, access to food is a survival need. And social thinkers have been considering this survival need for centuries.

Functionalists, for example, focus on the social role of food security and insecurity. Social philosopher Thomas Malthus (1826) first explored the social purpose of these unpleasant realities in his *Essay on Population*. In this essay, Malthus notes that human populations grew much faster than the food supply. As a result, occasional periods of food insecurity and starvation (along with war and disease) acted as a form of population control, which kept a population from disappearing. Within this framework, food insecurity is not only unavoidable, it is also socially useful.

Along similar lines, structural functionalists argue that poverty may play a key role in society because the threat of starvation and the lure of prosperity induce people to work hard, which benefits themselves, their families, and society as a whole. If we view hard work as a way to avoid starvation and achieve upward mobility, then we can think of inequality as promoting economic growth.

Conflict theory, on the other hand, sees poverty and starvation as socially harmful side effects of global capitalism. Today, multinational corporations (including agribusinesses) build up huge annual profits that are grossly out of line with the payments they offer their employees. This unequal distribution of wealth means that people can starve, or at least suffer continuing food insecurity, in communities and societies that produce a food surplus. Conflict theorists might point out that Walmart employees in the United States are paid so little that they qualify for food stamps, which they can trade in for food at Walmart (Frolik 2018). Walmart benefits from this arrangement twice: First, the government subsidizes the wages of their employees; second, they can trade the stamps in for even more cash.

As might be expected, conflict theorists are concerned with the social-structural and cultural causes of continued food insecurity. Food insecurity is commonplace in poor nations. These nations often focus on producing a particular agricultural crop—for example, sugar or bananas—and import most other food. People survive this way, but just barely. Many local people cannot afford to buy the food that is produced locally and exported at a profit to richer nations. Similarly, they cannot afford to buy the food that is produced elsewhere and imported. For example, in Cuba many people cannot afford to buy foreign food products or their own locally produced food. Instead, their well-educated population survives by exporting hard-working people who typically send monthly payments home to Cuba.

Symbolic interactionists, for their part, focus on the ways that people make sense of hunger and plenty. For example, they study the ways we interpret malnutrition, eating disorders, and obesity. They also study the ways that people who are hungry, malnourished, obese, or inclined to consume unhealthy foods (for example, huge soft drinks) are stigmatized. The public often sees eating habits as a reflection of a person's character. People in our society are inclined to view people who eat abnormally as morally weak and responsible for their own failure to eat good food. People who eat abnormally or look poorly fed, like those who are poorly dressed, are at a disadvantage at school and in the search for jobs. As a result, victims of food insecurity may be ridiculed or stigmatized, leading to further social disadvantage. Yet people eat abnormally for a variety of reasons, including food insecurity.

Feminists note that women have a particular concern with food insecurity, as "they are almost always responsible for taking care of nutrition in households" (Phillips 2009:495–6). Beyond this responsibility, many societies expect women to sacrifice food when it is scarce or insecure so that their partners and children can eat enough. Phillips (2009) notes women's relationship to food and nutrition "demonstrate a need for strong advocacy at both grassroots and international levels" (496).

Present-Day Food Insecurities

All humans, no matter where they live on the planet, need to eat roughly 2,300 calories a day. But these calories can't come from just one food source. Humans need variety in their diet to get all the nutrients they need to live healthy, active lives. For example, potassium, found in foods like spinach, lentils, and sweet potatoes, is so vital to organ function that a person would not be able to live long without it. Variety is not just the spice of life—it's a critical part of nutrition. That's why the variety of food intake is considered when examining food insecurity.

When people experience food insecurity, they feel it in various ways, as you may have already gathered from the quotes above. Most notably, a person who doesn't eat enough of the right foods almost immediately feels the physical discomfort of "hunger," which is painful and makes focusing difficult. But long-term hunger is more than just pain in the belly. A poor diet resulting from food insecurity can also cause or contribute to diabetes, heart disease, and other chronic illnesses. Besides these physical complications, food insecurity can produce social and psychological problems. Figure 7.1 shows the extra health-care costs incurred each year by food-insecure households. Note that hunger is expensive in many ways.

Consider the findings of noted Canadian food insecurity researcher Dr Valerie Tarasuk (2001b). She compiled responses from interviews with people experiencing routine hunger. Her respondents told her about the emotional elements of food insecurity. They described the monotony and feelings of deprivation caused by the limited selection of food in their diet. They also described a preoccupation with food—a constant worry about food insecurity that made focusing on other things difficult.

Beyond the stress and anxiety caused by food insecurity, there are also social dimensions to food insecurity. Much of eating is a social act. We gather to "break bread" and connect with friends and family over meals. Many cultural and religious traditions are

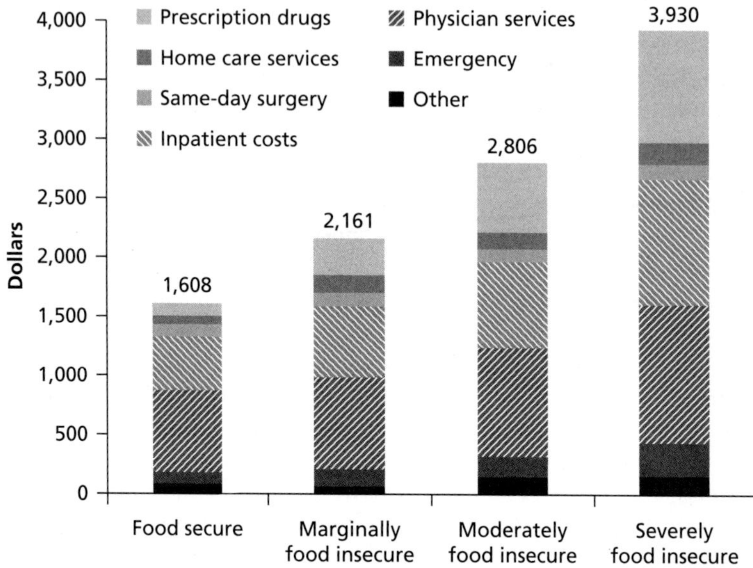

Figure 7.1 ◆ Average Healthcare Costs Associated with Food Insecurity
This graph shows the average healthcare costs for Ontarians over a 12-month period. Notice that costs in every category increase as food insecurity increases. As well, people with the most significant healthcare costs are the most likely to scrimp on food buying.

Source: Proof: Food Insecurity Policy Research n.d.

enacted with food and food rituals. Parents often use mealtimes to "check in" with their children and offer parental guidance. Preparing special meals for others communicates support, love, and respect. The routine of eating three meals a day offers a justified break from work and a moment to engage in self-care.

Households with high levels of food insecurity are often unable to gain these social benefits from food. They may not have enough food to prepare three meals a day, and, if necessary, parents will often forgo food so their children can eat. Children end up eating alone while parents occupy themselves with another task.

Food-insecure people may also feel social shame when trying to get food from charitable sources, friends, or even through less socially acceptable methods like theft. Feelings and experiences of social alienation, powerlessness, monotony, deprivation, preoccupation, stress, anxiety, shame, and guilt are often associated with food insecurity.

There are vast differences in food consumption patterns around the world. Culture deeply influences the kinds of food people choose. Someone from Britain might turn up her nose at the fish soup often served for breakfast in Vietnam. Vegemite and Marmite, popular sandwich spreads in the United Kingdom, New Zealand, and Australia, might disgust people in many other parts of the world. You might be surprised to learn that certain potato chip flavours, such as ketchup or dill pickle, that are adored in Canada flop south of the border.

Culture is not the only thing that controls the type, quality, and amount of food people eat around the world. There are also critical differences in food availability. For example, in poorer nations like Chad, Congo, and Burundi, food shortages mean there aren't enough calories for everyone to meet their daily requirement. So even if the food in these countries were evenly distributed, there still wouldn't be enough (Li 2012). Canada, on the other hand, has a surplus of available food; we have enough food for each person to eat an extra 1,200 calories a day. Despite this incredible surplus, food consumption in Canada is not equal. Also, all calories are not created equal. Many of the surplus calories available to Canadians are derived from "foods" we probably shouldn't be eating at all. As we will see in this chapter, many vulnerable populations in Canada are struggling to access enough of the *right* food.

Finally, there is much to be said about the impact of our collective food choices on the planet. We know that industrial agriculture, particularly meat production, is responsible for a significant percentage of global greenhouse gas emissions that have contributed to the climate crisis. If we are to limit climate change to a 2-degree Celsius target, most of us will have to dramatically change our diets. How will we achieve this on a global scale? Not easily, and not without changing availability, agricultural production strategies, transport, food processing and storage . . . but most of all, food *culture*.

Changing Trends in Access to Nutritious Food

Our methods of growing and delivering food are becoming increasingly efficient, yet more households in Canada are struggling with food security. Figure 7.2 shows, in graphic form, the most recent evidence on food insecurity.

But how do we know that food insecurity is a growing problem? One way of seeing changing trends in food insecurity is by looking at the number of people accessing food banks.

Food banks are usually good at tracking the types of people that need emergency food supplies. Thanks to their careful checking, we have access to statistics that show who is experiencing food shortages, why, and for how long. Some of these statistics challenge the assumptions that many people hold. Here are a few of them.

Many people think that food bank clients are homeless, but data from Food Banks Canada's 2018 HungerCount report shows the opposite is true: 89 per cent of the single-person households accessing food banks are "rental or social housing tenants, and 65 percent [cite] social assistance as their primary source of income" (11). These people spend about 70 per cent of their income simply keeping themselves sheltered.

Another misconception is the belief that **social assistance** or old age pensions are enough to cover basic living costs, including food expenses. However, nearly half of the households accessing food banks are recipients of social assistance (Food Banks Canada 2018). This suggests that social assistance payments are *not enough* for people to escape food insecurity.

social assistance Income support programs administered by the government and intended to help recipients cover the cost of food, shelter, clothing, and other daily necessities.

Another commonly held belief is that it is only single parents who seek support from food banks. Single parents do face chronic economic disadvantages and are overrepresented in the population seeking emergency help from food banks. However, households with two parents make up nearly 20 per cent of the families helped by food banks (Food Banks Canada 2018; see Figure 7.3).

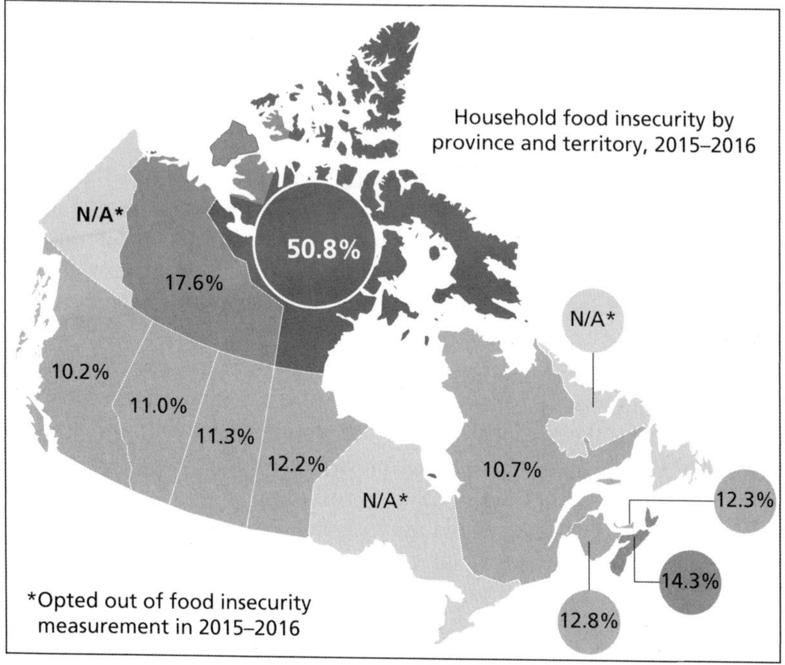
Household food insecurity by province and territory, 2015–2016
N/A*
50.8%
17.6%
N/A*
10.2%
11.0%
11.3%
12.2%
N/A*
10.7%
12.3%
14.3%
12.8%
*Opted out of food insecurity measurement in 2015–2016

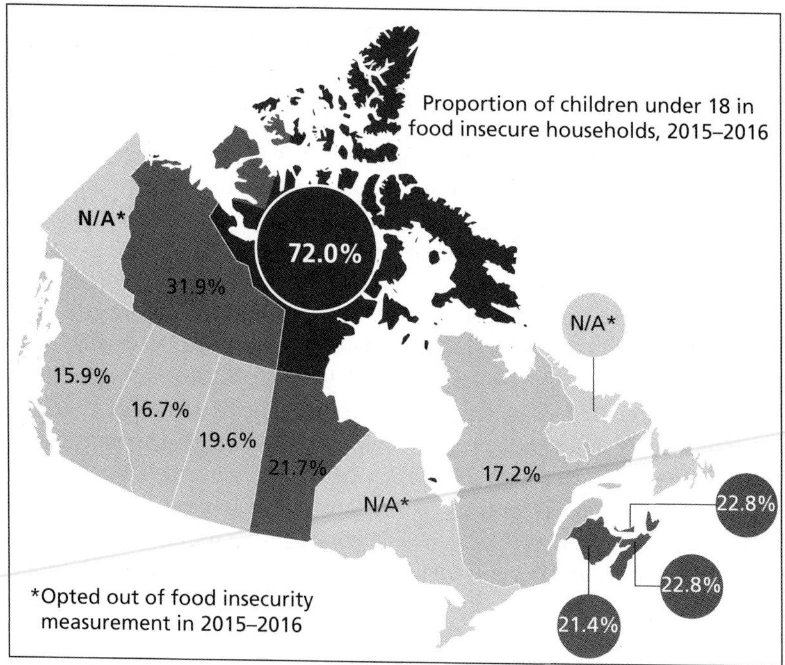
Proportion of children under 18 in food insecure households, 2015–2016
N/A*
72.0%
31.9%
N/A*
15.9%
16.7%
19.6%
21.7%
17.2%
N/A*
22.8%
22.8%
21.4%
*Opted out of food insecurity measurement in 2015–2016

(Continued)

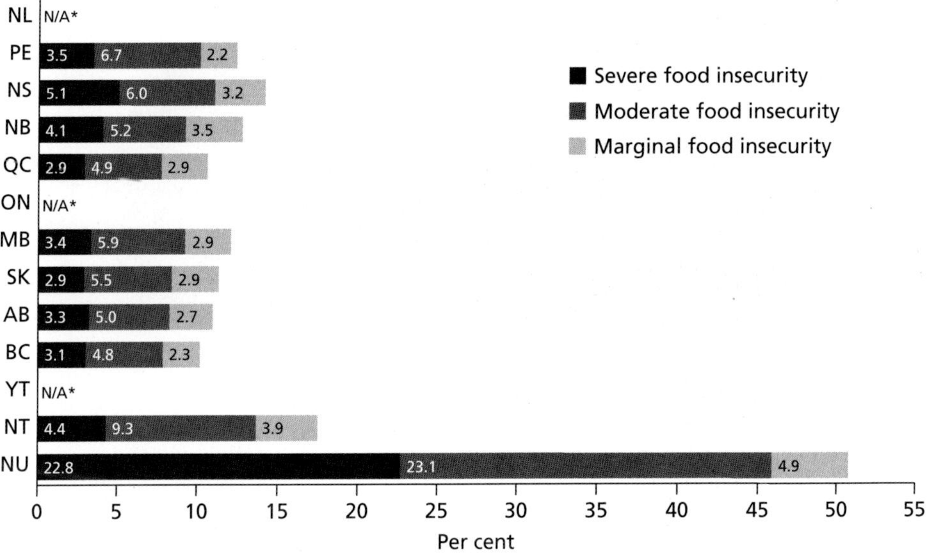

*Opted out of food insecurity measurement in 2015–2016

Figure 7.2 ◆ Food Insecurity in Canada: Facts

Source: Proof: Food Insecurity Policy Research 2018.

IN FOCUS ◆ History of Food Banks in Canada

Food banks emerged in Canada during an economic recession in the 1980s as a response to the inadequate support provided by unemployment insurance and provincial funds. The first food bank opened in Alberta in 1981. Currently, there are over 1700 food banks across Canada, which feed roughly 867,000 people per month, with 38 per cent of them being children or youth under the age of 18.

Food Banks Canada, the national organization representing Canadian food banks, released a report that notes food bank use has steadily risen across the country. Every province except Ontario and Manitoba saw a high increase in usage, and Nova Scotia saw an increase of over 20 per cent (Food Banks Canada 2016). Similarly, in its "HungerCount 2018" report, it is noted that over 501,000 households accessed food banks between 2017 and 2018 (6).

Food banks certainly help those who cannot afford food, but many have argued that they are a "bandage" solution that doesn't address larger issues. Food banks can create a public view that relieving hunger is a matter of charity, especially when corporate sponsors provide funds or food donations to a food bank. According to writer Graham Riches (2011), one way we can begin to address this problem is to remove what we call the "corporatization of hunger," which he argues allows the government to keep ignoring the problem.

Food Banks Canada admits the flaws of this system. One-third of food banks do not meet the nutritional needs of their clients. They may run out of food, give people less food out of fear of running out, or because they close too early in the day. The demand for food also usually exceeds the donations a food bank receives. Food banks, then, can only be seen as a starting point to ending hunger in Canada.

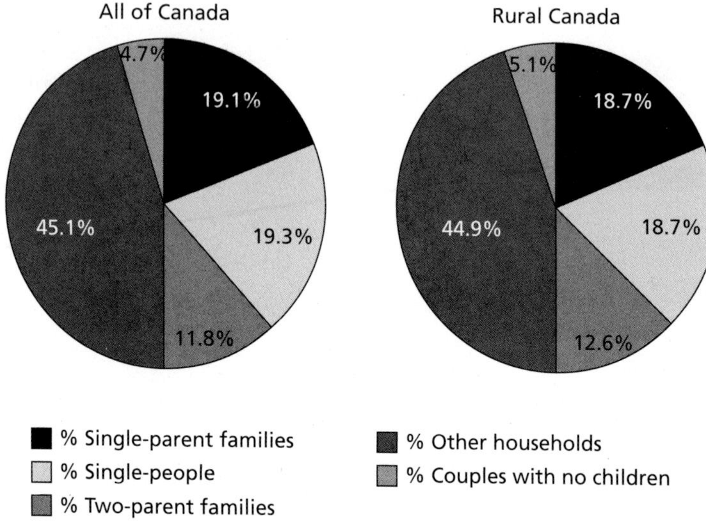

Figure 7.3 ◆ Food Bank Use, by Type of Household

Source: Food Banks Canada 2018.

Children add huge financial pressures to families: They don't bring any money into a home, but do they ever eat! That's probably why the lowest reported levels of food insecurity are found in adults without children (Statistics Canada 2019b). Children may not be seen standing in food bank lineups, but they are typically the largest population group to use food banks. More than 30 per cent of food bank users are children (Food Banks Canada 2018).

On their own, food bank statistics are not a perfect sign of how many families experience food insecurity in Canada. Some families may find other ways to cope with food insecurity. For example, some families may send children to another person's home for meals or buy food with credit cards and amass debt. They may also steal food or get it in other risky ways, such as by retrieving it from waste containers ("dumpster diving"). Or they may continually experience persistent, painful hunger.

Also, food banks are not equally distributed across Canada. Some have noted that as a person travels north in this country, food banks become harder to find despite the increasing need for them. Food Banks Canada (2018) reports that 46.8 per cent of households in Nunavut are food insecure. The fact there are fewer people accessing food banks in some regions of Canada may say less about levels of hunger and more about the scarcity of food banks.

The growing number of certain diet-related health problems is another sign that more families are experiencing food insecurity. In the past few decades, obesity, diabetes, and cardiovascular disease have been on the rise in Canada. The rise in prevalence of these diseases is another clue that people aren't eating enough of the right foods.

Taken altogether, the growing numbers of people using food banks and their reported experiences warrant the conclusion that more people in Canada are experiencing

◆ In Their Own Words ◆

Recently, the World Health Organization conducted an interview with food sociologist Marion Nestle, author of seven books on the socio-economic influences on food choices and the rising levels of obesity.

Q: Surely food companies have some level of responsibility to treat their consumers with a bit more respect?

A: A food company official I met . . . says his company has a vested interest in keeping people healthy because they'll buy more food for a longer period of time. Maybe . . . but when there's a conflict between corporate growth and making healthier foods, corporate growth wins out. Companies cannot go against their own economic interests . . . What's needed is a combination of public education [and] government restrictions on food industry marketing practices . . . so it is easier for people to eat more healthily.

Source: Jones 2012.

food insecurity. Why might that be? What are some factors influencing growing food insecurity?

Measuring food insecurity is more difficult than counting the number of Canadians visiting food banks, monitoring their physical health, or even asking about their experiences. For one thing, food prices are rising faster than the rate of inflation. The 2019 "Food Price Report" notes that food prices are rising in almost every category (see Table 7.1). It explains "the annual food expenditure for the average Canadian family is expected to increase by $411 in 2019 to around $12,157 for the year" (Charlebois et al. 2019:5). Most of this increase comes from the rising cost of fresh produce, making it difficult for families to continue purchasing fruits and vegetables. Likely, the COVID-19 epidemic will raise food prices even more.

Table 7.1 2019 Food Price Forecasts

Food Categories	Anticipated Increase (%)
Bakery	1–3
Dairy	0–2
Food	0–2
Fruits	1–3
Meat	(–3)–(–1)
Restaurants	2–4
Seafood	(–2)–0
Vegetables	4–6
Total Food Categories Forecast	**1.5–3.5**

Source: Somogyi 2018.

As well, studies have shown that the prices of unhealthy foods are less likely to increase compared with healthy foods like fruits and vegetables. One US study, for example, found that 1,000 calories of junk food cost $1.76, on average, while the same number of healthy calories cost $18.16. The head researcher on this study noted,

> if you have $3 to feed yourself, your choices gravitate toward foods which give you the most calories per dollar . . . Not only are the empty calories cheaper, but the healthy foods are becoming more and more expensive. Vegetables and fruits are rapidly becoming luxury goods. (Parker-Pope 2007)

Household food insecurity is also affected by macroeconomic factors like war and conflict. Impeded access to oil in Middle Eastern countries can affect food costs here in Canada (Charlebois et al. 2012). Oil is needed to ship foods and run the machinery on most farms, so when that becomes more expensive, the costs are passed down to the consumer. Likewise, global climate change has and will affect the cost of food. For example, the 2012 North American drought drove up prices for corn and soybeans, increasing the cost of grain for cattle and driving up meat prices.

Domestically, retail competition can drive food prices down as companies compete to attract customers with lower prices. But increasingly in Canada, small, independently owned farms that grow diverse crops are being squeezed out by large, single-crop farms operated by agri-business corporations. This reduces competition and can drive up prices. It also makes Canadians dangerously overreliant on a few food providers (many of which are headquartered outside of the country) instead of many local ones. When we rely on fewer and bigger suppliers, we are subject to the availability, quality, and price of what they give us, which can unpredictably rise and fall. We are also subject to how those few suppliers are affected by extreme weather events.

So far, we have sketched a picture of food insecurity in Canada and some factors influencing changing food trends. In the next section we will see how experiences of food insecurity are not evenly distributed among all populations in Canada. Specifically, we will address how low-income people, young people, women, seniors, Indigenous Peoples, and people with disabilities are more vulnerable to food insecurity than others. Other populations in Canada likely experience food insecurity because of systemic barriers, but for reasons of space we will not be discussing them here.

Low-Income People in Canada

Many sociologists who study food insecurity would point out that low or no income is the root of most food insecurity. Simply put, money equals food: Very few Canadians can feed themselves without spending money. To better understand the ways people are eating food, we need to understand how they get the money to buy it.

Income is most commonly gained from employment, so one common reason a person might experience food insecurity is unemployment. Not surprisingly, food bank use correlates with unemployment rates; when unemployment goes up in a community, so does the use of food banks (Food Banks Canada 2012). Figure 7.4 shows a correlation between food bank use and unemployment from the years 2004–14.

But not all people experiencing food insecurity are unemployed. In 2018, minimum wage workers represented 10 per cent of all employees (Morissette and Dionne-Simard 2018).

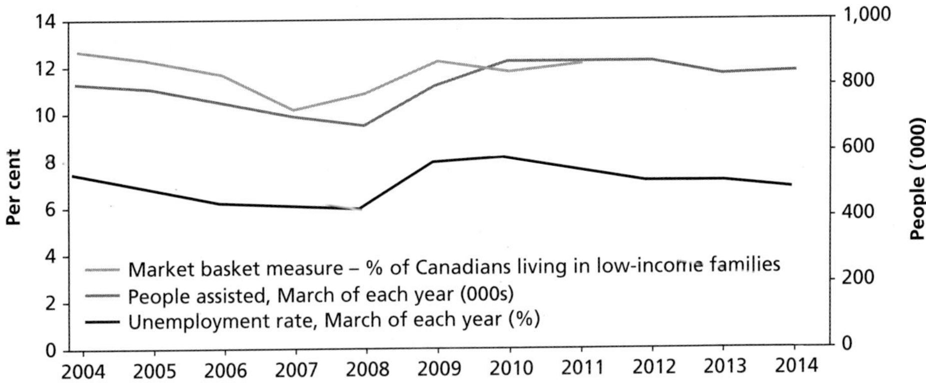

Figure 7.4 ◆ Food Bank Use, Unemployment, and Poverty in Canada, 2004–14

Source: https://www.broadbentinstitute.ca/en/post/food-bank-use-canada-now-25-higher-recession

Many of these low-income Canadians work full time and yet are members of the working poor. This means they fall below the low-income cut-off and struggle to meet their basic needs.

Income is most commonly gained from a job, but it can come from other sources as well. Many Canadians get income from social assistance programs, which as you'll recall from earlier in the chapter are income support programs designed—at least, in theory—to help people meet their basic needs.

employment insurance An income support program that offers temporary financial support to people who have lost a job through no fault of their own.

Employment insurance, for example, is a social assistance program that offers temporary financial support to people who have lost a job through no fault of their own. Another is the Canada Child Benefit that provides a monthly payment for each child in a family. There are also social assistance programs for people with disabilities who cannot work, either temporarily or permanently, and other programs for older, retired Canadians. What these programs have in common is that on their own they do not provide enough to allow recipients to live comfortably and eat enough nutritious food. Why is that?

There are competing beliefs about the amount the government should pay to those who need social assistance. Historically, the prevailing belief has been that social assistance should not exceed the amount that could be earned from a minimum wage job. This belief is founded on a functionalist notion that people are uncomfortable living in poverty and will therefore be motivated to seek employment and end their dependence on social assistance. The primary objective of social assistance, after all, is to get people working. A belief that someone drawing social assistance might choose to remain unemployed is widely thought to underpin the current rates set by the government. This belief contributes to negative stereotypes about Canadians on social assistance, especially the notion that they are "enjoying a free ride."

Another belief is that many people on social assistance are not motivated to seek work when the work available to them pays minimum wage and minimum wage is low. Instead of focusing on the rates of social assistance, many Canadians are calling for increases in minimum wage and childcare subsidies to encourage people to return to work. Some pilot studies have been conducted to test the truth of some of these beliefs. One of these—the Self-Sufficiency Project—is profiled in the box below.

Drawing Connections

A single mother returning to work at minimum wage would incur the cost of childcare. Recall from Chapter 4 that her childcare expenses would almost erase her net monthly earnings. She would be better off financially on social assistance! But as a result, she does not gather employment seniority, training, or experience. Does this benefit or hurt society?

IN FOCUS ◆ The Self-Sufficiency Project

In the 1990s, a not-for-profit Canadian research organization called the Social Research and Demonstration Corporation (2003) conducted an unusual social experiment. This organization wanted to test the theory that people on social assistance would be more likely to seek employment if they could earn a living wage doing so. The initiative was named the Self-Sufficiency Project.

The researchers guaranteed many single parents—90 per cent were women—a "top-up" to their earnings should they find a full-time job within one year. This top-up, which typically doubled the earnings these people would make in a full-time, minimum wage job, would taper off over three years as earnings rose. The theory was that at the three-year mark, participants would have progressed in their job to such an extent the subsidy was no longer a necessity.

The researchers also organized a control group. This control group consisted of a similar population—single parents on social assistance—but was not offered the top-up incentive. The employment rates in each group were measured over five years.

Do you think the single parents from the test group (receiving a minimum wage) were more likely to seek and secure employment? Which group do you think was more likely to be employed five years later? If you guessed that yes, people were more likely to seek work, you're right. The employment rates in the test group were almost double those in the control group within two years. The subgroup that was offered both a top-up and job skills training had the best result.

What does the Self-Sufficiency Project show us about food insecurity? The researchers note that some families used their higher income to buy basic needs, especially food and clothing. They also note that with a slightly higher income fewer families suffered from an inability to buy the groceries they needed. Five years later, however, after the experiment had ended, the rates of employment in both the control and test groups were largely the same. People who did not receive the employment income top-up were just as likely to find a job. Does that mean that income subsidies are ineffective? In other words, since both groups wound up in the same place within five years, why bother?

There are several reasons these findings suggest that income top-ups are worthwhile despite the employment parity five years later. For one thing, three years can matter a lot. In three years, a person can gain job skills that will increase their wages and job security. Three years also matter a lot for the parents of small children, whose lives—both current and future—will improve dramatically when household income increases. Also, an income top-up costs the government less than social assistance.

Another competing belief, which counters the strategy used by the Self-Sufficiency Project, is that focus should be placed on social assistance rates. Proponents believe the low rates of social support—and they are very low—are effectively preventing people from securing employment. First, take a look at Figure 7.5. It shows how, over the last two decades, social assistance has improved the well-being of low-income Canadians. Note, however, that despite social assistance, large proportions of Canadians continue to survive on low incomes.

Why would low social assistance rates prevent people from getting a job? For one thing, being poor can be hard work. Days are often spent "managing" poverty: seeking food, shelter, and other basic needs. We have learned that many people visiting food banks are on social assistance of some kind, and visiting a food bank takes time—time that could be spent searching for a job. And for a person on social assistance, the cost of Internet and a cellphone (for job hunting), professional clothing, and transportation to and from job interviews are large expenses.

In light of this, many Canadians suggest that increasing the rates of social assistance will help get people back to work. As well, increasing the rates of social assistance would have the added social benefit of keeping more of us safe and healthy.

It's true a guaranteed income program, such as the Mincome experiment, initially costs the government (and by extension, taxpayers) lots of money. And yet, there is money saved when fewer people are ill, fewer crimes are committed, and more people seek higher education and similarly are more likely to remain employed. A further cost–benefit analysis of initiatives like the one manufactured in Dauphin would tell us about the "true cost" of such programs. Sadly, one such experiment, launched in three Ontario communities in 2018, was abruptly cancelled when a new government took power. There was no chance for data to reveal the potential of this project to lift people out of poverty.

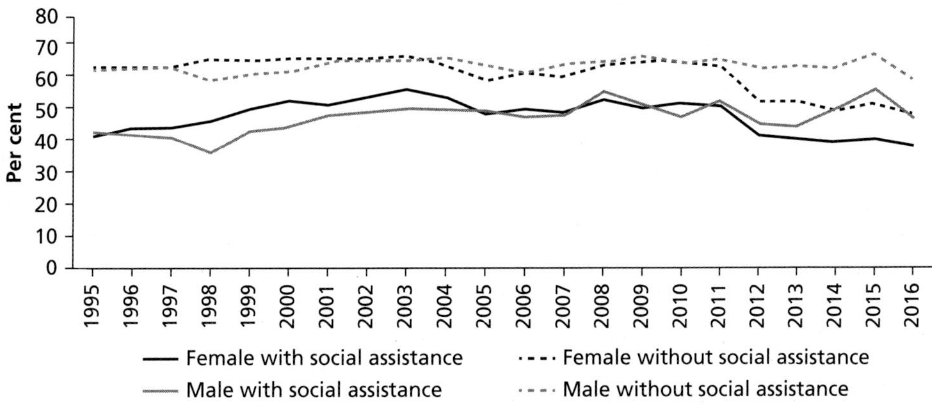

Figure 7.5 ◆ Low-Income Rates of Individuals Receiving and Not Receiving Social Assistance

Source: Statistics Canada 2018.

Jessie Golem

Read this testimonial closely. How does it connect the Basic Income project to food and nutrition? Voters might ask why elected politicians repeatedly put this successful experiment to an early death.

IN FOCUS ◆ Guaranteed Income

From 1974–8, Dauphin, Manitoba, was chosen as the site of a social experiment. In this experiment, residents who earned less than the low-income cut-off—working or non-working—were offered a "guaranteed income" cheque jointly funded by the provincial and federal governments to lift them out of poverty. This project was called "Mincome" (presumably a combination of the words "minimum" and "income"). Over 1,000 families took part in the experiment.

Facing a recession and some political shifts in power in the late seventies, both levels of government cancelled the Mincome project abruptly. Over 2,000 boxes of Mincome data then sat in storage for many years at Library and Archives Canada until professor Evelyn Forget from the University of Manitoba was granted access.

Her early review of the data demonstrated that residents of Dauphin showed better mental and physical health. They were less likely to drop out of school (the lower dropout rates persisted for a generation), had fewer accidents at work, and had fewer arrests and convictions. Moreover, only two populations in Dauphin worked less. They were mothers with newborns, who could suddenly afford to stay home with their babies, and teenagers, who elected to stay in school instead of work for pay.

Do these results surprise you? What does the guaranteed income experiment in Dauphin tell us about access to food? Remember, income is the most important determinant of food security. In 2009, the *Winnipeg Free Press* interviewed some people in Dauphin that had been assisted 40 years ago during the Mincome experiment (Reynolds 2009). Here is one excerpt from an interview with Hugh and Doreen Henderson, recipients of the Mincome cheques:

> "A couple of people came out and talked to us," says Doreen, 70. "We filled out forms, they wanted to see our receipts. We got to keep our family allowance." It was their children who benefited most . . . Doreen says the government should establish a similar program for seniors and young families. "Give them enough money to raise their kids. People work hard and it's still not enough," she says. "This isn't welfare. This is making sure kids have enough to eat."

Whether a person's income is derived from work, social assistance, or other sources, food is only one of the many costs of living. People need to pay for housing, clothing, transportation, electricity, and so on. As a result, episodes of food insecurity often result from cost increases or unexpected expenses, especially when a family's budget is already precariously balanced.

Take a look at Figures 7.6 and 7.7. These figures, compiled by Statistics Canada, show the changing costs of food in each province or territory. Figure 7.6 shows the share of overall spending on food by Canadian households. Figure 7.7 depicts the change in food prices between December 2017 and December 2018. During this time, food prices rose throughout all of Canada, with some of the largest increases experienced in Alberta, Ontario, and British Columbia.

Rent and mortgage payments can also be an enormous drain on a person's income if that income is already low. Most agree that a balanced budget requires a person to spend no more than 25 to 30 per cent on housing. Financial advisers caution that housing costs beyond that threshold of affordability will put undue pressure on a household. Despite

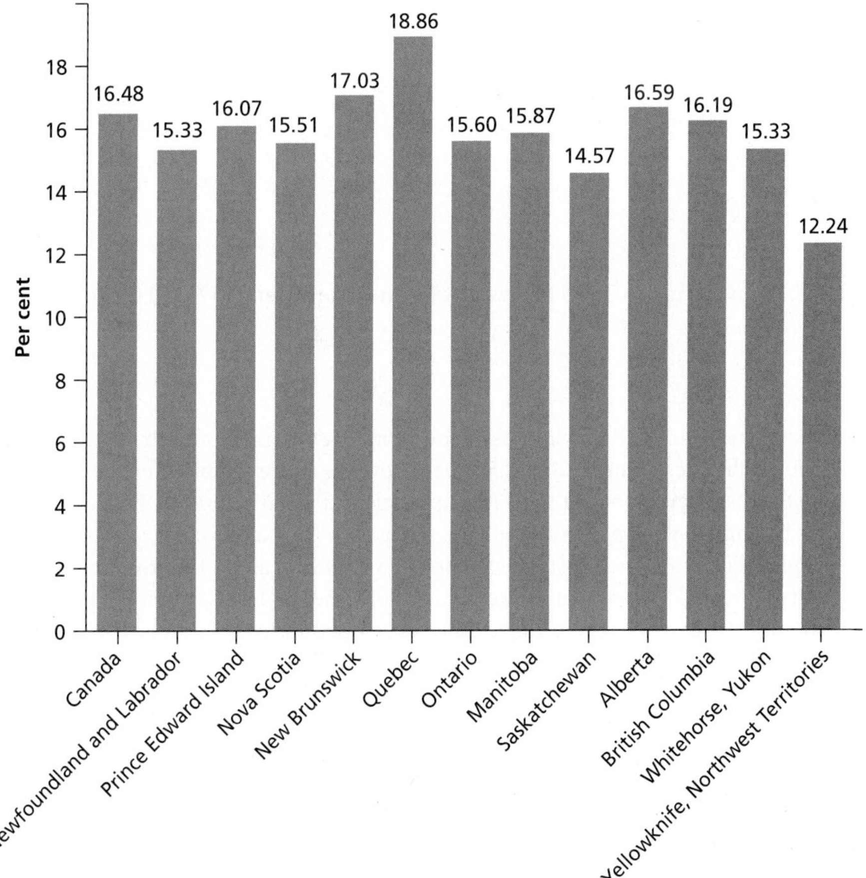

Figure 7.6 ◆ Percentage of Total Household Budget Spent on Food, 2018

Source: Statistics Canada 2019c.

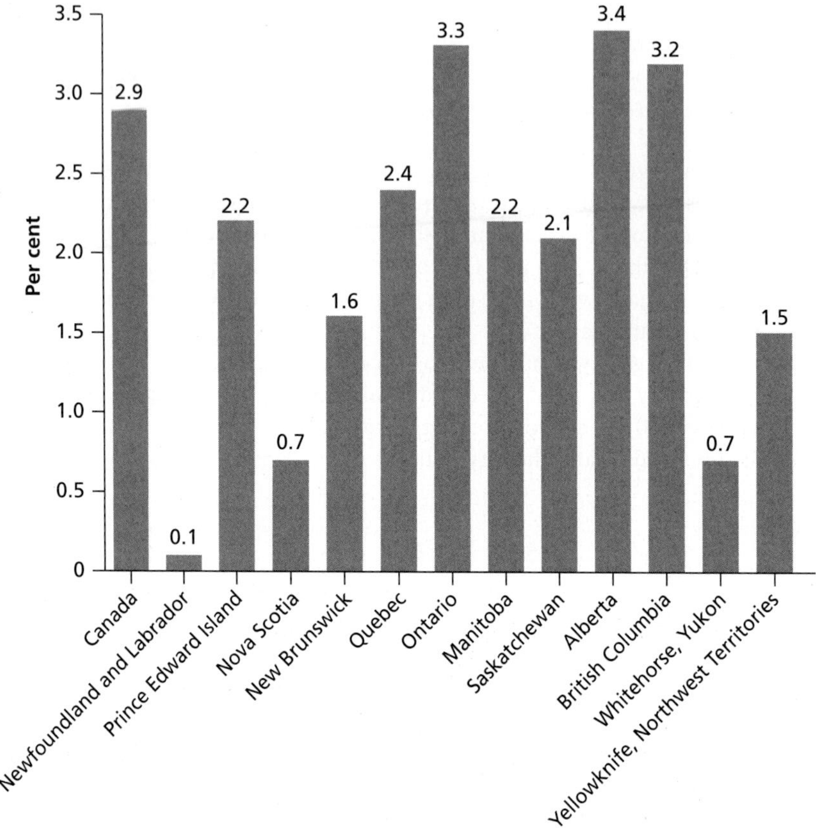

Figure 7.7 ◆ **Change in Food Prices between December 2017 and December 2018**

Source: Statistics Canada 2019c.

this advice, one-quarter of Canadians spend more than a third of their monthly income on housing (Statistics Canada 2016). Studies show the more people must spend on their housing, the less they spend on food (Kirkpatrick and Tarasuk 2007). Take a moment to calculate how much you spend on housing. Are you in the "safe zone"?

Cellphones are another cost to consider. Many would agree that owning a phone is a necessity, especially when you are seeking employment. However, people pay more for their phones in Canada than in most other developed nations (Harris 2018), and these high costs leave some Canadians choosing between eating and texting.

In 2014, 12 per cent of Canadian households were food insecure (Tarasuk, Mitchell, and Dachner 2016). Depending on the extent of their experiences, these households were further classified as being marginally food insecure (3.7 per cent), moderately food insecure (5.5 per cent), or severely food insecure (2.7 per cent). Slightly food-insecure households reported worrying about running out of food or having a limited selection of food. Moderately food-insecure households reported a compromise in the quality or the quantity of food consumed. Severely food-insecure households reported a drop in food intake that led to disrupted eating patterns, and in extreme cases going days without food.

For the first time in human history, obesity is a problem experienced by the poor in economically developed countries. Fruit and vegetable consumption is shown to be influenced by household income. The percentage of Canadians aged 12 or older who consumed fruits and vegetables at least five times daily was the lowest (27.4 per cent) in households within the lowest fifth of income earning households (Statistics Canada 2017). Typically, healthier food costs more at the grocery store. Food received from food banks also tends to be unhealthier, because it must be able to sit on the shelf for weeks or months without spoiling.

Researchers have also discovered geographic trends associated with health issues such as childhood obesity. One study found that children living in poorer neighbourhoods in Hamilton, Ontario, show twice the rates of obesity as those living in wealthier neighbourhoods (Moffat, Galloway, and Latham 2005). In low-income neighbourhoods, food availability may be an obstacle to healthy eating.

However, the jury is still out regarding the scarcity of healthy choices in poorer areas (sometimes called food deserts). A Montreal study found that median household income was unrelated to the density of fast-food outlets or grocery stores with a healthy selection of fruit and vegetables (Daniel, Kestens, and Paquet 2009). Another study examining 12 low-income neighbourhoods in Toronto found that availability doesn't matter anyway: Neighbourhood-level factors such as access to healthy food choices did not affect levels of food insecurity at all. Instead, household-level factors like income, education, and number of adults in the home had a greater effect on food insecurity (Kirkpatrick and Tarasuk 2009).

In short, food *availability* is not necessarily the problem for most food-insecure people in our society. Most people do not live in a distant village on the shores of Hudson Bay where fresh food needs to be flown in periodically at great cost and risk. Most people live physically near the food they need. The main problem is that low-income people can't afford nutrition. Said another way, they can only afford to buy cheap, infinitely available high-starch and high-sugar foods that are in every supermarket, convenience store, and gas station. Only this food will come close to filling their daily calorie needs at the price they can (nearly) afford. No wonder so many poor people—including people who live in dense urban settings surrounded by food outlets—are both malnourished and obese.

Young People in Canada

Most parents will tell you that their kids add joy and happiness to their lives. However, children are also a great burden, resource wise. They must be clothed, housed, supervised, and kept warm and dry. It's no surprise, then, that the population group in Canada most likely to be food insecure is families with children. In some provinces such as Manitoba and Saskatchewan, children make up nearly half of all food bank users (Food Banks Canada 2018). Often this is because the food insecurity of children is tied to the income insecurity of vulnerable populations who tend to have more children, such as Indigenous Peoples in Manitoba and Saskatchewan.

What are the effects of food insecurity in childhood? One study found that adolescents who experienced hunger as children were more likely to suffer from depression and show suicidal tendencies (McIntyre, Williams et al. 2012). Other effects include poor academic performance, cognitive delays, and negative effects on psychosocial development

(Bitton and Roth 2010). Children who experience food insecurity are also prone to obesity, which can lead to many other health problems, including an increased risk of broken bones, depression, diabetes, and many other problems (Taylor 2010). Others have found that experiences of hunger in childhood can lead to asthma (Kirkpatrick, McIntyre, and Potesio 2010).

How is childhood hunger addressed? Some of you may remember breakfast programs being offered at your elementary school; these were introduced in the 1990s and early 2000s. Most food banks or other food programs such as community kitchens or gardens—called **external coping strategies**—also target childhood food insecurity.

external coping strategies Programs offered outside of the home, such as community kitchens, food banks, and food programs, aimed at feeding children.

In the home, parents may use various coping strategies. These include skipping meals to feed their children and compromising on the quality and variety in the food they prepare. They also "stretch out" food (by adding water to dilute milk or juice), or rely on friends and family for support. These home-based measures are called **internal coping strategies**.

internal coping strategies Coping strategies within the home aimed at feeding children, such as stretching out food or relying on friends and family.

One Canadian study found that parents of children experiencing food insecurity are more likely to use internal, home-based coping strategies (McIntyre, Bartoo et al. 2012). The findings show that food-insecure families are more likely to compromise nutrition or skip meals than seek the help of a food bank or other charity. This is an alarming fact to consider when coupled with the increase in food bank use—how many families are struggling in secret? A study by Valerie Tarasuk and colleagues (2019) found that "most food-insecure households delayed bill payments and sought financial help from friends and family, but only 21.1 per cent used food banks." Other researchers speculated that "food insecurity and specifically, child hunger, are increasingly viewed as private matters that should stay within family boundaries" (McIntyre, Bartoo et al. 2012:431). What do you think? How are coping strategies affected by parents' feelings of shame and inadequacy?

Once again, the root of most childhood food insecurity is low household income. That's why many sociologists and other interested parties suggest that income supports for vulnerable households are a practical way to decrease levels of childhood hunger.

Women in Canada

Raising children on one income is a financial burden, and women are disproportionately responsible for feeding, clothing, and caring for children. This makes women uniquely vulnerable to food insecurity.

As we noted earlier, women are much more likely than men to be responsible for carework and nutrition. Feminist sociologists have been especially concerned about the factors that hinder women's abilities to carry out these tasks and the inequality that makes them women's unique responsibilities. The weight of these tasks and food insecurity is especially evident in households headed by single mothers (Tarasuk 2001b). Studies indicate that single mothers often forgo their own nutritional needs when there is a scarcity of food in the home. This means that when children are hungry, their mothers are likely to be even hungrier (McIntyre et al. 2003).

Why does this happen? One group of researchers speculated that "it may be that maternal self-deprivation of food is a socially acceptable practice . . . and mothers are taught to put their children's needs first" (McIntyre et al. 2003:691). How do social norms about mothering reinforce these behaviours?

Seniors in Canada

Earlier in this chapter you learned that people may get income from employment or other sources like social assistance. When a person is retired and can no longer work, they may get their income from social assistance.

There are two main income sources for people over the age of 65. The first source is personal savings and earnings. This might include money from a Registered Retirement Savings Plan, which is a special "locked" bank account into which a person can deposit money throughout their working life. Personal savings and earnings might also include an employee pension plan. Someone might also elect to save for retirement in other ways: a regular bank account, investments, or even a pickle jar buried in the backyard.

People over the age of 60 may also be entitled to the Canada Pension Plan (CPP). If you are employed, take a look at the small print on your next pay cheque and you'll see that roughly 5 per cent is taken away. That amount is matched by the government and put away for your retirement. Those who earn more contribute more, up to a maximum amount. This means the more comfortable your income is throughout your working life, the more comfortable your retirement will be—and vice versa.

Not everyone in Canada has personal savings or earnings like an employee pension plan, and not everyone is entitled to the CPP after the age of 65. For example, people who were stay-at-home caregivers for all of their working years or people who had precarious or under-the-table employment would likely not have access to these income sources post-retirement.

The government provides a second income source for seniors. The most common income source is Old Age Security, to which all Canadians are entitled. However, it is based on years of residency in Canada at the age of 65. If a person has lived in the country for 40 years, they will receive $601.45 per month (this is the 2019 rate—it increases slightly as the cost of living increases). On the other hand, if a person has lived in Canada for only 10 years, that person is entitled to only $150.36 per month. Note that new immigrants to Canada will receive far less than those who were born here.

And finally, the third income source for seniors is the Guaranteed Income Supplement. Canadian seniors are eligible if, after all income is calculated, they fall below a certain threshold. This amount depends on a person's income: The poorest seniors are entitled to more per month, and those closest to the threshold are entitled to practically nothing.

These various income sources help. In essence, seniors in Canada are provided with a guaranteed income (which we have discussed already in this chapter). In fact, Canada has one of the lowest elderly poverty rates among OECD countries, thanks in part to these stable, consistent income supports (Emery, Fleisch, and McIntyre 2013). Experiences of food insecurity often decrease by half among those who have reached the age of 65 and qualify for these income supports (McIntyre et al. 2016).

This doesn't mean that *all* seniors have enough food. Roughly 15 per cent of people over the age of 65 are considered low income (Statistics Canada 2017). And 7.4 per cent of elderly, unattached Canadians are struggling to meet their basic needs for safe, nutritious food (Tarasuk et al. 2016).

As we have seen in previous chapters, seniors are more prone to health complications. Most people visit doctors and require more healthcare in the final two years of their life than in the rest of their years combined. Seniors often develop health problems that require specialized diets. For example, diabetics need to monitor their intake of simple carbohydrates and ensure balanced, evenly distributed meals. Hypertensive seniors must eat a low-sodium diet. As you might imagine, seniors with food insecurity are less able to satisfy the dietary needs recommended by their doctors. An older study found that when seniors experience food insecurity, they compromise dietary quality first (Tarasuk 2001a).

The nutrition of Canada's seniors is not just important for people over the age of 65; it's of interest to *all* of us. Nearly half of our provincial healthcare budgets are spent treating chronic conditions. What's more, nearly half of those conditions are considered avoidable through lifestyle changes (exercising, drinking in moderation, not smoking), safe housing, and, of course, nutrition (Finlayson and Currie 2010). These chronic, preventable health problems are concentrated among seniors, whose care ends up being rather expensive. Ensuring they're eating well and staying healthy benefits us all.

Seniors, many have pointed out, are doing better in recent decades than in the mid- to late twentieth century. That is because of the advent and increase of previously mentioned government benefits. With the aging of the baby boomers, seniors have become—and will continue to be—a potent political force in Canada. Canada's 2019 election was the first time that baby boomers were outnumbered at the polls since their generation started voting. Seniors often vote against elected officials who fail to consider their particular needs. Seniors can be counted on to look into, and look after, their needs of income security and food security to a large extent. Historically, the same has not been true for young Canadians.

Indigenous Peoples in Canada

Indigenous Peoples in Canada make up only a small percentage of the total population and yet they are unequally represented in statistics describing food insecurity. Figure 7.8 shows how much more likely Indigenous Peoples are to report moderate to severe levels of food insecurity. Note that Inuit respondents demonstrate food insecurity nearly four times as often as non-Indigenous people in Canada.

Food insecurity is especially marked among Inuit. Among all Indigenous Peoples in Canada, those living in the northern regions are, statistically speaking, most likely to

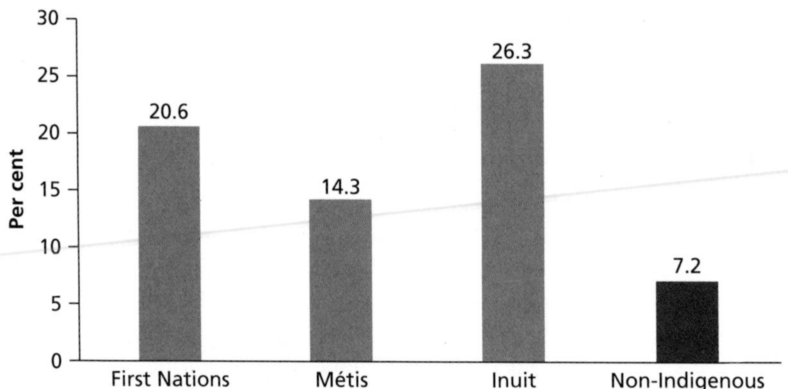

Figure 7.8 ◆ People in Canada Reporting Moderate to Severe Food Insecurity

Source: Statistics Canada 2019a.

experience food insecurity. Recall from earlier chapters that the Indigenous population is young and growing. In northern Indigenous communities, elementary school enrolment reflects this increase. Breakfast programs have become critical in some northern communities to address the needs of food-insecure students. A 2012 survey found that in Arctic Bay, a community on Baffin Island, 200 children—one-quarter of the community's total population—are fed every school day (Food Banks Canada 2012).

As we have seen in an earlier section of this chapter, both culture and environmental availability influence food choices. Traditionally, the diet of Inuit in Northern Canada comprises mainly **country food**: foods harvested and hunted from the surrounding area, like seal, whale, berries, and Arctic char. Some of these traditional foods, like seal and Arctic char, for example, offer a huge number of nutrients and are part of a healthy diet that has nourished northern populations for centuries.

country food Foods harvested and hunted from the surrounding area, like seal, whale, berries, and Arctic char in the North.

Hunting and gathering traditions surrounding country food continue to play a role in Indigenous diets. Figure 7.9 shows that many respondents report hunting and gathering as a source of food among First Nations Peoples in Canada. But sadly, there are increasing obstacles to this type of food sourcing. One barrier to traditional food gathering is the cost of hunting and fishing: Gas, hunting transportation such as boats and snowmobiles, and ammunition can be costly.

Another barrier is increasing contaminants in country food, especially in the North. Unfortunately, contaminants that originate in southern areas often concentrate

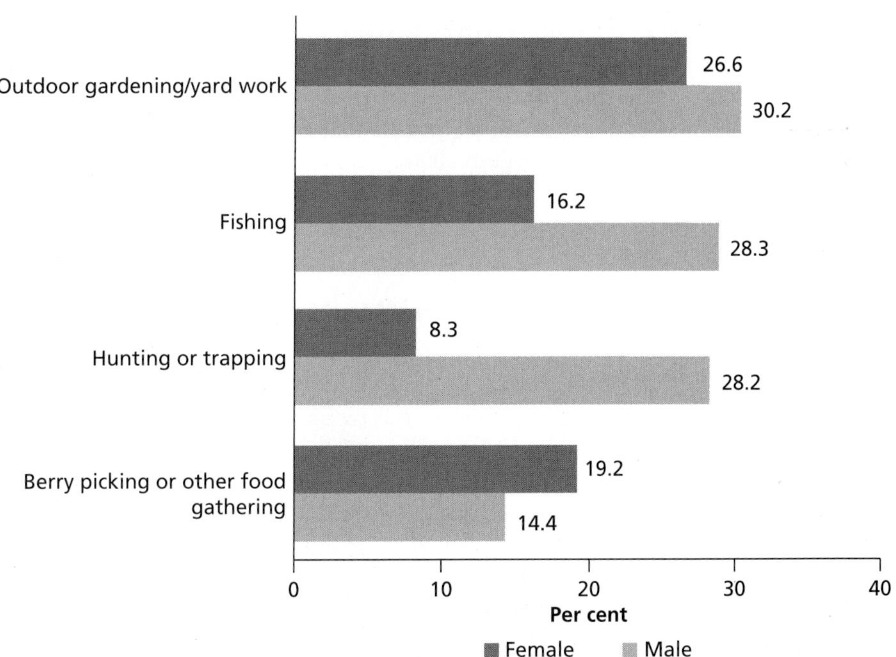

Figure 7.9 ◆ Percentage of First Nations Adults Who Participated in Various Food Sourcing Activities in the Three Months Prior to the Survey[1], by Sex

Source: First Nations Information Governance Centre 2018.

1. First Nations Regional Health Survey, Phase 3, vol. 2 (Ottawa: First Nations Information Governance Centre, 2018), page 72.

in the Arctic ecosystem. One large-scale study found unsafe levels of mercury in at least one-quarter of Inuit children's hair living in Nunavut (Tian et al. 2011).

Celebrated ethnobotanist Nancy Turner has written about the effects of environmental contaminants on the historic food sources of Indigenous Peoples in Canada. When a community avoids a particular food for one or two generations, "the knowledge related to harvesting and preparing these foods diminishes. Then, even if the quality of the food improves, its consumption may not be resumed" (Turner et al. 2008:3). Also, the small farmers who have traditionally harvested these crops stop production. As a result, these communities may turn to unhealthy processed food that is more readily available, free of (visible) pollutants, and cheap to buy.

Traditional cultural practices may contribute to better health among Indigenous Peoples in Canada. Health researchers Malcolm King, Alexandra Smith, and Michael Gracey (2009) found that some of the traditional food gathering and other cultural practices are associated with health and healing. And while the levels of these contaminants may be raised in some country foods, many agree the nutritional and cultural advantages of consuming country food outweigh the potential risks.

Another barrier is the skills required to effectively hunt and gather nutritious country food. These skills are under threat, and more people are getting their food from other sources. Many groups are recommending that steps be taken to preserve and promote traditional food gathering to lessen levels of food insecurity in isolated northern communities. At the end of this chapter, we will examine some exciting initiatives connecting northern residents with country food.

The changing climate is yet another barrier to traditional hunting and gathering, especially in the Far North. Thin ice makes some hunting and fishing especially dangerous, and changing temperatures may also affect the migration patterns or availability of animals like caribou. Some studies have also discovered changes in the availability of edible plant species like berries (Furgal and Seguin 2006).

As a result of these barriers, many traditional food alternatives have been replaced with processed and less nutritious food shipped from the south. These processed foods—such

◆ In Their Own Words ◆

The Inuit Tapiriit Kanatami and the Inuit Circumpolar Council report that:

> For Inuit in Canada the right to food extends far beyond economic, nutritional, and physical accessibility to include significant cultural importance. The hunting, harvesting, and sharing of country food is integral in providing social cohesion and cultural continuity for Inuit communities. Inuit livelihoods have historically been, and continue to be, defined by a deep relationship to the environment and the resources it provides. Despite the presence of market food in the modern Inuit diet, country food remains at the centre of Inuit identity and well-being.

Source: Inuit Tapiriit Kanatami and the Inuit Circumpolar Council 2010.

as Kraft cheese slices—tend to survive the trip to northern communities much better than, say, bananas or red peppers. As a result, the markets in the North often only offer low variety and poor-quality foods. One study found that the most commonly consumed foods are pop, Tang, white bread, potato chips, chocolate bars, and Kool-Aid (Lawn and Harvey 2003).

Food costs are extremely high in isolated northern regions; they are even higher than in low-income urban neighbourhoods. Why is this? Not only is it expensive to transport food to remote communities, but the storage of this food is also costly. This expense, not surprisingly, is passed onto the consumer.

There are also issues about the lack of competition in food provision. If a store is the only grocery store in town, they can adjust their prices accordingly. One study asked Northerners to comment on the affordability and scarcity of milk (Wendimu and Desmarais 2018). Here are some the testimonials from that study:

> "The North West Company buys milk in bulk. They get a big discount on that. Perimeter [an airline serving First Nations in northern Manitoba] also gives them a discount. In addition to that, they also get a subsidy from the federal government. But when the milk gets here the price is tripled. Why is that? Because there is no competition." (6)
>
> "They [Northern Store] have a monopoly and they can do whatever they want. If the government increases social assistance, they [Northern Store] also increase their prices." (7)

It can cost as much as \$360–\$450 a week to provide a nutritious diet for a family of four in an isolated northern community. By comparison, the cost of providing a similarly nutritious diet for a family of four in southern Canada is only \$200–\$250. It's true there are some income supports to help offset some of the added costs of living in isolated northern communities, but they are not enough.

For example, the Northern Living Allowance is offered through some employers (like the government) to help with costs of living and travel. The government also subsidizes some perishable foods to make them more affordable and provides tax credits for those living in prescribed zones. The average Canadian in southern provinces spends around one-tenth of their annual income on food. Meanwhile, residents of Nunavut spend on average a quarter of their annual income on food (Food Banks Canada 2012). Aside from the higher costs of living, this may also result from higher levels of unemployment, which influence household budgets for all basic needs.

When studying food insecurity in Indigenous communities, sociologists must bear in mind that culture plays a role in how people secure enough to eat. Researchers point out that some measurements of food insecurity might overlook important food sharing practices that are common in some communities. The First Nations Information Governance Centre (2018) points out that the forced implementation of reservations and European styles of agriculture, the Indian residential school system, and the laws underpinning the Indian Act have all played a part in decreasing participation in local food systems for many Indigenous Peoples. These forces, they argue, "continue to shape the types and amounts of foods that are eaten."

People with Disabilities in Canada

Ability and disability can impact vulnerability to food insecurity. A recent review of 106 articles found that disability is consistently associated with an increased risk of food insecurity across different populations and geographic settings (Schwartz, Buliung, and Wilson 2019).

One reason is income and a lack of it. Canadians with disabilities are vulnerable to being under- or unemployed. Some people with disabilities may face barriers when getting and preparing food. For some individuals, their disabilities produce pain, weakness, or fatigue, which can be a barrier to healthy eating (Nosek et al. 2004). Others may have specific and unique nutritional needs that can be challenging to meet, or have specific medical needs that divert funds away from food.

For individuals with disabilities, higher rates of food insecurity were associated with economic, social, and environmental barriers (Schwartz et al. 2019). Commonly reported barriers to food security included the cost of food or the lack of accessible features at food stores (for example, inaccessible entrances, placement of products, absence of accessible parking). Social norms also have an impact on food security for disabled individuals. Some may choose to shop alone and face the difficulties associated with shopping themselves rather than seeking help. However, those that seek help, from family or support workers, commonly reported feeling like a burden. Figure 7.10 shows the use of Greater Toronto Area food banks by people with disabilities. Note that the number of people who report having at least one disability increased over 10 years.

Finally, researchers have pointed to the many ways that food insecurity in itself is disabling. A lack of enough nutritious food can have negative effects on a person's health and can worsen an existing disability. Food security is a key social factor that shapes the experience of disability. Greater food security could make living with an impairment more manageable.

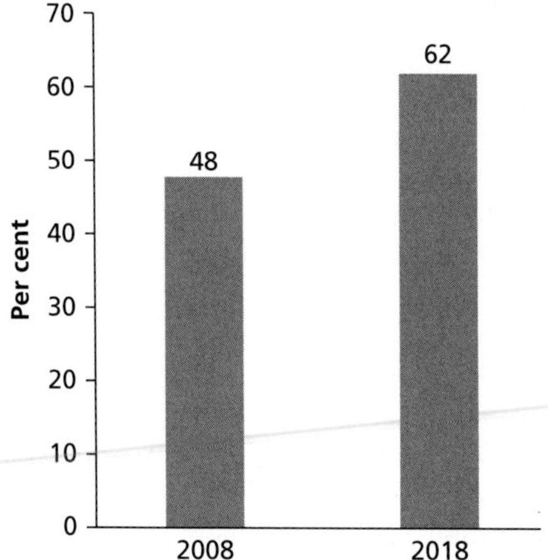

Figure 7.10 ◆ Use of Greater Toronto Area Food Banks by People with a Disability

Source: Daily Bread Food Bank 2018.

◆ In Their Own Words ◆

Here are some testimonies from researcher Juliet Gerbrandt's (2009) qualitative interviews with British Columbians with disabilities who were facing food insecurity. Try to identify some of the themes you've learned in this section in these testimonials. Look for difficulty using the grocery store, transportation issues, special diets, cost of food relative to income, and other themes.

Researcher: Can you elaborate a little bit on why it's hard [to get food]?

> "I am unable to access food banks because they don't at all meet the needs of special diets. I'm not allowed to have canned foods anymore because of the salt content."
>
> "In a store, if there is something I can't reach, pretty much 8 of the 10 times I'll just get mad and leave the store rather than simply say 'hey grab that down for me.'"
>
> "To get them on the bus, get them off at the bus stop, and then try to walk to my place with groceries, it was hard enough walking, but with the groceries it was just hell."
>
> "When I actually get the food home it can be very tiring and it can be very hard on my wrists. I might be too tired to chop it up and freeze it until tomorrow or the next day, depending on how my wrists are. So getting fresh cooked vegetables and meat can be quite difficult."
>
> "Since the cutbacks from government I no longer get homecare at all, period. I have to be careful what I buy, and if it's a food item I cannot slice or cut very well I have to rely on a neighbour to cut it for me."
>
> "I was eating food and I was getting food poisoning on a regular basis because I was thinking 'Well it's only been there three, four days.' I was too tired to cook more. I was too tired to get to the store to buy it. I didn't have the money to buy it."

Consequences of Unequal Access to Nutritious Food

Food insecurity is an enormous challenge for those who experience it, and it also has harmful effects for society as a whole. In this section, we will explore some of the various ways that food insecurity has negative social effects. Read the boxed quote for researcher Dr Valerie Tarasuk's take on the matter.

As we have discussed, food insecurity leads to health problems. And sick people are often unable to work and need medical care. A recent study found that "unhealthy eating constitutes a tremendous economic burden to Canada that is similar in magnitude to the burden of smoking and larger than that of physical inactivity" (Lieffers et al. 2018). We will take a deeper look at the impacts of poor health on social stability in the next chapter.

◆ In Their Own Words ◆

Food researcher Dr Valerie Tarasuk writes:

> [C]hronic and severe food insecurity predisposes individuals to poor health. However, it is also conceivable that poor health heightens the risk of household food insecurity and increases the likelihood of more severe food insecurity among low income groups. Alternatively, both the health of individuals and their household security status may be related to a third variable (for example, chronic poverty).

Source: Tarasuk 2001a.

The social cost of food deprivation is especially obvious in our most vulnerable populations. Older adults and chronically ill people deprived of food are more likely to die prematurely. Children are hardier, but hungry children do not learn as well as well-fed children, other things being equal. If we want a healthy, productive population, we need to start at the beginning. We need to ensure that all of our children are well educated, which means ensuring they are well fed when they arrive at school each day.

Canada's new food guide, as well as social researchers, stress the social significance of food deprivation for family rituals such as regular mealtimes. Families that sit down together for at least one meal a day—especially in the absence of televisions, smartphones, and tablets—tend to be better functioning than families that do not have this and other similar rituals. Poorly functioning families are more likely to break up and less likely to socialize their children effectively. For example, loss of family meal times created "disorganized eating patterns and jeopardized ritual [that] eroded the transfer of knowledge and practices; several others suggested it also hindered conviviality. Many mentioned that disrupted household dynamics decreased participation in social life" (Hamelin, Habicht, and Micheline 1999:527S).

So food insecurity is about more than simply a shortage of calories to a few scattered individuals. Hunger is socially structured and has deep social effects. Food-insecure people experience social exclusion, which erodes social cohesion (Tarasuk 2001a).

Strategies of Resistance

Government-Level Strategies of Resistance

An example of a government-level response to food insecurity is the Canada Prenatal Nutrition Program (CPNP). The CPNP began as a Public Health Agency of Canada initiative in 1994. It partners with local agencies to provide them with the reliable government funding they need to help low-income, young, or otherwise disadvantaged expecting mothers with prenatal programs (Tarasuk 2005). The main goal of the program is supporting pregnant women so they and their babies can preserve a healthy diet and environment. They must do so despite challenges like poverty, adolescent pregnancy, isolation, substance use, and domestic violence. Programs are also tailored to the cultural needs of immigrant and Indigenous women (Public Health Agency of Canada 2013).

Critical Thinking Question

This chapter highlights food banks as a strategy to confront growing food insecurity in Canada. Nick Saul, former director of The Stop Community Food Centre in Toronto, co-wrote an article in *The Walrus* suggesting "food banks may compound the very problems they should be solving." Do you agree?

> [Food banks] can serve as a valuable support in emergencies, but too many users are forced to rely on them regularly . . . Further, the poor—who receive mostly cheap processed items in their hampers—are disproportionately affected by such diet-related illnesses as diabetes, obesity, and heart disease. People are hungry . . . because of inadequate income supports, minimum wages that do not cover the bills, and the lack of affordable housing and childcare . . . It is time to have a frank conversation about the limitations of this [food bank] approach. (Saul and Curtis 2013)

The programs offered by the CPNP offer nutritional support in the form of counselling, food, coupons, and prenatal vitamins (Tarasuk 2005). Other services help prepare mothers to care for their new babies with breastfeeding education and food preparation classes. Some also provide classes on and support with infant care and child development (Public Health Agency of Canada 2013).

Estimates show that about 44,650 women accessed the programs provided by the CPNP in 2001–2. In 2008–9, 331 agencies across Canada provided CPNP programming (Public Health Agency of Canada 2010; Tarasuk 2005). One CPNP participant study found that recent immigrants, Indigenous women, low-income women, women who were drinking alcohol while pregnant, and teenagers were overrepresented at CPNP-funded programs (Public Health Agency of Canada 2010). This indicates that CPNP is reaching its desired population of "at-risk" mothers. The most recent statistics show that this program has had a favourable impact in helping mothers carry out a healthier pregnancy. The mothers have achieved this by taking prenatal vitamins, cutting back on smoking, and quitting drinking (Public Health Agency of Canada 2010). These changes lead to the birth of a healthier baby who has a mother with the tools and knowledge she needs to care for it.

Organization-Level Strategies of Resistance

Many organizations in Canada are addressing food insecurity. This excerpt from Food Banks Canada (2019) describes one organization that is attacking the problem from many angles:

> The Interfaith Food Bank Society of Lethbridge knew it needed to innovate to accommodate the growing demand for food bank use in its community. They launched several education programs within the food bank to support those in need.

"With these fresh ideas," says Danielle McIntyre, Executive Director, "the food bank was able to empower those we serve while strengthening our entire community."

The Interfaith Chinook Country Kitchen is a program that teaches participants how to cook healthy meals on a limited budget. The focus is to develop wholesome relationships with food while maximizing participant resources to put more nutritious meals on the table.

SHOP SMART is a complimentary two-hour workshop that teaches participants how to reduce the stress of visiting the grocery store. People are taught how to stretch their budget to make procuring food more affordable. All of these skills are taught to support nutritious meal planning.

The Collective Kitchen initiative teaches participants how to plan a menu, create a grocery list, and prepare 5–7 days of meals as a group. The food bank provides some ingredients, and participants share the cost of the rest. By cooking collectively, they are taught to expand on the skills they've learned through the SHOP SMART program. The result? New healthy eating habits are formed.

The Community Garden program allows participants to grow and tend to a garden as a group. They provide the care, and the garden provides fresh and nutritious food. Participants walk away with new knowledge about how to cultivate and grow a garden and a stronger sense of community.

The Project Protein is a program designed to help food bank clients source meat sustainably from local partners. Through partnerships with producers, farmers, ranchers, and feedlot operators, animal products are sourced, prepared, and distributed to families in need.

Like the Interfaith Food Bank Society of Lethbridge, food banks across Canada work with those they serve and their local communities to find innovative ways of addressing the stubborn problem of hunger in Canada.

Individual-Level Strategies of Resistance

As we have seen in this chapter, there are high levels of food insecurity and nutritional deficiency in remote northern communities. Importantly, many traditional, hunted foods are often available and nutritionally rich—but they are challenging for residents to access if they do not have the time, money, or ability to hunt. For the past several years, William Hyndman has been on a mission to change that. He is the founder of Nunavut's first Country Food Market, a market that allows hunters to sell their meat to residents.

This market has increased the variety and quantity of country foods available to the community. Residents like seniors, who cannot hunt country food on their own, can still consume it. Hunters can use the money they earn at the market to offset the cost of their fuel and hunting supplies. In this way, hunting for meat puts cash in the pockets of hunters and gives households more access to country foods (NAHO 2013). But there is a tension in this buy-and-sell arrangement: Some feel that hunted food should be shared, not sold—a model that reflects the traditional distribution patterns in many Inuit communities. That's why there have been efforts to develop a model that compensates hunters in a different way, perhaps by the government, like doctors and nurses (Kim 2016).

Closing Remarks

Like poverty, food insecurity has many definitions. Typically, governments decide its meaning, so food insecurity, like poverty, varies by society, within societies, and over time.

Some people think that food insecurity is caused by a pattern of damaging cultural habits (this is the so-called "culture of poverty" approach). Others believe it is simply caused by an unfair distribution of resources (the conflict approach). Functionalists believe that economic rewards are merit based, so poverty and food insecurity are mostly unavoidable. However, this standpoint cannot clarify why women, seniors, children, and Indigenous Peoples experience the most food insecurity.

Yet food insecurity does not merely mean that, at any given time, many Canadians are going hungry. It means that an even larger number of Canadians will move in and out of food insecurity over the course of their lifetimes.

With shifts in the economy, many people move in and out of poverty and food insecurity. Longer durations of poverty produce more harmful results, and children who are continuously poor, hungry, and malnourished have higher rates of antisocial behaviour than transiently hungry children. As we have seen, food insecurity—and poverty in general—has long-term effects for health, education, employment, employability, and mental health.

People who are more secure and prosperous may try to ignore these problems, but they will not solve themselves, nor will they only affect the lives of disadvantaged Canadians. There is plenty of hunger, unemployment, demoralization, and anger in our midst. To think otherwise is to live in a dream.

◆◆ Notable Thinkers ◆◆

Valerie Tarasuk

Valerie Tarasuk is a professor of nutritional sciences at the University of Toronto. Her research focuses on food insecurity and policies aimed at solving the problem in Canada. Her work often includes an examination of food banks and users, homeless youth, and low-income citizens.

One aspect of her research focuses on the correlation between nutrient inadequacies and food-insecure households. She cites differences in protein, vitamin A, thiamin, riboflavin, vitamin B-12, folate, magnesium, phosphorus, and zinc consumption. Food insecurity was associated with poorer diets among adults, which were indicated by significantly lower levels of milk, fruits, vegetables, and meat consumption (Kirkpatrick and Tarasuk) 2008). Tarasuk's research shows the many-sided aspects of food insecurity, revealing higher levels of poor functional health, restricted activity levels, chronic conditions, mental disorders (depression and distress), and less social support (Vozoris and Tarasuk 2003).

Further, low income is a striking barrier to receiving enough nutrition. Her analysis of 18 meals from charities in Toronto reveals a relationship between nutrient needs and food donations. On average, the meals were all below the energy and nutrient contents of the recommended average adult requirements. They included 2.6 servings of grains, 1.7 servings of meat and alternatives, 4.1 servings of fruits and vegetables, and 0.4 servings of milk products (Kirkpatrick and Tarasuk 2008).

Tarasuk's work offers a variety of suggestions, policies, and methods to ease the problem of food insecurity in Canada. She argues the government should encourage and set up more nutrition-related food marking and more effective communication tools to help consumers better understand good selection. They should also set up policies at the federal, provincial, and municipal levels to reduce economic and geographic barriers to food access (Tarasuk 2010). Further, her research has shown that household factors, such as income and income source, strongly correlate with food insecurity. This suggests and demonstrates the importance of neighbourhood-level interventions to improve access to food or social cohesion, which can help mitigate the issue of food insecurity (Tarasuk 2010).

Test Your Knowledge

1. What are some emotional elements of food insecurity?
2. In what ways do guaranteed income programs help save money for the government?
3. Which factors increase the odds of a Canadian child experiencing severe food insecurity?
4. Fill in the blank: One study that interviewed women experiencing food insecurity found that respondents listed the following coping strategies: ____________.
5. Why is it getting harder for Indigenous Peoples to get and eat country food?
6. How do the health problems and relative unemployment resulting from food security harm everyone in a society?
7. What are some social effects of food deprivation?
8. List the key points of each population group as highlighted in the chapter.

Population Group	Key Points (barriers, issues, and health outcomes related to food insecurity)
Low-income Canadians	
Seniors	
Young Canadians	
Parents	
Indigenous Peoples in Canada	

See the Answer Key online to check your answers.

Questions for Critical Thought

1. From a nutritional standpoint, do you think the rate of social assistance should be increased or decreased? Explain why.
2. Has increased food insecurity changed cultural and religious traditions associated with food and food rituals in Canada? Provide examples.
3. What are some reasons that explain why the prices of healthy foods are increasing while the prices of unhealthy foods remain cheap? Should efforts be taken to make healthier alternatives more affordable?
4. What are some problems that need to be addressed to equalize access to nutritious foods? Brainstorm ideas that extend beyond the realm of food.
5. Why should hunger be addressed as a social problem?

Additional Resources

Recommended Readings

Dachner, Naomi and Valerie Tarasuk. 2018. "Tackling Household Food Insecurity: An Essential Goal of a National Food Policy." *Canadian Food Studies* 5(3):230–47. As the title suggests, this article is an attempt to argue for a national food policy, centred on an understanding and appreciation of the need for universal food security throughout Canada.

Henry, Lisa. 2020. *Experiences of Hunger and Food Insecurity in College.* Basingstoke, UK: Palgrave Macmillan. This book explores the causes and consequences of food insecurity among college and university students, including the effects on academic performance, physical health, and mental health.

Scanlan, Stephen J. 2018. "Hunger and Food Insecurity." Pp. 423–40 in *The Cambridge Handbook of Social Problems*, edited by A.J. Trevino. Cambridge, U: Cambridge University Press. This is a masterful review of the current state of knowledge about food insecurity in the Western world.

Recommended Websites

Food Banks Canada

www.foodbankscanada.ca

Food Banks Canada is the national organization representing the community of food banks across Canada. Currently, they are striving to meet the short-term food demands while looking for longer-term methods to reduce hunger. They hope to do so through various activities such as running programs, setting up partnerships, creating awareness, and conducting research.

Food Secure Canada

http://foodsecurecanada.org

Food Secure Canada is an alliance of organizations and individuals based on three commitments: achieve and maintain zero hunger, develop a sustainable food system, and make healthy and safe foods easily and readily available. Together, the individuals and groups aim to advance food security in Canada by reaching out to different organizations and populations within Canada, such as the Indigenous population.

International Development Research Centre (IDRC)

www.idrc.ca

Through its Canadian International Food Security Research Fund, the IDRC aims to improve food security through research. This websites offers a variety of publications on food security to help alleviate hunger and poverty around the world.

Meal Exchange

www.mealexchange.com

Meal Exchange is a national student/youth-led charity that seeks to educate and mobilize youth to reduce local hunger and achieve food security by working within their communities. This website includes information to help youth gain more knowledge about food insecurity in Canada and the multifaceted nature of the issue as well information on how to take action.

The Working Group on Indigenous Food Sovereignty (WGIFS)

www.indigenousfoodsystems.org

WGIFS recognizes the importance of voicing and recognizing Indigenous perspectives in the food security movement across Canada. WGIFS aims to increase awareness of the issues, concerns, and strategies that impact the food systems and security of the Indigenous members of Canada and to mobilize communities along the way.

Recommended Films

Food Stamped. 2010. Directed by Shira Potash and Yoav Potash. United States: Summit Pictures. This documentary follows a couple as they attempt to eat a healthy, balanced diet on a food stamp budget—about one dollar per meal. The documentary includes appearances by activists, nutrition experts, politicians, and citizens who use food stamps to demonstrate the struggle low-income Americans face daily.

A Place at the Table. 2013. Directed by Kristi Jacobson and Lori Silverbush. United States: Participant Media. This documentary is about food insecurity in the United States that also offers potential solutions to this growing problem.

"Price Check: Why Are Grocery Prices in Canada's North so High?" 2019. *cbc Marketplace*. https://www.youtube.com/watch?v=gbm8_m4txKY&feature=youtu.be. This episode explores the reasons behind the staggering high food prices in Canada's North and why the Nutrition North subsidy, intended to fix the problem, has only made the crisis worst.

Wasting Away. 2014. Directed by Kathleen Martens. Canada: APTN Investigates. This short documentary exposes the harsh reality of food insecurity in Northern Canada. It also shows the failure of the Nutrition North subsidy program to live up to its promises of providing affordable and nutritious food to struggling communities such as Rankin Inlet, Nunavut.

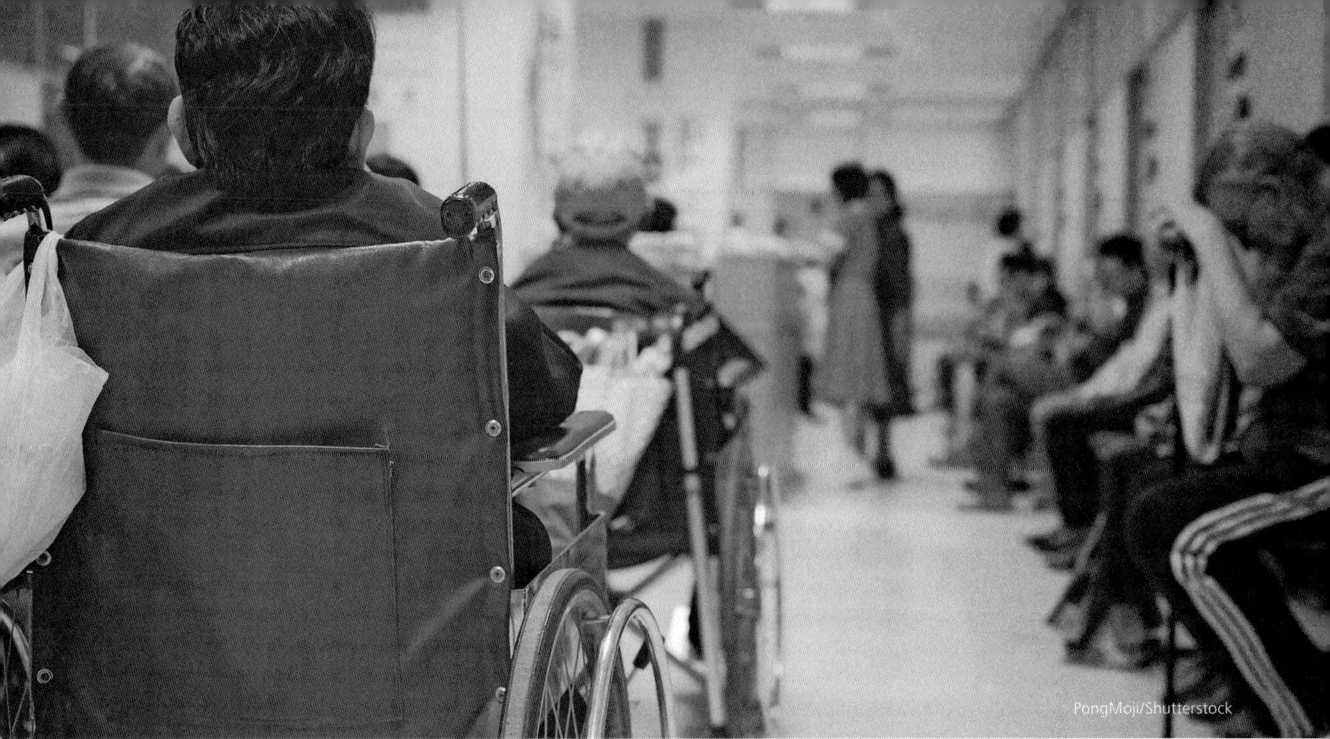
PongMoji/Shutterstock

8 Access to Good Health and Healthcare

Learning Objectives

- To compare different theoretical perspectives addressing health and healthcare disparities.
- To name and recognize the social determinants of health.
- To identify historical trends in Canadian health and healthcare.
- To list barriers that produce disparities in healthcare access.
- To name the effects of unequal access to healthcare.
- To evaluate the efforts undertaken to equalize access to good health and healthcare in Canada.

Introduction

No two humans are identical. Some are born without various parts, making functions such as breathing, digesting, thinking, or moving around more challenging. Some bodies have reduced organ function resulting from decades of smoking or poor nutrition. Other bodies are faster, leaner, and last longer, owing to hundreds of kilometres spent on the treadmill or hours spent on a yoga mat. Environments also influence bodies: Exposure to toxic chemicals, repetitive and painstaking work, and local climate creates physical differences between us. Our bodies are built differently and, just as our bodies influence our abilities and behaviours, our abilities and behaviours can influence our bodies.

social determinants of health (SDOH) The social factors, such as income, education, stress-related living, and working conditions, and social status that impact a person's health.

Because of all these variations, many sociologists spend their careers trying to understand the social factors that affect health, also known as the **social determinants of health (SDOH)**. The SDOH are not a person's genetic endowment passed on by their biological parents, although the expression of those genes can be affected by the social world. They are the living conditions that influence an individual's health status and are beyond the control of any single individual. They include income, education, and access to health services. Most sociologists believe that social determinants, and their potential to prevent illness, play a more significant role in shaping a population's overall health than genetic tendencies and lifestyle choices.

The "universal" system of healthcare that Canada is known for worldwide did not always exist. Before World War II, healthcare in Canada was private. In other words, people were expected to pay for their own healthcare expenses. Canada's system of universal healthcare was formalized in 1984 with the introduction of the Canada Health Act. Canada's healthcare system is designed to be universal—that is, to provide unlimited access and service to all Canadians. However, access to good health and healthcare remains an issue.

Theoretical Perspectives on Access to Healthcare

Functionalists assume that everyone thinks about good health the same way, that everyone wants good health, and that our social institutions routinely preserve good health. From this standpoint, healthcare is a social institution responsible for safeguarding the well-being of all members of society.

However, as Talcott Parsons (1951) suggested, it is also a form of social control. Illness, for its part, is a form of deviance that threatens the ability of society to work. The ill adopt a "sick role," allowing them to withdraw from society temporarily while they are recovering. During this time, they must obey the doctor's rules (for example, by continuing to take the medicine a doctor prescribed). Failure to do otherwise will result in social instability.

This approach to health and healthcare implies that society has a vested interest in keeping everyone healthy because an absence of good health leads to disorganization and deviance. In contrast, conflict theorists deny that society has a vested interest in keeping everyone in good health or that everyone has equal access to good health. Conflict theorists assume that good health is unequally distributed in society, just like every other valuable resource, and those with the most power will enjoy the best health. From this perspective, problems in the delivery of healthcare result from the capitalist economy, which treats medicine as a commodity to be produced and sold. Here, as in other domains, people struggle over scarce resources (in this case, medical treatment), and healthcare is affected by wealth, status, and power (or the lack thereof).

Conflict theory helps explain why, in many societies, poor people continue to have trouble paying for special health-related treatments, prescription pharmaceuticals, dental care, and extended care. By contrast, in societies committed to social legislation and equal treatment, socialized healthcare is the norm. This is the case for Canada, which introduced its first federally funded medical care system in 1968. And yet, as of the date of publication of this book, there is still no universal pharmacare or dental care program in Canada.

Feminist sociologists explore how gender impacts a person's health. They may point out that women are more prone to certain illnesses, like heart disease, for example, which kills more women in Canada than all forms of cancer combined. Yet women are often left off drug trials to treat these diseases. Feminist sociologists consider the way that pregnancy, childbirth, and even natural features like breast size or wrinkles can be "medicalized," framed as "diseases" and treated as such. Feminist sociologists might point out how the second shift (the tendency for women to take on more of the domestic labour in heterosexual partnerships) can take a toll on health. And they may also point out that despite all these things, men are, on average, unhealthier than women.

Sociologists working from a critical "race" perspective explore how ideas of racial inferiority have been used to justify mistreating some people in medical studies. Consider the example of the Tuskegee Syphilis study, when hundreds of Black Americans were deliberately left to suffer from a treatable illness so scientists could better understand how it progressed. In Chapter 10 you'll learn about the medical experiments conducted on Indigenous children in residential schools, who were deliberately deprived of dental care or dietary nutrients. These studies were permitted because of the prevailing racist belief that since some bodies were less human than others, and thus less worthy of fair treatment, they could be harmed to advance medical science.

Finally, symbolic interactionists focus their attention on social interactions and the ways people "perform" ideas of health and healthcare. The meanings of "health" and "sickness" vary from culture to culture and over time. Symbolic interactionists are also interested in the relations between sick people, family caregivers, and health professionals. They are involved in researching, for example, the ways that cultural expectations interfere with requests for care, the delivery of care, and compliance with doctors' treatment plans. This line of inquiry is especially important for Canada and its culturally diverse population.

From both the conflict and symbolic interactionist perspective, it is easy to understand "victim blaming." As the name suggests, victim blaming is when an illness is seen as the ill person's fault. This tendency is especially evident around lifestyle-related illnesses, such as obesity, addiction, and even HIV/AIDS.

Here, it makes sense to also introduce another theoretical perspective: the so-called *population health* perspective. This approach to health and illness analyzes society as a whole to ask why, in general, do certain kinds of people get sick or die more often than others? What is it about the way society is organized that increases the risk that some people will lead shorter, unhealthier lives than others?

Though rarely viewed in this light, we can think of Friedrich Engels as a founding figure of this approach. In his classic book *The Conditions of the Working Class in England*, Engels ([1845] 2009) showed how the dire conditions of disadvantage in Manchester affected the city's death rate. Engels recognized the importance of social conditions in producing these horrible results. Workers there were afflicted with substandard housing, lack of sanitation, inadequate diet and clothing, and harsh work environments. Three years later, the German doctor Rudolf Virchow, often credited as the "father of modern pathology," found the root causes of a typhus epidemic in Prussia were regional poverty, poor education, and inept government. Virchow famously remarked that "medicine is a social science" and asked, "Do we not always find the diseases of the populace traceable to defects in society?" (quoted in Rather 1985).

There is now enough evidence confirming Virchow's statements that people who are socially, economically, and politically disadvantaged suffer worse health than their well-off counterparts (Marmot 2005; Mackenbach and Bakker 2003). As we will see, these people include women, the elderly, ethnic minorities, homeless people, and others.

We begin this chapter with a brief discussion of the SDOH. Many, if not all, of these determinants overlap with what we have called forms of "survival capital." In this way, the social determinants of health are also the social determinants of survival.

The Social Determinants of Health

Education

The more education a person has, the healthier they are likely to be. It is not hard to see why. As Mikkonen and Raphael (2010) point out, "level of education is highly correlated with other social determinants of health such as the level of income, employment security, and working conditions." Better-educated individuals can also more readily access information about how to improve their health.

Employment and Job Security

Work provides income, a structure for people's daily lives, and a sense of identity. Unemployment, by contrast, leads to financial pressures as well as mental health issues, including stress and higher-than-average risks of depression, anxiety, and suicide. People who have lost their jobs may take up coping behaviours—smoking and drinking, for example—that have adverse effects on health.

The nature of one's work also affects health. Factors to consider include "employment security, physical conditions at work, work pace and stress, working hours, [and] opportunities for self-expression and individual development at work" (Mikkonen and Raphael 2010:20). Stressful jobs can increase the risk of both physical and **mental illness**.

mental illness Illness characterized by disturbances of emotion, thinking, or behaviour.

Early Childhood Development

What happens to us in childhood (and even before we are born) can hold serious outcomes for our health later in life. Sometimes childhood experiences can affect health throughout the life course, regardless of the socio-economic circumstances of a person's later life.

Food Insecurity

Chapter 7 discussed how levels of access to nutritious food deeply affect physical and mental health. It bears repeating here that, as Mikkonen and Raphael (2010) put it, "[p]eople who experience food insecurity are unable to have an adequate diet in terms of its quality or quantity. . . . People experiencing food insecurity consume fewer servings of fruits and vegetables, milk products, and vitamins than those in food-secure households" (26).

Housing

Not surprisingly, adequate shelter is a condition for health. Environments that are too crowded may promote the spread of infections and diseases. Even today, some Canadians (especially Indigenous Peoples living on reserves) lack access to clean drinking water. In addition, if housing is too expensive, people have less to spend on other basic needs.

Social Exclusion

People who are socially excluded or marginalized—for example, Indigenous Peoples, seniors, or recent immigrants—find it more difficult to secure good jobs and access social services, including healthcare. As a result, they run a higher risk of poor health and are less likely to be treated satisfactorily when they do fall ill.

Social Safety Net

Mikkonen and Raphael (2010) define the "social safety net" as the "benefits, programs, and supports that protect citizens during various life changes that can affect their health" (35). Such life changes include expected events, such as having children or retiring from work, and unexpected events, such as losing one's job or being injured in a car accident. If the social safety net is comprehensive, these events are less likely to result in permanent health problems.

Health Services

An important factor in keeping people healthy is access to good healthcare. A universal healthcare system like Canada's ensures low-income individuals have access to healthcare by spreading the costs across all members of society.

Other social determinants of health are income and income distribution, Indigenous status, gender, race, immigration status, and disability. They will be explored in more depth later in this chapter.

Changing Trends in Healthcare

We are much healthier as a society today than we used to be. Canadians live longer and enjoy less pain and a better quality of life. Vaccinations for smallpox, measles, tuberculosis, and polio are to thank for dramatic declines in these diseases, which accounted for most deaths in the past. Today, better treatments in chemotherapy and improvements in insulin injections give us higher survival rates from diseases like cancer and diabetes. Improved prenatal and postnatal care—mainly in the Global North—mean that more moms and babies survive childbirth. For example, the **infant mortality rate** in Canada has decreased from 10.9 deaths per 1,000 live births in 1979 to 4.5 per 1,000 in the last few years (Statistics Canada 2019b).

infant mortality rate The death rate of children under the age of 1, typically measured as deaths per year per 1,000 live births. Public health measures have great impacts on infant mortality rates.

One widespread trend in healthcare has been de-institutionalization: a tendency to shorten hospital stays and reduce the number of people with chronic conditions who are in long-term treatment facilities. This de-institutionalization started about 50 years ago and has continued rapidly, owing to several factors. First, the per-day cost of hospital care has grown continually over this period, so it is the most expensive way to care for people today. Second, the development and use of self-administered pharmaceutical drugs for a wide range of illnesses has allowed many people to remain active and at home, even while ill. Third, neoliberal governments, starting around 1980, were glad to download the costs of treatment to the patients themselves. Since Canadian healthcare does not routinely cover pharmaceuticals, shifting to pharmaceutical treatment meant shifting the treatment cost to sick people themselves (or their private insurance plans). Equally, homecare (rather than institutional care) meant shifting the caregiver burden from paid specialists to unpaid family members.

Finally, a concerted attack on psychiatrists and mental hospitals from the 1950s onward made the public widely sympathetic to de-institutionalizing mentally ill people. This attack on mental hospitals, in movies and elsewhere, included a widely read critique of "total institutions" by sociologist Erving Goffman (1961) in his classic work *Asylums*. At the time, people imagined that patients who had been de-institutionalized would receive suitable attention from families, friends, and health professionals. It was also imagined that they would regularly take their prescribed medications. In practice, however, many de-institutionalized patients were unable to get the help they needed from family and friends. Many also failed to take their prescribed medications, either because they couldn't afford them or they didn't like their side effects. And because neoliberal governments wanted to keep costs low, they did not fund a sufficient number of community-based health professionals (including nurses and social workers) to ensure that the de-institutionalized patients were doing well.

On the other hand, many public health measures have increased over the last 30 or so years. As a result, many unhealthy behaviours, like cigarette smoking and drunk driving, have decreased. In 1965, almost half of Canadians over the age of 15 smoked. By contrast, in 2014, less than one-fifth of Canadians aged 12 and over smoked (*CBC News* 2011; Government of Canada 2017; see Figure 8.1).

life expectancy at birth The expected duration of a person's life, considering age, time of birth, place of birth, sex, and so on.

Yet people do not equally enjoy these improvements in health. We can see this, for example, by comparing data on **life expectancy at birth**. At the time of their birth, we can

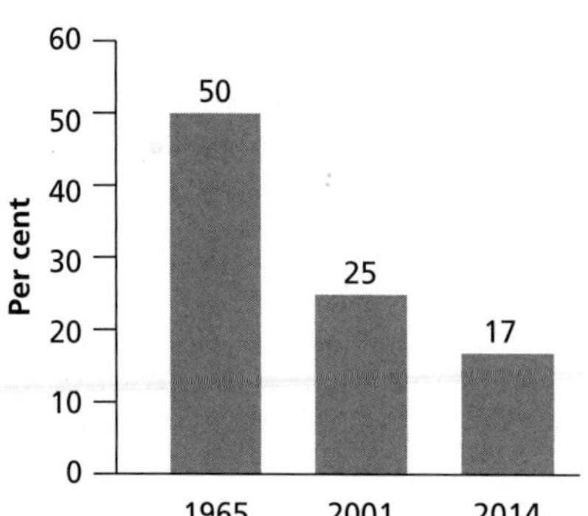

Figure 8.1 ◆ Daily or Occasional Smoking, Age 12 and Over

Source: Government of Canada 2017.

expect Canadian men to live, on average, 4.1 years less than Canadian females (Bushnik, Tjepkema, and Martel 2018). Indigenous Peoples in Canada, similarly, are expected to live 15 years less than the country's non-Indigenous population (Indigenous Services Canada 2018). Moreover, richer Canadians can expect to live longer than poorer Canadians (Government of Canada 2016). Lower life expectancies are typically found in regions with high rates of smoking, heavy drinking, and obesity (Greenberg and Normandin 2011). They are also found in regions of high unemployment, little education, and a relatively large Indigenous population.

The definitive proof that social inequality causes bad health is found in the so-called **Whitehall Studies**. These two studies were carried out by epidemiologists Marmot, Rose, Shipley, and Hamilton over the period 1967–88. They examined detailed health information on British civil servants. They found that death rates from chronic heart disease were three times higher among low-ranking civil servants than among high-ranking civil servants. Lower job status was also associated with a higher prevalence of significant health risks related to lifestyle. These included obesity, smoking, lessened leisure time, lower levels of physical activity, higher prevalence of underlying illness, higher blood pressure, and shorter height. Even after controlling for these lifestyle risks, a worker in the lowest job grade was still twice as likely to die of cardiovascular disease as a worker in the highest grade. These studies show that being on the bottom rung of the inequality ladder is dangerous for your health.

Whitehall Studies Two massive British studies carried out between 1967 and 1968 that showed how class inequality and health are correlated.

High social inequality correlates with social fragmentation, poor social relations, and a lack of autonomy for those in the lower ranks. These social stressors can cause or exacerbate mood disorders like depression, anxiety, and hostility, which compromise good health. Sometimes these issues are linked to cortisol, a hormone that is produced by the body as a response to stress. When cortisol is released into the body, the immune system is weakened (Segerstrom and Miller 2004). So the more stressed an individual is, the more cortisol is released, and the more vulnerable that person becomes to other kinds of illness.

Cortisol levels rise and fall over the day, and they respond to dangers (or stresses) in the environment. For example, in one study workers showed no significant difference in cortisol levels on awakening, regardless of their socio-economic position. However, within 30 minutes of being awake, the lower-employment grades showed significantly higher levels, especially on workdays. Presumably this was because they were anticipating chronic stress at work (Kunz-Ebrecht et al. 2004; Eller, Netterstrøm, and Hansen 2006).

In the second Whitehall Study, researchers tried to capture stress at work in three different dimensions: effort–reward imbalance, job strain, and organizational justice (Marmot 1991). Organizational justice refers to the fairness of decision making and social relationships in the workplace. All three signs of stress at work have been linked to coronary heart disease, with the risk of heart disease intensifying with increasing unfairness. Also, coronary heart disease has been linked to poor social support, low autonomy in the workplace, and depression, anxiety, and hostility.

The Whitehall Studies have been replicated many times and continue to be replicated today. In fact, similar findings are reported for many occupations. The Whitehall Studies are classic because they changed the way social scientists thought about health issues.

In this next section, we'll focus on populations in Canada that are vulnerable to poorer health. We will examine low-income people, women, men, seniors, immigrants, Indigenous Peoples, people from the LGBTQ+ community, and people with disabilities.

Low-Income People in Canada

How much money does a Canadian need to stay in good health? Nobody knows for sure. What we do know is that people who earn less are more likely to be unhealthy. Diet, exercise, and alcohol and tobacco use all vary by income, which also has a direct impact on other social determinants, including shelter, education, and early childhood development. In general, poverty poses a serious barrier to good health, both in Canada and elsewhere.

Researchers have noted many ways that poorer Canadians are unhealthier than wealthier Canadians. For one thing, Canadians residing in the lowest-income neighbourhoods live, on average, three years less than Canadians living in the highest-income neighbourhoods. We also see that lower-income Canadians are twice as likely to have a severe illness and die prematurely than higher-income Canadians. Further, when compared with the wealthiest 20 per cent of the Canadian population, the poorest 20 per cent have more than double the chance of having two or more chronic conditions such as heart disease or diabetes. Compared with affluent Canadians, low-income Canadians have less education, inferior food quality, and inadequate housing. Lower-income Canadians are less likely to be able to afford prescription medication. They are also less likely to be tested and diagnosed for medical problems early, which often leads to more severe health problems (Public Health Agency of Canada 2011).

And the health disparity goes beyond illness and disease. Children and teenagers in poorer neighbourhoods are more likely to be hospitalized from an unintentional injury such as poisoning, fire, cuts, or drowning (Oliver and Kohen 2010). The consistent correlation between poverty and ill health—and wealth and good health—is often referred to as the **social gradient in health**.

social gradient in health The correlation between social inequality and health—that is, between poverty and ill health, wealth and good health.

Why might health depend on wealth? One simple reason is that healthcare costs money. Yes, Canadians do enjoy a universal healthcare system that covers most—70 per cent—of a person's healthcare costs. And yet, 30 per cent of healthcare costs are not covered by health insurance (Mikkonen and Raphael 2010). Vision care, dental care, mobility aids like crutches, and homecare devices like adapted toilet seats are not covered. We hear politicians expressing support for a universal pharmacare program, and yet, as of the time this book was written, medication is not covered under most circumstances.

One study showed that "one in four lower income Canadians (24 percent) say they have delayed or stopped buying some prescription drugs, compared to 3 percent among those who earn more than $60,000" (Kondro 2012). Figure 8.2 compares heart-disease-related deaths in Canada to similar deaths in a few other countries. The critical difference between Canada and these other countries is the others have universal free medication programs and Canada does not.

Beyond the pure cost of healthcare, sociologists suggest several other social reasons for why wealth equals health. They include stress, education, and class discrimination.

When we think of the many resources needed for good health, we'd probably list access to nutritious food, regular medical checkups, effective and safe medicine, and access to clean, germ-free living environments. We may also list time for exercise and enough sleep. But low-income Canadians struggle to achieve all of these things. Some of the resources on that list, like suitable housing and nutritious food, are discussed in other chapters of this book. But another important and often overlooked element of good health is stress reduction.

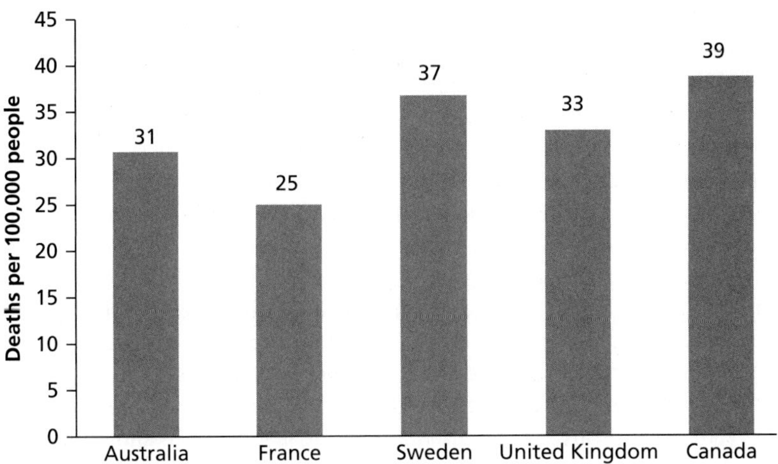

Figure 8.2 ◆ Deaths from Heart Disease

Source: Lopert, Docteur, and Morgan 2018.

◆ In Their Own Words ◆

I am a 31-year-old woman living with type 1 diabetes. I was diagnosed almost 10 years ago. I've lived in three different provinces since my diagnosis, and each has had unique challenges, barriers, and costs to accessing treatment, and none has been affordable by any measure. The cost of survival is astronomical. I was lucky enough to have been insured when I was diagnosed, but nevertheless, I've spent over $60,000 of my own money on insurance premiums, deductibles, insulin, prescribed test strips, ketone strip[s] and pumps. Best practices, such as using a continuous glucose monitor or test strip, are simply not affordable, even with coverage. Ironically, with my disease, the more stressed you are, the more difficult it becomes to keep glucose in range. For people like myself, who struggle to pay for supplies, the financial burden literally makes a person sicker. I can't imagine the consequences these costs have on people who are uninsured. I've reused needles and supplies, left infusion set in for longer than I should, all in an effort to decrease costs . . . Nobody chooses chronic illness, disability or disease. Yet we are expected to bear the burden of disease and daily management, in addition to the burden of cost in an effort to simply survive.

—Lily, Vancouver, British Columbia

Source: Lopert, Docteur, and Morgan 2018.

Everybody experiences some degree of stress. Some life circumstances, however, are much more stressful than others. It can be stressful to be poor. For example, research has shown the degree of control individuals have over stressful life circumstances, and how they cope with these circumstances, has a massive influence on health. Higher income usually gives people more control over situations and better coping skills for dealing with stress. It has also been shown that reduced control and poor coping skills have a biological effect. It increases vulnerability to many different diseases through pathways that involve the immune and hormonal systems (Government of Canada 2013).

On average, people with higher-than-average levels of stress have a higher susceptibility to illness and disease (Mikkonen and Raphael 2010). The effects of poverty-based stress may be felt even years after a person escapes poverty. One study out of Cornell University linked stress derived from childhood poverty to poor health in adulthood: "An early history of poverty appears to set children on a life-course trajectory of ill health" (Evans and Kim 2007:956). The researchers report that low-income children show increased blood pressure and stress hormones. Even as adults, they show a decreased ability to regulate those hormones adequately. So stress caused by poverty in childhood may, in adulthood, aggravate illnesses stemming from that same stress.

When examining health outcomes in Canada, some studies look at both educational attainment and income as measures of economic well-being. As you might guess, Canadians with postsecondary education are healthier on average than those without it (Statistics Canada 2019a). Take a look at Figures 8.3 through 8.7. They show how education and health are correlated on a range of dimensions: physical health, mental health, smoking, exercise, and nutritious food.

People with more education also live longer, on average (McIntosh et al. 2010). The correlation between education and health often comes down to income. The more educational credentials a person collects, the more likely they will find a safe, secure, and reasonably well-paid job, which leads to good health.

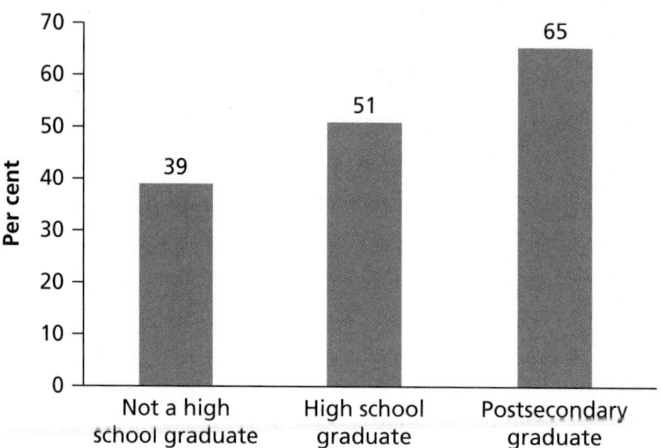

Figure 8.3 ✦ Self-Reported Health Status of "Very Good" or "Excellent" by Educational Attainment

From this figure, we can see that those with more education are more likely to report very good or excellent health.

Source: Statistics Canada 2019a.

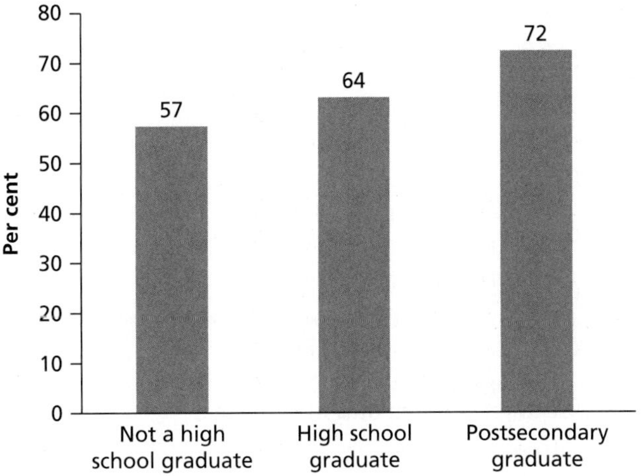

Figure 8.4 ◆ Perceived Mental Health as "Very Good" or "Excellent" by Educational Attainment

Source: Statistics Canada 2019a.

Education is also about learning how to get and use information. After all, managing one's health requires knowledge and a specific set of skills. One report on health literacy in Canada describes these skills as "prose literacy, document literacy and numeracy skills." These skills demand the ability to "find, understand, evaluate and communicate health-related information" (Canadian Council on Learning 2008:29). Educated Canadians are better able to take preventive measures to promote good health in themselves and their families because they know how to navigate the healthcare system effectively.

Finally, class discrimination may influence the healthcare low-income Canadians receive. In one recent study (Olah, Gaisano, and Hwang 2013), researchers pretended to be patients seeking a family doctor by "cold-calling" the offices of family physicians

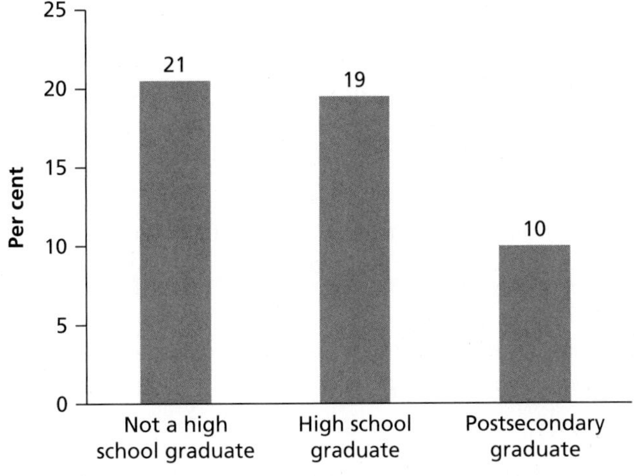

Figure 8.5 ◆ Current Daily Smoker by Educational Attainment

Source: Statistics Canada 2019a.

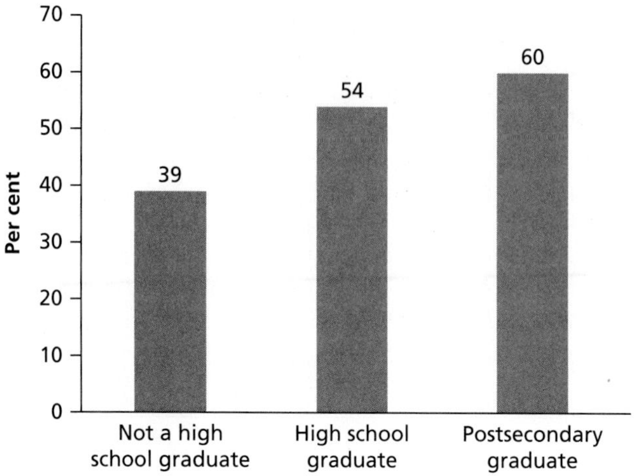

Figure 8.6 ◆ 150 Minutes of Exercise per Week by Educational Attainment

Source: Statistics Canada 2019a.

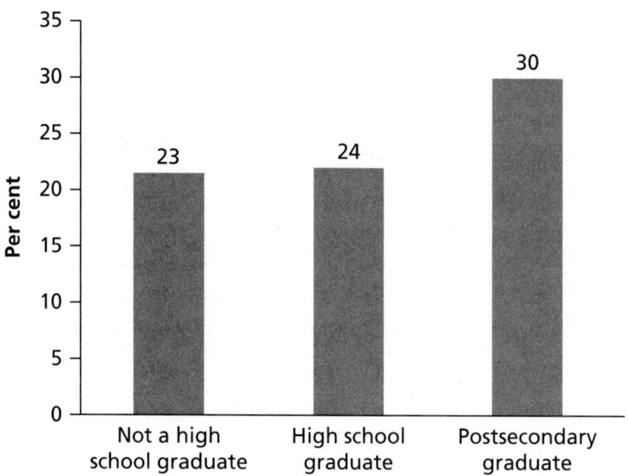

Figure 8.7 ◆ Five or More Servings of Fruit and Vegetables per Day by Educational Attainment

Source: Statistics Canada 2019a.

in Toronto. In their phone conversations with the office administrator, the researchers reported being either welfare recipients or bank employees. Here are excerpts from the scripts the researchers used:

> Hi. I was just transferred to Toronto with [name of major bank], and I need a family doctor for annual checkups. Is Dr ___________ accepting new patients?
>
> or
>
> Hi. I'm calling' cause my welfare worker told me that I need a family doctor for annual checkups. Is Dr __________ accepting new patients?

Which group of callers do you think was most likely to be granted a doctor's appointment? If you guessed the bank employees, you're right. Those pretending to be bank employees were over 50 per cent more likely to be granted an appointment than those pretending to be welfare recipients (Olah et al. 2013). The researchers offered some reasons why physicians may be less willing to treat low-income patients: "[P]hysicians have been shown to perceive patients with a low socioeconomic status more negatively in terms of their personalities, ability, behavioural tendencies and role demands" (E627). They might imagine poor patients are less informed about health issues, less likely to take good care of themselves, and less likely to stick to the treatment prescribed. To be sure, some of this is blatant prejudice, while some of it may be based on office experience. It is possible the economic barriers that prevent a person from being able to acquire medication and "follow through" with doctors' orders are also impacting the doctor's willingness to treat the patient.

Women in Canada

Given that more women are completing postsecondary education, some researchers theorize "the proportion of women reporting excellent health will continue to rise" (Turcotte 2012). That said, women have to deal with unique problems that can impact their health.

Consider single parenting. Recall from Chapter 4 that there are many challenges that come with being a single parent. Single parents are more likely to be women than men. Single mothers report higher levels of stress (Turcotte 2012), and stress is bad for health. It is tragically ironic that those who are least able to take a sick day off work—parenting work included—are the ones who may need one the most.

Women are also less likely to take part in leisure-time physical activity than men, which is harmful because it is an integral part of a healthy lifestyle (Turcotte 2012). This, in part, may be due to the distribution of labour in the home, which can impact a woman's leisure time (as highlighted in Chapter 4). Women are still putting in twice the numbers of hours on housework and carework than their male domestic partners.

Unemployment and low job security are correlated with poor health, and women are more likely to work in precarious jobs that may be characterized as "high strain." These are jobs with expectations that fall outside the responsibilities of that job. A good example would be a serving role. Often customers in a restaurant blame poor food experiences on their server, when, in reality, the kitchen is responsible for food quality. Servers get all the blame with none of the control: a perfect recipe for stress. High-stress jobs have been shown to increase a person's risk of health problems such as high blood pressure, depression, and anxiety. And while it is true that men are more likely to die from suicide, women are three or four times more likely to attempt it (Statistics Canada 2012b).

Women are also more likely than men to work **non-standard jobs**, so they are less likely to qualify for employment insurance. The lack of affordable childcare in Canada may force some women to choose to stay home with a child instead of work. As a result, women may have extended periods with little or no income, and as we saw in a previous section of this chapter, poverty is bad for a person's health.

non-standard job A job that is often characterized by part-time, temporary, on-call, contract, and self-employed work.

Further, cultural **appearance norms** that idealize certain features can be restrictive and even harmful to the health of both men and women. The media often advertise unattainable and extreme beauty ideals. There is pressure for all to fit in, as departures from

appearance norms Social "rules" that govern how people feel they should look to others.

these norms suggest poor genes, poor grooming, or a lack of self-discipline and self-worth. This media spotlight on body image is far more intense for women than for men. As a result, women experience more insecurity about their bodies and are much more likely to develop life-threatening eating disorders like anorexia, bulimia, or binge eating disorder.

Good healthcare requires good research. Good research helps healthcare professionals understand the unique health needs that attach to individual bodies. However, recent research has shown that most medical research is done on men. Usually, doctors assume the same findings automatically apply to women. Sometimes this assumption can be fatal to women when the wrong dosages are administered or a drug is wrongly combined with other drugs in an amount unsuited to women's bodies.

Let's expand this vital point a bit because it has been ignored for too long, at considerable risk to women. There are three gender- or sex-based issues when it comes to healthcare research. The first is that female bodies have historically been left out of relevant clinical research. One researcher from Stanford University, Dr Keith Humphreys, looked at the participants included in five alcohol addiction and treatment studies (Brandt 2007). He found that females (and racialized minorities) were routinely left out of participant pools.

Humphreys suggested that researchers may leave out these populations out of "habit or tradition" or efforts to produce desirable results in their research. Humphreys points out that "most researchers want women in the studies, but they don't realize the way they design the study undermines their intentions. For example, a researcher may not want anyone who is depressed in their alcohol study, and not stop to consider that, since the majority of people with depression are women, this choice might eliminate women from their study."

Second, the researchers that include women in their trials discover that their bodies respond differently to some drugs than men's bodies do. For example, women feel drowsier for a longer time after taking Ambien, a sleep aid, and react differently to antidepressants. Females also metabolize some drugs, like certain anxiety medications, faster than males and are less responsive to some painkillers and anesthetics (Edwards 2013). For these reasons, it is unwise and unhelpful to only test drugs on men's bodies.

Finally, women have different health needs than men. For one thing, women are more likely than men to experience chronic illness and disease. Women are also more susceptible to autoimmune diseases like multiple sclerosis and rheumatoid arthritis (Edwards 2013). They are more likely to experience pain, and yet one study showed that women were more likely to be ignored when complaining about their pain (Institute of Medicine 2011).

Significantly, women can also experience pregnancy. Pharmaceutical corporations are reluctant to include pregnant women in their drug trials owing to the possible liability of harm to fetuses. The resulting lack of data means that many people avoid taking necessary medications during pregnancy. There are safe and ethical ways to collect data about drug interactions during pregnancy. It may be more costly and time consuming, but increasingly research ethics boards are requiring that pregnant people not be excluded from research unless there is a clear reason they should be.

Health barriers faced by trans women are discussed later in this chapter.

Men in Canada

One of the primary objectives of this book is to introduce populations vulnerable to different forms of inequality. In a chapter on access to good health, there is a good reason to discuss men as a distinctly vulnerable population group. We'll review some of those reasons now.

Start with the most straightforward, most apparent fact: Men are less likely than women to visit doctors. Do you have a family doctor? If you answered yes to that question, and you visit your family doctor regularly, your odds of being in good health are better than those who don't. Family doctors play an essential role in building and maintaining good health. They treat minor illnesses, diagnose significant health issues in the critical early stages, and connect patients to relevant specialists who may diagnose and treat more complicated issues. Doctors are useful not only when you're sick but also when you want to *stay well.* People who do not have a family doctor are less likely to receive necessary preventive care, like a flu shot, mammograms, Pap tests, or colorectal screening (Statistics Canada 2019c).

But if you answered no to that question, you aren't alone. One in six Canadians do not have access to a regular family doctor, and this population is not randomly assigned (Statistics Canada 2012a). Men between the ages of 20 and 64 are significantly less likely than women to have a regular family doctor. Figure 8.8 shows how many people in Canada did not have a family doctor in 2017, organized according to age. Take a moment to compare the differences between men and women; you'll note that men are more likely to be without a family doctor in *every* age category.

Men do not fail to seek healthcare because they are naturally healthier than women. In fact, men are more likely to smoke and drink heavily and are less likely to make positive health changes such as improving their diet and exercising (Turcotte 2012). Men are also more likely to suffer from workplace accidents. In part, this results from the "gendering" of some professions. Men are more likely to work in dangerous workplaces, with heavy machinery and awkward surroundings (as on a construction site). However, Statistics Canada found that men were more likely to be injured even in management, business, or finance jobs—at twice the rate of women (Wilkins and Mackenzie 2008). So it seems that being a man in our society means taking risks and living with dangers and hazards.

But why are men more likely to take risks and less likely to seek the support of medical doctors? Dr Dennis Raphael, a health policy professor at York University writes "men's health is sometimes influenced—for the worse—by unhealthy constructs of masculinity that idealize aggressiveness, dominance and excessive self-reliance" (Mikkonen and

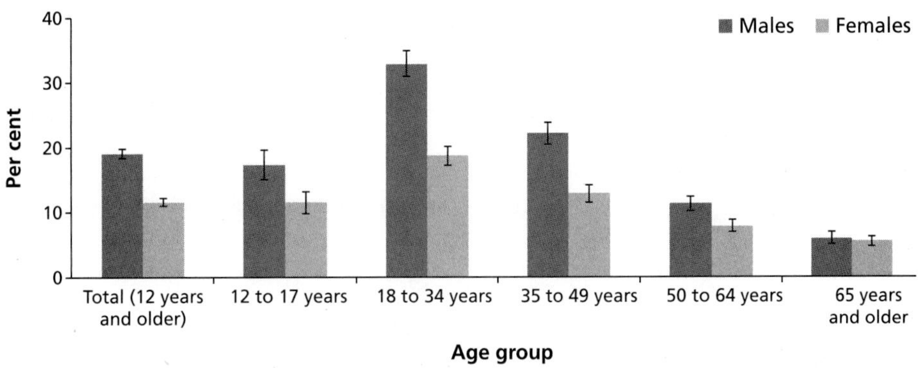

Figure 8.8 ◆ Percentage of Canadians without a Regular Healthcare Provider, by Sex

Source: Statistics Canada 2019c.

Raphael 2010). It is perhaps this excessive self-reliance and foolhardiness that keeps men from seeking the care they need.

Finally, men are more likely than women to suffer more extreme forms of social exclusion. Some studies have found that there are many more homeless young men than homeless young women in Canada. For example, a Canadian study on youth homelessness found that 57.6 per cent identified as male and 36.4 per cent as female (Gaetz et al. 2016). They are also three times more likely to die from suicide (Statistics Canada 2012b). It may be that the same preoccupation with self-reliance that keeps a man from visiting the doctor also keeps a socially isolated, even mentally ill man from seeking the help he needs.

Seniors in Canada

Everywhere and for everyone, good health usually declines as a person ages. Compared with young Canadians, Canadian seniors are more vulnerable to chronic illness, disease, and specific injuries. As a result, seniors typically need more healthcare than other age segments of the population. Figure 8.9 shows the average increase in healthcare costs as a person ages.

For example, many seniors require homecare. Homecare involves a friend, family member, or health professional visiting a senior's home to assist with bathing, dressing, meal preparation, transportation, or household chores. When compared to working-age adults with disabilities, seniors with disabilities are more likely to receive help with at least one everyday activity (Government of Canada 2009). Indeed, the older a senior is, the more likely they will require homecare (Gilmour 2018). Homecare needs are especially high among Canadian seniors with a disability.

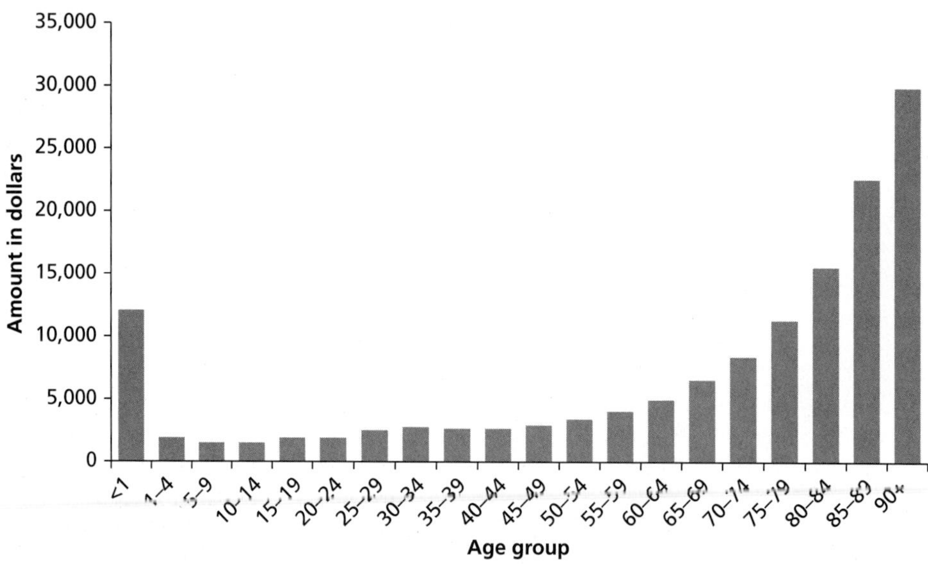

Figure 8.9 ◆ Provincial/Territorial Government Health Expenditure per Capita, by Age Group, 2017

Source: Canadian Institute for Health Information 2019.

Most seniors rely on friends and family for their homecare needs. These social support systems are sometimes called "informal" homecare, and they are essential for Canadian seniors. Roughly half of all Canadians, at some point in their lives, will provide care to a sick or aging loved one. Indeed, age-related health problems are the single most common problem requiring help from caregivers (Sinha 2015). Some seniors, for various reasons, may not have the same social support systems as others. A single senior, for example, cannot rely on the support of a spouse. Certain groups of seniors may be less likely to receive informal homecare and may also have weak social supports. They include seniors without children or grandchildren, seniors who live in rural or remote areas, and seniors who have recently arrived in Canada.

A smaller number of seniors rely on homecare provided by paid employees. These are typically professionals who provide medical support. But professional homecare often costs money, and seniors who can't afford this may have unmet homecare needs. In a recent survey, two-thirds of senior respondents credited their unmet homecare needs to cost. Seniors with a disability were 10 times more likely to report unmet homecare needs, and senior women were more likely than senior men to have this problem. This lack of homecare often results in avoidable injuries, increased risk of falls, depression, reduced self-care, and even premature death (Hoover and Rotermann 2012).

There are many social factors influencing the health of Canadian seniors. For example, studies have found that social engagement is correlated with well-being (Gilmour 2012; Carver et al. 2018). In part, this is because social activities may provide exercise and improve mental health. However, not all seniors are as socially engaged as they could be. In particular, low-income seniors are more isolated and unengaged. One study found that seniors from higher-income households were less likely to report feeling lonely (Gilmour 2012). Many factors play a part in this. For example, higher-income seniors are better able to afford specialized transportation like taxis to get from place to place or membership in clubs that offer welcoming programs.

As Canada's population ages, more seniors will need costly healthcare, and the availability of public dollars for healthcare is a growing concern. Canadians will have to admit that seniors with few social support systems have less chance of enjoying the health benefits of homecare and social engagement. The at-risk groups include low-income seniors, single seniors, disabled seniors, seniors living in remote regions, and newly immigrated seniors.

Immigrants in Canada

Consider, now, the place of new immigrants in Canadian society. Canadian immigrants are typically healthy when they arrive in Canada (Lu and Ng 2019); this is because they're not allowed into Canada if they're not.

People wishing to immigrate to Canada must undergo a medical examination to show that they will not pose a danger to public health. For example, they must show that they do not carry a dangerous virus that could spread in Canada. They also must show that they will not be a drain on the Canadian medical system. Under Canada's existing immigration policies, a person with a complicated long-term illness needing frequent medical treatment would not be an ideal candidate for immigration. That is largely why Canadian immigrants start off healthy. The exception is refugees, who are the immigrant type most likely to be unhealthy on arrival (Lu and Ng 2019). Researchers speculate that this is likely because refugees are "involuntary migrants who came to Canada to seek protection" from situations that are damaging to one's health—such as "wars, natural disasters, or persecution on the basis of race, religion, etc." (Lu and Ng 2019). We will discuss refugees later.

Healthy people are motivated to remain healthy, so it would be reasonable to assume the health status of Canadian immigrants would remain relatively stable. And yet studies show that this is not the case. Instead, many studies have shown that most immigrants report a decrease in good health within a few months of arriving in Canada. Their health status continues to decline over the following years (Lou and Beaujot 2005; Ng, Pottie, and Spitzer 2011; Statistics Canada 2005). These results are not unique to Canada. The same results are reported for immigrants to other, similar countries, like the United States and the United Kingdom. This suggests the decline in health is not unique to Canada but has something to do with migration.

Can you think of some reasons why Canadian immigrants might report a decline in their health status? Let's review a few of the possible reasons.

First, consider lifestyle adaptation. During the years of social adaptation and integration, some immigrants adopt unhealthy "Canadian" habits. Studies show, for example, the decline in immigrant health is associated with an increase in obesity rates (Statistics Canada 2005). Argys (2015) shows the same process occurring in all Global North countries. This is because "migration generally flows from low- to high-BMI countries," so the longer migrants stay, the more they "adopt natives' unhealthy lifestyles" and see a rise in their own body mass index, or BMIs (1).

Second, consider language. Language aptitude is another social determinant of health. Almost 40 per cent of immigrants have language challenges, and researchers have found that poorer language skills are associated with poorer health. Immigrants who speak one or both of Canada's official languages experience better health than immigrants who do not (Ng et al. 2011). Language skills are especially important when describing symptoms to a doctor, and they are essential when learning medication instructions. Language skills are also required for the kinds of social interaction and community involvement that promote good health.

The more social networks an immigrant has, the more likely they are to report being healthy (Zhao, Li Xue, and Gilkinson 2010). Think about how your own social networks keep you healthy. Social networks offer people stress-relieving opportunities. Friends provide free and well-delivered care when a person is ill, and friends help sick friends access and understand healthcare professionals. Forget about the life-giving effects of apples—sociologists have found that a good friend a day keeps the doctor away!

Where mental health is concerned, employment status is significant. Researchers Yimin Lou and Roderic Beaujot (2005) studied the factors influencing the mental health of immigrant populations. Doing so, they found that poor employment outcomes cause "poor status attainment and slower mobility in climbing up the socio-economic ladder" (3–4). They also list **alienation**, discrimination, feelings of isolation resulting from relocation, and the systematic and deliberate exclusion from opportunities or critical resources.

alienation The estrangement of individuals from one another or from a specific situation or process.

Though new immigrants consistently report better health conditions than the general Canadian-born population, over time this health advantage declines. Certain immigrant populations—including refugees and non-European immigrants—have a higher risk of transitioning to poorer health (Gushulak et al. 2011). As Mikkonen and Raphael (2010) note, "[r]acialized Canadians experience a whole range of adverse living circumstances that threaten not only their health but also the overall health and well-being of Canadian society" (47). These include lower-than-average incomes, persistent unemployment, and difficulty accessing high-quality healthcare. In short, being subjected to racism is bad for your health.

Yin Paradies (2006) reviewed 138 empirical studies to examine the link between experiences of racism and health consequences. Paradies reports stress, negative mental health outcomes, and even negative physical health outcomes (albeit less commonly) are preceded by self-reported experiences of racism. Paradies reminds us, however, that problems surrounding definition, data collection, and causal explanation must be solved before we can know the full extent of and reasons for this disturbing relationship.

Refugees and Undocumented or Non-status Immigrants in Canada

As noted above, a refugee is a person fleeing a dangerous or deadly circumstance in their home country. As soon as they land in Canada and declare their wish to stay as a refugee, they begin a lengthy process to settle their eligibility. During this time, they are called a **refugee claimant**.

refugee claimant An individual who has applied for refugee status in Canada and is waiting for the Immigration and Refugee Board to decide whether refugee status should be granted.

Most refugee claimants awaiting a decision on whether they will be officially designated as refugees are eligible for limited, temporary health insurance that is similar to provincial health coverage. However, there are barriers to healthcare that are unique to the refugee population.

For one thing, translation services are covered for mental healthcare, but not for other healthcare needs (like booking appointments or understanding drug information). The current coverage for mental healthcare includes clinical psychologists, registered psychotherapists, and counselling therapists, but not social workers, who could do much to reduce the long waitlist and support the waiting refugees. Any child born to a refugee claimant is covered by their provincial health plan, but many provinces do not provide free drugs to children. Their parent(s), in this case, would have to pay.

The extent of refugee healthcare has shifted with the changing governments in Canada; in just the past decade, the coverage has changed dramatically. For that reason, some doctors are unclear about whether they can treat refugees who are seeking medical care. In 2018, health and migration law scholar Brandon Chen and his colleagues (2018) published a study showing that "clear and accessible information about the [provision of refugee healthcare] appears to be lacking for patients and service providers alike." According to Chen, "the instability and complexity of the program during the years of cuts continue to cloud people's understanding" (98). This uncertainty no doubt compounds people's feelings of stress when they need care. It also reminds us that systems themselves can pose a barrier to healthcare when they become overcomplicated.

As we saw in earlier chapters, some people are not officially authorized to be here in Canada. Sociologists sometimes refer to this population as **undocumented or non-status Canadians**. They might be refugee claimants who have had their applications denied but did not leave. Or they might be temporary foreign workers who have stayed past the date covered by their visas. An undocumented Canadian does not carry a health card, will not be insured through provincial health insurance plans, and must pay to receive healthcare.

undocumented or non-status Canadians Refugee claimants who have had their applications denied or temporary foreign workers who have stayed past the date covered by their visa.

So what happens when an undocumented person in Canada gets sick? Some undocumented people without healthcare coverage visit volunteer-run, free clinics that serve this population. But these clinics are likely to be extremely busy and staffed by overworked doctors. The medication, which is mostly donated, sometimes runs out. In a newspaper article profiling one of these clinics, one doctor said "our clinic is at a sustainability crisis point. Everybody is under the gun here and we are swamped. Some nights, it's being crowd control" (Keung 2012).

As we said at the beginning of this chapter, sociologists vary in their perspectives on health, illness, and other aspects of survival. Some people, sociologists among them, view this treatment of undocumented people in Canada to be unfair, even inhumane. Others see it as a reasonable measure taken to protect the Canadian medical system from abuse and overuse by people who are not contributing tax dollars toward it.

Indigenous Peoples in Canada

Recent statistics have shown that Indigenous Peoples in Canada fare worse than the average Canadian when it comes to health. According to Health Canada, compared with the general population, the incidence of heart disease is 1.5 times higher in Indigenous Peoples than non-Indigenous people in Canada. Type 2 diabetes is 3 to 5 times higher, in part because obesity rates are higher among Indigenous populations, and tuberculosis infection rates are roughly 8 to 10 times higher for Indigenous Peoples. Moreover, roughly 15 per cent of all new HIV/AIDS infections occur among Indigenous Peoples (Health Council of Canada 2012). This is significant given that Indigenous Peoples make up only 4.9 per cent of the population. Indigenous Peoples are also more likely to drink and smoke (Statistics Canada 2018) and die prematurely (Park et al. 2015). And they are less likely to report good health than their non-Indigenous counterparts (Statistics Canada 2018).

Researchers have considered many reasons Indigenous Peoples have poorer health on average. We know that Indigenous communities struggle with disproportionately high levels of poverty, unemployment, and inadequate housing and that these factors all contribute to poor health. Sometimes the poor health of Indigenous Peoples is explained by the fact there are fewer healthcare professionals in remote areas where many Indigenous Peoples live. For example, statisticians Linda Gionet and Shirin Roshanafshar (2013) report that "most Inuit communities are served by a nursing station only and accessing hospital services can require extensive travel." The absence of healthcare professionals means a lack of healthcare. However, the way that health services are delivered can matter too. Studies have shown that, even where healthcare professionals are present, Indigenous populations report feeling marginalized, dismissed, or neglected (Green 2012).

residential instability Frequent residential movement of individuals from place to place.

As well, many Indigenous Canadians who live off-reserve often move from place to place. This movement has been referred to as **residential instability**, and researchers have found a correlation between high levels of residential uncertainty and poor health (King, Smith, and Gracey 2009). First, it's a challenge to complete an education when a person moves a lot. As we have seen, higher educational achievement is associated with better health. It is also challenging to set up healthy routines such as preparing nutritious food when a person has sporadic access to a kitchen and pantry. Finally, moving a lot puts pressure on loving relationships. Researchers have found that residential instability is associated with divorce and other forms of family instability, which also harm health (King et al. 2009).

Cultural factors are equally important to the health of Indigenous Peoples in Canada. Researchers have found that "colonization, globalization, migration, loss of language and culture, and disconnection from the land lead to the health inequalities of Indigenous peoples" (King et al. 2009). These particular determinants of health are uniquely—though not uniformly or universally—experienced by Indigenous Peoples in Canada. Recall, for instance, our discussion of food gathering practices in Chapter 7.

One continuing effect of colonization is the erosion of traditional cultural practices. This erosion may result from the displacement of Indigenous Peoples over centuries of colonization. Other factors include the social shaming—or even criminalization—of traditional cultural practices like potlatches, sun dances, and traditional forms of hunting and fishing. Finally, the sudden introduction of modern technology to remote, isolated communities may affect Indigenous Peoples' health and access to care.

However, cultural identities and cultural practices are dynamic. They change and adapt over time. This is true of all cultures. Many people even challenge the term *traditional*, which suggests a unique, genuine way of being against which other ways are measured. In fact, some sociologists point out that idealizing the term *traditional* stereotypes Indigenous Peoples as having a singular, unchanging identity. In turn, this view contributes to poor health results because it presumes Indigenous Peoples and their cultures cannot grow and find new ways to thrive.

Yet such growth is difficult to come by in the face of multiple barriers. In 2012, the Health Council of Canada promoted discussions with Indigenous Peoples across the country to understand their experiences in the healthcare system better. Participants described the racism and discrimination they had been subjected to while seeking medical care:

> They told stories of doctors who would not prescribe painkillers to Indigenous people (even when they were in severe pain) because of a mistaken and racist belief that Indigenous people are at high risk of becoming addicted . . . Other examples of racism included a staff member who used a code word to signal dismissively to a colleague the next patient was an Indigenous person; . . . and an Indigenous woman (and health care professional) who was told that she would not be included in the planning process for her family member's care because she "wouldn't understand." (Health Council Canada 2012)

In adults, experiences of residential schooling are "associated with increased probability of educational failure, marital instability, and unemployment" (Barton et al. 2005:309). Many residential school students lived with abuse, shame, and fear instead of love, acceptance, and support. Many have identified the ongoing trauma of residential schools as a factor contributing to elevated rates of mental illness in Indigenous communities (Government of Nunavut 2010; Truth and Reconciliation Commission 2015a).

Residential schools and other policies have marginalized Indigenous Peoples in Canada. These policies have denied them access to any position or symbol of power in society by separating them from their families, their communities, and Canadian society.

As a result, Indigenous Peoples in Canada disproportionately suffer from mental health issues. Depression, suicide, and addictions are much more prevalent in many Indigenous communities than in the general Canadian population, and **marginalization** and exclusion play an essential role. Another negative result of extreme mental distress is suicide. Suicide is especially common in Inuit communities in Northern Canada. In fact, Inuit show higher

marginalization A process that denies a group or individual access to important positions and symbols of economic, religious, or political power within any society.

◆ In Their Own Words ◆

The Truth and Reconciliation report chronicles the experiences of Colin Courtoreille and Mike Durocher, among others. Colin Courtoreille told of how rapidly one boy at the Grouard School was taken by pneumonia.

> "An Indian boy from Whitefish—he was in the next bed to me. He was coughing a lot—that was in February, about 1936. He got wet because he had a bad cold but we all had to play outside. He played in the snow and he got wet. At the time to go to bed—now we are in a dorm like in a hall—he was coughing and wheezing. I talked to the Sister—after I can talk a little bit of English, I always tried to help out—I said, 'George is really sick Sister, what's wrong with him?' She comes there and I can see her make a ginger in a cup. She gave it to him and sent him to bed. That boy died that night about 3 o'clock in the morning."

Mike Durocher, a student at Île-à-la-Crosse for nine years, said life was governed by "a regimental time clock dictated by Church functions." *Of the regimentation, a student from a different school said,* "We were trained like dogs—clap you get up—two claps you go eat—three claps maybe you go outside."

Source: Truth and Reconciliation Commission 2015b:43.

suicide rates than any other population in Canada. Inuit males aged 15–24 have a suicide rate 40 times greater than this age category in the rest of Canada (White 2011).

We know from Émile Durkheim's classic study of suicide that it points to a high degree of social disorganization and disintegration, and it may also reflect feelings of despair and hopelessness. So we should take the high rates of suicide among Indigenous Peoples in Canada seriously. The data show that Indigenous Peoples continue to deal with social integration following the impact of colonialism and cultural genocide on their communities. We cannot ignore this, nor can we ignore the ongoing impact of discrimination, poverty, high unemployment rates, high incarceration rates, and family disintegration.

A Statistics Canada study that shows exceptionally high rates of death by suicide among Canada's Inuit youth has drawn concern across the nation. This study examined the mortality rates of Inuit people aged 1–19 during a five-year period, 2004–8. In that age range, suicide was the most common cause of death, with youths from Inuit Nunangat 25 times more likely to commit suicide than young Canadians living elsewhere. The report also shows that during a period when Canada's overall suicide rate was declining, the suicide rate in Nunangat was climbing (Oliver, Peters, and Kohen 2012).

In most of Canada, people are more likely to commit suicide as they get older. However, in Canada's North, it's youth aged 15–24 who are at highest risk for committing suicide. Researcher Jack Hicks (2007) points out that Inuit youth face different kinds of problems, or risk factors, than older people. They include a lack of educational and occupational choices that, in turn, translate into limitations on marriage, childbearing, and homeownership.

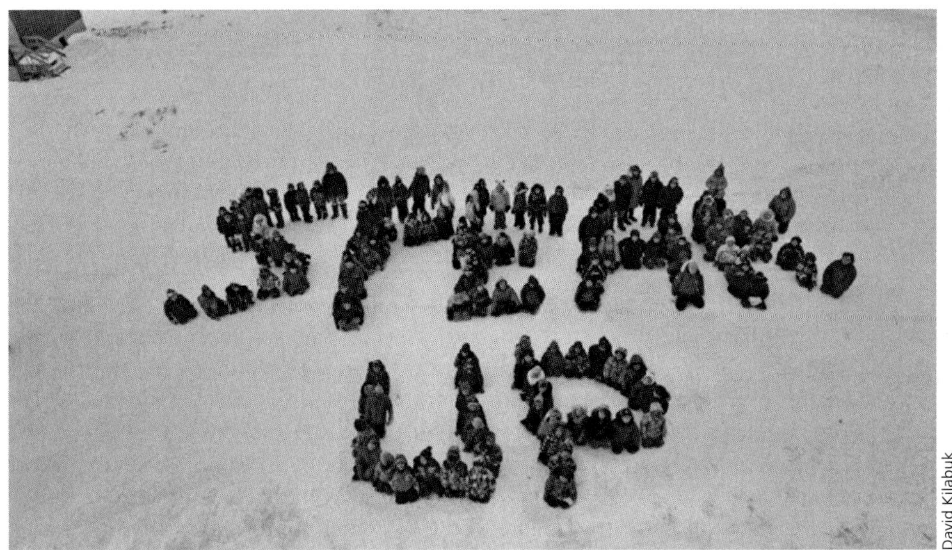

Children in Pangnirtung, Nunavut, send a living message with their bodies during an anti-bullying workshop in the community as part of the Embrace Life Council's suicide prevention work in the territory.

The same study discovered other alarming statistics that are important for understanding the relationship between Inuit youth, social determinants of health, and barriers to care. For instance, teenagers and children in Nunangat are 11 times more likely than other Canadians to die of infectious or parasitic diseases, and twice as likely to die from non-communicable illnesses. They're also 11 times more likely to die from injury than children and teenagers in the rest of Canada.

A report by the Standing Senate Committee on Indigenous and Northern Affairs (2017) notes that addressing SDOH "such as housing, educational attainment, poverty and unemployment" (1) are crucial to improving the day-to-day lives of Indigenous youth, ensuring their access to healthcare, and halting the increase in hopelessness and suicide in the North.

◆ In Their Own Words ◆

If the populations of "mainland" Canada, Denmark, and the United States had suicide rates comparable to those of their Inuit populations, national emergencies would be declared.

—Upaluk Poppel, Inuit Circumpolar Youth Council, 18 May 2005

More broadly, consider how we imagine "good health." Many Canadians think of "good health" as meaning freedom from illness, disease, or pain. However, King, Smith, and Gracey (2009) describe an alternate view shared among the Ojibway:

> The Anishinabek (Ojibway) word *mno bmaadis*, which translates into living the good life or being alive well, encapsulates beliefs in the importance of balance. All four elements of life, the physical, emotional, mental, and spiritual, are represented in the four directions of the medicine wheel. These four elements are intricately woven together and interact to support a healthy and robust person. (76)

Many factors interact to produce bad health for Indigenous Peoples in Canada. They include poverty, marginality, cultural demoralization, and geographical isolation, among others. Solutions that are generated by and within Indigenous communities are thought to be most effective and enduring than those imposed from "outside." Any initiative that infantilizes, disrespects, or otherwise marginalizes people is likely to worsen problems, not solve them. And we cannot overlook the significance of culture and the impact of historical injustices—such as the attempted erasure of Indigenous cultures. The attempted forcible Anglicization of Indigenous Peoples and the brutal and negligent ways it was carried out created a legacy of anxiety, distress, self-loathing, violence, and fractured families. The most direct measure of these problems was in the area of health, especially mental health and addiction.

It comes as no surprise, then, that the Truth and Reconciliation Commission's (2015a) 94 Calls to Action include multiple calls for reform in the area of health. The commission noted it is necessary to understand that the current state of Indigenous health results from policies from the Canadian government. Furthermore, it notes that identifying and overcoming barriers to good health and healthcare for Indigenous Peoples depends on changing the way we approach health broadly, to include more Indigenous Peoples working in the healthcare field, to appreciate and respect Indigenous approaches to health, and to improve training for healthcare workers so they can better help Indigenous Peoples seeking care.

LGBTQ+ People in Canada

The LGBTQ+ population in Canada is extraordinarily diverse. It reflects all manner of age, class, race, ethnicity, ability, and so on. It would be wrong to assume that all gay men experience the same barriers to good health and healthcare as do lesbian, bisexual, or trans-identified people in Canada. Likewise, one lesbian patient may have a different experience of health and healthcare than another. The experience a patient has depends on intersecting identities, such as immigration status, age, or membership in other vulnerable populations.

The last few decades have seen enormous political changes for the LGBTQ+ population. It may seem like ancient history, but there was once a time when a man or woman couldn't make important decisions about a same-sex partner who was critically sick or injured. Often, same-sex partners were not even able to visit their critically ill, hospitalized partners. Their status as "spouse" was not legally recognized until the early 2000s when the Supreme Court of Canada ruled the previous definition of spouse infringed on LGBTQ+ persons' rights and freedoms.

Many researchers have sought to understand the ways that sexual orientation or gender identity is a social determinant of health. Some have suggested that **heteronormativity** and **gender-normativity**—a set of assumptions that all people are, by default, heterosexual or the gender assigned by their sex at birth—might influence health. A heteronormative bias might cause healthcare professionals to overlook the sexual orientation of a patient, for example. A healthcare professional who doesn't ask important questions about sexual orientation, and instead assumes that everyone is straight, might miss a valuable opportunity to talk about health risks or treat illness. Similarly, a healthcare practitioner who overlooks or neglects to understand a patient's gender identity may neglect some crucial aspects of that patient's health, both physical and mental.

heteronormativity The societal assumption that all people are, by default, heterosexual and that heterosexuality is the normal state of being.

gender-normativity A set of assumptions that all people are, by default, the gender assigned by their sex at birth.

For example, if a doctor is treating a trans man who has had some form of gender-confirming surgery, and if this doctor doesn't know (or refuses to accept) that the patient was born with female sex characteristics, the doctor may fail to examine the patient's ovaries, cervix, and breast tissue. The doctor might equally neglect to note, when taking the patient's health history, that it is possible for him to have had several childbirths. Alternatively, it may be necessary for some trans women to have regular prostate exams, so doctors need to be mindful of and attentive to these needs.

Transphobia—that is, discrimination against trans-identified individuals—is a barrier to accessing medical care in Canada. Transphobia in the healthcare system encompasses a wide range of phenomena, including direct discrimination (for example, verbal abuse) or subtle forms of discrimination that make the environment hostile to the needs of trans patients (for example, gendered washrooms). Both subtle and direct expressions of transphobia act as barriers for general primary care (Bockting, Benner, and Coleman 2009; Green, Rachlin, and Lombardi 2008). They may also hinder mental healthcare (Avery, Hellman, and Sudderth 2001), substance and abuse treatment (Lombardi 2007), and HIV treatment (De Santis 2009; Kenagy 2005).

Much sociological work on trans experience with the healthcare system centres around the idea of *erasure*. Erasure refers to the systematic failure to notice and confirm trans identities (Snelgrove et al. 2012). Even healthcare programs directed at the LGBTQ+ community often fail to adequately meet the needs of their trans patients (Bauer et al. 2009).

Transphobia and erasure combine to create ill health results for trans people. Due to a lack of understanding, trans people (regardless of their sexual orientation) have a high rate of sexually transmitted infections and HIV. One study of male-to-female trans women in the United States found that 27.7 per cent of participants tested positive for HIV (Centers for Disease Control and Prevention 2013). As with other socially disadvantaged groups, mental health issues are prevalent in the trans population. One study found that trans people have a 30 per cent chance of attempting suicide (Kenagy 2005).

Like gender-normativity, heteronormativity can also negatively impact health. For example, a doctor might assume that just because a young woman doesn't report having a boyfriend she isn't sexually active. The doctor does not take the time to ask if the woman is a lesbian and does not promote an environment where the woman feels comfortable disclosing her sexual orientation. The result is the doctor may have missed an opportunity to discuss healthy sexual practices.

Perhaps for these reasons, lesbians are reportedly less likely than heterosexual women to consult a family doctor (Tjepkema 2008). One researcher speculated that some lesbians at first feel uncomfortable at the thought of discussing their sexual orientation with their family doctors. They may fear, based on previous experience, that disclosure may make them vulnerable to discrimination or otherwise inferior treatment. On the other hand, lesbians who have disclosed their sexual orientation to their family doctors usually make more use of the healthcare system (Tjepkema 2008). Studies show that **stigmatization** in medical settings can lead to "long-term rejection of the system, avoidance of regular examinations, failure to return for follow-up, reluctance to report health issues, and non-disclosure of sexual orientation to service providers" (Duncan et al. 2000:8).

stigmatization The process by which a person's status is diminished owing to a poorly regarded physical or social attribute.

People who are subject to social marginalization experience stress, which is bad for health. Many LGBTQ+ Canadians experience a unique, long-term form of social stigmatization that extends back to early childhood (Duncan et al. 2000). Unlike other vulnerable and marginalized groups, LGBTQ+ people are almost unique in having to deal with secrecy from an early age. A person of colour does not have to disclose to their parents that they're not white, risking their disappointment or rejection. But for many—perhaps most LGBTQ+ people—secrecy and "coming out" are significant concerns and sources of continuing stress, influencing the seeking and receiving of healthcare as well. This critical source of ill health will only be erased when the stigma attached to non-heterosexual sexual orientation is removed.

◆ In Their Own Words ◆

In 2011, the Trans Equality Society of Alberta gathered some testimonials from trans people seeking medical care. Trans individuals often describe their experiences of misgendering. They occur whenever a patient is addressed by a former, wrong name because the medical records are privileged over the preferences of the actual patient. Here is an example:

> I let the person at the desk know my name change, but the nurse called me by my former name, I didn't reply. The nurse called the former name again, I still didn't answer. Finally, the nurse shouted out Mister [female name]. The nurse blatantly refused to refer to me in a polite and professional manner.

In 2006, the Vancouver Coastal Health's Transgender Health Program published some suggested guidelines for healthcare professionals treating trans patients. Here are some sample scripts they recommend that doctors use. Do you think these "openers" would promote an inclusive environment?

> "Because so many people are impacted by gender issues, I have begun to ask everyone about it. Anything you do say about gender issues will be kept confidential. If this topic isn't relevant to you, tell me, and I'll move on."

> "Out of respect for my clients' right to self-identify, I ask all clients what gender pronoun they'd prefer I use for them. What pronoun would you like me to use for you?"

Discrimination and stigmatization may also show up in a lack of research into LGBTQ+-related health issues (Gapka and Raj 2003). For example, some LGBTQ+ health activists propose there are health issues unique to trans populations. They argue the long-term effects of hormone therapies often sought by transsexual people are underresearched because of systemic discrimination in the health research sector.

As noted, LGBTQ+ populations are diverse, and we don't want to suggest otherwise. But they share one common problem—stigmatization—that influences their health and healthcare. This stigmatization has declined dramatically in the last two or three decades, but we are still far from seeing an end to it, and to its health effects.

People with Disabilities in Canada

Disabilities can, of course, have an immediate impact on an individual's health, but the level of government support for people with disabilities is also important. Compared to many other developed countries, Canada lacks effective programs that provide support to people with disabilities, leading to isolation, increased vulnerability, and limited opportunities to participate within society (Council of Canadians with Disabilities 2009). Compared to many other developed countries, Canada underfunds programs that help people with disabilities. While Canada is not the worst among OECD nations in their support for disadvantaged groups, it is also far from best (OECD 2020).

This lack of action by the Canadian government can even affect the quality of care that people with disabilities receive as well as their ability to access healthcare. Sanmartin and Ross (2006) have found the presence of a physical disability increases the odds of failing to receive necessary routine care by more than 50 per cent. For people with physical disabilities, accessing care is more complicated than it is for people without disabilities. The physical arrangement of the doctor's office—for example, stairs and examining tables—can act as a disincentive or obstacle to accessing healthcare. So can the attitudes of healthcare providers toward people with disabilities, not to mention the expertise of healthcare providers.

The healthcare system responds to physical disabilities paradoxically. Veltman and colleagues (2001) report that one-fifth of doctors do not take enough account of their patients' disability, but another fifth credit everything to the disability. These latter doctors look at a patient's disability as an illness, whereas patients usually view their disability as a condition of life (Jorgensen 2005). Consider the consequences of this difference. Treatment for an illness aims to cure, but the same approach may not be needed to address a patient's life-long condition. Clinicians who view the patient's physical disability as an illness are likely to thrust the disabled person into the sick role. This adds further stigma to already challenging disabilities.

Learning that a child has an intellectual or physical disability disrupts the whole family. A common reaction for parents is psychological and emotional turmoil. Compared with mothers with non-disabled children, mothers whose children have cerebral palsy report higher rates of depression, anxiety, and stress (Begum and Desai 2010). Other parents with physically disabled kids were assessed for their mental health—44 per cent of parents had poor mental health. Mental health was adversely affected if children were of younger age, relied on help for activities of daily living, or had problems walking.

However, studies have found that having a child with a disability does not necessarily have a harmful influence on emotions. For example, an Alberta study showed mothers of children with disabilities were unusually adept at meeting their children's special caregiving needs. In this way, they could keep the disability from overwhelming the family. Mothers who preserved a positive view of their situations (for example, saying that family values improved because of the disability) had a much better-adjusted family (Trute et al. 2010).

The health status of people with intellectual disabilities is also poorer than that of the average Canadian (Emerson et al. 2010). Often this is because of problems people with intellectual disabilities have when accessing healthcare. Many factors, including recognizing signs of ill health and communicating health problems to others, act as barriers to accessing healthcare (Alborz et al. 2005; Krahn, Hammond, and Turner 2006). Many also rely on a third party to recognize health problems and take suitable action.

People with intellectual disabilities experience many of the same barriers faced by people with physical disabilities. For example, they must contend with the physical arrangement of offices, the negative attitudes of healthcare providers, and a tendency to credit health concerns to their disabilities. However, they also experience unique organizational barriers. These include the failure of care providers to adjust the environment (for example, by providing easy-read material or extending appointments; Emerson et al. 2010). Legal requirements about consent can also pose problems (Goldsmith, Skirton, and Webb 2008). That is, healthcare providers cannot assume that people with intellectual disabilities will find healthcare information as quickly or find it as accessible as those without the disability.

Thus, healthcare providers must make suitable adjustments to ensure their patients are fully aware of their choices and the risks associated with treatment so they can properly consent to a treatment plan. These adjustments include more accessible healthcare literature and better education on how to communicate difficult health information to people with intellectual disabilities.

Consequences of Health Inequality

Both health inequality and healthcare inequality have fuelled the national debate over healthcare reform. We know that sick people suffer, and that some people are more prone to illness than others. And yet everyone—even the healthiest among us—suffers to some degree when there are sick people in our society.

For example, sick people are also more likely to be absent from work. They often fail to contribute to their household and draw resources (for example, time) away from other household activities, such as childcare, cooking, cleaning, and relaxation. Sickness hurts the sick person, but it hurts their family, community, and the economy as well.

As you learned in Chapter 7, failing to feed people properly increases the likelihood they will get sick and need costly, often long-term healthcare. That is short-sighted and inhumane. Unemployed people often need social financial assistance and other social services. These programs, however stretched, underfunded, and inadequate they might be, can be vital to relieving poverty. However, they are expensive. Unemployed people do not contribute income tax because they don't have jobs. Nor are they investing and consuming at the same rate as people earning a steady income. At a societal level, the money spent ensuring the survival of unemployed people cannot be spent elsewhere on things like education, the arts, and research and development. This is one of the ways the impacts of food-related illnesses (and the later likelihood of unemployment) are felt throughout society.

As we know, sick people put pressure on medical care. They often need remedial healthcare, which can be more costly than preventive healthcare, which focuses on illness prevention.

Today, no one doubts that social inequality is at the root of some of the world's most pressing health and healthcare issues. For example, John Asafu-Adjaye (2014) concludes from panel data for 44 countries covering six periods that

> income inequality (measured by the Gini index) has a significant effect on health status when we control for levels of income, savings, and education. The relationship is consistent regardless of the specification of health status and income. (195)

One central concern has been the role for-profit health services can or should play in Canada's supposedly universal system (Contandriopoulos and Bilodeau 2009). This matter is especially pressing in underserviced areas like Northern Canada. The 2002 Royal Commission on the Future of Health Care in Canada called for targeted funding to improve care for Canadians living in smaller communities in rural and remote areas (Romanow 2002).

Medical school initiatives, such as BC's Northern Medical Program and the Northern Ontario School of Medicine, are explicitly designed for underserviced areas in Canada. They aim to produce young doctors who are trained to deliver healthcare services in northern, remote, and Indigenous communities and in francophone communities in English-speaking Canada.

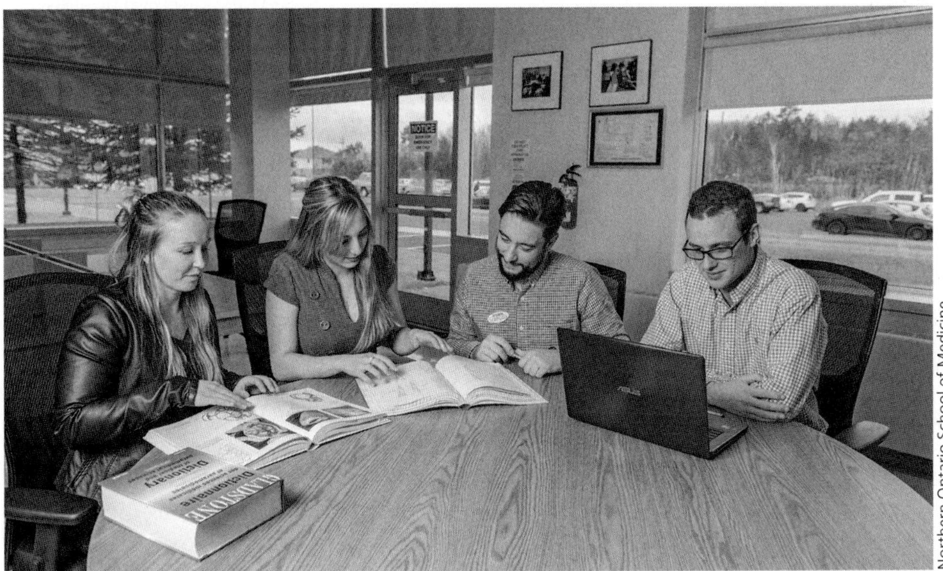

Northern Ontario School of Medicine

Francophone students studying at the Northern Ontario School of Medicine, which was designed to bring more doctors to underserviced areas of the province. Since opening, 69 per cent of all graduates have opted to work in remote and rural areas, particularly northern Ontario.

telehealth The use of computer and communications technologies to deliver healthcare, especially at a distance.

Because of the difficulties that remain in accessing healthcare, new healthcare delivery systems have been devised. **Telehealth**—the use of computer and communications technologies to aid healthcare delivery—is a growing industry that may revolutionize the medical profession's ability to service its patients. Specialists hundreds of kilometres away now routinely send out diagnostic images, such as X-rays, MRI scans, and pathology images electronically from rural or remote locations for review. Similarly, videoconferencing technology now allows medical consultations, mental health assessments, and observation of surgical procedures for educational purposes to take place over vast geographic distances (Sevean et al. 2009). This technology has the potential to reduce doctor and hospital visits and to ensure that emergencies are dealt with quickly and accurately.

Even with these efforts to improve access to healthcare, Statistics Canada reported that in 2016 15.8 per cent of Canadians aged 12 and older did not have a family doctor. In fairness, we should note that "[o]f the 4.8 million people without a primary health care provider, the most commonly reported reasons were that they had not tried to find one (28.7 per cent) or that they did not need one, but had a usual place of care (26.3 per cent)." However, Indigenous Peoples, as well as people living in poorer or more rural provinces, were more likely than other Canadians to be without a family doctor (Statistics Canada 2017).

Waiting Times

A significant concern about access to healthcare is "waiting time." Regrettably, our society cannot afford to provide immediate, high-quality care to everyone who needs it. This fact of economic life, in a society preoccupied with efficiency and speed, irritates many of us.

If we assume there will never be enough money to erase waiting, we need to consider why people react to waiting as negatively as they do. We also need to devise ways to make the unavoidable waiting more tolerable. However, sick people typically become frightened if their condition worsens or their pains increase while they are waiting for treatment (Fitzsimons et al. 2003). The longer patients remain on a waiting list, compared with how long they expected to wait, the more anxiety and depression they experience (Vermeulen et al. 2005; Conner-Spady et al. 2005a, 2005b). That said, men and women react to waiting differently (Parry et al. 2004). Among patients waiting for coronary bypass surgery, for example, men suffer much less anxiety during the wait than women do.

The importance of perceived waiting time suggests that healthcare providers need to work on improving people's expectations as much as on decreasing wait times. This may mean developing a better social organization of waiting. Here, sociologists need to study ways to organize the process of waiting more effectively to provide sympathetic "waiting communities." Waiting is more comfortable when people are aware of their position in the queue, know how fast the line is moving, and understand the reasons for delays.

Case management of waiting may solve the problem, for example, by giving every person in a queue a case manager to sympathetically answer questions, provide information, and connect with the relevant medical personnel. For disadvantaged people who are used to being ignored or mistreated, this could provide reassurance that their health is a priority and will be addressed, if not cured.

Strategies of Resistance

In this section, we review a few examples of efforts undertaken to equalize access to good health and healthcare. Even though healthcare is funded by the government in Canada, improving access to it needs work on the individual and organizational levels as well. Improvements will be most reliable when all three levels work in tandem to create more equal access for everyone.

Government-Level Strategies of Resistance

One crucial way in which the Government of Canada seeks to equalize access to good health and healthcare is by understanding it better. Health Canada, the federal government department that promotes healthy living, funds a vast number of research initiatives across the country. Consider, for example, the Centres of Excellence for Women's Health. These centres, spread across Canada, pull together academics, policymakers, and community organizations to produce research on topics related to women's health.

Health Canada also has programs that are specifically targeted to Indigenous Peoples in Canada. These programs include guides and information on environmental health both in the community and in natural environments, and their family health programs work to address problems particular to Indigenous Peoples. For example, the Indigenous Diabetes Initiative currently receives $50 million per year from the federal government to reduce the prevalence of diabetes in First Nations communities. By "using local knowledge, First Nations and Inuit communities are encouraged to develop innovative, culturally relevant approaches aimed at increasing community wellness and ultimately reducing the burden of type 2 diabetes" (Indigenous Services Canada 2013).

Organization-Level Strategies of Resistance

In this chapter, we have seen that Indigenous Peoples in Canada are a population vulnerable to poor health. We have seen that even when healthcare delivery is available, it does not always meet the diverse and unique needs of the Indigenous populations in Canada.

The All Nations Healing Hospital is an example of healthcare delivery that addresses the unique needs of the Prairie Indigenous populations. It is owned and operated by 16 First Nations governments and located near Regina, Saskatchewan. Besides acute and emergency care, the All Nations' Healing Hospital offers programs in diabetes management and prevention, nutrition, addictions counselling, and residential school survivors counselling. The hospital addresses the cultural needs of its clientele with traditional ceremonies and the involvement of Elders. In fact, it tries to include traditional components in all of its programs and activities.

The All Nations Healing Hospital also has programs designed especially for Indigenous women. The Women's Health Centre offers discreet and respectful health services to women while supporting their right to make well-informed decisions about their own bodies. The centre provides pre- and postnatal care, counselling services, and outreach programs to Indigenous communities. Most importantly, the centre offers care in a way that addresses the cultural, emotional, and physical needs that are unique to First

Nations' women. The centre runs alongside the All Nations Healing Hospital's Cultural Program, which

> promotes sharing and understanding of First Nation culture and its philosophics. It assists First Nations people in continuing the traditions of oral teachings and ensures the opportunity to integrate First Nations philosophies, beliefs and healing ways into a clinical setting. (Fort Qu'Appelle All Nations Hospital)

The cultural program organizes traditional ceremonies at the All Nations Healing Hospital and confers with First Nations Elders to ensure that traditional healing techniques are being administered properly.

Individual-Level Strategies of Resistance

All over Canada, there are individuals engaged in efforts to equalize access to good health and healthcare. Access to good healthcare is a fundamental right and should not be out of reach for any Canadian. It is crucial that we continue to work with and support initiatives that make healthcare more equitable. As we have seen, there is often significant overlap between the groups that have the least access to good healthcare (such as Indigenous Peoples and low-income Canadians). As a result, any strategy to address these flaws must adopt a holistic approach that considers the interlocking disadvantages.

Closing Remarks

As we have seen, some people have more or less chance to stay in good health. The chances that a person will be sick during their life depend in large part on social factors and not necessarily on character or choice.

As we've seen from the COVID-19 epidemic, other factors also affect the likelihood of illness or health. Consider how Canada fared during the epidemic, compared to our neighbour, the United States. Nothing illustrated better than COVID-19 the importance of public health leadership and universal healthcare. Canada had plenty of both, while the United States had too little of either.

Health is especially attractive to social scientists as a measure of social functioning—that is, whether society is working well or not. The overall health or sickness of a population is a sensitive measure of how well the government, the economy, the family, and other social institutions are fulfilling their expected roles. Health is a more responsive and secure signal than the currently popular measures of happiness or life satisfaction. Researchers have found that people's self-reports of their health are usually accurate.

However, under conditions of continued distress, both minds and bodies show signs of stress, decline, and decreased functioning. These signs include mental illnesses like anxiety and depression. They also include physical illnesses like chronic pain, psychosomatic disorders, and reduced cardiovascular functioning, among others. As a result, physical and mental illnesses are signs of social malfunctioning, whereas good health and the absence of disease is an indicator of happiness and life satisfaction, as mentioned above.

Researchers around the world continue to find that inequality makes a difference. Swedish research by Ulf Gerdtham and Magnus Johannesson used a random sample from the adult Swedish population of more than 40,000 individuals who were followed up for 10–17 years. The researchers found "that mortality decreases significantly as individual income increases" (228)

The dominant viewpoint among population health researchers is that social inequality causes poor health: Indeed, it is among the most potent social factors affecting health. So, in ending this chapter, it seems there is a stacked deck in Canadian society. People at the bottom have a much lower chance of achieving good health than people at the top. And as we have seen, there are many ways to get to the bottom.

◆◆ Notable Thinkers ◆◆

Richard Carpiano

Dr Richard Carpiano is a professor of sociology at the University of British Columbia whose research examines the impact of socio-economic conditions on health as well as its implications on health inequalities.

In one study, Carpiano and Polonijo (2013) examined two fundamental causes of health disparities, socio-economic and racial/ethnic minority status, on adolescent vaccine uptake. Low socio-economic and racial/ethnic minority parents were less likely to have knowledge of vaccination and less likely to get recommendations from health professionals. This resulted in a lower frequency of human papillomavirus vaccination, producing disparities in cervical cancer rates among adult populations in the future. In another study, he investigated the correlation between immigrant status and suicide (Pan and Carpiano 2013). He found that immigrants living among more racial minority immigrants had lower rates of suicide, which may be due to lower odds of depression and more community belonging. This was especially striking in rural communities, which had higher suicide rates because of less access to mental health services compared to urban regions and increased experiences of racism.

Further, Carpiano also examines the impact of social capital on health and health inequalities. He divides social capital into four forms: (1) social support, (2) social leverages (sharing information), (3) informal social control (safety procedures and norms), and (4) neighbourhood organization participation. In his study of neighbourhood social capital and adult health (Carpiano 2004), higher levels of social leverage and informal control were associated with lower odds of daily smoking and binge drinking. Social support was linked to higher likelihoods of both smoking and binge drinking.

Similarly, in another study, individual neighbourhood attachment was significantly associated with increased dental care use while social support was associated with lower dental care use (Chi and Carpiano 2013). Social support is often assumed to be positive and health promoting, but social interaction can also be hostile and unsupportive.

Test Your Knowledge

1. What is the social gradient in health?
2. What are three gender- or sex-based issues in healthcare research?
3. What problems that women face (more often than men) may affect their health?
4. Why are men less likely than women to visit the doctor?
5. Why is homecare for seniors often preferred over relocation to a seniors' home?
6. Can you identify at least three reasons that immigrants to Canada experience a decline in health?
7. Which two types of refugee claimants are eligible for public safety healthcare coverage? What does that coverage include?
8. How might a heternormative or gender-normative bias impact the healthcare received by the LGBTQ+ community?
9. List the key points of each population group as highlighted in the chapter:

Population Group within Canada	Main Issues in Health and Barriers in Getting Healthcare
Immigrants	
Refugees and undocumented or non-status immigrants	
Low-income Canadians	
Canadian seniors	
Men	
Indigenous Peoples	
LGBTQ+ people	
Women	

See the Answer Key online to check your answers.

Questions for Critical Thought

1. Should the efforts undertaken to equalize access to good health and healthcare address specific groups within the population or the entire Canadian population? Explain why.
2. Explain the quote "Medicine is a social science and politics is nothing but medicine on a large scale." Do you agree or disagree? Why?
3. Education attainment and wealth have been noted to have a positive impact on health. Explain why. Are there instances where education and income negatively impact health?
4. Should Canada provide healthcare to refugees and undocumented or non-status immigrants? Explain why or why not.
5. How does homelessness affect health? What potential solutions can solve health problems afflicting homeless people?

Additional Resources

Recommended Readings

Fisher, Sylvia K., Jeffery M. Poirier, and Gary M. Blau. 2012. *Improving Emotional and Behavioural Outcomes for LGBT Youth: A Guide for Professionals*. Baltimore, MD: Paul H. Brooks Publishing. This book offers recommended practices, interventions, and policies for professionals, policy-makers, program developers, and school psychologists for dealing with LGBTQ+ youth, with the aim of lessening their likelihood of developing mental illnesses.

Fitzpatrick, Kevin. 2013. *Poverty and Health: A Crisis among America's Most Vulnerable*. Westport, CT: Praeger. This book examines the physical health conditions of low-income and no-income men, women, and children in the United States, paying particular attention to issues of health-care delivery, access, and disparities among the poor.

Kronefeld, Jennie J. 2013. *Social Determinants, Health Disparities and Linkages to Health and Health Care*. Bingley, UK: Emerald Group Publishing Limited. This book examines social determinants and social inequalities of health and healthcare while encompassing the perspectives of patients, caregivers, and providers of care.

Parkes, M.W. and B. Poland (lead authors). 2018. "Ecological Determinants of Health in Public Health Education in Canada: A Scan of Needs, Challenges and Assets." Ecological Determinants Group on Education, June (https://www.cpha.ca/sites/default/files/uploads/about/cmte/EDGE-scan-needs-challenges-assets-2018-final.pdf). This report intends to promote the incorporation of ecological determinants of health into public health training and education in the Canadian context.

Smylie, Janet, Michelle Firestone, Michelle Spiller, and Tungasuvvingat Inuit. 2018. "Our Health Counts: Population-Based Measures of Urban Inuit Health Determinants, Health Status, and Health Care Access." *Canadian Journal of Public Health* 109:662–70. Unlike most surveys of Inuit health, this research studies urban Inuit in Ottawa. It finds a familiar pattern of poor living conditions, poor health, and poor healthcare.

World Health Organization Regional Office for Europe. 2012. "Social Determinants of Health and Well-being among Young People: Health Behaviour in School-Aged Children: International Report from the 2009/2010 Survey" (http://www.euro.who.int/en/publications/abstracts/social-determinants-of-health-and-well-being-among-young-people.-health-behaviour-in-school-aged-children-hbsc-study). This report studies the impact of social and demographic factors on the health of young people in 43 counties across Europe and North America.

Recommended Websites

Canada Without Poverty

https://cwp-csp.ca

Canada Without Poverty is a federally incorporated, not-for-profit charitable organization with the goal of combating and erasing poverty in Canada by producing new knowledge and influencing public policy. This website contains information and links to publications on the health effects correlated with living in poverty.

Canadian Mental Health Association (CMHA): Ontario: "Lesbian, Gay, Bisexual, Trans and Queer Identified People and Mental Health"

https://ontario.cmha.ca/documents/lesbian-gay-bisexual-trans-queer-identified-people-and-mental-health

CMHA is an initiative that aims to promote equal access to mental health services and reduce mental health inequalities. This site includes information on the health of the LGBTQ+ community, methods to promote the mental health of LGBTQ+ individuals, and information for health providers to better service LGBTQ+ individuals.

Centers for Disease Control and Prevention (CDC)

www.cdc.gov

The CDC is dedicated to promoting health and improving quality of life by preventing and controlling disease, injury, and disability. They have various publications that address social determinants on health, including the white paper, which addresses health disparities and aims to increase health equity.

National Collaborating Centre for Indigenous Health (NCCAH)

www.nccih.ca/28/Social_Determinants.nccah

The NCCAH was established by the Government of Canada with the aim of making the public health-care system more responsive to the First Nations, Inuit, and Métis peoples while addressing issues facing Indigenous health. This organization strongly focuses on social determinants of health, such as poverty, standard housing, and barriers to education caused by changes in culture, languages, land rights, and self-determination within the Indigenous community due to colonization.

Public Health Agency of Canada

https://www.canada.ca/en/public-health/services/health-promotion/population-health/what-determines-health.html

The Public Health Agency of Canada's website includes a page on social determinants of health. This website includes 12 key determinants, including income/social status, social support networks, education, employment, social environments, physical environments, and gender and its impact on health.

Truth and Reconciliation Commission: Calls to Action

https://nctr.ca/assets/reports/Calls_to_Action_English2.pdf

The commission made numerous calls for action in respect to health. This includes calls for recognition of government responsibility, establishment of measurable health goals, recognition of the need to respect the distinct health needs of the Indigenous Peoples, provision of sustainable funding for Indigenous healing centres, and recognition of the value of Indigenous healing practices.

World Health Organization (WHO)

www.who.int/social_determinants/en

The WHO is an organization within the United Nations responsible for providing leadership on global health matters, influencing health research, setting standards, sharing policy alternatives, and overseeing and assessing health trends. The WHO also publishes information on social determinants of health.

Recommended Films

Forever Young. 2017. Produced by the CBC. Canada (https://www.cbc.ca/firsthand/episodes/forever-young). This film challenges viewers to rethink how we view life, aging, and death. It visits Okinawa, Japan, and the island of Sardinia, examples of the world's "Blue Zones," which are geographic regions with extremely long life expectancies that are leaving demographers stumped.

One Nation Under Stress. 2019. Produced by HBO. United States. In this film, Dr Sanjay Gupta explores the link between stress and life expectancy in the United States. Life expectancy in the States continues to decrease and it is now shorter than all other major developed nations.

Unnatural Causes: Is Inequality Making Us Sick? 2007. Produced by California Newsreel. United States: Vital Pictures Inc. This four-hour PBS documentary examines the social determinants of health, especially race, in creating health inequalities and health disparities. It examines how inequalities in housing, wealth, jobs, and education can translate into bad health.

Reimar/Shutterstock

9 Access to Legal Representation and Social Services

Learning Objectives

- To compare different theoretical perspectives addressing social services and legal representation.
- To recognize the importance of equal access to social services and legal representation.
- To identify changing trends in the demand for social services and legal representation.
- To name barriers to equal access to social services and legal representation.
- To evaluate efforts to equalize access to social services and legal representation in Canada.

Introduction

Everybody needs help sometimes. That's why all three levels of government (federal, provincial, and municipal) dedicate tax revenue to **social services**. These are programs and interventions that aim to help people, such as income support or job training.

social services
Programs and interventions that seek to promote the general welfare of others.

Drawing Connections

Many of the types of survival capital we have explored in this book are also considered social services. For example, in Chapter 4 we explored childcare, which can be an important social service for many parents. Likewise, in Chapter 8 we explored how seniors face more complex health issues and often have unique healthcare needs. Barriers they face in accessing healthcare, then, also likely stand in their way of accessing other health-related social services. As you read this chapter, draw connections between what you already know about different populations, the barriers they face to survival capital, and what this means for their access to social services—especially for people who fall into more than one category and even experience the world differently within each category (for example, low-income, gender, racialized).

Not-for-profit organizations and non-governmental organizations (often with partial or complete government funding) like the YMCA or United Way also provide social services to Canadians. These services include supported housing, emergency food provision, and vital recreational and social opportunities.

Some social services are provided at no cost to the "consumer" (the word often used for the person in need). These include homeless shelters, in-school breakfast programs, parenting drop-in centres, or settlement programs for newcomers to Canada. Other programs are subsidized by the government to lessen the cost to consumers. For example, subsidies can reduce the cost of swimming lessons, childcare, rent for community housing, or home renovations needed to meet the needs of seniors or people with disabilities. Social services like these are theoretically available to everybody who shows a need.

Social services can be critical in emergencies. They pull people away from crisis and toward physical, emotional, and financial safety. They also help good communities become great communities. Libraries, recreation centres, and schools all play an important role in creating social cohesion and inclusion. They help make neighbourhoods safer, healthier, more productive, and more engaging places to live.

If you scan the news headlines, you've surely noticed that as government funding for some social services increases in one area ("Government Announces New Job Training Grant"), it is periodically slashed in others ("Homeless Shelter Closing"). This is because while many social programs are free or low cost to the consumer, they can be expensive to run. Often the programs that endure are either less costly or considered more useful than others.

Deciding whether a program runs or is cut often comes down to varying ideologies about how our country should be. For example, political disagreements surrounding the relative importance of housing the homeless versus providing emergency food relief for families can determine which program is funded (and which isn't). Figure 9.1 gives you an idea of how one Canadian province, Ontario, assigns funding for social programs.

We will also be discussing legal representation in this chapter. Legal representation is an important kind of survival capital for Canadians. In Canada, the right to legal counsel

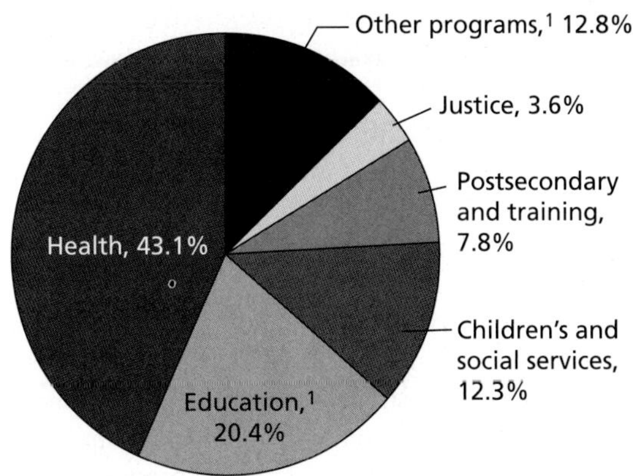

Figure 9.1 ◆ Program Expenses, Ontario

[1]Teachers' pension plan is included in other programs

Source: Government of Ontario 2018. © Queen's Printer for Ontario, 2018. Reproduced with permission.

is constitutionally protected by section 10 of the Charter of Rights and Freedoms. This means that every Canadian is entitled to legal help when they need it. However, many people struggle to secure satisfactory and suitable legal representation, typically due to cost. These people must often represent themselves or go without legal representation at all, often with negative results. That's why we'll also be focusing on legal representation and **legal aid** in this chapter.

legal aid Legal representation for those who cannot afford it.

Many people in Canada desperately need social services and legal representation, but not everyone has equal access to them. In this chapter, we will look at which populations in Canada face barriers to important social services and legal representation. We will explore why this unequal access hurts everyone, not just those directly involved. Finally, we will examine what some sociologists have to say about this problem and what governments and organizations can do to promote equal access to social services and legal representation.

Theoretical Perspectives on Access to Legal Representation and Social Services

Like access to daycare and higher education, access to legal representation is one of those things that tends to be ignored or minimized in a liberal welfare regime like Canada's. Provinces have the responsibility to supply legal aid to low-income people, and they vary somewhat in the services they pay for. But generally, Canadians who want access to the law—whether for a will, a deed, a contract, a divorce, or to defend themselves against criminal charges—have to pay for it out of their own pockets. And as with many other services in a market economy, you get what you are able to pay for.

Understanding inequality and access to legal representation and social services requires a larger discussion of law and legislation. What do law and legislation do for us, and why do they sometimes fail? Sociologists who study law have proposed many answers.

Through much of the nineteenth and early twentieth centuries, legal scholars viewed the legal system—indeed, government as a whole—as a system of written rules, rational decisions, and disinterested agents. However, in the 1930s, during the Great Depression, and again in the 1960s, during civil rights protests throughout the West, scholars became interested in how social inequality shaped and distorted the actual workings of the law and government.

Here is the problem they encountered: Law is based on rationality and reasonable behaviour. Lawyers and judges spend their time applying precedent and striving for logical consistency in their decisions. However, sociology is quite the opposite: It is the often study of non-rational behaviour. Sociologists frequently observe that people and institutions act non-rationally, even while justifying themselves on rational grounds.

More specifically, a piece of legislation may aim to accomplish one outcome, but for a variety of reasons sociologists discover it actually accomplishes a different one. Sociologists are interested in unanticipated consequences and how they often arise out of good, rational motives. So while the job of jurisprudence may be to devise and promote apparently consistent, rational decision making, the job of sociologists who study law is to find out whether these undertakings have the desired outcome. Often, they do not.

To some degree, this problem can be avoided by making sociological research, observation, and theory the basis of legal decision making. However, as Philip Selznick (1959) points out, this brings inevitable conflicts around what has been called "legal realism." Namely, sociologists would like to base laws (and social programs) on actual human behaviour. Indeed, humans desire and often adhere to norms of good behaviour that are present in reasoned systems of law. But humans also regularly break the rules and act against their own best interests. The law—and the sociology of law—must see how these opposing tendencies—rule abiding and rule breaking—play out and spur change in our legal system.

By the 1960s, as civil conflict began to ramp up throughout Western democracies, views of the sociology of law also began to change: They became less theoretical and more focused on practical problem solving. At this time, Jerome Skolnick (1963) argued that the sociology of law began to concern itself with addressing three social contradictions. First, the United States and Canada are self-declared egalitarian societies but in actuality are highly socially stratified (as John Porter famously pointed out in his classic sociological work *The Vertical Mosaic* [1965] 2015). Skolnick notes that the sociology of law investigates the impact of this stratification on the justice system. Second, many North Americans believe in individualism—that their individual vote allows them to participate directly in government and they have personal autonomy over their lives and societies. But as a whole, the United States (even more than Canada) prioritizes the national over the local and uses communication and social control systems that are increasingly depersonalized. In response, the sociology of law explores how individuals can obtain justice in a mass industrial society. Third, many North Americans view themselves as individual capitalists. This sentiment is particularly marked in suburbs, small towns, and rural regions, where even recently we have seen the strongest support for conservative and nativist political programs. But most economic power in North America—indeed, in the Global North—lies with large organizations, such as big businesses and the government. This means a few people at the top control the life chances of the masses at the bottom. In response, Skolnick notes that the sociology of law examines how laws have held up in private and public organizations. He concludes that these contradictions apply and need to be studied in a variety of regions, not only North America.

No one agrees more with Skolnick's assessment than Donald Black (1972, 1979), whose work concerned the connection between the law and social control, including the stratification system. On this matter, Black writes that we can learn a lot about the legal system as a whole by watching police behaviour. That is, the individual decisions and actions of a police person—an official who has been tasked with upholding the law—generally reflect larger patterns in our overall legal system. Conversely, we can predict and explain how police are likely to behave based on our understanding of those larger patterns in the system.

For this reason, Black urges scholars to adopt a zigzag (or what Robert Merton called "middle range"; Merton and Merton 1968) approach to studying the connection between law and society. He urges us to move between low-level empirical observations (such as observations of police behaviour) and higher-level theoretical formulations about the legal system as a whole. This approach is significantly different from the European "sociology of law" scholarship of the nineteenth century.

Just as Black claims that we develop the sociology of law by watching what police officers do, Max Weber asserted that we develop the sociology of law by watching what social institutions with authority do regarding social control. Whereas Karl Marx focused on the battle between two contending classes in capitalist societies, Weber proposed that the people in a given society have a multitude of interests, not just class-based ones (Albrow 1975). Lawyers are just one group of individuals who have some shared interests (financial, intellectual) and unique, shared sources of power. Namely, they have special skills—the ability to reason, argue convincingly, and apply technical legal knowledge—that make them indispensable.

From a sociological standpoint, law depends on a historical, comparative, and systematic study of authority systems as they are created, interpreted, and enforced by people with specific legal responsibilities. They include the police, lawyers, judges, and rulers. All of this occurs within the larger context of a class system at a particular time and place.

Now let's extend this to take in social services. Publicly funded social services are based on formal legislation and administered by a professional bureaucracy. As Max Weber pointed out, the essence of bureaucracy is decision making based on written rules. The decision makers themselves—their personalities, values, and interests—are irrelevant; they are authorized only to apply written rules in a fair and systematic way. But as many sociologists since Weber have pointed out, bureaucracies do not always work the way they are expected to, precisely because of contending personalities, values, and interests within the bureaucratic organization. As well, the values and goals of elected politicians often distort the functioning of bureaucracies that deliver legal and social services.

Now let's jump ahead to the present. Today, functionalists still see legal and social services as tools that help society run more efficiently. From this standpoint, a society would be unable to function without a wide variety of social services, social safety nets, and access to legal aid. Functionalists see the development of modern-day social services as a response to popular demands and protests that challenged the existing social order, especially around the time of the Great Depression.

As mentioned earlier, all of Canada's social services, then, were developed to appease the masses and ensure the survival of the dominant capitalist order, yet they were not funded as generously as they were in social democratic regimes (as in the Nordic countries). Consider unemployment insurance—social assistance to people who are in the workforce but temporarily without a job—which reduces the likelihood that these people will become radicalized and demand significant changes to the government or economy. It reduces the likelihood of revolution, rebellion, or even political mobilization.

In short, functionalists—following Weber—see legal and social services as the result of an evolutionary process in which Canadian society willingly moved toward a more egalitarian society, using social welfare to redistribute wealth. Conflict theorists, on the other hand—following Marx—highlight the role of active, sometimes even violent, protest that brought about these dramatic changes. They focus on class differences more than on authority differences.

Conflict theorists note that the economic conditions of capitalism result in pervasive inequalities. From this perspective, legal and social services are superficial solutions to social problems—such as poverty, racism, and sexism—that need deeper, longer-term solutions. From this standpoint, people like lawyers, social workers, teachers, police officers, and nurses deal with problems that could have been minimized, if not prevented, if society had been organized better. With conflict theory, the problem keeps coming back to the political and economic organization of society—especially the class structure.

The symbolic interactionist approach, for its part, pays attention to the social construction of claims and narratives around social inequality. With respect to legal and social services, symbolic interactionists are interested in the ways the media, politicians, and other prominent figures present the legitimacy of claims to legal and social assistance. Since voters and legislators will only support legal and social services they think are necessary and justifiable, symbolic interactionists are interested in how people make and defend claims about the need for certain costly social services. They are also interested in how claims and arguments that resist such spending are constructed.

Another interest of symbolic interactionists is the way people interpret and use legal and social services. For example, many disadvantaged people are reluctant to use legal and social services they have a right to, which obviously influences those services' impact. The reasons for this are varied. Indigenous Peoples, for example, may think that non-Indigenous agencies do not have the cultural sensitivity required to attend to their needs and may resist seeking social services as a result. We will explore this in further detail later.

Changing Trends in the Demand for Legal and Social Services

The demand for legal and social services in Canada has intensified over the past few decades. To take a non-legal example, food bank use was 31 per cent higher in 2012 than in 2008 (Food Banks Canada 2012) and has remained high since then (Food Banks Canada 2018). The Government of Canada reports the increase in social service use is the result of many factors. They include "unstable family structure, family violence, child poverty, aging of the population, stress, alcoholism, drug addiction, gambling addiction, dropping out of school, behavioural problems, traumatic events, etc." (Service Canada 2013).

Another proposed reason for this trend is the increasing number of single-parent households. In 2016, there were 1,114,055 lone-parent families in Canada. From 2001 to 2016, the percentage of children aged 0 to 14 living in a single-parent household increased

IN FOCUS ◆ Single Mother Support Services

Being a single parent is hard. That's why the YWCA of Metro Vancouver (2020) offers Single Mothers' Support Services to "assist, empower and inform single moms." Part of this program involves a family resource worker meeting with single mothers at no cost to provide resources and referrals related to housing, legal aid, employment, and education.

from 17.8 per cent to 19.2 per cent (Statistics Canada 2017). In Canada, single-parent households made up 19.1 per cent of all food bank users (Food Banks Canada 2018).

Single parents who are not receiving enough child support payments must often survive on only one income. Social services play a role for these families, helping provide children with vital resources. Research shows that child poverty increases children's vulnerability to health issues, developmental delays, and behavioural disorders, as well as increases their likelihood of becoming low-income adults (Kornberger, Fast, and Williamson 2001; Finnie and Bernard 2004). Social services that fill in the gaps with recreational, educational, and nutritional help can be invaluable for these families, and the sooner they access them the better off children are and will be as adults.

Another reason that social service use is increasing is the rapid growth of the Canadian seniors population. In 2015, for the first time ever, there were more Canadians aged 65 and older than children aged 0 to 14 years; 16.1 per cent of the population was aged 65 or older. This number is expected to rise, with 20.1 per cent of the population predicted to be aged 65 or older by 2024 (Statistics Canada 2015). As this population increases, so too does the demand for specific social services. A report by the Conference Board of Canada (2015) states that if the current levels of senior care persist, costs will rise from $28.3 billion in 2011 to $62.3 billion in 2026. From competent homecare to help with errands and exercise, seniors benefit from a variety of social services. Indeed, social or recreational programs that help seniors stay connected to their communities have proven benefits for mental and emotional health.

Social services are also needed to address problems that were once kept private. The impact of stress and anxiety, addiction, mental health, and behavioural challenges on people's lives is now more publicly recognized than ever. This has led to a rise in social services that address these problems. Social services play two roles here. First, they help give voice to people struggling with these issues, normalizing them and building communities of support. Second, they help treat these problems by offering aid and helping the vulnerable to help themselves. Increased awareness of these issues has resulted in a greater need for social services in schools and workplaces. Early intervention has the potential to solve people's problems before they intensify.

Legal representation is also critically important for Canadians today, but the availability of legal services in Canada is not keeping pace with increasing demand. For example, Zemans and Amaral (2018) notes that declines in the real dollar value of funding for legal aid services has meant reduced access to lawyers for people who need them most. In many provinces, measures of financial eligibility have been out of line with official measures of poverty since at least the mid-1990s. Zemans and Amaral note further that it is too soon to tell whether new service providers (for example, paralegal practitioners and students) and new technologies will return the needed service to prior levels or merely slow the rate of decline.

Ironically, both social services and affordable, suitable legal representation are sometimes easily available for people who don't need them. Yet they are often out of reach for the people who need them the most. These include low-income Canadians, youth, seniors, Indigenous Peoples, and people with disabilities or **chronic illnesses**. In the following pages, we will explore why.

chronic illness A long-lasting condition that can be managed but not cured.

Low-Income People in Canada

We begin, as we often do in this book, with a consideration of low-income Canadians. Many low-income Canadians cannot access legal representation and social services—some of which are, ironically, specifically intended for those with low incomes. In this section, we will see why this is and how these barriers can contribute to persisting low income.

One barrier is location. For social services to adequately meet the needs of a vulnerable population, they should be located near those who need them, ideally within walking distance. Studies show that often social services that might be most useful in a low-income neighbourhood just aren't there!

One of the biggest problems facing disadvantaged people in Canadian cities is distance from and easy access to the services they need. Often the real estate closest to subway routes and key business, entertainment, and educational sites is the choicest and most expensive real estate. To remedy this, some of Canada's cities have started improving social and legal services in the less-affluent neighbourhoods that are farther from downtown.

For example, the City of Vancouver (2020) advertises that it is "Building liveable, sustainable, and inclusive communities." Vancouver is sometimes viewed as inhospitable to low-income people, in large part because of the explosion of home prices that foreign buyers ignited in an effort to park their money in stable Western real estate and perhaps to also gain Canadian citizenship. In 2016, this trend led to a foreign buyer's tax, and the Vancouver real estate market has settled down somewhat since its introduction. Perhaps with this improvement in mind, the city has asserted its intent to "work with community groups and other agencies to address critical social issues that affect us all, and to make sure that the needs of all residents are met." The city mentions creating social programs to achieve this goal, including senior care, capacity building for Indigenous Peoples, youth programs, and childcare and child development strategies.

However, accomplishing such goals requires a huge amount of civic will and public support—which Brunet-Jailly (2008) points out is something Vancouver, with its "activist, tolerant and entrepreneurial civic culture," might be well suited to muster.

As we have seen, having a social service nearby promotes and enables use. But other factors besides the simple closeness of a building also influence accessibility. These factors might include service language, whether the site is designed to serve people with disabilities, fees, hours of service, and waiting lists. There is also a host of less tangible factors to consider, such as whether a user feels welcome and respected.

Monkey Business Images/Shutterstock

In this picture, Vancouver looks like the perfect city, and certainly a sustainable city wedged beautifully between the mountains and the ocean. Social planning is needed to make this perfect picture a reality.

What's the first thing you think about when you imagine yourself embroiled in a drawn-out legal battle? Probably the excessive cost! Did you know that it's not unusual for a lawyer to charge $500 to $1,000 for an early consultation and want a further $10,000 or more as a retainer to be paid upfront? See Figure 9.2 for some examples of legal services and associated fees for a law firm in Calgary. As you might expect, costs like these are a burden for many Canadians. Other barriers include a lack of knowledge of the legal system, which is notoriously dense and difficult to navigate for anyone without a formal education in law.

The high cost of legal representation is precisely why each province and territory in Canada provides some form of legal aid. However, the Canadian Bar Association (2015) reports the demand for legal aid far exceeds the supply. Additionally, the association points to discrepancies in coverage among jurisdictions and fragmented coverage within a legal aid program (see Figure 9.3). Worst of all, it produces a disproportionate impact of legal aid on different populations like women and Indigenous Peoples, who are overrepresented among the poor. As funding for these programs is increasingly limited, the eligibility requirements become more and more narrow. For example, in some jurisdictions only the poorest or unemployed qualify for legal aid, effectively leaving out the one in five Canadians who make up the working poor. Or, sometimes, only one part of a client's legal

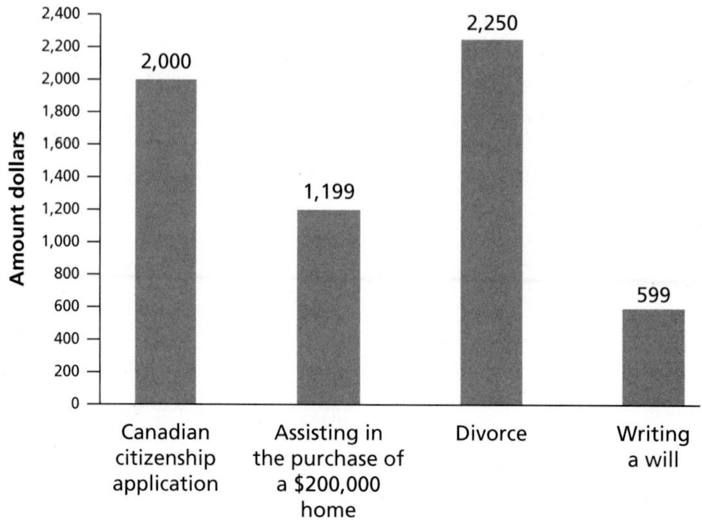

Figure 9.2 ◆ Legal Fees, Calgary, 2019

Source: Kahane Law 2019.

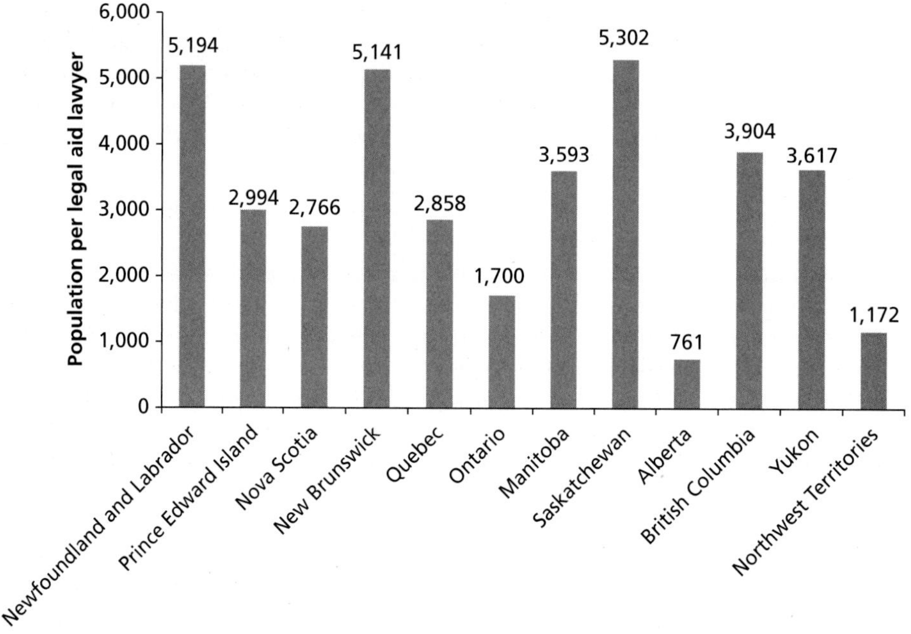

Figure 9.3 ◆ People per Legal Aid Lawyers in Each Province or Territory,* 2017–18

*Nunavut data unavailable

This figure shows the ratio of the total number of people in each province or territory to the number of legal aid lawyers and private lawyers providing legal aid services. What is quite evident in this chart is the wide variation between jurisdictions.

Source: Statistics Canada 2018a, 2018c.

service is funded, resulting in incomplete or unresolved cases. Many also point out the lawyers in this sphere of law are typically overworked, underpaid, and underresourced.

So while low-income Canadians are less likely to secure quality legal representation—mostly because of cost—studies show they are more likely to need it. This is not because people from poor neighbourhoods are more likely to commit crime; rather, poverty can amplify problems (such as unemployment, stress, conflict, substance abuse, and domestic violence) that can lead to crime.

The Criminal Justice System

In any discussion of legal aid, we also need to consider the criminal justice system. Because of the unequal structuring of our society, the people most likely to be caught up in the criminal justice system, either as offenders or victims, are also most likely to need legal aid.

Many advantaged Canadians never experience the criminal justice system, so they may think that harsh sentencing effectively punishes and deters crime. However, the reality is that imprisonment is costly and ineffective. It can cost roughly $100,000 to imprison one adult for a single year (Office of the Parliamentary Budget Officer 2018). The salaries of prison guards and administrative costs account for most spending, with food and shelter making up a small fraction of the budget.

Besides being expensive, imprisonment is not particularly effective for deterring crime. The damaging experiences prisoners endure leave them less able to deal with life on the outside after they are released. **Prisonization**, as Donald Clemmer (1950) explains, produces prisoners who have been effectively socialized into prison life. After becoming people who fit perfectly into the inmate society, they cannot live effectively outside it. As their release dates approach, inmates often feel great stress. Once released, many commit new crimes—sometimes even more violent crimes—and return to prison in a process known as recidivism. The extent of recidivism is difficult to measure, but studies consistently find large numbers of offenders returning to the criminal justice system—some over and over.

prisonization The process by which a person becomes socialized into prison life.

Recidivism may also be a product of the reduced life chances of inmates after release. The stigma of a criminal conviction, decreased human capital because of absence from the workforce, and weakened social connections all limit the job opportunities open to former prisoners. Jobs needing high levels of trust, skills, or credentials are largely out of reach. Former inmates are channelled into the secondary labour market where employment is precarious and there are few prospects for mobility. In this way, the penal system reinforces social disadvantage.

Low-income people are more likely to need legal representation because they are more likely to get caught. Twenty years ago, the National Council of Welfare (2000) reported that "for the same criminal behaviour, the poor are more likely to be arrested; if arrested, they are more likely to be charged; if charged, more likely to be convicted; if convicted, more likely to be sentenced to prison; and if sentenced, more likely to be given longer prison terms than members of the middle and upper classes." This is still the case today.

One reason for this is because illegal acts committed by low-income people are more likely to come to the attention of law enforcement personnel. To begin with, low-income people and their families have fewer resources to draw on to avoid arrest and imprisonment. For instance, wealthy parents might be able to pay for costs incurred by their child damaging property, thereby avoiding any charges. Or there might be greater police presence in lower-income or rapidly gentrifying neighbourhoods, which increases the likelihood of arrests (and decreases the likelihood of arrests in richer, unsupervised neighbourhoods).

Low-income people are also more likely to be the targets of random "stop and check" operations, often called *carding*. Often this is related to what we will discuss in Chapter 10 as racial profiling. For example, Brownfield, Sorenson, and Thompson (2001), using data from the Seattle Youth Study, find the odds of being arrested are similar for gang and non-gang members, controlling for the nature and level of self-reported delinquency. However, being Black or lower income increases a youth's odds of being arrested, independent of delinquency or the frequency with which youth hang out with their best friends.

Thus, both wealthy-looking and poor-looking people may take part in illegal activities. However, the latter are more likely to catch the attention of law personnel and thus need legal representation.

Compared to middle-income and wealthy citizens, low-income people are more likely to be detained when arrested, charged by the police, denied bail, and be convicted of their charges. Once released from prison, low-income Canadians face more difficulties accessing safe housing, employment, and social supports. This increases their chances of recidivism and, therefore, their need for quality legal representation (John Howard Society 2014). As you might expect, being without legal representation can worsen social exclusion. People with criminal records struggle to find employment, which contributes to a lifetime of poverty. On the other hand, prompt and affordable legal support "can play a role in helping people move out of some of the worst experiences of social exclusion" (Canadian Bar Association Access to Justice Committee 2013). Many people become trapped in an endless cycle of unemployment, desperation, and repeated criminal behaviour. Far more than legal aid is needed to prevent this: Family and community supports and jobs are needed too. However, legal help can play an important role in minimizing the effects of the police-and-court juggernaut.

Racialized People in Canada

Racialized populations often note that government, police, and public service providers treat them unfairly. Indeed, there is clear evidence there is differential treatment of and prejudice against racialized people when compared to white people of the same socio-economic class. Much of the evidence of this comes from the United States, which has a long and bitter history of race relations. However, research has found similar discrimination in the treatment of Black Canadians by police, courts, and other official organizations. In a report for Correctional Service Canada, esteemed researcher Dr Emerson Douyon (2016) wrote:

> Indigenous and Black people are indeed overrepresented in the criminal justice system in Canada. This is emphasized *ad nauseam* in reports, as if to suggest a hypothetical genetic predisposition in these two minority groups . . . The stark truth of the statistics creates a recurring malaise, but what do those figures conceal? What is needed here is context.

To put the matter simply, we need to consider the role of socio-economic conditions, but we also need to consider the role of cultural circumstances, social circumstances, and family circumstances. Context challenges the myth that certain individuals are "predisposed" toward criminality. What's more, all of these contextual and individual factors are shaped by history. The criminal justice system is as much a product of past and present conditions as the individual lawbreaker is.

For a variety of current and historical, economic, cultural, social, and familial factors, young Black people are both more likely to attract police attention than white people and to receive harsher sentences if convicted (Wortley and Tanner 2005). The proportion of Black people in federal prisons, which is 9 per cent overall, is three times that in the Canadian population overall (roughly 3.5 per cent). In Ontario's Joyceville Institution, Black prisoners make up more than a third of the total prison population (Office of the Correctional Investigator 2013). Once released from prison, many former convicts struggle to secure a job, as most employers conduct criminal record checks on potential hires and refuse to employ former convicts. Researchers have found that this hiring bias impacts Black job applicants more than other racialized groups (Hall et al. 2017; Uggan 2000). This perpetuates a cycle of unemployment and imprisonment, which fuels further distrust of police and the criminal justice system.

Discrimination (or the fear of discrimination) may deter racialized populations from accessing social services. For example, Enang (2001) found that Black women who feared receiving poor treatment based on their race, class, and gender were reluctant to access healthcare services. Similarly, in a study of Asian immigrants, Li and Browne (2000) found that immigrants who have previously experienced racial discrimination are often hesitant to access mental health services. Likewise, in a study of Indigenous Peoples in Canada, racism was noted as a major barrier that impeded their use of mental health services. Accessing help was often delayed for long periods of time due to previous experiences with racial profiling, racist assumptions, and stereotyping (Kafele 2004).

When it comes to legal aid, racialized people face barriers that are often the result of multiple intersecting identities. An example of this is the remand process. After arrest, people may be remanded into custody while awaiting trial or may be allowed in the community on bail. Racialized people are far more likely than white people to be held in remand.

Young People in Canada

Canadian youth are socio-economically diverse. So social services targeting this particular population group are also diverse. Just a few examples of youth-oriented social services might be job training, breakfast programs, recreational programs, or counselling services. Have you or someone you know ever made use of these social services?

Many key social services target youth homelessness. An estimated 20 per cent of homeless Canadians are young people. This means that up to 40,000 young people are homeless or living in shelters at some point every year (Gaetz et al. 2106). If you're having difficulty imagining how many people this is, picture the Montreal Canadiens' home ice, the Bell Centre, completely filled . . . twice!

Recall the various pathways to homelessness we explored in Chapter 6. A complicating factor for homeless youth is that they need official ID to access many social services like healthcare, shelters, and food banks. If a young person has their ID stolen, a risk that comes with living on the street, they may be unable to access some of these services.

Shelters are an important social service for homeless youth. To address their unique needs, some shelters earmark beds especially for youth, but currently the need outweighs the availability. In Canada as a whole in 2018, there were limited numbers of beds available for youth: according to Statistics Canada (2018b), only 1,442 beds for emergency circumstances and 1,410 beds for transitional housing.

Studies show that in some cities, like New York, 40 per cent of homeless youth are part of the LGBTQ+ community (Hunter 2008). The number may even be higher, as young Canadians are often reluctant to identify as LGBTQ+ to interviewers or staff working at shelters (Abramovich 2014). Homeless LGBTQ+ youth face additional challenges when accessing a safe place to shelter. That's why there are a handful of shelters in Canada for this population specifically, including Sprott House in Toronto.

Shelters are often ill equipped and inexperienced in dealing with trans issues, such as hormones, transition-related surgery, and name changes. Trans youth are often hesitant to seek refuge in shelters because of the violence and discrimination they may face by staff or other residents (Abramovich 2014)—50 per cent of LGBTQ+ youth have reported incidents of physical aggression in shelters (Bar 2013). As a result, many LGBTQ+ youth feel safer remaining in parks on the street.

Indigenous youth living in Canada are also at an increased risk of becoming homeless and are overrepresented in the Canadian youth homeless population. For example, Indigenous youth only make up 2 per cent of Canada's entire population, but they represent 30 per cent of the street youth population (Gaetz et al. 2016).

One way to lessen the number of homeless youth is to ensure they can get and keep satisfactory, stable housing. According to Carson, Clement, Crane, and Karabanow (2010), employment is key to helping homeless youth transition from the streets to a stable home and develop a sense of self and form self-esteem. Unfortunately, homeless youth face great difficulties in getting and keeping employment. And don't forget other problems as well, such as the fact that children under a certain age legally have to stay in school. They cannot receive employee's compensation, and some provinces have a lower minimum wage for younger workers. Three-quarters of homeless youth are not employed (Gaetz et al. 2016).

Social services like drop-in employment centres and life skills workshops have proven to be effective in helping youth secure employment. Homeless youth in Toronto, for example, continue to reveal a shortage of employment services and support programs designed for this population. According to the Homeless Hub (Aleman 2016), homelessness makes it hard to get and keep formal employment. Though we often take it for granted, people need both an address to put on a résumé and a place to prepare for interviews. As well, to be effective workers, they need a place to sleep, eat, shower, relax, and so on. They need a place where they and their belongings are secure. As well, homeless people who find employment often have to settle for precarious, unsafe, or poorly paid work. In particular, homeless young people face problems of age discrimination and weak social and human capital.

Homeless people also have difficulty accessing employment enrichment programs, especially if language barriers are present. As well, the lack of employment centres able to help youth with substance abuse issues or mental health programs is also cited as a barrier to employment. In short, homelessness poses huge problems for people, especially for young people.

Women in Canada

Being a woman in Canada, especially when combined with other socially disadvantageous statuses, can also hinder efforts to access social services and legal representation.

The percentage of homeless women in Canada is significantly lower than homeless men, and their experiences differ in several ways. For example, women often face abuse precisely where they try to escape it. Shelters can be unsafe spaces for women. Gaetz and colleagues (2013) explain that "many women will go to lengths to avoid the shelter system, including staying in dangerous and unhealthy relationships and/or making arrangements to move in with a partner (even when that situation is unsafe) rather than submit to the incredible risk of violence and exploitation on the streets."

In a typical year, shelters offer refuge to about 100,000 women in Canada. However, the beds available for women in 2018 were quite limited. According to Statistics Canada (2018b), there were only 2,029 beds for women requiring emergency support, 1,492 beds for women requiring transitional housing, and 7,494 beds for women who had suffered and fled domestic violence.

Homeless shelters aren't the only social service that Canadian women sometimes struggle to access. Compared to their male counterparts, women in Canada face greater difficulties in accessing Canada's employment insurance (EI) program, the monthly income that supports a person who is out of work. To qualify for EI, a person must show that they have worked a certain number of hours in the year before being laid off. This exact number depends on the rate of unemployment in the region. For example, in a region with low unemployment—say, 6 per cent—a person would need to amass 700 hours of employment, about 13 hours per week.

Can you guess why it might be more difficult for women to qualify for EI? Think back to Chapter 3. There we saw that women are more likely to work in non-standard or precarious jobs, like part-time, temporary, casual, or contract work; "under the table"; in non-insured work; or self-employment. Employment insurance programs do not cover most self-employed people. Women are more likely to leave paid employment temporarily to care for dependants, abandoning the hours they might have otherwise collected. Many women return to work after an absence of two years—not unusual for a woman who has elected to stay home with her young children. Doing so, they must sometimes amass twice the number of hours as their colleagues to qualify for EI. And as you may recall, in Canada women who work for pay still do most of the childcare at home. This limits their ability to collect overtime hours, which might otherwise enable them to qualify for EI in a shorter number of weeks (Townson and Hayes 2007).

Here, as in many other parts of this book, we are reminded of the truth of feminism's central premise: Social experiences are gendered in ways that impact people's access to different forms of survival capital. One example of this has to do with legal representation.

Women and Legal Representation

Studies show that women and men often have different legal needs. Women's need for legal representation is more likely to be in family law and civil law, whereas men are more likely to need representation in criminal law. When legal aid budgets are tight, and certain areas of legal aid are cut or cancelled, women can suffer the effects more than men. For example,

◆ In Their Own Words ◆

Read these women's experiences representing themselves in court. They were collected by West Coast LEAF, a Legal Education and Action Fund.

> "After being denied legal aid in 2002, I represented myself twice in court. I did not know what I was doing and it felt like nobody listened to me. My ex-partner's lawyer was brutal towards me. No one in the courtroom recognized that I was representing myself or that English is not my first language. This new judge . . . disregarded the other judge's decision. She said that my children could go back to overnight visits. The judge said my ex-partner's actions were 'just different parenting.' I had practiced going to court and representing myself, but this did not matter because I cannot argue with a lawyer. I am not a lawyer. I am just a mother."

> "After I became self-represented I had to draft my own court documents such as the Notices of Motion and Notices of Hearing. I had to do my own research and present my own evidence in the court . . . Dealing with this case became like a part time job for me because it was taking up so much of my time . . . Because of the time I had to spend working on this case I lost a job working at a restaurant because I didn't have the time to do both the job and prepare for court appearances."

Source: Brewin and Stephens 2004.

in the early 2000s, legal aid for family law was slashed in British Columbia. Women were unduly affected by these changes.

People who seek legal aid must meet certain criteria. Sometimes legal aid is only available for a person who is fearful for the safety of herself or her children. This has negative ramifications for women who need legal aid but aren't ready to come forward with a disclosure of abuse. For women who do receive legal aid, their situation is not always much better. Reduced funding for legal aid means that fewer lawyers make clients on legal aid their priority or take on these cases at all. So women who receive legal aid have fewer choices when deciding on a lawyer to handle their case and have greater difficulty accessing them (Osachoff 2008).

Despite these negative results, access to legal representation can improve women's quality of life, especially those experiencing domestic violence. This is seen in the results of a 2008 workshop on legal aid for women seeking help from **Battered Women Support Services** (BWSS) in British Columbia. The results show that between 2007 and 2008, the few women at BWSS who were granted legal aid could achieve results like full or joint custody of their children, child and spousal support, and safe access to and for their children.

Battered Women Support Services
An organization in British Columbia that seeks to free girls and women from violence through educational and training programs.

In contrast, women unable to get legal aid representation had to share the care of their children with their violent ex-partners. Often they did not receive fair child- and spousal-support payments and were forced into having unsafe access to their children with their violent ex-partners. As well, such women usually have to do their own research and help themselves in addressing complex legal issues that should be dealt with by legal professionals. The effects of cuts to legal aid funding can disrupt women's lives (see Arendell 1987; Burnham 2001; Greatbatch 1989).

Seniors in Canada

As mentioned earlier, the elderly population is the fastest growing group in Canada by a wide margin. Social services that meet the unique needs of this population are important today and will be even more important tomorrow.

In addition to encountering financial trouble, many seniors are infirm, so they need help with tasks that require strength, dexterity, and good eyesight. Similarly, they may require in-home care as they age and encounter health challenges. Moreover, in the last quarter of their lives, people are likely to develop a disability. Many of the barriers faced by disabled people therefore also prevent seniors from fully accessing available social services. We will explore these barriers in further detail later in this chapter.

Immigrants in Canada

Of all population groups described in this chapter, newcomers to Canada are most broadly in need of social services. It's true that some immigrants hit the ground running. These are people that easily secure housing and employment and hold a recognized array of qualifications. Many speak one or both of Canada's official languages and have a settled social or cultural community. However, many more arrive in Canada in need of settlement services and legal support. These may range from job skills training, pre- and postnatal care, language instruction, counselling, housing support, seniors' services, and many more.

As with many other issues we consider in this book, we are forced to recall the adage that an ounce of prevention may be better than a pound of cure. Preventing problems is costly in the short run, but it is often cheaper (as well as more humane) in the long run. Here, the first step to using the available social services is to learn they exist.

Communication barriers add to this problem. Immigrants who do not speak English—or do not speak English well—may lack the communication skills necessary to learn about or engage with the available services in their community. For example, interpreters are not provided in British Columbia for the important meetings people need to have with their lawyers to establish the parameters of the legal work to be done, despite being offered for criminal and family matters in the Provincial Court and Supreme Court, and family matters in the Supreme Court. And even when interpreters are available, some question whether good-quality—and fair—legal services can be delivered via an interpreter. See Figure 9.4 for a snapshot of how many and what type of legal aid services were offered to immigrants in Ottawa between 2016 and 2017.

Sometimes a social service may exist, but its delivery doesn't work for some populations in need. One clear example occurs when food banks limit consumers to food that is religiously or culturally inappropriate, or food that a family is unaccustomed to preparing or eating.

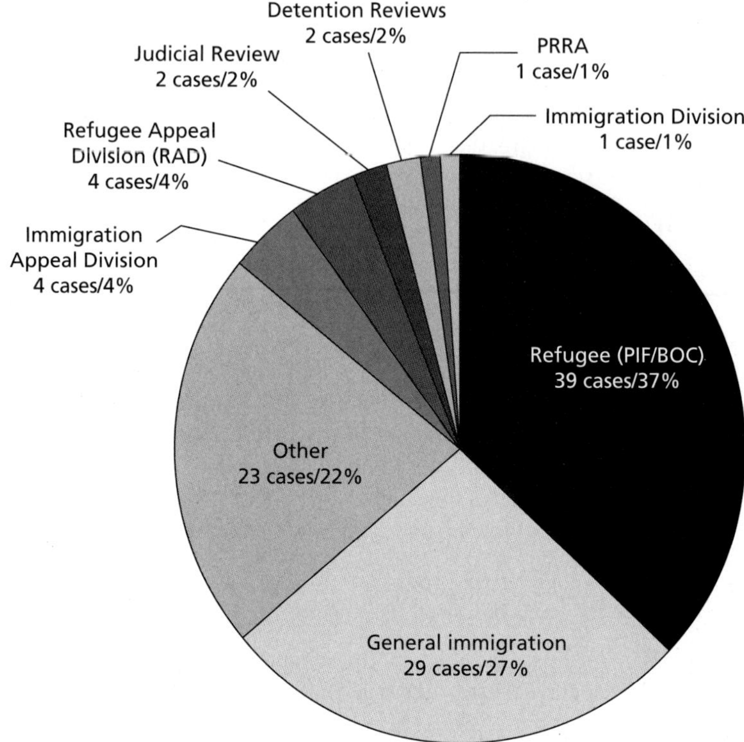

Figure 9.4 ◆ Legal Aid Services Offered to Immigrants

Note that refugee cases are the most common legal aid service offered to immigrants. Why do you think refugees are most likely to need and be granted legal aid?

Source: Legal Aid Ontario 2016.

◆ In Their Own Words ◆

In 2009, the Centre for Addiction and Mental Health in Toronto and the Mental Health Commission of Canada co-authored a study called "Improving Mental Health Services for Immigrant, Refugee, Ethno-Cultural and Racialized Groups." One of their participants had the following to say:

> Language and culture play an important role in mental health service delivery. For example, if I go to a service provider who doesn't know my language and is not familiar with my culture, first of all I will not be able to explain my problem to him/her as I want to say it. Secondly, even if he/she gets me, will still not be able to provide me with culturally appropriate treatment, which is very important. (2)

Source: Centre for Addiction and Mental Health and Mental Health Commission of Canada 2009.

As with many other populations discussed in this chapter, another factor that limits immigrants' access to services is eligibility requirements. Federally funded settlement services for immigrants are, in most provinces, only available to permanent residents and refugees. This means that temporary workers, foreign students, or non-status immigrants may live in Canada for years before they are eligible to use these services, especially since permanent immigration status is increasingly difficult to secure. Of this group, non-status immigrants are the most vulnerable, largely because they are not protected by provincial health insurance and are vulnerable to abuse, exploitation, and poor health.

If you guessed that fear of detention or deportation may deter non-status immigrants from accessing social services, you're right. Many organizations ask about immigration status and seek documentation like a permanent residency card, a passport, or refugee papers. And without papers, non-status parents aren't eligible for social services like childcare subsidies or even public transportation that allows wheelchairs. Since the government funds many social service organizations, there may be limits on how funds are used and which groups can access services. That means permanent residents receive priority over non-status immigrants in service delivery (Social Planning Toronto 2013). Finally, given their relative obscurity, gathering reliable data about the unique needs of non-status immigrants is a challenge. The less visible they are, the less we know about them, making social services irrelevant and inaccessible, which further marginalizes non-status immigrants, and the cycle continues.

◆ In Their Own Words ◆

In 2006, a group of researchers set out to examine the experiences of undocumented people in Toronto and their access to social services. They did so by interviewing the social service providers, many of whom were exhausted and disillusioned with their inability to serve this population. Here are some of their testimonies:

> "My referrals are embarrassing. I refer people to more barriers. They report back to me consistently: 'I went to that agency you referred me to and the minute they asked me for my documents, I just walked out the door.'"

> "A woman came into our office. She was visibly physically assaulted and reporting also sexual abuse by a man she knew but was not partnered with. She had no [legal immigrant] status and was obviously in crisis. She decided to [risk involving the police] in hopes the police would not get to the immigration question, but they did. And after the forensic testing was done at the hospital, she was taken to the police station [and] she was incarcerated. They called immigration and then she was questioned by immigration officers several hours later and now she has a deportation that is pending the trial against the man who raped her."

Source: Berinstein et al. 2006.

Indigenous Peoples in Canada

Indigenous Peoples make up only small percentage of the entire Canadian population. However, they have an outsized need for social services and legal representation compared to other groups. That is because of the combination of past and present disadvantages they experience.

As we have seen in previous chapters, they are overrepresented as both offenders and victims of crime (Office of the Correctional Investigator 2019). Between 2005 and 2015, the number of Indigenous women in federal custody doubled (Office of the Correctional Investigator 2015). They also receive longer sentences than average, even when individual criminal histories and the severity of the offences are considered (Jeffries and Stenning 2014). For Indigenous youth, they are eight times more likely than non-Indigenous youth to be imprisoned (Corrado, Kuehn, and Margaritescu 2014). Between 2012–18, Statistics Canada tracked a steadily declining trend in all adult incarcerations (Malakieh 2019). However, the trend is going in the opposite direction for Indigenous Peoples. Indigenous Peoples make up only 4 per cent of the general population but nearly 30 per cent of admissions to federal and provincial prisons, up from 20 per cent a decade earlier. In Manitoba and Saskatchewan, these numbers are even higher; in these places, Indigenous adult men make up a staggering three-quarters of admissions to custody. Young Indigenous people make up only 8 per cent of the Canadian youth population, but they account for nearly half of admissions to custody (Malakieh 2019).

Suggestions for reducing imprisonment rates among Indigenous populations include reconsidering culturally insensitive laws. The justice system has historically overlooked opportunities to practise more cultural sensitivity when dealing with Indigenous Peoples. For example, throughout the 2000s, the Kitchenuhmaykoosib Inninuwug (KI) First Nation of Ontario tried to prevent a mining company from drilling on what the KI considered to be their property. The judge admitted the KI were trying to protect their land, culture, and beliefs, but in the end ruled the company was allowed to drill anyway (Tomm 2013). Another example is child apprehension; there are more Indigenous children in state care now than during the height of the residential school system (Legal Aid Ontario 2015). Any legal strategy enabling safe reunification of parents and children must grow out of an understanding of the historic (and present-day) systemic maltreatment of Indigenous families and communities.

Given their overrepresentation as offenders and victims of crime, higher likelihood of being low-income, and higher vulnerability to child apprehension, Indigenous Peoples have a significant need for legal aid. This has led to developing Indigenous-specific criminal justice programs and services. They include the Indigenous Courtwork Program, Indigenous-specific services and initiatives in Correctional Service Canada, and an Indigenous justice strategy in Canada's Department of Justice (Brzozwski, Taylor-Butts, and Johnson 2006). Despite these efforts, Indigenous Peoples in Canada are still in more need of legal services and face unique barriers in accessing quality legal representation compared with their non-Indigenous counterparts.

The many barriers to getting appropriate legal service grow out of Canada's long history of systemic marginalization of Indigenous Peoples. Struggles over land ownership and treaty rights, intellectual property, traditional governance, and resource harvesting, all of which were largely negotiated through the legal system, have often left Indigenous

Peoples out in the cold. Lawyer and Indigenous rights supporter Ardith Walkem (2007) argues, "not surprisingly, the legacy of this history is that Indigenous people continue to be disproportionately enmeshed with Canadian law and legal systems . . . To many Indigenous people, the legal process continues this history of interference, domination, and control, and its operation is far removed from any concept of justice or fairness" (1).

Many Indigenous Peoples prefer to speak and work with Indigenous legal agencies that provide culturally sensitive services and lawyers who understand the unique issues they face (Reid and Malcolmson 2008; Rahman 2009). Indeed, Indigenous Peoples and groups have challenged these limitations and worked to find new, culturally safe ways of doing things. For example, they have established community centres in many towns and cities where they can meet other Indigenous Peoples. Many have embraced traditional medicine and healing practices. Many have pressed for justice reform that recognizes the value of restorative justice, rather than retribution. And, not least, many have pressed for family services that respect and protect Indigenous family life, despite the lingering effects of the residential school system and the Sixties Scoop.

The difficulty finding and accessing legal representation is greatest for those living in rural regions or on reserves. There are fewer affordable legal services available in rural provinces, and those living there often have less knowledge of the available legal resources. For instance, in Queen Charlotte, a town located in British Columbia with 7,000 inhabitants, only two lawyers are available; while in Dawson Creek, a town of around 12,000, only one lawyer accepts legal aid referrals. There is also less outreach to most Indigenous communities in rural regions and on reserves, which reduces the spread of information about legal services (Reid and Malcolmson 2008).

Also, because there are only a limited number of legal services on reserves, Indigenous Peoples seeking legal support must travel great distances to get the help they need. Difficulties with accessing cars, phones, or public transportation can make matters worse (Bressan and Coady 2017:11). According to one lawyer, "Many of my clients have to hitch hike for court. I'm talking about people coming in 100 to 130 km away" (Reid and Malcolmson 2008:56). This distance from legal services and court has been shown to increase Indigenous Peoples' likelihood of pleading guilty.

Unfortunately, their difficulties with the legal system do not end there. Indigenous Peoples in Canada also face particular difficulties in correctional services. According to Correctional Service Canada, First Nations, Métis, and Inuit inmates are often classified as higher security risk than non-Indigenous inmates. They are released later in their sentences, are more likely to have their conditional release rights revoked, and are more likely to be placed in segregation. This limits their access to "rehabilitation" programs, which in turn increases the likelihood of future offending (Sapers 2013).

In the *Washington Post*, former correctional investigator Howard Sapers argued that Canada's correctional system is "an artifact of colonial contact" resulting from "systemic bias built into many of the decision points and many of the process points in our criminal justice system . . . [These policies] end up being discriminatory in application, and that helps keep spinning the revolving door of [Indigenous] people coming in and out of the system" (Coletta 2019).

Setting up Indigenous-specific programs, such as the Ma Mawi/Stony Mountain Project, can be highly effective in interrupting this revolving door. The Ma Mawi/Stony Mountain Project helped Indigenous inmates learn to understand and control their use of violence (Zellerer 2003). Such a program can help Indigenous inmates, but the Canadian Office of the Correctional Investigator found that many Indigenous-specific programs have not yet been completely implemented (Mann 2013). As well, programs are often not carried out nationally (only locally) and cannot be reached by Indigenous inmates in time. Thus, these programs stand to help many Indigenous Peoples, but often they *can't* because of barriers to access.

So far we've focused on legal representation, given that it is a subject of great concern for this population. However, Indigenous Peoples in Canada face difficulties when accessing and using other social services as well. Despite the high rates of issues relating to mental health and addictions among the population, rehabilitation and mental health services are both difficult to access and often ineffective. DeVerteuil and Wilson (2007) compared seven drug addiction treatments centres across Canada. They found that all but one showed an indifference to and a lack of willingness to create dedicated Indigenous spaces for healing, despite the importance of cultural and spiritual elements for recovery. Similarly, many mental health services lack culturally specific programs, and this defect often reduces the effectiveness of treatment. Difficulty getting a diagnosis, communication issues, stigma, and transportation issues also hinder Indigenous Peoples' access to mental health services (Misener, Rudderham, and Vukic 2009).

◆ In Their Own Words ◆

Here are quotes taken from elderly Métis women in Saskatchewan.

About relying on their family to access social services:

> Yeah the transportation: for you to go to the hospital or go to the city you can't go by taxi or ambulance, your kids have to take you, right? So you have trouble with that. Cause if you didn't have kids, who would take you? Nobody!

About the pension provided by Old Age Security:

> And they think you are getting such a big cheque at the end of the month because you're not, if that's what it comes down to most of these people don't even have enough to last till the fifteenth of the month, even the ones that don't smoke, that don't drink, they still have to eat.

About the availability of social services:

> There's a lot of things she can get help with they don't have here because with homecare we only have two workers. They have to go all through the whole community. The same with our physical therapist. She can't come in cause there's not enough physical therapists, there is only one, so she can't get her therapy.
>
> It would be good if they had someone who could talk to them in Cree about mental problems like say psychology, because there's a lot

of things they don't know, how to cope. Like myself I understand Cree, but she don't understand English. Some have communication problems. When I'm mad at her she misunderstands and takes it the wrong way, see because I can't talk Cree.

Source: Krieg, Martz, and McCallum 2007.

The underresourcing of Indigenous Peoples on-reserve is also a social problem—one that has been recently recognized by the Canadian Human Rights Tribunal. In 2019, the tribunal ordered the federal government to pay billions of dollars in compensation to First Nations families who were negatively impacted by an underfunded child welfare system. As of publication, the case is still before the court of appeal.

People with Disabilities in Canada

The Government of Canada supports some social services for those with a disability or a chronic illness. These services range from postage-free literature for those who are visually impaired, to grants for students seeking postsecondary education, to funding for adjustments to homes and workplaces.

The most-cited form of social support for people who develop a disability that prevents them from working is the **Canada Pension Plan for Disability Benefits**. As long as a person has contributed to the Canada Pension Plan in the past and is under the age of 65, they are eligible for a monthly payment from the government. However, many find it is not enough to live on. For example, in 2018 the average monthly payment was $971.23. Most people in Canada would find it challenging, if not impossible, to meet all their basic needs on that income alone.

Canada Pension Plan for Disability Benefits
A taxable monthly payment that is available to people who have contributed to the Canada Pension Plan and cannot work regularly at any job because of a disability.

Critical Thinking Question

Estimate your monthly expenses for the following things:

- Rent or mortgage payment
- Transportation (gas, public transit, and so on)
- Food
- Heat and hydro
- Phone
- Internet
- Clothing
- Medicine
- Leisure activities
- Other expenses

Add them up. Do you think you could live on $971.23 per month?

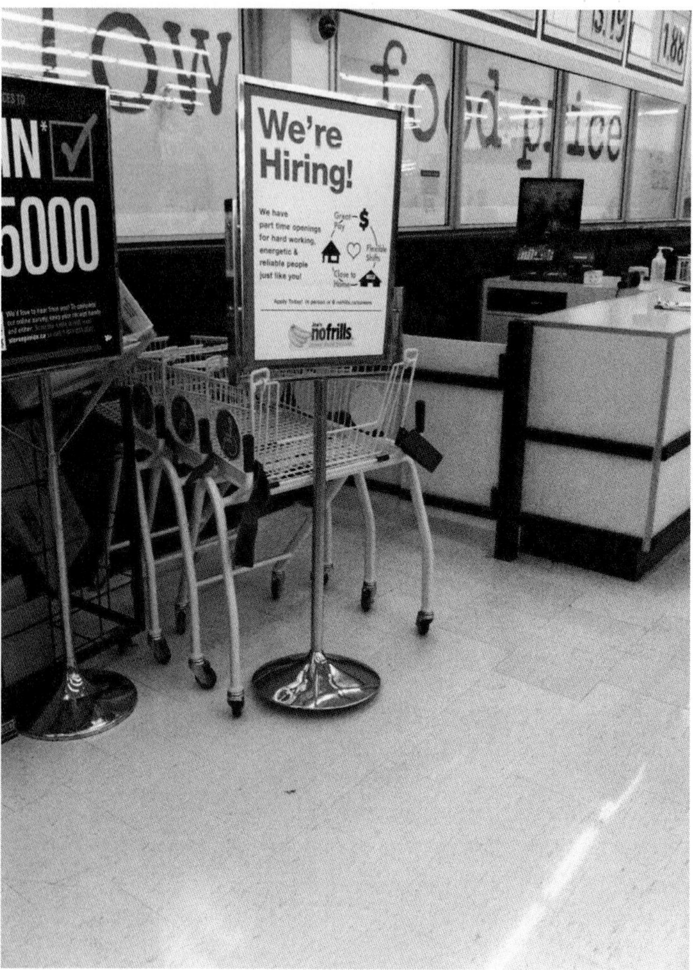

This large chain grocery store may provide wheelchair-adapted carts, but anyone with a mobility issue will have trouble moving the big sign that's blocking their access to the carts.

Canadians with a disability or chronic illness are more likely to need social services, but they face more barriers to accessing them and, thus, have more unmet needs. To begin with, physical barriers such as stairs, cramped hallways, and narrow doorways may hinder someone's ability to physically access health and social services (McColl 2005). Sanchez and colleagues (2000) found that when a mobility-impaired person phoned ahead to ensure that a service centre was accessible, staff would respond that it was, even if it was not. Perhaps it had a wheelchair ramp but lacked accessible bathrooms, examination tables that could be lowered, and so on. In light of this, specific training is needed to address the diverse needs of clients with disabilities.

Studies have shown that doctors systematically exclude people with disabilities from their roster of patients, especially those with mental illness or pain disorders (McColl, Aiken, and Schaub 2015). Those with disabilities are often reluctant to access health and social services because of the fear of being forced to pay staggering bills out of pocket.

Indigenous Peoples with a disability experience additional barriers to health and social services. One reason why is that many Indigenous Peoples in Canada are financially supported in part by transfer funds from the Canadian government. These funds, which are used for upgrading academic skills, vocational training, or retraining programs, are often granted only for those living on-reserve. When a person moves to an urban, off-reserve setting (possibly in pursuit of better support for a disability), they are less likely to be eligible for those social services (Senese 2013).

What we know is that accessing social services is one way to decrease the negative effects of a disability or chronic illness. Kelley-Moore and Schumacher (2006) conducted a study that examined elderly self-perception and the qualities that make one disabled. She discovered that a loss of control and agency was positively correlated with identification as disabled. The most-cited instances are the inability to drive and the need for homecare. Conversely, a varied and dense social network dramatically reduced the **self-perception** of disability (Kelley-Moore and Schumacher 2006). When people feel accepted, they are more likely to take part and contribute to their communities and the economy. That's one powerful reason making proper social services free and equally accessible to everyone with a disability matters.

self-perception
The processes by which people come to think about and know themselves.

IN FOCUS ◆ Youth Homelessness

The long-term social and economic costs of youth homelessness are many but often ignored (Varney and Van Vliet 2008). Thus, the decision to underfund services for homeless youth is also a decision to pay much higher costs in the decades that follow.

Homelessness—living in a shelter—appears to have more harmful, longer-term effects on young children than older ones. However, the ways in which services are provided to families also affect how well children develop, since it affects how they cope with the stresses of insecure housing.

Research on supportive housing programs for formerly homeless families reveals gaps in service provision. From the data, researchers conclude that supportive housing programs need to be tailored to the children's type and level of need. However, we need to better understand the needs of youth who do not use formal services and their reasons for not doing so. This means we need a better understanding of the "hidden" population of homeless youth, which requires focusing on the structural causes of youth homelessness. This balance of low-level observation and attention to structural causes demonstrates the "zigzag approach" mentioned earlier in this chapter; without it, we cannot hope to provide interventions that work.

Consequences of Unequal Access to Social Services and Legal Representation

We have noted throughout this book that informal social supports from family, friends, and other community members are often important in helping people deal with their difficulties related to inequality. That said, these informal supports cannot replace specialized services that all people—and especially, disadvantaged people—occasionally need. Chief among these are legal services when dealing with welfare, immigration, the police, or other arms of the government. So a lack of access to quality, affordable legal and social services compounds the disadvantage these people already experience.

It is true that specialized, professional services are costly. However, they help correct and prevent problems that, if untreated, will fester and become even more costly in both financial and human terms.

Strategies of Resistance

Government-Level Strategies of Resistance

We started out by acknowledging that, in the realm of legal and social services, there is a large gap between *what is* and *what is supposed to be.* Idealized notions of "law" and "bureaucracy" are founded on the expectation that reason will prevail and decision makers will fairly apply the written rules. Actual legal systems and bureaucracies, however, are imperfect. Like economic markets, which are also thought to operate fairly and for the benefit of all, legal systems and bureaucracies often reflect the power structure of society.

That said, the state is able to redress inequalities of power and make legal and social services work the way they are ideally supposed to work. For example, the Canadian government can make social services and legal representation more accessible by creating new programs and policies that promote inclusiveness. Consider the idea of setting up more support services for cultural sensitivity training. This practice may have secondary benefits: For example, it might encourage Indigenous Peoples to use mental health services or immigrant women who are dealing with domestic violence to seek help (Miedema and Wachholz 2012). The government could also develop outreach and follow-up services for these groups to ensure their problems are addressed and any improvements made are long lasting.

To address the issue of limited access to legal aid for many groups of Canadians, the government can do a couple of things. First, increasing the funding for legal aid would allow more people to get the legal support they need. The federal government could also ensure that legal aid is more accessible to Canadians by making access a constitutional right. A case in support of this notion was brought to the Supreme Court in 2005: The Canadian Bar Association asked the courts to declare that denying legal aid to "poor people" violated their rights to equality before and under the law. They sought the recognition of legal aid as a right protected by the Constitution. The courts ruled against the request, commenting that the Canadian Bar Association was not the right organization to bring forward a claim for "poor people." However, this means that another organization could bring the court a different argument and achieve a better result. It is still possible the denial of legal aid will be found unconstitutional, but further efforts to prove it will be needed.

Bear in mind that the reason funding for legal aid is so limited is because it is part of a larger package of underfunded programs that, together, make up the liberal welfare regime. And in turn, this liberal regime is supported by neoliberal philosophies of government—namely, less government is better than more because lower taxes on the rich are better than higher taxes. So to change access to legal representation on the government level will mean shifting closer to a social democratic welfare regime. In turn, this will mean garnering support for social democratic philosophies, policies, and parties.

Organization-Level Strategies of Resistance

Many strategies are available to provide people with better access to social services and legal representation. For example, legal representation for low-income youth in and around Toronto is available from Justice for Children and Youth (JFCY). JFCY is a not-for-profit legal aid clinic that focuses on providing legal services to those in conflict with the legal, education, social services, or mental health systems (Gaetz, O'Grady, and Buccieri 2010). They provide legal advice and support to youth and their parents as well as professionals and groups in communities throughout Ontario. For those who struggle to get legal aid because of eligibility requirements or other factors discussed in this chapter, JFCY offers a way to overcome the obstacles that hinder access to legal representation.

JFCY helps homeless youth in particular through their outreach and education program Street Youth Legal Services (SYLS). Offering workshops and one-on-one consultations, this program delivers free legal advice and referrals to homeless youth between the ages of 16 and 24 in Toronto. Youth on the streets often have multiple, interrelated legal issues. In addition, multiple barriers may stand in their way of accessing legal representation, such as being socially isolated and lacking money.

IN FOCUS ◆ The Food Bank as a Centre for Tax Advice

The Saskatoon Food Bank and Learning Centre is delivering a variety of critical services, including a tax centre. For over 20 years this service has helped low-income earners get expert advice on income tax issues that they couldn't otherwise afford.

In this way, the food bank helps people access funds they may not have realized were owing to them. They are likely to discover their eligibility for the Canada Child Benefit, Saskatchewan Low-Income Tax Credit, and provincial social services. By increasing their access to additional income, the food bank helps clients solve an even more fundamental problem than the lack of food: the lack of sufficient income.

In 2018, the Community Volunteer Income Tax Program helped over 7,000 people file tax returns. In doing so, they put $19.2 million back into the hands of low-income people in Saskatoon. It could not have done it without the unpaid work of over 50 knowledgeable volunteers who wanted to improve their community.

Source: Adapted from Food Banks Canada 2018.

An effective way to address such issues is to target several of them at once—and this is exactly what SYLS does. For example, SYLS fights the problem of social isolation among youth with multiple legal issues by bringing legal resources directly to youth. These are provided at drop-in centres, homeless shelters, and street youth programs where homeless youth go to get healthcare, food, and counselling. Reaching out to youth in places where they are comfortable and easily accessible is an efficient way of using SYLS's resources; moreover, it is a strategy that other organizations should consider adopting.

In a way, food banks have an easier time of attracting a clientele. While not everyone is familiar with the law and lawyers, everyone is familiar with eating and the need to eat. Some food banks have capitalized on this natural constituency by combining the supply of free food with the supply of other free, useful services.

Individual-Level Strategies of Resistance

In 2011, Chief Justice Beverley McLachlin spoke out against the inequities of the Canadian legal system in her keynote address at a colloquium at the University of Toronto (Benmor 2014). With more than 100 legal experts gathered, McLachlin expressed her disappointment in the inaccessibility of the Canadian legal system to the middle and lower classes (Ciccocioppo 2011). She compelled the lawyers and younger legal generation in the audience to use their skills for good. She said, "If you're the only one who can provide a fundamental social need from which you benefit, I think it follows that you have to provide it . . . And I don't think it's enough to say we are providing for the rich and the corporations. You have to find a way to provide it for everybody" (Makin 2011).

Several solutions were suggested during the conference, including creating a legal insurance plan, improving and increasing legal advice hotlines, as well as creating live websites where legal experts could give advice online. Other ideas focused on prevention techniques for the most common legal situations that middle-class people face: debt repayment, divorce, and custody proceedings. Some proposed adding warnings and reality checks about debt to credit statements to remind credit card holders. Others offered counselling to new couples about the financial realities of divorce, prenuptial agreements, custody battles, and so on (Makin 2011).

McLachlin's speech at this conference touched on a striking issue in legal accessibility in Canada and sparked a national discussion on the topic with a feature in the *Globe and Mail* and other major news outlets.

Closing Remarks

In this chapter, we've seen how crucial social services and legal representation are beyond the reach of many Canadians. What makes matters worse is that it's often the people who need these resources the most who are least able to access them. People who are poor, abused, chronically ill, and otherwise disadvantaged often find their own circumstances hinder fitting in with societal rules and norms. When they try to seek help to improve their problems, they are often further disadvantaged by the social institutions in place to help them.

Issues around domestic violence were recently aggravated by the long period required to shelter from COVID-19. During this period of prolonged social isolation, widespread unemployment, increased childcare, and domestic violence reportedly increased, in part a consequence of more drinking and substance abuse.

Breaking down the barriers to accessing these types of survival capital is essential. To do this, there must be a greater recognition that such barriers exist. The people who are most knowledgeable about these issues—that is, people who experience unequal access to services—aren't always able to effect positive change in their lives and the lives of others. Many of them are just trying to survive, which leaves them little time and few resources to call for change. Those who can make a difference, however, are those who are aware of the unequal access to social services and legal representation and who are in positions to institute change. Sociologists like you know the facts, but it is acting on these facts that will make all the difference for reducing inequality.

Notable Thinkers

Daniel Béland

Social problems call for corrective policies and programs, and few Canadian sociologists have been as dedicated as Daniel Béland in studying the policymaking process, both in Canada and elsewhere.

In the last 10 years, political sociologist and Canada Research Chair in Public Policy Daniel Béland has studied the convergence of certain key themes in political sociology. These have included power, ideas, language, debate, and public policy. In a 2009 paper titled "Ideas, Institutions, and Policy Change," Béland draws on political science literature to discuss three ways in which ideas influence policy change. First, he notes that ideas help to frame the problems and issues that enter policy agendas. Second, they shape the assumptions that affect the content of reform proposals. Third, they can become ideological weapons that shape reform activities. Yet institutional constraints also shape the politics of ideas and policy change. National institutions remain central to the politics of policymaking and interact with transnational actors and ideas to bring about change.

Consider, for example, the role of ideas about welfare change, as discussed in Béland's 2011 paper "The Politics of Social Policy Language." Here, he notes that key social policy ideas like "welfare state" are both vague and problematic. Focusing on social policy debate in the United States and France, Béland discusses the development of the ideas of "social security"/"sécurité sociale" and "welfare state"/"état-providence" in both countries. These ideas have long been controversial, in part because they are caught up in the inherently political drawing and redrawing of the contested boundaries of state action.

Some have said there is nothing as practical as a good theory. By making good theories about policymaking, Béland reminds us to pay close attention to both the unspoken assumptions of the people making policy and the needs of the people it serves.

Test Your Knowledge

1. What did Kelley-Moore and Schumacher's (2006) study on elderly self-perception and the qualities that make one disabled reveal?
2. What are some barriers Indigenous Peoples face in accessing legal services?
3. What are some barriers faced by immigrants in accessing social services?
4. How have budget cuts in Canada limited battered women's access to legal aid?
5. What are the similarities between legal and social services? What are the key differences?
6. Why don't legal systems work the way they are "supposed to"? Why don't bureaucracies work the way they are "supposed to"?
7. Why did concerns about the gap between "ideal" and "real" legal services arise in the 1930s and then again in the 1960s? Why did they diminish or disappear during the 1940s and 1950s?
8. Think of some ways that greater cultural sensitivity might improve legal or social services for Indigenous Peoples, new immigrants, or to other disadvantaged people.

See the Answer Key online to check your answers.

Questions for Critical Thought

1. Do you think there are enough social services in your community? If you answered no, what social services are missing?
2. Should undocumented or non-status immigrants and refugees be entitled to the social services and legal aid offered by the Canadian government? Explain why or why not.
3. Should families be obliged to take care of the elderly to lessen the burden on the Canadian government? Explain why or why not.

4. Should companies be required to hire a certain number of Canadians with disabilities? Why or why not?
5. There is little research into the experiences of the LGBTQ+ population and their access to social services and legal representation in Canada. Why do you think that is?

Additional Resources

Recommended Readings

Erkulwater, Jennifer. 2006. *Disability Rights and the American Social Safety Net*. Ithaca, NY: Cornell University Press. Erkulwater describes some of the successes made in developing social welfare policies for people with disabilities in the United States. She examines the disability rights movement, disability benefits, and disability programs that have enabled the severely disabled to work and become less dependent on welfare.

Klassen, Thomas. 2014. *Retirement in Canada (Issues in Canada)*. Toronto, ON: Oxford University Press. Klassen discusses the retirement-related changes that are taking place in Canada, as well as what we can predict about the future state of retirement. This book covers topics such as income security for older Canadians, how pensions will change in the coming years, as well as the debate about compulsory retirement.

Little, Bruce. 2008. *Fixing the Future: How Canada's Usually Fractious Governments Worked Together to Rescue the Canada Pension Plan*. Toronto, ON: University of Toronto Press. This book follows the development of the Canada Pension Plan, from the huge deficits faced in 1993 to its present state. Little discusses how the pension policy has succeeded in overcoming the large governmental deficits of the past as well as the reforms that have occurred. He interviews over 50 politicians, government officials, and other people who have worked closely with the reforms.

Tolley, Erin and Robert Young. 2011. *Immigrant Settlement Policy in Canadian Municipalities (Fields of Governance: Policy Making in Canadian Municipalities)*. Montreal, QC: McGill-Queens University Press. This book examines the policies, programs, and services for Canadian immigrants. Tolley and Young recommend methods to address the challenges related to governmental co-operation, delivery of services for immigrants, and overall immigrant well-being. As well, this book reveals some of the gaps and problems in the system and what governments are doing to aid immigrants' integration.

Vlasic, Pamela. 2008. *The Lives Behind the Numbers: Understanding the Disproportionate Representation of Indigenous Women in the Canadian Legal System*. Riga, Latvia: VDM Verlag Dr Müller Publishing. This book examines why Canadian Indigenous women are overrepresented in the legal system compared with non-Indigenous women. To better explain this social problem, Vlasic interviewed social services professionals and women who encounter trouble with the law.

Recommended Websites

Aboriginal Legal Services (ALS)

www.aboriginallegal.ca

ALS is dedicated to strengthening the ability of Indigenous communities and its citizens in dealing with the legal system as well as providing culturally suitable legal alternatives. They approach issues of justice in an assertive, helpful, and respectable manner. The organization also helps youth and adult Indigenous Peoples learn about their rights and offers various programs and aids in connecting people with other services that may be useful.

Council of Canadians with Disabilities (CCD)

www.ccdonline.ca/en/socialpolicy/actionplan/accessible-canada

The CCD is an organization for people with disabilities and aims to make Canada inclusive and accessible. They strive to increase disability-related supports, reduce poverty, and increase employment opportunities for the disabled. They also promote humans rights and ensure the elements of the UN Convention on the Rights of Persons with Disabilities is carried out. This is done through law reforms, litigation, educating the public, as well as communicating with key decision makers.

Legal Aid Ontario

www.legalaid.on.ca/en

Legal Aid Ontario is a not-for-profit organization that runs the legal aid program of Ontario. They seek to provide quality legal services in an efficient and cost-effective manner to low-income Canadians. This website includes information that can aid people in locating legal help, resources for lawyers, as well as up-to-date publications and resources.

Ontario Ministry of Education

www.edu.gov.on.ca/childcare/paying.html

This website provides information about the variety of services available for parents who are seeking help in paying for childcare. It covers information about the Child Care Subsidy, Ontario Child Benefit, Universal Child Care Benefit, and Canada Child Tax Benefit.

Service Canada

www.servicecanada.gc.ca/eng/services/pensions/cpp/disability/benefit/index.shtml

This website provides information about the Canada Pension Plan Disability Benefit as well as information about the application process, eligibility requirements, and types of benefits and services available.

Youth Employment Services (YES)

www.yes.on.ca

YES is an organization that seeks to help kids and encourage their empowerment, which is key to a safe and healthy community. YES provides innovative programs that help disadvantaged and vulnerable youth to become independent and contributing citizens. This website provides aid to youth looking for employment, various publications, as well as resources for employers looking to hire employees.

LeonWang/Shutterstock

10 Access to Safety

Learning Objectives

- To compare different theoretical perspectives on crime and access to safety.
- To name common misconceptions about crime and victimization.
- To explain how conceptions of crime are socially constructed.
- To list the ways that safety is affected by income level.
- To identify the barriers to safety faced by immigrants.
- To compare the differences in male and female victimization.
- To explain why younger Canadians are victimized more than others.
- To understand why Indigenous Peoples in Canada make up a large proportion of victims of violence.
- To name the effects of unequal access to safety.
- To identify approaches to reducing disparities in safety.

Introduction

This chapter is called "Access to Safety," but it could equally be called "Freedom from Victimization." **Victimization** is the singling out of an individual or a group for criminal or unfair treatment. Put another way, victims have compromised access to a critical type of survival capital: safety.

victimization The targeting of an individual or a group for subjection to crime, unfair treatment, or another wrong.

Victimization and the fear of becoming victimized prevent people from living happy, healthy lives. Beyond that, the victimization of some people has negative results for many. That is, societies where victimization is more likely to occur are unpleasant places to live for everyone, not only for those who are victimized. We will focus on the negative societal effects of victimization near the end of this chapter.

Victimization takes many forms. **Criminal victimization** happens when someone is the victim of a crime, such as homicide, assault, robbery, fraud, or theft. When these crimes are reported and the perpetrator is charged, we can track the frequency and nature of this victimization. What we know is that different populations in Canada are uniquely vulnerable to certain types of criminal victimization, and certain populations are also overrepresented among convicted offenders. Mostly, we will focus on criminal victimization in this chapter.

criminal victimization The targeting of an individual or a group for subjection to a crime, for example, homicide, assault, robbery, fraud, or theft.

Another type of victimization happens, ironically enough, at the hands of the people and social structures designed to protect Canadians from crime: the police, the courts, and even the media. All of these contribute to social problems like the overpenalization of some populations in Canada. For example, while we like to think of prisons as places where people are safely confined and rehabilitated, victimization happens there as well.

Victimization even occurs in the places we like to think are the safest: schools, hospitals, treatment facilities, and even our homes. Generally, our unwillingness as a society to satisfactorily regulate these places contributes to the widespread problem of insecurity. To some degree, we do this because we cling to some sacred myths about family, neighbourhood, school, and so on.

Not all victims are victims of "official" crimes. Consider people who suffer because the government has failed to regulate dangerous activities. These activities include the continued, unregulated pollution of the environment and the non-enforcement of many consumer safety or workplace safety laws. There are people not yet born who will be, in a sense, victimized by our gross maltreatment of the planet—by the laws of our economic systems and the values of overconsumption. They also include the non-regulation of financial activities that resulted in the meltdown of the world's economy in 2008. Once again, there are populations in Canada (and around the world) that suffer the ill effects of this kind of victimization more than others.

Theoretical Perspectives on Access to Safety

The functionalist approach to crime and victimization views crime as normal, universal, and unavoidable—in short, it is to be expected in any society. As a result, victimization is also to be expected in any society.

In his **strain (anomie) theory**, social theorist Robert Merton (1943) argues that crime arises when people cannot achieve culturally defined goals via legitimate means. In our society and others, many people work hard and still can't secure a top-shelf education or a

strain (anomie) theory Robert Merton's theory that many types of crime and deviant behaviour are necessary and natural adaptations to the gap between people's common goals and their unequal opportunities to gain them.

high-paying job. Often this is the result of inequalities stemming from class, gender, race, age, health, disability, or sexual orientation—inequalities we have faced often in this book. Not everyone winds up with enough money, power, or status to achieve the "good life."

Merton's theory has elements of both a conflict approach and functionalist approach, because it seeks to explain the survival of capitalism despite its most egregious features of inequality. Merton argues that capitalism survives because people learn to adapt to what he calls "anomie," the gap between learned success goals and limited opportunities. Rebellion is only one form of adaptation, and most people adapt in other ways, like conformity, robotic repetition of daily activities, retreating from daily life, or criminal behaviour.

Not everyone becomes a criminal. A strong social bond prevents most people from succumbing to the temptation to engage in criminal activities. Some adjust their goals to more modest ones and conform. However, people who are more associated with criminals are more likely to learn the values and skills (that is, illegitimate means) that simplify criminal behaviour.

differential association theory Proposes that people, through simple association, are socialized into their criminal environment and reproduce the prevailing order.

Differential association theory, credited to Edwin Sutherland (1946), looks at how people are socialized into their criminal environments and reproduce them. It proposes that people are social and copy one another to gain acceptance and approval. It views crime as resulting from too much of the "wrong kind" of organization, not too little of the "right kind" of organization (Kissner and Pyrooz 2009). Associating with criminals or witnessing crime, especially if it goes unpunished, teaches people not only the techniques of crime, but also the motives for, rationalizations of, and attitudes of such a lifestyle. In this sense, jails can be graduate schools for crime.

social disorganization theory Proposes that crime and other social pathologies (including suicide) result from a breakdown in social norms and social integration.

Social disorganization theory provides another perspective on the causes of crime. In many neighbourhoods, a breakdown in social norms and social integration can cause common, widespread criminality. This breakdown typically results from rapid social change and its resultant organizational problems. For example, it may result from rapid increases in population size, cultural diversity, and turnover that is common in an urban industrial society. Social disorganization leads to the loss of social cohesion—a central concern of functionalist theory. Other things being equal, the risk of robbery and assault near a person's home and of robbery and assault by strangers increases with declines in community social cohesion (Lee 2000). Also, random violence and exposure to the continual use of guns and knives in the community produces children who are more likely to act violently themselves (Scott 1999).

Conflict theorists might concede that crime and victimization are found in every society, but they would part with functionalists on two key points. First, they would deny that this universality proves that crime and victimization are functional to the survival of society. Second, they would point out that, however universal they may be, crime and victimization are distributed unequally in every society. Some kinds of people are more likely than others to be criminals, and some people are more likely than others to be victims. We cannot understand this fact unless we understand the connection between crime, victimization, and inequality.

Conflict theories of crime and violence point to inequalities in society as the cause of such deviant behaviour. Therefore, they would predict that as inequality increases in a society, crime also will increase, as will efforts to control it. As well, people who are most subject to inequality and disadvantage are the most likely to commit what are seen to be crimes.

Though largely correct, this theory ignores white-collar crimes. Conflict theory would explain largely unnoticed and unpunished white-collar crime by noting that, in general, rich and powerful people do what they want without consequences. Sometimes, they rewrite laws to decriminalize or deregulate their actions, often with dire social effects.

The conflict perspective notes that people in privileged positions work to preserve their status. Both the dominant ideology and formal laws—social constructs shaped and upheld by the ruling class—help the powerful to stay on top. They ensure, for example, that most people in society will view street crimes, such as public drug use and vagrancy, which are more common among the disadvantaged, as deviant. At the same time, corporate crimes that profit the wealthy but harm far larger numbers of people continue to be hidden from the mass media, the public, and policymakers. The conflict theorist's view is that people in power benefit from criminal laws, like those that protect their property, while people without power do not.

Social constructionism, an outgrowth of symbolic interactionism, looks at how deviant behaviours come to be defined as "deviant." This perspective stresses that no behaviours are inherently right or wrong: They become wrong, deviant, or criminal only when someone in power attaches a moral label to them.

Constructionist theories clarify the ways in which the notions of crime, violence, and criminality are built up and continued. However, there is no agreement on how best to depict crime and violence, if our goal is to prevent or deter such acts. For example, stories about violence against women that depict incidents as somehow routine or unavoidable may lead to a "culture of resignation." This sense of resignation is as dangerous in its own way as a **moral panic**. In short, while few researchers would deny that violent crime—domestic and otherwise—is problematic in society, the extent to which there is a "crime problem" is always open to debate.

moral panic A widespread feeling of fear—sometimes out of proportion—that something or someone will negatively destabilize society.

Feminist sociologists consider the ways in which gender makes someone more or less likely to be victimized by crime, or more or less likely to commit it. Consider Canadians' annual commemoration of the Montreal Massacre. On 6 December 1989, 14 women were shot and killed while attending L'Ecole Polytechnique. The shooter purposefully separated the women from the men before shooting them, saying he was "fighting feminism." In Canada, the massacre has become emblematic of the social problem of violence against women and continues to prompt calls for study and policy reform regarding how gender, crime, and violence intersect.

For example, women and girls in Canada are much more likely to be victims of sexual assault. They are also vulnerable to the most extreme forms of intimate partner violence, including violent acts that result in death. And yet overall, men are more likely to be victimized by assault and physical violence, largely at the hands of other men. Feminist sociologists consider the crimes that women are more likely to commit, if they commit crimes. They also examine the interplay of gender roles and imprisonment and consider the effect a woman's imprisonment has on her family and wider social network.

Three Things to Know about Crime and Victimization

1. "Crime" Is Social

Sociologists accept the notion that ideas of deviance (and, by extension, crime) are socially constructed. We see clear evidence of this when we see different norms of behaviour from society to society.

For example, in some places same-sex partnerships are illegal. In those societies, LGBTQ+ people risk social ridicule, imprisonment, and even execution if they are public with their identities. In other societies, same-sex marriage is legally supported and (increasingly) socially sanctioned, with politicians, public figures, and ordinary people openly celebrating their unions. We also see cultural differences in behaviours surrounding drug use, prostitution, traffic rules, and even dress.

While no society is fully risk-averse, some are more inclined to shy away from risk and expect more safety of self and security of property. For example, Canadians usually expect consistent, fair, and professional treatment from police officers and are shocked and upset when these expectations aren't met. Other societies, like those in which bribing authorities is common, expect far less consistency from their police.

Another reason sociologists believe that crime is socially constructed is that ideas of deviance change over time. Some behaviour, like smoking, has become more deviant over time. Some colleges and universities still have ancient ashtrays in the armrests of chairs in lecture halls, vestiges of the days when students—and professors—puffed away during lectures! Today, smokers often complain of being treated like outcasts, subjected to dirty looks and sneers, and reduced to stealing moments in dark, cold, inhospitable corners to enjoy their cigarettes. Other behaviours, like topless sunbathing and breastfeeding, have become less deviant and more accepted over time.

Ideas of crime often go hand in hand with ideas of victimization. Countries like the United States, for example, are highly litigious, meaning that lawsuits are filed much more often (and prison populations are proportionally large). Other societies do not demand the same "justice" for victims of crime. Some victims are invited to take part in deciding the fate of the offender, such as in the restorative justice models used by some Indigenous communities in Canada.

The differences in the involvement of victims reflect diverse ideas about whether an offence is against a person or an entire community. They also reflect whether the actions taken are designed to promote victims' healing or prevent further victimization of others by the offender. Some involvement is intended to rehabilitate offenders or deter others from committing similar offences.

2. What We Think about Crime Doesn't Always Match with What We Know

Popular notions about the frequency and nature of crimes, criminals, and victims sometimes do not match the facts. For example, after steadily decreasing—indeed, plummeting—for nearly 30 years, the crime rate across Canada has increased slightly in the past three years.

Crime rates can be affected by various things. For example, the increase in the total crime rate featured in Figure 10.1 is partially due to an increase in reports of sexual assault. Given that sexual assault in one of the crimes least likely to be reported to the police (Statistics Canada 2018a), the increase in number may not show an actual increase in sexual assaults. Instead, it may reveal the greater likelihood that victims came forward, thanks in part to the #MeToo movement. It could also have been affected by changing policing attitudes that encouraged disclosure and subsequent action.

In 2017, Quebec showed a 25 per cent increase in homicides. That's a significant jump; politicians could easily employ this statistic to bolster support for "tough on crime"

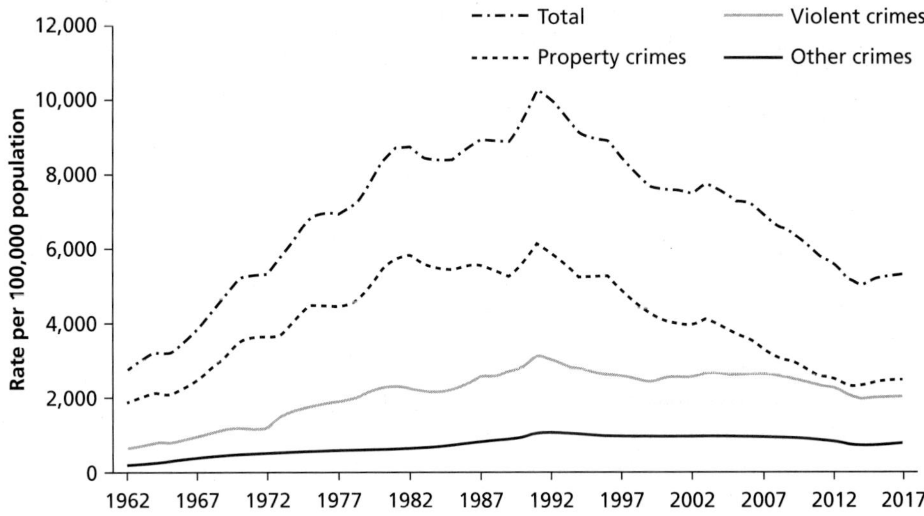

Figure 10.1 ◆ Crime Rates in Canada per 100,000 Population

Source: Statistics Canada 2018e.

initiatives (which often negatively impact the poor, racialized people, or religious minorities). And yet, if we peer behind the statistic, we see that this increase resulted from the Quebec City mosque shooting, in which a man opened fire in a mosque, killing six worshippers and injuring 40 others in an act of anti-Muslim brutality (Beattie, David, and Roy 2018).

Those of you who have moved from a small town to a bigger city might have been warned that cities are dangerous, crime-ridden places, yet this is not always the case. When we consider both the volume (per capita) and the severity of crime, Toronto—often thought of as being the most dangerous city in Canada—ranks 124th in a ranking of 229 municipalities. That puts Toronto far behind smaller cities like Guelph, Ontario, Laval, Quebec, and Canmore, Alberta (*Maclean's* 2018). In fact, in 2017, crime was 30 per cent higher in rural districts than in urban ones (Statistics Canada 2018d).

Why don't our ideas about crime match what's actually going on? Some argue that our understanding of crime is influenced by mainstream media exposure. This dramatic overrepresentation of the rate of crime in Canada is low by international standards. Stories about crime can outnumber other kinds of news stories, and the crime stories that get the most news coverage are those featuring violence. One study found that in a sample of Canadian newspapers, over 50 per cent of crime stories focused on violent crime (Landau 2006). How does this compare with the actual rate of violent crime? In Canada, violent crime makes up less than 6 per cent of reported offences.

Such inaccurate depictions may give viewers the wrong idea about crimes that are occurring. Often, the news will prominently feature stories related to violent crimes committed by strangers. These crimes do happen occasionally. However, in Canada it is more likely that people will be victimized by someone they know—for example, a spouse or family member.

IN FOCUS ◆ What Threatens Children More than Strangers in the Park at Night?

The nightly news might suggest that teaching children to avoid strangers is the best way to keep them safe. However, statistics tell us that children—and their parents—would be better served by lessons in water safety. Backyard pools and bathtubs are responsible for far more deaths than abductions by strangers. Helmets, seatbelts, and proper child-proofing of poisonous household substances are other safety measures that keep kids alive. Statistically speaking, the real dangers are lurking in our backyards and bathrooms, not necessarily down dark alleys or on deserted city streets.

Because of the emphasis on strangers, news consumers may imagine that crime only happens in dark alleys—not in their own kitchens or bedrooms. And according to Brazeau and Brzozowski (2008), "[i]n 2004, nearly 7 in 10 violent incidents did not involve a weapon. Among different types of violent offences, robberies were most likely to involve the use or presence of a weapon (45%). With sexual assaults, the vast majority (91%) did not involve a weapon." So, it may not be the stranger in the alley brandishing a switchblade that we need to worry about.

3. Media Portrayals of Victims Are Often Misleading

By focusing on certain kinds of victims, the media reinforce an idea that crime only happens to certain kinds of people. The media also reinforces a view that some victims are more or less deserving of the crime itself or of our sympathy.

Often, children, the elderly, or white, middle- to upper-class women who are violently victimized in public places by strangers are featured more prominently in news coverage of crime. It's true that violent crime can happen to members of these population groups. However, it is far more common among other groups, as we will see in the rest of this chapter. This tendency to grant victim status to some and not others is sometimes referred to as the **hierarchy of victimization**. Typically, people at the margins of society—the mentally or physically ill, the drug or alcohol addicted, the sexually divergent, the racialized communities, or the poor—get less attention when they are victimized by crime.

hierarchy of victimization The tendency to grant victim status to some people and not others.

This tendency by the media to overemphasize the experiences of a narrow slice of victims while neglecting others reinforces a notion that certain victims deserve what they get. This is often seen in gang-related shootings, which often fly under the public radar, or sexual assault cases where the "promiscuous" clothing of the victim is held up as evidence the attack was invited or provoked.

It is well supported, statistically speaking, that "a large proportion of all victimization incidents are experienced by a small number of victims" (Perreault, Sauve, and Burns 2010). To make matters worse, this small number of people are often victimized repeatedly. For example, only 2 per cent of Canadians accounted for 60 per cent of all the reported acts of violent victimization. Yet 40 per cent of people who reported being the victim of a crime said that they had been victimized more than once (Perreault et al 2010).

Some believe that people invite victimization—either single or repeat instances—into their lives. This might be through verbal provocation, engaging in antisocial behaviour,

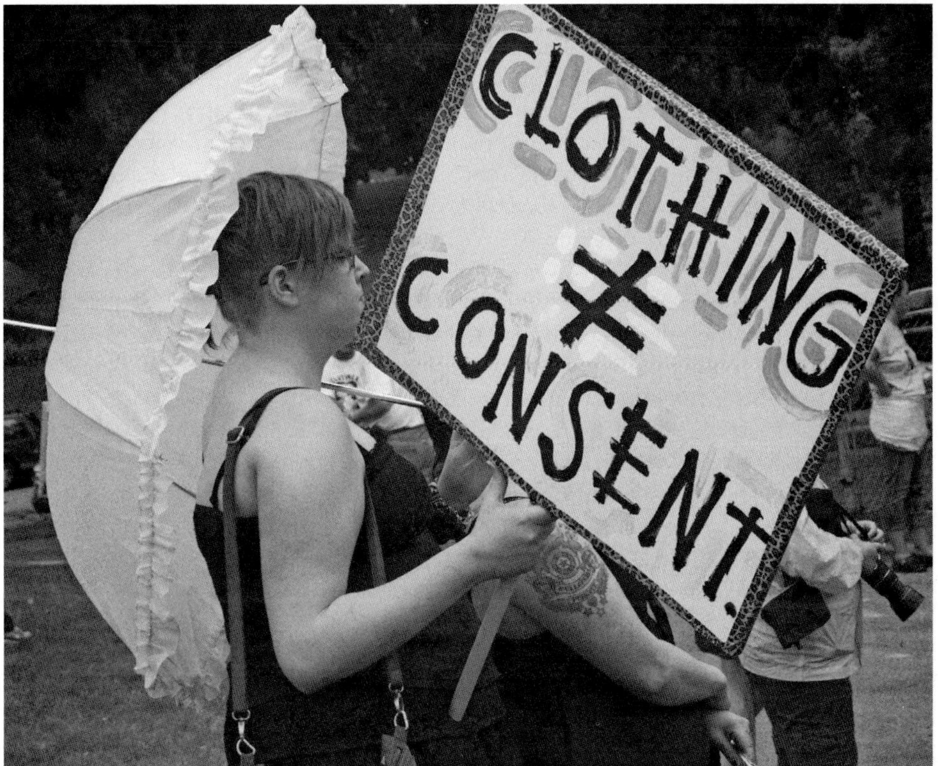

This sign protests some people's tendency to blame the victim of a sexual assault because of what she was wearing at the time. But is she responsible for the way someone else behaves?

or by wearing certain types of clothes. We often hear "blaming the victim" happening in cases of sexual violence. This is where the behaviour or outfit worn by the (typically female) victim is scrutinized to find out if the perpetrator was somehow responding to an active or passive "invitation to assault." This approach often holds a female victim responsible for the bad things that happen to her.

When "blaming the victim," people seek individualistic explanations of life experiences rather than structural explanations. Research has shown that no single variable distinguishes between women who experience sexual violence and those who do not (Moor 2009). Instead, many are calling for more research into the reasons that men sexually assault women. These reasons likely stem from society rewarding sexually dominant, aggressive male behaviour and of widespread female oppression, as opposed to women's behaviour or an outfit acting as an "invitation to assault." As early as 1975, sociologist Diana Russell theorized that sexual violence grew out of an "overconformity" to (not a deviance from) dangerous masculinity norms.

An alternate sociological theory to explain why the same people are victimized repeatedly is that they live in, work in, or visit neighbourhoods that are dangerous or violent. Per this theory, the repeated victimization is not due to a flaw in the victim but rather flaws in their social environment. The victim may be powerless to leave this environment, either for economic or social reasons.

So far, we have noted that what frames crime is socially determined, and what we think about crime doesn't always match what we know about crime. As we have seen, Canadians experience crime unequally. Some are more likely to be victimized, and victimized repeatedly, than others. For the rest of this chapter, we will expand on the third of those three points by describing some populations in Canada that are most vulnerable to victimization. As you read on, we urge you once again to bear in mind the principle of interlocking disadvantages discussed in earlier chapters.

Low-Income People in Canada

Crime studies in Canada have shown that people who live in low-income households are more likely to experience violent victimization than those in upper-income households (Perreault 2014). For Canadians living in households with annual incomes between $140,000 and $179,999, the rate of violent crime was 54 for every 1,000 people. However, for Canadians earning less than $20,000 this rate was much higher, at 79 victims for every 1,000 people.

Why do you think low-income Canadians experience increased rates of victimization and report higher levels of fear and distrust? Why are the poor residents of low-income neighbourhoods more likely to be frequent victims of certain kinds of crime and not others? Sociologists have speculated that higher rates of victimization in low-income neighbourhoods are the result of unfavourable social conditions. Let's consider some of them.

First, let's explore residential instability. As you may recall from Chapter 6, low-income Canadians are more likely to rent their homes and move often. And what we know is that crime rates are usually higher in neighbourhoods where people rent their homes (Kong 2005) and among people who have recently arrived in the neighbourhood (Savoie 2008).

So what does residential instability have to do with crime rates? As sociologist Edwin Sutherland (1947) argued way back in the 1940s, neighbourhoods with high levels of residential instability never have the chance to form close social bonds. Nobody gets to know each other long enough to share meals, lend lawn mowers, or trade childcare. The protective qualities granted by strong social bonds—the watchful eyes, the safe harbour in moments of crisis, the guardianship and loyalty provided by friends—are harder to find in places with high residential instability. In this vacuum, crime flourishes. And conversely, neighbourhoods with higher crime rates result in greater residential instability as people move to escape crime (Boggess and Hipp 2010).

The longer a person stays in a neighbourhood, the better they will know their neighbours. One study found that after one year, 4 per cent of residents in a neighbourhood reported knowing their neighbours. This edges up to 9 per cent after two to three years and 14 per cent for three to four years. Finally, over one-quarter of people report neighbourly relations after five years (Kong 2005). Figure 10.2 compares rates of residential instability among offenders and non-offenders in Saskatchewan.

A second crime-producing characteristic of low-income neighbourhoods is the lack of **socially positive opportunities**. Illegitimate (or criminal) opportunity theory posits that people are more likely to commit crimes when they have a better chance of making a living through crime than they do by non-criminal means. Communities that have fewer-than-average employment opportunities also tend to have fewer social resources like parks, community centres, and other safe and inviting places for people to congregate. Instead, they have multiple opportunities to steal, destroy, injure, and engage in other antisocial acts.

socially positive opportunities Social incentives to make a living by non-criminal means.

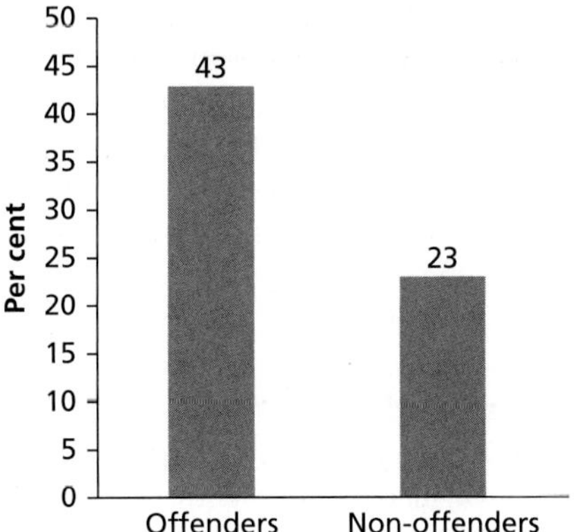

Figure 10.2 ◆ Residential Instability in Saskatchewan, 2009–10

Source: Statistics Canada 2018b.

We've noted in earlier chapters that unemployment concentrates in low-income neighbourhoods. This is because unemployed people cannot afford to live in more expensive neighbourhoods. Also, there are often few legitimate job choices in low-income neighbourhoods. For example, a grocery store that might employ 30 or 40 people is more likely to set up in a neighbourhood with a reliable customer base. It will not set up in a poor neighbourhood where people can't afford to shop. That means the low-income neighbourhood loses out on both the food choices and the jobs.

It is worth noting the population most at risk of both offending and victimization—young males aged 15–24—is also twice as likely to experience unemployment as the average Canadian (Kong 2005). As a result, there is a rough though weak correlation between unemployment rates and crime (Andresen 2012; Cantor and Land 1985; see Figure 10.3). People will usually do what they have to do to stay alive: If they are deprived of legitimate ways of making a living, they will turn to illegitimate ways.

One extreme consequence of low income is homelessness, and homeless people experience levels of victimization that are much, much higher than the average Canadian population. Why do you think this is? For one thing, homeless people do not usually have

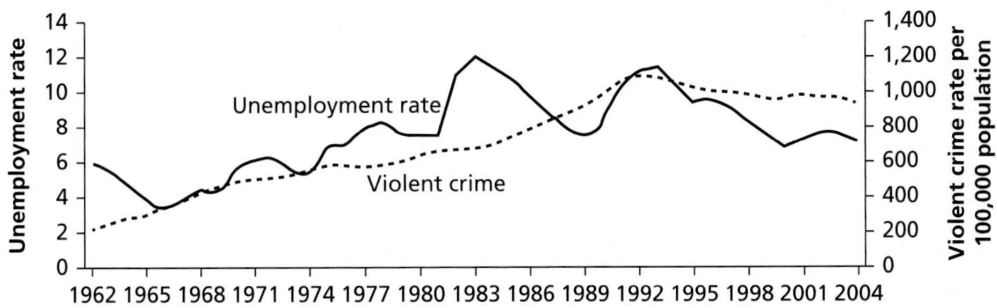

Figure 10.3 ◆ Comparison over Time in Rates of Violent Crime and Unemployment, 1962–2004

Source: Pottie Bunge and Johnson 2005.

conventional employment. Instead, they are often forced to take part in high-risk activities necessary for their survival. These might include begging, stealing, selling or transporting illegal drugs, or sex work. These jobs place people in close contact with violence and vigilante justice and often require people to spend time in unsupervised locales and form dangerous relationships.

However, the precise rates of victimization among people taking part in these high-risk activities are notoriously difficult to track. Often these incidents of victimization go unreported. Victims may fear that involving the authorities will lead to unpleasant personal results, whether it is at the hands of the law or in the exposed street environment where a perpetrator may seek retaliation.

Homeless people experience higher-than-average levels of victimization for other reasons, too. Homelessness is often correlated with other challenges, such as addiction or substance abuse, childhood victimization, previous imprisonment, or disability. These things make homeless people more prone to victimization because they have no safe place to call their own. They may also have low self-worth, poor social relationships, and may put themselves in unnecessarily risky situations. Furthermore, physical, emotional, or intellectual challenges are worsened by hunger, sleeplessness, exposure, and desperation. One study of over 200 homeless women found that "respondents reporting a history of childhood sexual abuse were four times more likely to report being sexually assaulted as adults and were [over two] times more likely to report being physically assaulted as adults" (Hudson et al. 2010).

Finally, homeless people are too often viewed as not fully human, and for that reason not fully deserving of safety or protection. This may place them on the receiving end of a random stranger's violent impulses. Researchers noted this in one UK lawsuit against three teen boys who beat a homeless man to death "on a dare" (*Huffington Post UK* 2013).

◆ In Their Own Words ◆

Some homeless people describe the harassment experienced from the public in a study by Williams and Stickley (2011):

> "They look at you when your homeless and think right you're just like a piece of shit in the gutter . . ." (Bill)
>
> "People take offence as you look dirty and just decide to beat you up because you are homeless which happens quite often now . . ." (John)
>
> "I feel like I don't have many rights . . . You're just a different citizen, a different person you're not treated like a person, you're treated like a bit of trash really . . ." (Shaun)
>
> "I have had quite a few things happen to me. I've had people throw up on me when I've been asleep, urinate on me . . ." (Jane)

This attitude that "homeless people don't matter" justifies their exclusion from standard measures of protection, and also reinforces the idea that homeless people are partially (or fully) to blame for any victimization they experience. This contempt for the homeless may lie behind the failure of the Vancouver police to adequately protect vulnerable women from serial killer Robert Pickton. Pickton evaded arrest for years but was eventually charged with the deaths of 27 women (though he admitted to killing 49).

An inquiry into the handling of Pickton's case found the RCMP did little in the early stages of their investigation to prevent further harm to women in Vancouver's downtown eastside. These women were low income, often homeless, and often racialized. The former judge who led the inquiry reported that investigating police forces treated the victims like "nobodies." "When I talk about systemic bias," he said, "I had to ask myself one question: would the reaction of the police and the public [have] been any different if the missing women had come from Vancouver's west side? The answer is obvious" (Dhillon and Bailey 2012). Many of the women who were killed by Pickton were Indigenous; we will discuss Indigenous women's vulnerability to violence later in this chapter.

Spotlight on People in Dangerous or Precarious Occupations

We have seen that victimization is not evenly distributed among Canadians and that some people are more likely to experience crime—and experience it repeatedly—than others.

There are also places where crime concentrates, like bars, airports, and tourist attractions—even private homes and institutions (especially in low-income neighbourhoods.) Sociologists call these areas **hot spots** and are curious about what makes them so. They might note, for example, that some hot spots invite more police scrutiny. This may result in more arrests, further cementing the area's criminal reputation. After all, people usually find what they're looking for only in the places they look for it!

hot spots Places where crime tends to concentrate, like bars, airports, tourist attractions—even private homes and institutions.

Workplaces are also hot spots of victimization. A Statistics Canada study (Léséleuc 2007) found that one-fifth of all incidents of violent victimization, including physical assault, sexual assault, and robbery, occurred in the victim's workplace. Seven out of 10 incidents of workplace violence were physical assaults, and men and women were equally likely to report having experienced workplace violence.

Violence in the workplace was found to be especially common in certain employment sectors. For example, one-third of all violent workplace incidents involved a victim who worked in social assistance or healthcare services, such as hospitals, nursing homes, or residential-care institutions. Victimization rates were also high among people working in accommodation (that is, hotel) or food services, retail or wholesale trade, or educational services. Other workers uniquely prone to victimization but who may not report it are those here because of temporary foreign worker programs. They include live-in caregivers or migrant agricultural workers, who fear deportation if they report abuse.

However, there is one job that is largely performed by women and carries with it the increased risk of violent victimization: sex work. In Canada, the sale of sex is legal but purchasing it is not. However, street soliciting is illegal, so most transactional communication may be hidden. Similarly, "living off the avails" (profiteering from) someone else's sex work is illegal. The purpose of these laws is to reduce exploitation and trafficking, but they also limit roles like bouncers, drivers, and bodyguards—people whose job it is to keep sex workers safe. They may also limit the protective opportunities of working together in a group.

◆ In Their Own Words ◆

Here is a testimony from Tamara O'Doherty's (2011) interviews with women in Canada's off-street sex industry. How does this account compare to those given by the homeless in Williams and Stickley's (2011) study?

> There are many different types of people in this industry and unfortunately what people think of is the darkness and the pimping and the street walking and that is where the problem is . . . It's almost as though society creates the risk because of the stigma that's attached. (Interviewee #9)

Sex workers in Canada are at a high risk of being criminally victimized, especially by physical and sexual assault. As sociologists note, sex workers spend much time in areas known for high rates of crime, increasing their risk of victimization. They also run a continuing risk of violence throughout their lives (Surratt et al. 2004). And like homeless people, attitudes that sex workers do not deserve society's protection contribute to their continued victimization.

Racialized People in Canada

hate-motivated crime Any crime motivated by bias, prejudice, or hate based on race, national or ethnic origin, language, colour, religion, sex, age, or any other similar factor.

Every once in a while, we hear about a person in Canada charged with a **hate-motivated crime**. What is a hate crime? Hate crimes may take many forms: physical assault, uttering threats, vandalism, and harassment, to name a few. Notably, a hate crime occurs when the victims are targeted "for whom they are, not because of anything they have done" (*CBC News* 2011). Hate crimes are different from other kinds of violence, however. That's because these acts make environments toxic, dangerous, and inhospitable for not just the victim but for all who share an important feature with the victim, like race, religious affiliation, ethnicity, immigration status, and so on.

Hate-motivated crimes are increasing in Canada (see Figure 10.4). In 2017, police-reported hate crimes rose by 47 per cent, with 2,073 hate-motivated crimes reported (664 more than in 2016; Statistics Canada 2018c). Nearly half of all hate-motivated crimes in 2017 resulted from the hatred of a person's race or ethnicity.

Recent surveys show that hate-motivated crimes against the Black population are the most common (Statistics Canada 2018c; see Figure 10.5). Hate-motivated crimes against LGBTQ+ people are also treading upwards and are most likely to be violent instead of property related.

racial profiling Any action taken for reasons of safety, security, or public protection that relies on stereotypes about race, colour, or other features rather than on a reasonable suspicion to single out individuals for different treatment.

Spotlight on Racial Profiling

Are you a racialized person? If so, have you ever been stopped and questioned by the police for no clear reason? You may have been the victim of a social phenomenon known as **racial profiling**. The Ontario Human Rights Commission defines racial profiling as "any action undertaken for reasons of safety, security or public protection, that relies on stereotypes about race, colour, ethnicity, ancestry, religion, or place of origin, or a combination

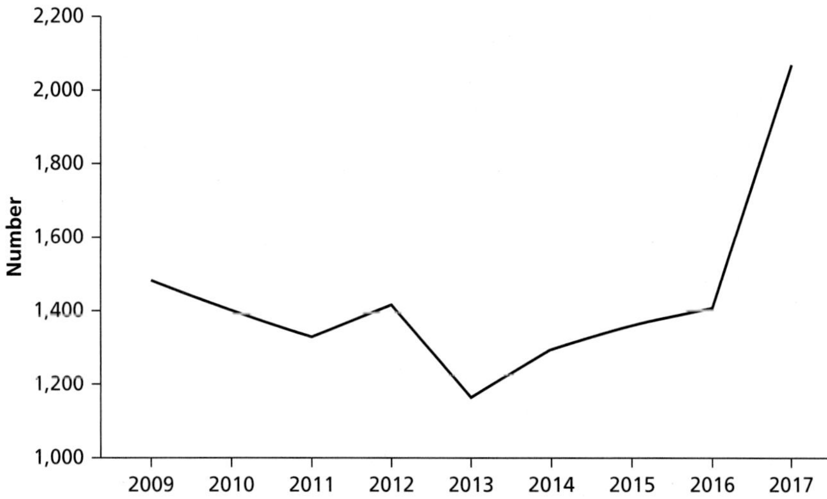

Figure 10.4 ◆ Police-Reported Hate Crimes in Canada

Source: Statistics Canada 2018c.

of these, rather than on a reasonable suspicion, to single out an individual for greater scrutiny or different treatment" (Ontario Human Rights Commission n.d.).

Racial profiling has often been alleged when police officers watch, search, or stop and question racialized people for no clear reason. A recent study in Calgary found that 96 per cent of Black respondents reported having experienced at least one incident of racial profiling in 2017 (Van Ngo et al. 2018). It also found that Black or Hispanic respondents (both at 40 per cent) were the most likely to report experiencing racial profiling six or more times during the one-year period.

Racial profiling at the hands of law enforcement is a type of victimization, and it is partly to blame for the overpenalization of racialized populations in Canada. As we've

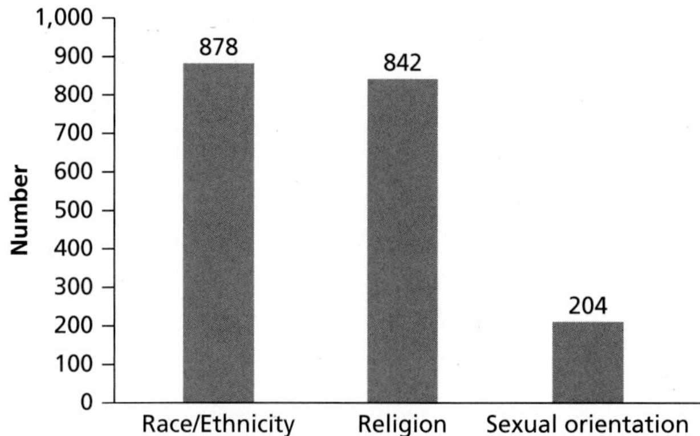

Figure 10.5 ◆ Number of Police-Reported Hate Crime According to Motivation, 2017

Source: Statistics Canada 2018c.

◆ In Their Own Words ◆

Journalist Desmond Cole reflects on what it is like to be stopped by police for being Black.

> I have been stopped, if not always carded, at least 50 times by the police in Toronto, Kingston and across southern Ontario. By now, I expect it could happen in any neighbourhood, day or night, whether I am alone or with friends. These interactions don't scare me anymore. They make me angry. Because of that unwanted scrutiny, that discriminatory surveillance, I'm a prisoner in my own city.
>
> . . . After years of being stopped by police, I've started to internalize their scrutiny. I've doubted myself, wondered if I've actually done something to provoke them. Once you're accused enough times, you begin to assume your own guilt, to stand in for your oppressor. It's exhausting to have to justify your freedoms in a supposedly free society. I don't talk about race for attention or personal gain. I would much rather write about sports or theatre or music than carding and incarceration. But I talk about race to survive. If I diminish the role my skin colour plays in my life, and in the lives of all racialized people, I can't change anything.

Source: Cole 2015.

mentioned before, people usually find what they're looking for in the places they are looking for it. If police routinely stop more Black teenagers than white teenagers, they will, for example, find more illegal drugs in the pockets of the Black teenagers. This doesn't mean white teenagers don't use drugs; it means fewer people are looking in their pockets.

Direct and indirect experiences with racial profiling can affect the way different racialized populations view racial profiling. One Toronto study found that Black people were more likely to be stopped and searched by the police. They were also more likely to have experienced racial profiling vicariously through friends and family than white or Asian people (Wortley and Owusu-Bempah 2011). This would explain why the Black respondents of the study were more likely to see racial profiling as a significant problem, whereas others were more likely to see it as a helpful instrument to fight crime.

Spotlight on Incarceration Rates of Black People in Canada

It's not only in their victimization that we see unequal experiences between Black people and other populations. Black people are overrepresented in Canadian prisons. According to the most recent available data, they account for nearly 10 per cent of the total prison population despite accounting for a mere 3 per cent of the general Canadian population. They are also the fastest growing population in the federal prison system (Sapers 2013).

IN FOCUS ◆ Black Women in Prison

In 2014, more than half of Black women in jail were there for drug charges. Take a look at this excerpt from a study commissioned by the Office of the Correctional Officer. Consider the intersections between race, poverty, and gender here.

> Many indicated that they willingly chose to carry drugs across international borders, primarily as an attempt to rise above poverty. There were some who reported having been forced into these activities with threats of violence to their children and/or families . . . Though many Black women . . . were incarcerated for drug trafficking, conviction for this type of offence does not necessarily translate into having a drug addiction or substance abuse problem.

Why do you think these women were required to complete a mandatory substance abuse program, despite any evidence of addiction or another identified therapeutic need?

Source: Office of the Correctional Investigator 2014.

Does this overrepresentation mean that Black people are committing more crimes than other people? Does this indicate racism in police surveillance and arrests? Does it reflect racist tendencies among juries and sentencing authorities? There is no single answer to these questions. In fact, it is likely a combination of several factors, such as higher crime rates (because of poverty and inequality) and prejudiced law enforcement (among police, courts, and juries).

What we know for certain is that Black people feel as though they are victims of prejudice and discrimination by the justice system. For example, in 2011–12, the Office of the Correctional Investigator (a federal agency that assesses the performance of the correctional system in Canada) conducted a study of the unique experiences of Black inmates. Nearly all the Black inmates who were interviewed for the study reported experiences of discrimination and covert racism by prison staff, such as being ignored, isolated, marginalized, and disregarded. One respondent noted that correctional officers "look right through me and say nothing. They just look right through me like I am not standing right in front of them" (Office of the Correctional Investigator 2014).

The study also revealed that Black inmates were overrepresented in "discretionary" prison charges, such as disrespecting staff and disobeying orders. Conversely, Black inmates were underrepresented in prison charges that required proof of infraction, such as a charge of being in possession of stolen property. As correctional investigator Howard Sapers (2013) notes, the experience of racial profiling "follows Black Canadians into prisons."

Young People in Canada

Younger Canadians—especially those between the ages of 15 and 18—are the most likely perpetrators of both property crimes and violent crimes in Canada. This correlation between youth and crime is displayed in an especially interesting way: As teenaged populations increase in one area, so too do crime rates. And as they decrease, crimes rates tend to correspondingly decrease (Kong 2005).

The correlation between youth and crime does not justify drawing generalizations that effectively criminalize all people under the age of 20. Rather, it means that of the small population of Canadians who commit crimes, a larger proportion of this group happens to be young. Yet being young is also a significant risk factor for being victimized.

For police-reported sexual assaults, one-quarter of victims were children aged 13 or younger, which is more than four times greater than the proportion of child victims of physical assault (Rotenberg 2017). Studies have shown that children, especially younger children, are most likely to experience this type of victimization at the hands of someone they know. In 55 per cent of sexual assault cases against children, the perpetrators were family members (Rotenberg 2017).

Just like the victimization of other people, the victimization of children takes several forms. Children can be physically and sexually assaulted, robbed, harassed, and killed. Given that young children are dependent on the care of a guardian, they are also vulnerable to maltreatment or neglect. There is suggestive evidence that patterns of child abuse, including child sexual abuse, are different for boys and girls, in biological families versus foster families, and in families of different socio-economic levels.

When we compare one generation to the next, we see that rates of reported abuse are decreasing. We also see that boys are more likely to be physically abused than girls, and that parents are the people most likely to abuse their children (Hango 2017).

The victimization of children happens in all kinds of homes, with all types of families, from all socio-economic classes. Studies have shown the younger the child, the more vulnerable they are to violence by a parent. And our data on the frequency of victimization of younger children may hide the reality. Statistics Canada reports that "younger victims are unique in that they may be unaware that they are being victimized, may not know how to seek help, may be unable to report their victimization or may be dependent on the perpetrator. Factors such as these may make their victimization more likely to be hidden and difficult to detect, particularly in the context of family violence" (Conroy 2017).

In her report on the victimization of children in Canada, researcher Lucie Ogrodnik (2010) shines the spotlight on the influence of new technology. She notes that the Internet and mobile phones have given young people new opportunities for bullying through social networking sites, online chat lines, personal webpages, emails, text messages, and the transmission of images. Unlike earlier forms of bullying, cyberbullying distributes and replicates information almost instantaneously, while protecting the anonymity of the bully.

After following a sample of Canadian Grade 5 and 6 students over the course of the year, Holfield and Leadbeater (2015) found that a minority of children reported experiencing cyberbullying or victimization—despite their high levels of access to phones and computers. The students usually did not attribute nasty motives to people making fun of others if they viewed it as "joking around." However, after a few years, the intentions and consequences of cyberbullying are clearer to students. A study of Canadian middle and high school students by Mishna (2012) found nearly one-third of the students were involved in cyberbullying as either victims or perpetrators. One in four of the students reported having been involved in cyberbullying as *both* the bully and the victim during the previous three months. Compared with traditional bullying, where victims are few and especially vulnerable, in cyberbullying the victims are many and varied. Girls are more likely than boys to be victims of cyberbullying, while the reverse is true for traditional bullying. Generally, the more hours per day a student used their computer, the more likely that student was to bully or be bullied.

Children who experience victimization suffer more than just the immediate or lingering physical and emotional effects. They may also experience long-term effects that

◆ In Their Own Words ◆

Nineteen-year-old Kestrel McNeill was bullied mercilessly—both online and on social media—during her last year of high school in Windsor, Ontario:

> My senior year of high school was the darkest time of my life . . . I suffered from severe depression, anxiety and suicidal thoughts. I was tormented and harassed. They'd mock me and tease me when I would raise my hand in class . . . I was told I needed a trip to the hospital . . . It made me feel so isolated. I started losing friends, I thought maybe it was my fault . . . what did I do to make this happen?

Source: Noseworthy 2016.

show up in emotional or psychological disorders (Abada, Hou, and Ram 2008). Some of the people who victimize others are themselves past victims—victimization can therefore produce new generations of victimizers. However, a past experience of neglect or abuse does not guarantee abusive parenting; many other factors come into play, not least of which is the role of the other parent. There are particular situations where abuse moves from one generation to the next, but such a detailed discussion is beyond the scope of this book.

Young people are victimized more often than other people in part because they are vulnerable. They have fewer resources to protect themselves than, say, their parents and other adults. At the same time, they are also likely to be victimized by other young people, and young people are likely victimizers. That is because they often have less "stake in conformity" than older people with jobs, families to care for, and mortgages to pay. As well, they often fail to assess the likely consequences of their actions; that is, with less experience under their belts, they have poorer judgment about the significance of what they are doing.

Women in Canada

Men and women experience fairly similar rates of violent crimes, but there are gender differences to be observed in the types of crimes they experience. For example, in 2017 there were 660 homicides in Canada. Three-quarters of victims were men, and a quarter were women (Statistics Canada 2018d). What makes the violent victimization of men different from that of women is of great interest to many sociologists.

And yet there are some types of crimes against women that are worthy of our attention. The first is the sheer unevenness of sexual assault. In 2017, 9 out of 10 victims of (police-reported) sexual assault were women. Nearly a third of victims were under the age of 25, and 65 per cent of victims had a business relationship with the accused. According to the 2014 General Social Survey, in that year the majority (83 per cent) of sexual assaults were not reported to police. In fact, only 5 per cent of sexual assaults were reported

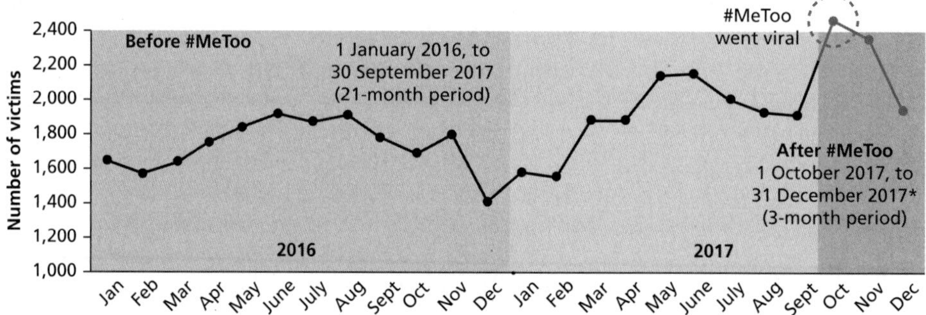

Figure 10.6 ◆ The #MeToo Movement's Influence on the Reporting of Sexual Assault

*Most recent data available

Note: Includes founded incidents only.

Source: Statistics Canada 2018a.

(Department of Justice 2019). However, the #MeToo movement (2017–18) appears to have influenced the number of women who reported their sexual victimization to the police (see Figure 10.6).

Despite the #MeToo movement's impact, there are still many women to do not report their victimization. It should also be noted that people who experienced sexual violence are also called "survivors," not "victims." This is to remind us that we all have agency, even in the face of atrocious attacks.

Sometimes, the places people consider the safest, like the home, are the most dangerous. This is especially true for many women in heterosexual spousal relationships who are victimized at the hands of their male partners. Conroy (2017) reports that in Canada, "regardless of the type of offence, girls and young women were most commonly victimized on private property and, of those who were, nearly two-thirds were victimized in their own homes."

◆ In Their Own Words ◆

It's time for society to tackle head-on the issues underpinning sexual violence against women. One way to start is for rape survivors to speak out about their experiences, [Professor Karyn] Freedman says [. . .] "It's a very difficult thing for women to come forward and identify themselves as victims of sexual violence, and for many complicated reasons. There are deeply ingrained taboos around talking about it, and many survivors struggle with feelings of embarrassment and shame, as I did. [. . .] As long as women are pressured to remain silent about their experiences, we will not get to see the problem on the scale that it is."

Source: University of Guelph 2014.

Yet our understanding of how much and what kind of domestic violence happens in Canada is incomplete. This is because many who experience it do not report it to the authorities. There are many reasons for this. For example, they may fear that their children will be removed from them or that they will have nowhere to live or no money. Or they may fear they will face more severe abuse as a form of "punishment" for disclosing their victimization to the police. They may also fear the penalty their abusive partner may face.

Both men and women report spousal victimization in the form of "threats of being hit with something, having something thrown at them that could hurt them, being pushed, grabbed or shoved or being slapped" (Kong 2005). Men are most often physically assaulted by strangers or people outside their families, but women are most likely to be victimized by someone with whom they had a current or former intimate relationship (Vaillancourt 2010). Finally, women are twice as likely to be killed by their domestic partner as men are (Hotton Mahoney 2011).

What is encouraging to note, perhaps, is that far fewer women are dying at the hands of their male partners today than 30 years ago. Researcher Tina Hotton Mahoney (2011) suggests that "[s]ome of the decline in rates of spousal homicide may be attributed to, among other factors, an increase in resources available to abused women, increased public awareness, and improvements in women's social and economic status that may enable them to leave abusive relationships at earlier stages." And yet, women are still being turned away each day from already-full shelters that could offer safe harbour from their abuser (Figure 10.7).

IN FOCUS ◆ Rural Women

Rural women living with violence share similar experiences with all women who face violence, but they face added barriers specific to living in rural areas. Consider the following:

- A rural woman may not have phone or Internet service.
- Usually no public transportation exists, so if she leaves she must take a family vehicle or find other means of transportation.
- Police and/or medical response may take a longer time.
- Rural areas have fewer resources for women, such as jobs, childcare, housing, healthcare, or shelters. Often, easy access to them is limited by distance.
- Extreme weather such as cold, snow, and mud regularly affect life in rural areas and may extend periods of isolation with an abuser;
- Poor roads or lack of roads may make transportation difficult.
- There may be no access to ferries or planes during parts of the year because of weather conditions.
- Seasonal work may regularly mean months of unemployment and result in women being trapped with an abuser for long periods.
- Hunting weapons are common to rural homes and everyday tools like axes, chains, pitchforks, and saws are potential weapons in violent situations.
- Travelling to urban areas and leaving their homes may be a barrier to rural women.

Source: Adapted from Purple Ribbon Campaign n.d.

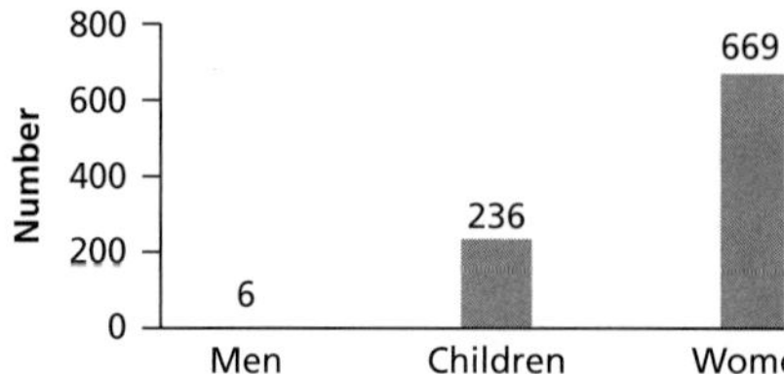

Figure 10.7 ◆ Who Was Turned Away from Canadian Shelters on a Snapshot Day in 2018?

Source: Moreau 2019.

Immigrants in Canada

As we have seen, immigrants to Canada encounter many barriers to survival capital. We've already discussed difficulties securing gainful and stable employment and the resulting vulnerability to housing and food insecurity. Many of the same attitudes that block newcomers from freely entering the workforce can also result in generalized feelings of alienation and the creation of closed-off ethnic communities. Another result is persistent discrimination in the form of widespread beliefs that immigrants are "lesser thans" who are undeserving of respect, power, protection, and safety. It would not be unreasonable—or uncommon—to think that immigrants are also vulnerable to higher rates of violent crime victimization stemming from similar discriminatory ideas. You may be surprised to learn the data do not support this conclusion. Data from the 2014 General Social Survey showed that immigrants experienced lower rates of violent victimization than the Canadian-born population. In fact, this survey showed that immigrants experience less than half as many violent crimes like sexual assault, robbery, and assault (Ibrahym 2018).

Now, let's use our sociological imaginations. Why do you think immigrants experience less violent crime victimization than the Canadian-born population? What is the usual connection between criminal behaviour and criminal victimization, and what is the known or estimated rate of criminal behaviour by immigrants? How do demographic factors affect the likelihood of criminal behaviour and victimization?

First, youth is a factor that sociologists often see associated with violent victimization. The immigrant population in Canada tends to be a little older than the Canadian-born population, making them less vulnerable to violent crime. Low income and low levels of education have also been identified as risk factors for violent victimization. It takes resources and education to immigrate to Canada, so these characteristics among immigrants might decrease vulnerability to some degree. Figure 10.8 compares rates of violent victimization of immigrants and non-immigrants. You'll note a decreasing trend over the last 10 years.

As we have already stated, there are many different types of victimization, and violent victimization is just one. So while immigrants are less likely to be victims of violent crimes, they are twice as likely than Canadian-born residents to report having been a victim of discrimination. They report this occurred when applying for a job, on the street, or in a store; those surveyed believed that this discrimination was due to their ethnic

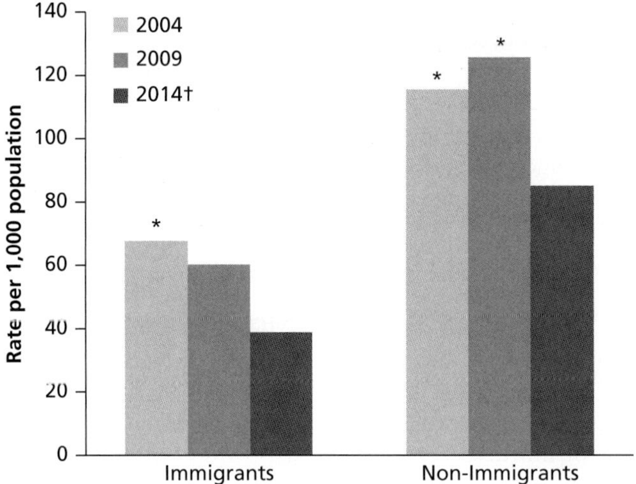

Figure 10.8 ◆ Violent Victimization Rates of Immigrants and Non-immigrants

*Significantly different from reference category ($p < 0.05$)

†Reference category

Source: Ibrahym 2018.

origin, culture, or skin colour (Ibrahym 2018). This might explain why immigrants were less likely to report feeling "very safe" when walking alone after dark, using public transportation, or when being alone in their home at night (Ibrahym 2018).

As we have seen, it is difficult to find reliable data on the victimization experienced by non-status immigrants and refugees, including undocumented workers. Their desire to remain "under the radar" of the authorities makes them less likely to report it when they have been the victim of a crime.

Many undocumented workers are here against their will. The practice of recruiting, selling, or transporting people across borders for forced labour is referred to as **human trafficking**, and it's a big problem in Canada. The victims may be children, teens, and women from poor families in the Global South. They or their families are lured with promises that better opportunities await them in Canada (or another destination). Some are kidnapped or otherwise coerced. Once arrived, victims are often stripped of their documents (both falsified and legitimate), effectively preventing them from returning home. They may be forced to work in the sex trade or other forms of high-risk labour, in factories, in commercial agriculture, or domestic work.

human trafficking
The export and import of humans—often women and children—for profitable exploitation in other countries through prostitution or slavery.

Indigenous Peoples in Canada

In Canada, overall rates for both violent and household victimization are significantly higher among Indigenous Peoples compared to non-Indigenous people. In 2014, the overall rate of violence among Indigenous Peoples was double that of non-Indigenous people. The overall rate of household victimization was more than one and a half times higher for Indigenous households than non-Indigenous households. Further, the rates of both sexual and physical assault are significantly higher for Indigenous Peoples compared with non-Indigenous people (Boyce 2016). In 2017, for example, while Indigenous Peoples made up only 5 per cent of the total population, they made up almost a quarter of homicide victims (Statistics Canada 2018d).

It is tragic, and socially dysfunctional, that Indigenous Peoples in Canada are victimized at rates that are much higher than the general population. What is also tragic is when no one seems especially concerned about it.

Spotlight on Missing and Murdered Indigenous Women and Girls

As mentioned in Chapter 2, for decades there has been evidence of an overrepresentation of Indigenous women and girls in homicide and disappearance statistics. In 2010, the Native Women's Association of Canada (2010) confirmed 582 cases since 1990. In 2013, legal researcher and civil servant Maryanne Pearce identified 824 Indigenous missing or murdered women and girls (Marks 2014). The incidents were so numerous in some parts of Canada that a stretch of road between Prince Rupert and Prince George in British Columbia was named the "Highway of Tears." In 2013, the RCMP confirmed 1,181 cases of "police-recorded incidents of Aboriginal female homicides and unresolved missing Aboriginal females between 1980 and 2012" (National Inquiry 2019).

The lack of police protection of Indigenous women and girls is often touted as a reason behind their victimization. Lorimer Shenher (2019), former Vancouver Police Department detective and lead investigator of Vancouver's missing women investigation, recalls his experience researching the victimization of Indigenous women and girls:

> I very quickly learned police officers informally categorized women as those who are "truly missing"—women and girls, usually students or working jobs, who went missing from the lives police perceive as "normal"—and those they referred to as "not actually missing." This latter group, whose motives for a sudden absence supposedly could not be assessed as sinister, due to living lives of marginalization and, in a bizarre marriage of stereotyping and flawed logic, high levels of risk for victimization by violence, unfathomably generated little concern and even less investigation from police.

Finally, in response to "mounting pressure from grassroots family members and survivors, community organizations and national Indigenous organizations, international human rights organizations, and the Truth and Reconciliation Commission of Canada" (National Inquiry 2019), a public inquiry supported by the federal government was launched in 2016—the first of its kind in Canada. Three years later, in June 2019, the final report was released. It included over 2,380 testimonials from Indigenous women and girls. This report outlines the many ways in which violence against Indigenous women and girls grows out of the historic maltreatment of Indigenous Peoples and uses a powerful word to describe that treatment: *genocide*.

Genocide is defined in the United Nations Convention on the Prevention and Punishment of the Crime of Genocide as "the deliberate and systematic destruction in whole or

◆ In Their Own Words ◆

Rebecca Moore is an I'nu woman born and raised in the Kjipuktuk district of Mi'kma'ki (so-called Halifax, Nova Scotia). She was a member of the National Family Advisory Circle for the Inquiry:

> Being an Indigenous woman means living under a society and "civilization" that benefits from your voicelessness, invisibility, disappearance, non-existence, and erasure. Because if we don't exist, then Canadians—while claiming to live an earnest and honest living—are free to steal and exploit what is rightfully ours by loosening the "Rule of Law" for themselves and tightening it to extinguish our existence and resistance.

Source: National Inquiry into Missing and Murdered Indigenous Women and Girls. 2019.

in part, of an ethnic, racial, religious or national group." This use of this term in the final report of the inquiry was notable, and some Canadians felt it didn't apply in this particular case. Others felt the opposite way. In an article for the *Globe and Mail,* Anishinaabe activist, artist, and television host Sarain Fox (2019) wrote: "All of my relatives already know this to be true because of what we've experienced. We're intimately aware of the reality that Canada doesn't want us to exist. All of the policies that govern our relationships with Canada were created with the goal (intentional or otherwise) to get us out of the way and remove us from the land."

The final report notes the many efforts and actions to undermine Indigenous women in Canada. They include trauma, social, and economic marginalization, maintaining the status quo and institutional lack of will, and ignoring the agency and expertise of Indigenous women, girls, and LGBTQ+ people. The report also issues 231 calls to justice.

Here's an important excerpt from the report:

> This genocide has been empowered by colonial structures, evidenced notably by the Indian Act, the Sixties Scoop, residential schools, and breaches of human and Inuit, Métis and First Nations rights. Taken together, they have led directly to the current increased rates of violence, death, and suicide in Indigenous populations.
>
> Settler colonialist structures enabled this genocide, which takes into account both immediate policies and actions and "the intergenerational effects of genocide, whereby the progeny of survivors also endure the sufferings caused by mass violence which they did not directly experience."

It is impossible to know precisely how many Indigenous women and girls have been murdered since the 1970s. Likely, it is in the thousands—possibly up to 4,000. While the inquiry took place, another 130 Indigenous women went missing or were murdered. As well, it is impossible to know in the cases of many missing murdered women who killed

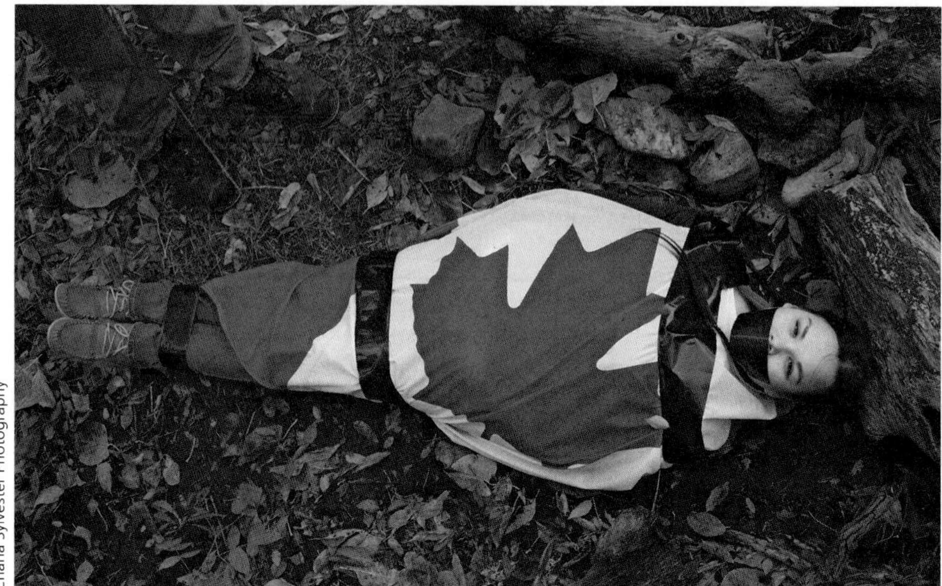
Charla Sylvester Photography

Photography student Charla Sylvester, from Beausoleil First Nation, uses her art to spotlight missing and murdered Indigenous women and girls.

or abducted these women—whether the perpetrators were Indigenous people or non-Indigenous people. The report implies a direct connection between "settler" behaviour and Indigenous murders, thus implying non-Indigenous people are responsible, but figures are not provided.

A great many factors are identified as contributing to this crisis of missing and murdered Indigenous women and girls. In Chapter 2 we considered the role of colonialism. Some commentators even suggest a connection with the climate crisis. Others point to the role of resource development projects, such as those in the oil and gas sector and the "man camps" of workers there. The report tells of the influx of transient workers with high salaries who are relatively anonymous in the community. They generally work in isolation for weeks and then "blow off steam" in nearby communities, spending money and getting drunk. These episodes are characterized by higher incidents of sexual violence and harassment of Indigenous women and girls.

Additionally, rotational shift work puts pressure on local families, increasing levels of domestic violence. Workplaces are male dominated and "hyper-masculine." Indigenous women report difficulty in securing employment in the extractive economy beyond the lowest-paid positions. This fuels gender-based income inequality, which may inhibit women from leaving abusive spouses or reporting on-the-job harassment.

Domestic violence and abusive spouses likely play a part in the story of murdered and missing Indigenous women. However, as Robert Innes (2015) points out in his analysis of this "moose on the loose," even domestic violence in Indigenous communities has a link to colonialism and the mistreatment of Indigenous Peoples in Canada.

LGBTQ+ People in Canada

In Chapter 5, you read about the unique victimization that LGBTQ+ youth face in school and how this can be a barrier to an education. In this chapter, you learned what a hate-motivated crime is. Sexual orientation, as a social characteristic deserving of protection, was included in the relevant sections of the Criminal Code only in 2003. So in 2004, Statistics Canada began, for the first time, to collect national data on the victimization rates of gay, lesbian, and bisexual people in Canada.

They find the "odds of being a victim of violent victimization [are] two times higher among lesbian, gay or bisexual Canadians than among their heterosexual counterparts" (Simpson 2018). This is true even after controlling for "other factors such as age, marital status, past history of homelessness, and childhood abuse." They are also much more likely—79 per cent compared with 2 per cent—to report that they had experienced discrimination on the basis of sexual orientation (Simpson 2018). Anti-gay, lesbian, or bisexual hate crimes also tend to be more violent in nature. And 86 per cent of victims reported that the offender was male.

Statistics Canada does not yet collect information about violence against trans people. We do know, however, that around the world trans people (particularly transwomen, who suffer from what is called **transmisogyny**) are disproportionally victims of hate-motivated crimes. Osmel Guerra Maynes, executive director of a trans-support service in British Columbia, says that this lack of representation in the data is an act of "erasure." It signals that Canadians tolerate trans people but don't really accept them or understand them (Green 2018).

transmisogyny
Prejudice against and abusive treatment of transgender women, resulting in hate crimes.

People Who Live in Residential Institutions

We often hope that large-scale institutions like prisons, schools, nursing homes, and hospitals are safe places for people who need unique care, protection, or rehabilitation. Unfortunately, this is not always the case.

As you have learned, one example of Canada's institutional history is the maltreatment of Indigenous children in the residential school system. Residential schools were established in the later 1800s to "civilize" and assimilate Indigenous children into white, Western culture. Contact with residents' family members was suppressed along with expressions of Indigenous culture (such as language and values). Residential school survivors recall frequent incidences of physical, emotional, and sexual abuse.

Recently, evidence of yet another type of abuse at residential schools for Indigenous children surfaced. For example, it has come to light the Government of Canada used over 1,300 children in residential schools as experimental subjects in a long-term study on human nutrition. The study involved intentionally depriving many children of key nutrients or dental care to observe the effects on the human body. As sociologist Erving Goffman (1961) pointed out in his classic work *Asylums*, living in a "total institution" isn't good for anyone's health, no matter how benign the founder's intentions. Few groups suffered more from their forced residence in total institutions than Indigenous children forced to attend residential schools.

◆ In Their Own Words ◆

Following the news that Indigenous children living in residential schools were the subjects of cruel nutritional experiments, Shawn Atleo (2013), former National Chief of the Assembly of First Nations, responded publicly in the Globe and Mail:

> My father attended one of the schools where these experiments took place. My family and countless others were treated like lab rats, some even being deprived of necessary nutrition and health care so researchers could establish a "baseline" to measure the effects of food and diet. The experiments are part of a long, sad pattern of federal policy that stretches through residential schools, forced relocations and the ultimate social experiment, the Indian Act, which overnight tried to displace ways of life that had been in place for generations. All of these experiments are abject failures.

The societal beliefs that permitted these experiments include notions that Indigenous Peoples are not fully human, not capable of self-determination, and not deserving of safety and protection. Such beliefs, if they persist today, would contribute to the overrepresentation of Indigenous Peoples in both victimization statistics and prison populations.

There is another institutionalized population that is uniquely vulnerable to victimization in Canada: people diagnosed with intellectual disabilities who live in residential institutions. These institutions are not as common as they once were. In the past, they housed children and adults who were deemed unfit to live independently or needed care that family members were unwilling or incapable of providing.

In 2010, former residents of the Huronia Regional Centre filed a class-action lawsuit. The centre, a residential institution for people—mostly children—with intellectual disabilities, operated in Orillia, Ontario, from 1945 to 2009. The plaintiffs in the suit described repeated, daily, long-term physical, emotional, and sexual abuse at the hands of the institutions' employees. These were the people whose very job it was to keep them safe and promote their healthy growth and development. On 17 September 2013, the government of Ontario avoided court by reaching a $35 million settlement with the former residents of the Huronia Regional Centre. Each of them was eligible for individual payouts of up to $42,000 (*CBC News* 2013). The Huronia Regional Centre is just one example of residential institutionalization in Canada. However, health historians Clarkson and Rossiter (2013) note this case is typical of the treatment of residents of institutions throughout Ontario.

When people are poor, subject to official profiling, and unable to get good legal representation, they are more likely to end up in prison—another type of total institution. So we will briefly discuss the prison risks of vulnerable people in our society. Incarceration

IN FOCUS ◆ The Moose Hide Campaign

In 2011, Cindy Gladue, a 36-year-old Indigenous woman, died from a laceration in her vagina. The man responsible admitted to his actions but said he didn't intend to kill her. The jury found him not guilty of murder.

Many were shocked by the outcome of Gladue's trial. Protests soon followed the news that Gladue's killer would walk free. Many saw this trial as one more example of the dehumanizing treatment of Indigenous victims of violence. As scholar and Indigenous advocate Dr Sarah Hunt and Naomi Sayers (2015) put it, Gladue's sex work experience was made "the origin of the violence she faced instead of placing fault in the violent actions of the assailant."

All too often, women—and particularly Indigenous women—are blamed for inviting violence into their lives. Simultaneously, Indigenous women are expected to head up the initiatives to end this violence. Too rarely are men—almost always the source of violence—made central in these conversations.

One Indigenous-led initiative is seeking to change this conversation: the Moose Hide Campaign. This initiative, started in 2011 by Paul Lacerte, calls on men to take action against the violent victimization of Indigenous women. The campaign has spread across the country and culminates every year in a gathering in Victoria. This initiative joins the actions by men of other backgrounds across the country who are calling for an end to violence against women.

The Moose Hide Campaign names residential schools, racism against Indigenous Peoples, and colonization as contributing factors in violence against women.

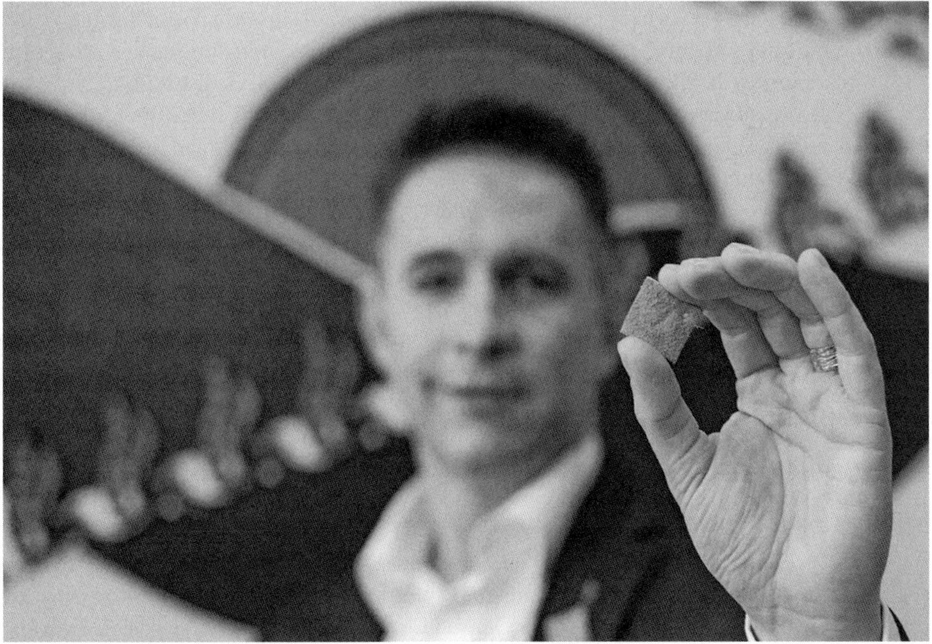

Arnold Lim

Paul Lacerte, founder of the Moose Hide Campaign, holds a moose hide square that signifies an effort to raise awareness against violence toward Indigenous women and children.

(or imprisonment) rates for some populations in Canada dramatically exceed their representation in the general Canadian population. Here are some examples:

- Black inmates account for approximately 10 per cent of the overall inmate population, and yet they represent only 3 per cent of the general Canadian population (Sapers 2012).
- Indigenous Peoples make up 5 per cent of Canada's population but about 20 per cent of the prison inmate population (Statistics Canada 2006). Regardless of sex, the proportion of Indigenous offenders incarcerated is substantially higher than that of non-Indigenous offenders. Regardless of the type of release, the proportion of Indigenous offenders who were granted parole is substantially lower than that of non-Indigenous adult offenders (Canadian Human Rights Commission 2010).

Earlier in this chapter, we pointed to research that suggests victims can become victimizers. One survey, for example, found that 85 per cent of incarcerated women in Canada reported a history of physical abuse and 68 per cent reported a history of sexual abuse (MacCharles 2012).

We also see a much higher-than-average number of people struggling with mental illness or addictions in prison. This number is on the increase as the amount of alternative community support services decline. Many—indeed, most—prisons do not have the support services to aid these people. In many cases, prison itself and its living conditions (for example, segregation units) can create or exacerbate mental illness.

Prisons, not surprisingly, are especially dangerous places for violent victimization. Prisoners are at particular risk of physical assault by other inmates, as well as theft of personal property. Common offences against prisoners include assault, robbery, threats of violence, theft from cells, and verbal abuse. For example, from 2005 to 2010, "the number of inmate assaults involving a maximum security woman at the five regional facilities has fluctuated between 5 and 23 per year, reaching its peak in 2009–2010" (Sapers 2012).

If you found yourself in prison, the most obvious effect this would have on your life is the loss of personal freedom. And yet another significant consequence is the loss of your voice; the shrinking likelihood that anybody will listen to you should you need to be heard. For this reason, it's difficult to know how common victimization in prisons is. However, in June 2012, Ontario Ombudsman André Marin released a report documenting abuses at the hands of correctional officers. "This report is not pretty," Marin noted in an interview. "It reveals some shocking stories—not just of violence within the provincial correctional system but of ugly conspiracies to cover up that violence" (Perkel 2011). The report describes several extreme instances of abuse. One involved an inmate code-named "Colin" who was restrained by six officers with handcuffs and leg restraints, then beaten "to a pulp, leaving his head swollen, his face and body battered" (Perkel 2011).

Marin's report supports fears that incidents of force might be swept under the carpet. He described that in the incident involving "Colin," guards "initially claimed the prisoner hit his head on the floor." The culture of silence among prison staff prevents the authorities—and the public—from having full knowledge of the scope of prisoner victimization. Marin's research "exposes corruption and a malignancy within the correctional system that has long been lamented but never eradicated: the code of silence" (Perkel 2011).

Crime as a Consequence of Inequality and the Consequences of Crime

What we have seen so far from this chapter is that the effects of crime are felt unequally, meaning some populations in Canada are more vulnerable to victimization and repeated victimization. Everyone experiences victimization differently, and it's virtually impossible to precisely measure the full physical, emotional, and financial dimensions of victimization in Canada. And yet we know that when a person or population is victimized, they are held back, pushed down, and further distanced from the life chances that support health and happiness. In this way, crime worsens inequality.

It's a vicious cycle, because crime and victimization is also the *result* of inequality. British researcher Richard Wilkinson (Wilkinson and Pickett 2009) shows that countries with greater inequality experience higher rates of violent crime. For example, he points out that more unequal countries have five times more murder than more-equal countries. Take a look at Figure 10.9. Compare the homicide rates of the United States, a country with a high level of income inequality, with Japan, a country with low levels. You'll note that Japan has a much lower homicide rate.

Wilkinson suggests that crime results from inequality because in unequal societies people lose trust in each other. The huge gap in living standards and lifestyles means that people are competing against one another for positions "at the top." Just like the data on

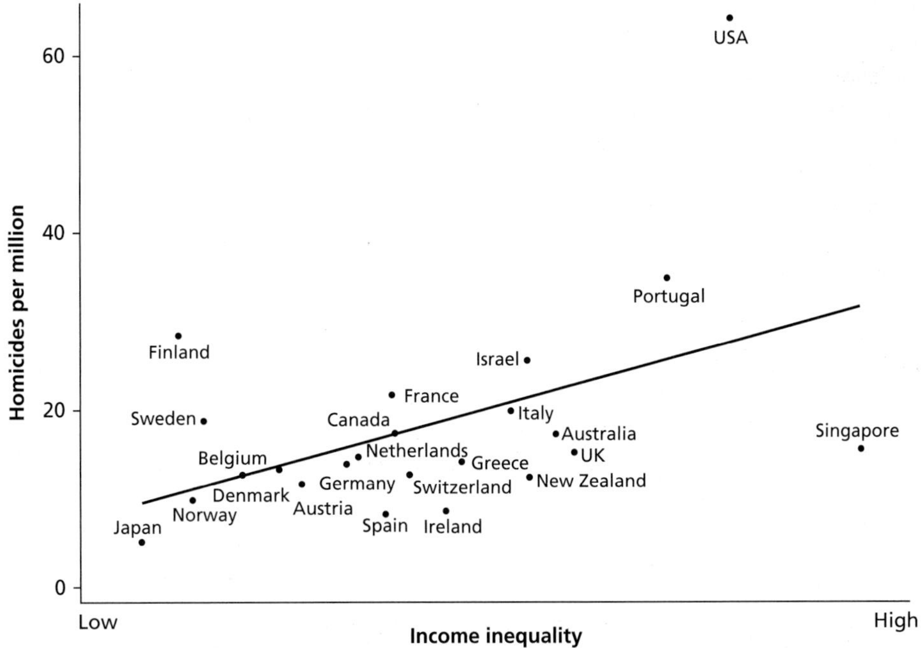

Figure 10.9 ◆ Homicide Rates and Income Inequality: Selected Countries

Source: Wilkinson and Pickett 2009.

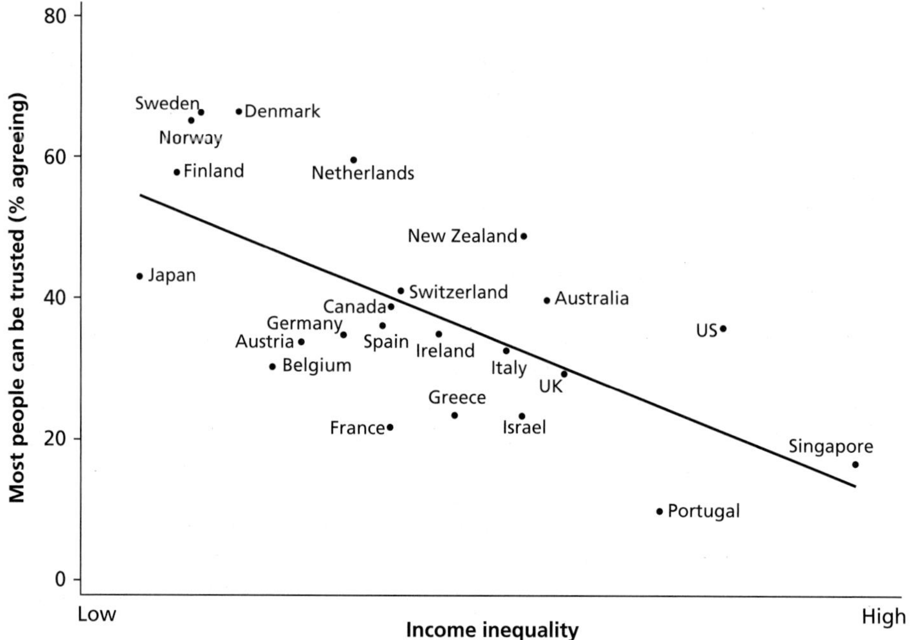

Figure 10.10 ◆ Correlations between Income Inequality and Interpersonal Trust, OECD Countries

Source: Wilkinson and Pickett 2009.

crime rates, we see that countries with higher levels of inequality also demonstrate low levels of trust (see Figure 10.10). What this means is that there appears to be some connection between trust, crime, and inequality.

Higher crime rates mean more people committing crime and more people being punished for their crimes (and punishments may be erroneous or excessive). The more crimes that are being committed, the more vulnerable everyone is to being victimized—and the more they may fear victimization. And finally, life is more difficult in a society where no one trusts each other. General social interactions are at best disrupted and at worst impossible when everyone lives in fear. This affects everyone in society.

◆◆ Notable Thinkers ◆◆

Rosemary Gartner

Rosemary Gartner is a professor emerita of criminology at the University of Toronto.

Much of Gartner's work has revealed important insights about women and their experiences of crime. In her 2008 paper, "Female Violent Offenders: Moral Panics or More Serious Offenders?" (Kruttschnitt and Gartner 2008), she studies whether and how the crimes committed by incarcerated females have changed in 40 years. They find that female offenders have not become more dangerous over time, contrary to popular belief. What has changed are certain characteristics of female crime.

For example, women are now more likely to act with an accomplice when committing violent crime or use a gun when committing homicide. Their crimes are also more motivated by the goal of obtaining money or drugs than they were in the past. One consistency over time, however, is the types of victims in homicides by women. Females most often commit homicide against their intimate partners.

Gartner has also examined how interpersonal violence has evolved in human history. Her article "Historical Patterns in Interpersonal Violence" (2011) combines the input of a number of scholars to trace the changes in interpersonal violence over centuries. They find that men have always accounted for a greater proportion of victims and perpetrators of violence and that one cause of interpersonal violence has been competition for scarce resources. Gartner notes that there has been a long-term decrease in interpersonal violence rather than an increase. She attributes this, in part, to the growth of institutions in society—with these institutions regulating violence, fewer people are willing or able to commit violent crime.

Strategies of Resistance

Government-Level Strategies of Resistance

In 2002, Bill C-24 came into effect. It officially defined the term "criminal organization" to help identify gang and youth gang problems in Canada. The bill also classified social situations that do and do not constitute a criminal organization or gang.

Following the lead of this bill and the recent emergence of youth and street gangs, the Halifax police and Nova Scotia Department of Justice (n.d.) partnered in devising a plan for gang prevention. A resource published by the initiative notes that street gang members can come from any social background and that street gang activity is driven by nothing deeper than a desire for profit and power.

The guide also discussed possible gang markers, but stressed that clothing and fashion markers are not a good way to identify gang members as these can often correspond to widespread fashion trends. A list of traits common to gang members is also provided in this pamphlet, which revealed the systematic nature of gang mentality. Traits included poverty, experience of domestic violence and substance use in the home, lack of family and community support, and a history of criminal activity in the family. This resource stressed working together with struggling families, teaching multicultural awareness and tolerance, and being an ally in general.

This approach to gang prevention avoids unnecessary violence and confrontation that could lead to the unfortunate imprisonment of troubled youth. Furthermore, it acknowledges gangs and gang violence as a systematic issue that involves police, school, and families.

Organization-Level Strategies of Resistance

In the summer of 2013, questions of racial tensions and the use of lethal force by police were raised when 18-year-old Sammy Yatim was fatally shot nine times and tasered on an empty streetcar in Toronto.

Through eyewitness statements and video shot with smartphones it was learned that Yatim exposed himself to others on the streetcar while brandishing a three-inch knife. Yatim ordered alarmed streetcar riders to first stay on the tram; then, allegedly in a confused state, ordered them to get off the tram. Police intervened in the situation. Several cellphone videos have shown that after warning Yatim not to come any closer, three shots were fired at him, causing Yatim to fall to the floor of the tram. Despite this, Yatim was shot at six more times, suffering a total of eight gunshot wounds, and was then tasered (Mahoney 2013).

The public responded with outrage and bewilderment at the seemingly disproportionately violent response of Toronto Police Constable James Forcillo. Multiple rallies, marches, and protests were held demanding "Justice for Sammy." Yet in 2016 Constable Forcillo was found not guilty of second-degree murder; instead, he was found guilty of attempted murder and sentenced to six years in prison.

Immediately after Forcillo shot Yatim, the Urban Alliance on Race Relations reminded Toronto of similar situations from the not so distant past, where police shot racialized mentally ill men without sufficient reason (Pieters and Goossen 2013). In June 2000,

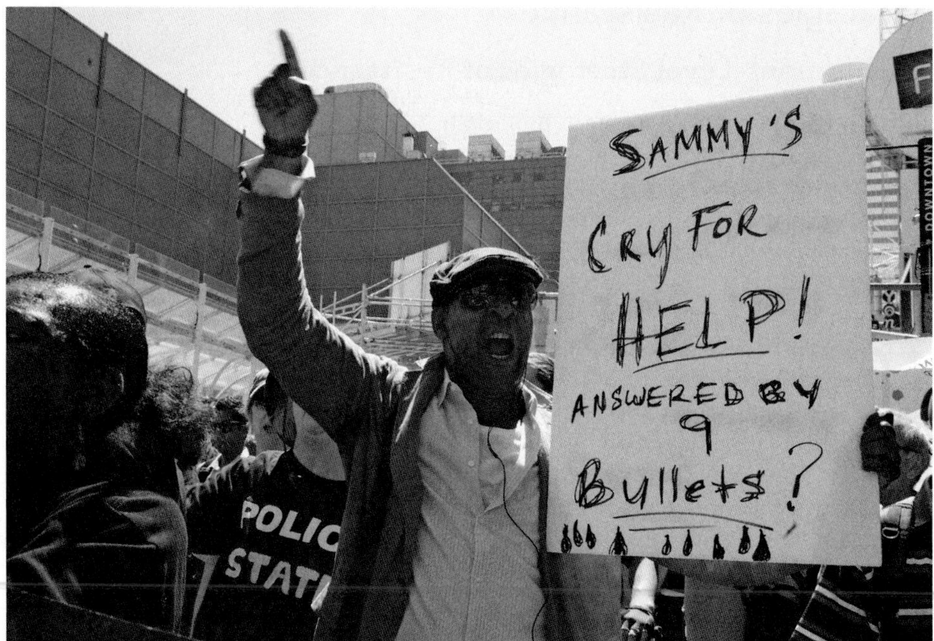

Victor Biro/Alamy Live News

Following the death of Sammy Yatim, marching protestors in downtown Toronto called for reform of the way police use force, particularly against young Black offenders.

in response to recent police shootings of Lester Donaldson and Edmond Yu, the Urban Alliance on Race Relations collaborated with the Queen Street Patients Council to address this problem with a conference entitled "Saving Lives: Alternatives to the Use of Lethal Force by Police." From this conference a report was developed that recommended officer training in the use of non-lethal technology to diffuse high-stress situations such as tasers and pepper spray (Pieters and Goossen 2013).

From these and similar cases, it seems clear that police in many cities have not yet been trained in ways to deal non-violently with people in distress, and especially people in distress who are also marginalized.

Individual-Level Strategies of Resistance

What can individual people do to fight for their rights to safety from violence? One example of an individual-level strategy of resistance is the case of *Jane Doe v. Metropolitan Toronto Commissioners of Police.*

In 1986, a serial rapist known as the "Balcony Rapist" was at large in Toronto. The man, later identified as Paul Callow, victimized five Toronto women in their low-rise apartments all in the same neighbourhood by entering through their unlocked balcony doors (Savino and Turvey 2011, SGM Law 2015). Callow's fifth and final victim is known only as Jane Doe. When she discovered that the police had known of a serial rapist in the area prior to her attack, she launched a suit at the Board of Commissioners of Police. Doe claimed the police had failed to take the testimonies of other victims seriously. They had also failed to warn other women in the community once they had determined the existence of an active serial rapist.

In 1998, Jane Doe's triple lawsuit was successful and the Board of Commissioners of Police was found to have been negligent and in violation of Doe's Charter rights to equality. It has also infringed on Doe's right to security of the person (Savino and Turvey 2011, SGM Law 2015). The Toronto police had failed to secure the safety of Toronto women by failing to take claims of sexual assault and rape seriously in investigating such claims. As well, the police failed all the female citizens of Toronto in assuming they would only react in panic and hysteria if warned of a perpetrator in their area. For this reason, they were required to offer a formal public apology.

Jane Doe's win was a massive victory for all sexual assault survivors in Canada; it raised the public's expectations for how the Ontario Provincial Police should respond to rape claims in the future. Doe's story sparked discussion about rape culture in Canada—an environment that blames victims for being raped instead of rapists for raping. In a speech she gave in 2003, Doe also proposed that had she been a member of a marginalized group, her claims likely would have received an even worse response: "Horrifying as it is, imagine for the poor woman who is raped who is Black, lesbian, disabled, drunk, a prostitute. They wouldn't be treated the same" (McCooey 2003).

Today, the federal Department of Justice (2017) reports that 83 per cent of sexual assaults are not reported to police. The *Doe* case suggests police have been often—perhaps usually—remiss in protecting women from the dangers of assault. So if the previous paragraphs suggest optimism can be drawn from the legacy of the *Doe* case, then this statistic undercuts it somewhat.

Closing Remarks

We have seen in this chapter that some people are victims of crime; in large part, this victimization is due to criminal behaviour, which is (in part) a result of social inequality. It also reflects inadequate access to legal protection, which is another result of unequal access to a vital form of survival capital: safety.

As Émile Durkheim (1895) suggested in an early essay on the "normality of crime," we can be victimized by too little social order (as crime-ridden communities show) or by too much social order (as the Spanish Inquisition showed). In neither instance is the problem that human beings are naturally bad; rather, it is that some forms of social organization are better than others for preventing victimization.

It is no wonder, then, that debate continues about control and punishment, about whether to tolerate deviance we cannot control or try to eliminate it through harsh, if usually ineffective, means. Briefly, the debate is about harm reduction versus standing on principle. Some would argue that we should make every effort, through laws and punishments, to show our disapproval of crime and other rule breaking. In other words, we must stand on principle to see that wrong is punished, even if these laws and punishments fail to achieve the desired result or deter further crime.

Others would argue that proposed harm-reduction strategies, such as the decriminalization and legalization of some offences, are preferable. They would reduce the danger to society—reduce victimization—and reduce recidivism among violators. These strategies will not appear as principled as strict rules and harsh punishments, but they can be more effective.

The job of sociologists who study deviance, crime, and control is to understand our society's needs and goals and to think clearly about how these might be satisfied legally. Equally, however, we must recognize that crime and victimization are, in large part, inevitable results of social inequality. We might do well to address the problem of inequality if we are to reduce the extent of victimization.

Test Your Knowledge

1. What is the hierarchy of victimization? Who is at the bottom of the hierarchy?
2. According to Edwin Sutherland (1947), how does residential instability affect crime rates?
3. Why are undocumented workers less likely to report experiences of victimization?
4. What are hate-motivated crimes, and which populations experience them most frequently?
5. True or false: The crime rate in Canada is increasing.
6. True or false: Immigrants are vulnerable to higher rates of violent crime victimization stemming from discriminatory ideas.
7. True or false: The victims of human trafficking in Canada tend to be children, teens, and women from poor families in the Global South.

8. True or false: Men and women experience fairly similar rates of violent crimes, but there are gender differences to be observed in the types of crimes they experience.
9. Match the theoretical perspective with its main points:

Theoretical Perspective	Main Points
1. Social disorganization theory	a. Crime is normal, universal, and unavoidable.
2. Social constructionist perspective	b. The gap between what people want and what they can get by legitimate means leads people to commit crime.
3. Conflict theory	c. The ways people, through simple association, are socialized into their criminal environment and reproduce the prevailing order affect criminal activity.
4. Functionalist perspective	d. Rapid social change leads to a breakdown in social norms and social integration, which results in crime.
5. Differential association theory	e. No behaviours are inherently right or wrong; they become wrong, deviant, or criminal only when someone in power attaches a moral label to them.
6. Strain theory	f. As inequality increases in a society, crime will also increase; those most subject to inequality are most likely to commit crimes.

See the Answer Key online to check your answers.

Questions for Critical Thought

1. What can be done to debunk the common misconceptions about crime and victimization? What community-level and national-level strategies might dismiss these myths?
2. What role does poverty play in producing crime? Brainstorm methods that a society might use to counter the effects of poverty on crime.
3. How does one's lifestyle affect their risk of victimization? What changes can be made by the government to reduce these risks?
4. What effect does gender have on unequal access to safety? Do you think crimes like domestic violence and sexual assault will continue to be gendered? Why or why not?
5. Which of the theoretical perspectives on unequal access to safety do you subscribe to? Can you relate any of these perspectives to real-life experiences?

Additional Resources

Recommended Readings

Agnew, R. and T. Brezina. 2019. "General Strain Theory." Pp 145–60 in *Handbook on Crime and Deviance*, edited by M.D. Krosh, A.J. Lizotte, and G.P. Hall. Switzerland: Springer. Derived from Merton's earlier strain theory, general strain theory specifies the major types of strains, identifies the types of strains that are most likely to cause crime, explains why these strains cause crime, and explains why only some strained individuals resort to criminal coping.

Akers, R. 2017. *Social Learning and Social Structure: A General Theory of Crime and Deviance*. New York: Routledge. Provides an overview of Akers's social learning theory, including its theoretical foundations and four central explanatory concepts of differential association, definitions, differential reinforcement, and imitation. An elaboration of Sutherland's earlier theory of differential association.

Bittle, S., L. Snider, S. Tombs, and D. Whyte. 2018. *Revisiting Crimes of the Powerful: Marxism, Crime and Deviance*. New York: Routledge. This book traces the evolution of research on crimes of the powerful since 1976, showing how critical scholars have integrated new theoretical insights derived from post-structuralism, feminism, and critical race studies.

Finkelhor, David. 2008. *Childhood Victimization: Violence, Crime, and Abuse in the Lives of Young People*. New York: Oxford University Press. This book explains the experiences, prevention, and treatment of juvenile victims by tracing the effects of victimization over the course of childhood. It discusses the categorizations of childhood victimizations as well as the risks and impacts of victimization on juveniles and their families.

Meloy, Michelle L. and Susan L. Miller. 2010. *The Victimization of Women: Law, Policies, and Politics*. New York: Oxford University Press. This book analyzes research on victimization, violence, and victim politics affecting women. It offers a historical look at violence against women, as well as responses from the media, social services, and the legal justice system.

Wortley, Scot. 2009. "The Immigration–Crime Connection: Competing Theoretical Perspectives," *Journal of International Migration and Integration* 10(4):349–58. This article discusses four theoretical models to view the immigration–crime connection and their corresponding policy implications.

Recommended Websites

Canadian Resource Centre for Victims of Crime

http://crcvc.ca

This resource centre is a national, non-governmental agency that advocates for victims of serious crime. This website informs victims of the rights, services, and financial assistance available to them in their province or territory, as well as crime prevention strategies.

Children and Youth Crime Prevention Through Social Development

www.ccsd.ca/resources/CrimePrevention/index.htm

This organization aims to promote well-being through measures that address the social, health, and educational factors affecting children and youth crime. This site outlines possible social challenges, social interventions, and policies for crime prevention.

Office of the Federal Ombudsman for Victims of Crime

www.victimsfirst.gc.ca/index.html

The Office of the Federal Ombudsman works to ensure that the responsibilities of the federal government to victims of crime are met. This website provides information on federal services available to victims and advice on navigating the criminal justice system.

Public Safety Canada
www.publicsafety.gc.ca

The purpose of this website is to promote safety at both the national and community levels in Canada. Included are a list of strategies to counter crime and related publications and reports on the subject.

Recommended Films

Not in Our Town: Light in the Darkness. 2011. Produced by Patrice O'Neill. United States: The Working Group. This one hour PBS documentary spotlights a town in New York uniting against anti-immigrant violence in their community. The film follows the brother of a hate crime victim as he and other community residents examine the causes of and steps to prevent hate crime.

Shawn Goldberg/Shutterstock

11 Respect and the Reproduction of Inequality in Popular Discourse

Learning Objectives

- To differentiate theoretical perspectives on respect and inequality.
- To explain how lack of respect or status can worsen marginalization.
- To compare and contrast the effects of erasure, stereotyping, and representation in popular media.
- To identify gender scripts in everyday life and how they influence our behaviour.
- To critically apply the idea of "othering" and name the conscious or unconscious use of this process to bolster power structures.
- To recognize the importance of discourse in shaping our view of the world.
- To identify approaches to increasing respect for all people in society.

Introduction

This chapter is different from the others because it proposes there is a non-tangible type of survival capital: respect.

When we think of what we need to live long, happy, healthy lives, we think of food, water, clothing, shelter, and medicine. And these types of survival capital are critical. As we have seen in the previous chapters, these resources are not equally accessible or available in Canada, and this is a significant social problem. Compromised access to this survival capital can dramatically affect people's life chances. It can decrease their opportunities, make them sick and unhappy, and shorten their lives. Similarly, disrespect can harm people socially, psychologically, economically, and culturally. We have already seen some evidence of this.

In Chapter 8, we mentioned cultural appearance norms (the "ideal way" that someone should look) and the socially constructed nature of beauty "standards." We noted that women often feel the pressure of these norms more than men do and can react to in extreme ways (developing eating disorders, for example). This pressure stems in part from the mass media, which dictate appearance norms. These norms affect how people see themselves and others. Often, people whose appearance falls outside the norm have poor self-esteem and are subject to disrespect and psychological and emotional abuse from others. So the way the mass media represent populations, especially vulnerable ones, can have deep, lasting effects on their well-being.

We also learned about psychological abuse emerging from a lack of respect in earlier chapters. In Chapter 5 we looked at the effect of residential schools on Indigenous Peoples in Canada. We saw how the trauma from residential schools, which were the product of a fundamental lack of respect for Indigenous Peoples and their culture, has had long-lasting effects on survivors and their communities. These effects are common for most children who have been psychologically abused; abuse reduces life chances and continues to affect victims well into adulthood. For all these reasons, sociologists argue that psychological abuse stemming from a lack of respect is not an isolated, individual problem. Instead, it is one that negatively affects society as a whole.

In 1943, psychologist Abraham Maslow first put forward his theory of human needs and motivations called **stage theory**. It was in this theory that he highlighted the importance of respect for human development. The theory's underlying assumption is that people cannot develop healthily and satisfy higher needs until they have fully satisfied lower-level needs. Maslow put these needs into a hierarchy based on the stages that people move through when developing. Within **Maslow's hierarchy of needs**, people must first satisfy their physiological and safety needs (such as food, shelter, and stability) before fulfilling self-esteem and self-actualization needs (such as respect and creativity; see Figure 11.1).

The fourth level in Maslow's hierarchy of needs—self-esteem—is the one that interests us most in this chapter. This is the stage where people satisfy their need for appreciation, respect, esteem, and approval. They are motivated by a need to feel that they are valued by and valuable to other people. Those in the fourth stage try to satisfy this need by taking part in various activities: as members of a team, a profession, a community, a family, or even through personal hobbies.

Those who successfully gain self-esteem, respect, and the approval of others feel good enough about themselves to crave for or strive for the next and final stage: the search for

stage theory Human cognitive and social development follows a pattern of successive stages. Each stage is characterized by specific needs that must be satisfied before an individual can progress to the higher levels of development.

Maslow's hierarchy of needs A psychological theory developed by Abraham Maslow that organizes human needs in rising stages. His theory suggests that more basic needs must be met before an individual will crave for or strive to satisfy higher-level needs.

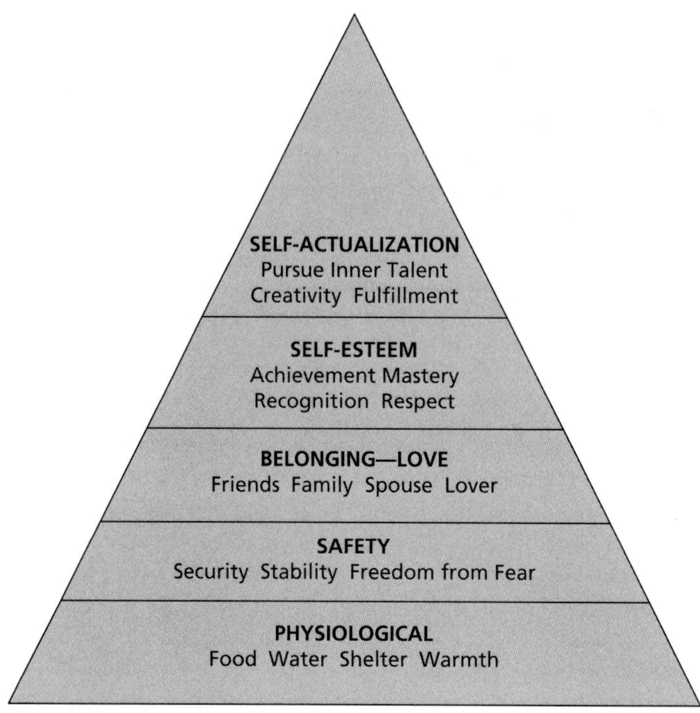

Figure 11.1 ◆ Maslow's Hierarchy of Needs

self-actualization. Those who fail to achieve self-esteem develop feelings of inferiority and often remain stuck at level four. In short, they cannot gain a full sense of self.

Studying respect and how it is distributed is worthwhile in a book about inequality. For one thing, disrespect has an immediate effect on the disrespected person; they feel slighted, hurt, or defeated. As well, a lack of respect for particular categories of people helps produce and reproduce degrading messages. These messages work to justify and therefore prolong their maltreatment, their systemic exclusion, or their compromised access to other types of survival capital.

Theoretical Perspectives on Respect and Inequality

There are different theoretical perspectives on the issue of unequal access to respect. Functionalists focus on the functionality, or social value, of unequal access to respect. They argue that depriving people of the money, authority, and respect they want makes these rewards more valuable and desirable. As a result, people gain more education and work harder to get these rewards, which benefits all of society.

Yet there are different kinds of "respect" in our society, and they cannot all be accessed through study and hard work. Someone cannot work or study hard enough to be considered beautiful by social standards, for example. Conflict theorists see unequal access to respect as the result of efforts by the wealthy and powerful to deny others the respect they covet. They alone, not society as a whole, benefit from the unequal access to respect. They take advantage of this inequality by basking in the fame, prestige, and public esteem the mass media provide to them. They operationalize the disrespect of others to strengthen their grip on power and resources by defining themselves as more naturally worthy of respect and pointing to others' failure to live up to their standard as evidence.

As conflict theorists know, this unequal access to respect has social results. It affects people's self-esteem and, in turn, their motivation to work hard and strive for acceptance. At the extreme, it results in what Marx, in his critique of capitalism, called "alienation." This is a feeling of distance from oneself, one's activities, one's colleagues, and humanity in general. Thus, the denial of respect can be destructive for both individuals and society as a whole.

Sociologists who take the symbolic interactionist approach focus on face-to-face exchanges in which people seek and receive respect. They study conversations and interactions between people of different social status and note how people in superior positions respond to displays of respect and disrespect. Those who study a social phenomenon called *stereotype threat* have found that people who believe they have been labelled as "deviants" are more likely to act antisocially.

As young people are the first to notice, shows of respect and disrespect can be subtle, and sometimes even unintentional. The way someone talks, together with their body language, words, and actions, can all demonstrate disrespect. Some people master speaking and behaving in disrespectful ways while obeying the rules of visible politeness. Consider a teacher overly praising a racialized student for their work; in this case, disrespect comes from the racist presumption that racialized students are not as high achieving as white students.

Defining Our Terms

But what do we mean by respect, esteem, and approval? The *Oxford Dictionary of Philosophy* states that respect forbids "treating a person as a mere means to an end" or "ignoring their personhood or their humanity." In other words, people are disrespected when they are treated as someone who is lesser than another.

In addition to being non-tangible, respect (also esteem and approval) is different from the other types of survival capital in that, at least in theory, respect is unlimited. There may be limited amounts of housing, employment, and nutritious food in some parts of Canada, and this means that when some people have more, others must have less. Respect isn't like that; there can always be more than enough to go around. And yet still it may be scarce.

People are disrespected in many places: their workplaces, their places of worship, their classrooms, and even the privacy of their bedrooms. In this chapter, however, we explore disrespect in popular discourse. The term **discourse** means "conversation." But sociologists (and others) include more than just spoken words when using the term. Works of art, photography, film, and even dance can be a form of conversation. When we qualify the term by adding "popular," we have in mind conversations and messages that are readily available and widely distributed—messages you see on your way to school, when you open Facebook or Instagram, or when you flip open a magazine in the dentists' waiting room.

Sociologists have been studying "respect" for a long time, often in relation to **status.** Status is a measure of social standing or respectability and can be inborn or earned. Often people of a similar status gather as members of "status groups," which are groups that

discourse The communication of information, thoughts, and ideas. It includes language, art, and all forms of expression. Discourse influences how we experience and view the world around us.

status A degree of social standing and respectability. It implies a social hierarchy in which people of different statuses enjoy different legal, political, and cultural rights.

celebrate and protect their common characteristic—whether ethnicity, race, or religion. Max Weber is well known for his emphasis on status. Recall from Chapter 1 we explored his theory on power and how status groups (people who share the same rank) tend to work together to seize and control essential resources. They achieve this by marrying each other, working with one another, and otherwise creating cultural boundaries that keep out people with a different or lesser status.

Status is also a term sociologists use to describe a person's social rank or position. Everyone holds many statuses at once. For example, a person could be a mother, doctor, friend, athlete, and neighbour at the same time. Altogether, a person's multiple statuses are known as a *status set*. The *Oxford Dictionary of Sociology* notes

> in American sociology, the concept of status . . . came to mean . . . a person's subjective evaluation of his or her position in the status hierarchy (that is "prestige"). The conflicting and competitive features of status-group relations were translated into the idea of status seeking by individuals (as in "prestigious roles," "prestige ranking," and so forth). Among many American sociologists, class and status came to be used interchangeably . . . to measure subjective evaluations of positions in a system of social stratification.

Within any society, some statuses carry power, prestige, wealth, and comfort, while others are popularly understood as "bad" or deceitful. They may even be viewed as causing and thus deserving their own misfortunes. For example, sex workers and people experiencing homelessness are often considered this way. Both achieved status (ones gained through the life course) and ascribed statuses (those that people are born into, largely outside of their control) play a large part in controlling social rewards like respect.

It is not only social rewards like respect, smiles, trust, and job opportunities that are distributed based on ideas about status. When resources appear limited, money may be diverted from people that society views as less worthy or deserving. For example, consider the continued failure to dedicate resources to address the lack of safe drinking water and decent housing in many Indigenous communities. Consider the lack of will to fund a universal childcare program for Canada's youngest citizens. Or consider the lack of real action to address the urgency of the climate crisis, which, as we have pointed out, impacts the poorest and most vulnerable first. In this way, a person's status, through no fault of their own, may influence their chances for a healthy, happy, and fulfilling life.

And like a harmful bacterial cell that divides and multiplies, damaging ideas about status reproduce across society. And every time these notions are repeated, they become more entrenched, making them even harder to challenge. And so in this sense, the production and reproduction of messages that certain "kinds" of people are less worthy than others further perpetuates the inequality. In other words, disrespect—denying a person's personhood—creates and perpetuates inequality.

Racialized People in Canada

When we think of the term *disrespect*, we often think of disparaging remarks, cruel jokes, and hurtful words and expressions. Disrespect, in all of its forms, reinforces negative notions about people's social value. Another type of disrespect is the unrealistic—and damaging—representation of vulnerable populations in popular media. We will first examine how racialized people are represented in media with the help of a much-cited cultural critic, Edward Said (1935–2003).

In his best-known book, *Orientalism* (1978), Said presents an analysis of how the West inaccurately represents the Middle East. He asked, what are the West's beliefs about the East? Are they grounded in truth? What are their effects? Said contends that these representations are influenced by colonial and post-colonial attitudes. He notes that they show a "subtle and persistent Eurocentric prejudice against Arabo-Islamic peoples and their culture" (12).

Said shows that when represented in works of fiction—or even on the nightly news—the religiously and culturally diverse people of Middle Eastern countries are often falsely grouped into a few "types." Most significantly, they are depicted as the "Other," a separate, backwards, opposite, and inferior population. This **othering** serves an essential purpose: It justifies colonial or imperial ambitions. Othering also extends well beyond its application to colonial relationships. It applies to all superior and subordinate relationships (for example, relations between genders).

othering The process by which an individual (the Other) is characterized as different from and alien to the norm. It places the "Other" firmly in the out-group and highlights the differences between the in-group and out-group. It marks the in-group as powerful and virtuous and the out-group as frail and insidious.

The *Oxford Dictionary of Social Work and Social Care* describes "othering" as follows:

> Placing a person or a group outside or in opposition to what is considered to be the norm. A concept developed by Simone de Beauvoir (1908–1986) in *The Second Sex* (1972) to analyze how women are constructed by patriarchal culture as not merely different from men but as negative, inferior, and abnormal in comparison with men. While men are "the One," beings in and of themselves, women are "the Other," being defined only in relation to men; they are what men are not, for example, men are rational, women are emotional. She saw this as a pervasive myth on which men build a society and which women internalize, accepting their otherness: "One is not born a woman; one becomes one." This concept has been extended in social work (and elsewhere) to other social divisions, such as age, disability, ethnicity, and sexuality.

Said's theories are 40 years old, but they are still relevant today. After the bombing of the World Trade Center in 2001, anti-Muslim and anti-Arab sentiment grew in the West. Many noted that terms like *Arab* or *Muslim* immediately became synonymous with terrorist—even though the word *terrorist* was unclear and selectively applied. False assumptions and outright lies about the Middle East were widely circulated.

The impact of these falsehoods persists today. A 2016 survey on Canadians' perception of discrimination in Canada by Abacus Data found the following:

- Seventy-nine per cent of Canadians say there is "some" or "a lot" of discrimination against Muslims, and 67 per cent say the same about discrimination towards Indigenous Peoples.
- Roughly equal-sized majorities see (some or a lot of) discrimination toward Black people and gay or lesbian people.
- Fifty-one per cent say women face discrimination, 45 per cent say people of the Jewish faith face discrimination, and 44 per cent say people of Asian descent face discrimination.
- Only 29 per cent see discrimination against Evangelical Christians, and only 22 per cent see discrimination against white people. (Anderson and Coletto 2016)

Another well-known sociologist who has examined representations of race and ethnicity is British cultural theorist Stuart Hall (1932–2014). Hall's work explores race and media representation (see Hall 1996). He shows that despite the diversity around the world in people's appearance, people get placed in just a few discrete racial categories with fixed characteristics.

Hall proposes that people with the power to define what is "normal" and what is marginal manipulate these categories. Hall highlights the role the media plays in defining what race is, for example. Images of race produced and reproduced in the media reinforce people's ideas about what someone from a particular racial category can or cannot do or will or won't be. He also looks at what it means, socially, to be classified into a racial category and how this classification is used to justify the unequal treatment of particular groups of people.

You may find another example of racial marginalization by looking in your wallet—that is, if you carry $100 bills. In 2012, a new design for the Canadian $100 bill was proposed. The first design featured what appeared to be an Asian woman scientist peering into a microscope. When the design was taken to focus groups, participants had concerns the scientist appeared to be Asian. As the *Financial Post* reported, the Bank of Canada "ordered the image redrawn, imposing what a spokesman called a 'neutral ethnicity' for the woman scientist who, now stripped of her 'Asian' features, appears on the circulating note. Her light features appear to be Caucasian" (Beeby 2012). The imagined "neutrality" of white skin—the belief that "whiteness" is not a race—is a practice called **invisibilizing** whiteness. This reinforces ideas that being white is "normal" and being non-white is odd or different.

invisibilizing The representation of specific characteristics (typically whiteness, heterosexuality, and skinniness) as standard or neutral and all other characteristics as deviant. This leads to a negative perception of those who do not fit the norm and leads to their marginalization.

"Othering" and stereotypical representations of racialized people in the media are forms of disrespect. They reduce the social value of racialized people, thus producing and preserving inequality. These forms of disrespect encourage us to fear and shun people

IN FOCUS ◆ Deggans' Rule

One rule that tests the portrayal of people in movies is Deggans' Rule. Deggans' Rule states that enduring films are those that (1) feature at least two racialized characters in the central cast and (2) include these characters in a plot that is not only about race (TV Tropes n.d.).

IN FOCUS ◆ Racism in the Media

Navigate to the address below, where you will find a Nivea advertisement in which a clean-cut Black man prepares to throw a bearded, afro-sporting version of his head with the caption: "Re-civilize yourself." What harmful stereotypes does this advertisement promote?

Source: https://i.huffpost.com/gen/332477/NIVEA-AD-RACIST.jpg

Critical Thinking Question

Some say that stock photographs reflect social norms. In groups of two, take out your cellphone and do a quick Google image search with search terms like "man driving a car" or "woman at the library." In your search, note how often these "everyday people" are white. What does this say about the invisibility of whiteness?

Critical Thinking Question

Take a moment to imagine a university lecture hall, with rows and rows of seats, coliseum-style. At the imaginary podium is an imaginary professor, imparting wisdom in a gripping, well-researched presentation. Your eyes dart from the podium to your notebook and back again as you take furious notes to capture the essence of this respected professor's lecture.

Now, take notice of how the professor looks in your mind's eye. Is this professor white? Is this professor a man? Is this professor older? If you answered yes to all of these questions, you may consider how popular depictions of wisdom and experience in postsecondary institutions might be influencing your assumptions!

about whom we know little, and to imagine—even exaggerate—their strengths and weaknesses. All of us, no matter how well-intentioned, are likely to do this with groups of unfamiliar people. That's why we have to avoid forming hasty judgments about unfamiliar groups. We need to reject stereotypes and instead seek more information, so we can base our ideas on good information and firsthand experience.

Women in Canada

So far, we have seen how forms of disrespect include disparaging remarks, "othering," and stereotypical representations in media. Another essential type of disrespect is indifference, which is a clear lack of interest or concern. People who are disrespected in this way are pushed to the side, left out of conversations, and ignored. Historically, this has happened to people in many social statuses. In this section, we will examine how it happens to women.

One place to examine the popular representation of women is in Hollywood movies. In the past few decades, sociologists and others have turned their attention to how the sheer lack of quality roles for women reflect beliefs about women's status in real life. Some "tests" and "rules" have been devised to analyze the inequality displayed in popular discourse.

The Bechdel Test

In 1985, cartoonist Alison Bechdel drew the cartoon featured below. In it, two characters are discussing a "test" for a movie worth seeing. First, the film has at least two women in it. Second, the women talk to each other. Third and finally, the conversation is about something other than a man.

In the years since this comic strip was published, the Bechdel test (comprising these three criteria) has become a popular tool for rating the representation of women in film. Despite the test's low standard, few blockbuster Hollywood movies pass. Here's a short list of famous failures:

- *Free Solo*
- *Gravity*
- *Moonlight*
- *The Wolf of Wall Street*
- *La La Land*
- *12 Years a Slave*
- *Toy Story 1 and 2*
- *Deadpool 2*
- *The Avengers*
- *A Star Is Born*
- *Star Trek: Into Darkness*
- The entire *Lord of the Rings Trilogy*

Of the movies you've seen this past year, which of them pass the Bechdel test?

Excerpted from Bechdel, Alison. "The Rule." *Dykes To Watch Out For.* Online Collection.

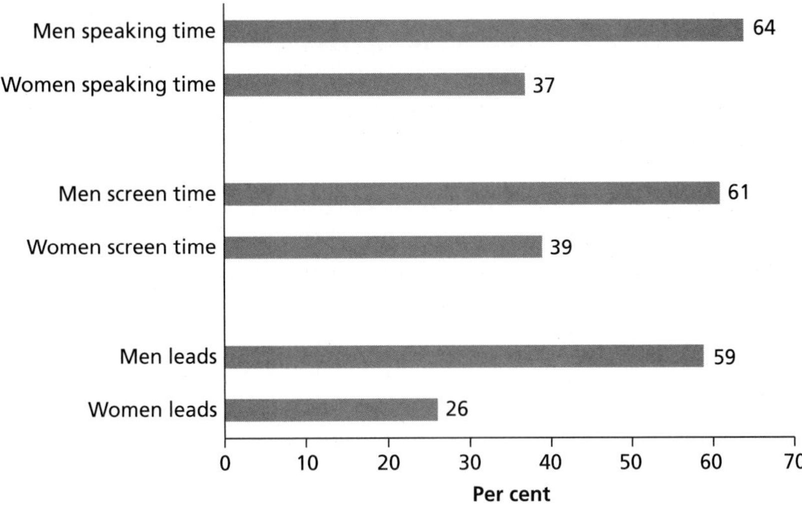

Figure 11.2 ◆ Representations of Men and Women in the 100 Top Grossing Movies of 2017

Source: Geena Davis Institute on Gender and Media 2018.

The Geena Davis Institute on Gender and Media (2018) examined the 100 top grossing family films in 2017 and noted a discrepancy between men and women in character screen and speaking time: on average, men got more screen time and more speaking time than women (see Figure 11.2).

Women in blockbuster movies or prime-time television are often cast in one of just a few roles. Media researcher Dr Stacey Smith found that women are more likely than men to be portrayed as parents. They are also more likely than men to be depicted in committed romantic relationships and are far more likely to be shown wearing sexy clothes that reveal their skin. Other characters are likely to reference women according to their sexual desirability, not their intelligence or skills. Women are less likely than men to be portrayed as employed, and they are less likely to hold high-prestige positions like presidents, CEOs, or politicians (Smith et al. 2013).

Some suggest the poor representation of women stems from industry beliefs about what audiences want to see. They think that audiences won't find women in high-power, high-skill jobs believable or appealing. Yet films that featured strong, complex female

Critical Thinking Question

Is the Bechdel test the best way to discover if a movie depicts women as interesting, realistic, intelligent, and complex human beings? Discuss the value of a test that sets the bar so low. Then try to come up with a better test for blockbuster movies. Compare your updated test with the one on page 362.

◆ In Their Own Words ◆

Some filmmakers commit to equal representation in film. Here are some filmmakers responding to the question "Why do you write strong female characters?"

> "I try to write parts for women that are as complicated and interesting as women are."
>
> —Nora Ephron, screenwriter of *When Harry Met Sally*

> "[I want] men to come away from it going, like, 'I'm not afraid of two women being funny' . . . These are just two funny people and you're just going to laugh for almost two hours."
>
> —Paul Feig, director of *Bridesmaids*

> "I wanted a female lead who has the equal force as the male leads. She's not going to be a sex kitten, she's not going to come out in cutoff shorts and a tank top, and it's going to be a real, earnestly drawn character . . ."
>
> —Guillermo del Toro, director of *Pan's Labyrinth*

> "Because you're still asking me that question."
>
> —Joss Whedon, creator of *Buffy the Vampire Slayer*

IN FOCUS ◆ Updated Bechdel Test

Writer Roxanne Gay devised a new six-point checklist for the equitable portrayal of women in film and TV. What do you think of it?

1. A woman's story is being told. She is not relegated to the role of sidekick, romantic interest, or bit player.
2. Her world is full of intelligent women who also have stories worth telling, even if their stories aren't the focus of the movie.
3. If she must engage in a romantic storyline, she doesn't have to compromise her sanity or common sense for love.
4. At least half the time, this woman needs to be a woman of colour or a transgender woman or a queer woman because all these women exist! She is different, but her story should not focus solely on this difference because she is a sum of her parts. She is not the token. She has friends who look like her, so they need to show up once in a while.
5. She cannot live in an unexplainably perfect apartment in an expensive city with no visible means of affording said unexplainably perfect apartment.
6. She doesn't have to live up to an unrealistic feminist standard. She can and should be human. She just needs to be intelligent and witty and interesting in the way women, the world over are, if we ever got a chance to know them on the silver screen. (Waldman 2014)

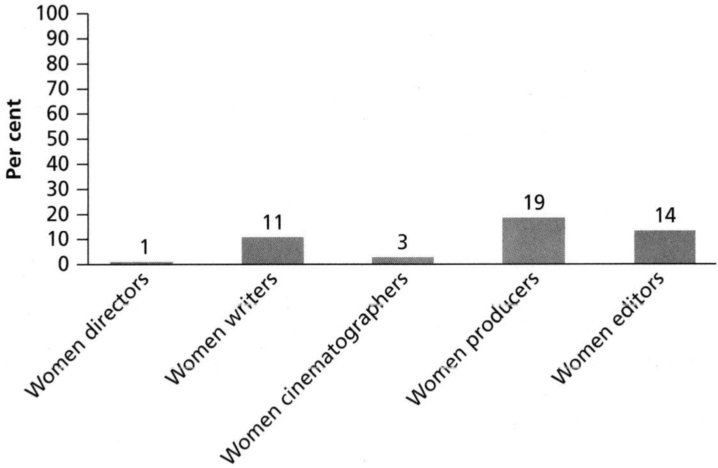

Figure 11.3 ◆ Women Making Films

Source: Women and Hollywood 2018.

characters (like *Captain Marvel*, starring Brie Larson; *Wonder Woman*, starring Gal Gadot; and *Arrival*, starring Amy Adams) fared better than most at the box office. In fact, they gross about 40 per cent more than average male-led films. Perhaps that's why the number of films with female leads has doubled in the past four years (Geena Davis Institute 2018).

Others suggest the lack of women in film stems from the lack of women *making* films (see Figure 11.3). Other commentators may argue the lack of realistic, "three-dimensional" women proves that movies are patriarchal. The sidelining, stereotyping, and sexualization of women is a weapon of powerful males aiming to preserve their power.

Essayist Katha Pollitt (1991) notes that in most popular storylines, "boys are the norm, girls the variation; boys are central, girls peripheral; boys are individuals, girls types. Boys define the group, its story and its code of values. Girls exist only in relation to boys." In other words, the male character, who is usually white and straight, is the default, the norm, the character against which all others are measured for their difference.

◆◆ Notable Thinkers ◆◆

Michel Foucault

People are judged according to how "normal" they are—that is, where they stand on conventional norms of behaviour, ability, appearance, and so on. This idea was brought to our attention by the French social theorist Michel Foucault (1926–1984). He is often touted as a founder of postmodern sociology, though Foucault worked in many different academic fields, including philosophy, history, psychology, gender studies, and literary criticism (see Taylor 2009).

Continued

One of his many contributions is the unsettling of the term *normal*. Foucault points out that ideas about normality are dynamic, meaning they change over time. Behaviour that is well regarded and rewarded at one point in history—like the physical abuse and control of wives by their husbands—is at other points viewed as deviant and abnormal.

Foucault suggests that society defines normal through the abnormal; in other words, what is considered "normal" are the leftover ideas once all the "abnormal" has been locked up and tucked away out of sight. People who are named "normal" get to keep all the power to themselves. They get to loudly assess, analyze, and often control the fate of those who are named "abnormal." Foucault theorized that this occurs not only in pop culture representations of society but everywhere we look. Not only do we judge people as normal or abnormal in this way—we also judge ourselves this way.

Critical Thinking Question

Video gaming is often associated with male teenagers, but did you know that nearly half of all gamers are women? Oddly, only 22 per cent of game designers are women, according to a survey of 3,000 game design professionals in 2015—nearly double the percentage 10 years earlier. How might that affect the playing experience? Can you apply Foucault's theories of abnormality to the representation of women in video games, another form of mass media?

Source: De Clercq 2016.

Notable Thinkers

Laura Mulvey

In the 1970s, British film theorist Laura Mulvey proposed that Hollywood cinema uses what she referred to as "the male gaze." This is a technique by which the viewer is forced into a "masculine subject position." By using careful camera angles, movie-makers force viewers to "see" the fictional world through the eyes of the male protagonist, turning the female characters into passive objects. This theory created some controversy. What do you think of Mulvey's idea?

In an episode of *The Mindy Project*, central character Mindy Lahiri is treated to a striptease from love-interest Danny Castellano. Viewers commented the way the scene was shot reversed the typical male gaze by making the camera angle suggest Mindy's point of view. Often, the camera is precisely at the level of Mindy's eyes.

Summing up, in hopes of gaining social approval, we usually follow **gender scripts**—generally understood rules for how "normal" males and females behave in our society. Our aim in doing this is to gain social acceptance and avoid disapproval. In short, we want to win and keep the respect of others. But these gender scripts are limiting, and performing them often feels like wearing shoes that are just a little too tight, and sometimes downright painful.

gender scripts The generally understood rules for how people of different genders "normally" behave in our society. Gender scripts are negotiated between people based on how society collectively imagines gender.

Some may think that the underrepresentation of three-dimensional female characters in horror movies or action films has little impact on the lives of real women. In her fascinating book *Invisible Women: Data Bias in a World Designed for Men*, journalist Caroline Criado Perez (2019) considers the dangerous implications of the "absent presence"—in other words, the invisibilizing of women. She notes, for example, that consumer products like smartphone keypads, pianos, ambulance equipment, and heavy doors are often designed to fit bigger bodies. As another example, astronaut suits presume that the default

IN FOCUS ◆ Size Discrimination

The term *fat-shaming* has been used to describe a particular attitude toward large people (mostly women). Some have pointed out that ridiculing "fatness," or depicting people with this body type as being unintelligent, unlovable, or undesirable, is still considered acceptable in many television shows, video games, and movies. Underneath these depictions, we see specific ideas of beauty (for example, thinness) valued over others.

In October 2018, plus-size model Tess Holliday was featured on the cover of Cosmopolitan UK. Many praised the cover for its inclusiveness and for its flattering and attractive depiction of a fat body. Others criticized the magazine for "glamorizing" obesity and promoting unhealthy lifestyles. This criticism is a typical response to positive representations of fat women in the media. Fat men rarely receive the same criticism. Activists of the Body Positive movement point out that other, visibly unhealthy behaviours like drinking or smoking are rarely shamed to the same extent. They also point out that making women feel good about themselves and their bodies does not encourage women to eat more or become fat. Instead, positive representation helps women feel more comfortable in their skin and improves their mental health, which is just as important as physical health.

COSMOPOLITAN UK

The Cosmopolitan cover featuring plus-size model Tess Holiday prompted mixed reactions. Some praised the magazine for its body positivity while others criticized it for promoting obesity.

What do you think? Does depicting fat women and men in a positive light promote obesity?

human body is a larger, male body. She reports that crash test dummies are typically artificial "male bodies," resulting in incomplete safety data that could assist women in car crashes. Hard hats slip off women's heads. Artificial intelligence has voice-activation software that doesn't register higher voices. All of these are real-life, harmful implications of a world that *just doesn't see* women.

Importantly, someone cannot work/study their way out of invisibility. In this way, it reminds us of Bourdieu's notion of "embodied capital"—cultural or economic capital that is embodied in a person's appearance and other people's perceptions of their appearance.

Immigrants in Canada

The mischaracterization of newcomers to Canada is a common form of disrespect in popular discourse. For example, immigrants to Canada are usually better educated and in possession of more professional qualifications than Canadian-born people. Yet politicians and media often depict immigrants as unskilled, lazy, uneducated, and a drain on society. When mainstream news media tells this story, they shape public opinion accordingly.

Even though Canadians hold some damaging beliefs about immigrants, one survey showed that we rank near the top when it comes to positive perceptions of immigrants compared to other OECD countries. Take a look at Figure 11.4; it lists countries from most accepting to least accepting. This Gallup poll (2017) asked people from around the world the same three questions: Is it a good thing or a bad thing that immigrants: (1) live in their country; (2) become their neighbours; and (3) marry a close relative. High numbers mean people are willing to get socially close to newcomers—to welcome them as residents, neighbours, and family members.

Negative portrayals of immigrants show a lack of information and firsthand familiarity with the people in question. Often, it also arises in periods of economic difficulty among groups of people who feel they are in competition with immigrants for jobs, housing, social services, and other social benefits. This connects directly with the conflict theory approach to understanding ethnic and racial conflict as having a material or economic basis.

People have a hard time uniting with others they view as endangering their access to survival capital. The people in power often promote such conflict and characterize it as a conflict about race or religion, or even a "clash of civilizations." However, at bottom, it is a clash over the opportunity to survive.

Some immigrants are also mischaracterized as criminals. Evidence has not shown a strong correlation between high immigration rates and high crime rates. While data on the ethnicity or national origin of offenders is not routinely collected in Canada, studies in the United States have shown immigrants have lower overall crime rates when compared to the domestic-born population (Ellis, Beaver, and Wright 2009). Poverty and social disorganization are what cause crime, not immigration.

Consider a content analysis study conducted in 2011 by sociologist Wendy Chan (2013). Chan collected and analyzed 650 newspaper articles on the subject of immigration written between 1990 and 2005. Chan found that in these articles, immigrants were largely depicted as criminals or illegally in the country. She noted that in the body of the articles, the word *criminal* was mentioned 1,231 times, whereas the word *victim* was mentioned only 73 times. Other words commonly used to describe immigrants in the articles were *illegal*, *terrorist*, *violent*, *dangerous*, and *smugglers*.

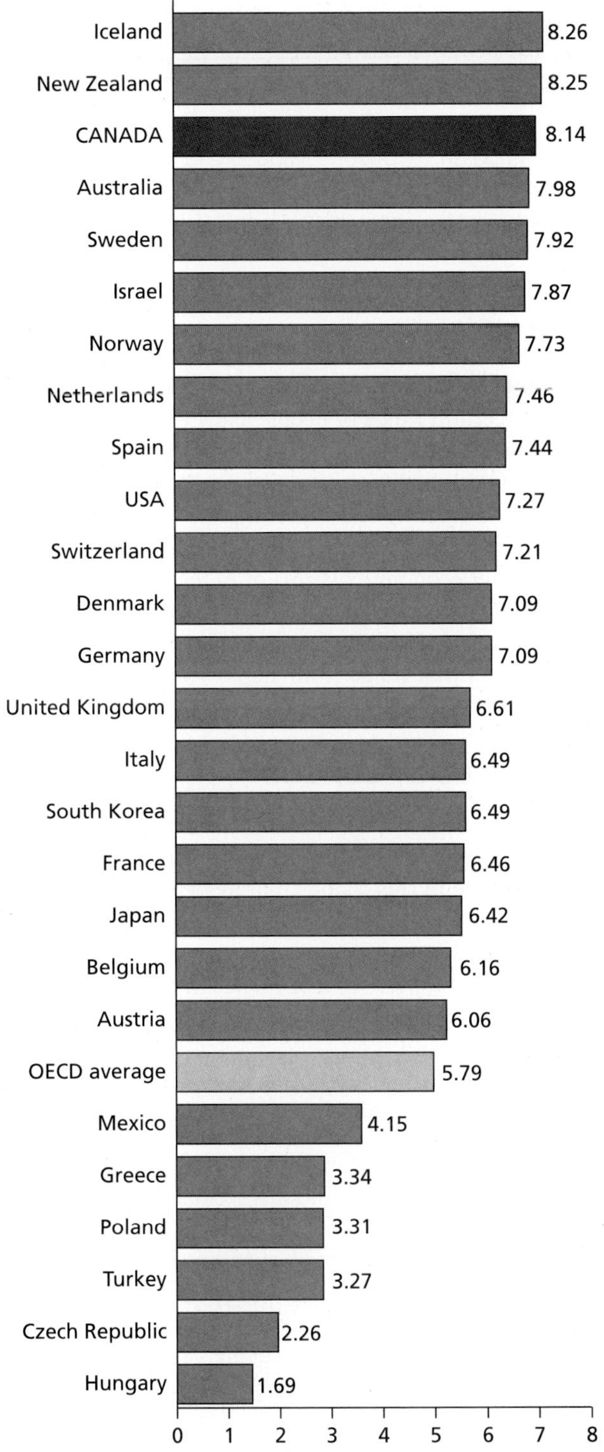

Figure 11.4 ◆ Migrant Acceptance Index

Source: Environics Institute for Survey Research 2018.

IN FOCUS ◆ Immigrants as Criminals

Depicting immigrants as criminals is not a trend of the past. During his 2016 presidential campaign, President Donald Trump made many disrespectful remarks about Mexican immigrants. His statement that "they're bringing drugs, they're bringing crime, they're rapists," was met with roaring applause. Despite widespread condemnation and no supporting evidence for this claim, Trump's election largely under his promise to "Build a Wall" underscores public views about immigrants in America.

underrepresentation The act of consciously or unconsciously reinforcing ideas of abnormality or deviance by ignoring or overlooking certain kinds of people. These groups are depicted in media (such as film or television) at a rate that does not reflect their prevalence in society.

In this chapter, we've discussed the lack of representation of racialized people and women in mass media. This **underrepresentation** can reinforce ideas of abnormality by ignoring or overlooking certain kinds of people. Now consider the social implication of overrepresentation: The effects of telling the same stories, again and again, about a specific population. As Chan (2013:42) points out, the cumulative effect of mainly negative accounts of immigrants is distorting and degrading.

Again, people are often ready to form quick judgments about unfamiliar groups, especially under conditions of economic distress or other causes of social anxiety. For example, in Canada and elsewhere, fears about terrorism have fuelled negative assumptions about immigrants from the Middle East. This lack of respect, as we have noted, can have dangerously harmful effects that range from stereotyping to job discrimination, social exclusion, and hate crimes.

Indigenous Peoples in Canada

We often find misrepresentations of people in media forms like television or movies. But stereotyping and misrepresentation preceded the arrival of modern media. This is true for all the populations studied in this chapter, but in Canada it is perhaps most prevalent for Indigenous Peoples. In fact, since before Confederation, Indigenous Peoples have been

◆ In Their Own Words ◆

Sociologist Wendy Chan writes that:

> The singular focus on immigrant criminality in Canadian mainstream news media reinforces "us-and-them" beliefs about immigrants. They promote beliefs that frame immigrants as all-the-same, dangerous, and a drain on the system, instead of recognizing their essential and positive contributions to the country. These beliefs may justify harsher immigration policies or sweeping, simplistic solutions to what are seen as simple social problems. The individual experiences, needs, and abilities of immigrants are reduced or ignored. Instead, immigrants "are non-persons and objects to be managed."

Source: Chan 2013:37.

negatively characterized by European settlers in places like novels, on postcards, and in early colonial newspapers. Consider this depiction of Indigenous Peoples from the *British Columbian* (1863). The editorial about the first residential school in British Columbia stated "[i]t would be manifestly impolitic and productive of harm to put the uncivilized and unchristianized Indians of this country in possession of all the rights and privileges of citizenship . . . If anyone should dispute our right to impose upon the natives a state of tutelage, we answer that it is an absolute necessity in order that the state may perform those duties toward them to which it became morally bound in taking possession of the country."

Indigenous media historian Robert Harding (2006) points out that editorials like this one reinforce a binary relationship ("us and them") between white, European settlers and Indigenous Peoples. The language frames the "re-education" of Indigenous Peoples as a kind act and reduces them to inferior, childlike beings. The Indigenous view is absent from this editorial and many, many others like it. Disrespectful images of Indigenous Peoples continue to abound in the media, in sports, in cartoons, and on social media.

Throughout this book we have seen some of the negative, distorted representations that have been historically circulated about Indigenous Peoples. Writer Thomas King (2012) has said "the only truth of the thing is the lie itself" (54). We use the term *Imagined Indian* to describe the artificial, two-dimensional people these misrepresentations depict. They are imaginary because these characterizations bear little resemblance to reality. Cultural studies theorist Jennifer Adese (2012) offers this description of the Imagined Indian:

> Constructions of Indigenous peoples as the Indian of travellers' journals, captivity narratives, dime-store novels, and other colonialist written records talk of wild frontiers, "noble braves" and "savages," and accommodating (albeit silent) "squaws" that ride on horseback and dress in feathers and buckskin. Indigenous men have often been constructed as "noble savages" who have an enduring spiritual connection with nature and who will inevitably die out because they are frozen in a "precontact primitive," "premodern" state. They have also been figured as "ignoble savages" who are "violent, emotionally cold, lazy and/or drunk." Similarly, Indigenous women have been constructed as tragic "primitives," matronly "squaws" who are destined to "die out" as they try (sometimes in their Disneyfied, Pocahontasesque sexualized way) to bring "harmony among the races." Indigenous women have also been portrayed as lazy, dirty, drunk, [and] sexually promiscuous . . . (483)

The systematic de-humanizing—disrespecting—of Indigenous Peoples throughout colonization is what sociologists call a strategy of **differentiation**. In other words, these characterizations produce a view that a population is inherently different than another. This, too is an example of "othering." Differentiation leads to narratives of blame; stories are told about the "different" population being fundamentally flawed, unintelligent, uncivilized, and deserving of maltreatment. These two processes grease the wheels of oppression and inequality. It's easier to accept the abuse of people who are understood to be different and deviant.

differentiation The social and cultural identification, then performance, of social differences, as between men and women, old and young, and so on.

Ideas that the oppression of Indigenous Peoples was somehow acceptable, just, and right conveniently supported colonial agendas. And these ideas, alive and well in popular discourse, continue to support this agenda today. In 1996, the Government of Canada's Royal Commission on Aboriginal Peoples stated:

> When the media address Indigenous issues, the impressions they convey are often distorted . . . Canada's Indigenous peoples are, in general, badly served by national and local media . . . The country's large newspapers, TV and radio news shows often contain misinformation, sweeping generalizations and galling stereotypes about Natives and Native affairs . . . The result is that most Canadians have little real knowledge of the country's Native peoples, or of the issues which affect them. (Vol. 5:103)

One place to examine the representations of Indigenous Peoples is the three Canadian Olympic Games. In each Olympics, the organizing committees chose to feature Indigenous Peoples prominently and proudly in the opening or closing ceremonies. This was to send a message to the world that Canada celebrated its "harmonious relationship" with the First Peoples of the land and to underline its commitment to multiculturalism, a long-upheld part of Canada's "brand." And yet each of the Olympics has been criticized for its "beads and feathers" characterizations of Indigenous Peoples.

For example, in a move that many would find shocking today, Indigenous Peoples were not consulted or included in the choreographic decision making in the Montreal Olympics (1976). In fact, most of the dancers featured in the Indigenous scene were not Indigenous, nor were the so-called "traditional dances" rooted in any known Indigenous traditions. At the Calgary Games (1988), Indigenous Peoples were represented in a lone figure, "the Native." He shared the stage with a Cowboy and a Mountie in a visual suggestion that these relationships were historically equal and peaceful. The Vancouver Games (2010) were the first to formally engage Indigenous consultants. Yet organizers "drew on

◆ In Their Own Words ◆

Over the centuries, many have challenged negative mischaracterizations of Indigenous Peoples in advertising, novels, Canadian tourism materials, and, most overtly, in Western-style movies and television programs. In his article, "Cowboys and Indians: Toys of Genocide, Icons of American Colonialism" (2004), Mandan, Hidatsa, and Arikara scholar Dr Michael Yellow Bird (2004) writes of his early memories of watching Westerns:

> As a child I observed that whenever the TV Indians battled with the TV cowboys, not only did we spectacularly lose, but to add insult to this injury we were also presented as screaming, grunting, unreasonable savages who unjustly assaulted and/or killed what seemed like the most helpless, likeable, and innocent white people in the world. The TV Indians were the poorest of war tacticians, buffoons, who would unfailingly ride directly into a great volley of bullets only to be killed over and over again in movie after movie. As I grew older, it crossed my mind the white stuntmen playing Indians who were repeatedly shot from their horses must have hated us whenever their back problems or arthritis flared up in their later acting years.

◆ In Their Own Words ◆

An aspiring participant in the Olympic Opening Ceremonies reflects that:

> Having my moccasins, my Métis sash, and my dad's moosehide jacket, I wasn't sure that even with all this and my "Homeland Security: Fighting Terrorism Since 1492" T-shirt I'd be "Indigenous enough" to be selected, and I wasn't sure that I wanted to find out—or that I wanted anyone affiliated with the Olympic organizing committee to decide whether or not I was.

Source: Quoted in Adese 2012.

language that posited First Nations as a singular entity and as a willful partner in the establishment of the nation" (Adese 2012).

Dr Jennifer Adese (2012) contends these misrepresentations, cloaked in the rhetoric of multiculturalism, mask an effort to "re-narrate" the story of Canada's colonial past. It does so by obscuring the history of forced cultural and religious assimilation, residential schools, political marginalization, physical displacement or relocation, and human rights violations. She asks, "What is Canada trying to say about itself by insisting on Indigenous presence within the Olympic ceremonies when in so many other spaces in Canadian society, we are purposefully invisibilized?"

Another site to examine the depictions of Indigenous Peoples is professional sports, where many teams have adopted mascots and team names that recall the Imagined Indian figure. Many feel that names like "the Braves," "the Redskins," and "the Chiefs" support and reproduce negative stereotypes of Indigenous Peoples. Moreover, fan traditions such as "the Tomahawk Chop" cheer or "Half-time Pow-wows" degrade and trivialize sacred customs.

Increasingly, teams have been called on to change their names and mascots. Detractors typically respond with one of three arguments. The first is that it's been this way for many years, and no one has ever complained. The second is that no harm is meant by these names and imagery. And the third is the use of Indigenous-themed names and mascots "pays tribute" to Indigenous Peoples.

In response, American political activist Ward Churchill (1996) asks us to imagine if Germany named its professional sports teams "the Jews." Or imagine if other historically oppressed people like Black Americans or the LGBTQ+ population were similarly "honoured" with derogatory team names and cheers. In this case, these discriminatory practices become so ingrained and normalized that many fail to see them for what they are.

IN FOCUS ◆ Indigenous Imagery in Professional Sports

Watch this television ad that challenges the controversial practice of using Indigenous names and imagery in professional sports: www.nytimes.com/2018/01/29/sports/baseball/cleveland-indians-chief-wahoo-logo.html.

LGBTQ+ People in Canada

Just a few decades ago, it was rare to see a normalized representation of LGBTQ+ people in popular discourse. Depictions were typically negative, showing LGBTQ+ people as "sexual deviants" or sick, depraved, and dangerous individuals looking to ensnare unsuspecting straight people.

Some of these mischaracterizations were challenged in the 1990s, especially in mainstream television with gay, lesbian, and bisexual characters in shows like *Ellen* and *Will and Grace*. While these characters played an important role in normalizing homosexuality in popular discourse, they were never shown being sexual and rarely shown kissing or even touching a love interest. Professor of media studies Guillermo Avila-Saavedra (2009) has noted:

> Homosexual images are presented in a way acceptable for heterosexual audiences by reinforcing traditional values like family, monogamy and stability. Most of the erotic connotations of homosexuality have been eliminated. Gay male characters, in particular, are only welcomed in mainstream mass media as long as they do not infer any sexual desires and practices. (8)

Today, there are more LGBTQ+ characters in mainstream television shows. You're probably familiar with *Queer Eye for the Straight Guy*, *Riverdale*, *Modern Family*, *Sex Education*, *Orange Is the New Black*, and more. In fact, the US-based Gay and Lesbian Alliance Against Defamation (GLAAD 2019) reports that in 2018–19 there was a record high of 8.8 per cent LGBTQ+ characters on mainstream television. Increasingly, these characters have regular story arcs. They struggle with the typical challenges of television characters instead of being defined only by their sexual preferences. Figure 11.5 shows how many gay, lesbian, and bisexual people were counted among the LGB characters. GLAAD notes that

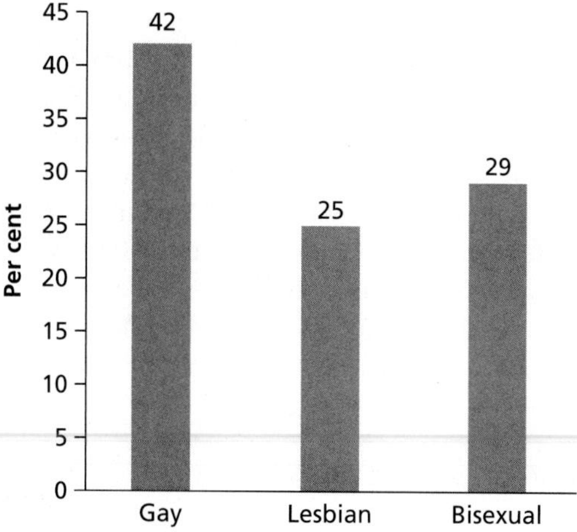

Figure 11.5 ✦ LGB Characters, 2018–19

Source: GLAAD 2019.

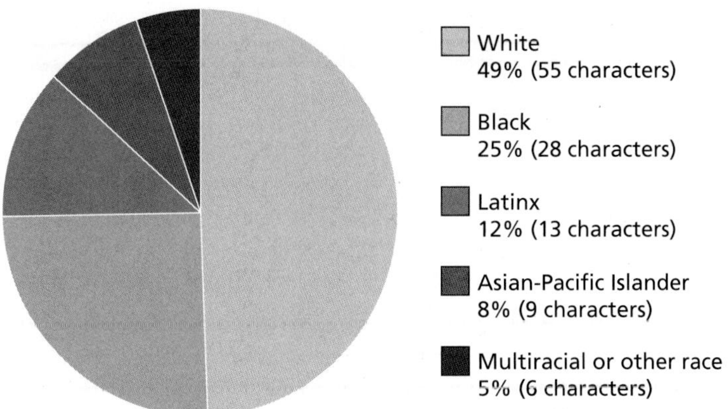

Figure 11.6 ◆ Racial Diversity of LGBTQ+ Characters on Broadcast Television

Source: GLAAD 2019.

often, LGB characters are killed off in the stories lines in a (sadly) predictable plot development they refer to as "Bury your Gays."

However, racialized LGBTQ+ people, or those with a disability, are almost absent from pop culture. This serves to reinforce the belief that homosexuality is a young, white, male experience. As Fred Fejes (2000) writes, gay characters are overwhelmingly "young, white, Caucasian, preferably with a well-muscled, smooth body, handsome face, good education, professional job, and a high income" (18). Figure 11.6 shows the breakdown of racialized LGBT characters in American broadcast television. You'll note that most are white.

Another population that is either largely ignored or negatively depicted in popular discourse is trans people. In their review of LGBTQ+ characters in 2018–19, GLAAD (2019) counted only six trans characters in broadcast television (and about the same number in

IN FOCUS ◆ The Russo Test

The Russo Test is named after Vito Russo, the co-founder and film historian for GLAAD. The Russo Test examines the representation of LGBT people in film. To pass the Russo test, the film must do the following:

1. Contain a character that is identifiably lesbian, gay, bisexual, and/or transgender (LGBT).
2. That character must not be solely or mainly defined by their sexual orientation or gender identity. That is, the character is made up of the same sort of unique character traits commonly used to distinguish straight characters from one another.
3. The LGBT character must be tied into the plot in such a way their removal would have a significant effect. Meaning they are not there to provide colourful commentary, paint urban authenticity, or (most commonly) set up a punchline; the character should matter.

Source: GLAAD 2013.

IN FOCUS ◆ Re-Editing Soaps

The popular American soap opera *As the World Turns* made history in 2007 when it featured the first mainstream soap opera kiss between two male characters, Luke Snyder and Noah Mayer. This event may have been promising at the time, but sadly soap operas have not been known for their broad and normalizing representation of LBGTQ+ people. However, a practice of fan-produced re-editing of soap operas and posting these creations to YouTube has been identified as a new way of challenging heteronormative storylines in soap operas (Dhaenens 2012).

How does this work? As you probably recall, soap operas typically feature multiple storylines playing out simultaneously. It may be common to see just one out of six or seven storylines featuring a same-sex romantic couple. Consider the case of *Christian and Oliver*, a fan-produced series based on the German soap opera *Forbidden Love*. Here, fans carefully go through each episode and cut out just the gay storyline, then edit it together. The mini-episode becomes entirely dedicated to this couple instead of including all the heterosexual storylines. You can watch an episode here: www.youtube.com/watch?v=elLu6-oA4MY.

streaming and cable platforms). Major film studios are slowly beginning to incorporate trans people, but their gender identity is often the most significant part of their character. The Netflix series *Orange Is the New Black* featured Sophia, a trans lead character played by trans actor Laverne Cox.

In an interview with *V* magazine (Defebaugh 2014), Cox said:

> I think that before Sophia, for the most part, representations of trans folks were comic relief. We've been victims, we've been mostly talked about in terms of our transition and being trans, but in a lot of ways Sophia gets to be just another woman in Litchfield, with a different experience and a different story.

Sophia is paving the way for other trans characters on television, characters with rich, relatable storylines and experiences.

Canadians consume a lot of American television, so we have focused on American television in this section. However, we are seeing an increase in the numbers of LBGTQ+ characters in Canadian-made television too, such as on *Schitt's Creek*, *Orphan Black*, and *Degrassi*. People want to see themselves reflected in the culture they consume, and Canadian networks and media production companies are recognizing the economic opportunities in giving people what they want. Though we don't usually think of respect as a form of survival capital, it does contribute to people's will to live. In this way, it is something sociologists, public health researchers, teachers, and policymakers need to consider all the time.

Laverne Cox played the role of Sophia in *Orange Is the New Black*. Only in the past ten or so years have the mainstream media begun to portray trans characters with sensitivity or depth.

People with Disabilities in Canada

The definitions and implications of disability are socially constructed—they are products of our ideas. One way to understand this is to note how these ideas change over time and from society to society. Historically, attitudes about disability ranged from outright fear to fascination. Some disabilities, like autism, for example, have only been popularly understood in recent decades. And while stigma has been associated with disability for centuries—millennia, even—the degree of stigmatization has decreased in many parts of the world.

And yet in Canada today, many disabled bodies are still not viewed as "whole" or "healthy." As a result, disabled bodies can be feared, degraded, or stigmatized. Even the term used to describe this difference—*disability*—defines a person by what they *can't* do instead of what they *can*. By contrast, bodies read as non-disabled are attributed with higher statuses.

As we have seen in the preceding chapters of this book, our beliefs about disability have real-life effects. In other words, it's not just the disability itself that makes life more challenging, it's the social marginalization derived from the disability. Beliefs create inaccessible architecture and public transportation, limit employment choices for people with disabilities, and privilege certain types of body functionality over others. That's why it's essential to examine how and why we form our beliefs about disability and how these beliefs are reproduced in popular discourse.

Like many of the other people in this chapter, the population of people with disabilities—though vast and increasing—are often ignored in popular culture. Blogger Anchel Krishna (2014), who is a mom to a child with cerebral palsy, wondered why advertisers are reluctant to feature families like hers:

> Is it because the general public can't handle seeing kids of different abilities? Is it too sad an image? Does it depict their worst fears in a visual way and that idea is just too scary?
>
> As a parent of a child who has a visible disability, let me tell you that our existence is not sad, tragic or filled with fear. We have the same ups and downs as any family—we likely just tend to celebrate the ups a little more. We know that our story could have been different and had an ending that didn't leave us with our spunky little girl. So whether I'm right or wrong, I feel entitled to having my experience of parenthood acknowledged and included. I want to see parents like me and kids of all abilities in the media.

Recently, *Today's Parent* magazine featured a child with Down syndrome on its cover. In a follow up to the photograph, the editors of the magazine pointed out the "media creates and molds our perception of the world, so what conclusion can a family reach when they rarely see similar people represented? They are invisible, marginalized, forgotten" (Emmons 2014).

Historically, people with disabilities in popular discourse have been defined by their disabilities. That is, their disability is a vital part of their role and a significant part of their story arc. All too often, the roles are based on a limited list of unfavourable tropes and tired, disparaging clichés.

The website "Disability Movies" (2014) reviews the portrayal of people with disabilities in feature films. Over the years, they've collected many "disability movie stereotypes and clichés." Their list is presented below. What do you think of this list? Do you have any stereotypes and disabilities to add? What kind of impression might moviegoers form of people with disabilities when they are bombarded with messages like these ones?

1. The disabled person spends the entire movie whining about how they want to die.
2. The disabled person dies immediately after passing on a life lesson, inspiring the non-disabled to live their lives to the fullest.
3. The disabled person offs themselves so they won't be a burden to others.
4. The disabled person was faking it all along!
5. Disability, especially disfigurement, is used to show that a character is the villain.
6. The disabled person needs non-disabled people to teach them their life isn't over.
7. People with disabilities can cure themselves through sheer force of will.
8. If disabled people are included on a team or in a group, it shows they're expected to fail.
9. Disabled people are filled with a murderous rage. Especially amputees.
10. If a disabled person shows up on a blind date, the other person will be terrified and try to escape.
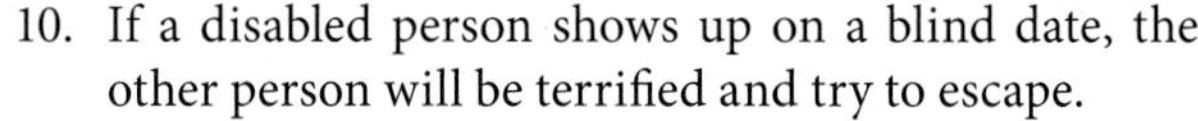
11. If marriage is proposed to a disabled person, they must turn down the offer and flee to avoid burdening the potential spouse.
12. Blind people have superhuman hearing and can use echolocation.
13. Blind people always want to feel everyone's face.
14. Deaf people can always lip read.
15. Need to make a non-disabled actor look disabled? Give them a bad haircut!

Kathy Hutchins/Shutterstock

Characters with a disability are only rarely portrayed by actors with that disability. As one exception, Micah Fowler, a young actor with cerebral palsy, had a starring role in the ABC comedy series *Speechless*.

The best way to address the poor mass media representation of disability is the subject of some debate. Some movies and television shows (such as *The Upside* and *Glee*) cast a non-disabled actor to play a person in a wheelchair. In fact, many Oscars have been awarded to non-disabled portrayals of disability. Some feel these roles—few as they are—should be filled by actors with a disability. Storme Toolis, a young actor who uses a wheelchair and was cast in *The Inbetweeners* film, says "I have an understanding of the character which only a disabled actor would. It's not only the physical things—the way I move my hands and feet, even how I speak, which even the best non-disabled actor couldn't capture" (Birkett 2011)

When directors defend the practice of casting non-disabled actors to play people with disabilities, they often point to a lack of available talent. This suggests the problems start even earlier, in acting schools, in high school drama classes, and in the television shows themselves. A lack of disability on TV underscores the myth that people with a visible disability don't belong at auditions.

What we know is that accurate and realistic depictions of people with disabilities in popular discourse are useful in equalizing opportunities. As always, familiarity and first-hand experience are essential in dispelling unfair treatment and stereotypical opinions. For example, one study examined the views about disability that a class of young children held. After many children's books featuring sensitive, realistic portrayals of disability were incorporated into their curriculum, the children's views changed. Children who had previously been resentful or feared disability were more likely to show compassion and understanding (Adomat 2014).

Thanks to modern medicine, people with disabilities are leading longer and more productive lives. That alone means we need to change our opinions of "normality" and we will all be better off when we do so.

◆ In Their Own Words ◆

Comic books have been one place where "othered" bodies, or disabilities, have historically been represented. DC Comics introduced Doctor Midnight, a visually impaired doctor, in 1940. Since then, others have followed: amputee Misty Knight in 1975, hearing impaired Echo in 1999, wheelchair-using Oracle, visually impaired Daredevil, and more recently, a mobility-impaired character in Archie. Comics, some have pointed out, celebrate different bodies by reinterpreting them as special superhuman powers.

Chip Reece's graphic novel Metaphase *features a character with Down syndrome. Here's an excerpt from an interview with Reece:*

> [Interviewer]: How did *Metaphase* come to be?
>
> Chip Reece: Basically, I was inspired by my son Ollie, who has Down's [*sic*] Syndrome, and his superhero-like strength through several major medical ordeals, including three open-heart surgeries. When I started to dig for comic book characters he could relate to as a person with Down's Syndrome, there wasn't much out there, and absolutely no superheroes. I found this odd, given how much my son and other kids with Down's Syndrome go through. Fifty percent of all kids born w/DS have congenital heart defects (Ollie had two), one scary health fact out of many. I wanted my son to have a comic book character that was like him, heroic, inspirational and full of endless potential. That's when I started to pursue the idea. (Reece 2014)

Do you think comic books have offered enough space for people with disabilities to find inspiration and raise their social status? Or are they unrealistically—and unfairly—representing unattainable, unbelievable images of disability?

Consequences of Unequal Access to Respect

It is worthwhile thinking about De Cremer and Mulder's (2007) conclusions about respect at this point:

> [First,] respect is a means to an end. Indeed, receiving respectful treatment signals relational appreciation and satisfies important human motives such as belongingness and reputation concerns. (445)

In other words, respect is vital in social relationships. Everyone likes to receive respect and wants to associate with people who show them respect. So by giving respect, we assure ourselves of continued social relationships.

> [Second,] respect can also be seen as an end in itself . . . The enactment of respect itself makes us authentic and moral human beings . . . "Respect as an end in itself" represents a call from the society as a whole to ensure the morality of the collective we live in.

As we noted at the beginning of this chapter, respect is a way of treating people as "ends in themselves," not mere instruments for the achievement of our own goals. This is similar to the well-known Golden Rule—namely, treat people as you would like to be treated yourself.

Strategies of Resistance

Government-Level Strategies of Resistance

If we understand respect as a non-tangible form of survival capital, then much like remedial mental healthcare and addictions support, respect helps us prevent people from falling into harmful and even fatal spirals of behaviour.

With this in mind, many disadvantaged groups have worked to remedy misconceptions, increase co-operation, and encourage mutual shows of respect. But when these efforts fail, remedial steps are needed. Consider this example: In early 2015, the Assembly of First Nations presented a mental wellness continuum they had devised. This project, in collaboration with Health Canada and First Nations and Inuit mental health leaders, allowed them to set their own priorities for mental healthcare locally. The goal of this framework is to address the long-standing gaps in the mental healthcare and addictions services available to Indigenous individuals, families, and communities in Canada (Assembly of First Nations 2015).

Because of a combination of social, historical, and economic disadvantages, the Indigenous population in Canada struggles with mental health. Statistics from 2006 show Indigenous men, women, and youth are at much higher risk of dying by suicide than the general population. This is likely because of a combination of factors. However, the disproportionately high rates of depression in First Nations individuals and post-traumatic stress disorder in residential school survivors may be significant contributors.

Addictions to drugs and alcohol are also common among First Nations and Inuit people. According to the Assembly of Manitoba Chiefs (2018), "[s]ubstance abuse is more common in northern and remote communities as a result of a history of colonization, isolation, poverty, and language barriers. These First Nations are also more vulnerable to suicide, violence, and poor performance in schools."

The First Nations Mental Wellness Continuum Framework aims to improve programs for Indigenous mental health by making them more consistent throughout the federal, provincial, and territorial governments. By having a more standardized system of care, mental health programming can better address the unique obstacles faced by Indigenous Peoples in Canada. On a smaller scale, this framework seeks to empower local mental health service providers to alter their programs according to the specific needs of their community (Health Canada 2015).

This innovative framework offers a way to improve the standard of mental healthcare for Canada's Indigenous population, while still accounting for locally based issues.

Organization-Level Strategies of Resistance

Reel Injun is a 2009 documentary directed by Cree filmmaker Neil Diamond and co-produced by the National Film Board of Canada and the CBC. This exploratory documentary looks at the way Indigenous groups in North America have been portrayed in American cinema. As we have noted, these portrayals have spurred stereotypes and myths about Indigenous Peoples. *Reel Injun* seeks to deconstruct the image of Indigenous Peoples created and preserved by Hollywood since the 1930s.

One of the main points of this eye-opening film is how gullible viewers can be in believing what they see in the movies. *Reel Injun* exposes the portrayal of Indigenous Peoples for what it is: racist misrepresentation. These misrepresentations range from inaccurate costuming to red-face makeup in films like *Dances with Wolves* and other films (often Westerns) revered as classics (Woodend 2010). As an alternative to these misrepresentations, *Reel Injun* offers the possibility of an era in cinema in which Indigenous Peoples make their own films from their own points of view. *Reel Injun* was well received and won multiple awards.

The widespread support and acknowledgment of this film is a significant step forward in Indigenous Peoples' efforts to represent their true selves, on their own terms, in popular discourse. More generally, what is needed is more organizational support for Indigenous cinema and filmmaking.

Individual-Level Strategies of Resistance

Anita Sarkeesian challenges the way women are represented in pop culture in her educational video web series "Feminist Frequencies" available on YouTube. Sarkeesian covers the representation of women in various platforms. However, her primary focus is on women in video games in her subseries called "Tropes vs. Women in Video Games" (YouTube.com/feministfrequency). A trope is a cliché used in creative contexts, including writing, film, and art. An image, plot, phrase, or character becomes a trope when it becomes overused to the point of instant recognition from the audience.

Sarkeesian defines, exposes, and provides examples of damaging tropes. They include the manic pixie dream girl, women in refrigerators, the Smurfette principle, the evil demon seductress, the mystical pregnancy, and the straw feminist. One of her series explores the damsel-in-distress character always played by women.

After the success of her web series, which is still active today, Sarkeesian has lectured and presented internationally at universities, conferences, and game development studios. She has also received recognition for her work from various game developer award committees and has been featured in multiple mainstream publications (Feminist Frequency 2012).

Closing Remarks

As even Abraham Maslow (1943) was ready to admit, respect is not a matter of immediate life and death. People can live without respect, though they cannot live without food, water, shelter, and physical safety. That is why Maslow listed respect and self-esteem as needs of a higher order, to be satisfied after the more primary needs have been taken care of.

However, that doesn't mean that respect is trivial. People who lack respect are likely to suffer reduced self-esteem. And a lack of self-esteem is likely to lead to other undesirable results. We might even say that people who lack self-esteem are socially incapacitated—unable or unlikely to set their sights high and strive for the goals they value most. They are more likely than others to settle for a second-best education, second-best job, second-best marriage, and second-best life. They are more likely than others to give up easily when faced with adversity.

Perhaps worst of all, they are less likely than others to demand equal access to the resources we have discussed in this book: to a good job, good health, a good education, and so on. This allows society to continue in its unequal way; without the self-esteem or worth to advocate for change, future generations of the same populations are also exploited, excluded, lessened, and denied respect.

And when specific identities are continually disrespected in popular discourse—when they are derided, debased, and ignored—it acts to confirm and therefore justify inequality. These repeated mischaracterizations say, why bother ourselves about the suffering of people who are less important, less intelligent, or less worthy? Why bother worrying about inequality at all?

In the end, respect may in fact be one of the most critical resources if our goal is to improve society and erase the inequalities we have discussed in this book. Respect is one of those things—like wisdom and imagination—that can't be seen but is nonetheless essential to everyone. In this chapter, we have seen that this invisible resource is denied to many Canadians, and in a great many instances, popular discourse—mass media, sports, social media—is to blame. So, reforming the way mass media present us to ourselves may be an excellent place to start fixing the problem of unequal respect in our society.

Test Your Knowledge

1. Name, in order, the categories that Maslow identified in his hierarchy of needs. How do they relate to the study of respect?
2. How does respect affect inequality?
3. What is othering? How does it influence inequality?

4. What is the Bechdel test? Analyze something (a movie, television episode, video game, or novel) you've seen recently using this test. Does it pass or fail?
5. What is a trope? What does the study of tropes tell sociologists about respect?
6. True or false: The Russo test is used to find out whether a film positively represents characters with a disability.
7. True or false: Sociologists who embrace the conflict approach dismiss the idea that social inequality benefits society as a whole.
8. One of the non-verbal ways that people can show disrespect—sometimes intentionally using this to disrespect someone through their words—is through ___________.

See the Answer Key online to check your answers.

Questions for Critical Thought

1. Can you imagine the sequence by which a person who has been disrespected can fall into behaviour patterns that are self-harming that results, finally, in illness or even death? Describe one such sequence.
2. How can the process of "othering" be used to manipulate political events? Can you think of any contemporary examples? How might we prevent this from happening in the future?
3. This chapter discussed a number of groups that are under- or misrepresented in mainstream media. Can you think of any other groups that face these challenges? How are they similar and how are they different from the ones discussed in this chapter?
4. Do you think underrepresentation of certain groups in the media has increased or decreased during the past decade? Why is this? What are the most significant barriers to increasing the visibility of these groups?
5. What does it mean for something to be "normal"? Is being "normal" even possible?

Additional Resources

Recommended Readings

Fuchs, S. 2001. *Against Essentialism: A Theory of Culture and Society.* Cambridge, MA: Harvard University Press. This book presents a sociological theory of culture. This interdisciplinary and foundational work deals with fundamental issues common to current debates in social theory, including society, culture, meaning, truth, and communication.

Holtzman, L. and L. Sharpe. 2014. *Media Messages: What Film, Television, And Popular Music Teach Us about Race, Class, Gender, And Sexual Orientation.* Armonk, NY: M.E. Sharpe. This book analyzes how the media we consume affects our understanding of different groupings in society. The analysis is not only theoretical but is also supported with many examples of television shows, movies, and songs from popular culture.

Said, E. 1978. *Orientalism.* New York: Pantheon. In this book, Edward Said clarifies his idea of "othering" in relation to how the Middle East is viewed and portrayed by Western societies. This is a seminal book about how the West treats other cultures and deals with many of the themes discussed in this chapter.

Recommended Websites

Bechdel Test

http://bechdeltest.com

This website allows you to see how a wide range of movies stand up to the Bechdel test. You may be interested to see which movies have passed the test and the ratio to those that have not.

Disability News Service

http://disabilitynewsservice.com

This website seeks to address the underrepresentation of people with disabilities in the news and the lack of news stories on issues that affect their lives. It is an excellent example of equitable reporting and focuses on issues of respect and status in society.

National Film Board

www.nfb.ca

A repository of filmed Canadian culture, including short documentaries about and films made by groups we have discussed in this chapter, including films about and by Indigenous Peoples.

Women's Media Center

www.womensmediacenter.com

The Women's Media Center works to increase the visibility of women in the media we consume. The website contains literature and statistics about how women are underrepresented in the media, as well as articles and blogs about feminist issues.

HerrBullermann/Shutterstock

12 How Canada Compares

A Snapshot of Inequality around the World

Learning Objectives

- To name and explain some global trends in social inequality.
- To explain the meaning of Gini index (or coefficient) scores.
- To identify specific ways other countries have addressed social inequality.
- To compare international approaches to education, early childhood education, housing, and healthcare.
- To make connections between global levels of inequality and life in Canada and vice versa.

Introduction

In earlier chapters, we saw how different types of survival capital—including healthcare, nutritious food, housing, and education—are shared in Canada. We have also considered some of the social reasons that explain why vulnerable populations in Canada have unequal access to these interconnected survival capital. For example, a shortage of education can worsen the shortage of income from employment, which can lead to a shortage of nutritious food or housing. As we have discovered, people need all of these types of survival capital to lead long, healthy, happy lives.

And we have also discovered that Canadians, on average, are better off than many—most—people in the world. In this chapter, we step back from our country for a global perspective on inequality.

Gini index The statistical representation of income inequality between the rich and the poor. It expresses inequality on a scale of 0 to 1, with 1 being perfect (or complete) inequality and 0 being perfect equality.

Let's begin by noting that inequality—at least, income inequality and wealth inequality—is well measured throughout the world today. Everywhere, people use the **Gini index** (or coefficient) to measure inequality, compare inequality from country to country, and watch how inequality is changing over time.

Evidence suggests that inequality is a growing concern worldwide and is made worse by social forces that extend beyond national borders. Today's problems include nuclear spread, biodiversity loss, and the climate crisis; all of these global problems are worsened by (and in turn, worsen) inequality. We will start by reviewing some basic facts about global inequality today. Then we'll spend time comparing Canada with other, similar countries.

In the last half of the chapter, we will look at some of the smart, innovative solutions that are being deployed in different countries to level the playing field. Some of the initiatives we will read about might not work in Canada, for various reasons. Other initiatives might work here, but they aren't happening as much as they could. The important thing to understand is that inequality is something we can correct, or at least adjust, through social legislation. The job of the sociologist is to examine this variation, explain it, and analyze how it affects people's lives for better or worse.

Basic Facts about Global Inequality: The Poor

There are 7.5 billion of us on this planet—twice as many as there were in 1960. It is estimated that we'll reach 10 billion by the 2080s, if not sooner. The most rapid population growth happens in the world's poorest countries, partly because women in these countries don't have access to education, effective and safe birth control, or a living wage. These conditions are usually correlated with higher birth rates.

Conversely, studies have shown that in the developed world women usually have fewer children the more education they get, the more time they spend in the paid labour force, and the higher income they earn. This is easy to understand: childbearing carries heavy "opportunity costs" for women. They could otherwise be earning large amounts of money and gaining independence and pleasure through their work (see, for example, United Nations 2017). In much of the world, women lack this choice. They may be unable to gain access to higher education, high-paying jobs, or contraceptive technology, leading to more births.

extreme poverty Living on a budget of less than US$1.90 per day. People living in extreme poverty are often faced with chronic malnutrition and often die from treatable diseases because of a lack of available or affordable medical care.

Poverty is common around the world. In 2016, almost 10 per cent of the world's workers and their families lived on less than US$1.90 per person per day (United Nations 2016). This is considered **extreme poverty**.

Extreme poverty and malnutrition go hand in hand. One in 10 people in the world are "chronically malnourished": They aren't getting enough food, or the food they are eating lacks vital nutrients. Globally, one in six children under the age of five is underweight, and even more show signs of stunted growth owing to the effects of malnutrition (United Nations 2018).

It is common for people living in extreme poverty to die of preventable, treatable diseases. Treatable diseases like tuberculosis, cholera, polio, or measles kill hundreds of thousands of people in developing nations every year. Malaria, for example—which is preventable, easily diagnosed, and curable (for the low, low cost of $1)—kills one child every minute.

Children, mostly babies, die in developing countries much more often than in wealthier countries. In 2017, 15,000 children died each day, mostly due to preventable, treatable conditions like pneumonia, diarrhea, and malnutrition. In the poorest regions of sub-Saharan Africa, 1 in 13 children die before the age of five (UNICEF 2018).

The death of children and babies is so common in some parts of the world that it skews statistics on life expectancy. Chad, for example, has a life expectancy of only 50 years, largely because of the early deaths of babies and children.

A preventable death of a child in Canada is so rare that it often makes the headlines. By contrast, the many who perish in developing countries "die quietly in some of the poorest villages on earth, far removed from the scrutiny and the conscience of the world" (UNICEF 2018). Let's put this in perspective: Think of 13 children you know. Now picture losing one of them to pneumonia and imagine the resulting impact that would have on families, neighbourhoods, and communities.

Death, disease, and starvation are not the only daily realities for the world's poorest people. The global overexploitation of the environment has led to huge losses of biodiversity and increases in extreme weather, otherwise known as the climate crisis. People in developing countries, especially those living in extreme poverty, feel these changes first and most severely. These are people whose homes are less equipped to handle erratic, extreme weather or whose livelihoods depend on healthy rivers, marine stocks, and forests. In 2018, the United Nations first officially used the term *climate refugee*, stating that "climate, environmental degradation and natural disasters increasingly interact with the drivers of refugee movements." Most of the world lives in a nation *from* which people will flee or a nation *to* which they will flee, which means that all of us will have to confront the human realities of the climate crisis.

In Chapter 5, we mainly focused on barriers to postsecondary education since all children in Canada receive a free education until the end of secondary school. This is not the case in many countries in the world where families are expected to pay tuition for their children, even in primary school. In poorer communities, these expenses—especially when combined with ingrained patriarchal beliefs about the roles and value of women—mean that girls are much less likely to receive a primary education than boys. In the poorest countries, girls have less than a 50 per cent chance of completing primary school.

The same patriarchal beliefs that deprive women of an education also play out at the highest levels of government, where women are much less likely to participate in change making. In a 2018 global analysis, the rate of women's representation in parliament was only 24 per cent. In a quarter of these governments, women constituted 10 per cent or less of the membership (Inter-Parliamentary Union 2019). Interestingly, Rwanda—not as developed or wealthy as many countries—had the highest percentage of women in government: 61 per cent! The United Nations has addressed the lack of women in government. It points out that "whether in the public or private sphere, from the highest levels of government decision-making to households, women continue to be denied equal opportunity with men to participate in decisions that affect their lives" (United Nations 2013:5).

IN FOCUS ◆ Malala Yousafzai

> Let us pick up our books and our pens. They are our most powerful weapons. One child, one teacher, one book, and one pen can change the world.

Malala Yousafzai has become a heroic figure in the fight for girls' education. This young activist from Pakistan survived a 2012 assassination attempt during which she was shot in the head by Taliban militia. After spending months in recovery, she came back on the international scene louder than ever, bravely defending the right to education. Malala was the youngest person ever awarded the Nobel Peace Prize.

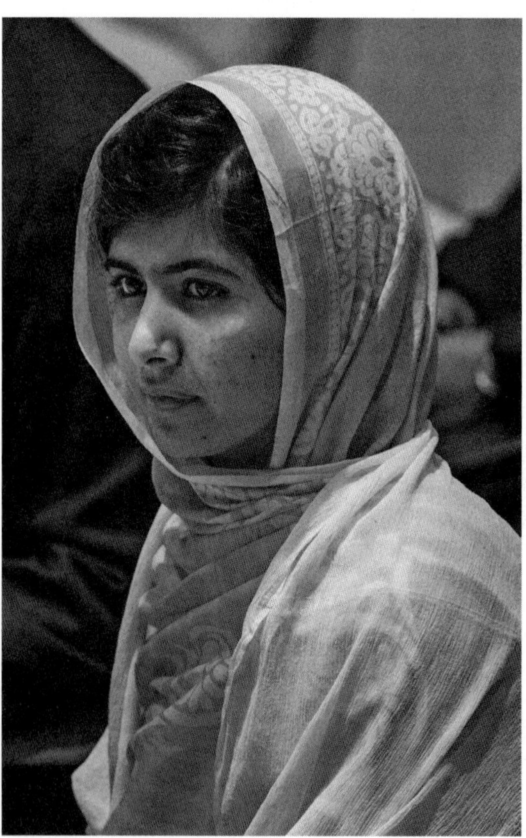

Malala Yousafzai is a heroic advocate for female education in developing, often misogynistic countries. She is the youngest person to be awarded the Nobel Peace Prize.

Organisation for Economic Co-operation and Development (OECD) An international organization comprising 36 member-states committed to researching and proposing solutions for economic, social, and environmental problems.

The good news is the number of people living in extreme poverty is shrinking. The mortality rate for children under five has fallen dramatically in the last 20 years. More people have access to clean water and safe toilets. More children are attending school. This doesn't mean the poorest are getting rich, or even comfortably middle class—it means the "extremely poor" in most emerging economies are bumping up ever so slightly to "very poor."

At the same time, we are seeing an increase in the gap between the rich and the poor in both developed and developing countries.

Basic Facts about Global Inequality: The Rich

One way that economists understand and compare economic inequality, country by country, is by measuring how much richer the richest are than the poorest. What they have noticed is the gap between the rich and the poor is increasing in most countries around the world. The **Organisation for Economic Co-operation and Development (OECD)**, an important international organization that compares 36 similar countries, reports that

> Income inequality in OECD countries is at its highest level for the past half century. The average income of the richest 10% of the population is about nine times that of the poorest 10% across the OECD, up from seven times 25 years ago. Only in Turkey, Chile, and Mexico has inequality fallen, but in the latter two countries the incomes of the richest are still more than 25 times those of the poorest. (OECD 2019a)

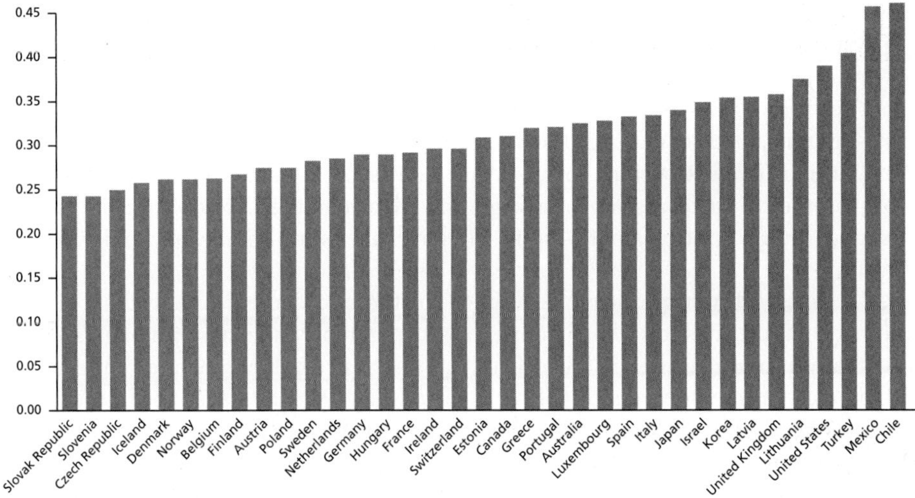

Figure 12.1 ◆ Income Inequality in OECD Countries

Source: OECD 2020.

The mission of the OECD is to find solutions to common economic, social, and environmental problems. The OECD also serves as a research hub; it measures and compares social data collected from all the member countries (and others!) and recommends changes based on that data. When examining inequality around the world, OECD data sets are a great place to start.

Seven out of 10 people on the planet live in a country that has seen increased inequality over the past 30 years (World Top Incomes Database 2017). However, we also see big differences from country to country. In some Nordic countries, for example, the richest slice of the population is only about five times richer than the poorest. In Mexico and Chile, the richest slice of the population is 27 times richer than the poorest. Similarly, large emerging economies like China and India show higher (and growing) inequality.

In Chapter 1 we introduced the Gini index, which researchers use to measure inequality, compare inequality from country to country, and watch how inequality is changing over time. The Gini index provides a helpful basis for visualizing levels of inequality in different countries. Figure 12.1 doesn't list all the countries in the world, but it shows a representative sample. Notice that Canada sits near the middle: more equal than countries like Mexico and the UK, but less equal than Finland and Ireland.

It is important to realize that on a global scale fewer people are controlling the world's wealth. Consider this: Today, half of the world's wealth is now owned by only 1 per cent of the population. In 2018, the world's 26 richest people owned the same amount of wealth as the world's 3.8 *billion* poorest people—half of the total world population (Oxfam 2019).

Why Is Higher Inequality Happening?

Imagine if a time traveller from the year 800 were to land in, say, a thousand years later in the year 1800. They would probably recognize many of the same familiar social structures. People were still being born, living, and dying in small, mostly rural communities. They were still providing for themselves and their families with local employment and subsistence agriculture and bartering for goods and services.

And yet if that time traveller set the dial on the time machine for 200 years beyond that—the year 2000—they might think they had landed on a different planet. In a short period of time, many of our social structures have become unrecognizable.

Consider manufacturing: Today, people and factories spread out across the globe work together to make, assemble, package, and sell a computer. Your computer probably has more stamps on its passport—or, its shipping paperwork—than you could ever hope to collect!

Or consider banking: The money used to buy those computers is rarely cash. Instead, another computer deducts a sum from an abstract number in an abstract bank account. Eventually another number is "deposited" into the abstract bank account of the factory owner and the transaction is complete. The age when like was traded for like, or when paper money *represented* value rather than being valuable itself, is long gone for many of people. The same can be said about small, local, independent banks managing their communities' money. Today, wealth is managed by huge, global, and "too big to fail" banks.

Now let's consider information technology: Ships used to deliver handwritten letters from one continent to the other. Today, over 100 billion emails are sent every day, their messages circling the planet in mere seconds. This revolutionary speed and volume of communication means that we can produce a lot more a lot faster.

And finally, consider labour migration: National borders are becoming increasingly porous as people move from country to country to work or live.

While there is no single driving force behind the increases in inequality around the world, "globalization" has produced conditions that hasten the concentration of wealth. Globalization has resulted in the creation of international organizations like the United Nations, whose objectives are to promote peace and security for everyone in the world. Other large international organizations like the World Bank and the International Monetary Fund coordinate large-scale lending and borrowing between countries. Historically, some of these loans have come with strings attached and required borrowing countries to "shrink" their governments to reduce their fiscal imbalances. These "strings attached loans" are often identified as a driver behind the growing international inequality.

To qualify for the much-needed loan, a government might be obliged to sell publicly owned assets, like railroads and water treatment plants, to private (and often foreign) buyers. This **privatization** of public assets means that money that might otherwise stay within a country is sent to bank accounts elsewhere. Instead of being used to provide education or healthcare, money is drained out of the pockets of the poorest, out of the country, and redistributed to foreign interests.

And even if profits were earned by a resident of the country, these people could dodge paying domestic taxes on this income by banking in **tax havens** like Switzerland or the Cayman Islands. Today, *trillions* of dollars are sitting in tax havens. This means that governments cannot use this tax revenue to fund programs that would equalize opportunities for the poorest in their countries. That's one reason organizations like the Tax Justice Network work to reform tax havens to make it more difficult for the wealthiest to escape fair taxation.

Wealth often accompanies (and produces) power. This means the wealthiest can influence politicians to bend or create laws that favour them and remove laws that impede

privatization The process of transferring ownership of a business, enterprise, agency, public service, or public property from the public sector (government) to a business that works for a profit or to a not-for-profit organization. It may also mean government transfer of services or jobs to private firms, for example, revenue collection, law enforcement, and prison management.

tax havens A state, country, or territory where money can be stored at a low rate of taxation or even tax free and where little or no information is shared with foreign tax authorities.

them. For example, the wealthiest often lobby against labour laws that oblige employers to pay their workers a living wage. They may fight against any efforts to decrease or wipe out greenhouse gas emissions, protect ecosystems and species habitats, and guarantee safe and fair working conditions.

Many of the big changes in the last few decades are technological in nature. Technological change often privileges higher-skilled workers because it takes some skill—like literacy, for example—to adapt to new technology. Lower-skilled workers are also more vulnerable to being replaced by robots. High-tech work is called **skills biased work**, and it often limits opportunities and worsens life chances for the unskilled.

skills biased work Technological work that requires skills like literacy that are typically learned in school environments.

Job choices for unskilled workers around the world are limited. Often, unskilled workers in emerging economies end up in manufacturing, which we've noted has become increasingly globalized. To attract big factories and the thousands of jobs that come with them, many emerging economies will relax employment rules. "We've got workers desperate for work—build here!" they say. This has resulted in high employment rates in otherwise poor communities.

However, in these places, workers receive low wages (sometimes less than 30 cents an hour). They also receive few or no health benefits and are often employed part time or on short-term contracts to save their employers money. This strategy is sometimes known as a **race to the bottom**—meaning the company that "wins" is the one that reduces the most costs. These practices make the poorest even more vulnerable. Big corporations may also

race to the bottom Progressively lowering standards, especially wages and working conditions, to undercut the competition. In other words, trying to "win" by losing the most.

If you were to check the tags on the clothing you're currently wearing, would you find that most items were made in North America? Probably not. To save money, many companies today make their products in developing economies with low wages and unsafe working conditions.

"shop around" to see which state, province, or country will want them to pay the lowest taxes. They do this in exchange for setting up a job-creating headquarters.

Another interesting driving force of inequality is the change in household structure. Families with multiple earners can pool their resources and live more efficiently (heating a room costs the same whether there is one or two people living in it). Today, there are far more single-headed households around the world than there were three decades ago, which lessens the concentration of wealth. Another trend that has influenced wealth concentration is the increased tendency to marry within one's income bracket (for example, lawyers marrying lawyers instead of lawyers marrying assistants or clerks). This practice, known as **assortative mating**, affects the otherwise-more-equal distribution of earnings from income.

assortative mating A social trend in which individuals marry within their socio-economic bracket.

Different Actions to Combat Inequality

In the previous section, we described a few of the driving forces of global inequality. In this section, we will look at some actions that countries are taking—or not taking—to combat inequality and increase equitable access to survival capital. Specifically, we compare Canada with the United States, Japan, Sweden, Germany, Ireland, Finland, and Norway. These countries are all considered **high-income economies**, which the World Bank defines as countries with a per capita income of $12,000 or more. The countries we're about to compare are not characterized by extreme poverty. They are also all member-states of the OECD, and they are all market-driven economies supported by democratically elected governments.

high-income economies Countries with a per capita income of $12,000 or more.

Let's begin with a simple but powerful generalization: The conditions under which humans live in the world today—that is, under the sway of capitalism, globalization, and automation—do not tend naturally toward greater equality. Indeed, as Thomas Piketty (2014) and other economic historians have observed, they tend toward increasing, ever-more-extreme inequalities of wealth and power.

This means that equality, if we are to have it, must be won against enormous odds; and throughout this book we have seen that the Nordic countries—Norway, Sweden, Denmark, Finland, and Iceland—have succeeded best in this battle. As Gøsta Esping-Andersen (1990) explained, they have done this by adopting what he calls a "social democratic welfare regime." This regime is a set of social and political institutions that cover almost every aspect of daily life and seek to redistribute wealth and power. They also seek to reduce suffering and raise the most vulnerable members of society socially and economically.

This Nordic social welfare regime took decades to develop, and its development required skilful, dedicated political leadership and a strong political mandate. This, in turn, required strong public support for the practices of social democracy and for the idea of social equality. This, in turn, meant that the cultures of these countries had to be sympathetic to and compatible with these egalitarian practices. Countries with liberal or traditional or mixed welfare regimes (like Canada) did not and do not have compatible cultures, strong public support for equality, suitable political leadership, or a network of appropriate social and political institutions that achieving equality would require.

All this being said, as we have hinted throughout this book and will note more directly in the pages below, the Nordic countries are not heaven on earth. They are imperfect, and they struggle to avoid backsliding into greater inequality as a result of capitalism, globalization, and automation. Beyond that, they have not been fully successful—not as successful as Canada, for example—in welcoming into their lives and assimilating ethnic and racial minorities. In comparative terms, they excel at promoting income and gender equality but have a way to go in promoting equal citizenship for ethnic and racial minorities. So we will need to consider, among other things, whether the full package—income and gender equality, as well as a full slate of social equalities—is possible for any existing society. At present, the full package does not exist.

With this said, let's review what we have discovered about the state of the stacked deck in different comparison societies.

Income from Employment

As we read in Chapter 3, many Canadians struggle to find safe, stable, and reasonably paid work, especially when their experience of inequality is compounded by interlocking disadvantages. One of the major reasons behind this inequality is employment discrimination. This means that some people in Canada are more likely to be denied jobs, to be laid off, and are the last to be promoted. But employment inequality begins long before the job hunt. Evidence shows that certain populations in Canada have unequal access to key employment prerequisites like education or training.

In Chapter 3, we explored models that sought to explain employment inequality. The "common sense" perspective suggests that people earn what they deserve; those who work harder are paid more, so **wage gaps** exist. The functional theory of stratification proposes that income inequality exists because some jobs need more intensive and expensive training; higher wages encourage people to seek these more challenging and socially valuable occupations. As we saw in Chapter 3, critics of this theory point out social disagreement about the value of different jobs (for example, highly paid celebrities). Similarly, this theory doesn't do much to justify inherited wealth.

wage gap The difference in the earnings of different demographics, expressed as a percentage of the dominant groups' earnings. It can help us better understand wage equality or inequality among different groups and populations.

Two more models worth noting are the ethnicity model and equity model. Related to functionalism, the ethnicity model states that if immigrants cannot secure work, it is because they have yet to conform to the Canadian work environment. Conversely, the **equity model** is part of conflict theory and claims that institutional barriers cause employment inequality. The workplace itself is designed to promote the interests of a few—those at the top—while not catering to others—those at the bottom. As a result, the rich stay rich and the poor stay poor.

equity model A theory that explains employment inequality as a product of institutional barriers that make finding work more difficult for certain demographics and keep wealth concentrated at the top.

The equity model creates interesting discussions about social mobility: How can low-income populations climb up the income ladder if social institutions are designed to cater to those at the top? Questions like this one fuelled the "Occupy Wall Street" movement in 2011, a series of protests emerging in the United States that quickly spread around the world. One of the goals of this movement was to draw attention to the concentration of wealth in the hands of few at the expense of many (Byrne 2012).

This trend is especially pronounced in the United States, where social mobility and income inequality are an increasing problem. The Occupy Wall Street movement revealed some stark realities: Since the 1980s, income inequality has risen sharply in the United States. As we showed in Figure 12.1, the United States has the fourth-highest inequality of all OECD member-states (OECD 2019a).

Why is income inequality so prevalent in the United States, even after taxes and transfers? Explanations vary widely. In this next section, we compare the United States and Sweden and focus on how policies related to employment can impact inequality. Some begin by pointing out the US tradition of high **worker–CEO pay ratios** (see Figure 12.2). In the United States in 2018, the average pay of the top CEOs was 312 times as much as an average American worker (Rushe 2018). In Canada, CEOs earn a more modest 209 times as much as the average Canadian worker (Macdonald 2018).

worker–CEO pay ratios The amount CEOs earn compared to their average or lowest-paid employee.

The pay of American CEOs is largely determined by "executive compensation committees," which are appointed or overseen *by* the CEOs. In hopes of discouraging this practice, the US Securities and Exchange Commission is trying to compel CEOs to disclose exactly how much they earn.

In 2018, a report by the Canadian Centre for Policy Alternatives found the average compensation for the 100-highest paid CEOs in Canada was $10.4 million. This amount was 209 times higher than the average wage in Canada, which is just under $50,000 (Macdonald 2018).

We have noted that racialized people in Canada report experiencing discrimination in the workplace. This is also true in the United States. Perhaps one of the most notable historic periods of employment discrimination based on race or ethnicity emerged after the 9/11 attacks in 2001. In the nine weeks following the attacks, 800 incidents of workplace discrimination were reported. According to opinion polls, anyone of Arabic descent was viewed as most "foreign" and "unsociable" when compared to Black Americans and Hispanic Americans, two other marginalized racial groups in the United States (Sides and Gross 2013).

Scholars have also studied American employment discrimination patterns on grounds of gender identity (James et al. 2016), sex (Torres Sevilla-Quiñones de León 2014), class (Rivera and Tilcsik 2016), age (Johnson and Gosselin 2018), and weight (Roehling, Pichler, and Bruce 2013).

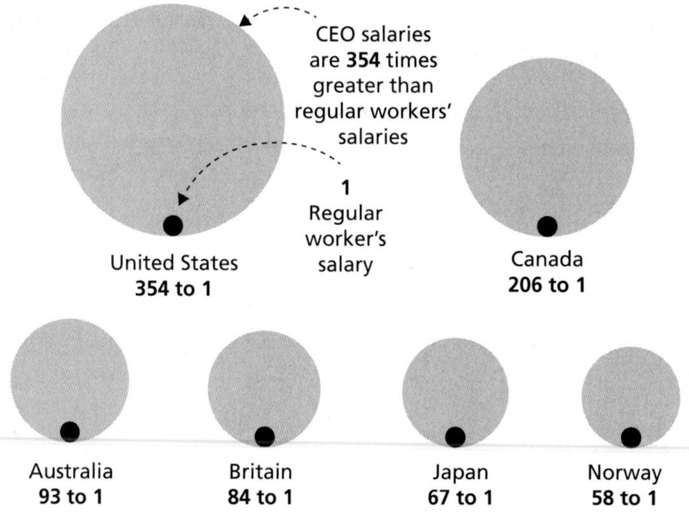

Figure 12.2 ◆ Global CEO-to-Worker Pay Ratios
This image uses bubbles to compare CEO-to-worker pay ratios around the world.

Source: *Maclean's* 2014.

While no country has fully equal opportunities for employment, Sweden is largely considered one of the most equitable First World economies, ranking eleventh of the OECD countries. What has Sweden done differently from the United States (ranked thirty-first) and Canada (ranked nineteenth)? For one thing, university is state-funded through taxes in Sweden, which means university is free for Swedes. Swedish citizens also have broader access to many other important forerunners to employment, including quality, low-cost, or free early childhood education and job search and training services. In contrast to Americans and Canadians, Swedish citizens are willing to pay high taxes in return for these public social services. Perhaps that's why the Swedish word for "tax" also translates as "treasure" (Government of Sweden 2019).

For decades, Sweden has focused on promoting higher labour participation rates for women as part of its broader plan to address gender equality. Parental leave policies that seek to equalize parenting responsibilities are one of the ways of doing so. In 1974, Sweden became the first country to grant men and women equal access to paid parental leave (now parents receive 16 months of paid parental leave). Most notably for employment equality, in 1995 Sweden introduced a non-transferable leave plan. In 2019, this means that 3 of the 18 months of subsidized leave are allocated for a second parent on a "use-it-or-lose-it" basis. This encourages both parents to share the burden (and joy!) of childcare. With the exception of Quebec, Canada has no policy offering parental leave specifically for second parents.

In Europe, there has been a noted attitude shift whereby the care of young children is increasingly accepted as a father's activity. A study of men in 27 European countries, for example, showed that men who had taken paternity leave were significantly more likely to be involved in housework and carework after the leave had ended (Meil 2013).

Sweden equalizes employment opportunities through their relatively fast routes for immigrants to secure employment. In the 2000s, Sweden decreased the number of years of residency needed to apply for citizenship, reduced the waiting period for citizenship, abolished the language skill test, and recognized dual citizenship. These changes made it easier for immigrants to gain citizenship, an important stepping-stone to secure employment.

Citizenship signals to employers that a person is planning to stay in the country. In Sweden, gaining citizenship also provides access to the European Union, basic social security, legal rights in the workplace, and protection from deportation (Bevelander and Pendakur 2012). The easier acquisition of citizenship for immigrants opens more opportunities and gives immigrants the same legal status as everyone else in the workplace, theoretically guaranteeing safe and reasonably compensated jobs.

Many different factors contribute to employment inequality—far more than we have explored here. Not all initiatives can be broadly applied in all political and cultural contexts, and no country has managed to fairly dole out employment to all those who need it. Some countries, like the United States, have a lot to do to mitigate the inequality of employment. Others, like Sweden, have taken measures that appear to have had some effect.

Housing and Transportation

In Chapter 6, we saw that housing is unequally available to everyone in Canada. And yet housing is so important: Humans all need shelter, of course, but housing also affects how and to what degree we access other important resources. It's challenging to get and keep a job, for example, without a fixed address. Also, our sense of dignity and belonging are tied up in our homes. As gentrification, bulk-housing takeovers by large private equity firms, and ghettoization trends continue, more housing inequalities appear.

Indeed, Canada is not the only country to struggle with housing inequality. As a result, we can see different national approaches to housing characterized by various types of housing taxation, land use, and rental rules. Social housing is one strategy that addresses housing inequality. That's because these homes are typically rented at below market cost and are assigned based on need.

Social housing—housing provided by government agencies or not-for-profit organizations—is common around the world. What varies from country to country are the degree and scope of social housing; some countries have more social housing and others have less. For example, social housing makes up only 5 per cent of total housing stock in Korea, Norway, Switzerland, Australia, and Italy. By contrast, social housing makes up around 20 per cent of total housing stock in Denmark, the Netherlands, and Austria. The most available data suggest that, in Canada, roughly 10 per cent of total housing stock is social housing.

residential segregation The concentration of similar socio-economic brackets in one geographic area.

targeted social housing system The grant of social housing to those who show the greatest financial need.

Depending on the approach, social housing can worsen **residential segregation** by crowding together housing units in districts with poorer educational opportunities and employment. This tendency is most common in a **targeted social housing system**, which prioritizes those who display the most financial need.

Germany has taken a creative spin on social housing with its house rental-sharing program (Fox 2014). First, a senior or person with a disability is identified. They are eligible if they do not need (or do not qualify for) formal social care but have their own home and a spare room. This individual is matched with a "homesharer" who needs affordable accommodation and is willing and able to help out with the house. The homesharers are usually from lower socio-economic status, like a foreign student or someone starting a modestly paid career who would otherwise be vulnerable to housing insecurity.

This homeshare scheme finds compatible matches, helping both parties take responsibility for each other and improve their quality of life. After Germany's success, many other countries have started to use this model to address the housing inequality problems in their own countries.

Another kind of German house sharing happens between elders and young children (Oltermann 2014). The *Mehrgenerationenhäuser*, or "multigenerational house," combines the nursery and the sitting room, creating both a kindergarten as well as a social centre for the elderly and young children. Pensioners volunteer to read books to the children once a week and run a "rent-a-granny" service to relieve and help exhausted young parents. At the same time, teenagers offer to show elderly people how to use new technologies, such as computers and mobile phones. All generations benefit from this creative residential design.

These initiatives do more than provide housing: They also fulfill other important social needs. Surely there is more that can be done in Canada to equalize housing access and provide vulnerable people with shelter, a measure of dignity, and a place to call home.

Daycare and Early Childhood Education

As you learned in Chapter 5, many disadvantaged people are especially vulnerable to unequal access to quality early childhood care and education.

Recall that, in Canada, paid childcare is market determined, meaning it may be offered by businesses like any other "commodity." There is a shortage of government-regulated childcare. Unregulated childcare of varying quality is available, and many desperate parents are forced to take whatever is available. Both regulated and unregulated childcare is costly (in some places, it is more expensive than university tuition).

At the moment, Canada is one of just a few First World economies without a national program that offers quality, low-cost public childcare (see Figure 12.3). Early childhood education and care should ideally align with parental leave allowances. Free and universal care should kick in around the same time parental leave expires, so parents can transition seamlessly back to work.

Countries where childcare is publicly delivered perform better on UNESCO, OECD, UNICEF, and other benchmark rankings. And in countries where all children are entitled to childcare and that care is funded by the government, participation is higher. For examples, in Denmark, less than 1 per cent of families opt out of childcare because of cost.

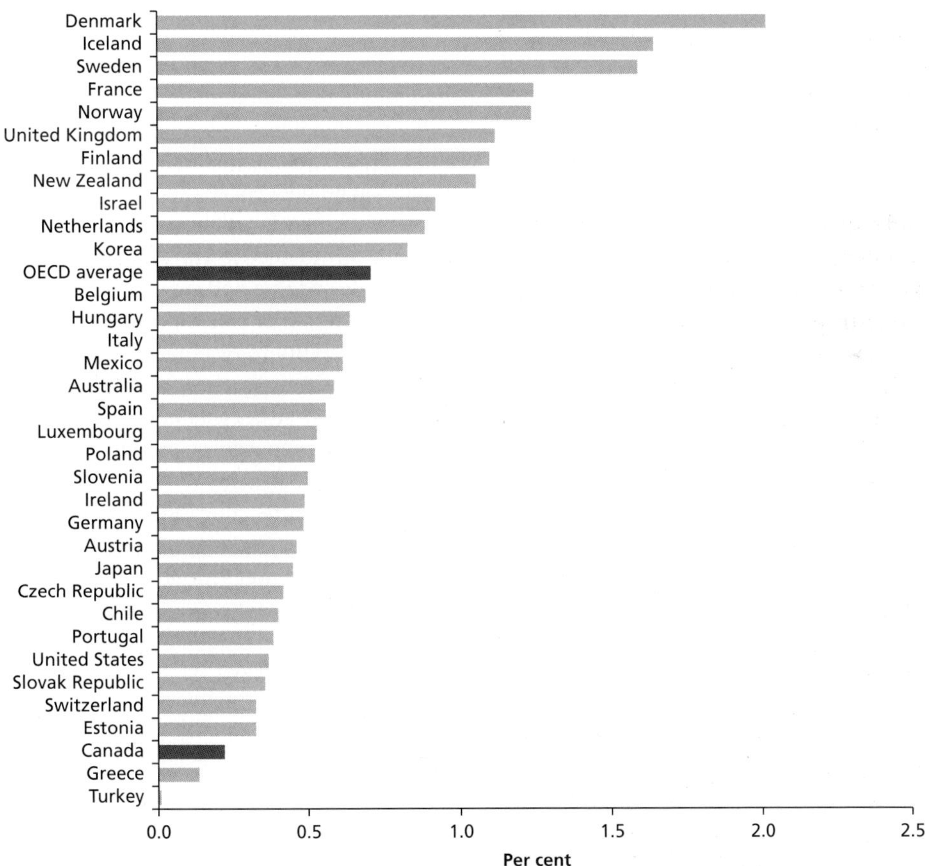

Figure 12.3 ◆ How Much Do Countries Spend on Early Childhood Care and Education?

Source: OECD 2019b.

IN FOCUS ◆ Focus on Finland

When 35 OECD countries are ranked according to educational achievement of 15 year olds, Finland comes in first place. It's true the Finnish primary and secondary education systems are excellent. And yet, it's Finland's excellent *preschool* programs that many credit for the country's high educational standing. Here's Peter Adamson, a researcher for UNICEF, describing what gives Finland its preschool edge over similar countries:

> Finland spends considerably more than the OECD average on early years care and education, [and] has exceptionally high minimum qualification requirements for preschool teaching staff and the highest standards of staff-to-child ratios of any advanced economy (1:3 for children under three years old, and 1:8 for children three and over). Most commentators on Finland's outstanding record of educational achievement cite the quality of the country's early years' education. (OECD 2016b)

Compare that to 22 per cent of families in the United Kingdom who can't afford care (UNICEF 2019).

Let's compare two countries: Norway and the United States. In Norway, parents can take up to 49 weeks of *paid* parental leave or 59 weeks at 80 per cent of their salary. Fifteen weeks of this is earmarked for the second parent on a use-it-or-lose-it basis. Centre-based, preschool childcare is provided for *all* children aged 1–5 who need it, and fees for this care are heavily subsidized; specific fees are based on family income and never exceed 6 per cent of parental income (while single parents pay nothing). The control of these centres is the authority of the local town, giving the centres the ability to respond to local needs, such as culturally suitable care for Indigenous Sami children. Teachers must be specifically trained with at least a university degree. A federal act states that childcare centres have a duty to meet the needs of both child and parent by encouraging parental involvement whenever suitable.

Early childhood care and education is only one factor in the educational success of a nation. That said, as of 2015, Norway scores above the United States in science, reading, and math, and children show a greater sense of belonging and lower school-related anxiety (OECD 2018).

Now let's move from a comparison of early childhood care and education to a consideration of when people typically complete the rest of their education.

Postsecondary Education

Canada has one of the best education systems in the world, and all children in Canada can attend quality public elementary and secondary schools for free. In fact, Canada fares well internationally in education achievement by the age of 15. In a 2015 OECD survey of 72 member and non-member nations, Canada ranked seventh overall (OECD 2018). When we examine postsecondary education, however, we begin to see some major barriers. Recall the inequalities pointed out in Chapter 5: Youth from lower-income families are less likely to seek postsecondary education than their counterparts from higher-income families (Frenette 2017).

But cost alone is not the only barrier to education. Older students, students with disabilities, racialized students, new immigrant students, Indigenous students, and LGBTQ+ students all face diverse, multiple, and overlapping barriers to education in Canada.

Another country that shares Canada's low postsecondary participation ranking is the United States. As in Canada, students entering colleges and universities in the United States have to pay tuition, and the US rates are among the highest in all the OECD countries (OECD 2013). Over the past 30 years, the average tuition rate for a degree at a public university in the United States has increased by more than 250 per cent. Today, tuition at private universities like Harvard and MIT can be upwards of US$45,000 per year. This severely limits aspiring students from low-income families.

In recent years, the United States has experienced a problem called **educational undermatching**. Undermatching occurs when a capable, talented, and bright student from a low-income family does not apply to Ivy League colleges like Harvard, Princeton, or Yale. In fact, one study showed most low-income high achievers do not apply to any college at all.

educational undermatching A circumstance in which a capable, talented, and bright student from a low-income family does not apply to Ivy League (or "selective") colleges like Harvard, Princeton, or Yale.

Why aren't they applying? Hoxby and Avery (2013) found that, in part, the low-income high achievers attended high schools where they were not likely to meet teachers, guidance counsellors, or older students who had attended an Ivy League school. Without this important contact, these high achievers were less likely to imagine these schools as a possibility.

As we've mentioned, Canada ranks high in international comparisons of educational achievement by age 15. This is, in part, because of our universal public elementary and secondary school system. Recall that not all countries in the world have publicly funded school for children and teens. In some places, families must pay tuition fees even for a six year old to attend the equivalent of our Grade 1.

One way to increase Canada's postsecondary enrolment, however, would be to copy countries like Norway, Sweden, Finland, and most recently Germany. These countries have scrapped tuition fees for postsecondary education. Why? One German government official argued that "Tuition fees are socially unjust . . . they particularly discourage young people who do not have a traditional academic family background from taking up studies" (Charter 2014).

IN FOCUS ◆ How Would You Like to Be Paid to Go to School?

In Denmark, over 300,000 students benefit from government grants—grants, not loans (although Danish education loans are also widely available). These grants aim to cover a portion of students' living expenses while they are enrolled in higher education. The eligible amount grows or shrinks for students working while in school, students living with parents, students struggling with ill health, and new mothers and fathers who must balance school with parenting. The grants even allow for students to change their course of study midway through their program and extend their grants for another 12 months!

Of course, tuition is never truly "free"—in these countries, the cost of offering postsecondary education is borne by the taxpayers, an arrangement not everyone readily accepts. But while the private returns for the university-educated student are obvious—better health, higher income, and more job choices—the **public returns** for a country are also worth noting. An educated population means greater social contributions and tax revenues.

public returns The public benefits, such as improved population health and higher literacy rates, that are derived from investment in institutions such as education.

In fact, the OECD (2013) has calculated the net public return on investment in postsecondary education as follows: "The net public return on investment for a man in [postsecondary] education is over USD$100 000 across OECD countries—almost three times public investment in that man's education. For a woman, the public return is around USD$60 000, which is almost twice the amount of public investment." Put that way, the added tax load seems justifiable.

Offering free postsecondary education would be one way to equalize access to education in Canada. However, recall that cost is not the only barrier; we also have to address systemic discrimination of other forms that inhibit populations in Canada from full academic participation. What we know is that postsecondary achievement can work, over generations, to lift families out of poverty, enable social mobility, and increase life chances. However, it will only have that effect if we can get the children of low-income, low-education families to aspire to higher education.

Healthcare

All societies are troubled with the task of caring for the sick. However, satisfactory access to healthcare remains a challenge for people in many parts of the world, including Canada. In Chapter 8, we discussed how social status, education level, age, gender identity, and sexual orientation may impede or simplify access to satisfactory healthcare. We discovered that some people have a greater need for healthcare. Consider living conditions: We know that some unsafe homes—usually the homes of low-income earners—make their residents more vulnerable to particular illnesses. And some elements of healthcare, like prescription medication, and some elements of sickness prevention, like gym memberships, cost more money than many can afford to spend.

Typically Canadians are proud of our universal healthcare system, and we don't rank too poorly among other OECD countries in terms of healthcare delivery. Wait times are a problem, to be sure. In international comparisons of other publicly funded healthcare systems, we have ranked near the bottom in timeliness of care (CIHI 2017). In other words, Canadians typically wait longer to see doctors when compared to other publicly funded healthcare systems. When we do get to see a doctor, however, we report higher-than-average satisfaction with the care we receive.

When we look for poor health around the world, we find that poverty and poor health go together. For example, the World Health Organization (2019) calculates there is a 36-year gap between life expectancy in the richest counties and the poorest countries. They write, "A child born in Malawi can expect to live for only 47 years while a child born in Japan could live for as long as 83 years."

However, while poverty is one contributing factor to poor health, inequality is another. Citizens in countries that are comparable, economically speaking, may fare better or worse depending on the distance between the poorest and the richest. For example, when relative inequality is considered, education levels matter even more. In more-equal

Sweden, mortality among men with the least education is less than twice that of highly educated men. In less-equal Hungary, the Czech Republic, and Poland, mortality among the least-educated men is four times greater than mortality among the most-educated men.

It's hard to identify a First World economy that solves the problem of health inequality, but Sweden might be a good place to start. Globally, Sweden is considered a leader in preventive healthcare practices and policies. In Sweden, the life expectancy at birth is 82 years, which is two years higher than the OECD average of 80 years (OECD 2016a).

In Sweden, more equitable healthcare is actively pursued in various ways. First and most important, better healthcare and equality of access to healthcare is a formal goal and principle of its health policies (Bürstrom 2002). Also important is Sweden's **decentralized** health system: County (regional) councils can make decisions about work arrangements that best address their needs. This flexible and innovative model allows for better-funded and specialized hospitals and more personalized patient care (Rae 2005). While Canada's health system is also decentralized, provinces, rather than smaller regional (or county) units, are responsible for funding and providing care.

decentralization The distribution of administrative powers or roles over a less concentrated or specialized area.

Sweden's fully decentralized health system means that individual clinical centres have more autonomy and patients have more choices in their healthcare treatments. That's because they can shop around for a clinic that best meets their needs. On top of all of this, Sweden collects data on diagnoses, treatment, and effects of diseases gathered from complete records of every case. This data is shared and used to grow knowledge about illness and healthcare delivery (Rae 2005). Canada, by comparison, has no national

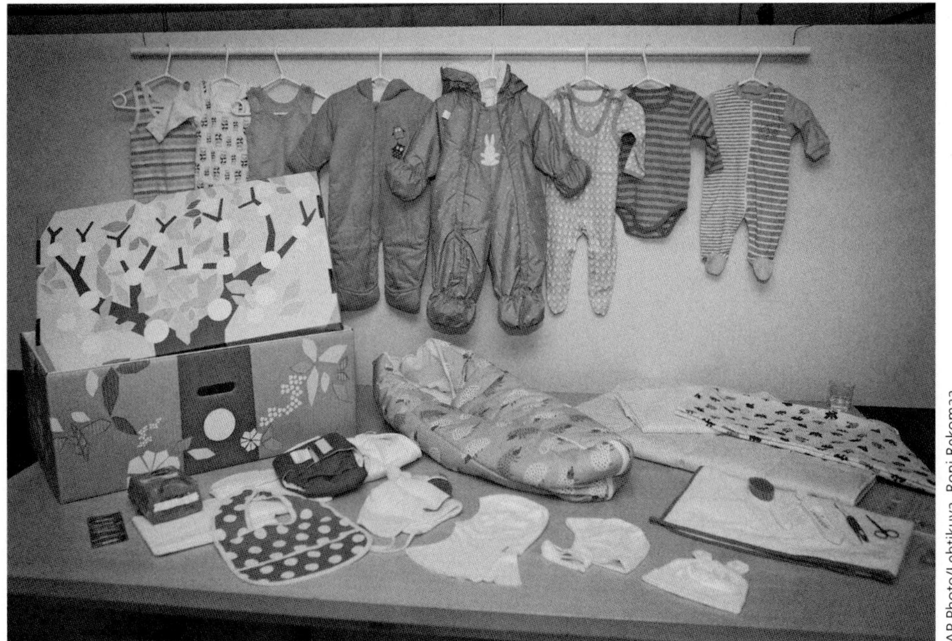

AP Photo/Lehtikuva, Roni Rekomaa

In Finland, this maternity package is sent to every expectant mother, providing her with the necessities for her newborn. The box it comes in even doubles as a crib.

healthcare electronic database, and many of the provinces are still creating even the most basic databases.

Another example of a country that has seen improvements in overall health by improving access to basic needs is Finland. Evidence shows that good health in the first months of life pays off over a lifetime. To ensure that all Finnish citizens have an equally healthy start, the government of Finland sends all expectant mothers a **Finnish Maternity Package** filled with just about everything a new baby needs. The kit, a tradition that dates back 75 years, includes a high-quality sleep sac, clothing, outdoor gear, cloth diapers, bedding, and even bathing products: more gear than many low-income families could ever afford. Popular clothing designers are hired to create the cute and fun patterns, and parents eagerly anticipate the latest look their youngster will sport. The best thing of all: The cardboard box even has a mattress at the bottom so it cleverly doubles as a bed! (Lee 2013)

Finnish Maternity Package A box containing the necessities for a baby's first year of life and delivered to all expectant mothers who are citizens in Finland.

In all societies, socio-economic inequalities result in widening health inequalities. In a publicly funded system like Canada's, all citizens pay to care for sick people, and all citizens benefit when fewer people get sick. There is value in watching how other societies are equalizing access to this most important survival capital.

Equality, Prosperity, and Happiness

Research on happiness has consistently shown that certain specifiable conditions make people happy. These include a secure and sufficient income, good health, a family household, a safe neighbourhood, a source of meaning (whether from religion, a job, or otherwise), and the feeling of belonging to a community.

With these things in mind, Canada usually scores in the top 10 happiest countries in the world (see Table 12.1). However, people in other countries are consistently even happier than Canadians. Specifically, people in Nordic countries—Finland, Norway, Denmark, Iceland, and Sweden—are happier than people in Canada. In the world happiness rankings, Canada currently scores seventh, well ahead of the United States and the United Kingdom but still behind most of the Nordic countries.

Table 12.1 World's Happiest and Least Happy Countries, 2019

World's Happiest Countries, 2019	World's Least Happy Countries, 2019
1. Finland	1. South Sudan
2. Norway	2. Central African Republic
3. Denmark	3. Afghanistan
4. Iceland	4. Tanzania
5. Switzerland	5. Rwanda
6. Netherlands	6. Yemen
7. Canada	7. Malawi
8. New Zealand	8. Syria
9. Sweden	9. Botswana
10. Australia	10. Haiti

Source: Sustainabe Development Solutions Network 2019.

It seems the Nordic countries have found happiness by lessening inequality through a social democratic welfare regime. There is a clear (negative) correlation between the average happiness of a country's citizens and its income inequality, as measured by the Gini index. As well, income equality correlates with other kinds of equality—for example, with legislation that protects the equal treatment of men and women or people of different religions, ages, and sexual orientations. In general, income equality accompanies other civil rights and broad protections of human dignity. It also correlates with progressive social programs, anti-discrimination laws, and social welfare achieved through taxation and wealth redistribution. In short, income equality signals a culture of citizenship that protects and promotes general well-being.

When discussing the egalitarianism of Nordic culture, some mention *Janteloven* or the law of Jante (Bendixen, Bringslid, and Vike 2018). *Janteloven* is not a codified law so much as a cultural philosophy defined by the Danish novelist Aksel Sandemose. It refers to the focusing of attention on the well-being of the collective, not on the achievements and well-being of the individual (Trotter 2015). Such a collectivist philosophy will shape the culture of a society. However, the link between the law of Jante and Nordic egalitarianism remains anecdotal.

Many aspects of Nordic culture and society interact at the individual, local, and institutional levels to prevent harm. As mentioned, this relies in part on the economic redistribution of wealth through taxation. The relative prosperity of Nordic countries allows their governments to spend lavishly on health, education, safety, and infrastructure.

Nordic countries follow an economic model called the social democratic welfare regime, and sometimes fittingly called the Nordic model. Greve (2007) characterizes this model as very decentralized, with many protections for families and workers. Decentralized decision making in the Nordic model means various influences at the local and regional levels manage the economy. This lack of national hierarchy shows a willingness of Nordic governments to focus on the specific, varying needs of people throughout their respective countries. Though there are no minimum wage laws in the Nordic model, wage levels are largely controlled by trade unions, so they are worker friendly. This fact underscores the importance of trade unions to the Nordic model. Not only do the unions protect their workers, but they also safeguard minimum wage levels and job security in general.

Another critical factor in the success of Nordic countries is good governance—that is, skilled leadership and well-conceived institutions. Good governance is hard to define, but the World Bank has developed a set of six worldwide governance indicators to measure it. Included in these measures are political stability, control of corruption, the rule of law, and regulatory quality. Each of these elements contributes to personal well-being. According to Gaygisiz (2010), high regulatory quality, or the ability of a government to make and enforce laws, is directly correlated with greater well-being. For example, it correlates with lower injury rates on the roads, in workplaces, and at home.

Another quality central to good government and social well-being is the rule of law. The rule of law refers to the equality of every person before the law, meaning that one's power, prestige, or status has no impact on the chance or effects of prosecution. It is especially important in reducing or preventing the harm that is caused by the neglect of the law. Again, take the example of accidents: Proper enforcement of traffic laws will reduce the chance of traffic accidents because of speeding or driving under the influence. Said another way, the rule of law—and thus, the benefits that flow from the rule of law—is most secure where power is shared most equally.

Where the rule of law is enforced and there is a willingness to obey the law, people are less willing to take dangerous risks. In a society with a high degree of egalitarianism, people with more power than others are less able to get away with infractions. Equality makes people less likely to commit those infractions. We see the benefits of this even in accident rates. Countries with less inequality have lower road traffic injury rates. This benefit stems from a combination of good governance, a just judicial system, and a general willingness to obey the law. These institutional qualities, in turn, result from greater social equality.

Conversely, high rates of income inequality, as measured by the Gini index predict high rates of road traffic injuries in OECD countries (Gaygisiz 2009). High rates of income inequality also predict high rates of injury at home, with the highest rates among children who live in substandard housing (Sengoelge et al. 2013).

Rianne Mahon (1991, 2002) proposes that Denmark and Sweden might be the egalitarian blueprint for a Canadian childcare policy. As noted, the Nordic countries follow a welfare state model. Unlike other welfare states, the Nordic countries apply a welfare regime that needs the co-operation of both governments and citizens. Their welfare state embraces three broad policies: a large investment in health and education, universal transfer payments for social security, and a strong commitment to full employment and job retraining programs (Lane and Ersson 2008).

Now let's pause for a moment to catch our breath. You may be asking, "How does happiness and Nordic models/perspectives relate to Canadians' experiences of inequality? How does it relate to the concept of interlocking disadvantages and to the unique challenges different marginalized groups in Canada face?"

These are interesting questions that are perhaps too complicated for an introductory book like this one. We started this section by noting that people around the world tend to value and desire the same things. The same things make them happy, but poor and powerless people in unequal countries have less access to these happiness-producing things than rich and powerful people do. Their jobs are less secure, their bodies less healthy, their family life less comfortable and relaxing. They have less confidence their government is looking after their well-being, and they have less trust in public institutions.

Of course, we know from the study of interlocking disadvantages that income inequality and poverty are not the only unhappiness-producing problems people face. People who face barriers to their acquisition of survival capital will be less happy than people who do not. This is true whether the barriers they face are due to income inequality and poverty, racism, sexism, homophobia, or otherwise. However, no one has done a systematic comparison of the happiness levels (or deficits) of different marginalized groups—this is an area that needs further study. We do know (see Tepperman and Gheihman 2013) that different kinds of inequalities are related and found in the same places. We are more likely, for example, to find racism and sexism and homophobia in countries with high income inequality (for example, the United States) than in countries with lower income inequality (for example, Canada and the Nordic countries).

Could Canada become more like the Nordic countries—that is, less unequal and therefore happier? If so, at what cost (if any) could it accomplish this goal? That question is addressed in Tepperman and Finnsdottir's forthcoming book *Canada's Place in a Shrunken World*, which compares Canada with 16 other similar countries (including the Nordic countries). At this point, our best guess is that Canada may be hampered in its ability to achieve Nordic happiness by four main factors: its large geographic size, its large population, its high degree of cultural diversity, and its high rates of immigration. We may find that it is easier to promote co-operation, consensus, and sharing in a small, homogeneous, fairly static society (like Norway) than in a large, diverse, and rapidly changing society (like Canada). This means that Canada must consider our sprawling geography and our large, diverse, and ever-changing population if we wish to adopt Nordic strategies of promoting equality of condition. Take, for example, childcare: It's expensive to run an entire centre in a remote area for very few children, and in a diverse urban centre it's a challenge to meet the cultural needs of all the children who attend. These are some of the challenges unique to a country like Canada.

Unlike many industrial societies that promote (or claim to promote) equality of opportunity, the Nordic countries promote equality of condition. Equality of condition means that everyone has a (more) similar amount of wealth and power. Equality of opportunity means that everyone has a similar chance (or "liberty") to attain unequal amounts of wealth and power. Ironically, research shows that the two are connected: People in countries with more equality of condition typically also have more equality of opportunity.

As we have noted many times, in their social values, Nordic countries favour social democracy, which is oriented to equality of condition. This is different from the more profit-oriented values of the United States, a country that claims to favour equality of opportunity. Where US culture views fairness or equity as being in competition with efficiency and profitability, the Nordic countries view equity and fairness as promoting both efficiency and profitability as well as social justice (Falkenberg 1998). The Nordic concern with equality of condition promotes the development of social justice in both politics and daily social life.

This outlook is nothing new. Equality legislation has a long history in Nordic countries—many wrote gender equality into anti-discrimination and equality legislation in the 1970s (Reisel 2014). For example, in 1978, Norway adopted the Gender Equality Act, which covers all parts of social life. In 1979, Sweden passed the Equal Opportunities Act, which includes gender equality in the labour market (though not in other domains).

The growth of the European Union (EU) has significantly influenced thinking and legislation throughout Europe. Two EU directives, the Race Equality Directive and the Employment Equality Directive, provide anti-discriminatory protections on grounds other than gender (Kantola 2014). The Nordic countries have gradually expanded the grounds of discrimination in their anti-discrimination legislation and widened the policy area of "equality" (Reisel 2014; Skjeie and Langvasbråten 2009). This widening is clear from Sweden's adoption of the Act on Prohibition of Discrimination in 2005, the revised Work Environment Act in 2006, and the Discrimination Act in 2009. Other Nordic countries have moved in similar legislative directions.

Corporatism, which combines a capitalist economy with extensive state control and trade union involvement, is critical for Nordic politics and influences program planning, policymaking, and policy implementation in Nordic countries. Lane and Ersson (2008) note that key corporations take part in significant policy planning activities and central government agencies.

However, labour unions also play an essential part in forming egalitarian policies in Scandinavia. Historically, labour unions have promoted equal pay to lessen gender inequality in the labour market. As early as 1957, the Swedish Trade Union Confederation and the Swedish employers' confederation both demanded a wage system based on skills and performance rather than gender. The successful implementation of equal pay in Sweden encouraged the Norwegian Equal Pay Committee and the union for clerical workers in Denmark to seek and achieve an equal-pay agreement shortly after (Roseberry 2002).

All the Nordic countries are prosperous by any standard we might apply. Finland, Norway, Iceland, and Sweden occupy the top four places in the World Economic Forum Gender Gap Index, and Denmark ranks seventh. As well, the Nordic model is a benchmark for the international promotion of gender equality. Under their welfare regimes, the Nordic countries combine a sizable public sector with a dual breadwinner model. In the private sphere, this dual breadwinner model assumes that both partners in families do wage work. However, this produces a great need for extensive childcare services and maternity and parental leave. In the public sphere, this model assumes a high percentage of women in elite political positions and gender equality in all public debate, politics, and private lives of citizens (Siim and Mokre 2013). A gender-inclusive model of citizenship allows both men and women to become earners and carers in Nordic societies. This model is consistent with Nancy Fraser's (1994) universal caregiver model, in which men shoulder the responsibility of caregiving just as much as women do.

As noted earlier in this chapter, universal daycare systems, "working mother" policies, and parental leave policies break the gendered imbalance of childcare responsibility between men and women. Likewise, the Nordic welfare states also value harmony between work and family life and preserve a gender-neutral policy of child or homecare allowances, showing they recognize the value of homecare. Lone mothers taking care of children are treated as workers and are provided generous benefits. The policy of homecare allowances recognizes the importance of childcaring mothers, providing economic support for mothers to continue their independent lives and improve their status. Acker (1992) suggests that paying wages to stay-at-home mothers in Scandinavia should be a benchmark for North American countries to address gender inequality at home and at work.

With increasing numbers of immigrants, the Nordic countries face a new challenge to equality: The problem of addressing interlocking disadvantages in the face of rapidly rising ethnic, racial, religious, and linguistic diversity. Canada, as we know, has embraced diversity and multiculturalism as central goals of the Canadian state and society. The Nordic countries, less experienced in dealing with immigration and diversity, have had a harder time adjusting public thinking to the new reality. As a result, Siim and Skeje (2008) note the relative exclusion of diverse ethnic minorities in the labour market, politics, and society.

Nationalist politicking can account for some of the increasing tensions between the dominant group and minority groups in Nordic countries. Nationalism is a sentiment that produces a feeling of national superiority and excludes social groups that do not fit within the homogenous national identity (Meijer 2015). Post-colonial feminist scholars argue that the ideas of exclusive national identities have been built on a notion of being grounded in ethnicity (Liinason and Meijer 2018). Such national belonging reinforces the distinctions between immigrants and the majority population.

Critical race scholars argue the Nordic countries, though historically innocent of colonialism, quickly internalize the superiority of whiteness in their accounts of nationhood (Liinason and Meijer 2018). Sverigedemokraterna (SD), the Sweden Democrats party, is an example of a radical right-wing populist party that supports nationalism, increasing the tensions between the dominant group and "the others." Jimmie Åkesson, the leader of SD, has built a hierarchy of religious respectability, giving top priority to Swedish Lutheranism and opposing Islam (Norocel 2013). This approach has increased the "otherness" of Muslims in Sweden and destabilized ethnic and religious equality in the state.

Many Nordic people think that language and culture are inseparable in the nation and necessary for national belonging. This view drives the Nordic countries to stress the education of immigrants in the majority language. In some Nordic countries (though not Sweden) minority languages are discouraged, producing an implicit notion of "otherness" among immigrants and other minorities. The issues of discrimination in education spill over across boundaries and destabilize Europe as a whole. To solve this problem, the EU rather than national states may have to listen more closely to the voices of minorities and develop a non-ethnocentric curriculum at the broadest level (Gundara 2000). Canadian provinces have done the same in recent years.

To sum up, the Nordic countries perform excellently in income equality, gender equality, and good government. Arguably, that is a key reason why people who live in Nordic countries are happier than people who live in (most) other countries. The combination of economic prosperity, social democracy, and good government is a recipe for happiness that any country—Canada included—might want to emulate.

Nordic happiness is due mainly to the priority they give to gender and income equality in legislation and extensive public services, as well as widespread social values on equality. However, their emphasis on gender and income equality may undermine the solution of other inequalities in society, such as racial, religious, and linguistic inequality. With this in mind, the Nordic states are gradually recognizing the need for an intersectional approach, though they are facing various barriers in making the change.

Closing Remarks

Our world has changed significantly in the last century. While national borders are still important, we are seeing ever more interconnectedness and globalization in every domain.

Increasingly, we are seeing regional problems like the spread of diseases (for example, Ebola or COVID-19); the flight of millions of war, economic, and climate refugees; and growing threats of cyberattacks that menace economic and political stability. We are also seeing global-scale problems like the climate crisis, biodiversity loss and cascading species extinction, and resource scarcity that need global solutions.

Evidence shows that worsening inequality is a global problem, not just a problem in Canada. Many countries in the world—in fact, most countries—face a growing gap between the richest and the poorest of their citizens. And countries themselves are unequally arrayed, so the richest members of the richest countries live like gods compared to the poorest members of the poorest countries.

In this chapter, we've asked you to take a step back from your examination of inequality within Canada. First, we directed your attention to what inequality looks like on a global scale, focusing on how much richer the richest are and what effects extreme poverty have on individuals and on society as a whole. Next, we discussed some of the strategies that other countries are using to equalize access to employment, housing, early childhood care and education, postsecondary education, and healthcare.

Not all measures work equally well in all societies. Canada may not be able to adopt the strategies that, say, Denmark has used to such great success. Our cultures and histories, not to mention population sizes and geography, may be too different, though we can't be sure without further study.

Repeating what has now been made obvious, Canada may not be able to forget its heritage of violence against Indigenous Peoples. The United States may not be able to put its centuries' old history of slavery and racism behind it. The United Kingdom may not be able to mend the rift between England, Scotland, Wales, and Ireland—the latter three being historic victims of conquest and colonial occupation. Similarly, throughout Europe separatist movements continue to incite unrest, and racism against Jews, the Roma, and other minority populations continue to resurface. Worldwide, tribalism, sectarianism, and nationalism threaten political order. We know this just by reading the news.

Underneath all of this seething discontent we find the marks and scars of inequality; there will never be peace, co-operation, and coordination of the kind the world needs until inequality is addressed on a global scale.

In the recent COVID-19 epidemic, people around the world had their lives disrupted by the new and seemingly invincible disease. Yet, as usual, people with more money, influence, and power were safer—less likely to contract the illness and less likely to die from it—than less advantaged people. This is always true of natural disasters, including epidemics, climate change, and others.

Humanity is facing its greatest challenges today—challenges that, if unsolved, may result in destroying the human race through biodiversity loss, environmental degradation, famine, disease, or global war. That means humanity needs to use all the knowledge at our disposal to solve this problem. Everyone will have to become part of the solution if we are to avoid the costs of inaction. And it will only be by studying one another's experiments with equality, justice, co-operation, and trust that we, humanity, will secure the future. This book is a small start in that direction.

Knowledge can make us powerful, and as we have seen, wrong information, in the form of stereotypes and rumours, can produce much social harm. Good information, in the form of social research, can transform society for the better. As educated people, we must learn to distinguish between fact and fantasy. It is our job as sociologists to understand and, if possible, describe reality so we can all act usefully and rationally. Armed with good understanding of the social problems we face, we can seek solutions together.

As this book has shown, problems of inequality and exclusion, ignorance, and misinformation keep humanity from reaching its potential. Our human future will depend on better understanding inequality and reducing the problems it creates. Cyberspace may provide new, exciting opportunities to create communities across borders and to see human life in every part of the world. But cyberspace also plunges us into a larger, more crowded pond than we have ever known, and it brings untold risks of misinformation panic and dangerous folly. As with all technological advancements in the last two centuries, the development of cyberspace may lead to more egalitarian and productive social life. But it will also allow us to tell one another more lies more quickly (and more persuasively) than ever before. How we will survive this "ordeal by information" remains to be seen. Like our colleagues in the past, we must continue to imagine and struggle to create a new society.

Test Your Knowledge

1. True or false: A Gini index of 0 means that a country has perfect equality; a Gini index of 1 represents complete inequality.
2. True or false: Evidence shows that poor people are perfectly happy so long as they can enjoy equality of opportunity.

3. What are some social conditions that correlate with women having fewer babies?
4. What measures has Sweden taken to increase access to employment income?
5. Describe the creative solutions for housing inequality in Germany that are featured in this chapter.
6. Which non-Nordic countries are in the top 10 happiness list? What data might you collect to explain their high level of happiness?
7. Fill in the blank: Housing provided by government agencies or not-for-profit organizations is called _______________, and _______________ gives priority to those that show the most financial need through narrow eligibility criteria.
8. Fill in the blank: _______________ is a social trend in which individuals marry within their socio-economic bracket.

See the Answer Key online to check your answers.

Questions for Critical Thought

1. Despite being a long way away from perfect social equality, Canada remains among the most equitable countries in the world. Why is it that Canada ranks so well?
2. We've examined social inequality within individual countries. What do you think is responsible for inequality *between* countries? For example, why is the standard of living higher in New Zealand than in Namibia?
3. Is social inequality something that should be addressed by all countries jointly or is it something that each country should try to tackle by itself?
4. What can Canada learn from other countries in terms of addressing social inequality? Which countries could learn from Canada, and what should they take away?
5. What are the biggest barriers to addressing social inequality worldwide in the categories discussed in this chapter?

Additional Resources

Recommended Readings

Gornick, J. 2013. *Income Inequality: Economic Disparities and the Middle Class in Affluent Countries*. Stanford, CA: Stanford University Press. While income and wealth inequality across all populations is the primary focus, the contributions to this book pay special attention to the middle class. The research also casts important light on how economic inequality affects and is affected by gender disparities, labour markets, institutions, and politics.

Grusky, D. 2006. *Inequality: Classic Readings in Race, Class, and Gender*. Boulder, CO: Westview Press. The field of inequality emerged out of a classic set of texts that continue to be read and to inform ongoing research. This work brings together 20 classic readings in the field and provides an introduction to fundamental concepts, theories, and empirical results.

Svallfors, S. 2005. *Analyzing Inequality: Life Chances and Social Mobility in Comparative Perspective*. Stanford, CA: Stanford University Press. This book summarizes key issues in global inequality, addressing a broad range of international sociological issues. The chapters, each written by a distinguished social scientist, are of interest to both scholars and students.

Recommended Websites

National Geographic: "The New Face of Hunger"

www.nationalgeographic.com/foodfeatures/hunger

National Geographic sent photographers to document hunger in three different parts of the United States, "to give face to the same statistics: one-sixth of Americans don't have enough food to eat."

OECD Library

www.oecd-ilibrary.org

This website has information and statistics on various indicators of social equality for all members of the OECD, including Canada.

Tax Justice Network

www.taxjustice.net

This website, established in 2003, contains research, analysis, and advocacy on the topics of international tax and financial regulation, including information about existing tax havens.

UNESCO

http://en.unesco.org

The United Nations Educational, Scientific and Cultural Organization's website has lots of information about global inequality. It examines individual countries and data across regions.

World Bank

http://data.worldbank.org

The World Bank's data page includes economic statistics about countries all over the world. You can find more information about the Gini index here, as well as other indicators of economic well-being and social equality.

Recommended Films

The Price We Pay. 2014. Directed by Harold Crooks. Canada. This documentary examines the issue of tax avoidance and the use of tax havens by multinational corporations.

The Story of a T-Shirt. 2013. Produced by Alex Blumberg. This film tells the story of a simple T-shirt—from its manufacture to distribution—that shows how the world is tied together through flows of raw materials, labour, and finished goods in ways we would hardly imagine. http://apps.npr.org/tshirt/#/title

Swedish Dads. Enjoy Swedish photographer Johan Bavman's documentary about fathers who elect to use Sweden's parental leave program: www.johanbavman.se/swedish-dads

Why Poverty? The Why Foundation has videos about poverty as experienced in particular places around the globe. It also has some videos that look at the systemic, global forces that cause global inequalities. www.whypoverty.net

13 Conclusion

This book has explored Canadian people's unequal access to survival capital and the idea of the "stacked deck." When we talk about a stacked deck, we mean society has been pre-arranged in a particular way to benefit some people—the advantaged and privileged—and hinder the rest.

Continuing the production and promotion of inequality creates the unequal opportunities that we all confront and, often, learn to live with. Yet inequality carries enormous costs, from heightened risks of illness and mortality to crime and punishment and violent conflict within and between nations. Inequality between nations enables rich corporations to exploit the human labour, Indigenous land management, and ecosystems of poorer nations. These patterns of consumption and exploitation are antithetical to environmental sustainability and worsen the climate crisis.

Given the harmful effects of social inequality, why does it persist? Some who stand to benefit have successfully convinced many people that inequality is natural and unavoidable. According to them, inequality exists to reward hard workers for their dedication and perseverance. Lessening inequality would decrease the incentive for people to work hard and carry out demanding jobs that are vital to society as a whole.

How, then, do we begin to convince the wealthy, influential advantaged Canadians—the primary decision makers in our society—to put corrective measures in place? Most people would likely approve of more equality if they realized its advantages. By presenting empirical evidence, we have hoped to make a compelling case that we can take practical action to lessen the degree of inequality in Canada today. Like nineteenth-century German philosopher Friedrich Nietzsche (2017) in his essay, *On the Genealogy of Morality*, we recognize that two moralities or worldviews exist when it comes to examining inequality. Nietzsche equated the so-called "master morality" to classical Greek and Roman values. This value system prized strength, pride, and nobility, unlike the so-called "slave morality" of Christian values, which prized sympathy, kindness, humility, and forgiveness.

Like Nietzsche, we recognize these two "moralities" represent different cultural systems—one pre-industrial and aristocratic, the other modern and democratic. As Nietzsche points out, the master morality confidently views the self as the source of all values: "What is good for me is good." This view suggests that what benefits some will benefit all, a belief that, in its more recent incarnation, some have named the "trickle down" theory of economics. If so, individuals should be able to accrue great wealth and power and pass it along to others. The slave morality, created in opposition to the master morality, is, on the other hand, obsessed with freedom, equality, and the collective good.

In short, the master morality tolerates inequality as unavoidable, while the slave morality does not. In their simplest outline, functionalist theories of inequality are closest to the former point of view, since functionalist theories view inequality as unavoidable and necessary to the survival of society. Other sociological theories we have discussed—conflict theory, feminist theory, critical race theory, and symbolic interactionism (especially social constructionism)—do not see inequality as unavoidable or necessary, though recognizing the persistence and universality of inequality.

Thus, the debate about inequality—its causes and effects—has been going on a long time, though under different names and guises. Unlike Nietzsche, we do not view the democratic "slave morality" as weak or degraded, or the aristocratic "master morality" as pure and preferable. Indeed, we believe the opposite. We live in a society persuaded by democratic values and so-called "slave morality," and we think a rational case can be made for the social benefits of democratic equality. Besides, research has proved the "trickle down" theory of economics invalid: For many reasons, economies and societies do not automatically improve when the rich get richer. For these reasons, we mount an argument against "aristocratic" and self-centred, advantaged Canadians. But like Nietzsche, we do understand that in the modern world there are (at least) two worldviews or moralities that need to understand each other and agree on issues of inequality. To help bring about this understanding, we think, is the role of the sociologist.

Because advantaged Canadians influence public policy more than marginalized Canadians, their views have played a significant role in shaping social assistance programs in Canada over the past several decades. We know that advantaged people often oppose equalizing measures such as **redistributive progressive taxation**. Many advantaged Canadians argue that high incomes and comfortable lifestyles are just rewards for their hard work. They see no reason to sacrifice their own standard of living to improve that of lower-income, marginalized Canadians. Even some marginalized Canadians have adopted views opposing redistributive policies from which they stand to gain.

redistributive progressive taxation A tax system that requires a higher-income earner to pay more taxes than a lower-income earner.

An improved social support system would improve their quality of life, as well as mitigating the harmful effects of inequality on health, crime, and conflict. Yet some have come to believe that such a system would be unfair, damaging to the economy, or impossible to put in place. But these beliefs are wrong, even though many politicians may campaign—and win—with platforms that promote this way of thinking. The ability of these politicians to convince people to vote against their own interests brings to mind an oft-cited proverb: "The forest was shrinking, but the trees kept voting for the axe because its handle was made of wood, so they thought it was one of them."

In other societies, leaders have convinced their citizens of the benefits of a robust social support system. These societies have prospered by setting up just such a system (as in Sweden, for example, which you learned about in Chapter 12). Setting up a stronger social support system here in Canada, however, would need a shift in values. Only in societies where most people think that financial results are beyond the control of any single individual do we find strong support for redistribution. The challenge is to carry out a similar "mind shift" here in Canada.

As funding for social support programs has been cut, scholars have explored how these changes affected marginalized Canadians. Many sought to find out whether lower taxes on the wealthy actually stimulated economic growth. Research shows it does not. In fact, undertaxing the wealthy harms the economy. Researchers have found that lower net inequality stimulates economic growth and promotes more prolonged periods of economic expansion (Beltrame 2014). Redistributive taxation does not hold back growth, contradicting the belief that such redistribution compromises economic prosperity by deterring well-off, self-styled "job creators" from continuing to work hard and invest.

Social assistance programs in Canada fail to provide satisfactory benefits and don't do enough to offset the negative health effects of poverty (Nelson 2013; Shahidi et al. 2019). It has also become increasingly challenging to garner support for these programs, however meager they already are. In sum, then, academics offering evidence-based opinions that have shown social support in today's Canada is far from "generous." Some argue that social programs providing, at most, subsistence-level benefits will motivate marginalized Canadians to find jobs as quickly as possible. However, researchers have shown that more generous welfare support *promotes* job finding.

Canadians who receive the maximum unemployment benefits available will eventually enjoy longer-term job stability. These recipients can afford to carry out longer job searches, allowing them to find positions better suited to their skills and education (Pollmann-Schult and Buchel 2005). Rather than a "hammock" that promotes learned helplessness and dependency, unemployment benefits and other forms of social assistance serve as springboards. They propel recipients into better jobs and better, healthier, and more productive lives.

Yet this does not always happen; some marginalized people internalize the victim-blaming narratives spread by the powerful. Others do believe they are disadvantaged because of systemic inequalities and barriers hindering their upward mobility. These people are, therefore, invested in restructuring the status quo. They recognize that redistributive policies and social assistance programs have been put in place to that end but tell us that these measures are not adequately addressing their problems.

Because it is inadequate, many people do not rely on social assistance for extended periods (with the exception of disability benefits; Ayala and Rodriguez 2006). More often, low-income earners transition in and out of dependence on social support as their work arrangements change (Bäckman and Bergmark 2011; Hansen and Wahlberg 2009).

Class inequalities are a little different than other inequalities, however. To address racism, sexism, ageism, ableism, and so on we need to address discrimination. To address class differences, we need to change how we divide our wealth. Class inequalities are more readily noted than those related to sex, race, age, and sexuality and easier to measure in quantifiable terms. Certain parts of the population obviously enjoy greater material comfort than others. Because they cannot deny its existence, advantaged Canadians try to justify the present system of class inequality, arguing that people merely get what they deserve. In considering inequalities grounded in sex, race, age, and sexuality, advantaged people claim that enough has already been done to address the discrimination at the root of these inequalities. Further efforts are unnecessary, they think. We think otherwise.

This book has explored many laws, programs, and policies that aim to protect marginalized Canadians. These are intended to limit or erase discrimination, remove barriers to advancement, and promote overall well-being and social integration. Citing these initiatives as evidence, some advantaged people hold that Canadians have successfully built an inclusive, tolerant society. Here, they imagine, everyone is equal or at least enjoys equal opportunities to get ahead with hard work. Others disagree with this assessment. People who suffer the disadvantages of social inequalities say the discussion is far from closed. We still have a great distance to go before enjoying the egalitarian society advantaged Canadians think already exists.

How are we to resolve these conflicting viewpoints? First, let's use what we have learned from academic researchers. Academics have provided empirical data showing that social inequalities persist. You have learned about some of these researchers and their findings throughout this book. Their research can—and does—influence policy. Many of these researchers are also members of marginalized populations and have dedicated their careers to reminding us of social problems and uplifting others like them. For example, in this book you have learned about multiple barriers faced by Indigenous Peoples in Canada. Indigenous scholars, activists, Elders, lawyers, teachers, community builders, parents, and others have been at the forefront of the impressive and innovative solutions to problems of inequality facing their communities. Their contribution is critical because their voices have been historically silenced. As well, the solutions that emerge from their research are the ones that, in many cases, are most likely to work.

This book has addressed the facts of inequality and pointed to both the many competing narratives put forward about inequality and the reasons—often self-serving— why some people approve some accounts over others. Considering these narratives alongside academic data challenges the belief that they are true statements of fact. This comparative exercise has practical value: The first step in any change is to become conscious of our currently unconscious attitudes and beliefs. Only by recognizing there are many views of and potential solutions for inequality can we begin to address it.

To that end, we must become more aware of our tendency to distinguish between different "kinds" of people. The habit of classifying people based on characteristics like gender and gender identity, sex, age, race, ethnic ancestry, social class, disability, and sexual orientation overlaps with how we ascribe unequal value to them.

By showing that these categories, like the power of traditionally dominant groups, are socially constructed, we can better value the standpoints and opinions of marginalized Canadians. To come to grips with the enduring issue of inequality, we must first recognize its existence. Equally important, marginalized Canadians must guide solutions when they tell us how they would like these problems to be addressed. For some, this book may inspire further research and action. And for others, this book will urge you to do a little more listening.

Glossary

absolute poverty versus relative poverty Absolute poverty refers to how much difficulty a person has satisfying their daily survival needs. Relative poverty describes that person's economic condition compared to the average in their community.

ageism Discrimination, or the holding of irrational and damaging views about individuals or groups, based on their age.

agency An individual's ability to make choices.

alienation The estrangement of individuals from one another or from a specific situation or process.

appearance norms Social "rules" that govern how people feel they should look to others.

assortative mating A social trend in which individuals marry within their socio-economic bracket.

Battered Women Support Services An organization in British Columbia that seeks to free girls and women from violence through educational and training programs.

bourgeoisie Those who own and control the means of production in a capitalist society.

built environment The city design (for example, zoning), housing, and associated transportation infrastructure that enables us to get from place to place.

Canada Pension Plan for Disability Benefits A taxable monthly payment that is available to people who have contributed to the Canada Pension Plan and cannot work regularly at any job because of a disability.

carer strategy Part-time employment, plus assistance, is considered the best way for women to combine work and care.

chain migration Migration to communities or countries that results from information about opportunities received from friends and relatives.

choice strategy Women are given many opportunities to exercise choice to either provide care or engage in full-time employment.

chronic illness A long-lasting condition that can be managed but not cured.

class consciousness An ability to see what is in the best interests of one's social class.

class politics Political speech focused on class position, as distinct from "identity politics," which focuses on gender, racial, regional, or other non-class affiliations.

common (collective) conscience A shared state of mind, including common values, in a small stable community.

country food Foods harvested and hunted from the surrounding area, like seal, whale, berries, and Arctic char in the North.

credentialism The organization of education to ensure that students receive the formal qualifications (that is, diplomas and degrees) they need to get jobs.

criminal victimization The targeting of an individual or a group for subjection to a crime, for example, homicide, assault, robbery, fraud, or theft.

critical theory An analysis of politics and society, based in Marxian theory, that focuses on the historical and ideological forces that influence culture and human behaviour.

critical race theory (CRT) A form of analysis that explores the way that beliefs about race organize all social structures.

cultural capital Knowledge, material objects, and credentials that elevate status, distinguish one group from another, and perpetuate inequality.

cycle of opportunity The set of factors or events by which advantage, once started, is likely to continue unless there is outside intervention.

cycle of poverty (or deprivation) The set of factors or events by which poverty, once started, is likely to continue unless there is outside intervention.

decentralization The distribution of administrative powers or roles over a less concentrated or specialized area.

de-professionalization The tendency for immigrants to occupy jobs that underutilize their experience and qualifications.

differential association theory Proposes that people, through simple association, are socialized into their criminal environment and reproduce the prevailing order.

differentiation The social and cultural identification, then performance, of social differences, as between men and women, old and young, and so on.

disability The condition of having difficulty carrying out familiar tasks, according to the Canadian Survey on Disability. This includes being limited in normal daily activities because of a long-term health condition or health-related problem.

disability rights movement A Canadian movement that spoke for the respect, full citizenship, and inclusion of disabled people in society.

discourse The communication of information, thoughts, and ideas. It includes language, art, and all forms of expression. Discourse influences how we experience and view the world around us.

discrimination The unjust or prejudicial treatment of different categories of people, especially on the grounds of race, age, sex, or sexual orientation.

earner-carer strategy Unpaid care work and paid work are equally shared between men and women.

earner strategy Men and women are equally encouraged to participate in the labour market through policies against gender discrimination in employment.

economies of scale The per-unit cost advantage of building something bigger rather than smaller.

educational undermatching A circumstance in which a capable, talented, and bright student from a low-income family does not apply to Ivy League (or "selective") colleges like Harvard, Princeton, or Yale.

emotional work Paid work that demands not only face-to-face contact with customers but also the continued expression or non-expression of certain emotions; also known as "commodified emotions."

employment discrimination Refers to the unequal treatment by employers based on ascriptive characteristics such as gender, race, ethnicity, accent, and skin colour.

employment insurance An income support program that offers temporary financial support to people who have lost a job through no fault of their own.

equity model A theory that explains employment inequality as a product of institutional barriers that make finding work more difficult for certain demographics and keep wealth concentrated at the top.

external coping strategies Programs offered outside of the home, such as community kitchens, food banks, and food programs, aimed at feeding children.

extreme poverty Living on a budget of less than US$1.90 per day. People living in extreme poverty are often faced with chronic malnutrition and often die from treatable diseases because of a lack of available or affordable medical care.

false consciousness An inability to see what is in the best interest for one's class, compounded by an erroneous belief that may hinder change, supporting the status quo.

feminization The increasing presence and influence of women in previously male-dominated jobs or institutions.

feminization of education The growing educational focus on developing skills of girls and women in middle and higher education, which risks alienating and disadvantaging boys and men.

feminization of poverty The overrepresentation of women among the poor.

Finnish Maternity Package A box containing the necessities for a baby's first year of life and delivered to all expectant mothers who are citizens in Finland.

food insecurity When a household does not have consistent access to enough safe, nutritious food.

food security When a household has consistent access to enough safe, nutritious food.

gender scripts The generally understood rules for how people of different genders "normally" behave in our society. Gender scripts are negotiated between people based on how society collectively imagines gender.

gender-normativity A set of assumptions that all people are, by default, the gender assigned by their sex at birth.

gentrification When property in old downtown areas is bought by businesses and middle-class homeowners and upgraded to better condition and attractiveness, pushing out long-time residents who are often low-income people.

ghettoization Occurs when certain neighbourhoods are settled mainly by people of one particular class, race, or ethnic group.

Gini index The statistical representation of income inequality between the rich and the poor. It expresses inequality on a scale of 0 to 1, with 1 being perfect (or complete) inequality and 0 being perfect equality.

hate-motivated crime Any crime motivated by bias, prejudice, or hate based on race, national or ethnic origin, language, colour, religion, sex, age, or any other similar factor.

heteronormativity The societal assumption that all people are, by default, heterosexual and that heterosexuality is the normal state of being.

hierarchy of victimization The tendency to grant victim status to some people and not others.

high-income economies Countries with a per capita income of $12,000 or more.

hot spots Places where crime tends to concentrate, like bars, airports, tourist attractions—even private homes and institutions.

housing discrimination Any practice or policy that systemically causes harm through inequitable access to housing based on prejudiced or biased assumptions about would-be residents.

human capital The skills, knowledge, and credentials that can be shared from one person to another and contribute to the productivity of society.

human trafficking The export and import of humans—often women and children—for profitable exploitation in other countries through prostitution or slavery.

infant mortality rate The death rate of children under the age of 1, typically measured as deaths per year per 1,000 live births. Public health measures have great impacts on infant mortality rates.

institutional completeness A community characteristic featuring a full array of necessary services and goods, including schools, churches, and media.

institutionalized When beliefs and behaviours are formally established in an organization and guide behaviour accordingly.

interactions Reciprocal behaviours between two or more people producing shared and evolving realities.

interlocking disadvantages The ways in which multiple identity characteristics can overlap and intersect to worsen life chances.

internal coping strategies Coping strategies within the home aimed at feeding children, such as stretching out food or relying on friends and family.

intersectionality The interaction or combination of social factors that makes inequality more than the result of additive disadvantages, resulting in disadvantages that combine in unique ways.

invisibilizing The representation of specific characteristics (typically whiteness, heterosexuality, and skinniness) as standard or neutral and all other characteristics as deviant. This leads to a negative perception of those who do not fit the norm and leads to their marginalization.

knowledge economy An economic system based on intellectual capital.

labelling theory A theory that asserts people create social realities (like "crimes," for example) when they label them as such.

latent functions Unintended consequences of the norms of a particular social institution.

lateral violence Violence directed "sideways" at peers instead of at oppressing groups or individuals.

legal aid Legal representation for those who cannot afford it.

LGBTQ+ An acronym referring to people who identify as lesbian, gay, bisexual, trans, queer/questioning. The + indicates that the acronym can encompass many other identities, such as Two-Spirit, intersex, pansexual, and so on. The LGBTQ+ community can encompass people who have diverse experiences of disadvantages.

life chances A term credited to Max Weber, referring to the opportunities people have to gain wealth, power, and prestige.

life expectancy at birth The expected duration of a person's life, considering age, time of birth, place of birth, sex, and so on.

manifest functions These are the stated, intended purposes of a particular social institution.

marginalization A process that denies a group or individual access to important positions and symbols of economic, religious, or political power within any society.

market-basket measure (MBM) The method used to measure low income in Canada that calculates how much income a household requires to meet its needs. These include subsistence needs (such as basic food and shelter) and the needs to satisfy community norms.

market-determined childcare model An arrangement under which childcare providers sell childcare to parents and guardians, just like any other providers of goods and services on the open market.

Maslow's hierarchy of needs A psychological theory developed by Abraham Maslow that organizes human needs in rising stages. His theory suggests that more basic needs must be met before an individual will crave for or strive to satisfy higher-level needs.

mechanical solidarity Social integration or cohesion that is rooted in a common conscience.

mental illness Illness characterized by disturbances of emotion, thinking, or behaviour.

moral panic A widespread feeling of fear—sometimes out of proportion—that something or someone will negatively destabilize society.

non-standard job A job that is often characterized by part-time, temporary, on-call, contract, or self-employed work.

opportunity costs The value of opportunities a person forgoes to take advantage of other opportunities.

organic solidarity Social integration or cohesion that is rooted in a recognition and appreciation of difference and interdependence.

Organisation for Economic Co-operation and Development (OECD) An international organization comprising 36 member-states committed to researching and proposing solutions for economic, social, and environmental problems.

othering The process by which an individual (the Other) is characterized as different from and alien to the norm. It places the "Other" firmly in the out-group and highlights the differences between the in-group and out-group. It marks the in-group as powerful and virtuous and the out-group as frail and insidious.

phase out The process of gradually exiting a workforce, so an individual works part time or part year before leaving the workforce.

political will The desire and ability to mobilize people politically behind a particular policy or program.

positivism A belief that social truths can be discovered through the application of scientific methods of research.

precarious employment Non-standard employment that is poorly paid, insecure, and unprotected.

prisonization The process by which a person becomes socialized into prison life.

privatization The process of transferring ownership of a business, enterprise, agency, public service, or public property from the public sector (government) to a business that works for a profit or to a not-for-profit organization. It may also mean government transfer of services or jobs to private firms, for example, revenue collection, law enforcement, and prison management.

proletariat People who exchange their labour for wages and work for the bourgeoisie in a capitalist society.

public returns The public benefits, such as improved population health and higher literacy rates, that are derived from investment in institutions such as education.

race to the bottom Progressively lowering standards, especially wages and working conditions, to undercut the competition. In other words, trying to "win" by losing the most.

racialization The social processes of distinguishing or classifying people according to their believed race or ethnicity.

racialized stratification The process by which the membership of an individual or a group to a race becomes the basis for social stratification.

racial profiling Any action taken for reasons of safety, security, or public protection that relies on stereotypes about race, colour, or other features rather than on a reasonable suspicion to single out individuals for different treatment.

redistributive progressive taxation A tax system that requires a higher-income earner to pay more taxes than a lower-income earner.

refugee claimant An individual who has applied for refugee status in Canada and is waiting for the Immigration and Refugee Board to decide whether refugee status should be granted.

Registered Indians (or Status Indians) Indigenous Peoples who are registered with the Government of Canada and entitled to some rights and benefits as outlined in the Indian Act. Interestingly, there is no federal register for Inuit or Métis.

regulation Official oversight ensuring that childcare centres meet health, safety, and educational standards.

Reserve Army of Labour Marx and Engels's term for a pool of unemployed people seeking work.

residential instability Frequent residential movement of individuals from place to place.

residential segregation The concentration of similar socio-economic brackets in one geographic area.

role Refers to the dynamic element of status and the way in which status is performed.

sandwich generation Middle-aged adults who are caring for both their elderly parents and their own young children.

self-perception The processes by which people come to think about and know themselves.

senescence The natural decline of physical and mental abilities during the aging process.

sense of agency A person's feeling of confident independence.

skill obsolescence The degree to which professionals lack the up-to-date knowledge or skills necessary to preserve effective performance in their current or future work roles.

skills biased work Technological work that requires skills like literacy that are typically learned in school environments.

social assistance Income support programs administered by the government and intended to help recipients cover the cost of food, shelter, clothing, and other daily necessities.

social capital Advantageous relationships that enable better access to key social and economic resources.

social construction A term used to describe how something has meaning only because it is made up or seen as such—it is not real (or biological) in nature.

social determinants of health (SDOH) The social factors, such as income, education, stress-related living, and working conditions, and social status that impact a person's health.

social disorganization theory Proposes that crime and other social pathologies (including suicide) result from a breakdown in social norms and social integration.

social gradient in health The correlation between social inequality and health—that is, between poverty and ill health, wealth and good health.

socially positive opportunities Social incentives to make a living by non-criminal means.

social mobility The ability of individuals to move within a social hierarchy; often used in terms of job or class.

social networks Patterns of social relationships among individuals based on face-to-face interaction or mediated communication.

social reproduction The biological reproduction of the labour force, including the provision of food, shelter, clothing, and healthcare.

social services Programs and interventions that seek to promote the general welfare of others.

socialization The processes surrounding the internalization and learning of culture, most of which occurs during childhood.

sociological imagination Refers to the ability to see the interconnections between individual experiences and larger societal patterns, trends, or forces.

socio-economic status (SES) An important determinant of health that considers income, class, social networks, cultural capital, education, and other achieved credentials.

stage theory Human cognitive and social development follows a pattern of successive stages. Each stage is characterized by specific needs that must be satisfied before an individual can progress to the higher levels of development.

status A degree of social standing and respectability. It implies a social hierarchy in which people of different statuses enjoy different legal, political, and cultural rights.

stigma Visible or invisible social distinctions that disqualify individuals from full social acceptance.

stigmatization The process by which a person's status is diminished owing to a poorly regarded physical or social attribute.

strain (anomie) theory Robert Merton's theory that many types of crime and deviant behaviour are necessary and natural adaptations to the gap between people's common goals and their unequal opportunities to gain them.

structural discrimination Any set of rules or practices that disadvantages some groups while advantaging other groups.

survival capital The resources and opportunities people in a modern urban society need to survive and, perhaps, thrive.

targeted social housing system The grant of social housing to those who show the greatest financial need.

tax havens A state, country, or territory where money can be stored at a low rate of taxation or even tax free and where little or no information is shared with foreign tax authorities.

telehealth The use of computer and communications technologies to deliver healthcare, especially at a distance.

transmisogyny Prejudice against and abusive treatment of transgender women, resulting in hate crimes.

underemployment Employment in a job that needs far less education and preparation than an individual has earned.

underrepresentation The act of consciously or unconsciously reinforcing ideas of abnormality or deviance by ignoring or overlooking certain kinds of people. These groups are depicted in media (such as film or television) at a rate that does not reflect their prevalence in society.

undocumented or non-status Canadians Refugee claimants who have had their applications denied or temporary foreign workers who have stayed past the date covered by their visa.

victimization The targeting of an individual or a group for subjection to crime, unfair treatment, or another wrong.

wage gap The difference in the earnings of different demographics, expressed as a percentage of the dominant groups' earnings. It can help us better understand wage equality or inequality among different groups and populations.

walkable neighbourhood A neighbourhood that is safe enough to walk around at almost any time of day or night.

wealth deciles Wealth expressed in terms of tenths of the population, ranked from bottom to top; so the wealthiest Canadians are in the top decile of the population.

Whitehall Studies Two massive British studies carried out between 1967–88 that showed how class inequality and health are correlated.

worker CEO pay ratios The amount CEOs earn compared to their average or lowest-paid employee.

working poor Low-income individuals who may be drawing an income from a part-time job or other forms of precarious work.

References

Chapter 1

Becker, Howard S. [1963] 2008. *Outsiders*. New York: Simon and Schuster.

Blum, William. 2004. *Killing Hope: U.S. Military and CIA Interventions since World War II*. Monroe, ME: Common Courage Press.

Blumer, Herbert. (1971). Social Problems as Collective Behavior. *Social problems* 18(3):298–306.

Bourdieu, Pierre. 1970. *Reproduction in Education, Society, and Culture*. Paris: Editions de Minuit.

———. [1979] 1984. *Distinction: A Social Critique of the Judgement of Taste*. Translated by Richard Nice. Cambridge, MA: Harvard University Press.

———. 1986. "The Forms of Capital." Pp. 241–58 in *Handbook of Theory and Research for the Sociology of Education*, edited by J. Richardson. New York: Greenwood.

Carbado, Devon W. 2013. "Colorblind Intersectionality." *Signs: Journal of Women in Culture and Society* 38(4):811–45.

Choo, Hae Yeon and Myra Marx Ferree. 2010. "Practicing Intersectionality in Sociological Research: A Critical Analysis of Inclusions, Interactions, and Institutions in the Study of Inequalities." *Sociological Theory* 28(2):129–49.

Collins, Randall. 1974. *Conflict Sociology*. New York: Academic Press.

Crenshaw, Kimberlé. 1991. "Mapping the Margins: Intersectionality, Identity Politics, and Violence against Women of Color." *Stanford Law Review* 43(6):1241–99.

———. 2015. "Why Intersectionality Can't Wait." *Washington Post*, September 24 (https://www.washingtonpost.com/news/in-theory/wp/2015/09/24/why-intersectionality-cant-wait).

Dahrendorf, Ralf. 1959. *Class and Class Conflict in Industrial Society*. London, UK: Routledge & Kegan Paul.

Davis, Kathy. 2008. "Intersectionality as Buzzword: A Sociology of Science Perspectives on What Makes a Feminist Theory Successful." *Feminist Theory* 9:67–85.

Davis, Kingsley and William Moore. 1945. "Some Principles of Stratification." *American Sociological Review* 10:242–9.

Elliott, Larry. 2019. "Worlds 26 Richest People Own as Much as Poorest 50%, Says Oxfam." *The Guardian*, January 21 (https://www.theguardian.com/business/2019/jan/21/world-26-richest-people-own-as-much-as-poorest-50-per-cent-oxfam-report).

Fukuyama, Francis. 2004. *State-Building: Governance and World Order in the 21st Century*. Ithaca, NY: Cornell University Press.

Geerts, Evelien and Iris Van Der Tuin. 2013. "From Intersectionality to Interference: Feminist Onto-epistemological Reflections on the Politics of Representation." *Women's Studies International Forum* 41(3):171–8.

Hancock, Ange-Marie. 2007. "Intersectionality as a Normative and Empirical Paradigm." *Politics and Gender* 3(2), 248–54.

Haraway, Donna. 1988. "Situated Knowledges: The Science Question in Feminism and the Privilege of Partial Perspective." *Feminist Studies* 14(3):575–99.

Hardaway, Cecily R. and Vonnie C. McLoyd. 2009. "Escaping Poverty and Securing Middle Class Status: How Race and Socioeconomic Status Shape Mobility Prospects for African Americans during the Transition to Adulthood." *Journal of Youth and Adolescence* 38(2):242–56.

Herman, Edward S. and Noam Chomsky. 1988. *Manufacturing Consent: The Political Economy of the Mass Media*. New York: Pantheon Books.

Hinton, Pita. 2014. "Situated Knowledges' and New Materialism(s): Rethinking a Politics of Location." *Women: A Cultural Review* 25(1):99–113.

James, Carl E. 2009. "African-Caribbean Canadians Working 'Harder' to Attain Their Immigrant Dreams: Context, Strategies, and Consequences." *Wadabagei: A Journal of the Caribbean and its Diaspora* 12(1):92.

Jolly, Margaret. 2012. *Studies in Anthropology and History*. Vol. 12, *Women of the Place: Kastom, Colonialism and Gender in Vanuatu*. Abingdon, UK: Taylor & Francis.

Lindsay, Keisha. 2009. "(Re)reading Intersectionality and Identity in the Discourse on Marginalized Black Men." Ph.D. diss., University of Chicago.

Lipset, Seymour M. and Reinhard Bendix. [1959] 1991. *Social Mobility in Industrial Society*. Piscataway, NJ: Transaction Publishers.

Longino, Helen. 1993. "Feminist Standpoint Theory and the Problems of Knowledge." *Signs* 19(1):201–12.

Marx, Karl and Friedrich Engels. [1848] 2017. *The Communist Manifesto*. London, UK: Pluto Press.

McClintock, Anne. 1995. *Imperial Leather: Race, Gender, and Sexuality in the Colonial Contest*. New York: Routledge.

Mills, C. Wright. 1959. *The Sociological Imagination*. New York: Oxford University Press.

Moshman, David. 2007. "Us and Them: Identity and Genocide." *Identity: An International Journal of Theory and Research* 7(2):115–35.

Nash, Jennifer C. 2008. "Re-thinking Intersectionality." *Feminist Review* 89:1–15.

Owen, David S. 2007. "Towards a Critical Theory of Whiteness." *Philosophy & Social Criticism* 33(2):203–22.

Porter, John. [1965] 2015. *Vertical Mosaic: An Analysis of Social Class and Power in Canada, 50th Anniversary Edition*. Toronto: University of Toronto Press.

Rousseau, Jean-Jacques. [1755] 2009. *Discourse on the Origin and Basis of Inequality among Men*. Auckland, NZ: Floating Press.

Scott, John ed. 2006 *Fifty Key Sociologists: The Contemporary Theorists*. London, UK: Routledge.

Smith, Dorothy E. 1990. *The Conceptual Practices of Power: A Feminist Sociology of Knowledge*. Toronto, ON: University of Toronto Press.

Wittfogel, Karl A. 1957. *Oriental Despotism: A Comparative Study of Total Power*. New Haven, CT: Yale University Press.

Wollstonecraft, Mary. [1792] 1972. *A Vindication of the Rights of Woman: With Strictures on Political and Moral Subjects*. London, UK: Printed for J. Johnson.

Wood, Julia. 2005. "Feminist Standpoint Theory and Muted Group Theory: Commonalities and Divergences." *Women and Language* 28(2):61–4.

Wright, Eric Olin. 1997. *Class Counts: Comparative Studies in Class Analysis*. Cambridge, UK: Cambridge University Press.

Chapter 2

Angeles, L. 2007. "Income Inequality and Colonialism." *European Economic Review* 51(5):1155–76

Arriagada, Paula. 2016. "First Nations, Metis, and Inuit Women. Women in Canada: A Gender-Based Statistical Report." Statistics Canada, catalogue no. 89-503-X (https://www150.statcan.gc.ca/n1/pub/89-503-x/2015001/article/14313-eng.htm).

Auger, M.D. (2016). "Cultural Continuity as a Determinant of Indigenous Peoples' Health: A Metasynthesis of Qualitative Research in Canada and the United States." *International Indigenous Policy Journal*, 7(4).

Axelsson, P., Kukutai, T., and Kippen, R. 2016. "The Field of Indigenous Health and the Role of Colonisation and History." *Journal of Population Research* 33(1):1–7.

Bachar E., M. Cale, J. Eisenberg, and H. Dasberg. 1994. "Aggression Expression in Grandchildren of Holocaust Survivors: A Comparative Study." *Israel Journal of Psychiatry and Related Sciences* 31:41–7.

Barker, B., Sedgemore, K., Tourangeau, M., Lagimodiere, L., Milloy, J., Dong, H., Hayashi, K., Shoveller, J., Kerr, T. & DeBeck, K. 2019. "Intergenerational Trauma: The Relationship Between Residential Schools and the Child Welfare System Among Young People Who Use Drugs in Vancouver, Canada." *Journal of Adolescent Health* 65(2):248–54. doi:10.1016/j.jadohealth.2019.01.022

Bauer, G.R. and A. Scheim. 2015. "Transgender People in Ontario, Canada: Statistics to Inform Human Rights Policy." London, ON: Trans PULSE Project. Retrieved January 13, 2019 (http://transpulseproject.ca/wp-content/uploads/2015/06/Trans-PULSE-Statistics-Relevant-for-Human-Rights-Policy-June-2015.pdf).

BMO Financial Group. 2013. "Canadian Businesses Slow to Hire People with Disabilities: BMO" (http://newsroom.bmo.com/press-releases/canadian-businesses-slow-to-hire-people-with-disab-tsx-bmo-201310240906438001).

Bombay, A., K. Matheson and H. Anisman. 2014. "The Intergenerational Effects of Indian Residential Schools: Implications for the Concept of Historical Trauma." *Transcultural Psychiatry* 51(3):320–38. doi:10.1177/1363461513503380

Burlock, A. 2017. "Women with Disabilities. Women in Canada: A Gender-Based Statistical Report." Statistics Canada, catalogue no. 89-5034-X (https://www150.statcan.gc.ca/n1/pub/89-503-x/2015001/article/14695-eng.htm).

Butt, Daniel. 2013. Colonialism and postcolonialism. Pp. 892–8 in *International encyclopedia of ethics*, edited by H. LaFollette. Oxford, UK: Blackwell.

Canadian Press. 2017. "Census Data Expected to Shed Light on Shrinking Marriage Stats." *CBC News*, August 1 (https://www.cbc.ca/news/canada/montreal/census-marriage-statistics-1.4218799).

CARP. 2013. "CARP Launches New Elder Abuse Paper and Recommendations on the International Day to End Elder Abuse" (http://www.carp.ca/2013/06/14/carp-launches-new-elder-abuse-paper-and-recommendations-on-the-international-day-to-end-elder-abuse).

CBC News. 2010. "Bullying and Sexual Orientation by the Numbers." October 29 (http://www.cbc.ca/news/canada/bullying-and-sexual-orientation-by-the-numbers-1.909444).

Clark, W. 2007. "Delayed Transitions of Young Adults." Statistics Canada (https://www150.statcan.gc.ca/n1/pub/11-008-x/2007004/10311-eng.htm).

Cranswick, Kelly and Donna Dosman. 2008. *Eldercare: What We Know Today*. Statistics Canada, Catalogue no. 11-008-X. Retrieved May 14, 2020 (https://www150.statcan.gc.ca/n1/pub/11-008-x/2008002/article/10689-eng.htm).

Elias, B., Mignone, J., Hall, M., Hong, S.P., Hart, L., & Sareen, J. 2012. "Trauma and Suicide Behaviour Histories Among a Canadian Indigenous Population: An Empirical Exploration of the Potential Role of Canada's Residential School System." *Social Science & Medicine* 74(10):1560–9. doi:10.1016/j.socscimed.2012.01.026

Employment and Social Development Canada. 2019. "Canada Reaches Lowest Poverty Rate in History." Retrieved May 13, 2020 (https://www.canada.ca/en/employment-social-development/news/2019/03/canada-reaches-lowest-poverty-rate-in-history.html).

Environics Institute. 2018. "Canadian Public Opinion about Immigration, Refugees, and the USA." *Focus Canada* Fall 2018 (https://www.environicsinstitute.org/docs/default-source/default-document-library/focus-canada-fall-2018---final-report.pdf?sfvrsn=fe91cb12_0).

Fanon, Frantz. 1961. *The Wretched of the Earth*. New York: Grove Press.

First Nations Centre. 2005. *First Nations Regional Longitudinal Health Survey (RHS) 2002/03: Results for Adults, Youth, and Children Living in First Nations Communities*. Ottawa, ON: First Nations Centre.

Fondation Jasmine Roy. 2018. "LGBT+ Realities Survey" (https://fondationjasminroy.com/en/initiative/lgbt-realities-survey).

Fossion, P., M.C. Rejas, L. Servais, I. Pelc, and S. Hirsch. 2003. "Family Approach with Grandchildren of Holocaust Survivors." *American Journal of Psychotherapy* 57(4), 519–27.

Frank, Andre G. 1976. *Economic Genocide in Chile: Equilibrium on the Point of a Bayonet*. Nottingham, UK: Spokesman.

Gaetz, S., J. Donaldson, T. Richter, and T. Gulliver. 2013. *The State of Homelessness in Canada 2013*. Toronto, ON: Canadian Homelessness Research Network Press.

Galabuzi, G. 2006. *Canada's Economic Apartheid: The Social Exclusion of Racialized Groups in the New Century*. Toronto, ON: Canadian Scholar's Press.

Galarneau, D., R. Morissette, and J. Usalcas. 2013. *Insights on Canadian Society—What Has Changed for Young People in Canada?* Ottawa, ON: Statistics Canada.

Gone, J.P., W.E. Hartmann, A. Pomerville, D.C. Wendt, S.H. Klem, and R.L. Burrage. 2019. "The Impact of Historical Trauma on Health Outcomes for Indigenous Populations in the USA and Canada: A Systematic Review." *The American Psychologist* 74(1):20–35. doi:10.1037/amp0000338

Government of Canada. 2013a. "Aboriginal Peoples and Communities." Aboriginal Affairs and Northern Development Canada (https://www.aadnc-aandc.gc.ca/eng/1100100013785/1304467449155).

Government of Canada. 2013b. "Six Selection Factors—Federal Skilled Workers." Citizenship and Immigration Canada (https://www.cic.gc.ca/english/immigrate/skilled/ apply-factors.asp).

Government of Canada. 2018. "What Is Indian Status? Aboriginal Affairs and Northern Development Canada (https://www.aadnc-aandc.gc.ca/eng/1100100032463/1100100032464).

Guerra, Ricardo O., Beatriz Eugenia Alvarado, and Maria Victoria Zunzunegui. 2008. "Life Course, Gender and Ethnic Inequalities in Functional Disability in a Brazilian Urban Elderly Population." *Aging Clinical and Experimental Research* 20(1):53–61.

Hartmann, W.E. and J.P. Gone. 2014. "American Indian Historical Trauma: Community Perspectives from Two Great Plains Medicine Men." *American Journal of Community Psychology* 54:274–88. http://dx.doi.org/10.1007/s10464-014-9671-1

Hendry, L. 2018. "'I Didn't Come Here to Live This Kind of Life': Skilled Immigrants on Desperate Hunt for Jobs in Quebec." *CBC News*, September 25 (https://www.cbc.ca/news/canada/montreal/quebec-immigration-skilled-workers-election-1.4833739).

Hudon, T. and A. Milan. 2016. "Visible Minority Women. Women in Canada: A Gender-Based Statistical Report." Statistics Canada, catalogue no. 89-503-X (https://www150.statcan.gc.ca/n1/pub/89-503-x/2015001/article/14315-eng.htm).

Hughes, Everett. 1939. *French Canada in Transition*. Chicago, IL: University of Chicago Press.

Israel, Solomon. 2017. "StatsCan on Gender Pay Gap: Women Earn 87¢ to Men's $1." *CBC News*, March 8 (https://www.cbc.ca/news/business/statistics-canada-gender-pay-gap-1.4014954).

Kellerman, N. P. (2001). "Psychopathology in Children of Holocaust Survivors: A Review of the Research Literature." *Israel Journal of Psychiatry and Related Sciences*, 38(1), 36–46.

Marsh, T.N., Coholic, D., Cote-Meek, S., & Najavits, L.M. 2015. "Blending Aboriginal and Western Healing Methods to Treat Intergenerational Trauma with Substance Use Disorder in Aboriginal Peoples Who Live in Northeastern Ontario, Canada." *Harm Reduction Journal* 12(1):14. doi:10.1186/s12954-015-0046-1

Matthews, Richard. 2016. "The Cultural Erosion of Indigenous People in Health Care." *Canadian Medical Association Journal* 189(2):E78–9. doi:10.1503/cmaj.160167

Maxwell, K. 2014. "Historicizing Historical Trauma Theory: Troubling the Trans-generational Transmission Paradigm." *Transcultural Psychiatry* 51(3):407–35. doi:10.1177/1363461514531317

Mazor, A. and I. Tal. 1996. "Intergenerational Transmission: The Individuation Process and the Capacity for Intimacy of Adult Children of Holocaust Survivors." *Contemporary Family Therapy* 18(1):95–112.

McKee, Virginia. 1999. "Seniors Survey Identifies Double Discrimination for Senior Lesbians." *Herizons* Spring:9.

Morris, Stuart, Gail Fawcett, Laurent Brisebois, and Jeffrey Hughes. 2018. "A Demographic, Employment and Income Profile of Canadians with Disabilities aged 15 Years and Over, 2017." Statistics Canada (https://www150.statcan.gc.ca/n1/en/catalogue/89-654-X2018002).

Moynihan, Daniel. 1965. *The Negro Family: The Case for National Action*. Washintgon, DC: Office of Policy Planning and Research: United States Department of Labour.

National Council of Welfare. 2012. *Poverty Profile: Special Edition* (https://www.canada.ca/content/dam/esdc-edsc/migration/documents/eng/communities/reports/poverty_profile/snapshot.pdf).

National Council of Welfare. 2013. *Poverty Profile: Special Edition: A Snapshot of Racialized Poverty in Canada* (https://www. esdc.gc.ca/eng/communities/reports/pover- ty_profile/snapshot.pdf).

National Inquiry into Missing and Murdered Indigenous Women and Girls. 2019. *Reclaiming Power and Place: Final Report of the National Inquiry into Missing and Murdered Indigenous Women and Girls* (https://www.mmiwg-ffada.ca/wp-content/uploads/2019/06/Final_Report_Vol_1a-1.pdf).

Norris, Doug. 2017. "Canada Is Home to More Seniors than Children." Environics Institute. Retrieved May 14, 2020 (https://environicsanalytics.com/resources/blogs/ea-blog/2017/05/03/canada-is-home-to-more-seniors-than-children).

Okazaki, S., David, E. J. R., and Abelmann, N. 2008. "Colonialism and Psychology of Culture." *Social and Personality Psychology Compass* 2(1):90–106.

O'Neill, L., T. Fraser, A. Kitchenham, and V. McDonald. 2018. "Hidden Burdens: A Review of Intergenerational, Historical and Complex Trauma, Implications for Indigenous Families." *Journal of Child & Adolescent Trauma* 11(2):173–86. doi:10.1007/s40653-016-0117-9

Okazaki, S., David, E. J. R., & Abelmann, N. (2008). Colonialism and psychology of culture. *Social and personality psychology compass*, *2*(1), 90-106.

Pasma, C., and R. Sears. 2010. *Bearing the Brunt: How the 2008–2009 Recession Created Poverty for Canadian Families.* Ottawa, ON: Citizens for Public Justice.

Pearce, M.E., W.M. Christian, K. Patterson, K. Norris, A. Moniruzzaman, K.J.P. Craib, M.T. Schechter, and P.M. Spittal. 2008. "The Cedar Project: Historical Trauma, Sexual Abuse and HIV Risk among Young Aboriginal People Who Use Injection and Non-injection Drugs in Two Canadian Cities." *Social Science & Medicine* 66(11):2185–94. doi:10.1016/j.socscimed.2008.03.034

Porter, John. [1965] 2015. *The Vertical Mosaic: An Analysis of Social Class and Power in Canada.* Toronto, ON: University of Toronto Press.

Raj, A. 2012. "Same Sex Marriage Canada Census 2011: Census Shows New Picture of Couples' Unions." *Huffington Post Canada*, September 19.

Ravanera, Z.R. and F. Rajulton. 2007. *Changes in Economic Status and Timing of Marriage of Young Canadians. Canadian Studies in Population [ARCHIVES]* 34(1):49–67.

Royal Canadian Mounted Police. 2014. "Missing and Murdered Indigenous Women: A National Operational Overview." May 27 (http://www.rcmp-grc.gc.ca/pubs/mmaw-faapd-eng.htm).

Rogow, Sally. 2002. "The Disability Rights Movement: The Canadian Experience." *International Journal of Special Education* (http://citeseerx.ist.psu.edu/viewdoc/download?doi=10.1.1.597.3857&rep=rep1&type=pdf).

Sagi-Schwartz, A., Van IJzendoorn, M. H., & Bakermans-Kranenburg, M. J. (2008). Does Intergenerational Transmission of Trauma Skip a Generation? No Meta-Analytic Evidence for Tertiary Traumatization with Third Generation of Holocaust Survivors." *Attachment & Human Development*, 10(2), 105–21.

Savage, Laura. 2017. "Section 3: Police-Reported Family Violence against Seniors in Canada, 2017." Statistics Canada (https://www150.statcan.gc.ca/n1/pub/85-002-x/2018001/article/54978/03-eng.htm).

Statistics Canada. 2007. "2006 Census: Families, Marital Status, Households and Dwelling Characteristics." *The Daily*, September 12 (https://www.statcan.gc.ca/daily-quotidien/070912/ dq070912a-eng.htm).

———. 2010. "Projections of the Diversity of the Canadian Population" (https://www.statcan.gc.ca/pub/91-551-x/91-551-x2010001-eng.pdf)

———. 2012. "A Profile of Persons with Disabilities among Canadians Aged 15 Years or Older, 2012." Catalogue no. 89-654-X (https://www150.statcan.gc.ca/n1/pub/89-654-x/89-654-x2015001-eng.htm).

———. 2013a. "Canadian Survey on Disability, 2012." *The Daily*, December 3 (https://www.statcan.gc.ca/daily-quotidien/131203/ dq131203a-eng.htm).

———. 2013b. "Disability in Canada: Initial Findings from the Canadian Survey of Disability" (https://www150.statcan.gc.ca/n1/en/catalogue/89-654-X2013002).

———. 2014. "Number and Percentage of People Living in Low Income by Family Type." 2014 Canada Income Survey. CANSIM table 206-0042. Retrieved January 13, 2019 (https://www.canada.ca/en/employment-social-development/programs/poverty-reduction/backgrounder.html).

———. 2016. "Census of Population" (https://www12.statcan.gc.ca/census-recensement/2016/dp-pd/prof/details/page.cfm?Lang=E&Geo1=PR&Code1=01&Geo2=&Code2=&SearchText=Canada&SearchType=Begins&SearchPR=01&B1=All&TABID=1&type=0).

———. 2017a. "Aboriginal Peoples in Canada: Key Results from the 2016 Census." Retrieved January 16, 2019 (https://www150.statcan.gc.ca/n1/daily-quotidien/171025/dq171025a-eng.htm).

———. 2017b. "Analysis: Population by Age and Sex." Retrieved May 15, 2020 (https://www150.statcan.gc.ca/n1/pub/91-215-x/2017000/sec2-eng.htm).

———. 2017c. "Census Profile, 2016 Census." Catalogue no. 98-316-X2016001. Retrieved January 11, 2019 (https://www12.statcan.gc.ca/census-recensement/2016/dp-pd/prof/index.cfm?Lang=E).

———. 2017d. "Children Living in Low-Income Households" (https://www12.statcan.gc.ca/census-recensement/2016/as-sa/98-200-x/2016012/98-200-x2016012-eng.cfm).

———. 2017e. "Individual MBM Low-Income Status (6) and Economic Family Characteristics of Persons (25) for the Population in Private Households of Canada, Provinces and Territories, Census Metropolitan Areas and Census Agglomerations." 2016 Census. Catalogue no. 98-400-X2016148. Retrieved January 11, 2019 (https://www12.statcan.gc.ca/census-recensement/2016/dp-pd/dt-td/Rp-eng.cfm?LANG=E&APATH=3&DETAIL=0&DIM=0&FL=A&FREE=0&GC=0&GID=0&GK=0&GRP=1&PID=110727&PRID=10&PTYPE=109445&S=0&SHOWALL=0&SUB=999&Temporal=2016,2017&THEME=119&VID=0&VNAMEE=&VNAMEF=).

———. 2017f. "Same-Sex Couples in Canada in 2016: 2016 Census in Brief." Retrieved January 16, 2019 (https://www12.statcan.gc.ca/census-recensement/2016/as-sa/98-200-x/2016007/98-200-x2016007-eng.cfm).

———. 2017g. "Visible Minority and Population Group Reference Guide." Census of Population, 2016. Retrieved January 13, 2019 (https://www12.statcan.gc.ca/census-recensement/2016/ref/guides/006/98-500-x2016006-eng.cfm).

———. 2018a. "Canadian Survey on Disability, 2017." *The Daily*, November 28 (https://www150.statcan.gc.ca/n1/daily-quotidien/181128/dq181128a-eng.htm).

———. 2018b. "Population Growth in Canada: From 1851–2061." Retrieved May 14, 2020 (http://www12.statcan.gc.ca/census-recensement/2011/as-sa/98-310-x/2011003/fig/fig3_1-1-eng.cfm).

———. 2018c. "Senior Victims of Police-Reported Family and Non-Family Violence, by Victim Sex and Relationship of Accused to Victim, Canada, 2017" (https://www150.statcan.gc.ca/n1/pub/85-002-x/2018001/article/54978/tbl/tbl3.1-eng.htm).

Truth and Reconciliation Commission of Canada. 2015. *Final Report of the Truth and Reconciliation Commission of Canada.* Winnipeg, MB: Truth and Reconciliation Commission of Canada.

United Nations. 2014. "Country Reports: Canada." Office of the High Commissioner for Human Rights.

Van Ijzendoorn, M. H., Bakermans-Kranenburg, M. J., & Sagi-Schwartz, A. (2003). "Are Children of Holocaust Survivors Less Well-Adapted? A Meta-Analytic Investigation of Secondary Traumatization." *Journal of Traumatic Stress*, 16(5), 459–69.

Wallerstein, Immanuel. 1992. "The West, Capitalism, and the Modern World-System." *Review* 15(4):561–619.

Wesley-Esquimaux, C.C. and M. Smolewski. 2004. *Historic Trauma and Aboriginal Healing.* Ottawa, ON: Aboriginal Healing Foundation.

Chapter 3

Anderson, Karen. 2012. *Thinking about Sociology: A Critical Introduction.* Don Mills, ON: Oxford University Press.

Antecol, H., A. Jong, and M. Steinberger. 2008. "The Sexual Orientation Wage Gap: The Role of Occupational Sorting and Human Capital." *Industrial and Labor Relations Review* 61:518–43.

Block, Sheila, and Grace-Edward Galabuzi. 2011. *Canada's Colour Coded Labour Market: The Gap for Racialized Workers.* Wellesley Institute (https://www.wellesleyinstitute.com/wp-content/uploads/2011/03/Colour_Coded_Labour_MarketFINAL.pdf).

———. 2018. *Persistent Inequality: Ontario's Colour-Coded Labour Market.* Canadian Centre for Policy Alternatives (https://www.policyalternatives.ca/sites/default/files/uploads/publications/Ontario%20Office/2018/12/Persistent%20inequality.pdf).

Boulet, Virginie and Nadine Badets. 2017. "Early Motherhood among Off-Reserve First Nations, Métis and Inuit Women." Insights on Canadian Society. Statistics Canada, catalogue no. 75-006-X (https://www150.statcan.gc.ca/n1/en/catalogue/75-006-X201700154877).

Brown, A.D. 2017. "Identity Work and Organizational Identification." *International Journal of Management Reviews* 19(3):296–317.

Burke, M. 2008. "Aboriginal People Are Wanted in the Trade Industry." *Windspeaker,* February:24.

Canadian Mental Health Association. n.d. "Stigma and Discrimination." *Workplace Mental Health Promotion: A How-To Guide* (https://wmhp.cmhaontario.ca/workplace-mental-health-core-concepts-issues/issues-in-the-workplace-that-affect-employee-mental-health/stigma-and-discrimination).

Clance, Pauline R. and Suzanne A. Imes. 1978. "The Imposter Phenomenon in High Achieving Women: Dynamics and Therapeutic Intervention." *Psychotherapy: Theory, Research & Practice* 15(3):241.

Creese, G. and B. Beagan. 2009. "Gender at Work: Strategies for Equality in Neo-Liberal Times." Pp. 224–36 in *Social Inequality in Canada: Patterns, Problems, and Policies*, 5th edn, edited by E. Grabb and N. Guppy. Toronto, ON: Pearson Prentice Hall.

Delphy, C. and D. Leonard. 1984. *Close to Home: A Materialist Analysis of Women's Oppression.* Amherst, MA: University of Massachusetts Press.

Desmarais, S. and J. Curtis. 1997. "Gender and Perceived Pay Entitlement: Testing for Effects of Experience with Income." *Journal of Personality and Social Psychology* 72(1):141.

Dharssi, Alia. 2016. "Skilled Immigrants Wasting Their Talents in Canada." *Calgary Herald,* September 14 (https://calgaryherald.com/news/national/skilled-immigrants-wasting-their-talents-in-canada).

Doucet, Andrea. 2012. "Gender Equality and Gender Difference." In *Reading Sociology: Canadian Perspectives, edited by* L.T. Kalyta. Don Mills, ON: Oxford University Press.

Dress for Success Vancouver. 2011. *Annual General Report 2011.*

Duxbury, Linda and Christoper Higgins. 2012. "Revisiting Work-Life Issues in Canada: The 2012 National Study on Balancing Work and Caregiving in Canada" (https://newsroom.carleton.ca/wp-content/files/2012-National-Work-Long-Summary.pdf).

Ferguson, Sarah J. and Shunji Wang. 2014. "Graduating in Canada: Profile, Labour Market Outcomes and Student Debt of the Class of 2009–2010." Statistics Canada (https://www150.statcan.gc.ca/n1/en/catalogue/81-595-M2014101).

Finnie, R. and R. Meng. 2002. "Are Immigrants' Human Capital Skills Discounted in Canada?" Business and Labour Market Analysis Division, Statistics Canada.

Fong, Francis. 2012. "The Plight of Younger Workers." *TD Economics*, March 8, 1–3.

———. 2018. "We Don't Know the Extent of Precarious Work." *Policy Options* (https://policyoptions.irpp.org/magazines/january-2018/we-dont-know-the-extent-of-precarious-work).

Gates, Trevor G. and Pamela A. Viggiani. 2014. "Understanding Lesbian, Gay, and Bisexual Worker Stigmatization: A Review of the Literature." *International Journal of Sociology and Social Policy* 34(5/6):359–74.

Gobel, C. and T. Zwick. 2012. "Age and Productivity: Sector Differences." *De Economist* 160:35.

Government of Canada. 2011. "*Employment Equity Act: Annual Report 2010.*" Ottawa, ON: Her Majesty the Queen in Right of Canada.

Grant, H. and G. Wong Grant. 2002. "Age Discrimination and the Employment Rights of Elderly Canadian Immigrants." The Law Commission of Canada (https://pdfs.semanticscholar.org/3727/9882661bf03b4f63a77d3106528c214be610.pdf).

Gunderson, M. 2003. "Age Discrimination in Employment in Canada." *Contemporary Economic Policy* 23(1):318.

Guimond, E., N. Robitaille, and S. Senécal. 2009. "Aboriginal Populations in Canadian Cities: Why Are They Growing so Fast?" Indigenous and Northern Affairs Canada (https://www.aadnc-aandc.gc.ca/eng/1352402108618/1352402154515).

Hango, D. and P. de Broucker. 2007. *Education-to-Labour Market Pathways of Canadian Youth: Findings from the Youth in Transition Survey.* Ottawa, ON: Ministry of Industry and Statistics Canada.

Hardy, Vincent, Marton Lovei, and Martha Patterson. 2018. "Recent Trends in Canada's Labour Market: A Rising Tide or a Passing Wave?" Statistics Canada, August 31 (https://www150.statcan.gc.ca/n1/pub/71-222-x/71-222-x2018001-eng.htm).

Hiltz, R. 2012a. "Canadians Believe Employers Discriminate Against Older Applicants: Poll." *Vancouver Sun*, July 23 (http://www.vancouversun.com/life/canadians+believe+employers+discriminate+against+older+applicants+poll/6975266/story.html).

Hiltz, R. 2012b. "Hard to Teach, But Older Workers Are Highly Valued: Poll." *Vancouver Sun,* July 23 (http://www.vancouversun.com/news/national/hard+teach+older+workers+highly+valued+poll/6977392/story.html).

Hossain, B. and L. Lamb. 2012. "The Impact of Human and Social Capital on Aboriginal Employment Income in Canada." *Economic Papers: A Journal of Applied Economics and Policy* 31(4):440–50.

Hou, F. and Y. Lu. (2017). "International Students, Immigration and Earnings Growth: The Effect of a Pre-immigration Canadian University Education." Statistics Canada, August 22 (https://www150.statcan.gc.ca/n1/pub/11f0019m/11f0019m2017395-eng.htm).

Ivie, R., S. White, and R.Y. Chu. 2016. "Women's and Men's Career Choices in Astronomy and Astrophysics." *Physical Review Physics Education Research* 12(2):020109. doi:10.1103/PhysRevPhysEducRes.12.020109

Jencks, Christopher. 1988. "Whom Must We Treat Equally for Educational Opportunity to Be Equal?" *Ethics* 98(3):518–33.

Kimle, P.A. and M.L. Damhorst. 1997. "A Grounded Theory Model of the Ideal Business Image for Women." *Symbolic Interaction* 20(1):45–68.

Kurtz, D.L. 2012. "Roll Call and the Second Shift: The Influences of Gender and Family on Police Stress." *Police Practice and Research* 13(1):71–86. doi:10.1080/15614263.2011.596714

Kwon, Y.H. 1994. The influence of appropriateness of dress and gender on the self-perception of occupational attributes. *Clothing and Textiles Research Journal* 12(3):33–39.

Lewis, Oscar. 1961. *The Children of Sanchez: Autobiography of a Mexican Family.* New York: Random House.

Liu, Shuping. 2013. "Postsecondary Education Latecomers: Profile and Labour Market Outcomes of Ontario PSE Graduates." Higher Education Quality Council of Ontario (http://www.heqco.ca/sitecollectiondocuments/pse%20latecomers%20eng.pdf).

Maclean's. 2012. "Cultivating Tomorrow's Aboriginal Leaders." June 25:24.

Marni, L. and A.A. Kosny. 2012. "A National Scan of Employment Standards, Occupational Health and Safety and Workers' Compensation Resources for New Immigrants to Canada." *Canadian Journal of Public Health* 103(1):53.

Marshall, S.K., Y.A. Richard, A. Stevens, W. Spence, S. Deyell, and A. Easterbrook. 2011. "Adolescent Career Development in Urban-Residing Aboriginal Families in Canada." *The Career Development Quarterly* 59:539.

Massimino, P.M. and K. Turner. 2017. "Business Etiquette and Career Advancement: Do Manners Still Matter?" *Proceedings of the Northeast Business & Economics Association.*

Mills, S. 2011. "The Difficulty with Diversity: White and Aboriginal Women Workers' Representations of Diversity Management in Forest Processing Mills." *Labour/Le Travail* 67:45–76.

Morris, S., G. Fawcett, L. Brisebois, and J. Hughes. 2018. "A Demographic, Employment and Income Profile of Canadians with Disabilities Aged 15 Years and Over, 2017." Canadian Survey on Disability Reports.

Moyer, Melissa and Amanda Burlock. 2018. "Time Use: Total Work Burden, Unpaid Work, and Leisure." Statistics Canada (https://www150.statcan.gc.ca/n1/pub/89-503-x/2015001/article/54931-eng.htm).

Moyser. M. 2017. "Women and Paid Work." Statistics Canada (https://www150.statcan.gc.ca/n1/pub/89-503-x/2015001/article/14694-eng.htm).

Office of the Fairness Commissioner. 2012. "Licensing Outpaces Employment for Internationally Educated Professionals" (http://www.fairnesscommissioner.ca/files_docs/content/pdf/en/Licensing_outpaces_employment_for_internationally_educated_professionals.pdf).

O'Rourke, D. 2012. "*#GenerationFlux: Understanding the Seismic Shifts that Are Shaking Canada's Youth.*" Community Foundations of Canada (https://www.communityfoundations.ca/wp-content/uploads/2019/04/GenerationFlux-2012.pdf).

Oxfam. 2019. *Public Good or Private Wealth?* (https://oxfamilibrary.openrepository.com/bitstream/handle/10546/620599/bp-public-good-or-private-wealth-210119-summ-en.pdf).

Parkinson, David. 2019. "Non-Standard Workers Make up 31 Per Cent of Canada's Workforce." *Globe and Mail,* May 1 (https://www.theglobeandmail.com/business/commentary/article-non-standard-workers-make-up-31-per-cent-of-canadas-workforce).

Parnell, Martha K., Suzanne H. Lease, and Michael L. Green. 2015. "Perceived Career Barriers for Gay, Lesbian, and Bisexual Individuals." *Journal of Career Development* 39(3):248–68.

Peluchette, J.V. and K. Karl. 2007. "The Impact of Workplace Attire on Employee Self-Perceptions." *Human Resource Development Quarterly* 18(3):345–60. doi:10.1002/hrdq.1208.

———. 2018. "'She's got the look': Examining Feminine and Provocative Dress in the Workplace." PP. 116–28 in *Research Handbook of Diversity and Careers*, edited by A.M. Broadbridge and S.L. Fielden. Cheltenham, UK: Edward Elgar Publishing.

Peluchette, J.V., K. Karl, and K. Rust. 2006. "Dressing to Impress: Beliefs and Attitudes Regarding Workplace Attire." *Journal of Business and Psychology* 21(1):45–63. doi:10.1007/s10869-005-9022-1.

Pratt, M.G. and A. Rafaeli. 1997. "Organizational Dress as a Symbol of Multilayered Social Identities." *Academy of Management Journal* 40(4):862–98.

Public Service Alliance of Canada. 2017. "History in the Making" (http://psacunion.ca/sites/psac/files/attachments/pdfs/10_-_equity_at_work_-_handouts_-_en.pdf).

Rafaeli, A. and M.G. Pratt. 1993. "Tailored Meanings: On the Meaning and Impact of Organizational Dress." *Academy of Management Review* 18(1):32–55.

Ragins, B.R. 2004. "Sexual Orientation in the Workplace: The Unique Work and Career Experiences of Gay, Lesbian, and Bisexual Workers." *Research in Personnel Human Resources Management* 23:35–120.

Retail Council of Canada. 2020. "Minimum Wage by Province" (https://www.retailcouncil.org/resources/quick-facts/minimum-wage-by-province).

Robson, Karen and Jean Wallace. 2001. "Gendered Inequalities in Earnings: A Study of Canadian Lawyers." *Canadian Review of Sociology* 38(1):75–95.

Roth, A., J. Kim, and D. Kincade. 2017. "Businesswomen's Choice of Professional Dress: Model Development for Dress Perception." *Journal of Global Fashion Marketing* 8(4):313–25.

Sani, Giulia M. 2014. "Men's Employment Hours and Time on Domestic Chores in European Countries." *Journal of Family Issues* 35(8):1023–47.

Statistics Canada. 2009. "Study: Quality of Employment in the Canadian Immigrant Labour Market." *The Daily,* November 23 (http://www.statcan.gc.ca/daily-quotidien/091123/dq091123b-eng.htm).

———. 2011. "Study: Aboriginal People and the Labour Market." *The Daily* (http://www.statcan.gc.ca/daily-quotidien/111123/dq111123b-eng.htm).

———. 2012a. "Study: How the Older Unemployed Look for Work, 2006 to 2010." *The Daily (*http://www.statcan.gc.ca/daily-quotidien/120822/dq120822c-eng.htm).

———. 2012b. "Women in Canada: A Gender-Based Statistical Report" (http://www.statcan.gc.ca/pub/89-503-x/89-503-x2010001-eng.htm).

———. 2014. *Towards a Poverty Reduction Strategy: A Background on Poverty in Canada.* Retrieved February 17, 2019 (https://www.canada.ca/en/employment-social-development/programs/poverty-reduction/backgrounder.html#wb-cont).

———. 2015a. "Personal Networks and the Economic Adjustment of Immigrants." Statistics Canada (https://www150.statcan.gc.ca/n1/pub/11-008-x/2011002/c-g/11592/c-g01-eng.htm).

———. 2015b. "Status of Women in Canada" (https://www.swc-cfc.gc.ca/initiatives/wesp-sepf/fs-fi/es-se-eng.html).

———. 2016. *2016 Census of Population.* Statistics Canada, catalogue no. 98-400-X2016192.

———. 2017a. "Canada [Country] and Canada [Country]." 2016 Census. Statistics Canada, catalogue no. 98-316-X2016001. Retrieved March 10, 2019 (https://www12.statcan.gc.ca/census-recensement/2016/dp-pd/prof/index.cfm?Lang=E).

———. 2017b. "Study: Low Income among Persons with a Disability in Canada, 2014." *The Daily,* August 11 (https://www150.statcan.gc.ca/n1/daily-quotidien/170811/dq170811a-eng.htm).

———. 2017c. "Working Seniors in Canada." November 29 (https://www12.statcan.gc.ca/census-recensement/2016/as-sa/98-200-x/2016027/98-200-x2016027-eng.cfm).

———. 2017d. "Women in Paid Work" (https://www150.statcan.gc.ca/n1/daily-quotidien/170308/dq170308b-eng.htm).

———. 2018a. *"Aboriginal Population Profile."* 2016 Census. Catalogue no. 98-510-X2016001. Retrieved March 10, 2019 (http://www12.statcan.gc.ca/census-recensement/2016/dp-pd/abpopprof/index.cfm?Lang=E).

———. 2018b. "The Canadian Immigrant Labour Market: Recent Trends from 2006 to 2017" (https://www150.statcan.gc.ca/n1/pub/71-606-x/71-606-x2018001-eng.htm).

———. 2018c. "Percentage of Paid Workers Covered by a Registered Pension Plan (RPP)" (https://www150.statcan.gc.ca/n1/daily-quotidien/180627/t002e-eng.htm).

———. 2018d. "Unionization Rates Falling" (https://www150.statcan.gc.ca/n1/pub/11-630-x/11-630-x2015005-eng.htm).

———. 2019. "Labour Force Characteristics of Immigrants by Educational Attainment, Annual" (https://www150.statcan.gc.ca/t1/tbl1/en/tv.action?pid=1410008701&pickMembers%5B0%5D=2.6&pickMembers%5B1%5D=4.8&pickMembers%5B2%5D=5.1&pickMembers%5B3%5D=6.2).

———. 2020a. "Distribution of Employment Income of Individuals by Sex and Work Activity, Canada, Provinces and Selected Census Metropolitan Areas, Annual." Canadian Income Survey. Table 206-0053 (https://www150.statcan.gc.ca/t1/tbl1/en/tv.action?pid=1110024001).

———. 2020b. "Income of Individuals by Age Group, Sex and Income Source, Canada, Provinces and Selected Census Metropolitan Areas, Annual." Canadian Income Survey. Table 2016-0052 (https://www150.statcan.gc.ca/t1/tbl1/en/tv.action?pid=1110023901).

Struijf-Mandishora, L. 2012. "From Intake to Employment—An ISANS Journey." *ISANS* (http://www.isans.ca/from-intake-to-employment-an-isis-journey).

Sweetland, S.R. 1996. "Human Capital Theory: Foundations of a Field of Inquiry." *Review of Educational Research* 66(3):341–59.

Thomas, D. 2015. *"Personal Networks and the Economic Adjustment of Immigrants."* Statistics Canada (http://www.statcan.gc.ca/pub/11-008-x/2011002/article/11592-eng.htm#a8).

Triana, M.D.C., M. Jayasinghe, J.R. Pieper, D.M. Delgado, and L. Li. 2019. "Perceived Workplace Gender Discrimination and Employee Consequences: A Meta-Analysis and Complementary Studies Considering Country Context." *Journal of Management* 45(6):2419–47.

Turcotte, M. 2015. "Persons with Disabilities and Employment." Statistics Canada (https://www150.statcan.gc.ca/n1/pub/75-006-x/2014001/article/14115-eng.htm#a9).

Uppal, S. and S. LaRochelle-Cote. (2014). "Overqualification among Recent University Graduates in Canada." *Insights on Canadian Society.* Statistics Canada, catalogue no. 75-006-X (https://www150.statcan.gc.ca/n1/pub/75-006-x/2014001/article/11916/citation-eng.htm).

Usher, A. 2018. "Do the Math: Tuition Fees Are Not Out of Control." *Globe and Mail*, August 30 (https://www.theglobeandmail.com/business/commentary/article-do-the-math-tuition-fees-are-not-out-of-control).

White, J., P. Maxim, and S. Obeng Gyimah. 2003. "Labour Force Activity of Women in Canada: A Comparative Analysis of Aboriginal and Non-Aboriginal Women." *Canadian Journal of Regional Science* 40(4):391–415.

Wallace, Jean. 2006. "Can Women in Law Have It All? A Study of Motherhood, Career Satisfaction and Life Balance." *Research in the Sociology of Organizations 24*:283–306.

Wilkinson, Richard and Kate Pickett. 2010. *The Spirit Level*. London, UK: Penguin.

Williams, C. 2006. "*Disability in the Workplace.*" Perspectives on Labour and Income, Statistics Canada (http://www.statcan.gc.ca/pub/75-001-x/10206/9096-eng.htm).

Wright, Teresa. 2018. "Concerns Raised Over High Fees Charges to Temporary Foreign Workers." Canadian Press, May 23 (https://toronto.citynews.ca/2018/05/28/concerns-raised-over-recruiting-fees-charged-to-temporary-foreign-workers).

Chapter 4

Abedi, Maham. 2019. "How Canadian Provinces Are Taking on Affordable Child Care—And How It Compares to the World. *Global News*, March 26 (https://globalnews.ca/news/5097254/canada-affordable-child-care-world).

Adamson, Peter. 2008. "*The Childcare Transition: A League Table of Early Childhood Education and Care in Economically Advanced Countries.*" UNICEF (https://www.unicef-irc.org/publications/507-the-child-care-transition-a-league-table-of-early-childhood-education-and-care-in.html).

Ainsworth, Mary D. 1969. "Object Relations, Dependency, and Attachment: A Theoretical Review of the Infant-Mother Relationship." *Child Development* 40(4):969–1025.

Ainsworth, M.D.S., M.C. Blehar, E. Waters, and S. Wall. 1978. *Patterns of Attachment: A Psychological Study of the Strange Situation.* Hillsdale, NJ: Erlbaum.

Akbari, E. and K. McCuaig. 2019. "Early Childhood Education Report." Atkinson Centre for Society and Child Development at the Ontario Institute for Studies in Education/University of Toronto (http://ecereport.ca/media/uploads/2017-report-pdfs/ece-report2017-en-feb6.pdf).

Barbeau, Carole. 2001. "Work-Related Child-Care Centres in Canada." Human Resources Development Canada, Labour Program.

Belsky, Jay and Michael Pluess. 2011. "Differential Susceptibility to Long-Term Effects of Quality of Child Care on Externalizing Behavior in Adolescence?" *International Journal of Behavioral Development* 36(1):2–10

Berrueta-Clement, J.R., L.J. Schweinhart, W.S. Barnett, A.S. Epstein, and D.P. Weikart. 1984. "Changed Lives: The Effects of the Perry Preschool Program on Youths through Age 19." *Monographs of the HighScope Educational Research Foundation* 8. Ypsilanti, MI: HighScope Press.

Bowlby, J. 1960. "Separation Anxiety." *International Journal of Psychoanalysis* 41:89–113

———. 1973. Separation: Anxiety and Anger. *New York: Basic Books.*

Broadbent Institute. 2012. "*Towards a More Equal Canada: A Report on Canada's Economic and Social Inequality.*" October (https://www.broadbentinstitute.ca/towards_a_more_equal_canada).

Bruning, Gwennaële and Janneke Plantenga. 1999. "Parental Leave and Equal Opportunities: Experiences in Eight European Countries." *Journal of European Social Policy* 9(3):195–209.

Carson, A. 2013. "How Do You Feel to Be a Mom Who Works Outside of the Home?" June 19, J. Ball, Interviewer, Toronto, Ontario.

CBC News. 2010. "Rural Daycares Could Have Trouble Meeting Numbers." June 1 (http://www.cbc.ca/news/canada/prince-edward-island/story/2010/06/01/pei-daycare-rural-reaction-584.html).

CBC News. 2013. "Unlicensed Daycares Operate Free from Oversight: Majority of Canadian Children Can't Get into Licensed Daycare." *Marketplace, February 21 (http://*www.cbc.ca/news/canada/story/2013/02/21/marketplace-unlicensed-daycare.html).

City of Toronto. 2017. "Toronto's Licensed Child Care Growth Strategy for Children under 4 2017–2026" (https://www.toronto.ca/legdocs/mmis/2017/cd/bgrd/backgroundfile-102626.pdf).

City of Calgary. 2018. "2018 Compensation Disclosure List" (http://www.calgary.ca/CA/cmo/Documents/2018-Compensation_disclosure_list.pdf).

Cleveland, G. and M. Krashinsky. 2003. "*Fact and Fantasy: Eight Myths about Early Childhood Education and Care.*" Toronto, ON: Childcare Resource and Research Unit.

Crowe, R. 2018. "Welcome to the Mommune: 20 Stories from Women Who Chose to Co-Mother Their Kids." Moms (https://www.moms.com/welcome-to-the-mommune-20-stories-from-women-who-chose-to-co-mother-their-kids).

CTV News. 2018. "Daycare Fees Continue to Rise across Canada" (https://www.ctvnews.ca/features/analysis-daycare-fees-continue-to-rise-across-canada-1.3940099).

Decter, A. 2011. "*Educated, Employed and Equal: The Economic Prosperity Case for National Childcare.*" YWCA Canada (https://ywcacanada.ca/wp-content/uploads/2018/10/Educated-Employed-and-Equal-2011.pdf).

Durkheim, Emile. 1897. *Le Suicide*. Paris: Félix Alcan, Éditeur.

Ebbels, Kelly. 2008. "Daycare Collective Provides Radical Child Care." *McGill Daily*, March 17 (https://www.mcgilldaily.com/2008/03/daycare_collective_provides_radical_child_care).

Esping-Andersen, Gøsta. 1990. *The Three Worlds of Welfare Capitalism*. Cambridge, UK: Polity Press.

Ferns, C. and M. Friendly. 2014. The State of Early Childhood Education and Care in Canada 2012." The Moving

Childcare Forward Project (https://www.childcarecanada .org/sites/default/files/StateofECEC2012.pdf).

Fortin, N., B. Bell, and M. Böhm. 2017. "Top Earnings Inequality and the Gender Pay Gap: Canada, Sweden and the United Kingdom." Discussion Paper Series, IZA Institute of Labour Economics (http://ftp.iza.org/dp10829.pdf).

Friendly, M. and S. Halfon, S. 2012. "Why Universal Childcare Is Essential for a More Equal Canada." Rabble.ca, July 12 (http://rabble.ca/blogs/bloggers/child-care-canada-now/2012/07/why-universal-childcare-essential-more-equal-canada).

Friendly, M. and S. Prentice. 2009. *About Canada. Childcare.* Black Point, NS: Fernwood Publishing.

Friendly, M., B. Grady, L. Macdonald, and B. Forer. 2015. "Early Childhood Education and Care in Canada 2014." Childcare Resource and Research Unit. Retrieved March 27, 2019 (https://www.childcarecanada.org/sites/default/files/ECEC-2014-full-document-revised-10-03-16.pdf).

Glass, Jennifer and Tetsushi Fujimoto. 1995. "Employer Characteristics and the Provision of Family Responsive Policies." *Work and Occupations* 22(4):380–411.

Government of British Columbia. n.d. "Affordable Child Care Benefit" (https://www2.gov.bc.ca/gov/content/family-social-supports/caring-for-young-children/child-care-funding/child-care-benefit).

Harvard University. 2010. "*The Foundations of Lifelong Health Are Built in Early Childhood: Summary of Essential Findings.*" Boston, MA: Centre on the Developing Child.

Hope Irwin, S. 2009. *The SpeciaLink Early Childhood Inclusion Quality Scale.* Sydney, NS: Breton Books.

HRSDC. 2012. *Public Investments in Early Childhood Education and Care in Canada.* Gatineau, QC: Government of Canada.

Immerman, Ronald S. and Wade C. Mackey. 1999. "The Societal Dilemma of Multiple Sexual Partners: The Costs of the Loss of Pair-Bonding." *Marriage & Family Review* 29(1):3–19.

Kohen, Dafna, Clyde Hertzman, and J. Douglas Willms. 2002. "The Importance of Quality Child Care." *Vulnerable Children*:261–76.

Lamb, Michael E. and Lieselotte Ahnert. 2006. "Nonparental Child Care: Context, Quality, Correlates, and Consequences." Pp. 73–134 in *Handbook of Child Psychology: Child Psychology in Practice,* 5th edn, edited by I.E. Spiegel and K.A. Renniger. New York: Wiley.

Lappegard, Trude. 2008. "Changing the Gender Balance in Caring: Fatherhood and the Division of Parental Leave in Norway." *Population Research and Policy Review* 27(2):139–59.

Lareau, Annette. 2003. *Unequal Childhoods.* Berkeley, CA: University of California Press.

Leclair, Anne. 2017. "Majority of Families Denied Quebec Supplement for Children with Exceptional Needs." *Global News,* November 21 (https://globalnews.ca/news/3873636/majority-of-families-denied-quebec-supplement-for-children-with-exceptional-needs).

Lee, Jann. 2018. "Telecommuting Becoming Standard in Canadian Workplaces: Survey." Benefits Canada, November 28 (https://www.benefitscanada.com/news/telecommuting-becoming-standard-in-canadian-workplaces-survey-122266).

Macdonald, David and Martha Friendly. 2014. "*The Parent Trap: Child Care Fees in Canada's Big Cities.*" Ottawa, ON: Canadian Centre for Policy Alternatives.

———. 2018. "Developmental Milestones: Child Care Fees in Canada's Big Cities." Ottawa, ON: Canadian Centre for Policy Alternatives.

Misra, Joya, Michelle J. Budig, and Stephanie Moller. 2007. "Reconciliation Policies and the Effects of Motherhood on Employment, Earnings and Poverty." *Journal of Comparative Policy Analysis* 9(2):135–55.

Oakley, Ann. 1974. *Housewife.* London, UK: Allen Lane.

OECD. 2003. "*Early Childhood Education and Care Policy: Canada Country Note.*" OECD Directorate for Education.

———. 2016. "OECD Urges Canadian Governments to Increase Funding for Childcare" (http://www.oecd.org/canada/oecdurgescanadiangovernmentstoincreasefundingforchildcare.htm).

Ontario NDP. 2018. "Horwath's $12 per Day Child Care Plan Is Change for the Better of Families." May 16 (https://www.ontariondp.ca/news/horwaths-12-day-child-care-plan-change-better-families).

Osborne, Cynthia, Wendy Manning, and Pamela Smock. 2007. "Married and Cohabiting Parents' Relationship Stability: A Focus on Race and Ethnicity." *Journal of Marriage and Family* 69(5):1345–66. doi:10.1111/j.1741-3737.2007.00451.x

Parsons, Talcott and Robert Freed Bales. 1955. *Family Socialization and Interaction Process. New York: Free Press of Glencoe.*

Prentice, Susan. 2007a. "Childcare, Justice and the City: A Case Study of Planning Failure in Winnipeg." *Canadian Journal of Urban Research* 16(1):92–108.

———. 2007b. "Less Access, Worse Quality." *Journal of Children and Poverty* 13(1):57–73.

Reardon, Sean. 2013. "No Rich Child Left Behind." *New York Times,* April 27 (https://opinionator.blogs.nytimes .com/2013/04/27/no-rich-child-left-behind).

Richards, Elizabeth. 2019. "Who Are the Working Women in Canada's Top 1%?" Statistics Canada (https://www150 .statcan.gc.ca/n1/pub/11f0019m/11f0019m2019002-eng.htm).

Riley, Joellen. 2013. "The Gender Agenda: Gaining Momentum." International Women's Day Address, March 8 (http://sydney.edu.au/news/84.html?newscategoryid=12&newsstoryid=11127).

Saltman, Jennifer. 2019. "B.C. Budget 2019: Increase to Child-Care Funding, New Child Benefit Introduced." *Vancouver Sun,* February 19 (https://vancouversun.com/news/local-news/b-c-budget-2019-minor-increase-to-child-care-funding-new-benefit-introduced).

Shonkoff, J. and D. Phillips. 2000. "From Neurons to Neighborhoods: The Science of Early Childhood Development." National Research Council and Institute of Medicine. Washington, DC: National Academy Press.

Sinha, Marie. 2015. "Child Care in Canada." Statistics Canada, catalogue no. 89-652-X (https://www150.statcan.gc.ca/n1/pub/89-652-x/89-652-x2014005-eng.htm).

Smith, Adam. [1776], 1991. *The Wealth of Nations*, Vol 1. New York, NY: Prometheus Books.

Statistics Canada. 2008. "Analytical Paper: Participation and Activity Limitation Survey 2006: Families of Children with Disabilities in Canada." Ottawa, ON: Author

———. 2015. "Generational Change in Paid and Unpaid Work." Catalogue no. 11-008-X (https://www150.statcan.gc.ca/n1/pub/11-008-x/2011002/article/11520-eng.htm).

———. 2016a. "Labour Force Survey, December 2016" (https://www150.statcan.gc.ca/n1/daily-quotidien/170106/dq170106a-eng.htm).

———. 2016b. "Workplace and Employee Survey." Catalogue 92-135-GWE (https://www12.statcan.gc.ca/census-recensement/2011/ref/92-135/surveys-enquetes/workplace-empl-milieutravailempl-eng.cfm).

———. 2020a. "Part-Time Employment by Reason, Annual." Table 14-10-0029-01 (http://www.statcan.gc.ca/pub/11-008-x/2011002/c-g/11520/c-g001-eng.htm).

———. 2020b. "Proportion of Children Aged 0 to 5 Participating in Child Care, Provinces and Territories" (https://www150.statcan.gc.ca/n1/daily-quotidien/190410/cg-a001-eng.htm).

Tencer, Daniel. 2018. "Look How Much Smaller Canada's Economy Would Be without Women." *Huffington Post*, March 8 (https://www.huffingtonpost.ca/2018/03/08/women-workforce-canada_a_23380416).

TD. 2012. "*Early Childhood Education Has Widespread and Long Lasting Benefits*." Special Report, TD Economics.

Tierney, A.L. and C.A. Nelson. 2009. "Brain Development and the Role of Experience in the Early Years." *Zero to three* 30(2):9–13.

YMCA. 2020. "Toronto YMCA Daycare Fees" (https://ymcagta.org/find-a-y/toronto-pinnacle-ymca-child-care-centre).

United Nations. 2006. Convention on the Rights of Persons with Disabilities. *Treaty Series* 2515:3.

Vincent, Carole. 2013. "Why Do Women Earn Less than Men?" *CRDCN Research Highlight* 1/5 (http://ir.lib.uwo.ca/crdcn_rccdr/vol1/iss5/1).

Waite, Linda J. 2000. "The Family as a Social Organization: Key Ideas for the Twenty-First Century." *Contemporary Sociology 29(3)*:463–69.

Wiart, L., H. Kehler, G. Rempel, and S. Tough. 2011. "Alberta Inclusive Child Care Project." Alberta Centre for Child, Family and Community Research (http://www. research-4children.com/public/data/documents/AICCPFINALREPORTDecember2011pdf.pdf).

World Bank. 2013. "Early Child Development" (https://www.worldbank.org/en/topic/earlychildhooddevelopment).

Chapter 5

Abraham, C. 2010a. "Part 1: Failing Boys and the Powder Keg of Sexual Politics." *Globe and Mail, October 15* (https://www.theglobeandmail.com/news/national/time-to-lead/part-1-failing-boys-and-the-powder-keg-of-sexual-politics/article4081751).

———. 2010b. "Part 2: The Endangered Male Teacher." *Globe and Mail, October 18* (https://www.theglobeandmail.com/news/national/time-to-lead/part-2-the-endangered-male-teacher/article4330079).

Andruska, Emily, Jeanne Hogarth, Cynthia N. Fletcher, Gregory Forbes, and Darin Wohlgemuth. 2014 "Do You Know What You Owe? Students' Understanding of Their Student Loans." *Journal of Student Financial Aid* 44(2):Article 3.

Arkorful, V. and N. Abaidoo. 2014 "The Role of e-Learning, the Advantages and Disadvantages of Its Adoption in Higher Education." *International Journal of Education and Research* 2:397–410.

Association of Universities and Colleges of Canada. 2011. *Trends in Higher Education: Vol. 1: Enrolment.* Ottawa, AU.

Block, K., A. Croft, and T. Schmader. 2018. "Worth Less? Why Men (and Women) Devalue Care-Oriented Careers." *Frontiers in Psychology* 9:1353. doi:10.3389/fpsyg.2018.01353

Breton, Raymond. 1974. "Social and Academic Factors in the Career Decisions of Canadian Youth." *Social Forces* 52(3):425–6.

Byrom, T. and N. Lightfoot. 2013. "Interrupted Trajectories: The Impact of Academic Failure on the Social Mobility of Working-Class Students." *British Journal of Sociology of Education* 34(5/6):812–28.

Canadian Council on Learning. 2009. "*Post-Secondary Education in Canada: Who Is Missing Out?*" April 1 (https://www.tru.ca/__shared/assets/CCL_2009_Post_Secondary_Canada_Whos_Missing_Out23674.pdf).

Canadian Federation of Students. n.d. "Fight the Fees" (https://cfs-fcee.ca/campaigns/fight-the-fees).

Canadian Paediatric Society. 2018. "ADHD in Children and Youth: Part 1—Etiology, Diagnosis, and Comorbidity" (https://www.cps.ca/en/documents/position/adhd-etiology-diagnosis-and-comorbidity).

CBC News. 2019. "'Nothing Ever Stays the Same': Minister Defends Tuition, Student Fee, OSAP Changes." January 21 (https://www.cbc.ca/news/canada/toronto/ontario-minister-tuition-cut-student-fees-opting-out-osap-changes-1.4986612).

Chalifoux, Thelma, chair. 2003. "*Urban Aboriginal Youth: An Action Plan for Change: Final Report.*" Standing Senate Committee on Aboriginal Peoples (https://sencanada.ca/content/sen/committee/372/abor/rep/repfinoct03-e.pdf).

Chen, W. and F. Hou. 2019. "Intergenerational Education Mobility and Labour Market Outcomes: Variation among the Second Generation of Immigrants in Canada." Statistics Canada (https://www150.statcan.gc.ca/n1/pub/11f0019m/11f0019m2019006-eng.htm).

Chiose, S. 2016. "Colleges and Universities Face Mental-Health Crisis, Study Says." *Globe and Mail*, September 9 (http://ezproxy.humber.ca/login?url=https://search-proquest-com.ezproxy.humber.ca/docview/1817717756?accountid=11530).

Cho, S.H., Y. Xu, and D.E. Kiss. 2015. "Understanding Student Loan Decisions: A Literature Review." *Family and Consumer Sciences Research Journal* 43(3):229–43

College Student Alliance, Ontario Student Trustees Association, and Ontario Undergraduate Student Alliance. 2011. *"Breaking Barriers: A Strategy for Equal Access to Higher Education." February 9* (https://www.ousa.ca/submission_equal_access_to_higher_education).

Coleman, James. 1962. *The Adolescent Society.* New York: The Free Press of Glencoe.

Combs, A.E. 2016. "Does Close Count in Higher Education? Estimating the Effect of Distance on Degree Completion in Kentucky" (https://aefpweb.org/sites/default/files/webform/41/Does%20close%20count%20in%20higher%20education.pdf).

Davies, S. and N. Guppy. 2010. *The Schooled Society: An Introduction to the Sociology of Education,* 2nd edn. Don Mills, ON: Oxford University Press.

Desimone, L. and D. Long. 2010. "Teacher Effects and the Achievement Gap: Do Teacher and Teaching Quality Influence the Achievement Gap Between Black and White and High- and Low-SES Students in the Early Grades?" *Teachers College Record* 112(12):3024–72.

Dillabough, J.A. and M. Arnot. 2002. "Recasting Educational Debates about Female Citizenship, Agency and Identity." *School Field* 13(3/4):61–90.

Education Without Borders. 2013. "The Situation of Non-Status Migrants." *Education for All* (http://www.solidarityacrossborders.org/en/solidarity-city/solidarity-city-journal/education-for-all).

Early Development Instrument. 2020. "About" (https://edi.offordcentre.com/about).

Esping-Andersen, Gøsta. 1990. *The Three Worlds of Welfare Capitalism.* Cambridge, UK: Polity Press.

Faught, E.L., J.P. Ekwaru, D. Gleddie, K.E. Storey, M. Asbridge, and P.J. Veugelers. 2017. "The Combined Impact of Diet, Physical Activity, Sleep and Screen Time on Academic Achievement: A Prospective Study of Elementary School Students in Nova Scotia, Canada." *International Journal of Behavioral Nutrition and Physical Activity* 14(1):29.

Fernald, A., V.A. Marchman, and A. Weisleder. 2013. "SES Differences in Language Processing Skill and Vocabulary Are Evident at 18 Months." *Developmental Science* 16(2):234–48. doi:10.1111/desc.12019

Fedewa, A.L. and S. Ahn. 2011. "The Effects of Physical Activity and Physical Fitness on Children's Achievement and Cognitive Outcomes: A Meta-Analysis." *Research Quarterly for Exercise and Sport* 82(3):521–35.

Finnie, Ross and Richard Mueller. 2009. "Access to Post-Secondary Education in Canada among the Children of Canadian Immigrants." *Educational Policy Institute (*http://www.yorku.ca/pathways/literature/Access/finnie.mueller.immigrants.june.2008.pdf*).*

Finnie, Ross, Richard Mueller, and Andrew Wismer. 2012. "Access and Barriers to Post-Secondary Education: Evidence from the YITS." *Canadian Journal of Higher Education* 45(2):229–62.

Frederickson, Megan. 2018. "Canadian Professors Still Face a Gender Pay Gap." *Maclean's,* March 28 (https://www.macleans.ca/education/canadian-professors-still-face-a-gender-pay-gap).

Frenette, Marc. 2003. "Access to College and University: Does Distance Matter?" Statistics Canada catalogue number 11F0019MIE2003201 (https://www150.statcan.gc.ca/n1/en/catalogue/11F0019M2003201).

———. 2017. "Postsecondary Enrolment by Parental Income: Recent National and Provincial Trends." Statistics Canada (https://www150.statcan.gc.ca/n1/pub/11-626-x/11-626-x2017070-eng.htm).

Garner, R., J. Bootcheck, M. Lorr, and K. Rauch. 2006. "The Adolescent Society Revisited: Culture, Crowds, Climates, and Status Structures in Seven Secondary School." *Journal of Youth and Adolescence* 35:1023–35.

Gayle, G., I. Golan, and M.A. Soytas. 2018. "Intergenerational Mobility and the Effects of Parental Education, Time Investment, and Income on Children's Educational Attainment." *Third Quarter* 10(3):281–95. doi:10.20955/r.100.28195

Goto, S.T. and C. Martin. 2009. "Psychology of Success: Overcoming Barriers to Pursuing Further Education." *Journal of Continuing Higher Education* 57(1):10–21. doi:10.1080/07377360902810744

Government of Canada. 2018. "Student Loans and Grant Eligibility Assessment Thresholds." Retrieved May 3, 2019 (https://www.canada.ca/en/employment-social-development/services/education/student-loan-eligibility-assessment.html).

Hanushek, Eric A. and Ludger Woessman. 2008. "The Role of Cognitive Skills in Economic Development." *Journal of Economic Literature* 46(3):607–68.

Hart, D. and A. Kempf. 2015. "Public Attitudes towards Education Ontario 2015." The 19th OISE Survey of Education Issues (http://www.oise.utoronto.ca/oise/UserFiles/Media/Media_Relations/Final_Report_-_19th_OISE_Survey_on_Educational_Issues_2015.pdf)

Herrold, K. and K. O'Donnell. 2008. *"Parent and Family Involvement in Education, 2006–07 School Year."* The National Household Education Surveys Program of 2007. Washington, DC: National Center for Education Statistics.

Human Resources and Skills Development Canada (HRSDC). 2013. *"Indicators of Well-Being in Canada: Learning—School Drop-outs"* (https://www.homelesshub.ca/resource/indicators-well-being-canada-learning-%E2%80%93-school-drop-outs-0).

Iannelli, Cristina, Adam Gamoran, and Lindsay Paterson. 2011. Scottish Higher Education, 1987–2001: Expansion through Diversion." *Oxford Review of Education* 37(6):717–41. doi:10.1080/03054985.2011.636227

Jaggars, S.S., N. Edgecombe, and G.W. Stacey. 2013. "What We Know about Online Course Outcomes." Community

College Research Center, Teachers College, Columbia University..

Johnson, C.L., B. O'Neill, S.L. Worthy, J.M. Lown, and C.F. Bowen. 2016. "What Are Student Loan Borrowers Thinking? Insights from Focus Groups on College Selection and Student Loan Decision Making." *Journal of Financial Counseling and Planning* 27(2):184–98. doi:10.1891/1052-3073.27.2.184

Kershaw, P., L. Anderson, B. Warburon, and C. Hertzman. 2009. "15 by 15: A Comprehensive Policy Framework for Early Human Capital Investment in BC." Human Early Learning Partnership University of British Columbia (http://earlylearning.ubc.ca/media/publications/15by15-full-report.pdf).

Knighton, T., F. Hujaleh, J. Iacampo, and G. Werkneh. 2009. "Lifelong Learning among Canadians Aged 18 to 64 Years: First Results from the 2008 Access and Support to Education and Training Survey." Statistics Canada (http://www.statcan.gc.ca/pub/81-595-m/81-595-m2009079-eng.htm).

Lindsay, S., E. Cagliostro, and G. Carafa. 2018. "A Systematic Review of Barriers and Facilitators of Disability Disclosure and Accommodations for Youth in Post-Secondary Education." *International Journal of Disability, Development and Education* 65(5):526–56.

Lusardi, A. and O.S. Mitchell. 2011. "Financial Literacy around the World: An Overview." *Journal of Pension Economics and Finance* 10(4):497–508. doi:10.1017/S1474747211000448

Marsh, H.W. and S. Kleitman. 2005. "Consequences of Employment during High School: Character Building, Subversion of Academic Goals, or a Threshold?" *American Educational Research Journal* 42(2):331–69. doi:10.3102/00028312042002331

McCloy, U. and L. DeClou. 2013. "Disability in Ontario: Post-secondary Education Participation Rates, Student Experience and Labour Market Outcomes." Higher Education Quality Council of Ontario.

McIsaac, J.D., S.F.L. Kirk, and S. Kuhle. 2015. "The Association between Health Behaviours and Academic Performance in Canadian Elementary School Students: A Cross-Sectional Study." *International Journal of Environmental Research and Public Health* 12(11):14857–71. doi:10.3390/ijerph121114857

Meyer, Harold R. and Susan K. Lasky. 2017. "The ADD/ADHD Child and School—Not Always a Good Match." The ADD Resource Centre, August 25 (https://www.addrc.org/add-adhd-child-school).

Morris, S., G. Fawcett, L. Brisebois, and J. Hughes. 2018. "A Demographic, Employment and Income Profile of Canadians with Disabilities Aged 15 Years and Over, 2017." Statistics Canada, Canadian Survey on Disability Reports (https://www150.statcan.gc.ca/n1/pub/89-654-x/89-654-x2018002-eng.htm).

Neyt, B., E. Omey, D. Verhaest, and S. Baert. 2018. "Does Student Work Really Affect Educational Outcomes? A Review of the Literature." *Journal of Economic Surveys*, 33(3):896–921.

Noah, Timothy. 2012. "White House: Here's Why You Have to Care about Inequality." *New Republic*, January 13 (http://www.newrepublic.com/blog/timothy-noah/99651/white-house-heres-why-you-have-care-about-inequality).

O'Brien, Matthew. 2013. "'The Great Gatsby Curve': Why It's so Hard for the Poor to Get Ahead Today." *The Atlantic, June 18.*

OECD. 2015. "The ABCs of Gender Equality in Education: Aptitude, Behaviour, Confidence" (http://www.oecd.org/pisa/keyfindings/pisa-2012-results-gender-eng.pdf).

Ontario College of Teachers. 2004. "Narrowing the Gender Gap: Attracting Men to Teaching" (https://www.oct.ca/-/media/PDF/Attracting%20Men%20To%20Teaching/EN/Men_In_Teaching_e.pdf).

PEW Charitable Trusts. 2012. *Pursuing the American Dream: Economic Mobility Across Generations.* Washington, DC: Author.

Reardon, Sean. 2013. "No Rich Child Left Behind." *New York Times,* April 27 (https://opinionator.blogs.nytimes.com/2013/04/27/no-rich-child-left-behind).

Richards, John and Megan Scott. 2009. *"Aboriginal Education: Strengthening the Foundations."* CPRN Research Report (http://oaresource.library.carleton.ca/cprn/51984_en.pdf).

Savage, Dan and Terry Miller (eds.). 2011. It Gets Better: Coming Out, Overcoming Bullying, and Creating a Life Worth Living. New York: Penguin Books.

Scherger, S. and M. Savage. 2010. "Cultural Transmission, Educational Attainment and Social Mobility." *The Sociological Review* 58(3):406–28.

Sidhu, N. 2008. *"The Right to Learn: Access to Public Education for Non-Status Immigrants."* Toronto, ON: Community Social Planning Council of Toronto.

Standing Senate Committee on Social Affairs, Science and Technology. 2010. *"Accessibility of Post-Secondary Education in Canada."*

———. 2011. *"Opening the Door: Reducing the Barriers to Post-Secondary Education in Canada."*

Statistics Canada. 2006. "Study: Who Gets Student Loans?" *The Daily* (http://www.statcan.gc.ca/daily-quotidien/060324/dq060324c-eng.htm).

———. 2007. "Study: Postsecondary Attendance among Local Youth Following the Opening of a New University." *The Daily* (http://www.statcan.gc.ca/daily-quotidien/070125/dq070125a-eng.htm).

———. 2008. "2008 Access and Support to Education and Training Survey." 2008 Public Use Microdata File.

———. 2011. "Study: University Completion by Parents' Educational Attainment." *The Daily* (http://www.statcan.gc.ca/daily-quotidien/110824/dq110824d-eng.htm).

———. 2012. "University Tuition Fees, 2012/2013." *The Daily* (http://www.statcan.gc.ca/daily-quotidien/120912/dq120912a-eng.htm).

———. 2013a. "Public Postsecondary Enrolments and Graduates, 2010/2011." *The Daily* (http:/www.statcan.gc.ca/daily-quotidien/130123/dq130123a-eng.htm).

———. 2013b. "Study: Education and Retirement Saving Behaviours of Families." *The Daily* (http://www.statcan.gc.ca/daily-quotidien/110519/dq110519b-eng.htm).

———. 2015. "Proportion of Canadians Aged 18 to 64 Who Reported Various Reasons for Not Undertaking Further Education or Training between July 2007 and June 2008." Table A.2.2 (https://www150.statcan.gc.ca/n1/pub/81-595-m/2009079/t/tbla.2.2-eng.htm).

———. 2016. *2016 Census of Population*. Catalogue no. 98-400-X2016192.

———. 2017. "Canada [Country] and Canada [Country]." 2016 Census. Catalogue no. 98-316-X2016001. Retrieved March 10, 2019 (https://www12.statcan.gc.ca/census-recensement/2016/dp-pd/prof/index.cfm?Lang=E).

———. 2018a. "Canadian Postsecondary Enrolments and Graduates, 2016/2017." *The Daily,* November 28 (https://www150.statcan.gc.ca/n1/daily-quotidien/181128/dq181128c-eng.htm).

———. 2018b. "Education Indicators in Canada: An International Perspective" (https://www150.statcan.gc.ca/n1/pub/81-604-x/2018001/hl-fs-eng.htm).

———. 2018c. "Number and Salaries of Full-Time Teaching Staff at Canadian Universities." Table 37-10-0108-01 (https://www150.statcan.gc.ca/t1/tbl1/en/tv.action?pid=3710010801).

———. (2018d). "Tuition fees for degree programs, 2018/2019." September 5 (https://www150.statcan.gc.ca/n1/daily-quotidien/180905/dq180905b-eng.htm).

———. 2019a. "Distribution of Population Aged 25 to 64 (Total and with Aboriginal Identity), by Sex and Educational Attainment." Table 37-10-0100-01 (https://www150.statcan.gc.ca/t1/tbl1/en/tv.action?pid=3710010001).

———. 2019b. "National Graduates Survey, Student Debt from All Sources, by Province and Level of Study." Table 37-10-0036-01 (https://www150.statcan.gc.ca/t1/tbl1/en/tv.action?pid=3710003601).

Taylor, C. and T. Peter. 2011. "'We Are Not Aliens, We're People, and We Have Rights.' Canadian Human Rights Discourse and High School Climate for LGBTQ Students." *Canadian Review of Sociology* 48(3):275–312.

Taylor, C., T. Peter, C. Campbell, E. Meyer, J. Ristock, and D. Short. 2015. "The Every Teacher Project on LGBTQ-Inclusive Education in Canada's K-12 Schools: Final Report." Winnipeg, MB: Manitoba Teachers' Society.

Toronto District School Board. 2018. "2017 Student and Parent Census: Overall Findings." November (https://www.tdsb.on.ca/portals/0/research/docs/2017_Census.pdf).

UNESCO. (2017). "Six Ways to Ensure Higher Education Leaves No One Behind." Policy Paper 30 (https://unesdoc.unesco.org/ark:/48223/pf0000247862).

U of T News. 2019. "U of T to Implement Salary Increase for More Than 800 Women Faculty Members." April 26 (https://www.utoronto.ca/news/u-t-implement-salary-increase-more-800-women-faculty-members).

Walton, G. 2004. "Bullying and Homophobia in Canadian Schools: The Politics of Policies, Programs, and Educational Leadership." *Journal of Gay and Lesbian Issues in Education* 1(4):23–36.

Wollstonecraft, Mary. [1792] 1997. *A Vindication of the Rights of Woman*. Peterborough, ON: Broadview Press.

Zeitlin, Irving M. 2001. *Ideology and the Development of Sociological Theory,* 7th edn. Upper Saddle River, NJ: Prentice Hall.

Chapter 6

Alangh, A., M. Chiu, and B.R. Shah. 2013. "Rapid Increase in Diabetes Incidence among Chinese Canadians Between 1996 and 2005." *Diabetes Care* 36(10):3015.

Anaya, James. 2014 "The Situation of Indigenous Peoples in Canada." United Nations *Human Rights Council, Twenty-Seventh Session* (http://unsr.jamesanaya.org/country-reports/the-situation-of-indigenous-peoples-in-canada).

Andersen, H.S. 2010. "Spatial Assimilation in Denmark? Why Do Immigrants Move to and from Multi-Ethnic Neighbourhoods?" *Housing Studies* 25(3):281–300.

Aubry, T., F. Klodawsky, and D. Coulombe. 2012. "Comparing the Housing Trajectories of Different Classes within a Diverse Homeless Population." *American Journal of Community Psychology* 49(1/2):142–55.

Beattie, Sara and Hope Hutchins. 2015. "Shelters for Abused Women in Canada, 2014." Statistics Canada (https://www150.statcan.gc.ca/n1/pub/85-002-x/2015001/article/14207-eng.htm).

Belcher, J.R. and B.R. DeForge. 2012. "Social Stigma and Homelessness: The Limits of Social Change." *Journal of Human Behavior in the Social Environment* 22(8):929–46.

Breton, Raymond. 1964. "Institutional Completeness of Ethnic Communities and the Personal Relations of Immigrants." *American Journal of Sociology* 70(2):193–205.

Brown, Emily. 2016. "Overcoming the Barriers to Micro-Housing: Tiny Houses, Big Potential." University of Oregon (http://hdl.handle.net/1794/19948).

Bruce, D. 2003. "Housing Needs of Low-Income People Living in Rural Areas" (https://www.homelesshub.ca/resource/housing-needs-low-income-people-living-rural-areas).

Bux, Roman, Markus Parzeller, and Hansjürgen Bratzke. 2001. "Causes and Circumstances of Fatal Falls Downstairs." *Forensic Science International* 171:122–6.

Canadian Centre for Diversity and Inclusion. 2019. "Benchmarking Study, 2019" (https://ccdi.ca/media/1864/20190222-research-national-diversity-and-inclusion-benchmarking-study.pdf).

Canadian Centre of Economic Analysis and Canadian Urban Institute. 2019. "Toronto Housing Market Analysis: From Insight to Action" (https://www.toronto.ca/legdocs/mmis/2019/ph/bgrd/backgroundfile-124480.pdf).

Carr, S.C. and M. MacLachlan. 1998. "Actors, Observers, and Attributions for Third World Poverty: Contrasting Perspectives from Malawi and Australia." *Journal of Social Psychology* 138(2):189–202.

CBRE Group. 2019. "Global Living 2019." Retrieved May 14, 2019 (https://www.cbreresidential.com/uk/sites/uk-residential/files/property-info/FINAL%20REPORT.pdf).

CERA. 2008. *"Human Right in Housing: An Advocate's Guide."* Toronto, ON: Centre for Equality Rights in Accommodation.

———. 2009. *"Sorry, It's Rented": Measuring Discrimination in Toronto's Rental Housing Market.* Toronto, ON: Centre for Equality Rights in Accommodation.

———. 2011. *Know Your Rights: Housing Discrimination Is Against the Law.* Toronto, ON: Centre for Equality Rights in Accommodation.

CERA and MNO. 2015. "Northern Housing Rights" (http://www.equalityrights.org/wp-content/uploads/2010/04/NHR-FINAL-Public-Report-2015.pdf).

Cheung, C. 2018. "By the Numbers: Metro Vancouver's Increasing Inequality and Division." *The Tyee*, November 15 (https://thetyee.ca/News/2018/11/15/Metro-Vancouver-Inequality-Division).

CLEO. 2017. "Social Assistance Rules about Couples: What You Need to Know if You Live with Someone" (https://www.cleo.on.ca/en/publications/cohab-en).

CMHC. 2009. *Canadian Housing Observer.* Ottawa, ON: Canada Mortgage and Housing Corporation.

———. 2011. *Canadian Housing Observer.* Ottawa, ON: Canada Mortgage and Housing Corporation.

———. 2018. "Housing Conditions of Aboriginal Households Living On-Reserve" (https://www.cmhc-schl.gc.ca/en/data-and-research/data-tables/housing-conditions-aboriginal-households-living-on-reserve).

———. 2019 "A Stronger National Housing Strategy." April 11 (https://www.cmhc-schl.gc.ca/en/media-newsroom/news-releases/2019/stronger-national-housing-strategy).

Council to Homeless Persons. 2019. *Parity* 32(8) (https://www.homelesshub.ca/sites/default/files/attachments/Parity-October2019-Vol32-08.pdf).

Dion, K. 2001. "Immigrants' Perceptions of Housing Discrimination in Toronto: The Housing New Canadians Project." *Journal of Social Issues* 57(3):523–9.

Doberstein, C. 2012. "Applying European Ideas on Federalism and Doing It Better? The Government of Canada's Homelessness Policy Experiment." *Canadian Public Policy* 38(3):395–410.

Duncan, K.C., J. Clipsham, E. Hampson, C. Kreiger, J. MacDonnell, D. Roedding, K. Chow, and D. Milne. 2000. "Improving the Access to and Quality of Public Health Services for Lesbians and Gay Men: A Position Paper for the Ontario Public Health Association." June (https://opha.on.ca/OPHA/media/Resources/Position-Papers/2000-01_pp.pdf?ext=.pdf).

Durkheim, Émile. [1893] 2014. *The Division of Labor.* New York: Free Press.

Easton, Janet. 2017. "Are Tiny Houses a Big, Bad Idea? 77 Reasons Critics Don't Like Them." *The Oregonian*, April 10 (https://www.oregonlive.com/hg/2017/04/tiny_house_bad_idea_mistake.html).

Edwards, S. 2019. "The Push to Make Housing a Human Right Comes to HotDocs." *Now Magazine* (https://nowtoronto.com/movies/features/hot-docs-leilani-farha-push-housing).

Gaetz, S., E. Dej, T. Richter, and M. Redman. 2016. "The State of Homelessness in Canada 2016." The Homeless Hub (https://homelesshub.ca/sites/default/files/attachments/SOHC16_final_20Oct2016.pdf).

Gaetz, S., T. Gulliver, and T. Richter. 2014. "The State of Homelessness in Canada 2014." The Homeless Hub (https://homelesshub.ca/sites/default/files/SOHC2014.pdf).

Gans, Herbert J. 1982. *Urban Villagers.* New York : Simon and Schuster.

Giesbrecht, E., E. Smith, B. Mortenson, and W. Miller. 2017. "Needs for Mobility Devices, Home Modifications and Personal Assistance among Canadians with Disabilities." Statistics Canada (https://www150.statcan.gc.ca/n1/pub/82-003-x/2017008/article/54852-eng.htm).

Goering, P., S. Velhuizen, A. Watson, C. Adair, B. Kopp, E. Latimer, and A. Ly. 2012. *At Home/Chez Soi Interim Report.* Ottawa, ON: Mental Health Commission of Canada.

Gossage, Patrick. 2018. "Good Review (Mostly) for the National Housing Strategy." *Policy Options*, February 22 (https://policyoptions.irpp.org/magazines/february-2018/good-reviews-mostly-for-the-national-housing-strategy).

Government of Canada. 2019. "Ending Long-Term Drinking Water Advisories" (https://www.sac-isc.gc.ca/eng/1506514143353/1533317130660).

Grant, T.L., N. Edwards, H. Sveistrup, and C. Andrew. 2010. "Inequitable Walking Conditions Among Older People: Examining the Interrelationship of Neighbourhood Socio-economic Status and Urban Form Using a Comparative Case Study." *BMC Public Health* 10:677.

Gurin, Gerald and Patricia Gurin. 1970. "Expectancy Theory in the Study of Poverty." *Journal of Social Issues* 26(2):83–104.

Habitat for Humanity. 2013. "About Us" (http://www.habitat.ca).

Hamilton, Anita. 2014. "Portland Plan Tiny Houses for the Homeless." *Time* (http://time.com/3177905/tiny-houses-homeless-portland-oregon).

Hollis, S.A. 2004. "Blaming Me, Blaming You: Assessing Service Learning and Participants' Tendency to Blame the Victim." *Sociological Spectrum* 24(5):575–600.

Homeless Hub. 2016. "About Homelessness: How Many People Are Homeless in Canada?" (https://www.homelesshub.ca/about-homelessness/homelessness-101/how-many-people-are-homeless-canada).

Ibrahim, D. 2018. "Violent Victimization, Discrimination and Perceptions of Safety: An Immigrant Perspective, Canada, 2014." Statistics Canada (https://www150.statcan.gc.ca/n1/pub/85-002-x/2018001/article/54911-eng.htm).

Jones, A., T. Geilenkeuser, I. Helbrecht, and D. Quilgars. 2012. "Demographic Change and Retirement Planning: Comparing Households' Views on the Role of Housing Equity in Germany and the UK." *International Journal of Housing Policy* 12(1):27–45.

Kelley, Gil. 2017. "Memorandum: City of Vancouver 2016 Census—Income Data Release" (https://vancouver.ca/files/cov/2017-09-29-city-of-vancouver-2016-census-income-data-release.pdf).

Keung, N. 2012. "Exploitive Rent Demands 'a Norm' for Newcomers." *Toronto Star*, January 29 (https://www.thestar.com/news/investigations/2012/01/29/exploitive_rent_demands_a_norm_for_newcomers.html).

Klodawsky, F. 2006. "Landscapes on the Margins: Gender and Homelessness in Canada." *Gender, Place & Culture* 13(4):365–81.

Leo, C. and M. August. 2006. "National Policy and Community Initiative: Mismanaging Homelessness in a Slow Growth City." *Canadian Journal of Urban Research* 15(1):1–21.

Maki, K. 2017. "Housing, Homelessness, and Violence Against Women." Women's Shelters Canada (https://www.homelesshub.ca/sites/default/files/attachments/Housing%2C%20Homelessness%2C%20and%20VAW%20Discussion%20Paper%20Aug%202017.pdf)

Milan, A. 2016. "Diversity of Young Adults Living with Their Parents." Statistics Canada (https://www150.statcan.gc.ca/n1/pub/75-006-x/2016001/article/14639-eng.htm).

Morissette, R. 2019. "The Wealth of Immigrant Families in Canada." Statistics Canada (https://www150.statcan.gc.ca/n1/pub/11f0019m/11f0019m2019010-eng.htm).

Motz, T.A. and C.L. Currie. 2019. "Racially-Motivated Housing Discrimination Experienced by Indigenous Postsecondary Students in Canada: Impacts on PTSD Symptomology and Perceptions of University Stress." *Public Health* 176:59–67.

Murdie, Robert A. 2003. "Housing Affordability and Toronto's Rental Market: Perspectives from the Housing Careers of Jamaican, Polish and Somali Newcomers. *Housing, Theory and Society* 20(4):183–96.

———. 2008. "Pathways to Housing: The Experiences of Sponsored Refugees and Refugee Claimants in Accessing Permanent Housing in Toronto." *Journal of International Migration and Integration* 9(1):81–101.

Nangia, Parveen. 2013. "Discrimination Experienced by Landed Immigrants in Canada." RCIS Working Paper, Ryerson University (https://www.ryerson.ca/content/dam/rcis/documents/RCIS_WP_Parveen_Nangia_No_2013_7.pdf).

NGLTFPI. 2006. "*Lesbian, Gay, Bisexual and Transgender Youth: An Epidemic of Homelessness.*" New York: National Gay and Lesbian Task Force Institute Policy.

Novac, S., J. Darden, D. Hulchanski, and A.-M. Segu. 2002. "*Housing Discrimination in Canada: The State of Knowledge.*" Ottawa, ON: Canada Mortgage and Housing Corporation.

OHRC. 2008. "*Right at Home: Report on the Consultation on Human Rights and Rental Housing in Ontario.*" May 28 (http://www.ohrc.on.ca/en/right-home-report-consultation-human-rights-and-rental-housing-ontario).

Paradis, E., R.M. Wilson, and J. Logan. 2014. "Nowhere Else to Go: Inadequate Housing & Risk of Homelessness among Families in Toronto's Aging Rental Buildings." Cities Centre, University of Toronto (http://neighbourhoodchange.ca/documents/2014/04/paradis-et-al-2014-nowhere-else-to-go-inadequate-housing-risk-of-homelessness-among-families-in-torontos-aging-rental-buildings-rp231.pdf).

Patterson, Dennis Glen (chair) and Patricia Bovey (deputy chair). 2019. "Northern Lights: A Wake-Up Call for the Future of Canada." June (https://sencanada.ca/content/sen/committee/421/ARCT/reports/ARCTFINALREPORT_E.pdf).

Pflug-Back, Kelly Rose. 2016. "Racist Landlords Are Making Toronto's Housing Crisis Worse: Indigenous Tenants Tell Stories of Discrimination and Prejudice." Ricochet Media, March 30 (https://ricochet.media/en/1049/racist-landlords-are-making-torontos-housing-crisis-worse).

Premji, Stephanie. 2017. "Precarious Employment and Difficult Daily Commutes." *Relations Industrielles* 72(1):77–98.

Richter, S., K. Kovacs Burns, J. Chaw-Kant, M. Calder, S. Mogale, L. Goin, Y. Mao, and K. Schnell. 2011. "Homelessness Coverage in Major Canadian Newspapers, 1987–2007." *Canadian Journal of Communication* 36(4):619–35.

Robertson, Q.M. and I.O. Williamson. 2012. "Justice in Self-Managing Teams: The Role of Social Networks in the Emergence of Procedural Justice Climates." *Academy of Management Journal* 55:685–701.

Roos, L.E., N. Mota, T.O. Afifi, L.Y. Katz, J. Distasio, and J. Sareen. 2013. "Relationship Between Adverse Childhood Experiences and Homelessness and the Impact of Axis I and II Disorders." *American Journal of Public Health* 103(S2):S275–81.

Schneider, B., K. Chamberlain, and D. Hodgetts. 2010. "Representations of Homelessness in Four Canadian Newspapers: Regulation, Control, and Social Order." *Journal of Sociology & Social Welfare* 37(4):147–72.

Scott, John, ed. 2014. *Oxford Dictionary of Sociology*, 4th edn. Oxford, UK: Oxford University Press.

Simmel, Georg, and Kurt H. Wolff, eds. 1950. "The Metropolis and Mental Life." *The Sociology of Georg Simmel*. New York: Free Press.

Shaftoe, David and Judit Alcade. 1991. "Racial Discrimination and Rental Accommodation in Kitchener-Waterloo." Race Relations Committee.

Stastna, K. 2011. "Shacks and Slop Pails: Infrastructure Crisis on Native Reserves: Spending on Housing and Water in First Nations Communities Not Keeping Up with Need." *CBC News*, November 26 (http://www.cbc.ca/news/canada/story/2011/11/24/f-first-nations-infrastructure.html).

Statistics Canada. 2006. "Seniors' Access to Transportation." *The Daily* (http://www.statcan.gc.ca/daily-quotidien/061215/dq061215c-eng.htm).

———. 2016. "Diversity of Young Adults Living with Their Parents." Insights on Canadian Society, June 15 (https://www150.statcan.gc.ca/n1/pub/75-006-x/2016001/article/14639-eng.htm).

———. 2017. "Canada [Country] and Canada [Country]." 2016 Census, catalogue no. 98-316-X2016001. Retrieved

March 10, 2019 (https://www12.statcan.gc.ca/census-recensement/2016/dp-pd/prof/index.cfm?Lang=E).

Taylor, K. 2012. "*Risk of Developing Diabetes Higher in Neighbourhoods that Aren't Walk-friendly: Study.*" Toronto, ON: St Michael's Hospital.

Taylor, P. 2013. "A 'Massive Increase' in Diabetes." *Globe and Mail*, May 31:L6.

Teixeira, Carlos. 2008. "Barriers and Outcomes in the Housing Searches of New Immigrants and Refugees: A Case Study of 'Black' Africans in Toronto's Rental Market." *Journal of Housing and the Built Environment* 23(4):253–76.

———. 2011. "Finding a Home of Their Own: Immigrant Housing Experiences in Central Okanagan, British Columbia, and Policy Recommendations for Change." *Journal of International Migration and Integration* 12(2):173–97.

Teixera, Carlos and Jamie McEwan. 2012. "Doing Their 'Home' Work: A Case Study of University of British Columbia Okanagan Student Youth Rental Housing Experiences in the City of Kelowna, British Columbia, Canada." *BC Studies* 173

Tepperman, Lorne and Nicole Meredith. 2016. *Waiting to Happen: The Sociology of Unexpected Injuries.* Toronto, ON: Oxford University Press.

Toronto Community Foundation. 2012. "Toronto's Vital Signs: 2012 Report" (https://torontofoundation.ca/wp-content/uploads/2018/02/TVS12FullReport.pdf)

Wachocki, K. 2014. "Understanding Perceptions about Food Choices for Low Income Communities: Victim Blaming and Food Oppression." Doctoral dissertation, Kean University.

Waegemakers-Schiff, J., R. Schiff, A. Turner, and K. Bernard. 2015. "Rural Homelessness in Canada: Directions for Planning and Research." *Journal of Rural and Community Development* 10(4):85–106.

Wasfi, R., D. Levinson, and A. El-Geneidy. 2012. "Measuring the Transportation Needs of Seniors." *Journal of Transport Literature* 6(2):8–32.

Weissman, Eric, Jeannette Waegemakers-Schiff, and Rebecca Schiff. 2019. "Post-Secondary Student Homelessness (PSSH) and Canadian Youth: Stigma and Institutional Responses to Student Homelessness. *Parity* 32(8):32–4.

Wright, E.O., ed. 2005. *Approaches to Class Analysis.* Cambridge, UK: Cambridge University Press.

Zaretzky, K., P. Flatau, and M. Brady. 2008. "What is the (Net) Cost to Government of Homelessness Programs?" *Australian Journal of Social Issues* 43(2):231–54.

Chapter 7

Bitton, S. and J. Roth. 2010. "Addressing Food Insecurity: Freedom from Want, Freedom From Fear." *Journal of the American Medical Association* 304(21):2405–6.

Charlebois, S., E. McGuinty, V. Keselj, C. Mah, A. Giusto, J. Music, S. Somogyi, F. Tapon, P. Uys, E. Van Duren, J. Harris, and J. Son. 2019. "Canada's Food Price Report 2019." University of Guelph (https://cdn.dal.ca/content/dam/dalhousie/pdf/management/News/News%20&%20Events/Canada%20Food%20Price%20Report%20ENG%202019.pdf).

Charlebois, S., F. Tapon, M. Von Massow, E. Van Duren, W. Pinto, and R. Moraghan. 2012. "*Food Price Index 2013.*" University of Guelph (https://www.uoguelph.ca/cpa/Food-Index-2013.pdf).

Daily Bread Food Bank. 2018. "Who's Hungry?" (https://www.dailybread.ca/wp-content/uploads/2018/10/Whos-Hungry-2018-full-3.pdf).

Daniel, M., Y. Kestens, and C. Paquet. 2009. "Demographic and Urban Form Correlates of Healthful and Unhealthful Food Availability in Montréal, Canada." *Canadian Journal of Public Health* 100(3):189–93.

Emery, J.C.H., V.C. Fleisch, and L. McIntyre. 2013. "How a Guaranteed Annual Income Could Put Food Banks Out of Business." *School of Public Policy Research Papers* 37(6):1–20.

Finlayson, G.S. and R.J. Currie. 2010. "The Additional Cost of Chronic Disease in Manitoba." Manitoba Centre for Health Policy, Department of Community Health Sciences, University of Manitoba.

First Nations Information Governance Centre. 2018. "National Report of the First Nations Regional Health Survey Phase 3: Volume Two" (https://fnigc.ca/sites/default/files/docs/fnigc_rhs_phase_3_volume_two_en_final_screen.pdf).

Food Banks Canada. 2012 "*HungerCount 2012*" (https://foodbankscanada.ca/getmedia/3b946e67-fbe2-490e-90dc-4a313dfb97e5/HungerCount2012.pdf.aspx).

———. 2016. "Increasing Food Bank Use Shows Urgent Need for Federal Action on Poverty." November 15 (https://www.foodbankscanada.ca/Media/News-Releases/2016/Increasing-food-bank-use-shows-urgent-need-for-fed.aspx).

———. 2018. "HungerCount 2018" (https://foodbankscanada.ca/getmedia/241fb659-05f5-44a2-9cef-56f5f51db523/HungerCount-2018_FINAL_EN.pdf.aspx?ext=.pdf).

———. 2019. "HungerCount 2019" (https://hungercount.foodbankscanada.ca).

Frolik, C. 2018. "Walmart, McDonald's Tops in Ohio for Employees on Food Stamps." *Dayton Daily News*, January 12 (https://www.daytondailynews.com/news/local/walmart-mcdonald-tops-ohio-for-employees-food-stamps/cxqzF1NHn74uisiJNcpFFP).

Furgal, C. and J. Seguin. 2006. "Climate Change, Health, and Vulnerability in Canadian Northern Aboriginal Communities." *Environmental Health Perspective* 114(12):1964–70.

Gerbrandt, J.S. 2009. *The Experiences of People with Disabilities Who Are on Persons with Disabilities Benefits with Regard to Food Security.* Master's dissertation, University of British Columbia, Vancouver.

Hamelin, A.-M., J.-P. Habicht, and B. Micheline. 1999. "Food Insecurity: Consequences for the Household and Broader Social Implications." *Journal of Nutrition* 129(2Supp):525S–8S.

Harris, S. 2018. "Cellphone Services in Canada Are Comparable to Driving a Luxury Car, Report Author Argues."

CBC News, May 8 (https://www.cbc.ca/news/business/wireless-prices-cell-phone-plan-canada-1.4652550).

Inuit Tapiriit Kanatami and the Inuit Circumpolar Council. 2010. "Inuit and the Right to Food: Submission to the United Nations Special Rapporteur on the Right to Food for the Official Country Mission to Canada" (http://www.inuitcircumpolar.com/uploads/3/0/5/4/30542564/icc.itk.inuit_and_the_right_to_food-for_un_rapporteur_on_the_right_to_food.pdf).

Johnston, Josée and S. Baumann. 2014. *Foodies: Democracy and Distinction in the Gourmet Foodscape*. New York: Routledge.

Jones, B. 2012. "Counting the Cost of Calories." World Health Organization (http://www.who.int/bulletin/volumes/90/8/12-040812/en/index.html).

Kim, Alexander. 2016. "Tackling the Culture Clash over Country Food in Nunavut." *Artic Deeply*, August 5 (https://www.newsdeeply.com/arctic/articles/2016/08/05/tackling-the-culture-clash-over-country-food-in-nunavut).

King, Malcolm, Alexandra Smith, and Michael Gracey. 2009. "Indigenous Health Part 2: The Underlying Causes of the Health Gap." *Lancet* 374(9683):76–85.

Kirkpatrick, S., L. McIntyre, and M. Potestio. 2010. "Child Hunger and Long-Term Adverse Consequences for Health." *Archives of Pediatrics and Adolescent Medicine* 164(8):754–62.

Kirkpatrick, S. and V. Tarasuk. 2007. "Adequacy of Food Spending Is Related to Housing Expenditures among Lower-Income Canadian Households." *Public Health and Nutrition* 10(12):1464–73.

———. 2008. "Food Insecurity Is Associated with Nutrient Inadequacies among Canadian Adults and Adolescents." *Journal of Nutrition* 138(3):604–12.

———. 2009. "Food Insecurity and Participation in Community Food Programs among Low-Income Toronto Families." *Canadian Journal of Public Health* 100(2):135–9.

Lawn, J., and D. Harvey. 2003. "*Nutrition and Food Security in Kugaaruk, Nunavut: Baseline Survey for the Food Mail Pilot Project.*" Ottawa, ON: Department of Indian and Northern Affairs Canada.

Li, A. 2012. "Canada Ranks Eighth on Global Food Security Index: But Despite Abundance, Developed Countries Don't Get Right Nutrients." *Toronto Star*, July 11:A14.

Lieffers, J.R.L., J.P. Ekwaru, A. Ohinmaa, and P.J. Veugelers. 2018. "The Economic Burden of Not Meeting Food Recommendations in Canada: The Cost of Doing Nothing." *PloS One* 13(4):e0196333. doi:10.1371/journal.pone.0196333

Malthus, Thomas R. 1826. *An Essay on the Principle of Population, Vol. 1.* Online Library of Liberty.

McIntyre, L., A. Bartoo, J. Pow, and M. Potestio. 2012. "Coping with Child Hunger in Canada: Have Household Strategies Changed over a Decade." *Canadian Journal of Public Health*, 103(6):e428–32.

McIntyre, L., D.J. Dutton, C. Kwok, and J.C.H. Emery. 2016. "Reduction of Food Insecurity among Low-Income Canadian Seniors as a Likely Impact of a Guaranteed Annual Income." *Canadian Public Policy* 42(3):274–86. doi:10.3138/cpp.2015-069

McIntyre, L., T. Glanville, K.D. Raine, J.B. Dayle, B. Anderson, and N. Battaglia. 2003. "Do Low-Income Lone Mothers Compromise Their Nutrition to Feed Their Children?" *Canadian Medical Association Journal* 168(6): 689–91.

McIntyre, L., J. Williams, D. Lavorato, and S. Patten. 2012. "Depression and Suicide Ideation in Late Adolescence and Early Adulthood Are an Outcome of Child Hunger." *Journal of Affective Disorders* 150(1):123–9.

Moffat T., T. Galloway, and J. Latham. 2005. "Stature and Adiposity among Children in Contrasting Neighborhoods in the City of Hamilton, Ontario, Canada." *American Journal of Human Biology* 17(3):355–67.

Morissette, R. and D. Dionne-Simard. 2018. "Recent Changes in the Composition of Minimum Wage Workers." Insights on Canadian Society, Statistics Canada (https://www150.statcan.gc.ca/n1/pub/75-006-x/2018001/article/54974-eng.htm).

NAHO. 2013. "*Determinants of Health: Food Security, Profile 5.*" Inuit Tuttarvingat of NAHO (http://www.naho.ca/inuit).

Nosek, M.H., R.B. Hughes, C.A. Howland, M.E. Young, P.D. Mullen, and M. Shelton. 2004. "The Meaning of Health for Women with Physical Disabilities." *Family and Community Health* 27(1):6–21.

Orwell, George. [1933] 2001. *Down and out in Paris and London*. London, UK: Penguin.

Parker-Pope, T. 2007. "A High Price for Healthy Food." *New York Times, December 5 (*https://well.blogs.nytimes.com/2007/12/05/a-high-price-for-healthy-food).

Phillips, R. (2009). "Food Security and Women's Health: A Feminist Perspective for International Social Work." *International Social Work* 52(4):485–98.

PressProgress. 2014. "Food Bank Use in Canada Now 25% Higher than before the Recession." Broadbent Institute, November 4 (https://www.broadbentinstitute.ca/en/post/food-bank-use-canada-now-25-higher-recession).

Proof: Food Insecurity Policy Research. n.d. "The Impact of Food Insecurity on Health." University of Toronto, Department of Nutritional Sciences (http://proof.utoronto.ca/wp-content/uploads/2016/06/health-impact-factsheet.pdf).

———. 2018. "Latest Household Food Insecurity Data Now Available." June 25 (https://proof.utoronto.ca/new-data-available).

Public Health Agency of Canada. 2010. "Summative Evaluation of the Canada Prenatal Nutrition Program" (http://www.phac-aspc.gc.ca/about_apropos/evaluation/reports-rapports/2009-2010/cpnp-pcnp/index-eng.php).

———. 2013. "*About* CPNP" (http://www.phac-aspc.gc.ca/hp-ps/dca-dea/prog-ini/cpnp-pcnp/about-apropos-eng.php).

Reynolds, L. 2009. "Dauphin's Great Experiment: Mincome, Nearly Forgotten Child of the '70s, Was a Noble Experiment." *Winnipeg Free Press*, December 9 (https://www.winnipegfreepress.com/local/dauphins-great-experiment.html).

Riches, G. 2011. "*Why Governments Can Safely Ignore Hunger.*" Ottawa, ON: Canadian Centre for Policy Alternatives.

Saul, Nick and Andrea Curtis. 2003. "The Hunger Game: Food Banks May Compound the Very Problems They Should Be Solving." *The Walrus*, April 13 (https://thewalrus.ca/the-hunger-game).

Schwartz, N., R. Buliung, and K. Wilson. 2019. "Disability and Food Access and Insecurity: A Scoping Review of the Literature." *Health and Place* 57:107–21.

Social Research and Demonstration Corporation. 2003. "Learning What Works: Evidence from SRDC's Social Experiments and Research—What Happens When a Temporary Earnings Supplement Is Withdrawn?" Winter 2003 3(1):4.

Somogyi, S. 2018. "Pricey Produce Expected to Increase Our Grocery Bills in 2019, Says Canada's Food Price Report." December 4 (https://news.uoguelph.ca/2018/12/pricey-produce-expected-to-increase-our-grocery-bills-in-2019-says-canadas-food-price-report).

Statistics Canada. 2016. "Housing in Canada: Key Results from the 2016 Census" (https://www150.statcan.gc.ca/n1/daily-quotidien/171025/dq171025c-eng.htm).

———. 2017. "Fruit and Vegetable Consumption, 2015" (https://www150.statcan.gc.ca/n1/pub/82-625-x/2017001/article/14764-eng.htm).

———. 2018. "The Effect of Government Transfer Programs on Low-Income Rates: A Gender-Based Analysis, 1995 to 2016." *Income Research Paper Series,* November 6 (https://www150.statcan.gc.ca/n1/pub/75f0002m/75f0002m2018003-eng.htm).

———. 2019a. "Health Indicator Profile, by Aboriginal Identity and Sex, Age-Standardized Rate, Four Year Estimates." Table 13-10-0099-01 (https://www150.statcan.gc.ca/t1/tbl1/en/tv.action?pid=1310009901).

———. 2019b. "Household Food Security by Living Arrangement." Table 13-10-0385-01 (https://www150.statcan.gc.ca/t1/tbl1/en/tv.action?pid=1310038501).

———. 2019c. "Latest Snapshot of the CPI, April 2019" (https://www150.statcan.gc.ca/n1/pub/71-607-x/2018016/cpi-ipc-eng.htm).

Tarasuk, Valerie. 2001a. "*Discussion Paper on Household and Individual Food Insecurity.*" Ottawa, ON: Health Canada.

———. 2001b. "Household Food Insecurity with Hunger Is Associated with Women's Food Intakes, Health and Household Circumstances." *Journal of Nutrition* 131(10):2670–6.

———. 2005. "Household Food Insecurity in Canada." *Topics in Clinical Nutrition* 20(4):99–312.

———. 2010. "Policy Directions to Promote Healthy Dietary Patterns in Canada." *Applied Physiology, Nutrition and Metabolism* 35(2):229.

Tarasuk, V., J. Cheng, C. de Oliveira, N. Dachner, C. Gundersen, and P. Kurdyak. 2003. "Association between Household Food Insecurity and Annual Health Care Costs." *Canadian Medical Association Journal* 187(14):E429–36.

Tarasuk V., A.A.F. St-Germain, and R. Loopstra. 2019. "The Relationship between Food Banks and Food Insecurity: Insights from Canada." *Voluntas*. doi/org/10.1007/s11266-019-00092-w

Tarasuk, V., A. Mitchell, and N. Dachner. 2016. "Household Food Insecurity in Canada, 2014." Proof (https://proof.utoronto.ca/wp-content/uploads/2016/04/Household-Food-Insecurity-in-Canada-2014.pdf).

Tarasuk, V., A.A.F. St-Germain, and A. Mitchell. 2019. "Geographic and Socio-Demographic Predictors of Household Food Insecurity in Canada, 2011–12." *BMC Public Health* 19(1):12.

Taylor, B. 2010. "Poor and Fat: The Link between Poverty and Obesity in Canadian Children." *CBC News*, October 1 (https://www.cbc.ca/news/technology/poor-and-fat-the-link-between-poverty-and-obesity-in-canadian-children-1.972762)

Tian, W., G. Egeland, I. Sobol, and H. Chan. 2011. "Mercury Hair Concentrations and Dietary Exposure among Inuit Preschool Children in Nunavut, Canada." *Environment International* 37(1):42–8.

Turner, N.J., R. Gregory, C. Brooks, I. Failing, and T. Satterfield. 2008. "From Invisibility to Transparency: Identifying the Implications." *Ecology and Society* 13(2).

Vozoris, N., and V. Tarasuk, V. 2003. "Prenatal and Child Nutrition Programs in Relation to Food Insecurity." *Canadian Review of Social Policy* 51:67.

Wendimu, M. and A. Desmarais. 2018. "Why Is Milk so Expensive in First Nations Communities? Access to and Affordability of Milk in Northern Manitoba." Ottawa, ON: Canadian Centre for Policy Alternatives.

Chapter 8

Alborz, Alison, Rosalind McNally, and Caroline Glendinning. 2005. "Access to Health Care for People with Learning Disabilities in the UK: Mapping the Issues and Reviewing the Evidence." *Journal of Health Services Research & Policy* 10(3):173–82.

Argys, L. 2015. "Consequences of the Obesity Epidemic for Immigrants." *IZA World of Labor*:210.

Asafu-Adjaye, John. 2004. "Income Inequality and Health: A Multi-Country Analysis." *International Journal of Social Economics* 31(1/2):195–207.

Avery, A.M., R.E. Hellman, and L.K. Sudderth. 2001. "Satisfaction with Mental Health Services among Sexual Minorities with Major Mental Illness." *American Journal of Public Health* 91(6):990–1.

Barton, S.S., H.V. Thommasen, B. Tallio, and W. Zhang. 2005. "Health and Quality of Life of Aboriginal Residential School Survivors, Bella Coola Valley, 2001." *Social Indicators Research* 73:295–312.

Bauer, Greta R., Rebecca Hammond, Robb Travers, Matthias Kaay, Karin M. Hohenadel, and Michelle Boyce. 2009. "'I Don't Think This Is Theoretical; This Is Our Lives': How Erasure Impacts Health Care for Transgender People." *Journal of the Association of Nurses in AIDS Care* 20(5):348–61.

Begum, Rashida, and Ona Desai. 2010. "A Comparative Study to Evaluate Psychological Status of Mothers of Children with Cerebral Palsy and Mothers of Normal Children." *Indian Occupational Therapy* 42(2):3–9.

Bockting, Walter, Autumn Benner, and Eli Coleman. 2009. "Gay and Bisexual Identity Development among Female-to-Male Transsexuals in North America: Emergence of a Transgender Sexuality." *Archives of Sexual Behavior* 38(5):688–701.

Brandt, M. 2007. "Strict Eligibility for Medical Studies Can Omit Women, Blacks." *Stanford News*, May 30 (http://news.stanford.edu/news/2007/may30/med-leftout-053007.html).

Bushnik, T., M. Tjepkema, and L. Martel. 2018. "Health-Adjusted Life Expectancy in Canada." Health Reports, Statistics Canada, catalogue no. 82-003-X (https://www150.statcan.gc.ca/n1/pub/82-003-x/2018004/article/54950-eng.htm).

Canadian Council on Learning. 2008. "Health Literacy in Canada: A Healthy Understanding" (http://www.en.copian.ca/library/research/ccl/health/health.pdf).

Canadian Institute for Health Information. 2019. "National Health Expenditure Trends, 1975 to 2019" (https://www.cihi.ca/sites/default/files/document/nhex-trends-narrative-report-2019-en-web.pdf).

Carpiano Richard M. 2004. *The Forms of Social Capital: A Sociomedical Science Investigation of Neighborhood Social Capital as a Health Determinant Using a Bourdieu Framework*. ProQuest Dissertations Publishing.

Carpiano, Richard M. and Polonijo, Andrea N., 2013. "Social Inequalities in Adolescent Human Papillomavirus (HPV) Vaccination: A Test of Fundamental Cause Theory." *Social Science & Medicine* 82:115–25.

Carver, L., R. Beamish, S. Phillips, and M. Villeneuve. 2018. "A Scoping Review: Social Participation as a Cornerstone of Successful Aging in Place among Rural Older Adults." *Geriatrics* 3(4):75.

CBC News. 2011. "The Decline of Smoking in Canada." July 29 (https://www.cbc.ca/news/canada/story/2011/07/29/f-smoking-statistics.html).

Centers for Disease Control and Prevention. 2013. "HIV among Transgender People" (http://www.cdc.gov/hiv/group/gender/transgender).

Chen, Y.Y. Brandon, Vanessa Gruben, and Jamie Chai Yun Liew. 2018. "'A Legacy of Confusion': An Exploratory Study of Service Provision under the Reinstated Interim Federal Health Program." *Refuge* 34(2):94–102.

Chi, D.L. and R.M. Carpiano. 2013. "Neighborhood Social Capital, Neighborhood Attachment, and Dental Care Use for Los Angeles Family and Neighborhood Survey Adults." *American Journal of Public Health* 103(4):e88–e95.

Conner-Spady, Barbara, Angela Estey, Gordon Arnett, Kathleen Ness, John McGurran, Robert Bear, Tom Noseworthy, and Steering Committee of the Western Canada Waiting List Project. 2005a. "Determinants of Patient and Surgeon Perspectives on Maximum Acceptable Waiting Times for Hip and Knee Arthroplasty." *Journal of Health Services Research & Policy* 10(2):84–90.

Conner-Spady, Barbara L., Suren Sanmugasunderam, Paul Courtright, Drew Mildon, John J. McGurran, and Tom W. Noseworthy. 2005b. "The Prioritization of Patients on Waiting Lists for Cataract Surgery: Validation of the Western Canada Waiting List Project Cataract Priority Criteria Tool." *Ophthalmic Epidemiology* 12(2):81–90.

Contandriopoulos, Damien and Henriette Bilodeau. 2009. "The Political Use of Poll Results about Public Support for a Privatized Healthcare System in Canada." *Health Policy* 90(1):104–12.

Council of Canadians with Disabilities. 2009. "Building an Inclusive and Accessible Canada: Supporting People with Disabilities" (http://www.ccdonline.ca/en/socialpolicy/actionplan/accessible-canada).

De Santis, J.P. 2009. "HIV Infection Risk Factors among Male-to-Female Transgender Persons: A Review of the Literature." *Journal of the Association of Nurses in AIDS Care* 20(5):362–72.

Duncan, K., J. Clipsham, E. Hampson, C. Krieger, J. MacDonnell, D. Roedding, et al. 2000. *Improving the Access to and Quality of Public Health Services for Lesbians and Gay Men: A Position Paper for the Ontario Public Health Association.* Toronto, ON: Ontario Public Health Association.

Edwards, L. 2013. "The Gender Gap in Pain." *New York Times*, March 16 (https://www.nytimes.com/2013/03/17/opinion/sunday/women-and-the-treatment-of-pain.html).

Eller, N.H., B. Netterstrøm, and A.M. Hansen. 2006. "Psychosocial Factors at Home and at Work and Levels of Salivary Cortisol." *Biological Psychology* 73(3):280–7.

Emerson, E., S. Baines, L. Allerton, and V. Welch. 2010. "Health Inequalities and People with Learning Disabilities in the UK: 2010." *Durham: Improving Health & Lives: Learning Disabilities Observatory.*

Engels, Friedrich. [1845] 2009. *The Condition of the Working Class in England.* London, UK: Penguin Classics.

Evans, G.W. and P. Kim. 2007. "Childhood Poverty and Health." *Psychological Science* 18:11.

Fitzsimons, Donna, Kader Parahoo, S.G. Richardson, and Maurice Stringer. 2003. "Patient Anxiety While on a Waiting List for Coronary Artery Bypass Surgery: A Qualitative and Quantitative Analysis." *Heart & Lung: The Journal of Acute and Critical Care* 32(1):23–31.

Fort Qu'Appelle All Nations Hospital. n.d. (http://www.fortquappelle.com/anhh.html).

Gaetz, Stephen, Bill O'Grady, Sean Kidd, and Kaitlin Schwan. 2016. "Without a Home: The National Youth Homelessness Survey." Canadian Observatory on Homelessness Press (https://homelesshub.ca/sites/default/files/attachments/WithoutAHome-final.pdf).

Gapka, S., and R. Raj. 2003. *Trans Health Project: A Position Paper and Resolution Adopted by the Ontario Public Health Association.* Toronto, ON: Ontario Public Health Association.

Gerdtham, Ulf-G., and Magnus Johannesson. 2004. "Absolute Income, Relative Income, Income Inequality, and Mortality." *Journal of Human Resources* 39(1):228–47.

Gilmour, H. 2012. "*Social Participation and the Health and Well-being of Canadian Seniors.*" Statistics Canada (http://www.statcan.gc.ca/pub/82-003-x/2012004/article/11720-eng.htm).

———. 2018. "Unmet Home Care Needs in Canada." Health Reports, Statistics Canada, catalogue no. 82-003-X (https://www150.statcan.gc.ca/n1/pub/82-003-x/2018011/article/00002-eng.htm).

Gionet, Linda and Shirin Roshanafshar. 2013. "Health at a Glance: Select Health Indicators of First Nations People Living Off Reserve, Métis and Inuit." Statistics Canada (http://www.statcan.gc.ca/pub/82-624-x/2013001/article/11763-eng.htm).

Goffman, Erving. 1961. *Asylums: Essays on the Social Situation of Mental Patients and Other Inmates.* New York: Penguin.

Goldsmith, Lesley, Heather Skirton, and Christine Webb. 2008. "Informed Consent to Healthcare Interventions in People with Learning Disabilities—An Integrative Review." *Journal of Advanced Nursing* 64(6):549–63.

Government of Canada. 2009. "Advancing the Inclusion of People with Disabilities." 2009 Federal Disability Report. Human Resources and Skills Development Canada (https://www.canada.ca/content/dam/esdc-edsc/migration/documents/eng/disability/arc/federal_report2009/fdr_2009.pdf).

———. 2013. "What Makes Canadians Healthy or Unhealthy?" (https://www.canada.ca/en/public-health/services/health-promotion/population-health/what-determines-health/what-makes-canadians-healthy-unhealthy.html).

———. 2016. "Health Status of Canadians 2016: Report of the Chief Public Health Officer" (https://www.canada.ca/en/public-health/corporate/publications/chief-public-health-officer-reports-state-public-health-canada/2016-health-status-canadians/page-4-how-healthy-are-we-life-expectancy-birth.html).

———. 2017. "How Healthy Are Canadians?" (https://www.canada.ca/en/public-health/services/publications/healthy-living/how-healthy-canadians.html).

Government of Nunavut. 2010. "Nunavut Suicide Prevention Strategy." October (https://www.gov.nu.ca/sites/default/files/files/NSPS_final_English_Oct%202010(1).pdf).

Green, B.L. 2012. "Applying Interdisciplinary Theory in the Care of Aboriginal Women's Mental Health." *Journal of Psychiatric and Mental Health Nursing* 17:797–803.

Green, J., E. Lombardi, and K. Rachlin. 2008. "Utilization of Health Care among Female-To-Male Transgender Individuals in the United States." *Journal of Homosexuality* 54(3):243–58.

Greenberg, L. and C. Normandin. 2011. "Disparities in Life Expectancy at Birth." Health at a Glance, Statistics Canada, catalogue no. 82-624-X (https://www150.statcan.gc.ca/n1/pub/82-624-x/2011001/article/11427-eng.htm).

Gushulak, B.D., K. Pottie, J.H. Roberts, S. Torres, and M. DesMeules. 2011. "Migration and Health in Canada: Health in the Global Village." *Canadian Medical Association Journal* 183(12):E952–8.

Health Council of Canada. 2012. "Empathy, Dignity, and Respect: Creating Cultural Safety for Aboriginal People in Urban Health Care." December (https://healthcouncilcanada.ca/files/Aboriginal_Report_EN_web_final.pdf).

Hicks, J. 2007. "The Social Determinants of Elevated Suicide among Inuit Youth." *Indigenous Affairs 4*:32–7.

Hoover, M., and M. Rotermann. 2012. "Seniors' Use of and Unmet Needs for Home Care, 2009." *The Daily*, December 12 (http://www.statcan.gc.ca/pub/82-003-x/2012004/article/11760-eng.htm).

Indigenous Services Canada. 2013. "Diabetes: Aboriginal Diabetes Initiative" (https://www.sac-isc.gc.ca/eng/1569960595332/1569960634063).

———. 2018. "Improving Health Outcomes" https://www.canada.ca/en/indigenous-services-canada/news/2018/01/improving_healthoutcomes.html).

Jorgensen M. 2005. "A Disability Paradox." *Canadian Family Physician* 51:1474–6.

Kenagy, G.P. 2005. "Transgender Health: Findings from Two Needs Assessment Studies in Philadelphia." *Health & Social Work* 30(1):19–26.

Keung, N. 2012. "Volunteer Clinics Overwhelmed by Refugees with No Health Care." *Toronto Star, September 30* (https://www.thestar.com/news/gta/2012/09/30/volunteer_clinics_overwhelmed_by_refugees_with_no_health_care.html).

King, Malcolm, Alexandra Smith, and Michael Gracey. 2009. "Indigenous Health Part 2: The Underlying Causes of the Health Gap." *Lancet* 374(9683):76–85.

Kondro, Wayne. 2012. "Health Disparities among Income Groups Becoming More Pronounced." *Canadian Medical Association Journal* 185(13): E695–6.

Krahn, Gloria L., Laura Hammond, and Anne Turner. 2006. "A Cascade of Disparities: Health and Health Care Access for People with Intellectual Disabilities." *Mental Retardation and Developmental Disabilities Research Reviews* 12(1):70–82.

Kunz-Ebrecht, S.R., C. Kirschbaum, M. Marmot, and A. Steptoe. 2004. "Differences in Cortisol Awakening Response on Work Days and Weekends in Women and Men from the Whitehall II Cohort." *Psychoneuroendocrinology* 29(4):516–28.

Lombardi, Emilia. 2008. "Substance Use Treatment Experiences of Transgender/Transsexual Men and Women." *Journal of LGBT Health Research* 3(2):37–47.

Lopert, Ruth, Elizabeth Docteur, and Steve Morgan. 2018. "Body Count: The Human Cost of Financial Barriers to Prescription Medication." Canadian Federation of Nurses Unions (https://nursesunions.ca/wp-content/uploads/2018/05/2018.04-Body-Count-Final-web.pdf).

Lou, Y., and R. Beaujot. 2005. "What Happens to the 'Healthy Immigrant Effect': The Mental Health of Immigrants to Canada." *PSC Discussion Papers Series* 19:15.

Lu, Chaohui, and Edward Ng. 2019. "Healthy Immigrant Effect by Immigrant Category in Canada." Statistics Canada (https://www150.statcan.gc.ca/n1/en/catalogue/82-003-X201900400001).

Mackenbach, Johan P. and Martijntje J. Bakker. 2003. "Tackling Socioeconomic Inequalities in Health: Analysis of European Experiences." *Lancet* 362(9393):1409–14.

Marmot, M.S. 1991. "Health Inequalities among British Civil Servants." *The Whitehall II Study* 337:1387–93.

———. 2005. "Social Determinants of Health Inequalities." *Lancet* 365(9464):1099–104.

McIntosh, C.N., P. Finès, R. Wilkins, and M.C. Wolfson. 2010. "Income Disparities in Health-Adjusted Life Expectancy for Canadian Adults, 1991 to 2001." Statistics Canada (http://www.statcan.gc.ca/pub/82-003-x/2009004/article/11019-eng.htm#a4).

Institute of Medicine. 2011. *Relieving Pain in America: A Blueprint for Transforming Prevention, Care, Education, and Research*. Washington, DC: National Academies Press.

Mikkonen, J. and D. Raphael. 2010. *Social Determinants of Health: The Canadian Facts*. Toronto, ON: York University School on Health Policy and Management.

Ng, E., K. Pottie, and D. Spitzer. 2011. "Official Language Proficiency and Self-Reported Health among Immigrants to Canada." Statistics Canada (http://www.statcan.gc.ca/pub/82-003-x/2011004/article/11559-eng.htm).

OECD. 2020. "Public Spending on Incapacity." doi:10.1787/f35b71ed-en.

Olah, M.E., G. Gaisano, and S. Hwang. 2013. "The Effect of Socioeconomic Status on Access to Primary Care: An Audit Study." *Canadian Medical Association Journal* 185(6): E263–9.

Oliver, L.N. and D.E. Kohen. 2010. "Neighbourhood Variation in Hospitalization for Unintentional Injury among Children and Teenagers." Statistics Canada (http://www.statcan.gc.ca/pub/82-003-x/2010004/article/11351-eng.htm).

Oliver, L.N., P.A. Peters, and D.E. Kohen. 2012. "Mortality Rates among Children and Teenagers Living in Inuit Nunangat, 1994 to 2008." *Health Reports* 23(3):17–22.

Pan, S.W. and R.M. Carpiano. 2013. "Immigrant Density, Sense of Community Belonging, and Suicidal Ideation among Racial Minority and White Immigrants in Canada." *Journal of Immigrant and Minority Health* 15(1):34–42.

Park, Jungwee, Michael Tjepkema, Neil Goedhuis, and Jennifer Pennock. 2015. "Avoidable Mortality among First Nations Adults in Canada: A Cohort Analysis." Statistics Canada (https://www150.statcan.gc.ca/n1/pub/82-003-x/2015008/article/14216-eng.htm).

Parry, Odette, Elizabeth Peel, Margaret Douglas, and Julia Lawton. 2004. "Patients in Waiting: A Qualitative Study of Type 2 Diabetes Patients' Perceptions of Diagnosis." *Family Practice* 21(2):131–6.

Paradies, Yin. 2006. "A Systematic Review of Empirical Research on Self-Reported Racism and Health." *International Journal of Epidemiology* 35(4):888–901.

Parsons, Talcott. 1951. *The Social System*. New York: The Free Press of Glencoe.

Public Health Agency of Canada. 2011. "Reducing Health Inequalities: A Challenge for Our Times" (http://publications.gc.ca/collections/collection_2012/aspc-phac/HP35-22-2011-eng.pdf).

Rather, L.J., ed. 1985. *Rudolf Virchow: Collected Essays on Public Health and Epidemiology*, Vol. 1. Canton, MA: Science History Publications.

Romanow, R. 2002. *"Building on Values: The Future of Health Care in Canada: Final Report." Royal* Commission on the Future of Health Care in Canada.

Sanmartin, Claudia, and Nancy Ross. 2006. "Experiencing Difficulties Accessing First-Contact Health Services in Canada: Canadians without Regular Doctors and Recent Immigrants Have Difficulties Accessing First-Contact Healthcare Services." *Healthcare Policy* 1(2):103.

Segerstrom, Suzanne C. and Gregory E. Miller. 2004. "Psychological Stress and the Human Immune System: A Meta-Analytic Study of 30 Years of Inquiry." *Psychological Bulletin* 130(4):601.

Sevean, Pat, Sally Dampier, Michelle Spadoni, Shane Strickland, and Susan Pilatzke. 2009. "Patients and Families Experiences with Video Telehealth in Rural/Remote Communities in Northern Canada." *Journal of Clinical Nursing* 18(18):2573–9.

Sinha, Maria. 2015. "A Portrait of Caregivers, 2012." Statistics Canada (https://www150.statcan.gc.ca/n1/pub/89-652-x/89-652-x2013001-eng.htm).

Snelgrove, J.W., A.M. Jasudavisius, B.W. Rowe, E.M. Head, and G.R. Bauer. 2012. "Completely 'Out-At-Sea' with 'Two-Gender Medicine': A Qualitative Analysis of Physician-Side Barriers to Providing Healthcare for Transgender Patients." *BMC Health Services Research* 12(1):110.

Standing Senate Committee on Indigenous and Northern Affairs. 2017. "Breaking Point: The Suicide Crisis in Indigenous Communities." June (https://www.ourcommons.ca/Content/Committee/421/INAN/Reports/RP8977643/inanrp09/inanrp09-e.pdf).

Statistics Canada. 2005. "Dynamics of Immigrants' Health in Canada: Evidence from the National Population Health Survey" (http://www.statcan.gc.ca/daily-quotidien/050223/dq050223c-eng.htm).

———. 2012a. "Access to a Regular Medical Doctor, 2011" (http://www.statcan.gc.ca/pub/82-625-x/2012001/article/11656-eng.htm).

———. 2012b. "Study: Suicide Rates, an Overview, 1950 to 2009" (http://www.statcan.gc.ca/daily-quotidien/120725/dq120725a-eng.htm).

———. 2017. "Primary Health Care Providers, 2016" (https://www150.statcan.gc.ca/n1/pub/82-625-x/2017001/article/54863-eng.htm).

———. 2018. "First Nations People, Métis and Inuit in Canada: Diverse and Growing Populations" (https://www150.statcan.gc.ca/n1/pub/89-659-x/89-659-x2018001-eng.htm).

———. 2019a. "Health Characteristics, Annual Estimates, by Household Income Quintile and Highest Level of Education." Table 13-10-0097-01 (https://www150.statcan.gc.ca/t1/tbl1/en/cv.action?pid=1310009701).

———. 2019b. "Infant Deaths and Mortality Rates, by Age Group." Table 13-10-0713-01 (https://www150.statcan.gc.ca/t1/tbl1/en/tv.action?pid=1310071301).

———. 2019c. "Primary Health Care Providers, 2017" (https://www150.statcan.gc.ca/n1/pub/82-625-x/2019001/article/00001-eng.htm).

Tjepkema, M. 2008. "Health Care Use among Gay, Lesbian and Bisexual Canadians." *Health Reports* 19(1).

Trute, B., K.M. Benzies, C. Worthington, J.R. Reddon, and M. Moore. 2010. "Accentuate the Positive to Mitigate the Negative: Mother Psychological Coping Resources and Family Adjustment in Childhood Disability." *Journal of Intellectual and Developmental Disability* 35(1):36–43.

Truth and Reconciliation Commission of Canada. 2015a. *Canada's Residential Schools: The Final Report of the Truth and Reconciliation Commission of Canada: Vol. 1*. Montreal, QC: McGill-Queen's University Press.

———. 2015b. *Canada's Residential Schools: The Métis Experience: The Final Report of the Truth and Reconciliation Commission of Canada: Vol. 3*. Montreal, QC: McGill-Queen's University Press.

Turcotte, M. 2012. "*Women and Health*." Statistics Canada (http://www.statcan.gc.ca/pub/89-503-x/2010001/article/11543-eng.htm).

Veltman A., D.E. Stewart, G.S. Tardif, and M. Branigan. 2001. "Perceptions of Primary Healthcare Services among People with Physical Disabilities. Part 1: Access Issues." *Medscape General Medicine* 3:18.

Vermeulen, Karin M., Otto H. Bosma, Wim van der Bij, Gerard H. Koëter, and Elisabeth M. TenVergert. 2005. "Stress, Psychological Distress, and Coping in Patients on the Waiting List for Lung Transplantation: An Exploratory Study." *Transplant International* 18(8): 954–9.

White, P. 2011. "The Trials of Nunavut: Lament for an Arctic Nation." *Globe and Mail*, April 1 (https://www.theglobeandmail.com/news/national/nunavut/the-trials-of-nunavut-lament-for-an-arctic-nation/article547265).

Wilkins, K. and S.G. Mackenzie. 2008. "*Work Injuries*." Statistics Canada (http://www.statcan.gc.ca/pub/82-003-x/2006007/article/10191-eng.htm).

Zhao, J., X. Li Xue, and T. Gilkinson. 2010. "*Health Status and Social Capital of Recent Immigrants in Canada: Evidence from the Longitudinal Survey of Immigrants to Canada*." Citizenship and Immigration Canada (http://www.cic.gc.ca/english/resources/research/immigrant-survey/index.asp).

Chapter 9

Abramovich, A. 2014. "*Solutions: LGBTQ2 Youth Homelessness*." The Homeless Hub, June 23 (https://www.rondpointdelitinerance.ca/blog/solutions-lgbtq2-youth-homelessness).

Albrow, M. 1975. "Legal Positivism and Bourgeois Materialism: Max Weber's View of the Sociology of Law." *British Journal of Law and Society* 2(1):14–31

Aleman, Ambar. 2016. "Employment and Homelessness." Homeless Hub, July 11 (https://www.homelesshub.ca/blog/employment-homelessness).

Arendell, Terry J. 1987. "Women and the Economics of Divorce in the Contemporary United States." *Signs*:121–35.

Bar, J. 2013. "*'Hey Faggot': Understanding That the Current Homeless System, Planning Policy, and Land Use Planning Tools Is Not Designed to Address the Socialized and Institutionalized Disregard for the* LGBTQ *Homeless Youth Population*." Ryerson University (https://digital.library.ryerson.ca/islandora/object/RULA%3A2410).

Béland, D. 2009. "Ideas, Institutions, and Policy Change." *Journal of European Public Policy* 16(5):701–18.

———. 2011. "The Politics of Social Policy Language." *Social Policy & Administration* 45(1):1–18.

Benmor, Steven. 2014. "Is Legal Representation Only Available to the Very Rich and Very Poor?" *AdvocateDaily.com*.

Berinstein, C., J. Macdonald, P. Nyers, C. Wright, and S. Sahar Zerehi. 2006. "*'Access Not Fear': Non-Status Immigrants and City Services*." Toronto, ON: Joint Centre of Excellence for Research on Immigration and Settlement.

Black, Donald J. 1972. "The Boundaries of Legal Sociology." *Yale Law Journal* 81(6):1086–100.

———. 1979. "Common Sense in the Sociology of Law." *American Sociological Review* 44(1):18–27.

Bressan, A. and K. Coady. 2017. "Guilty Pleas among Indigenous People in Canada." Department of Justice Canada: Research and Statistics Division (http://publications.gc.ca/collections/collection_2018/jus/J4-62-2017-eng.pdf).

Brewin, A. and L. Stephens. 2004. "*Legal Aid Denied: Women and the Cuts to Legal Services in BC*." Vancouver, BC: Canadian Centre for Policy Alternatives, West Coast LEAF.

Brownfield, David, Ann Marie Sorenson, and Kevin M. Thompson. 2001. "Gang Membership, Race, and Social Class: A Test of The Group Hazard and Master Status Hypotheses." *Deviant Behavior* 22(1):73–89.

Brunet-Jailly, E. 2008. "Cascadia in Comparative Perspectives: Canada-US Relations and the Emergence of Cross-Border Regions." *Canadian Political Science Review* 2(2):104–24.

Brzozowski, J., A. Taylor-Butts, and S. Johnson. 2006. "*Victimization and Offending Among the Aboriginal Population in Canada*." Statistics Canada (http://www.statcan.gc.ca/pub/85-002-x/85-002-x2006003-eng.pdf).

Burnham, Linda. 2001. "Welfare Reform, Family Hardship, and Women of Color." *Annals of the American Academy of Political and Social Science* 577(1):38–48.

Carson, A., P. Clement, K. Crane, and J. Karabanow. 2010. *Leaving the Streets Stories of Canadian Youth*. Winnipeg, MB: Fernwood Publishing.

Canadian Bar Association. 2015. "Legal Aid in Canada" (http://www.cba.org/Sections/Legal-Aid-Liaison/Resources/Resources/Legal-Aid-in-Canada).

Canadian Bar Association Access to Justice Committee. 2013. "*Reaching Equal Justice: An Invitation to Envision and Act*" (https://www.cba.org/Publications-Resources/Resources/Equal-Justice-Initiative/Reaching-Equal-Justice-An-Invitation-to-Envisi-(1)).

Centre for Addiction and Mental Health and Mental Health Commission of Canada. 2009. "*Improving Mental Health Services for Immigrant, Refugee, Ethno-Cultural and Racialized Groups Issues and Options for Service Improvement.*" November 12 (https://www.mentalhealthcommission.ca/sites/default/files/Diversity_Issues_Options_Report_ENG_0_1.pdf).

Ciccocioppo, Lucianna. 2011. "There Is No Justice without Access to Justice: Chief Justice Beverly McLachlin." University of Toronto Faculty of Law, November 11 (https://www.law.utoronto.ca/news/there-no-justice-without-access-justice-chief-justice-beverley-mclachlin).

City of Vancouver. 2020. "Building Liveable, Sustainable, and Inclusive Communities" (https://vancouver.ca/people-programs/building-community.aspx).

Clemmer, Donald. 1950. "Observations on Imprisonment as a Source of Criminality." *Journal of Criminal Law and Criminology* 41(3):311–19.

Coletta, A. 2019. "Canada's Indigenous Population Is Overrepresented in Federal Prisons—And It's Only Getting Worse." *Washington Post* (https://www.washingtonpost.com/news/worldviews/wp/2018/07/01/canadas-indigenous-population-is-over-represented-in-federal-prisons-and-its-only-getting-worse).

Conference Board of Canada. 2015. "Future Care for Canadian Seniors: Demand and Expenditures Expected To Rise Dramatically By 2026 (https://www.conferenceboard.ca/press/newsrelease/15-11-03/Future_Care_For_Canadian_Seniors_Demand_And_Expenditures_Expected_To_Rise_Dramatically_By_2026.aspx?AspxAutoDetectCookieSupport=1).

Corrado, R.R., S. Kuehn, and I. Margaritescu. 2014. "Policy Issues Regarding the Overrepresentation of Incarcerated Aboriginal Young Offenders in a Canadian Context." *Youth Justice* 14(1):40–62.

DeVerteuil, G. and K. Wilson. 2010. "Reconciling Indigenous Need with the Urban Welfare State? Evidence of Culturally-Appropriate Services and Spaces for Aboriginals in Winnipeg." *Geoforum*, 41(3):498–507.

Douyon, Emerson. 2016. "Ethnocultural Minorities and the Canadian Correctional System." Correctional Service Canada (https://www.csc-scc.gc.ca/about-us/006-4000-eng.shtml#o).

Enang, J. 2001. "Black Women's Health: A Synthesis of Health Research Relevant to Black Nova Scotians." Halifax, NS: Dalhousie University.

Finnie, R. and A. Bernard. 2004. "The Intergenerational Transmission of Lone Mother and Low Income Status: Family and Neighbourhood Effects" (http://www.cerforum.org/conferences/200406/papers/Finnie-Bernard.pdf).

Food Banks Canada. 2012. "HungerCount 2012" (https://foodbankscanada.ca/getmedia/3b946e67-fbe2-490e-90dc-4a313dfb97e5/HungerCount2012.pdf.aspx).

———. 2018. "HungerCount 2018" (https://foodbankscanada.ca/getmedia/241fb659-05f5-44a2-9cef-56f5f51db523/HungerCount-2018_FINAL_EN.pdf.aspx?ext=.pdf).

Gaetz, S., J. Donaldson, T. Richter, and T. Gulliver. 2013. *The State of Homelessness in Canada 2013.* Toronto, ON: Canadian Homelessness Research Network.

Gaetz, S., B. O'Grady, and K. Buccieri, 2010. "Surviving Crime and Violence: Street Youth and Victimization in Toronto." Canadian Observatory on Homelessness (https://www.homelesshub.ca/resource/surviving-crime-and-violence-street-youth-and-victimization-toronto).

Gaetz, S., B. O'Grady, S. Kidd, and K. Schwan. 2016. "Without a Home: The National Youth Homelessness Survey." Canadian Observatory on Homelessness (https://www.homelesshub.ca/YouthWithoutHome).

Government of Ontario. 2018. "Public Accounts: 2016–2017 Annual Report" (https://www.ontario.ca/page/public-accounts-2016-17-annual-report).

Greatbatch, Jacqueline. 1989. "The Gender Difference: Feminist Critiques of Refugee Discourse." *International Journal of Refugee Law* 1(4):518–27.

Hall, A., S. Hickox, J. Kuan, and C. Sung. 2017. "Barriers to Employment: Individual and Organizational Perspectives." Pp 243–86 in *Research in Personnel and Human Resources Management: Vol. 35,* edited by M. Ronald Buckley, Anthony R. Wheeler, Jonathon R. B. Halbesleben. Bingley, UK: Emerald Publishing Limited.

Hunter, Ernst. 2008. "What's Good for the Gays Is Good for the Gander: Making Homeless Youth Housing Safer for Lesbian, Gay, Bisexual, and Transgender Youth." *Family Court Review* 46(3):543–57.

Jeffries, S. and P. Stenning. 2014. "Sentencing Aboriginal Offenders: Law, Policy, and Practice in Three Countries." *Canadian Journal of Criminology and Criminal Justice* 56(4):447–94.

John Howard Society. 2014. *The Counter Point: Issue 1* (https://johnhoward.on.ca/wp-content/uploads/2014/09/counter-point-1-poverty-and-crime-is-there-a-connection.pdf).

Kafele, K. 2004. *Racial Discrimination and Mental Health: Racialized and Aboriginal Communities.* Toronto, ON: Ontario Human Rights Commission.

Kahane Law. 2019. "Fees" (https://kahanelaw.com).

Kelley-Moore, J. and J. Schumacher. 2006. "When Do Older Adults Become 'Disabled'? Social and Health Antecedents of Perceived Disability in a Panel Study of the Oldest Old." *Journal of Health and Social Behavior* 47(2):126–41.

Kornberger, R., J.R. Fast, and D.L. Williamson. 2001. "Welfare or Work: Which Is Better for Canadian Children?" *Canadian Public Policy* 27(4):407–21.

Krieg, Brigtette, Diane J.F. Martz, and Lisa McCallum. 2007. "Access to Health Services for Elderly Métis Women in Buffalo Narrows, Saskatchewan." August (http://www.pwhce.ca/pdf/buffaloNarrowsAug07.pdf).

Legal Aid Ontario. 2015. "Report: Legal Aid Ontario's Aboriginal Justice Strategy" (https://www.legalaid.on.ca/en/publications/reports.asp).

———. 2016. "Refugee and Immigration Services, 2016/17" (https://www.legalaid.on.ca/en/publications/report-refugee-and-immigration-services-2016-17annualreport.asp).

Li, H. and A. Browne. 2000. "Defining Mental Illness and Accessing Mental Health Services: Perspectives of Asian Canadians." *Canadian Journal of Community Mental Health* 19:143–59.

Makin, Kirk. 2011. "Access to Justice Becoming a Privilege of the Rich, Judge Warns." *Globe and Mail*, February 10 (https://www.theglobeandmail.com/news/national/access-to-justice-becoming-a-privilege-of-the-rich-judge-warns/article565873).

Malakieh, J. 2019. "Adult and Youth Correctional Statistics in Canada, 2016/2017." Statistics Canada (https://www150.statcan.gc.ca/n1/pub/85-002-x/2018001/article/54972-eng.htm).

Mann, M. 2013. "Good Intentions, Disappointing Results: A Progress Report on Federal Aboriginal Correction." Office of the Correctional Investigator (http://www.oci-bec.gc.ca/cnt/rpt/oth-aut/oth-aut20091113-eng.aspx).

McColl, M.A. 2005. "Disability Studies at the Population Level: Issues of Health Service Utilization." *American Journal of Occupational Therapy* 59(5):516–26.

McColl, M.A., A. Aiken, and M. Schaub. 2015. "Do People with Disabilities Have Difficulty Finding a Family Physician?" *International Journal of Environmental Research and Public Health* 12(5):4638–51.

Merton, R.K. and R.C. Merton. 1968. *Social Theory and Social Structure*. New York: Simon and Schuster.

Miedema, Bauje and Sandra Wachholz. 2012. "A Complex Web: Access to Justice for Abused Immigrant Women in New Brunswick." *Review of Women's Studies* 11:1–2.

Misener, R.M., S. Rudderham, and A. Vukic. 2009. "A Community Partnership to Explore Mental Health Services in First Nations Communities in Nova Scotia." *Canadian Journal of Public Health*, 100(9):432.

National Council of Welfare. 2000. "Justice and the Poor." Spring (http://www.oaith.ca/assets/files/Publications/justice_andthe_poor.pdf).

Office of the Parliamentary Budget Officer. 2018. "Update on Costs of Incarceration" (http://publications.gc.ca/collections/collection_2018/dpb-pbo/YN5-152-2018-eng.pdf).

Office of the Correctional Investigator. 2013. "Annual Report of the Office of the Correctional Investigator 2012–2013" (https://www.oci-bec.gc.ca/cnt/rpt/annrpt/annrpt20122013-eng.aspx#s3).

———. 2015. "Annual Report of the Office of the Correctional Investigator 2014–2015" (https://www.oci-bec.gc.ca/cnt/rpt/annrpt/annrpt20142015-eng.aspx#s8).

———. 2019. "Aboriginal Issues" (https://www.oci-bec.gc.ca/cnt/priorities-priorites/aboriginals-autochtones-eng.aspx).

Osachoff, K. 2008. "A Women's Right to Legal Representation: A Critical Examination of Legal Aid in BC." Vancouver, BC: Battered Women Support Services.

Porter, John. [1965] 2015. *The Vertical Mosaic: An Analysis of Social Class and Power in Canada*. Toronto, ON: University of Toronto Press.

Rahman, S. 2009. "Mapping the Gap: Linking Aboriginal Women with Legal Services and Resources." *West Coast* LEAF (http://www.westcoastleaf.org/wp-content/uploads/2014/10/2011-REPORT-Mapping-the-Gap-Linking-Aboriginal-Women-with-Legal-Resources-and-Services.pdf).

Reid, G. and J. Malcolmson. 2008. "Voices from the Field: Needs Mapping Self-help Services in Rural and Remote Communities" (http://www.justiceeducation.ca/themes/framework/documents/Voices_from_the_Field_Final_August_2008.pdf).

Sapers, Howard. 2012. "Spirit Matters: Aboriginal People and the Corrections and Conditional Release Act." Office of the Correctional Investigator (https://www.oci-bec.gc.ca/cnt/rpt/oth-aut/oth-aut20121022-eng.aspx).

Sanchez, J., G. Byfield, T. Brown, K. LaFavor, D. Murphy, and P. Laud. 2000. "Perceived Accessibility versus Actual Physical Accessibility of Healthcare Facilities." *Rehabilitation Nursing* 25:6–9.

Selznick, P. 1959. "The Sociology of Law." *Journal of Legal Education* 12:521.

Senese, L.C. and K. Wilson. 2013. "Aboriginal Urbanization and Rights in Canada: Examining Implications for Health." *Social Science & Medicine* 91:219–28.

Service Canada. 2013. "*Social Workers." September 3 (*http://www.servicecanada.gc.ca/eng/qc/job_futures/statistics/4152.shtml.

Skolnick, Jerome H. 1965. "The Sociology of Law in America: Overview and Trends." *Social Problems* 13(Suppl 1):4–39.

Social Planning Toronto. 2013. "*Accessing Community Programs and Services for Non-Status Immigrants in Toronto" August 16 (*https://www.socialplanningtoronto.org/accessing_community_programs_and_services_for_non_status_immigrants_in_toronto_organizational_challenges_and_responses).

Statistics Canada. 2015. "Canada's Population Estimates: Age and Sex." *The Daily*, September 29 (https://www150.statcan.gc.ca/n1/daily-quotidien/150929/dq150929b-eng.htm).

———. 2017. "Portrait of Children's Family Life in Canada in 2016." *Census in Brief*, August 2 (https://www12.statcan.gc.ca/census-recensement/2016/as-sa/98-200-x/2016006/98-200-x2016006-eng.cfm).

———. 2018a. "Canada at a Glance 2018: Population." Table 1 (https://www150.statcan.gc.ca/n1/pub/12-581-x/2018000/pop-eng.htm).

———. Statistics Canada. 2018b. "Homeless Shelter Capacity, Bed and Shelter Counts for Emergency

Shelters, Transitional Housing and Violence against Women Shelters for Canada and Provinces." Table 14-10-0353-01 (https://www150.statcan.gc.ca/t1/tbl1/en/tv.action?pid=1410035301).

———. 2018c. "Legal Aid Service Delivery by Private Bar, Staff, and Other Lawyers, 2017–18, Total Lawyers Providing Legal Aid Services, 2017–18." Canadian Centre for Justice Statistics, Legal Aid Survey, Table 3 (https://www.justice.gc.ca/eng/rp-pr/jr/aid-aide/1718/p1.html#table3).

Tomm, M. 2013. "Public Reason and the Disempowerment of Aboriginal People in Canada." *Canadian Journal of Law & Society* 28(3):293–314.

Townson, M. and K. Hayes. 2007. "*Women and the Employment Insurance Program.*" Toronto, ON: Canadian Centre for Policy Alternatives.

Uggen, Christopher. 2000. "Work as a Turning Point in the Life Course of Criminals: A Duration Model of Age, Employment, and Recidivism." *American Sociological Review* 67:529–46.

Varney, D. and W. Van Vliet. 2008. "Homelessness, Children, and Youth: Research in the United States and Canada." *American Behavioral Scientist* 51(6):715–20.

Walkem, A. 2007. "*Building Bridges: Improving Legal Services Aboriginal Peoples.*" Vancouver, BC: Legal Services Society.

Wortley, S. and J. Tanner. 2005. "Inflammatory Rhetoric? Baseless Accusations? A Response to Gabor's Critique of Racial Profiling Research in Canada." *Canadian Journal of Criminology and Criminal Justice* 47(3):581–610.

YWCA of Metro Vancouver. 2020. "*Single Mothers' Support Services*" (https://ywcavan.org/programs/single-mothers-support-services).

Zellerer, E. 2003. "Culturally Competent Programs: The First Family Violence Program for Aboriginal Men in Prison." *The Prison Journal*, 171–90.

Zemans, F. and J. Amaral. 2018. "A Current Assessment of Legal Aid in Ontario." *Journal of Law and Society Policy* 29:1–28.

Chapter 10

Abada, T., F. Hou, and B. Ram. 2008. "The Effects of Harassment and Victimization on Self-Rated Health and Mental Health among Canadian Adolescents." *Social Science & Medicine* 67(4):557–67. doi:10.1016/j.socscimed.2008.04.006

Andresen, M.A. 2012. "Unemployment and Crime: A Neighborhood Level Panel Data Approach." *Social Science Research* 41(6):1615–28. doi:10.1016/j.ssresearch.2012.07.003

Atleo, S. 2013. "For Canada and First Nations, It's Time to End the Experiments." *Globe and Mail*, July 25 (https://www.theglobeandmail.com/opinion/for-canada-and-first-nations-its-time-to-end-the-experiments/article13400934).

Beattie, Sara, Jean-Denis David, and Joel Roy. 2018. "Homicide in Canada, 2017." Statistics Canada (https://www150.statcan.gc.ca/n1/pub/85-002-x/2018001/article/54980-eng.htm).

Boggess L.N. and J.R. Hipp. 2010. "Violent Crime, Residential Instability and Mobility: Does the Relationship Differ in Minority Neighborhoods?" *Journal of Quantitative Criminology* 26:351–70.

Boyce, J. 2016. "Victimization of Aboriginal People in Canada, 2014." Statistics Canada (https://www150.statcan.gc.ca/n1/pub/85-002-x/2016001/article/14631-eng.htm).

Brazeau, R. and J.-A. Brzozowski. 2008. "Violent Victimization in Canada." Statistics Canada (http://www.statcan.gc.ca/pub/89-630-x/2008001/article/10643-eng.htm#6).

Canadian Human Rights Commission. 2010. "Report on Equality Rights of Aboriginal People" (https://www.chrc-ccdp.gc.ca/eng/content/report-equality-rights-aboriginal-people).

Cantor, D. and K.C. Land. 1985. "Unemployment and Crime Rates in the Post-World War II United States: A Theoretical and Empirical Analysis." *American Sociological Review* 50(3):317–32. doi:10.2307/2095542

CBC News. 2011. "*What Is a Hate Crime?" June 17* (http://www.cbc.ca/news/canada/story/2011/06/15/f-hate-crimes.html).

CBC News. 2013. "Huronia Regional Centre Lawsuit Ends in $35M Settlement." September 17 (https://www.cbc.ca/news/canada/huronia-regional-centre-lawsuit-ends-in-35m-settlement-1.1857506).

Cole, Desmond. 2015. "The Skin I'm In: I've Been Interrogated by Police More than 50 Times—All Because I'm Black." *Toronto Life*, April 21 (https://torontolife.com/city/life/skin-im-ive-interrogated-police-50-times-im-black).

Conroy, S. 2017. "Section 1: Police-Reported Family Violence against Children and Youth in Canada, 2017." Statistics Canada (https://www150.statcan.gc.ca/n1/pub/85-002-x/2018001/article/54978/01-eng.htm).

Department of Justice. 2017. "JustFacts: Sexual Assault." May (https://www.justice.gc.ca/eng/rp-pr/jr/jf-pf/2017/may02.html).

———. 2019. "JustFacts: Sexual Assault." April (https://www.justice.gc.ca/eng/rp-pr/jr/jf-pf/2019/apr01.html).

Dhillon, S. and I. Bailey. 2012. "Inquiry Slams Police in Pickton Case." *Globe and Mail*, December 17 (https://www.theglobeandmail.com/news/british-columbia/inquiry-slams-police-in-pickton-case/article6477651).

Durkheim, Émile. 1895. "On the Normality of Crime." *The Rules of Sociological Method*. New York: Free Press

Fox, S. 2019. "The Genetics of Genocide: I'm Healing so My Future Daughter Doesn't Have To." *Globe and Mail*, June 6 (https://www.theglobeandmail.com/opinion/article-ill-tell-my-daughter-one-day-in-the-mmiwg-report-canada-finally).

Gartner, R. 2011. "Historical Patterns of Interpersonal Violence." In *Oxford Bibliographies Online: Criminology*, edited by R. Rosenfeld. New York: Oxford University Press.

Goffman, E. (1961). *Asylums: Essays on the Social Situation of Mental Patients and Other Inmates*. New York: Anchor.

Green, M. 2018. "Critical Data Is Still Missing on Transgender and Non-Binary Canadians: StatsCan." *Toronto Star*, May 31 (https://www.thestar.com/vancouver/2018/05/31/no-national-data-for-trans-people-advocates.html).

Halifax Regional Police and the Nova Scotia Department of Justice. n.d. "Gang Prevention: A Resource Guide on Youth and Gangs" (http://novascotia.ca/just/publications/documents/GangPrevention.pdf).

Hango, D. 2017. "Childhood Physical Abuse: Differences by Birth Cohort." Statistics Canada (https://www150.statcan.gc.ca/n1/pub/75-006-x/2017001/article/54869-eng.htm).

Holfeld, B. and B.J. Leadbeater. 2015. "The Nature and Frequency of Cyber Bullying Behaviors and Victimization Experiences in Young Canadian Children." *Canadian Journal of School Psychology* 30(2):116–35.

Hotton Mahoney, T. 2011. "*Women and the Criminal Justice System: A Gender Based Statistical Report.*" Statistics Canada.

Hudson, A., K. Wright, D. Bhattacharya, K. Sinha, A. Nyamathi, and M. Marfisee. 2010. "Correlates of Adult Assault Among Homeless Women." *Journal of Health Care for the Poor and Underserved*, 21(4):1250–62.

Huffington Post UK. 2013. "Teenagers Who Beat Homeless Man, Kevin Bennett, to Death Sentenced for His Murder." April 15.

Hunt, S., and Sayers, N. 2015. "Cindy Gladue Case Sends a Chilling Message to Indigenous Women." *Globe and Mail*, March 25 (https://www.theglobeandmail.com/opinion/cindy-gladue-case-sends-a-chilling-message-to-indigenous-women/article23609986).

Ibrahym, D. 2018. "Violent Victimization, Discrimination and Perceptions of Safety: An Immigrant Perspective, Canada, 2014." Statistics Canada (https://www150.statcan.gc.ca/n1/pub/85-002-x/2018001/article/54911-eng.htm).

Innes, Robert A. 2015. "Moose on the Loose: Indigenous Men, Violence, and the Colonial Excuse." *Aboriginal Policy Studies* 4(1).

Kissner, Jason and David C. Pyrooz. 2009. "Self-Control, Differential Association, and Gang Membership: A Theoretical and Empirical Extension of the Literature." *Journal of Criminal Justice* 37(5):478–87.

Kong, R. 2005. "Criminal Justice Indicators." Statistics Canada (http://www.statcan.gc.ca/daily-quotidien/040601/dq040601a-eng.htm).

Kruttschnitt, C., and R. Gartner. 2008. "Female Violent Offenders: Moral Panics or More Serious Offenders?" *Australian & New Zealand Journal of Criminology* 41(1):9–35.

Landau, T. 2006. *Challenging Notions: Critical Victimology in Canada.* Toronto, ON: Canadian Scholar's Press.

Lee, Matthew R. 2000. "Community Cohesion and Violent Predatory Victimization: A Theoretical Extension and Cross-National Test of Opportunity Theory." *Social Forces* 79(2):683–706.

Léséleuc, S. 2007. "Criminal Victimization in the Workplace, 2004." Canadian Centre for Justice Statistics, Statistics Canada (https://www.publicsafety.gc.ca/lbrr/archives/cnmcs-plcng/cn000033259112-eng.pdf).

MacCharles, T. 2012. "Federal Prison Population in Canada Growing." *Toronto Star*, October 23 (https://www.thestar.com/news/canada/2012/10/23/federal_prison_population_in_canada_growing.html).

Maclean's. 2018. "Canada's Most Dangerous Places 2018" (https://www.macleans.ca/canadas-most-dangerous-places).

Mahoney, Jill. 2013. "New Footage Reveals Further Details in Toronto Streetcar Shooting." *Globe and Mail*, July 30 (https://www.theglobeandmail.com/news/toronto/new-footage-reveals-further-details-in-streetcar-shooting/article13495500).

Marks, D. 2014. "How Can 824 Women Disappear without Raising an Alarm?" *Sudbury Star* (https://www.thesudburystar.com/2014/03/21/how-can-824-women-disappear-without-raising-an-alarm/wcm/64f78c4f-0d59-bf5c-a7fc-e13ac5934fea).

McCooey, Paula. 2003. "Jane Doe Book on Cop Attitudes towards Rape Victims." *Ottawa Citizen*, March 8.

Merton, Robert K. 1968. *Social Theory and Social Structure.* New York: Free Press.

Mishna, F. 2012. *Bullying: A Guide to Research, Intervention, and Prevention.* Toronto, ON: Oxford University Press.

Moor, A. 2009. "Prevalence of Exposure to Sexual Violence among Women in Israel: Preliminary Assessment." *Social Issues in Israel*:46–65.

Moreau, G. 2019. "Canadian Residential Facilities for Victims of Abuse, 2017/2018" Statistics Canada (https://www150.statcan.gc.ca/n1/pub/85-002-x/2019001/article/00007-eng.htm).

Native Women's Association of Canada. 2010. "Fact Sheet: Missing and Murdered Aboriginal Women and Girls" (https://www.nwac.ca/wp-content/uploads/2015/05/Fact_Sheet_Missing_and_Murdered_Aboriginal_Women_and_Girls.pdf).

National Inquiry into Missing and Murdered Indigenous Women and Girls. 2019. "Reclaiming Power and Place" (https://www.mmiwg-ffada.ca/wp-content/uploads/2019/06/Final_Report_Vol_1a.pdf).

Noseworthy, Kelly. 2016. "Cyberbullying Victim Speaks Out: 'It Was the Darkest Time of My Life.'" *CBC News*, March 30 (https://www.cbc.ca/news/canada/hamilton/headlines/cyberbullying-victim-speaks-out-it-was-the-darkest-time-of-my-life-1.3509284).

O'Doherty, Tamara. 2011. "Criminalization and Off-Street Sex Work in Canada." *Canadian Journal of Criminology and Criminal Justice* 53(2):217–45.

Office of the Correctional Investigator. 2014. "A Case Study of Diversity in Corrections: The Black Inmate Experience in Federal Penitentiaries: Final Report" (https://www.oci-bec.gc.ca/cnt/rpt/oth-aut/oth-aut20131126-eng.aspx).

Ogrodnik, Lucie. 2010. "*Child and Youth Victims of Police-Reported Violent Crime, 2008.*" Canadian Centre for Justice Statistics, Statistics Canada (https://www150.statcan.gc.ca/n1/pub/85f0033m/85f0033m2010023-eng.htm).

Ontario Human Rights Commission. n.d. "What Is Racial Profiling? (Fact Sheet)" (http://www.ohrc.on.ca/en/what-racial-profiling-fact-sheet).

Perkel, C. 2011. "'Shocking' Stories of Guards' Brutality Revealed in Ontario Ombudsman Report." *CTV News*, June 13 (https://ottawa.ctvnews.ca/shocking-stories-of-guards-brutality-revealed-in-ontario-ombudsman-report-1.1321393).

Perreault, S. 2014. "Criminal Victimization in Canada, 2014." Statistics Canada (https://www150.statcan.gc.ca/n1/pub/85-002-x/2015001/article/14241-eng.htm).

Perreault, S., J. Sauve, and M. Burns. 2010. *"Multiple Victimization in Canada, 2004."* Statistics Canada, January 6 (http://www.statcan.gc.ca/pub/85f0033m/85f0033m2010022-eng.htm).

Pieters, Gary and Tam Goossen. 2013. "Make Public Oversight of Police Training a Priority." *Toronto Star,* August 4 (https://www.thestar.com/opinion/commentary/2013/08/04/make_public_oversight_of_police_training_a_priority.html).

Pottie Bunge, Valerie and Holly Johnson. 2005. "Exploring Crime Patterns in Canada." Statistics Canada, catalogue no. 85-561-MWE2005005 (https://www150.statcan.gc.ca/n1/pub/85-561-m/85-561-m2005005-eng.htm).

Purple Ribbon Campaign, Newfoundland and Labrador. n.d. "Challenges for Rural Women" (http://www.respectwomen.ca/ruralchallenges.html).

Rossiter, K., and A. Clarkson. 2013. "Opening Ontario's 'Saddest Chapter': A Social History of Huronia Regional Centre." *Canadian Journal of Disability Studies* 2(3).

Rotenberg, C. 2017. "Police-Reported Sexual Assaults in Canada, 2009 to 2014: A Statistical Profile." *Juristat,* Statistics Canada (https://www150.statcan.gc.ca/n1/daily-quotidien/171003/dq171003a-eng.htm).

Russell, Diana E.H. 1975. *The Politics of Rape: The Victim's Perspective.* New York: Stein & Day.

Sapers, H. 2012. *"Annual Report of the Office of the Correctional Investigator 2011–2012."* Ottawa, ON: Office of the Correctional Investigator.

———. 2013. *"Annual Report of the Office of the Correctional Investigator 2012–2013."* Ottawa, ON: Office of the Correctional Investigator.

Savino, John O. and Brent E. Turvey, eds. 2011. *Rape Investigation Handbook.* Amsterdam: Elsevier Science.

Savoie, J. 2008. "Analysis of the Spatial Distribution of Crime in Canada: Summary of Major Trends." Canadian Centre for Justice Statistics, Statistics Canada, October 7 (http://www.statcan.gc.ca/pub/85-561-m/85-561-m2008015-eng.htm).

Scott, Charles L. 1999. "Juvenile Violence." *Psychiatric Clinics of North America* 22(1):71–83.

SGM Law. 2015. "Civil Litigation: *Jane Doe v. Metropolitan Toronto (Municipality) Commissioners of Police*." SGM *Notable Cases* (http://www.sgmlaw.com/en/about/JaneDoev.MetropolitanTorontoMunicipalityCommissionersofPolice.cfm).

Shenmer, L. 2019. "Will the MMIWG Inquiry's Report Change the Way We Police in Canada?" *Globe and Mail*, June 6 (https://www.theglobeandmail.com/opinion/article-will-the-mmiwg-inquirys-report-change-the-way-we-police-in-canada).

Simpson, L. 2018. "Violent Victimization of Lesbians, Gays and Bisexuals in Canada, 2014." Statistics Canada (https://www150.statcan.gc.ca/n1/pub/85-002-x/2018001/article/54923-eng.htm).

Statistics Canada. 2006. *"Aboriginal People Over-represented in Saskatchewan's Prisons" (*http://www41.statcan.ca/2006/2693/ceb2693_002-eng.htm).

———. 2018a. "Before and after #MeToo: A Look at Police-Reported Sexual Assaults in Canada" (https://www150.statcan.gc.ca/n1/pub/11-627-m/11-627-m2018036-eng.htm).

———. 2018b. "Economic Profiles of Saskatchewan Offenders, 2009/2010" (https://www150.statcan.gc.ca/n1/daily-quotidien/180906/dq180906d-eng.htm).

———. 2018c. "Number of Police-Reported Hate Crimes, Canada, 2009 to 2017." *The Daily* (https://www150.statcan.gc.ca/n1/daily-quotidien/181129/cg-a001-eng.htm).

———. 2018d. "Police-Reported Crime Statistics, 2017." *The Daily* (https://www150.statcan.gc.ca/n1/daily-quotidien/180723/dq180723b-eng.htm?indid=4751-2&indgeo=0).

———. 2018e. "Uniform Crime Reporting Survey (UCR)" (http://www23.statcan.gc.ca/imdb/p2SV.pl?Function=getSurvey&SDDS=3302).

Surratt, H.L., J. Inciardi, S. Kurtz, and M. Kiley. 2004. "Sex Work and Drug Use in a Subculture of Violence." *Crime and Delinquency* 50(1): 43–59.

Sutherland, Edwin. 1947. *Principles of Criminology.* New York: J. B. Lippincott Co.

University of Guelph. 2014. "Prof Uses Personal Story of Rape, Recovery to Address Gender Inequality." News release, April 9 (http://www.uoguelph.ca/news/2014/04/prof_uses_perso.html).

Vallaincourt, R. 2008. *"Gender Differences in Police-Reported Violent Crime in Canada, 2008."* Canadian Centre for Justice Statistics, Statistics Canada (https://www150.statcan.gc.ca/n1/pub/85f0033m/85f0033m2010024-eng.htm).

Van Ngo, H., K. Neote, C. Cala, M. Antonio, and J. Hickey. 2018. "The Experience of Ethno-Cultural Members with Racial Profiling." *Journal of Ethics and Culture Diversity in Social Work* 27(3):253–70.

Wilkinson R.G. and K.E. Pickett. 2009. *The Spirit Level.* New York: Penguin.

Williams, S. and T. Stickley. 2011. "Stories from the Streets: People's Experiences of Homelessness." *Journal of Psychiatric and Mental Health Nursing* 18(5):432–9.

Wortley, S., and A. Owusu-Bempah. 2011. "The Usual Suspects: Police Stop and Search Practices in Canada." *Policing and Society* 21(4):395–407.

Chapter 11

Adese, J. 2012. "Colluding with the Enemy? Nationalism and Depictions of 'Aboriginality' in Canadian Olympic Moments." *American Indian Quarterly* 36(4):479–502.

Adomat, D.S. 2014. "Exploring Issues of Disability in Children's Literature Discussions." *Disability Studies Quarterly* 34(3).

Anderson, Bruce and David Coletto. 2016. "Muslims and Indigenous People Face the Most Discrimination in Canada, According to Canadians." Abacus Data, December 29 (https://abacusdata.ca/muslims-and-indigenous-people-face-the-most-discrimination-in-canada-according-to-canadians).

Assembly of First Nations. 2015. "First Nations Mental Wellness Continuum Framework launched." January 28 (http://www.afn.ca/index.php/en/news-media/latest-news/first-nations-mental-wellness-continuum-framework-launched).

Assembly of Manitoba Chiefs. 2018. "Treatment Centres for Addiction Issues Urgently Needed for First Nations in Manitoba." October 30 (https://manitobachiefs.com/treatment-centres-for-addiction-issues-urgently-needed-for-first-nations-in-manitoba).

Avila-Saavedra, G. 2009. "Nothing Queer about Queer Television: Televized Construction of Gay Masculinities." *Media Culture Society* 31(1):5–21.

Beeby, D. 2012. "Bank of Canada Bans Image of Asian Woman from $100 Bill." *Financial Post*, August 12.

Birkett, D. 2011. "My Daughter Stars in The Inbetweeners Movie—And so Does Her Wheelchair." *The Telegraph*, August 5 (https://www.telegraph.co.uk/culture/film/starsandstories/8681292/My-daughter-stars-in-The-Inbetweeners-Movie-so-does-her-wheelchair.html).

British Columbian. 1863. "Our Relations with the Indians." June 13.

Chan, W. 2013. News Media Representations of Immigrants in the Canadian Criminal Justice System. Vancouver, BC: Metropolis British Columbia.

Churchill, Ward. 1996. "Let's Spread the 'Fun' Around: The Issue of Sports Team Names and Mascots." Pp. 439–43 in *A Native Son: Selected Essays on Indigenism, 1985–1995*. Boston, MA: South End Press.

De Beauvoir, S. 1972. *The Second Sex*, translated by H.M. Parshley. London, UK: Cape.

De Clercq, Lize. 2016. "Why Are There so Few Female Game Developers?" uniteIT, February 28 (http://www.unite-it.eu/profiles/blogs/why-are-so-few-women-developing-video-games).

De Cremer, David, and Laetitia B. Mulder. 2007. "A Passion for Respect: On Understanding the Role of Human Needs and Morality." *Gruppendynamik und Organisationsberatung* 38(4):439–49.

Defebaugh, W. 2014. Laverne Cox. *V Magazine*, September (http://www.out.com/entertainment/popnography/2014/08/22/exclusive-first-look-laverne-cox-honored-v-magazines-rebels).

Dhaenens, F. 2012. "Queer Cuttings on YouTube: Re-editing Soap Operas as a Form of Fan-Produced Queer Resistance." *European Journal of Cultural Studies* 15:442.

Disability Movies. 2014. "Disability Movie Stereotypes and Clichés" (http://disabilitymovies.com/disability-movie-cliches).

Ellis, L., K. Beaver, and J. Wright. 2009. *Handbook of Crime Correlates*. Cambridge, MA: Academic Press.

Emmons, S. 2014. "Why We Put this Little Girl on Our Cover." *Today's Parent*, June 6.

Environics Institute. 2018. "Canadian Public Opinion about Immigration and Minority Groups" (https://www.environicsinstitute.org/docs/default-source/project-documents/focus-canada-winter-2018---immigration-and-minority-groups/focus-canada-winter-2018-survey-on-immigration-and-minority-groups---final-report.pdf?sfvrsn=ede94c5f_2).

Fejes, Fred. 2000. "Making a Gay Masculinity." *Critical Studies in Mass Communication*, 17(1):113–17.

Feminist Frequency. 2012. "*Feminist Frequency: Conversations with Pop Culture*" (http://www.feministfrequency.com/about).

Geena Davis Institute on Gender and Media. 2018. "Gender and Race Representations in the Top Family Films of 2017" (https://seejane.org/research-informs-empowers/the-see-jane-100).

GLAAD. 2013. "*2013 Studio Responsibility Index*" (https://www.glaad.org/sri/2013).

———. 2019. "Where We Are on TV" (http://glaad.org/files/WWAT/WWAT_GLAAD_2018-2019.pdf).

Hall, S. 1996. *Race: The Floating Signifier*. Northampton, MA: Media Education Foundation

Harding, R. 2006. "Historical Representations of Aboriginal People in the Canadian News Media." *Discourse Society* 17:205.

Health Canada. 2015. "First Nations and Inuit Mental Health and Addictions–Cluster Evaluation 2005/06-2009/10" (http://www.hc-sc.gc.ca/ahc-asc/performance/eval/2012/fni-addiction-evaluation-pni-eng.php).

King, Thomas. 2012. *The Inconvenient Indian: A Curious Account of Native People in North America*. Toronto, ON: Doubleday Canada.

Krishna, A. 2014. "Special Needs in the Media: Why the Neglect?" *Today's Parent*, January 28.

Maslow, Abraham H. 1943. "A Theory of Human Motivation." *Psychological Review* 50(4):370–96.

Perez, Caroline Criado. 2019. *Invisible Women: Exposing Data Bias in a World Designed for Men*. New York: Random House.

Pollitt, Katha. 1991. "Hers; The Smurfette Principle." *New York Times*, July 7 (https://www.nytimes.com/1991/04/07/magazine/hers-the-smurfette-principle.html).

Royal Commission on Aboriginal Peoples. 1996. "Report of the *Royal Commission on Aboriginal Peoples*" (https://www.bac-lac.gc.ca/eng/discover/aboriginal-heritage/royal-commission-aboriginal-peoples/Pages/final-report.aspx).

Reece, C. 2014. "Chip Reece Builds the World of Metaphase." January 22 (http://www.comicosity.com/interview-chip-reece-builds-the-world-of-metaphase).

Said, Edward. 1978. *Orientalism*. New York: Pantheon.

Smith, S.L., M. Choueiti, A. Prescott, and K. Pieper. "*Gender Roles & Occupations: A Look at Character Attributes and Job-Related Aspirations in Film and Television.*" Geena Davis Institute on Gender in Media (https://seejane.org/wp-content/uploads/full-study-gender-roles-and-occupations-v2.pdf).

Taylor, D. 2009. "Normativity and Normalization." *Foucault Studies* 7:45–63.

TV Tropes. n.d. "Useful Notes: *Deggans' Rule*" (https://tvtropes.org/pmwiki/pmwiki.php/UsefulNotes/DeggansRule).

Waldman, K. 2014. "The Bechdel Test Sets the Bar Too Low. Let's Write a New One." *Slate*, January 7 (https://slate.com/human-interest/2014/01/the-bechdel-test-needs-an-update-weve-set-the-bar-for-female-representation-too-low.html).

Women and Hollywood. 2018. "What You Need to Know about Women in Hollywood in 2017" (https://womenandhollywood.com/infographic-what-you-need-to-know-about-women-in-hollywood-in-2017-a7e7321a125f).

Woodend, Dorothy. 2010. "Reel Injun and Salute." *The Tyee*, February 19.

Yellow Bird, Michael. 2004. "Cowboys and Indians: Toys of Genocide, Icons of American Colonialism." *Wicazo Sa Review* 19(2):33–48.

Chapter 12

Acker, J. (1992). "The Future of Women and Work: Ending the Twentieth Century." *Sociological Perspectives* 35(1):53–68.

Bendixen, S., M.B. Bringslid, and H. Vike, eds. 2018. *Egalitarianism in Scandinavia: Historical and Contemporary Perspectives*. London, UK: Palgrave Macmillan.

Bevelander, Pieter and Ravi Pendakur. 2012. "Citizenship, Co-Ethnic Populations, and Employment Probabilities of Immigrants in Sweden." *Journal of International Migration and Integration* 13(2):203–22.

Burström, Bo. 2002. "Increasing Inequalities in Health Care Utilisation across Income Groups in Sweden during the 1990s." *Health Policy* 62(2):117–29.

Byrne, Janet, ed. 2012. *The Occupy Handbook*. Boston, MA: Little, Brown.

Canadian Institute for Health Information. 2017. "How Canada Compares: Results from the Commonwealth Fund's 2016 International Health Policy Survey of Adults in 11 Countries—Accessible Report" (https://www.cihi.ca/sites/default/files/document/text-alternative-version-2016-cmwf-en-web.pdf).

Charter, D. 2014. "German Universities Scrap All Tuition Fees." Sunday Times, September 22 (https://www.thetimes.co.uk/article/german-universities-scrap-all-tuition-fees-thmnh5l0b2j).

Esping-Andersen, Gøsta. 1990. *The Three Worlds of Welfare Capitalism*. Cambridge, UK: Polity Press.

Falkenberg, A.W. 1998. "Quality of Life: Efficiency, Equity and Freedom in the United States and Scandinavia." *Journal of Socio-Economics* 27(1):1–28.

Fox, A. 2014. "We Need to Learn from Germany's Experiments in Shared Care." *The Guardian*, May 3 (https://www.theguardian.com/commentisfree/2014/may/03/learn-germany-experiments-shared-care).

Fraser, Nancy. 1994. "After the Family Wage: A Post-Industrial Thought Experiment." *Political Theory* 22(4):591–618.

Frenette, M. 2017. "Postsecondary Enrolment by Parental Income: Recent National and Provincial Trends." Statistics Canada (https://www150.statcan.gc.ca/n1/pub/11-626-x/11-626-x2017070-eng.htm).

Gaygisiz, E. 2009. "Economic and Cultural Correlates of Road-Traffic Accident Fatality Rates in OECD Countries." *Perceptual and Motor Skills* 109(2):531–45.

Government of Sweden. 2019. "Why Swedes Are Okay with Paying Taxes" (https://sweden.se/society/why-swedes-are-okay-with-paying-taxes).

Greve, B. 2007. "What Characterises the Nordic Welfare State Model?" *Journal of Social Sciences* 3(2):43–51.

Gundara, J. 2000. "Religion, Human Rights and Intercultural Education." *Intercultural Education* 11(2):127–36.

Hoxby, C. and C. Avery. 2013. "The Missing 'One-Offs': The Hidden Supply of High-Achieving, Low-Income Students." *Brookings Papers on Economic Activity*, Spring.

Inter-Parliamentary Union. 2019. "Gender Equality at a Glance" (https://www.ipu.org/resources/publications/about-ipu/2019-03/gender-equality-glance).

James, S.E., J.L. Herman, S. Rankin, M. Keisling, L. Mottet, and M. Anafi. 2016. "The Report of the 2015 U.S. Transgender Survey." National Center for Transgender Equality (https://www.transequality.org/sites/default/files/docs/USTS-Full-Report-FINAL.PDF).

Johnson, R.W. and P. Gosselin. 2018. "How Secure Is Employment at Older Ages?" Urban Institute (https://www.urban.org/sites/default/files/publication/99570/how_secure_is_employment_at_older_ages_2.pdf).

Kantola, J.E. 2014. "The Paradoxical Gendered Consequences of the EU Policy on Multiple Discrimination: The Nordic Case." *European Integration Online Papers* 18:Article 7.

Lane, J.E. and S. Ersson. 2008. "The Nordic Countries: Compromise and Corporatism in the Welfare State." Pp. 256–89 in *Comparative European Politics*. London, UK: Routledge.

Lee, H. 2013. "Why Finnish Babies Sleep in Cardboard Boxes." *BBC News Magazine*, June 4 (https://www.bbc.com/news/magazine-22751415).

Liinason, M. and C.M. Meijer. 2018. "Challenging Constructions of Nationhood and Nostalgia: Exploring the Role of Gender, Race and Age in Struggles for Women's Rights in Scandinavia." *Women's History Review* 27(5):729–53.

Macdonald, David. 2018. "Climbing Up and Kicking Down: Executive Pay in Canada." Canadian Centre for Policy Alternatives (https://www.policyalternatives.ca/publications/reports/climbing-and-kicking-down).

Maclean's. 2014. "Who Earns What: Global CEO-to-Worker Pay Ratios." September 27 (https://www.macleans.ca/economy/money-economy/global-ceo-to-worker-pay-ratios).

Mahon, Rianne. 1991. "From Solidaristic Wages to Solidaristic Work: A Post-Fordist Historical Compromise for Sweden?" *Economic and Industrial Democracy* 12:295–325.

———. 2002. "Child Care: Toward What Kind of 'Social Europe'?" *Social Politics: International Studies in Gender, State & Society* 9(3):343–79.

Meijer, A. 2015. "E-governance Innovation: Barriers and Strategies." *Government Information Quarterly* 32(2):198–206.

Meil, G. 2013. "European Men's Use of Parental Leave and Their Involvement in Child Care and Housework." *Journal of Comparative Family Studies* 44(5):557–70.

Norocel, O.C. 2013. "'Give Us Back Sweden!' A Feminist Reading of the (Re)Interpretations of the Folkhem Conceptual Metaphor in Swedish Radical Right Populist Discourse." *NORA: Nordic Journal of Feminist and Gender Research* 21(1):4–20.

OECD. 2013. "Education at a Glance 2013: OECD Indicators" (http://www.oecd.org/education/eag2013%20(eng)--FINAL%2020%20June%202013.pdf).

———. 2016a. "OECD Better Life Index: Country Reports" (https://www.oecd.org/newsroom/BLI2013-Country-Notes.pdf).

———. 2016b. "Starting Strong IV: Early Childhood Education and Care Data Country Note: Finland" (http://www.oecd.org/education/school/ECECDCN-Finland.pdf).

———. 2018. "Programme for International Student Assessment 2015: Results in Focus" (https://www.oecd.org/pisa/pisa-2015-results-in-focus.pdf).

———. 2019a. "Income Inequality (Indicator)" (https://www.oecd-ilibrary.org/social-issues-migration-health/income-inequality/indicator/english_459aa7f1-en).

———. 2019b. "Public Spending on Childcare and Early Education." Social Policy Division (https://www.oecd.org/els/soc/PF3_1_Public_spending_on_childcare_and_early_education.pdf).

———.2020. "Income inequality (Indicator)." doi: 10.1787/459aa7f1-en (Accessed on 30 April 2020).

Oxfam. 2019. "5 Shocking Facts about Extreme Global Inequality and How to Even It Up" (https://www.oxfam.org/en/even-it/5-shocking-facts-about-extreme-global-inequality-and-how-even-it-davos).

Oltermann, P. 2014. "Germany's 'Multigeneration Houses' Could Solve Two Problems for Britain." *The Guardian*, May 2 (https://www.theguardian.com/world/2014/may/02/germany-multigeneration-house-solve-problems-britain).

Piketty, Thomas. 2014. *Capital in the Twenty-First Century*. Cambridge, MA: Harvard University Press.

Rae, David. 2005. "Getting Better Value for Money from Sweden's Healthcare System." OECD Economics Department Working Papers (https://www.oecd-ilibrary.org/economics/getting-better-value-for-money-from-sweden-s-healthcare-system_082725005676).

Reisel, L. 2014. "Legal Harmonization and Intersectionality in Swedish and Norwegian Anti-Discrimination Reform. *Social Politics* 21(2):218–40.

Rivera, L.A. and A. Tilcsik. 2016. "Class Advantage, Commitment Penalty: The Gendered Effect of Social Class Signals in an Elite Labor Market." *American Sociological Review* 81(6):1097–131. doi:10.1177/0003122416668154

Roehling M.V., S. Pichler, and T.A. Bruce. 2013. "Moderators of the Effect of Weight on Job-Related Outcomes: A Meta-Analysis of Experimental Studies." *Journal of Applied Social Psychology* 43:237–52.

Roseberry, W. 2002. "Understanding Capitalism—Historically, Structurally, Spatially." Pp. 61–79 in *Locating Capitalism in Time and Space: Global Restructurings Politics and Identity*, edited by D. Nugent. Stanford, CA: Stanford University Press.

Rushe, Dominic. 2018. "US Bosses Now Ear 312 Times the Average Worker's Wage, Figures Show." *The Guardian*, August 16 (https://www.theguardian.com/business/2018/aug/16/ceo-versus-worker-wage-american-companies-pay-gap-study-2018).

Sengoelge, M., M. Hasselberg, D. Ormandy, and L. Laflamme. 2014. "Housing, Income Inequality and Child Injury Mortality in Europe: A Cross-Sectional Study." *Child: Care, Health and Development* 40(2):283–91.

Sides, J. and K. Gross. 2013. "Stereotypes of Muslims and Support for the War on Terror." *Journal of Politics* 75(3):583–98.

Siim, Birte and Monika Mokre, eds. 2013. *Negotiating Gender and Diversity in an Emergent European Public Sphere*. London: Palgrave Macmillan.

Siim, Birte and Hege Skeje. 2008. "Tracks, Intersections and Dead Ends: Multicultural Challenges to State Feminism in Denmark and Norway." *Ethnicities* 8(3):322–44.

Sustainable Development Solutions Network. 2019. "World Happiness Report, 2019" (https://worldhappiness.report/ed/2019).

Tepperman, L. and M. Finnsdottir. Forthcoming. *Canada's Place in a Shrunken World*. Oakville, ON: Rock's Mills Press.

Tepperman, L. and N. Gheihman. 2013. *Habits of Inequality*. Toronto, ON: Oxford University Press.

Torres Sevilla-Quiñones de León, Margarita. 2014. "The Scarring Effect of 'Women's Work': The Determinants of Women's Attrition from Male-Dominated Occupations." *Social Forces* 93(1):1–29.

Trotter, S.R. 2015. "Breaking the Law of Jante." *eSharp* 23:1–24.

United Nations. 2013. "The Millennium Development Goals Report 2013" (https://www.un.org/millenniumgoals/pdf/report-2013/mdg-report-2013-english.pdf).

———. 2016. "Ending Poverty" (https://www.un.org/en/sections/issues-depth/poverty/index.html).

———. 2017. "World Fertility Report 2015." Department of Economic and Social Affairs (https://www.un.org/en/development/desa/population/publications/pdf/fertility/wfr2015/worldFertilityReport2015.pdf).

———. 2018. "Report of the United Nations High Commissioner for Refugees" (https://www.unhcr.org/gcr/GCR_English.pdf).

UNICEF. 2018. "Levels and Trends in Child Mortality" (https://data.unicef.org/resources/levels-and-trends-in-child-mortality).

———. 2019. "Family-Friendly Policies in Rich Countries: How Canada Compares" (https://oneyouth.unicef.ca/sites/default/files/2019-06/UNICEF_ResearchBrief_Canadian-Companion_EN-FINAL_WEB.pdf).

World Health Organization. 2019. "World Conference on Social Determinants of Health" (https://www.who.int/sdhconference/background/news/facts/en).

World Top Incomes Database. 2017 (http://topincomes.g-mond.parisschoolofeconomics.eu).

Chapter 13

Ayala, L. and M. Rodríguez. 2007. "What Determines Exit from Social Assistance in Spain?" *International Journal of Social Welfare* 16(2):168–82.

Bäckman, O. and Å. Bergmark. 2011. "Escaping Welfare? Social Assistance Dynamics in Sweden." *Journal of European Social Policy* 21(5):486–500.

Beltrame, Julian. 2014. "Canada's Richest 86 Have as Much Wealth as Poorest 11 Million." *CTV News*, April 3 (http://www.ctvnews.ca/business/canada-s-richest-86-have-as-much-wealth-as-poorest-11-million-1.1758778).

Byrne, Janet, ed. 2012. *The Occupy Handbook*. New York: Back Bay Books.

Hansen, J. and R. Wahlberg. 2009. "Poverty and Its Persistence: A Comparison of Natives and Immigrants in Sweden." *Review of Economics of the Household* 7(2):105–32.

Nelson, K. 2013. "Social Assistance and EU Poverty Thresholds 1990–2008. Are European Welfare Systems Providing Just and Fair Protection against Low Income?" *European Sociological Review* 29(2):386–401.

Nietzsche, Friedrich. 2017. *Nietzsche: On the Genealogy of Morality and Other Writings*. Cambridge, UK: Cambridge University Press

Pollmann-Schult, M. and F. Büchel. 2005. "Unemployment Benefits, Unemployment Duration and Subsequent Job Quality: Evidence from West Germany." *Acta Sociologica* 48(1):21–39.

Shahidi, F.V., C. Ramraj, O. Sod-Erdene, V. Hildebrand, and A. Siddiqi. 2019. "The Impact of Social Assistance Programs on Population Health: A Systematic Review of Research in High-Income Countries." *BMC Public Health* 19(1): Article 2. doi:10.1186/s12889-018-6337-1

Index

Page numbers in *italics* indicate figures or illustrations.